T0181635

Lecture Notes in Computer Science 13218

More information about this series at https://link.springer.com/bookseries/558

Jong Hwan Park · Seung-Hyun Seo (Eds.)

Information Security and Cryptology – ICISC 2021

24th International Conference
Seoul, South Korea, December 1–3, 2021
Revised Selected Papers

 Springer

Editors
Jong Hwan Park
Sangmyung Universirsity
Seoul, Korea (Republic of)

Seung-Hyun Seo ⓘ
Hanyang University
Ansan, Korea (Republic of)

ISSN 0302-9743　　　　　　　　ISSN 1611-3349 (electronic)
Lecture Notes in Computer Science
ISBN 978-3-031-08895-7　　　　ISBN 978-3-031-08896-4 (eBook)
https://doi.org/10.1007/978-3-031-08896-4

This Springer imprint is published by the registered company Springer Nature Switzerland AG
The registered company address is: Gewerbestrasse 11, 6330 Cham, Switzerland

Preface

The 24th International Conference on Information Security and Cryptology (ICISC 2021) was held during December 1–3, 2021. This year's conference was hosted by the Korea Institute of Information Security and Cryptology (KIISC).

The aim of the ICISC conference is to provide an international forum for the latest results of research, development, and applications within the field of information security and cryptology. This year, we received 63 submissions and were able to accept 23 papers for presentation at the conference. The challenging review and selection processes were successfully conducted by Program Committee (PC) members and external reviewers via the EasyChair review system. For transparency, it is worth noting that each paper underwent a blind review by at least three PC members. Furthermore, to resolve potential conflicts concerning the reviewer's decisions, individual review reports were open to all PC members and the review phase was followed by detailed interactive discussions on each paper. For this LNCS post-proceedings, the authors of selected papers had a few weeks to prepare for their final versions, based on the comments received from the reviewers.

The conference featured two invited talks, given by Xiuzhen Cheng and Vadin Lyubashevsky. We thank the invited speakers for their kind acceptances and insightful presentations. We would like to thank all authors who submitted their papers to ICISC 2021, as well as all PC members. It was a truly wonderful experience to work with such talented and hardworking researchers. We also appreciate the external reviewers for assisting the PC members. Finally, we would like to thank all attendees for their active participation and the organizing members who successfully managed this conference. We look forward to seeing you again at next year's ICISC.

December 2021

Jong Hwan Park
Seung-Hyun Seo

Organization

General Chair

Jae-Cheol Ryu   Chung-Nam National University, South Korea

Organizing Chair

Jong-Hyouk Lee   Sejong University, South Korea

Program Chairs

Jong Hwan Park   Sangmyung University, South Korea
Seung-Hyun Seo   Hanyang University, South Korea

Program Committee

Dong-Guk Han   Kookmin University, South Korea
Sungwook Kim   Seoul Women's University, South Korea
Changhoon Lee   Seoul National University of Science and
                                 Technology, South Korea
Kwangsu Lee   Sejong University, South Korea
Mun Kyu Lee   Inha University, South Korea
Jooyoung Lee   KAIST, South Korea
Hyung Tae Lee   Chung-Ang University, South Korea
Dongyoung Roh   National Security Research Institute, South Korea
Seogchung Seo   Kookmin University, South Korea
Jae Hong Seo   Hanyang University, South Korea
Hwajeong Seo   Hansung University, South Korea
Jihye Kim   Kookmin University, South Korea
Changmin Lee   Korea Institute for Advanced Study, South Korea
Jongsung Kim   Kookmin University, South Korea
Yun Aaram   Ewha Womans University, South Korea
Taek-Young Youn   DanKook University, South Korea
Jung Yeon Hwang   Sungshin Women's University, South Korea
Minhye Seo   Duksung Women's University, South Korea
Heeseok Kim   Korea University, South Korea
Wenling Wu   Institute of Software, Chinese Academy of
                                 Sciences, Beijing
Zhenfu Cao   East China Normal University, China

Contents

Quantum Circuit

Efficient Implementation

Cryptographic Protocol I

Revocable Hierarchical Identity-Based Authenticated Key Exchange

Yuki Okano[1]([✉]), Junichi Tomida[1], Akira Nagai[1], Kazuki Yoneyama[2], Atsushi Fujioka[3], and Koutarou Suzuki[4]

[1] NTT Social Informatics Laboratories, Tokyo, Japan
{yuki.okano.te,junichi.tomida.vw,akira.nagai.td}@hco.ntt.co.jp
[2] Ibaraki University, Ibaraki, Japan
kazuki.yoneyama.sec@vc.ibaraki.ac.jp
[3] Kanagawa University, Kanagawa, Japan
fujioka@kanagawa-u.ac.jp
[4] Toyohashi University of Technology, Aichi, Japan
suzuki@cs.tut.ac.jp

Abstract. Identity-based authenticated key exchange (IB-AKE) would be considered to have an advantage in the sense that it does not require certificate management. However, IB-AKE has not both a key delegation functionality and a key revocation functionality. This leaves the problem of the burden to the private key generator when there are a large number of parties in the system, and the problem of the lack of a clear way to eliminate dishonest parties from the system. In this paper, we propose a new authentication mechanism called revocable hierarchical IB-AKE (RHIB-AKE), which can decentralize key generation and revocation performed by a PKG. We also propose a generic construction of RHIB-AKE from a revocable hierarchical identity-based key encapsulation mechanism (RHIB-KEM). We obtain the first RHIB-AKE schemes from pairings or lattices by our generic construction since RHIB-KEM is known to be constructed from them. For security, we show that our scheme resists against leakage of all combinations of master, static, current, and ephemeral secret keys except ones trivially break the security.

Keywords: Revocable hierarchical identity-based authenticated key exchange · rhid-eCK model · Revocable hierarchical identity-based key encapsulation mechanism

1 Introduction

Identity-based authenticated key exchange (IB-AKE) [5,10,16,27,34] is a cryptographic protocol and enables two parties to share a common session key via unauthenticated networks, where each party is identified with information called an identity (ID). IB-AKE succeeds in removing the management of certificates provided by a certificate authority in the ordinary public key infrastructure (PKI) based setting. Instead of that, it is necessary that an additional single

J. H. Park and S.-H. Seo (Eds.): ICISC 2021, LNCS 13218, pp. 3–27, 2022.
https://doi.org/10.1007/978-3-031-08896-4_1

authority called a private key generator (PKG) exists who extracts the secret key of each party corresponding to the identity of that party from its own secret key called the master secret key. On the contrary, it causes the problem of the burden to the authority if the number of parties belonging to the system is huge.

Hierarchical IB-AKE (HIB-AKE) [12,17,36] is one extension of IB-AKE and solves the above problem. HIB-AKE supports a key delegation functionality. Also, HIB-AKE only requires each party to trust the master public key generated by a single PKG when compared to a simple independent multiple PKG setting, in which each party must obtain the master public key of the PKG on another party without PKI. However, since HIB-AKE does not support a secret key revocation mechanism, there remains a problem with how to eliminate dishonest parties from the HIB-AKE system. Only this point is inferior to the PKI setting. Therefore, an efficient revocation mechanism is needed in the HIB-AKE system, assuming the case where the number of parties increases. It is natural to extend HIB-AKE to revocable HIB-AKE (RHIB-AKE).

As for identity-based encryption (IBE) systems, Boneh and Franklin [3] proposed a naive revocation method that requires the PKG to periodically regenerate secret keys of all parties. This method is not practical if the number of parties increases too much. Boldyreva et al. [2] use the complete subtree method to propose the first revocable IBE (RIBE) where the PKG workload is logarithmic of the number of parties in the system. In RIBE systems, ciphertexts cannot be decrypted directly from the secret key corresponding to the party's ID. The party needs a decryption key for each time period. PKG broadcasts key update information over a public channel every time period, and only non-revoked parties can obtain their own decryption key from key update information and their own secret key.

Seo and Emura [29] used Boldyreva's idea of RIBE to propose a new revocable hierarchical identity-based encryption (RHIBE) that is an extension of hierarchical identity-based encryption. RHIBE has both a key delegation functionality and a key revocation functionality. In other words, every non-leaf party in the hierarchical structure can revoke secret keys of low-level parties. Therefore, in HIB-AKE, it is a natural direction to achieve a key revocation with Boldyreva's idea of RIBE. However, it is not trivial to construct a secure RHIB-AKE satisfying desirable security requirements for AKE such as forward secrecy and security against master secret key leakage.

1.1 Related Works

Many RHIBE schemes have been proposed [8,19,23,24,29–31,33,35]. Each party has an ID corresponding to a node of a tree. A party of depth-ℓ in the tree has a level-ℓ ID, $(ID_1, ..., ID_\ell)$ and the parent node with a level-$(\ell - 1)$ ID being $(ID_1, ..., ID_{\ell-1})$. In the beginning, the party in the root node (or level-0) called PKG generates a master public key (MPK) and master secret key (MSK). A party that is not in the leaf nodes can generate static secret keys (SSKs) for lower-level parties from its own SSK (or MSK in case of PKG)[1]. The party can

---

[1] This means that all parties except those in leaf nodes can take a role as PKG. For convenience, however, we call only the party in the root node PKG in what follows.

also revoke lower-level parties according to time period by distributing (non-secret) key update information (KU) that the party generates from its SSK and a revocation list. Every party can generate a current secret key (CSK) for time period T from its own SSK and KU for T if the party is not revoked at T.[2] A valid ciphertext is associated with an ID, ID and a time period T, which can be decrypted by only CSK for ID and T.

1.2 Our Contribution

We put forward a new AKE mechanism named *Revocable Hierarchical Identity-Based AKE* (RHIB-AKE). RHIB-AKE allows for the revocation of secret keys that have been compromised or expired and having multiple PKGs by only trusting a single master public key generated by a single PKG. Formally, our contribution is two-fold: first, we introduce the concept of RHIB-AKE and formally define it; second, we present a generic methodology to construct an RHIB-AKE scheme. By our generic construction, we obtain the first RHIB-AKE schemes from pairings and lattices.

RHIB-AKE Model. In RHIB-AKE, the hierarchical ID structure and the key delegation/revocation mechanisms are the same as those in RHIBE. Instead of encryption and decryption in RHIBE, parties run an AKE protocol to create a secure channel. Concretely, in time period T, every pair of parties who have their CSK for T, that is, who are not revoked at T can run an AKE protocol to compute a shared key called session key (SK). In the protocol, each party generates an ephemeral secret key (ESK) and computes an SK from the ESK and the CSK for T.

Note that naively sending a session key via RHIBE does not satisfy desirable security requirements for AKE such as forward secrecy and security against MSK leakage. To capture these threats, we extend the id-eCK model [16], which is one of the strongest security models for IB-AKE, to the RHIB-AKE setting and formally define a security model for RHIB-AKE called the *rhid-eCK model*. Similar to the id-eCK model, we consider maximum exposure of secret information in the rhid-eCK model to capture the following threats. The secret information in RHIB-AKE consists of the MSK, SSKs, CSKs, ESKs, and SKs. The MSK may be exposed when the PKG is corrupted. SSKs may be revealed if a party stores them in an insecure storage while they must be generated in a tamper-proof module. CSKs may be revealed if they remain in memory without being securely erased before they are updated, and are read out by an adversary. ESKs may be guessed to an adversary if a pseudo-random number generator implemented in a system is poor. The SKs may be revealed if they are misused to encrypt messages with a vulnerable scheme.

---

[2] An SSK and a CSK are the names in the context of RHIB-AKE as defined in this paper, and in the context of RHIBE they are actually called a secret key and a decryption key, respectively.

RHIB-AKE Construction. We propose the first RHIB-AKE schemes that are secure in the rhid-eCK security model from pairings and lattices. Our starting point is the work by Fujioka et al. [11], who proposed a generic construction of a CK^+ secure AKE protocol from IND-CCA (indistinguishability against chosen ciphertext attack) secure public-key encryption[3]. Our observation is that while the CK^+ and the eCK model [22] are incomparable, their technique is applicable to the eCK model. Thus, our idea is that if we have an IND-CCA secure RHIBE scheme, we can generically construct a rhid-eCK secure RHIB-AKE scheme analogously to the work by Fujioka et al. Following the idea, we show that such a generic construction is possible and prove that if the underlying RHIBE is IND-CCA secure then the resulting RHIB-AKE is rhid-eCK secure.

A problem here is that no IND-CCA secure RHIBE scheme is known. Fortunately, we can easily achieve one by applying the Fujisaki-Okamoto transformation [13] to an IND-CPA secure RHIBE scheme, which can be constructed from pairings [8,33] or lattices [19,35]. Note that the BCHK transformation [18] is not applicable to RHIBE (see [18] for details, where they use the BCHK transformation in a non-black box manner). Thus, starting from these works, we can achieve RHIB-AKE schemes from pairings and lattices through our generic construction, where the latter is considered to be secure against quantum adversaries.

1.3 Organization

The rest of this paper is organized as follows. We introduce the definition of RHIB-AKE and its security model in Sect. 2. We propose our RHIB-AKE scheme in Sect. 3. We then give some instantiations of our RHIB-AKE scheme in Sect. 4. The conclusion and future works are finally given in Sect. 5.

2   Revocable Hierarchical Identity-Based Authenticated Key Exchange

In this section, we provide the definitions of an RHIB-AKE scheme and the rhid-eCK security model. Before describing the details, we give some notations.

Notations. $\mathbb{N}$ denotes the set of natural numbers. If S is a set, $s \in_R S$ denotes that s is chosen uniformly at random from S, and $|S|$ the number of elements in S. Let $a||b$ be the concatenation of a and b. Let $\lceil x \rceil$ denote the smallest integer greater than or equal to x. Let U_i be a party and $ID_i = (ID_{i,1}, \ldots, ID_{i,t})$ be the associated identity where $ID_{i,j} \in \{0,1\}^*$. An integer $|ID_i| := t$ denotes the hierarchical level of identity $ID_i = (ID_{i,1}, \ldots, ID_{i,t})$. The level-0 party with the special identity "pkg" is called the PKG. The order $ID_i' \succ ID_i$ between two identities

---

[3] Precisely, they use IND-CCA secure public-key encapsulation mechanism (PK-KEM) and IND-CPA (indistinguishability against chosen plaintext attack) secure PK-KEM as building blocks. For ease of exposition, we employ IND-CCA secure PKE here since it implies both IND-CCA secure PK-KEM and IND-CPA secure PK-KEM.

holds if $ID'_i = (ID_{i,1}, \ldots, ID_{i,k_1})$ and $ID_i = (ID_{i,1}, \ldots, ID_{i,k_1}, \ldots, ID_{i,k_2})$ for $1 \le k_1 \le k_2$. Especially, ID'_i is the parent of the identity ID_i, i.e., $ID'_i = pa(ID_i)$ if $k_1 + 1 = k_2$. Let $\mathcal{I}_{ID_i} := \{ID''_i \mid pa(ID''_i) = ID_i\}$ be a set of identities whose parent is ID_i and $\mathcal{I}_{\mathsf{pkg}} := \{ID''_i \mid pa(ID''_i) = \mathsf{pkg}\}$ be a set of identities whose parent is the PKG.

2.1 RHIB-AKE Scheme

In this subsection, we introduce a syntax of RHIB-AKE. All parties are modeled as a probabilistic polynomial-time (PPT) Turing machine. RHIB-AKE scheme Π consists of the following five algorithms and a key exchange protocol.

$\mathsf{ParGen}(1^\kappa, L) \to (MSK, MPK)$: It takes a security parameter, 1^κ, and the maximum depth of the hierarchy, $L \in \mathbb{N}$, which is a polynomial of κ as input, and outputs a master secret key, MSK, and a master public key, MPK. The PKG runs this algorithm.

$\mathsf{SSKGen}(MPK, ID'_i, ID_i, SSK_{ID'_i}) \to (SSK_{ID_i}, SSK'_{ID'_i})$: It takes MPK, two identities $ID'_i = pa(ID_i)$ and $ID_i = (ID_{i,1}, \ldots, ID_{i,t})$, and a static secret key, $SSK_{ID'_i}$, corresponding to ID'_i, and outputs SSK_{ID_i}, corresponding to ID_i and the updated $SSK'_{ID'_i}$ corresponding to ID'_i. The party associated with ID'_i runs this algorithm. If the party is the PKG, this algorithm takes the MPK, identity ID_i, and the MSK, and outputs SSK_{ID_i}, corresponding to ID_i and the updated MSK', i.e., $\mathsf{SSKGen}(MPK, ID_i, MSK) \to (SSK_{ID_i}, MSK')$.

$\mathsf{Rev}(MPK, T, RL_{ID_i, T-1}, Add) \to RL_{ID_i, T}$: It takes MPK, a time period, T, a revocation list, $RL_{ID_i, T-1}$, and a set of identities, $Add \subset \mathcal{I}_{ID_i}$, that are added to the revocation list, and outputs the updated revocation list, $RL_{ID_i, T}$. The party associated with ID_i runs this algorithm. Note that $RL_{ID_i, 0} = \emptyset$.

$\mathsf{KUGen}(MPK, T, SSK_{ID_i}, RL_{ID_i, T}, ku_{pa(ID_i), T}) \to (ku_{ID_i, T}, SSK'_{ID_i})$: It takes MPK, a time period, $T \in \mathbb{N}$, SSK_{ID_i} corresponding to ID_i, a revocation list, $RL_{ID_i, T} \subset \mathcal{I}_{ID_i}$, and parent's key update information, $ku_{pa(ID_i), T}$, and outputs $ku_{ID_i, T}$, corresponding to ID_i and the updated SSK'_{ID_i}. The party associated with ID_i runs this algorithm. If the party is the PKG, this algorithm takes MPK, a time period, T, and MSK, and a revocation list, $RL_{\mathsf{pkg}, T} \subset \mathcal{I}_{\mathsf{pkg}}$, and outputs $ku_{\mathsf{pkg}, T}$, and the updated MSK', i.e., $\mathsf{KUGen}(MPK, T, MSK, RL_{\mathsf{pkg}, T}) \to (ku_{\mathsf{pkg}, T}, MSK')$.

$\mathsf{CSKGen}(MPK, SSK_{ID_i}, ku_{pa(ID_i), T}) \to CSK_{ID_i, T} / \perp$: It takes MPK, SSK_{ID_i}, corresponding to ID_i, and parent's $ku_{pa(ID_i), T}$, outputs a current secret key, $CSK_{ID_i, T}$, or $\perp$ indicating that ID_i or some ID'_i such that $ID'_i \succ ID_i$ have been revoked.

Key Exchange Protocol. Parties U_A and U_B can share a session key in time period $T \subset \mathbb{N}$ by performing the two-pass protocol by using each of the following four algorithms in turn. U_A has SSK_A, and $CSK_{A,T}$, corresponding to ID_A, and U_B has SSK_B, and $CSK_{B,T}$, corresponding to ID_B.

InitEK($MPK, T, ID_A, SSK_A, CSK_{A,T}, ID_B$) → ($ESK_A, EPK_A$): Party U_A computes ephemeral keys by algorithm InitEK which takes the MPK, MPK, the time period, T, ID_A, SSK_A, $CSK_{A,T}$, ID_B, and outputs an ephemeral secret key, ESK_A, and an ephemeral public key, EPK_A. U_A sends EPK_A to party U_B.

ResEK($MPK, T, ID_B, SSK_B, CSK_{B,T}, ID_A, EPK_A$) → ($ESK_B, EPK_B$): Party U_B computes ephemeral keys by algorithm ResEK which takes MPK, the time period, T, ID_B, SSK_B, $CSK_{B,T}$, ID_A, and EPK_A, and outputs ESK_B, and EPK_B. U_B sends EPK_B to U_A.

ResSK($MPK, T, ID_B, SSK_B, CSK_{B,T}, ID_A, ESK_B, EPK_B, EPK_A$) → SK: Party U_B computes a session key by algorithm ResSK which takes MPK, the time period, T, ID_B, SSK_B, $CSK_{B,T}$, ID_A, ESK_B, EPK_B, and EPK_A, and outputs a session key, SK.

InitSK($MPK, T, ID_A, SSK_A, CSK_{A,T}, ID_B, ESK_A, EPK_A, EPK_B$) → SK: Party U_A computes a session key by algorithm InitSK which takes MPK, the time period, T, ID_A, SSK_A, $CSK_{A,T}$, ID_B, ESK_A, EPK_A, and EPK_B, and outputs SK.

Session. An invocation of a protocol is called a *session*. For a party, U_A, a session is activated via an incoming message of the forms, ($\Pi, \mathcal{I}, T, ID_A, ID_B$) or ($\Pi, \mathcal{R}, T, ID_A, ID_B, EPK_B$), where Π is a protocol identifier. If U_A is activated with ($\Pi, \mathcal{I}, T, ID_A, ID_B$) (resp. ($\Pi, \mathcal{R}, T, ID_A, ID_B, EPK_B$)), then U_A is the *initiator* (resp. *responder*). After activation, U_A switches the second element (or role) of the incoming message, appends an EPK, EPK_A, to it, and sends it as an outgoing response. If U_A is the responder, U_A computes a session key. If U_A is the initiator, U_A that has been successfully activated via ($\Pi, \mathcal{I}, T, ID_A, ID_B$) can be further activated via ($\Pi, \mathcal{I}, T, ID_A, ID_B, EPK_A, EPK_B$) to compute a session key.

An initiator U_A identifies its session via ($\Pi, \mathcal{I}, ID_A, ID_B, EPK_A$) or ($\Pi, \mathcal{I}, ID_A, ID_B, EPK_A, EPK_B$). If U_A is a responder, the session is identified via ($\Pi, \mathcal{R}, ID_A, ID_B, EPK_B, EPK_A$). The *matching session* of session sid = ($\Pi, \mathcal{I}, ID_A, ID_B, EPK_A, EPK_B$) is session sid$'$ = ($\Pi, \mathcal{R}, ID_B, ID_A, EPK_A, EPK_B$) and vice versa. We say that U_A is the *owner* of session sid if the third element of sid is ID_A, U_B is the *peer* of session sid if the fourth element of sid is ID_B, and a session is *completed* if its owner computes a session key.

2.2 Security Model

In this subsection, we define the rhid-eCK security model. This security model, like the definition of the id-eCK model, consists of the definition of an adversary and its capabilities, the definition of freshness, and the security experiment.

This security model is different from the id-eCK model in the following points: 1) an adversary also has access to CSKReveal and Revoke queries, the former capturing the reveal of CSKs of parties and the latter capturing system-wide revocation list updates and time period increments, and 2) the freshness condition is modified based on the additional queries.

Adversaries. Adversary $\mathcal{A}$ is modeled as a PPT Turing machine. It controls all communications between parties including session activation by performing the following query, where T_{cu} is the current time period initialized with 1.

- Send(message): The input message has one of the following forms: $(\Pi, \mathcal{I}, T_{cu}, ID_A, ID_B)$, $(\Pi, \mathcal{R}, T_{cu}, ID_B, ID_A, EPK_A)$, or $(\Pi, \mathcal{I}, T_{cu}, ID_A, ID_B, EPK_A, EPK_B)$. Adversary $\mathcal{A}$ obtains the response from the party.

Note that adversary $\mathcal{A}$ does not control the communication for delivery of either SSK or KU between each party and its parent.

A party's private information is not accessible to the adversary. However, leakage of private information is captured via the following adversary queries, where $\mathcal{ID}$ is a set of identities which the SSK is already generated.

- SKReveal(sid): The adversary obtains the session key for session sid, provided that the session is completed.
- ESKReveal(sid): The adversary obtains the ESK of the owner of session sid.
- SSKReveal(ID_i): The adversary learns the SSK corresponding to identity ID_i if SSK_{ID_i} is already generated.
- CSKReveal(ID_i, T): The adversary learns the CSK corresponding to ID_i and time period T if $T \leq T_{cu}$ and CSKGen($MPK, SSK_{ID_i}, ku_{pa(ID_i),T}$) = $CSK_{ID_i,T} \neq \perp$.
- MSKReveal(): The adversary learns the MSK of the system.
- EstablishParty(U_i, ID_i): This query allows the adversary to give an SSK corresponding to identity ID_i on behalf of party U_i if the SSK is not yet generated and the SSK corresponding to the parent identity of ID_i is already generated. Otherwise, $\perp$ is returned. When $\perp$ is not returned, the adversary controls party U_i. If a party is established by this query, then we call party U_i *dishonest*. If not, we call the party *honest*.
- Revoke(RL): If the following conditions are not satisfied for the set of identities $RL \subset \{ID \mid |ID| \geq 1\}$, then $\perp$ is returned.
    - For all $ID_i \in \mathcal{ID} \cup \{\mathsf{pkg}\}$, $RL_{ID_i, T_{cu}} \subset RL$.
    - For all $ID_i \in \mathcal{ID}$, $ID_i \in RL$ if $pa(ID_i) \in RL$.
  Otherwise, T_{cu} is incremented as $T_{cu} \leftarrow T_{cu} + 1$. Then, PKG's revocation list is updated as $RL_{\mathsf{pkg},T_{cu}} \leftarrow \mathsf{Rev}(MPK, T_{cu}, RL_{\mathsf{pkg},T_{cu}-1}, RL \cap \mathcal{I}_{\mathsf{pkg}})$ and $(ku_{\mathsf{pkg},T_{cu}}, MSK') \leftarrow \mathsf{KUGen}(MPK, T_{cu}, MSK, RL_{\mathsf{pkg},T_{cu}})$ is computed. For any party U_i with $ID_i \in \mathcal{ID}$, its revocation list is updated as $RL_{ID_i,T_{cu}} \leftarrow \mathsf{Rev}(MPK, T_{cu}, RL_{ID_i,T_{cu}-1}, RL \cap \mathcal{I}_{ID_i})$ and $(ku_{ID_i,T_{cu}}, SSK'_{ID_i}) \leftarrow \mathsf{KUGen}(MPK, T, SSK_{ID_i}, RL_{ID_i,T_{cu}}, ku_{pa(ID'_i),T_{cu}})$ is computed. The adversary obtains all key updated information $\{ku_{ID_i,T_{cu}}\}_{ID_i \in \mathcal{ID} \cup \{\mathsf{pkg}\}}$.

Freshness. Our security definition requires the notion of *freshness*. $\mathsf{sid}^* = (\Pi, \mathcal{I}, T^*, ID_A, ID_B, EPK_A, EPK_B)$ or $(\Pi, \mathcal{R}, T^*, ID_A, ID_B, EPK_B, EPK_A)$ be a completed session between honest party U_A with identity ID_A and U_B with identity ID_B. Let $\overline{\mathsf{sid}}^*$ be the matching session of sid^* if the matching session exists. We define session sid^* to be fresh if none of the following conditions hold:

1. Adversary $\mathcal{A}$ issues SKReveal(sid*), or SKReveal($\overline{\text{sid}^*}$) if $\overline{\text{sid}^*}$ exists.
2. $\overline{\text{sid}^*}$ exists and adversary $\mathcal{A}$ makes either of the following queries
   - both ESKReveal(sid*) and SSKReveal(ID) for identity ID such that $ID \succ ID_A$ and $ID \notin RL_{pa(ID),T^*-1}$,
   - both ESKReveal($\overline{\text{sid}^*}$) and SSKReveal(ID) for identity ID such that $ID \succ ID_B$ and $ID \notin RL_{pa(ID),T^*-1}$,
   - both CSKReveal(ID_A, T^*) and ESKReveal(sid*), or
   - both CSKReveal(ID_B, T^*) and ESKReveal($\overline{\text{sid}^*}$).
3. $\overline{\text{sid}^*}$ does not exist and adversary $\mathcal{A}$ makes either of the following queries
   - both ESKReveal(sid*) and SSKReveal(ID) for identity ID such that $ID \succ ID_A$ and $ID \notin RL_{pa(ID),T^*-1}$,
   - SSKReveal(ID) for ID such that $ID \succ ID_B$ and $ID \notin RL_{pa(ID),T^*-1}$,
   - both CSKReveal(ID_A, T^*) and ESKReveal(sid*), or
   - CSKReveal(ID_B, T^*).

Note that if adversary $\mathcal{A}$ issues MSKReveal(), we regard $\mathcal{A}$ as having issued SSKReveal(ID_A) and SSKReveal(ID_B).

Security Experiment. We consider the following security experiment. Initially, adversary $\mathcal{A}$ is given a set of honest parties and makes any sequence of the above queries. During the experiment, $\mathcal{A}$ makes the following query.

- Test(sid*): Session sid* must be fresh. Select a bit $b \in_R \{0,1\}$ and return the session key held by sid* if $b = 0$, and return a random key if $b = 1$.

The experiment continues until adversary $\mathcal{A}$ makes a guess b'. The adversary *wins* the game if the test session sid* is still fresh and if $\mathcal{A}$'s guess is correct, i.e., $b' = b$. The advantage is defined as $\text{Adv}_\Pi^{\text{RHIB-AKE}}(\mathcal{A}) = |\Pr[\mathcal{A} \text{ wins}] - 1/2|$. We define the security as follows.

Definition 1. *We say that RHIB-AKE scheme Π is secure in the rhid-eCK model if the following conditions hold:*

1. *If two honest parties complete matching sessions, then, except with negligible probability, they both compute the same session key.*
2. *For any PPT adversary $\mathcal{A}$, $\text{Adv}_\Pi^{\text{RHIB-AKE}}(\mathcal{A})$ is negligible.*

Moreover, we say that RHIB-AKE scheme Π is selective secure in the rhid-eCK model, if $\mathcal{A}$ outputs (T^*, ID_A, ID_B) at the beginning of the security experiment.

3   Our RHIB-AKE Scheme

In this section, we give a generic construction of selective rhid-eCK secure RHIB-AKE from key encapsulation mechanism (KEM) and revocable hierarchical identity-based KEM (RHIB-KEM). We define RHIB-KEM required for our construction. We show the instantiation of RHIB-KEM in Sect. 4.

3.1   Preliminaries

We recall the security definition for pseudorandom function (PRF), key derivation function (KDF), twisted PRF, and KEM.

Basic Cryptographic Functions. We give definitions of a pseudorandom function and a key derivation function [11,20].

Pseudorandom Function (PRF). Let $\mathcal{F} = \{F : \mathcal{K}_\kappa \times D_\kappa \rightarrow R_\kappa\}$ be a function family with respect to key $k \in \mathcal{K}_\kappa$. Let $\mathcal{RF}$ be the set of all functions from D_κ to R_κ. We say that $\mathcal{F}$ is a PRF (family) if for any PPT distinguisher $\mathcal{D}$ it holds that $\mathrm{Adv}_{\mathcal{F},\mathcal{D}}^{prf}(\kappa) = |\mathrm{Pr}[\mathcal{D}^{F_k(\cdot)}(1^\kappa) \rightarrow 1 \mid k \in_R \mathcal{K}_\kappa] - \mathrm{Pr}[\mathcal{D}^{f(\cdot)}(1^\kappa) \rightarrow 1 \mid f \in_R \mathcal{RF}]|$ is negligible for security parameter κ.

Key Derivation Function (KDF). Let $KDF : Salt_\kappa \times D_\kappa \rightarrow R_\kappa$ be a function. Function KDF is a key derivation function if for any PPT distinguisher $\mathcal{D}$, any distribution X_{D_κ} over D_κ with $H_\infty(X_{D_\kappa}) \geq \kappa$, and any salt $s \in Salt_\kappa$, it holds that $\mathrm{Adv}_{\mathcal{D}}^{KDF}(\kappa) := |\mathrm{Pr}[\mathcal{D}(s,y) \rightarrow 1 \mid y \in_R R_\kappa] - \mathrm{Pr}[\mathcal{D}(s, KDF(s,x)) \rightarrow 1 \mid x \leftarrow X_{\mathcal{D}}]|$ is negligible for security parameter κ.

Twisted PRF. We give a definition of a twisted PRF (TPRF). This function is used with the input of ESKs and CSKs to this function in order to ensure that our construction is resilient to ephemeral secret key exposure.

Definition 2 (Twisted Pseudorandom Function [21]). *Let $F' : LD_\kappa \times RD_\kappa \rightarrow R_\kappa$ be a function. Function F' is a TPRF if for any PPT distinguisher $\mathcal{D}$ and $\mathcal{D}'$ it holds that two difference $|\mathrm{Pr}[\mathcal{D}((b, F'(a,b))) \rightarrow 1 \mid a \in_R LD_\kappa, b \in_R RD_\kappa] - \mathrm{Pr}[\mathcal{D}((b, R)) \rightarrow 1 \mid b \in_R RD_\kappa, R \in_R \mathcal{R}_\kappa]|$ and $|\mathrm{Pr}[\mathcal{D}'((a, F'(a,b))) \rightarrow 1 \mid a \in_R LD_\kappa, b \in_R RD_\kappa] - \mathrm{Pr}[\mathcal{D}'((a, R)) \rightarrow 1 \mid a \in_R LD_\kappa, \mathcal{R} \in_R \mathcal{R}_\kappa]|$ are both negligible for security parameter κ.*

KEM. We recall the definition of IND-CPA security for KEM and the min-entropy of KEM keys. In our construction, session keys are computed from KEM keys via a KDF and a PRF. To use a KDF to obtain a PRF key computationally indistinguishable from a uniformly random PRF key, KEM keys need to have κ-min-entropy property.

A KEM scheme consists of three algorithms (wKeyGen, wEnCap, wDeCap) with two randomness spaces $\mathcal{R}_{wK}$ and $\mathcal{R}_{wE}$, and a key space $\mathcal{KS}$.

wKeyGen$(1^\kappa, r_g) \rightarrow (ek, dk)$: It takes a security parameter, 1^κ and randomness, $r_g \in \mathcal{R}_{wK}$, and outputs a pair of encapsulation and decapsulation keys, (ek, dk).

wEnCap$(ek, r_e) \rightarrow (K, C)$: It takes ek and randomness, $r_e \in \mathcal{R}_{wE}$, and outputs a pair of a key and a ciphertext, (K, C), where $K \in \mathcal{KS}$.

wDeCap$(dk, C) \rightarrow K$: It takes dk and C, and outputs $K \in \mathcal{KS}$.

We require the correctness condition. That is, we have $K = \mathsf{wDeCap}(dk, C)$ for any $r_g \in \mathcal{R}_{wK}$, $r_e \in \mathcal{R}_{wE}$, $(ek, dk) \leftarrow \mathsf{wKeyGen}(1^\kappa, r_g)$, and $(K, C) \leftarrow \mathsf{wEnCap}(ek, r_e)$.

Definition 3 (IND-CPA Security for KEM). *A KEM is IND-CPA secure if for any PPT adversary* $\mathcal{A} = (\mathcal{A}_1, \mathcal{A}_2)$, *it holds that* $\mathrm{Adv}_{\mathcal{A}}^{\mathsf{ind\text{-}cpa}}(\kappa) = |2\mathrm{Pr}[(ek, dk) \leftarrow \mathsf{wKeyGen}(1^{\kappa}), state \leftarrow \mathcal{A}_1(ek), b \in_R \{0, 1\}, (K_0^*, C_0^*) \leftarrow \mathsf{wEnCap}(ek), K_1^* \in_R \mathcal{KS}, b' \leftarrow \mathcal{A}_2(K_b^*, C_b^*, state), b' = b] - 1|$ *is negligible for security parameter* κ.

Definition 4 (Min-Entropy of KEM Key). *A KEM is* κ-*min-entropy KEM if for any encapsulation key* ek, *randomness* $r_e \in \mathcal{R}_{wE}$, *distribution* $D_{\mathcal{KS}}$ *of variable* K *defined by* $(K, C) \leftarrow \mathsf{wEnCap}(ek, r_e)$, *and distribution* D_{pub} *of public information,* $H_{\infty}(D_{\mathcal{KS}_{KEM}} | D_{pub}) \geq \kappa$ *holds, where* H_{∞} *denotes min-entropy.*

3.2   RHIB-KEM

We newly define RHIB-KEM and its two security notions: selective indistinguishability against chosen-ciphertext attacks (selective-IND-CCA), and min-entropy of RHIB-KEM keys. Our definition is based on Katsumata et al.'s definition of RHIBE and its security [19], and also includes adversary's access to the decapsulation oracle using the decapsulation key corresponding to the challenge time period and the challenge identity in the security game.

An RHIB-KEM scheme consists of six algorithms (Setup, SKGen, KeyUp, DKGen, EnCap, DeCap). The revocation list $RL_{ID,T}$ of a party with identity ID in the time period T is a subset of $\mathcal{I}_{ID}$, which contains the identities of its children. As in the definition of Katsumata et al., we do not explicitly introduce the revoke algorithm as part of our syntax since it is a simple operation of appending revoked party identities to a list. The above six algorithms have the following interfaces.

Setup($1^{\kappa}, L$) → (mpk, msk): It takes a security parameter, 1^{κ} and the maximum depth of the hierarchy, $L \in \mathbb{N}$, and outputs a master public key, mpk and a master secret key, msk.

SKGen($mpk, sk_{pa(ID)}, ID$) → ($sk_{ID}, sk'_{pa(ID)}$): It takes mpk, a parent's secret key, $sk_{pa(ID)}$, and an identity, ID, and outputs a secret key, sk_{ID} for ID and the parent's updated secret key, $sk'_{pa(ID)}$. Note that $sk_{pa(ID)} = msk$ if the PKG is the parent of ID.

KeyUp($mpk, T, sk_{ID}, RL_{ID,T}, ku_{pa(ID),T}$) → ($ku_{ID,T}, sk'_{ID}$): It takes mpk, a time period, $T \in \mathbb{N}$, sk_{ID} corresponding to ID, a revocation list, $RL_{ID,T} \subset \mathcal{I}_{ID}$, and a parent's key update information, $ku_{pa(ID),T}$, and outputs a key update information, $ku_{ID,T}$ and the updated sk'_{ID}. Note that $sk_{ID} = msk$, $RL_{ID,T} = RL_{\mathsf{pkg},T}$, and $ku_{pa(ID),T} = \perp$ if $ID = \mathsf{pkg}$.

DKGen($mpk, sk_{ID}, ku_{pa(ID),T}$) → $dk_{ID,T}$ or $\perp$: It takes mpk, sk_{ID} corresponding to ID, and a parent's $ku_{pa(ID),T}$, and outputs a decryption key, $dk_{ID,T}$ for the time period T or $\perp$ indicating that ID or some of its ancestors has been revoked.

EnCap(mpk, ID, T, r_e) → (K, C): It takes mpk, ID, a time period, T, and randomness, $r_e \in \mathcal{R}_E$, and outputs a key, $K \in \mathcal{KS}_{RH}$ and a ciphertext, C, where $\mathcal{R}_E$ is a randomness space, and $\mathcal{KS}_{RH}$ a key space.

$\mathsf{DeCap}(mpk, dk_{ID,T}, C) \to K'$: It takes mpk, $dk_{ID,T}$, and C, and outputs a key, $K' \in \mathcal{KS}_{RH}$.

We require the correctness condition. That is, we have $K = \mathsf{DeCap}(mpk, dk_{ID,T}, C)$ for any $\kappa \in \mathbb{N}$, $L \in \mathbb{N}$, and $(mpk, msk) \leftarrow \mathsf{Setup}(1^\kappa, L)$, any identity $ID = (ID_1, \ldots, ID_t)$, any time period T, any pair of a key and a ciphertext $(K, C) \leftarrow \mathsf{EnCap}(mpk, ID, T)$ if $ID' \notin RL_{pa(ID'),T}$ holds for any identity $ID' \succ ID$.

Security Definition. We give a formal security definition for RHIB-KEM. Let $\Sigma = (\mathsf{Setup}, \mathsf{SKGen}, \mathsf{KeyUp}, \mathsf{DKGen}, \mathsf{EnCap}, \mathsf{DeCap})$ be an RHIB-KEM. This security definition is defined via a game between an adversary $\mathcal{A}$ and a challenger $\mathcal{C}$. This game is parameterized by a security parameter κ and a polynomial $L = L(\kappa)$ representing the maximum depth of the identity hierarchy. The game also has the global counter T_{cu} initialized with 1, which denotes the current time period. The game proceeds as follows:

At the beginning, adversary $\mathcal{A}$ sends the challenge identity/time period pair (ID^*, T^*) to challenger $\mathcal{C}$. Next, $\mathcal{C}$ runs $(mpk, msk) \leftarrow \mathsf{Setup}(1^\kappa, L)$, and prepares two lists: SKList that initially contains (pkg, msk) and RevList $= \emptyset$. $\mathcal{C}$ also initializes cflag $= 0$. Challenger $\mathcal{C}$ then executes $(ku_{\mathsf{pkg},1}, sk'_{\mathsf{pkg}}) \leftarrow \mathsf{KeyUp}(mpk, T_{cu} = 1, sk_{\mathsf{pkg}}, \emptyset, \perp)$ for generating a key update information for the initial time period $T_{cu} = 1$ and gives $(mpk, ku_{\mathsf{pkg},1})$ to $\mathcal{A}$. After that, adversary $\mathcal{A}$ may adaptively make queries in Fig. 1. At some point, $\mathcal{A}$ outputs $b' \in \{0,1\}$ as its guess for b and terminates.

This completes the description of the game. In this game, $\mathcal{A}$'s advantage is defined by $\mathrm{Adv}_{\mathcal{A},L}^{\mathsf{s\text{-}ind\text{-}cca}}(\kappa) = |2\dot{\Pr}[b' = b] - 1|$.

If $\mathcal{A}$ never issues DeCap during this game, then the advantage is defined as $\mathrm{Adv}_{\mathcal{A},L}^{\mathsf{s\text{-}ind\text{-}cpa}}(\kappa)$ instead of $\mathrm{Adv}_{\mathcal{A},L}^{\mathsf{s\text{-}ind\text{-}cca}}(\kappa)$.

Definition 5 (Selective-IND-CCA Security for RHIB-KEM). *We say that an RHIB-KEM is selective-IND-CCA secure if for any PPT adversary $\mathcal{A}$, it holds that $\mathrm{Adv}_{\mathcal{A},L}^{\mathsf{s\text{-}ind\text{-}cca}}(\kappa)$ is negligible for security parameter κ.*

Definition 6 (Selective-IND-CPA Security for RHIB-KEM). *We say that an RHIB-KEM is selective-IND-CPA secure if for any PPT adversary $\mathcal{A}$, it holds that $\mathrm{Adv}_{\mathcal{A},L}^{\mathsf{s\text{-}ind\text{-}cpa}}(\kappa)$ is negligible for security parameter κ.*

Similar to KEM in Sect. 3.1, we define the min-entropy of RHIB-KEM key. We use RHIB-KEM keys as keys of PRFs via a KDF.

Definition 7 (Min-Entropy of RHIB-KEM Key). *An RHIB-KEM is κ-min-entropy RHIB-KEM if for any identity ID, any time period T, any randomness $r_e \in \mathcal{R}_E$, any distribution $D_{\mathcal{KS}}$ of variable K defined by $(K, C) \leftarrow \mathsf{EnCap}(ID, T, r_e)$, and any distribution D_{pub} of public information, $H_\infty(D_{\mathcal{KS}_{KEM}} | D_{pub}) \geq \kappa$ holds.*

3.3 Construction

Our construction is based on Fujioka et al.'s scheme [11] and generically consists of a selective-IND-CCA secure RHIB-KEM, an IND-CPA secure KEM, a PRF, a TPRF, and a KDF. This construction satisfies selective rhid-eCK security.

SecKeyGen(ID) :
    if $(ID, *) \in$ SKList $\vee (pa(ID), *) \notin$ SKList
        return $\perp$
    else
        $(sk_{ID}, sk'_{pa(ID)}) \leftarrow$ SKGen $(mpk,$
           $sk_{pa(ID)}, ID)$
        SKList $\leftarrow$ SKList $\cup \{(ID, sk_{ID})\}$
        if $|ID| \leq L - 1$
           $(ku_{ID,T_{cu}}, sk'_{ID}) \leftarrow$ KeyUp $(T_{cu}, sk_{ID}$
            , $\emptyset, ku_{pa(ID),T_{cu}})$
           return $ku_{ID,T_{cu}}$
        else
           return SUCCESS

SecKeyReveal(ID) :
    if $(T_{cu} \geq T^*) \wedge (ID \succ ID^*) \wedge (\forall ID' \succ ID,$
        $ID' \notin RL_{pa(ID'),T^*})$
        return $\perp$
    else
        $(ID, sk_{ID}) \leftarrow$ SKList
        RevList $\leftarrow$ RevList $\cup \{ID\}$
        return sk_{ID}

DecKeyReveal(ID, T) :
    if $(T > T_{cu}) \vee ((ID, T) = (ID^*, T^*)) \vee$
        $(ID \in RL_{pa(ID),T})$
        return $\perp$
    else
        $dk_{ID,T} \leftarrow$ DKGen $(mpk, sk_{ID},$
           $ku_{pa(ID),T})$
        return $dk_{ID,T}$

Update(RL) :
    if $\exists ID \in$ SKList$((RL_{pkg,T_{cu}} \not\subseteq RL) \vee$
        $(RL_{ID,T_{cu}} \not\subseteq RL) \vee (\exists ID' \succ ID, ID' \in RL$
        $\wedge ID \notin RL) \vee (ID \succ ID^* \wedge T_{cu} = T^* - 1 \wedge$
        $ID \in$ RevList $\wedge ID \notin RL))$
        return $\perp$
    else
        $T_{cu} \leftarrow T_{cu} + 1$
        KUList $= \emptyset$
        for $ID \in \{ID' \mid (ID', *) \in$ SKList, $ID' \notin RL,$
           $|ID'| \leq L - 1\} \cup \{pkg\}$
           $RL_{ID,T_{cu}} \leftarrow RL \cap \mathcal{I}_{ID}$
           $(ku_{ID,T_{cu}}, sk'_{ID}) \leftarrow$ KeyUp$(mpk, T_{cu}, sk_{ID},$
           $RL_{ID,T_{cu}}, ku_{pa(ID),T_{cu}})$
           KUList $\leftarrow$ KUList $\cup \{ku_{ID,T_{cu}}\}$
        return KUList

DeCap(ID^*, T^*, C) :
    if $C = C^*$
        return $\perp$
    else
        $K \leftarrow$ DeCap(mpk, dk_{ID^*,T^*}, C)
        return K

Challenge(ID^*, T^*) :
    if cflag $= 1$
        return $\perp$
    else
        $r_e \leftarrow \mathcal{R}_E$
        $(K_0^*, C^*) \leftarrow$ EnCap(mpk, ID^*, T^*, r_e)
        $K_1^* \leftarrow \mathcal{KS}_{RH}$
        $b \leftarrow \{0, 1\}$
        cflag $\leftarrow 1$
        return (K_b^*, C^*)

Fig. 1. Adversarial queries

Design Principle. We design our construction to solve three problems: 1) the exposure resistance of ESKs, 2) the exposure resistance of SSKs for already revoked identities, and 3) the exposure resistance of the MSK, SSKs, and CSKs.

For the first problem, we use a TPRF. In the construction, an ESK and a CSK are input to the TPRF. The output of the TPRF cannot be computed if the ESK is revealed but the CSK is not. We use the outputs of a TPRF as randomness to generate EPKs. This makes it impossible for an adversary to know the randomness since neither the ESK nor the CSK can be revealed by the freshness definition.

For the second problem, we use a selective-IND-CCA secure RHIB-KEM. It is difficult to obtain the RHIB-KEM key from the ciphertext associated with an identity even if an adversary obtains the RHIB-KEM secret key of the SSK such that the corresponding identity has already been revoked. In the construction, two-session parties use RHIB-KEM keys generated with each other's peer identity to compute a session key. Therefore, we can provide the exposure resistance of SSKs for already revoked identities.

For the third problem, we use an IND-CPA secure KEM. An initiator generates session-specific encapsulation and decapsulation keys of the KEM, and the responder generates a KEM key for the encapsulation key. The initiator and the responder use the KEM key to compute a session key. This allows our construction to satisfy the exposure resistance of the MSK, SSKs, and CSKs.

Our Generic Construction. We construct an RHIB-AKE scheme Π from an RHIB-KEM (Setup, SKGen, KeyUp, DKGen, EnCap, DeCap), a KEM (wKeyGen, wEnCap, wDeCap) with two randomness spaces $\mathcal{R}_{wK}$ and $\mathcal{R}_{wE}$. Let $\mathcal{KS}$ be the key space of the outputs of EnCap and wEnCap.

ParGen$(1^\kappa, L) \to (MSK, MPK)$: The PKG selects PRF $F : \mathcal{FS} \times \{0,1\}^* \to \{0,1\}^\kappa$ with key space $\mathcal{FS}$ of size κ, TPRF $G : LD_\kappa \times RD_\kappa \to \mathcal{R}_{wE}$ with $|LD_\kappa| = |RD_\kappa| = 2^\kappa$, and KDF $KDF : \{0,1\}^\kappa \times \mathcal{KS} \to \mathcal{FS}$ with randomly chosen public salt $s \in_R \{0,1\}^\kappa$. Moreover, the PKG generates master key pair $(mpk, msk) \leftarrow \mathsf{Setup}(1^\kappa, L)$. The PKG outputs $MSK = msk$ and $MPK = (F, G, KDF, s, mpk)$.

SSKGen$(MPK, ID'_i, ID_i, SSK_{ID'_i}) \to (SSK_{ID_i}, SSK'_{ID'_i})$: If $|ID| = 1$ i.e. the PKG is a parent of ID, the PKG generates $(sk_{ID}, msk') \leftarrow \mathsf{SKGen}(mpk, msk, ID)$ and outputs $SSK_{ID} = sk_{ID}$, $MSK' = msk'$. Otherwise, party $U_{pa(ID)}$ whose identity is the parent of identity ID generates key pair $(sk_{ID}, sk'_{pa(ID)}) \leftarrow \mathsf{SKGen}(mpk, sk_{pa(ID)}, ID)$ with its secret key $SSK_{pa(ID)} = sk_{pa(ID)}$ and outputs $SSK_{ID} = sk_{ID}$ and $SSK'_{pa(ID)} = sk'_{pa(ID)}$.

Rev$(MPK, T, RL_{ID_i, T-1}, Add) \to RL_{ID_i, T}$: Party U_i with identity ID_i outputs $RL_{ID_i, T} = RL_{ID_i, T-1} \cup Add$.

KUGen$(MPK, T, SSK_{ID_i}, RL_{ID_i, T}, ku_{ID'_i, T}) \to (ku_{ID_i, T}, SSK'_{ID_i})$: If the PKG runs this algorithm with its revocation list $RL_{\mathsf{pkg}, T}$, it runs $(ku_{\mathsf{pkg}, T}, msk') \leftarrow \mathsf{KeyUp}(mpk, T, msk, RL_{\mathsf{pkg}, T})$ and outputs $ku_{\mathsf{pkg}, T}$ and $MSK' = msk'$. Otherwise, party U_i with identity ID_i runs this algorithm with its revocation list $RL_{ID_i, T}$. U_i runs $(ku_{ID_i, T}, sk'_{ID_i}) \leftarrow \mathsf{KeyUp}(T, sk_{ID_i}, RL_{ID_i, T}, ku_{pa(ID_i), T})$ and outputs $ku_{ID_i, T}$ and $SSK'_{ID_i} = sk'_{ID_i}$.

CSKGen$(MPK, SSK_{ID_i}, ku_{pa(ID_i), T}) \to CSK_{ID_i, T} / \bot$: Party U_i with identity ID_i runs this algorithm. U_i runs $dk_{ID_i, T} \leftarrow \mathsf{DKGen}(mpk, sk_{ID_i}, ku_{pa(ID_i), T})$ with its SSK $SSK_{ID_i} = sk_{ID_i}$ and generates $\sigma_{ID_i, T} \in_R LD_\kappa$ uniformly at random. U_i outputs its CSK $CSK_{ID_i, T} = (dk_{ID_i, T}, \sigma_{ID_i, T})$.

Key Exchange Protocol. We describe our key exchange in Fig. 2. Here, we describe the detail. In the time period T, initiator U_A with identity ID_A and CSK $CSK_{A,T} = (dk_{A,T}, \sigma_{A,T})$, and responder U_B with identity ID_B and CSK $CSK_{B,T} = (dk_{B,T}, \sigma_{B,T})$ performs the following algorithms.

$$\boxed{\begin{array}{l} \textbf{Common public parameter}: F, G, KDF, s, mpk \\ \textbf{Current keys for party } U_A : CSK_A := (dk_{A,T}, \sigma_{A,T}) \\ \textbf{Current keys for party } U_B : CSK_B := (dk_{B,T}, \sigma_{B,T}) \end{array}}$$

Party U_A (Initiator)   **Party U_B (Responder)**

$$\tau_A \in_R RD_\kappa; \ r_A \in_R \mathcal{R}_{wK}$$
$$(K_A, C_A) \leftarrow$$
$$\quad \mathsf{EnCap}(mpk, ID_B, T, G(\sigma_{A,T}, \tau_A))$$
$$(ek_E, dk_E) \leftarrow \mathsf{wKeyGen}(1^\kappa, r_A) \xrightarrow{ID_A, ID_B, C_A, ek_E}$$

$$\tau_B \in_R RD_\kappa; \ r_B \in_R \mathcal{R}_{wE}$$
$$(K_B, C_B) \leftarrow$$
$$\mathsf{EnCap}(mpk, ID_A, T, G(\sigma_{B,T}, \tau_B))$$
$$\xleftarrow{ID_A, ID_B, C_B, C_E} (K_E, C_E) \leftarrow \mathsf{wEnCap}(ek_E, r_B)$$

$$K_B \leftarrow \mathsf{DeCap}(mpk, dk_{A,T}, C_B)$$
$$K_E \leftarrow \mathsf{wDeCap}(dk_E, C_E)$$
$$K_A' \leftarrow KDF(s, K_A); \ K_B' \leftarrow KDF(s, K_B)$$
$$K_E' \leftarrow KDF(s, K_E)$$
$$ST := (ID_A, ID_B, T, C_A, ek_E, C_B, C_E)$$
$$SK = F(K_A', ST) \oplus F(K_B', ST)$$
$$\oplus F(K_E', ST)$$

$$K_A \leftarrow \mathsf{DeCap}(mpk, dk_{ID_B, T}, C_A)$$
$$K_A' \leftarrow KDF(s, K_A); \ K_B' \leftarrow KDF(s, K_B)$$
$$K_E' \leftarrow KDF(s, K_E)$$
$$ST := (ID_A, ID_B, C_A, ek_E, C_B, C_E)$$
$$SK = F(K_A', ST) \oplus F(K_B', ST)$$
$$\oplus F(K_E', ST)$$

Fig. 2. Our key exchange

$\mathsf{InitEK}(MPK, T, ID_A, SSK_A, CSK_{A,T}, ID_B) \to (ESK_A, EPK_A)$: Party U_A generates random elements $\tau_A \in_R RD_\kappa$ and $r_A \in \mathcal{R}_{wK}$, and computes a pair of a key and a ciphertext $(K_A, C_A) \leftarrow \mathsf{EnCap}(mpk, ID_B, T, G(\sigma_{A,T}, \tau_A))$ of the RHIB-KEM, and a pair of an encapsulation key and a decapsulation key $(ek_E, dk_E) \leftarrow \mathsf{wKeyGen}(1^\kappa, r_A)$ of the KEM. U_A sets $ESK_A = (\tau_A, r_A)$ as its ESK and sends EPK $EPK_A = (ID_A, ID_B, T, C_A, ek_E)$ to U_B.

$\mathsf{ResEK}(MPK, T, ID_B, SSK_B, CSK_{B,T}, ID_A, EPK_A) \to (ESK_B, EPK_B)$: Party U_B generates random elements $\tau_B \in_R RD_\kappa$ and $r_B \in \mathcal{R}_{wE}$, and computes a pair of a key and a ciphertext $(K_B, C_B) \leftarrow \mathsf{EnCap}(mpk, ID_A, T, G(\sigma_{B,T}, \tau_B))$ of the RHIB-KEM, and a pair of a key and a ciphertext $(K_E, C_E) \leftarrow \mathsf{wEnCap}(ek_E, r_B)$ of the KEM. U_B sets $ESK_B = (\tau_B, r_B)$ as its ESK and sends EPK $EPK_B = (ID_A, ID_B, T, C_B, C_E)$ to U_A.

$\mathsf{ResSK}(MPK, T, ID_B, SSK_B, CSK_{B,T}, ID_A, ESK_B, EPK_B, EPK_A) \to SK$: Party U_B decrypts $K_A \leftarrow \mathsf{DeCap}(mpk, dk_{ID_B, T}, C_A)$ and computes $K_A' \leftarrow KDF(s, K_A)$, $K_B' \leftarrow KDF(s, K_B)$, and $K_E' \leftarrow KDF(s, K_E)$. U_B computes session key $SK = F(K_A', ST) \oplus F(K_B', ST) \oplus F(K_E', ST)$ with session transcript $ST = (ID_A, ID_B, T, C_A, ek_E, C_B, C_E)$.

$\mathsf{InitSK}(MPK, T, ID_A, SSK_A, CSK_{A,T}, ID_B, ESK_A, EPK_A, EPK_B) \to SK$: Party U_A decrypts $K_B \leftarrow \mathsf{DeCap}(mpk, dk_{A,T}, C_B)$ and $K_E \leftarrow \mathsf{wDeCap}(dk_E, C_E)$, and computes $K_A' \leftarrow KDF(s, K_A)$, $K_B' \leftarrow KDF(s, K_B)$, and $K_E' \leftarrow KDF(s, K_E)$. U_A computes session key $SK = F(K_A', ST) \oplus F(K_B', ST) \oplus F(K_E', ST)$ with session transcript $ST = (ID_A, ID_B, T, C_A, ek_E, C_B, C_E)$.

Theorem 1. *If RHIB-KEM* (Setup, SKGen, KeyUp, DKGen, EnCap, DeCap) *is selective-IND-CCA secure and is κ-min-entropy RHIB-KEM, KEM* (wKeyGen, wEnCap, wDeCap) *si IND-CPA secure and is κ-min-entropy KEM, function F is a PRF, function G is a TPRF, and function KDF is a KDF, then RHIB-AKE scheme Π is selective secure in the rhid-eCK model.*

We show the proof of Theorem 1 in Appendix A. We give an overview of the security proof. We consider the following six maximal exposure patterns in the rhid-eCK model and the presence of the matching session: a) both SSKs or both CSKs, b) the SSK or CSK of U_A, the ESK of U_B, and the SSK of U_B such that ID_B has been revoked, c) the SSK or CSK of U_A and the ESK of U_B, d) the SSK or CSK of U_B and the ESK of U_A, e) the ESK of U_A, the ESK of U_B, and the SSK of U_B such that ID_B has been revoked, and f) both ESKs.

In case a), K_E is protected by the security of KEM since r_A and r_B are not exposed. In case b), τ_A is not exposed and dk_B is not generated. Therefore, $G(\sigma_{A,T}, \tau_A)$ is hidden and K_A is protected by the security of RHIB-KEM. In case c), τ_A and dk_B are not exposed. Therefore, $G(\sigma_{A,T}, \tau_A)$ is hidden and K_A is protected by the security of RHIB-KEM. In case d), τ_B and dk_A are not exposed. Therefore, $G(\sigma_{B,T}, \tau_B)$ is hidden and K_B is protected by the security of RHIB-KEM. In case e), σ_A is not exposed and dk_B is not generated. Therefore, $G(\sigma_{A,T}, \tau_A)$ is hidden and K_A is protected by the security of RHIB-KEM. In case f), σ_A and dk_A are not exposed. Therefore, $G(\sigma_{A,T}, \tau_A)$ is hidden and K_A is protected by the security of RHIB-KEM.

Then, we transform the rhid-eCK security game so that the session key in the test session is randomly distributed. First, we change the output of the TPRF into a randomly chosen value since one input of the TPRF is hidden from the adversary; therefore, the randomness of the protected RHIB-KEM can be randomly distributed. Second, we change the protected RHIB-KEM key or KEM key into a random key; therefore, the input of KDF is randomly distributed and has sufficient min-entropy. Third, we change the output of KDF into randomly chosen values. Finally, we change one of the PRFs (corresponding to the protected RHIB-KEM or KEM) into a random function. Therefore, the session key in the test session is randomly distributed; thus, there is no advantage to the adversary. We can show a similar proof in non-matching cases.

4   Instantiations

In this section, we provide some RHIB-AKE schemes as concrete instantiations based on the pairings and lattices from our construction in Sect. 3. We consider instantiations of selective-IND-CCA secure RHIB-KEM and IND-CPA secure KEM from Theorem 1. Note that a PRF can be instantiated with HMAC [1] or a block cipher such as AES [7] and both TPRF and KDF can be constructed from a PRF [6,11]. To the best of our knowledge, no selective-IND-CCA secure RHIB-KEM has ever been proposed, but selective-IND-CPA secure RHIBE does exist. We give a method for constructing a selective-IND-CCA secure RHIB-KEM from a selective-IND-CPA secure RHIBE. We then give instantiations of selective-IND-CPA secure RHIBE and IND-CPA secure KEM.

4.1   Construction of RHIB-KEM

We construct a selective IND-CCA secure RHIB-KEM $\Sigma = $ (Setup, SKGen, KeyUp, DKGen, EnCap, DeCap) from a selective IND-CPA secure RHIBE scheme

$\Sigma' = (\mathsf{Setup}, \mathsf{SKGen}, \mathsf{KeyUp}, \mathsf{DKGen}, \mathsf{Enc}, \mathsf{Dec})$. The syntax and security definition of RHIBE follows Katsumata et al. [19]. RHIBE differs from RHIB-KEM in Enc and Dec, and Enc is an algorithm that takes the input to EnCap of RHIB-KEM and a message as additional input, and outputs a ciphertext, while the input and output of Dec is the same as DeCap of RHIB-KEM. The selective-IND-CPA security game for RHIBE is identical to the selective-IND-CPA security game for RHIB-KEM except that instead of an adversary distinguishing a real KEM key and a random key, the adversary distinguishes a ciphertext in one of two messages of its choice.

Let the randomness space of Enc in Σ' be $\mathcal{R}_{Enc}$, $H : \{0,1\}^* \rightarrow \mathcal{R}_{Enc}$ be a hash function with an appropriate output length, modeled as a random oracle. The construction is as follows: Setup, SKGen, KeyUp, and DKGen are the same as Setup', SKGen', KeyUp', and DKGen' respectively.

$\mathsf{EnCap}(mpk, ID, T, r_e) \rightarrow (K, C)$: It chooses K from $\mathcal{KS}_{RH}$ uniformly at random. It computes $C \leftarrow \mathsf{Enc}(mpk, ID, T, K||ID||T||r_e, H(m||ID||T||r_e))$ and outputs K, C.

$\mathsf{DeCap}(mpk, dk_{ID,T}, C) \rightarrow K'$: It computes $K'||ID'||T'||r'_h \leftarrow \mathsf{Dec}(mpk, dk_{ID,T}, C)$. If $C = \mathsf{Enc}(mpk, ID', T', K'||ID'||T'||r'_h, H(K'||ID'||T'||r'_h))$ holds, it outputs K'. Otherwise, it outputs $\bot$.

This construction is the Fujisaki-Okamoto transformation [13] of Σ'. Therefore, RHIB-KEM Σ is selective-IND-CCA secure in the random oracle model if RHIBE Σ' is selective-IND-CPA secure. It is also κ-min-entropy RHIB-KEM when the size of the keyspace is larger than 2^κ and keys are chosen uniformly at random. Note that when encrypting a κ-bit key with a 1-bit encryption scheme such as some lattice-based RHIBEs [19,35], we can encrypt all bits to κ ciphertexts, which can be seen as a ciphertext of a κ-bit key.

4.2 Pairing-Based Instantiations

We can apply selective-IND-CPA secure RHIBE schemes to our RHIB-AKE from the symmetric external Diffie-Hellman (SXDH) assumption [8,9,33] and the ElGamal KEM as an IND-CPA KEM to our RHIB-AKE from the decisional Diffie-Hellman (DDH) assumption. We compared our instantiations of RHIB-AKE scheme with some RHIBEs and the ElGamal KEM in terms of the computational costs and the communication sizes in Table 1 for reference, where $e : \mathbb{G}_1 \times \mathbb{G}_2 \rightarrow \mathbb{G}_T$ is the asymmetric pairing with prime order p used in those RHIBEs, the ElGamal KEM is the scheme on group $\mathbb{G}_1$, ℓ is the hierarchical level of initiator and responder IDs, $D = \lceil \log_2 N \rceil$ for the integer N which is the maximum number of child nodes in each node, P means pairing operation, E_t $(t = 1, 2, T)$ means exponentiation operation on $\mathbb{G}_t$, $\mathrm{len}(g_t)$ $(t = 1, 2, T)$ is the length of a group element of $\mathbb{G}_t$, and $\mathrm{len}(p)$ is the length of a field element of the prime field $\mathbb{Z}_p$. We use Emura et al.'s scheme [8] instantiated by Chen and Wee's hierarchical identity-based encryption (HIBE) scheme [4], Emura et al.'s basic scheme [9] instantiated by Chen and Wee's HIBE scheme [4], and Takayasu's

Table 1. Comparison of our instantiations

Instantiation of RHIBE	Computation (per party)	Communication size
Emura et al. [8] + Chen and Wee [4]	$2((\ell + 4)E_1 + E_T)$ + 3P + 2E_1	$8\text{len}(g_1) + 2\text{len}(g_T)$
Emura et al. [9] + Chen and Wee [4]	$2(\ell(D + 1) + 1)$ $\times ((\ell + 4)E_1 + E_T)$ + 3$(\ell + 1)$P + 2E_1	$2(3\ell(D+1)+4)\text{len}(g_1)$ $+2(\ell(D+1)+1)\text{len}(g_T)$
Takayasu [33]	$2((\ell + 7)E_1 + E_T)$ + (4P + 4E_2) + 2E_1	$10\text{len}(g_1) + 2\text{len}(g_T)$ + 4len(p)

scheme [33] as RHIBEs. In our construction, both initiator and responder need to perform one encapsulation and one decapsulation algorithm of selective-IND-CCA secure RHIB-KEM to perform a key exchange. In other words, they need to perform two encryption algorithms and one decryption algorithm of selective-IND-CPA secure RHIBE. In addition, they require two exponentiation operations on $\mathbb{G}_1$ to be performed in the process of using the ElGamal KEM. The communication size in Table 1 is the sum of the sizes of two ciphertexts of the RHIB-KEM scheme, one encapsulation key of the KEM, and one ciphertext of the KEM, excluding the size of initiator and responder IDs and the time period in the EPKs, sent by them.

In Appendix B, we estimate the performance of implementing instantiated RHIB-AKE scheme as shown in Table 1 on Raspberry Pi3, which is a well-known IoT device. If the hierarchical level ℓ is small (i.e., $\ell = 2$ or 3) and the device is the same spec as the Raspberry Pi3, using RHIB-AKE is quite practical.

4.3 Lattice-Based Instantiations

We can apply selective-IND-CPA secure RHIBE schemes to our RHIB-AKE from the learning with errors (LWE) assumption [19,35]. We can easily obtain IND-CPA secure KEMs with min-entropy κ from IND-CPA secure public-key encryption (PKE) scheme with the message space size larger than 2^{κ}. We can use lattice-based IND-CPA secure PKEs from the (Ring-)LWE assumption [25, 26,28,32]. Estimating performance of instantiated schemes in the same way as pairing-based schemes is a future work.

5 Conclusion

We gave the first definition of an RHIB-AKE scheme and its security model called the rhid-eCK model. An RHIB-AKE scheme allows parties under different PKGs to share a session key by simply trusting a master public key generated by the PKG at the root node, and also allows parties to be revoked. The rhid-eCK security implies that a scheme resists against leakage of all combinations of master, static, current, and ephemeral secret keys except ones trivially break the security. We also proposed the first construction of RHIB-AKE that satisfies the rhid-eCK model and its instantiations based on the parings and lattices.

In this work we only estimated the performance of pairing-based RHIB-AKE schemes. Therefore it is necessary to actually implement schemes and check the performance as future works. We also leave implementing and evaluating the performance of lattice-based RHIB-AKE schemes which are essential to realizing post-quantum authentication.

We believe that our RHIB-AKE scheme can be built as an authentication system consisting of a huge number of IoT devices. Password-based authentication with default or weak passwords is widely used in IoT systems, and we consider replacing such insecure methods with RHIB-AKE will be a new remedy.

A Proof of Theorem 1

In the rhid-eCK security experiment, we suppose that sid^* is the session identifier for the test session and that at most μ sessions are activated. Let κ be the security parameter, and $\mathcal{A}$ be a PPT (in κ) bounded adversary. We also suppose that $\mathcal{A}$ outputs (T^*, ID_A, ID_B) at the beginning of this experiment, where ID_A (resp. ID_B) is party U_A's (resp. U_B's) ID. Suc denotes the event that $\mathcal{A}$ wins.

We consider 14 events covering all cases of $\mathcal{A}$'s behavior: 8 events when the test session has no matching session, and 6 events when it has a matching session. The former can be divided into two main cases, depending on whether the session owner is an initiator or a responder. In each case, we consider the following exposure patterns: 1) the CSK or SSK of the owner and the SSK of the peer such that the peer has been revoked, 2) the ESK of the owner and the SSK of the peer such that the peer has been revoked, 3) the CSK or SSK of the owner, and 4) the ESK of the owner. We consider the event where the owner of the test session is an initiator and the exposure pattern in 1) occurs. That is,

E_1: U_A is the initiator and the owner of sid^*, sid^* has no matching session $\overline{\mathsf{sid}^*}$, $\mathcal{A}$ issues $\mathsf{CSKReveal}(ID_A, T^*)$ or $\mathsf{SSKReveal}(ID)$ for some $ID \succ ID_A$, and $\mathcal{A}$ issues $\mathsf{SSKReveal}(ID)$ such that $ID \succ ID_B$ and $ID \in RL_{pa(ID),T^*-1}$.

We can evaluate the probability of an adversary winning if the other seven events occur as well as if E_1 occurs. The latter, i.e. the events where the test session has a matching session, consists of the six exposure patterns shown in the overview of the proof for Theorem 1 of Sect. 3. We consider the following event.

E_2: There exists a matching session $\overline{\mathsf{sid}^*}$ of sid^*, and $\mathcal{A}$ issues $\mathsf{CSKReveal}(ID_X, T^*)$ or $\mathsf{SSKReveal}(ID)$ for some $ID \succ ID_X$, where $X = A, B$.

We can evaluate the probability of an adversary winning if the other five events occur as well as if E_1 or E_2 occurs. Therefore, we evaluate $|2\Pr[Suc \mid E_i] - 1|$ given the event E_i for $i = 1, 2$ to finish the proof.

Event E_1. We change the interface of oracle queries and the computation of the session key. These instances are gradually changed over hybrid experiments, depending on specific sub-cases. In the last hybrid experiment, the session key in the test session does not contain information of the bit b. Thus, $\mathcal{A}$ only outputs a random guess. Let $\mathbf{H}_0, \ldots, \mathbf{H}_6$ be these hybrid experiments, S_i be the event that $\mathcal{A}$ wins in $\mathbf{H}_i$, T_{cu} be the current time period, and s_A be the number of sessions of U_A which have been activated, which is initialized with 0.

Hybrid Experiment $\mathbf{H}_0$. This experiment is the real experiment for rhid-eCK security and in this experiment, the environment for $\mathcal{A}$ is as defined in the scheme. Thus, $|2\Pr[Suc \mid E_3] - 1| = |2\Pr[S_0 \mid E_3] - 1|$.

Hybrid Experiment $\mathbf{H}_1$. If session identifiers in two sessions are identical, the experiment halts, a bit b' is randomly selected, and $\mathcal{A}$ is considered to output b'. Two session identifiers are identical if and only if the initiators and responders of the two sessions match and the EPKs (C_A, ek_E, C_B, C_E) output by the two sessions are equal. When ek_E and C_E are equal in the two sessions, these K_E are also equal by the correctness of KEM. The probability that these K_E are equal is at most $1/2^\kappa$ by the κ-min-entropy property of KEM. Therefore, $|\Pr[S_0 \mid E_3] - \Pr[S_1 \mid E_3]|$ is negligible for κ.

Hybrid Experiment $\mathbf{H}_2$. The experiment selects an integer $i \in [1, \mu]$ randomly in advance. If $\mathcal{A}$ issues Test query to a session except i-th session of party U_A, the experiment halts, a bit b' is randomly selected, and $\mathcal{A}$ is considered to output b'. Since guess of the test session matches with $\mathcal{A}$'s choice with probability $1/\mu$, $|2\Pr[S_1 \mid E_3] - 1| = \mu \cdot |2\Pr[S_2 \mid E_3] - 1|$.

Hybrid Experiment $\mathbf{H}_3$. The computation of (K_A^*, C_A^*) in the test session is changed. Instead of computing $(K_A^*, C_A^*) \leftarrow \mathsf{EnCap}(mpk, ID_B, T^*, G(\sigma_{A,T}, \tau_A))$, it is changed as $(K_A^*, C_A^*) \leftarrow \mathsf{EnCap}(mpk, ID_B, T^*, R)$, where $R \in_R \mathcal{R}_E$.

Adversary $\mathcal{A}$ does not issue $\mathsf{ESKReveal}(sid^*)$ from the freshness definition. Hence, we construct a distinguisher $\mathcal{D}$ between $(\sigma_{A,T}, G(\sigma_{A,T}, \tau_A))$ and $(\sigma_{A,T}, R)$ for TPRF G from $\mathcal{A}$ in $\mathbf{H}_2$ or $\mathbf{H}_3$. $\mathcal{D}$ simulates obeying the scheme, except that $\mathcal{D}$ computes $(K_A^*, C_A^*) \leftarrow \mathsf{EnCap}(mpk, ID_B, T^*, R)$ for $\mathsf{Send}(\Pi, \mathcal{I}, T^*, ID_A, ID_B)$, where R is either the output of TPRF G or random element. From $\mathcal{A}$'s point of view, the simulation by $\mathcal{D}$ is same as $\mathbf{H}_2$ if R input to $\mathcal{D}$ is the output of TPRF G. Otherwise, the simulation by $\mathcal{D}$ is the same as $\mathbf{H}_3$. Thus, $|\Pr[S_2 \mid E_3] - \Pr[S_3 \mid E_3]|$ is negligible for κ since the advantage of $\mathcal{D}$ is negligible.

Hybrid Experiment $\mathbf{H}_4$. The computation of K_A^* in the test session is changed again. Instead of computing $(K_A^*, C_A^*) \leftarrow \mathsf{EnCap}(mpk, ID_B, T^*, R)$, it is changed as choosing $K_A^* \leftarrow \mathcal{KS}_{RH}$ randomly.

We construct a selective-IND-CCA adversary $\mathcal{B}$ against RHIB-KEM from $\mathcal{A}$ in $\mathbf{H}_3$ or $\mathbf{H}_4$. $\mathcal{B}$ synchronizes the time period in the selective-IND-CCA game with the time period in the rhid-eCK game. $\mathcal{B}$ performs the following steps.

Adversary $\mathcal{B}$ gives the challenge identity/time period pair (ID_B, T^*) to challenger $\mathcal{C}$ and receives a master public key mpk and the key update information $ku_{PKG,1}$ in $T_{cu} = 1$. Then, $\mathcal{B}$ chooses a PRF $F : \mathcal{FS} \times \{0,1\}^* \to \{0,1\}^\kappa$ with key space $\mathcal{FS}$, a TPRF $G : LD_\kappa \times RD_\kappa \to \mathcal{R}_{wE}$ and a KDF $KDF : \{0,1\}^\kappa \times \mathcal{KS} \to \mathcal{FS}$ with randomly chosen public salt $s \in \{0,1\}^\kappa$. $\mathcal{B}$ also sets $MPK = (F, G, s, KDF, mpk)$. $\mathcal{B}$ choose a set of identities $\mathcal{ID}$ for honest parties, including ID_A and ID_B, issues SecKeyGen(ID) for all $ID \in \mathcal{ID}$, and gives $\{ku_{ID,1}\}_{ID\in\mathcal{ID}}$ answered by the oracle to $\mathcal{A}$. $\mathcal{B}$ then gives $MPK, \mathcal{ID}$, and $\{ku_{ID,1}\}_{ID\in\mathcal{ID}}$ to $\mathcal{A}$.

In preparation for $\mathcal{A}$'s oracle queries, $\mathcal{B}$ creates a list $\mathcal{L}_S$ of sessions, a list $\mathcal{L}_{SK}$ of completed session sid and session key SK pairs, and a list $\mathcal{L}_{NCS}$ of non-completed sessions. Initially, these lists are empty sets. $\mathcal{B}$ simulates oracle queries by $\mathcal{A}$ as Fig. 3. When $\mathcal{A}$ outputs a guess b', if $\mathcal{A}$'s guess is correct, $\mathcal{B}$ answers that K^* received by the challenge query is the real key, otherwise it answers that K^* is the random key.

From $\mathcal{A}$'s point of view, the simulation by $\mathcal{B}$ is the same as $\mathbf{H}_3$ if K^* that $\mathcal{B}$ received in the challenge was the real key. Otherwise, the simulation by $\mathcal{B}$ is the same as $\mathbf{H}_4$. Thus, $|\Pr[S_3 \mid E_3] - \Pr[S_4 \mid E_3]|$ is negligible for κ since the advantage of $\mathcal{B}$ is negligible.

Hybrid Experiment $\mathbf{H}_5$. The computation of K'^*_A in the test session is changed. Instead of computing $K'^*_A \leftarrow KDF(s, K^*_A)$, it is changed as choosing $K'^*_A \in \mathcal{KS}$ randomly. K^*_A has sufficient min-entropy since it is randomly chosen in $\mathbf{H}_4$. Thus, $|\Pr[S_4 \mid E_3] - \Pr[S_5 \mid E_3]|$ is negligible for κ by the definition of the KDF.

Hybrid Experiment $\mathbf{H}_6$. The computation of SK^* in the test session is changed. Instead of computing $SK^* = F(K'^*_A, ST) \oplus F(K'^*_B, ST) \oplus F(K'^*_E, ST)$, it is changed as $SK^* = x \oplus F(K'^*_B, ST) \oplus F(K'^*_E, ST)$ where $x \in \{0,1\}^\kappa$ is chosen randomly. We construct a distinguisher $\mathcal{D}'$ between PRF F and a random function from $\mathcal{A}$ in $\mathbf{H}_5$ or $\mathbf{H}_6$. $\mathcal{D}$ simulates the security game obeying the scheme, except that $\mathcal{D}$ computes $SK^* = x \oplus F(K'^*_B, ST) \oplus F(K'^*_E, ST)$ for Send($\Pi, \mathcal{I}, T^*, ID_A, ID_B$), where x is either of the output of F or RF. From $\mathcal{A}$'s point of view, the simulation by $\mathcal{D}'$ is the same as $\mathbf{H}_5$ if the oracle it accesses is PRF F. Otherwise, the simulation by $\mathcal{D}'$ is the same as $\mathbf{H}_6$. Thus, $|\Pr[S_5 \mid E_3] - \Pr[S_6 \mid E_3]|$ is negligible for κ since the advantage of $\mathcal{D}'$ is negligible.

The session key in the test session is perfectly randomized in $\mathbf{H}_6$. We have $\Pr[S_6 \mid E_3] = 1/2$ since $\mathcal{A}$ cannot obtain any advantage from Test query. Thus, $|2\Pr[Suc \mid E_3] - 1|$ is negligible for κ.

Event E_2. We change the interface of oracle queries and the computation of the session key as in the case of E_1. Let $\mathbf{H}'_0, \ldots, \mathbf{H}'_5$ be these hybrid experiments and S'_i be the event that $\mathcal{A}$ wins in experiment $\mathbf{H}'_i$. Hybrid experiments $\mathbf{H}'_0$, $\mathbf{H}'_1$, and $\mathbf{H}'_2$ are the same as $\mathbf{H}_0$, $\mathbf{H}_1$, and $\mathbf{H}_2$ in E_1 respectively.

Hybrid Experiment $\mathbf{H}'_3$. The computation of K^*_E in the test session is changed. Instead of computing $(K^*_E, C^*_E) \leftarrow$ wEnCap(ek^*_E, r_B), it is changed as choosing $K^*_E \in_R \mathcal{KS}_{RH}$ randomly.

We construct an IND-CPA adversary $\mathcal{B}$ from $\mathcal{A}$ in $\mathbf{H}_2'$ or $\mathbf{H}_3'$. $\mathcal{B}$ simulates obeying the scheme, except that $\mathcal{B}$ sets $K_E^* = K^*$ for $\mathsf{Send}(\Pi, \mathcal{R}, T^*, ID_B, ID_A, (C_A^*, ek_E^*))$ and $\mathsf{Send}(\Pi, \mathcal{I}, T^*, ID_A, ID_B, (C_A^*, ek_E^*), (C_B^*, C_E^*))$. From $\mathcal{A}$'s point of view, the simulation by $\mathcal{B}$ is same as $\mathbf{H}_2'$ if K^* received in the challenge is the real key from wEnCap. Otherwise, the simulation by $\mathcal{B}$ is same as $\mathbf{H}_3'$. Thus, $|\Pr[S_2' \mid E_2] - \Pr[S_3' \mid E_2]|$ is negligible for κ since the KEM is IND-CPA secure.

Hybrid Experiments $\mathbf{H}_4'$ *and* $\mathbf{H}_5'$. Hybrid experiments $\mathbf{H}_4'$ and $\mathbf{H}_5'$ are similar to $\mathbf{H}_5$ and $\mathbf{H}_6$ in E_1 respectively, except that the computation of K'^*_E and $F(K'^*_E, ST)$ are changed. Therefore, both $|\Pr[S_3 \mid E_2] - \Pr[S_4 \mid E_2]|$ and $|\Pr[S_4 \mid E_2] - \Pr[S_5 \mid E_2]|$ are also negligible for κ in the same way as E_1.

The session key in the test session is perfectly randomized in $\mathbf{H}_5$. We have $\Pr[S_5 \mid E_2] = 1/2$. Thus, $|2\Pr[Suc \mid E_2] - 1|$ is negligible for κ.

B Estimation

In this appendix, we estimate the performance of our proposed protocol by using our cryptographic library. Our software cryptographic library is written in C, using OpenSSL C library for operations of a multiple precision integer. We used the Gallant–Lambert–Vanstone (GLV) [15] and Galbraith–Lin–Scott (GLS) [14] techniques for the scalar multiplication. We also applied the optimal ate pairing on Barreto-Naehrig curve to the pairing operation. In this work we chose the parameters at the 128-bit security level.

Table 2. Execution environment

CPU	ARMv8 Cortex-A53
Clock	1.2 GHz
RAM	1 GB
Development Board	Raspberry Pi3
OS	32-bit Raspbian

Table 3. Experimental results (msec)

Scalar Mult. on G_1	9.838
Scalar Mult. on G_2	18.661
Pairing	57.088

We summarize our execution environment for our experiment in Table 2. Table 3 contains the average time (in milliseconds) of 100 iterations, and also shows the timing of computing pairing and scalar multiplication on G_1, G_2. An estimated total time for instantiations of RHIB-AKE in Table 1 is within 1 s when the hierarchical level ℓ is small (i.e., $\ell = 2$ or 3). In conclusion, if the device is the same spec as the Raspberry Pi3, using RHIB-AKE is quite practical.

$\mathsf{Send}(\Pi, \mathcal{I}, T_{cu}, ID_\alpha, ID_\beta)$:

    if $(T_{cu} = T^*) \wedge (\alpha = A) \wedge (\beta = B) \wedge (s_A = i - 1)$

        $s_A \leftarrow s_A + 1$

        $(K^*, C_A^*) \leftarrow \mathsf{Challenge}(ID_B, T^*)$

        $r_A^* \leftarrow \mathcal{R}_{wK}$

        $(ek_E^*, dk_E^*) \leftarrow \mathsf{wKeyGen}(1^\kappa, r_A^*)$

        $\mathcal{L}_S \leftarrow \mathcal{L}_S \cup \{(\Pi, T^*, ID_A, ID_B, C_A^*, ek_E^*)\}$

        return $(ID_A, ID_B, T^*, C_A^*, ek_E^*)$

    else

        $(ESK_\alpha, EPK_\alpha) \leftarrow \mathsf{InitEK}(MPK, T_{cu},$

            $ID_\alpha, SSK_\alpha, CSK_{\alpha,T}, ID_\beta)$

        $\mathcal{L}_S \leftarrow \mathcal{L}_S \cup \{(\Pi, T_{cu}, ID_\alpha, ID_\beta, C_\alpha, ek_E)\}$

        if $(\alpha = A)$

            $s_A \leftarrow s_A + 1$

        return EPK_α

$\mathsf{Send}(\Pi, \mathcal{R}, T_{cu}, ID_\beta, ID_\alpha, (C_\alpha, ek_E))$:

    if $(T_{cu} \geq T^*) \wedge (\beta = B)$

        $(ESK_B, EPK_B) \leftarrow \mathsf{ResEK}(MPK, T_{cu},$

            $ID_B, SSK_B, CSK_{B,T_{cu}}, ID_\alpha, EPK_\alpha)$

        $\mathcal{L}_{NCS} \leftarrow \mathcal{L}_{NCS} \cup \{(\Pi, T_{cu}, ID_B, ID_\alpha,$

            $C_\alpha, ek_E, C_B, C_E)\}$ /* $\mathcal{B}$ cannot

compute the session key since ID_B has
been revoked.*/

        return EPK_B

    else

        $(ESK_\beta, EPK_{beta}) \leftarrow \mathsf{ResEK}(MPK, T_{cu},$

            $ID_\beta, SSK_\beta, CSK_{\beta,T_{cu}}, ID_\alpha, EPK_\alpha)$

        if $\exists ID \succ ID_\beta (ID \in RL_{pa(ID), T_{cu}-1})$

            $\mathcal{L}_{NCS} \leftarrow \mathcal{L}_{NCS} \cup \{(\Pi, T_{cu}, ID_\beta,$

              $ID_\alpha, C_\alpha, ek_E, C_\beta, C_E)\}$

        else

            $SK \leftarrow \mathsf{ResSK}(MPK, T_{cu}, ID_\beta, SSK_\beta,$

              $CSK_{\beta,T_{cu}}, ID_\alpha, ESK_\beta, EPK_\beta, EPK_\alpha)$

            $sid \leftarrow (\Pi, T_{cu}, ID_\beta, ID_\alpha, C_\alpha, ek_E,$

              $C_\beta, C_E)$

            $\mathcal{L}_{SK} \leftarrow \mathcal{L}_{SK} \cup \{(sid, SK)\}$

        return EPK_β

$\mathsf{SKReveal}(sid)$:

    if $(sid, SK) \in \mathcal{L}_{SK}$

        return SK

    else

        return $\perp$

$\mathsf{ESKReveal}(sid)$:

    parse $sid =: (*, *, ID_\alpha, *, *, *)$

    find ESK_α

    return ESK_α

$\mathsf{Send}(\Pi, \mathcal{I}, T_{cu}, ID_\alpha, ID_\beta, (C_\alpha, ek_E), (C_\beta, C_E))$:

    if $((\Pi, T_{cu}, ID_\alpha, ID_\beta, C_\alpha, ek_E) \notin \mathcal{L}_S) \vee (\perp \leftarrow$
$\mathsf{DecKeyReveal}(ID_\alpha, T_{cu}))$

        $\mathcal{L}_{NCS} \leftarrow \mathcal{L}_{NCS} \cup \{(\Pi, T_{cu}, ID_\alpha, ID_\beta,$

            $C_\alpha, ek_E, C_\beta, C_E)\}$

        return $\perp$

    else if $(T_{cu} = T^*) \wedge (\alpha = A) \wedge (\beta = B) \wedge (s_A = i)$

        $K_A^* \leftarrow K^*$

        $K_B^* \leftarrow \mathsf{DeCap}(mpk, dk_{A,T^*}, C_B^*)$

        $K_E^* \leftarrow \mathsf{wDeCap}(dk_E^*, C_E^*)$

        for $X = A, B, E$

            $K'^*_X \leftarrow KDF(s, K_X^*)$

        $SK \leftarrow F(K'^*_A, ST) \oplus F(K'^*_B, ST) \oplus$

            $F(K'^*_E, ST)$

        $sid \leftarrow (\Pi, T^*, ID_B, ID_A, C_A^*, ek_E^*,$

            $C_B^*, C_E^*)$

        $\mathcal{L}_{SK} \leftarrow \mathcal{L}_{SK} \cup \{(sid, SK)\}$

    else

        $SK \leftarrow \mathsf{InitSK}(MPK, T_{cu}, ID_\alpha, SSK_\alpha,$

            $CSK_{\alpha,T_{cu}}, ID_\beta, ESK_\alpha, EPK_\alpha, EPK_\beta)$

        $sid \leftarrow (\Pi, T_{cu}, ID_\alpha, ID_\beta, C_\alpha, ek_E, C_\beta, C_E)$

        $\mathcal{L}_{SK} \leftarrow \mathcal{L}_{SK} \cup \{(sid, SK)\}$

    return SUCCESS

$\mathsf{SSKReveal}(ID_\alpha)$:

    $sk_\alpha \leftarrow \mathsf{SecKeyReveal}(ID_\alpha)$

    return sk_α

$\mathsf{CSKReveal}(ID_\alpha, T)$:

    $dk_{\alpha,T} \leftarrow \mathsf{DecKeyReveal}(ID_\alpha, T)$

    $\sigma_{\alpha,T} \leftarrow LD_\kappa$

    return $(dk_{\alpha,T}, \sigma_{\alpha,T})$

$\mathsf{EstablishParty}(\alpha, ID_\alpha)$:

    if $(pa(ID_\alpha) \in \mathcal{ID}) \wedge (ID_\alpha \notin \mathcal{ID})$

        issue $\mathsf{SecKeyGen}(ID_\alpha)$

        $sk_\alpha \leftarrow \mathsf{SecKeyReveal}(ID_\alpha)$

        $\mathcal{ID} \leftarrow \mathcal{ID} \cup \{ID_\alpha\}$

        return sk_α

$\mathsf{Revoke}(RL)$:

    $\{ku_{ID,T_{cu}}\}_{ID \in \in \mathcal{ID} \setminus RL} \leftarrow \mathsf{Update}(RL)$

    return $\{ku_{ID,T_{cu}}\}_{ID \in \in \mathcal{ID} \setminus RL}$

$\mathsf{Test}(sid)$:

    $(sid, SK_1) \leftarrow \mathcal{L}_{SK}$

    $SK_0 \leftarrow \{0, 1\}^\kappa$

    $b \leftarrow \{0, 1\}$

    return SK_b

Fig. 3. Query simulation

References

1. Bellare, M., Canetti, R., Krawczyk, H.: Keying hash functions for message authentication. In: Koblitz, N. (ed.) CRYPTO 1996. LNCS, vol. 1109, pp. 1–15. Springer, Heidelberg (1996). https://doi.org/10.1007/3-540-68697-5_1
2. Boldyreva, A., Goyal, V., Kumar, V.: Identity-based encryption with efficient revocation. In: Proceedings of the 15th ACM Conference on Computer and Communications Security, CCS 2008, pp. 417–426. Association for Computing Machinery, New York (2008). https://doi.org/10.1145/1455770.1455823
3. Boneh, D., Franklin, M.: Identity-based encryption from the Weil pairing. In: Kilian, J. (ed.) CRYPTO 2001. LNCS, vol. 2139, pp. 213–229. Springer, Heidelberg (2001). https://doi.org/10.1007/3-540-44647-8_13
4. Chen, J., Wee, H.: Dual system groups and its applications – compact HIBE and more. Cryptology ePrint Archive, Report 2014/265 (2014). https://eprint.iacr.org/2014/265
5. Chen, L., Cheng, Z., Smart, N.P.: Identity-based key agreement protocols from pairings. Int. J. Inf. Secur. **6**(4), 213–241 (2007). https://doi.org/10.1007/s10207-006-0011-9
6. Dachman-Soled, D., Gennaro, R., Krawczyk, H., Malkin, T.: Computational extractors and pseudorandomness. In: Cramer, R. (ed.) TCC 2012. LNCS, vol. 7194, pp. 383–403. Springer, Heidelberg (2012). https://doi.org/10.1007/978-3-642-28914-9_22
7. Daemen, J., Rijmen, V.: The Design of Rijndael: AES-Advanced Encryption Standard. Springer, Cham (2002). https://doi.org/10.1007/978-3-662-60769-5
8. Emura, K., Takayasu, A., Watanabe, Y.: Adaptively secure revocable hierarchical IBE from k-linear assumption. Cryptology ePrint Archive, Report 2020/886 (2020). https://eprint.iacr.org/2020/886
9. Emura, K., Takayasu, A., Watanabe, Y.: Generic constructions of revocable hierarchical identity-based encryption. Cryptology ePrint Archive, Report 2021/515 (2021). https://eprint.iacr.org/2021/515
10. Fujioka, A., Hoshino, F., Kobayashi, T., Suzuki, K., Ustaoglu, B., Yoneyama, K.: ID-ECK secure ID-based authenticated key exchange on symmetric and asymmetric pairing. IEICE Trans. Fundam. Electron. Commun. Comput. Sci. **E96.A**(6), 1139–1155 (2013). https://doi.org/10.1587/transfun.E96.A.1139
11. Fujioka, A., Suzuki, K., Xagawa, K., Yoneyama, K.: Strongly secure authenticated key exchange from factoring, codes, and lattices. Des. Codes Crypt. **76**(3), 469–504 (2014). https://doi.org/10.1007/s10623-014-9972-2
12. Fujioka, A., Suzuki, K., Yoneyama, K.: Hierarchical ID-based authenticated key exchange resilient to ephemeral key leakage. In: Echizen, I., Kunihiro, N., Sasaki, R. (eds.) IWSEC 2010. LNCS, vol. 6434, pp. 164–180. Springer, Heidelberg (2010). https://doi.org/10.1007/978-3-642-16825-3_12
13. Fujisaki, E., Okamoto, T.: How to enhance the security of public-key encryption at minimum cost. In: Imai, H., Zheng, Y. (eds.) PKC 1999. LNCS, vol. 1560, pp. 53–68. Springer, Heidelberg (1999). https://doi.org/10.1007/3-540-49162-7_5
14. Galbraith, S.D., Lin, X., Scott, M.: Endomorphisms for faster elliptic curve cryptography on a large class of curves. J. Cryptol. **24**(3), 446–469 (2011). https://doi.org/10.1007/s00145-010-9065-y
15. Gallant, R.P., Lambert, R.J., Vanstone, S.A.: Faster point multiplication on elliptic curves with efficient endomorphisms. In: Kilian, J. (ed.) CRYPTO 2001. LNCS, vol. 2139, pp. 190–200. Springer, Heidelberg (2001). https://doi.org/10.1007/3-540-44647-8_11

16. Huang, H., Cao, Z.: An ID-based authenticated key exchange protocol based on bilinear Diffie-Hellman problem. In: Proceedings of the 4th International Symposium on Information, Computer, and Communications Security, ASIACCS 2009, pp. 333–342. Association for Computing Machinery, New York (2009). https://doi.org/10.1145/1533057.1533101

17. Ishibashi, R., Yoneyama, K.: Adaptive-ID secure hierarchical ID-based authenticated key exchange under standard assumptions without random oracles. In: Sako, K., Tippenhauer, N.O. (eds.) ACNS 2021. LNCS, vol. 12726, pp. 3–27. Springer, Cham (2021). https://doi.org/10.1007/978-3-030-78372-3_1

18. Ishida, Y., Watanabe, Y., Shikata, J.: Constructions of CCA-secure revocable identity-based encryption. In: Foo, E., Stebila, D. (eds.) ACISP 2015. LNCS, vol. 9144, pp. 174–191. Springer, Cham (2015). https://doi.org/10.1007/978-3-319-19962-7_11

19. Katsumata, S., Matsuda, T., Takayasu, A.: Lattice-based revocable (hierarchical) IBE with decryption key exposure resistance. In: Lin, D., Sako, K. (eds.) PKC 2019. LNCS, vol. 11443, pp. 441–471. Springer, Cham (2019). https://doi.org/10.1007/978-3-030-17259-6_15

20. Krawczyk, H.: Cryptographic extraction and key derivation: the HKDF scheme. In: Rabin, T. (ed.) CRYPTO 2010. LNCS, vol. 6223, pp. 631–648. Springer, Heidelberg (2010). https://doi.org/10.1007/978-3-642-14623-7_34

21. Kurosawa, K., Furukawa, J.: 2-pass key exchange protocols from CPA-secure KEM. In: Benaloh, J. (ed.) CT-RSA 2014. LNCS, vol. 8366, pp. 385–401. Springer, Cham (2014). https://doi.org/10.1007/978-3-319-04852-9_20

22. LaMacchia, B., Lauter, K., Mityagin, A.: Stronger security of authenticated key exchange. In: Susilo, W., Liu, J.K., Mu, Y. (eds.) ProvSec 2007. LNCS, vol. 4784, pp. 1–16. Springer, Heidelberg (2007). https://doi.org/10.1007/978-3-540-75670-5_1

23. Lee, K., Kim, J.S.: A generic approach to build revocable hierarchical identity-based encryption. Cryptology ePrint Archive, Report 2021/502 (2021). https://eprint.iacr.org/2021/502

24. Lee, K., Park, S.: Revocable hierarchical identity-based encryption with shorter private keys and update keys. Des. Codes Cryptogr. **86**(10), 2407–2440 (2018). https://doi.org/10.1007/s10623-017-0453-2

25. Lindner, R., Peikert, C.: Better key sizes (and attacks) for LWE-based encryption. In: Kiayias, A. (ed.) CT-RSA 2011. LNCS, vol. 6558, pp. 319–339. Springer, Heidelberg (2011). https://doi.org/10.1007/978-3-642-19074-2_21

26. Lyubashevsky, V., Peikert, C., Regev, O.: On ideal lattices and learning with errors over rings. In: Gilbert, H. (ed.) EUROCRYPT 2010. LNCS, vol. 6110, pp. 1–23. Springer, Heidelberg (2010). https://doi.org/10.1007/978-3-642-13190-5_1

27. McCullagh, N., Barreto, P.S.L.M.: A new two-party identity-based authenticated key agreement. In: Menezes, A. (ed.) CT-RSA 2005. LNCS, vol. 3376, pp. 262–274. Springer, Heidelberg (2005). https://doi.org/10.1007/978-3-540-30574-3_18

28. Peikert, C., Waters, B.: Lossy trapdoor functions and their applications. In: Proceedings of the Fortieth Annual ACM Symposium on Theory of Computing, STOC 2008, pp. 187–196. Association for Computing Machinery, New York (2008). https://doi.org/10.1145/1374376.1374406

29. Seo, J.H., Emura, K.: Efficient delegation of key generation and revocation functionalities in identity-based encryption. In: Dawson, E. (ed.) CT-RSA 2013. LNCS, vol. 7779, pp. 343–358. Springer, Heidelberg (2013). https://doi.org/10.1007/978-3-642-36095-4_22

30. Seo, J.H., Emura, K.: Revocable hierarchical identity-based encryption. Theor. Comput. Sci. **542**, 44–62 (2014)

31. Seo, J.H., Emura, K.: Revocable hierarchical identity-based encryption: history-free update, security against insiders, and short ciphertexts. In: Nyberg, K. (ed.) CT-RSA 2015. LNCS, vol. 9048, pp. 106–123. Springer, Cham (2015). https://doi.org/10.1007/978-3-319-16715-2_6

32. Stehlé, D., Steinfeld, R., Tanaka, K., Xagawa, K.: Efficient public key encryption based on ideal lattices. In: Matsui, M. (ed.) ASIACRYPT 2009. LNCS, vol. 5912, pp. 617–635. Springer, Heidelberg (2009). https://doi.org/10.1007/978-3-642-10366-7_36

33. Takayasu, A.: More efficient adaptively secure revocable hierarchical identity-based encryption with compact ciphertexts: achieving shorter keys and tighter reductions. Cryptology ePrint Archive, Report 2021/539 (2021). https://eprint.iacr.org/2021/539

34. Tomida, J., Fujioka, A., Nagai, A., Suzuki, K.: Strongly secure identity-based key exchange with single pairing operation. In: Sako, K., Schneider, S., Ryan, P.Y.A. (eds.) ESORICS 2019. LNCS, vol. 11736, pp. 484–503. Springer, Cham (2019). https://doi.org/10.1007/978-3-030-29962-0_23

35. Wang, S., Zhang, J., He, J., Wang, H., Li, C.: Simplified revocable hierarchical identity-based encryption from lattices. In: Mu, Y., Deng, R.H., Huang, X. (eds.) CANS 2019. LNCS, vol. 11829, pp. 99–119. Springer, Cham (2019). https://doi.org/10.1007/978-3-030-31578-8_6

36. Yoneyama, K.: Practical and exposure-resilient hierarchical ID-based authenticated key exchange without random oracles. IEICE Trans. Fundam. Electron. Commun. Comput. Sci. **E97.A**(6), 1335–1344 (2014). https://doi.org/10.1587/transfun.E97.A.1335

Towards Witness Encryption Without Multilinear Maps

Gwangbae Choi[1]([✉]) and Serge Vaudenay[2]

[1] Fasoo, Seoul, Korea
gwangbae.choi@hotmail.com
[2] Ecole Polytechnique Fédérale de Lausanne (EPFL), Lausanne, Switzerland
serge.vaudenay@epfl.ch

Abstract. Current proposals of extractable witness encryption are based on multilinear maps. In this paper, we propose a new construction without.

We propose the notion of hidden group with hashing and make an extractable witness encryption from it. We show that the construction is secure in a generic model. We propose a concrete construction based on RSA-related problems. Namely, we use an extension of the knowledge-of-exponent assumption and the order problem. Our construction allows to encrypt for an instance of the subset sum problem (actually, a multi-dimensional variant of it) for which short solutions to the homogeneous equation are hard to find. Alas, we do not propose any reduction from a known NP-complete problem.

Keywords: Witness key encapsulation mechanism · Subset sum problem

1 Introduction

Witness encryption was first proposed by Garg et al. [10]. The idea is that a secret is encrypted together with an instance x of an NP language. The resulted ciphertext can be decrypted by using a witness ω for the instance, which is verified by a relation $R(x, \omega)$.

Witness encryption based on an NP-complete language is a powerful primitive as it implies a witness encryption based on any NP language. Anyone can encrypt a message for anyone who could solve a given equation $R(x, .)$. This is very nice to encrypt a bounty. It can also be used to send secrets to the future [14].

There are several kinds of witness encryption schemes. Regular schemes offer IND-CPA security when the encryption key x does *not* belong to the language. However, in that case, decryption is not possible either. Extractable schemes are such that for any efficient adversary, there must exist an efficient extractor such that either it is hard for the adversary to decrypt, or it is easy for the extractor having the same inputs to produce a witness. Like obfuscation, existing constructions of extractable witness encryption are based on multilinear maps which are currently heavy algorithms. To mitigate their complexity, offline schemes allow efficient encryption but have an additional setup algorithm which does the heavy part of the scheme.

Cramer and Shoup proposed the notion of Hash-proof systems which is also based on NP languages [5]. Those systems use a special hash function which has a public key and a secret key. We can hash an instance x either with its witness ω together with the public key, or with the secret key alone. Somehow, the secret key is a wildcard for a missing witness. Hash-proof systems are used to build *CCA-secure KEM* [6]. We encapsulate by picking a random (x, ω) pair in the relation R and hashing x to obtain a key $K = h_{\mathsf{pk},\omega}(x)$ and it encapsulates into $\mathsf{ct} = x$. We decapsulate using the secret key: $K = h_{\mathsf{sk}}(\mathsf{ct})$. In witness encryption, the construction is upside down: we encapsulate with x by generating a fresh key pair $(\mathsf{sk}, \mathsf{pk})$ for the hash-proof system and we hash using the secret key: $K = h_{\mathsf{sk}}(x)$ and $\mathsf{ct} = \mathsf{pk}$. We decapsulate by hashing with a witness and the public key: $K = h_{\mathsf{ct},\omega}(x)$ One problem is to build a hash-proof system with extractable security for an NP-complete problem.

The notion of security with extractor of the witness encryption is non-falsifiable [15]. There exist other non-falsifiable notions which use extractors. For instance, the knowledge-of-exponent assumption (KEA) was proposed by Damgård in 1991 [7]. It says that for any efficient adversary, there must exist an efficient extractor such that given (g, g^y) in a given group, it is hard, either for the adversary to construct a pair of form (g^x, g^{xy}), or for the extractor having the same input not to produce x. KEA can be proven in the *generic group model* [1,8].

Witness encryption can be achieved using obfuscation: the ciphertext is an obfuscated program which takes as input ω and releases the plaintext if $R(x, \omega)$ holds. As shown by Chvojka et al. [3], this can also be turned into an offline witness encryption scheme. An alternate approach from Faonio et al. [9] relies on *predictable arguments of knowledge*. It was used by Barta et al. [2] to construct a solution based on the approximation problem for the minimal distance of a linear code.

Our Contribution. In this paper, we construct an efficient witness encryption scheme[1] WKEM for a variant of the subset sum problem. Concretely, an instance is a tuple $x = (x_1, \ldots, x_t, s)$ of vectors x_i and s, a witness is a vector $\omega = (a_1, \ldots, a_t)$ of non-negative *small* integers a_i, and $R(x, \omega)$ is equivalent to the vectorial equation $a_1 x_1 + \cdots + a_t x_t = s$. In the regular subset sum problem, all a_i must be boolean and the vectors x_i and s are actually scalars (i.e. the dimension is $d = 1$). Here, we require the a_i to be polynomially bounded and vectors have some dimension d. We also require the homogeneous equation $a_1' x_1 + \cdots + a_t' x_t = 0$ to have no small integer solution a_i' (positive or negative), which is a severe

---

[1] Actually, we construct a KEM.

limitation of our construction. So, we require x to belong to a language $L_1 \cap L_2$ with $L_1 \in$ NP (the Multi-SS problem) and $L_2 \in$ coNP (the co-HLE problem). Alternately, we require such homogeneous relation to be hard to find.

Our encryption scheme is based on the following idea which we explain for $d = 1$ as follows: encryption generates a (n, ℓ, g, k) tuple such that g has multiplicative order ℓ modulo n and k is invertible modulo ℓ. The values k and ℓ are not revealed. Then, the ciphertext consists of $(n, g, y_1, \ldots, y_t)$ with $y_i = k^{x_i} \bmod \ell$ and the encapsulated key is $h = g^{k^s} \bmod n$. It is believed that given a set of $(x_i, k^{x_i} \bmod \ell)$ pairs with large x_i, it is hard to recover a multiple of ℓ, even when given (n, g, h), and unless a linear relation with small coefficients is known about the x_i. The decryption rebuilds $h = g^{y_1^{a_1} \cdots y_t^{a_t}} \bmod n$ from the ciphertext and the witness. The key idea in the security is that the operations need to be done in the hidden group of residues modulo ℓ. The product $y_1^{a_1} \cdots y_t^{a_t}$ can only be done over the integers since ℓ is unknown, and is feasible because the a_i's are small. However, the basis-g exponential reduces it modulo ℓ in a hidden manner.

Interestingly, computing the products $y_1^{a_1} \cdots y_t^{a_t}$ from reduced y_i values resembles to the notion of *graded encoding*, which is the basis of currently existing multilinear maps. In our construction, a 1-level encoding of x is $k^x \bmod \ell$. Hence, each y_i is a 1-level encoding of x_i and $y_1^{a_1} \cdots y_t^{a_t}$ is an encoding of $a_1 x_1 + \cdots + a_t x_t$ of level $a_1 + \cdots + a_t$. The level of encoding is somehow proportional to the size of the integer.

Our construction is based on a homomorphism mapping x_i to y_i from $\mathbb{Z}^d$ to the hidden group $\mathbb{Z}_\ell^*$. This hidden group is included in a larger structure $\mathbb{Z}$. We can do multiplications in $\mathbb{Z}$ which are compatible with the hidden group. However, we later need to reduce elements in a compatible and hidden manner. We call this reduction operation *hashing*. In our construction, it is done by the $y \mapsto g^y \bmod n$ function. We formalize the notion of hidden group with hashing (HiGH).

To be able to prove security, we need an assumption which generalizes the knowledge-of-exponent assumption: we need to say that computing h implies being able to write it as the exponential of some (multiplicative) linear combination of the y_i's with known exponents. To do so, we must make the group sparse over the integers (so that we cannot find element by chance). For that, we duplicate the basis-k exponential like in the Cramer-Shoup techniques [4]. Then, we formulate two computational assumptions. The first one, which we call the *kernel assumption* says that it is hard to find a non-zero vector x mapping to 1 by the homomorphism, with only public information (i.e., the ciphertext). We show that it is equivalent to the order assumption for the RSA modulus ℓ: given a random $k \in \mathbf{Z}_\ell^*$, it is hard to find a multiple of the order of k. The second one, which is non-standard, is similar to the knowledge of exponent assumption, and so is non-falsifiable. The game will be defined as the HiGH-KE game in the paper. A simplification of this game (in dimension $d = 1$) for our favorite instance looks like what follows:

Input: x:
1: parse $x = (x_1, \ldots, x_t, \mathsf{aux})$
2: pick RSA moduli ℓ and $n = pq$ such that ℓ divides $p - 1$ and $q - 1$
3: pick g of order ℓ in $\mathbf{Z}_n^*$
4: pick $k \in \mathbf{Z}_\ell^*$ and $\theta \in \mathbf{Z}_{\varphi(\ell)}^*$
5: $y_i \leftarrow (k^{x_i}, k^{\theta x_i}) \bmod \ell$, $i = 1, \ldots, t$
6: $\mathcal{A}'(x_1, \ldots, x_t, y_1, \ldots, y_t, n, g, \mathsf{aux}) \rightarrow h$
7: **if** there is no ξ such that $h = (g^{k^\xi}, g^{k^{\theta\xi}}) \bmod n$ **then** abort
8: set ρ to the random coins used by $\mathcal{A}'$
9: $\mathcal{E}'(x_1, \ldots, x_t, y_1, \ldots, y_t, n, g, \mathsf{aux}, \rho) \rightarrow (1^{a_1}, \ldots, 1^{a_t})$
10: **if** $h = (g^{k^{a_1 x_1 + \cdots + a_t x_t}}, g^{\theta(a_1 x_1 + \cdots + a_t x_t)}) \bmod n$ **then return** 0
11: **return** 1

Essentially, we want that for every adversary $\mathcal{A}'$, there exists an extractor $\mathcal{E}'$ such that if $\mathcal{A}'$ succeeds to forge the exponential of a pair of form $(k^\xi, k^{\theta\xi})$, then the extractor finds ξ as a linear combination $\xi = a_1 x_1 + \cdots + a_t x_t \bmod \ell$ with small non-negative integers a_i. In other words, the only way to forge such a pair is to pick some small a_i and to compute $y_1^{a_1} \cdots y_t^{a_t}$ over the integers (because ℓ is not hidden).

We prove the security in a generic HiGH model. We also propose an RSA-based HiGH for which we prove security (under our non-standard but realistic assumptions but without the generic model) for instances x which have no $a_1 x_1 + \cdots + a_t x_t = 0$ relation with small a_i.

Structure of this Paper. We start with preliminaries in Sect. 2. We define NP languages, the subset sum problem SS, the multidimensional subset sum problem Multi-SS, and the homogeneous linear equation problem HLE. In Sect. 3, we define WKEM, a witness key encapsulation mechanism. We define the extractable security notions extractable-OW and IND-extractable. We show that IND-extractable is a stronger security notion than extractable-OW and we show how to construct an IND-extractable WKEM from an extractable-OW WKEM using a random oracle. In Sect. 4, we define our notion of Hidden Group With Hashing (HiGH). We prove basic properties and define two security notions for HiGH: the knowledge exponent assumption (HiGH-KE) and the kernel assumption (HiGH-Ker). In Sect. 5, we propose a generic construction of an extractable WKEM from a HiGH satisfying both properties. In Sect. 6, we propose a construction of a HiGH based on RSA. We finally conclude. Due to lack of space, some proofs are provided in the full version of this paper. Our full version also includes a definition for a generic HiGH model and prove security in this model.

2   Preliminaries

We denote the indicator function by $\mathbb{1}_r$. We consider "words" as bitstrings (i.e. we use a binary alphabet) and $|x|$ denotes the bit length of x. 1^a is the bitstring of length a with all bits set to 1. $\#S$ denotes the cardinality of the set S. $\mathsf{negl}(\lambda)$

denotes any function f such that for all $c > 0$, for any sufficiently large λ, we have $|f(\lambda)| < \frac{1}{\lambda^c}$. Similarly, $\mathsf{Poly}(\lambda)$ denotes any function f such that there exists $c > 0$ such that for any sufficiently large λ, we have $|f(\lambda)| < \lambda^c$. For simplicity, all advantages are considered as a function of λ which is omitted.

Definition 1 (NP language). *Let L be a language. The language L is in the class NP if there exists a predicate R and a polynomial P such that L is the set of all words x for which there exists a witness ω satisfying $R(x, \omega)$ and $|\omega| \leq P(|x|)$, and if we can compute R in time polynomially bounded in terms of the size of x.*

It is important to stress that in what follows, the predicate is actually more important than the language itself.

Our construction will be based on a variation Multi-SS of the subset sum problem SS. We first define the subset sum problem. Intuitively, the subset sum problem is a problem of finding a subset of a given set of integers whose sum is equal to a target value. The Subset Sum (SS) NP language is defined by:

Instance: a tuple $x = (x_1, \ldots, x_t, s)$ of non-negative integers.
Witness: a tuple $\omega = (a_1, \ldots, a_t)$ of bits $a_i \in \{0, 1\}$, $i = 1, \ldots, t$.
Predicate $R(x, \omega)$: $a_1 x_1 + \cdots + a_t x_t = s$.

It is well-known that SS is NP-complete [13]. We extend SS to the Multi-SS predicate R in dimension d by:

Instance: a tuple $x = (x_1, \ldots, x_t, s)$ of *vectors* of non-negative integers in $\mathbb{Z}^d$.
Witness: a tuple $\omega = (1^{a_1}, \ldots, 1^{a_t})$ with non-negative integers a_i, $i = 1, \ldots, t$.
Predicate $R(x, \omega)$: $a_1 x_1 + \cdots + a_t x_t = s$.

In Multi-SS, we write $\omega = (1^{a_1}, \ldots, 1^{a_t})$ to stress that the a_i must be polynomially bounded in terms of $|x|$. It is easy to show that for $d \geq 1$, over the space $\mathbb{Z}^d$, the problem is NP-complete. We give here a similar reduction as the one by Groth et al. [12]:

1. Start from SAT which is NP-complete.
2. Reduce to a system of Boolean equations, all of form u NOR $v = w$.
3. Reduce to a system of linear equations over $\mathbb{N}$ with positive integral coefficients.
   - Each Boolean literal z is mapped to a pair of unknowns (z_+, z_-) coming with a linear equation $z_+ + z_- = 1$.
   - Each u NOR $v = w$ equation is mapped to a pair of unknowns (g_+, g_-) coming with a linear equation $g_+ + g_- = 1$.
   - Each u NOR $v = w$ equation is mapped to a linear equation $u_+ + v_+ + g_+ + 2w_- = 2$.
4. Reduce to Multi-SS by writing the system of equations as $X \times a = s$ where X is a $d \times t$ matrix of coefficients in $\{0, 1, 2\}$, a is a vector of t unknowns, and s is a vector of d coefficients in $\{1, 2\}$.

Hence, Multi-SS seeks vectors a_i of non-negatives as opposed to Booleans a_i for SS. Unfortunately, this reduction introduces short solutions to the homogeneous problem like $z_+ = g_+ = +1$ and $z_- = g_- = -1$ for all z and g. The problem is that such solution will make our construction insecure. Namely, we consider the *Homogeneous Linear Equation* problem (HLE):

> **Instance**: a tuple $x = (x_1, \dots, x_t)$ of *vectors* in $\mathbb{Z}^d$.
> **Witness**: a tuple $\omega = (1^{a_1}, \dots, 1^{a_t}, b_1, \dots, b_t)$ with non-negative integers a_i and bits $b_i \in \{0, 1\}$, $i = 1, \dots, t$, with $(a_1, \dots, a_t) \neq (0, \dots, 0)$.
> **Predicate** $R(x, \omega)$: $(-1)^{b_1} a_1 x_1 + \cdots + (-1)^{b_t} a_t x_t = 0$.

3   Primitives of Witness Key Encapsulation Mechanism

We adapt the primitives of witness encryption from Garg et al. [10] so that we have a key encapsulation mechanism instead of a cryptosystem.

Definition 2 (Witness key encapsulation mechanism (WKEM)). *Let R be an NP predicate. A witness key encapsulation mechanism for R consists of the following two algorithms and a domain $\mathcal{K}_\lambda$ defined by a security parameter λ:*

- Enc$(1^\lambda, x) \rightarrow K, $ct*: A probabilistic polynomial-time algorithm which takes a security parameter λ and a word x as inputs, and outputs a plaintext $K \in \mathcal{K}_\lambda$ and a ciphertext* ct*.*
- Dec$(\omega, ct) \rightarrow K/\bot$*: A deterministic polynomial-time algorithm which takes a witness ω and a ciphertext* ct *as inputs, and outputs a plaintext K or $\bot$ which indicates the decryption failure.*

Then, the following property is satisfied:

- **Correctness***: For any security parameter λ, for any word x and witness ω such that $R(x, \omega)$ is true, we have*

$$\Pr_\gamma \left[\mathsf{Dec}(\omega, \mathsf{ct}) = K | (K, \mathsf{ct}) \leftarrow \mathsf{Enc}(1^\lambda, x; \gamma) \right] = 1.$$

Based on the security notions of extractable witness encryption [11] and KEM [6], we define extractable indistinguishability as follows.

Definition 3 (Extractable indistinguishability). *Let $(\mathcal{K}_\lambda, \mathsf{Enc}, \mathsf{Dec})$ be a WKEM for R. Given an adversary $\mathcal{A}$, we define the following game with $b \in \{0, 1\}$:*

Game IND-EWE$^b_\mathcal{A}(1^\lambda, x)$*:*

> *1:* Enc$(1^\lambda, x) \rightarrow K_1, $ct
> *2: pick a random $K_0 \in \mathcal{K}_\lambda$*
> *3:* $\mathcal{A}(x, K_b, \mathsf{ct}) \rightarrow r$
> *4:* **return** *r*

We define the advantage of $\mathcal{A}$ by

$$\mathsf{Adv}_{\mathcal{A}}^{\mathsf{IND\text{-}EWE}}(x) = \Pr[\mathsf{IND\text{-}EWE}_{\mathcal{A}}^{1}(x) \to 1] - \Pr[\mathsf{IND\text{-}EWE}_{\mathcal{A}}^{0}(x) \to 1]$$

We say that WKEM *is extractable indistinguishable for a set X of instances x if for any probabilistic and polynomial-time* IND-EWE *adversary $\mathcal{A}$, there exists a probabilistic and polynomial-time extractor $\mathcal{E}$ such that for all $x \in X$, $\mathcal{E}(x)$ outputs a witness of x with probability at least $\mathsf{Adv}_{\mathcal{A}}^{\mathsf{IND\text{-}EWE}}(x)$ or at least $\frac{1}{2}$ up to a negligible term. More precisely,*

$$\forall x \in X \quad \Pr[R(x, \mathcal{E}(x))] \geq \min\left(\mathsf{Adv}_{\mathcal{A}}^{\mathsf{IND\text{-}EWE}}(x), \frac{1}{2}\right) - \mathsf{negl}(\lambda)$$

Note that if no witness exists for x, $\mathcal{E}(x)$ outputs a witness with null probability. Hence, it must be the case that $\mathsf{Adv}_{\mathcal{A}}^{\mathsf{IND\text{-}EWE}}(x) = \mathsf{negl}(\lambda)$. This property for all x without witness is actually the weaker (non-extractable) security notion of witness encryption [10].

Ideally, we would adopt this definition for the set X of all possible words. The reason why we introduce X is to avoid some "pathological" words making our construction insecure, which is a limitation of our construction. As pathological words are also characterized by an NP relation, X can be seen as a common subset of NP and coNP languages. Decryption requires a witness for x belonging to the NP language.

Chvojka et al. [3] requires $\Pr[R(x, \mathcal{E}(x))]$ to be "non-negligible" (without defining what this means). In our notion, we require more. Namely, we require extraction to be as effective as the attack.

The reason why the extractor extracts with probability "at least $\mathsf{Adv} - \mathsf{negl}$ or at least $\frac{1}{2}$" is that when $\mathsf{Adv}_{\mathcal{A}}^{\mathsf{IND\text{-}EWE}}$ is close to 1, we do not care if the extractor is not as good as the adversary, which could be unnecessarily hard to prove. We only care that it is either "substantially good" (i.e. at least $\frac{1}{2}$) or at least as good as $\mathcal{A}$. This will become necessary when we will need to amplify the probability of success of an extractor, as it will be the case in the proof of Theorem 6.

Faonio et al. [9, Def. 3] use instead $\Pr[R(x, \mathcal{E}(x))] \geq \frac{1}{2}\mathsf{Adv}_{\mathcal{A}}^{\mathsf{IND\text{-}EWE}}(x)$ which is probably more elegant but not tight.

We define extractable one-way security, which is a weaker security notion than extractable indistinguishability. Later, we show that an extractable one-way scheme can be transformed into an extractable indistinguishable one by generic transformation. Hence, we will be able to focus on making an extractable one-way WKEM.

Definition 4 (Extractable one-wayness). *Let $(\mathcal{K}_{\lambda}, \mathsf{Enc}, \mathsf{Dec})$ be a* WKEM *for R. Given an adversary $\mathcal{A}$, we define the following game:*

Game $\mathsf{OW\text{-}EWE}_{\mathcal{A}}(1^{\lambda}, x)$:

1: *(ROM only) pick a random function H*
2: $\mathsf{Enc}(1^{\lambda}, x) \to K, \mathsf{ct}$
3: $\mathcal{A}(x, \mathsf{ct}) \to h$
4: **return** $\mathbb{1}_{h=K}$

In the random oracle model (ROM), the game starts by selecting a random hash function H and Enc, Dec, *and* $\mathcal{A}$ *are provided a secure oracle access to H. We define the advantage of* $\mathcal{A}$ *by*

$$\mathsf{Adv}_{\mathcal{A}}^{\mathsf{OW\text{-}EWE}}(x) = \Pr[\mathsf{OW\text{-}EWE}_{\mathcal{A}}(x) \to 1]$$

We say that WKEM *is extractable one-way for a set X of instances x if for any probabilistic and polynomial-time* OW-EWE *adversary* $\mathcal{A}$, *there exists a probabilistic and polynomial-time extractor* $\mathcal{E}$ *such that for all* $x \in X$, $\mathcal{E}(x)$ *outputs a witness of x with probability at least* $\mathsf{Adv}_{\mathcal{A}}^{\mathsf{OW\text{-}EWE}}(x)$ *or at least* $\frac{1}{2}$ *up to a negligible term:*

$$\forall x \in X \quad \Pr[R(x, \mathcal{E}(x))] \geq \min\left(\mathsf{Adv}_{\mathcal{A}}^{\mathsf{OW\text{-}EWE}}(x), \frac{1}{2}\right) - \mathsf{negl}(\lambda)$$

As for IND-EWE, we observe that security implies $\mathsf{Adv}_{\mathcal{A}}^{\mathsf{OW\text{-}EWE}}(x) = \mathsf{negl}(\lambda)$ when x has no witness.

Indistinguishable Implies One-Way. As a warm-up, we show the easy result that extractable indistinguishable implies extractable one-way.

Theorem 5. *Let* $(\mathcal{K}_\lambda, \mathsf{Enc}, \mathsf{Dec})$ *be a* WKEM *for R. We assume that* $1/|\mathcal{K}_\lambda|$ *is negligible. If* WKEM *is extractable indistinguishable for a set X of instances x,* WKEM *is also extractable one-way for X.*

The proof is given in the full version of this paper.

Strongly Secure from Weakly Secure Transform. We now propose a generic WKEM transformation from OW-EWE-secure to IND-EWE-secure. The construction uses a random oracle. Let $\mathsf{WKEM}_0 = (\mathcal{K}_\lambda^0, \mathsf{Enc}_0, \mathsf{Dec}_0)$ be an OW-EWE-secure WKEM and H be a random oracle from $\mathcal{K}_\lambda^0$ to $\mathcal{K}_\lambda$. Our transformation is $\mathsf{WKEM} = (\mathcal{K}_\lambda, \mathsf{Enc}, \mathsf{Dec})$ as follows:

$\underline{\mathsf{Enc}(1^\lambda, x):}$
1: $\mathsf{Enc}_0(1^\lambda, x) \to h, \mathsf{ct}$
2: $K \leftarrow H(h)$
3: **return** K, ct

$\underline{\mathsf{Dec}(\omega, \mathsf{ct}):}$
4: $\mathsf{Dec}_0(\omega, \mathsf{ct}) \to h$
5: $K \leftarrow H(h)$
6: **return** K

The intuition behind this transformation is the hardness of guessing an input to the random oracle H from the output.

Theorem 6. *If* WKEM_0 *is extractable one-way for a set X of instances, then* WKEM *from the above transformation is extractable indistinguishable for X in the random oracle model.*

The proof is given in the full version of this paper.

4   Hidden Group with Hashing

We define a new structure HiGH with correctness and security notions.

4.1   Definitions

We define the hidden group with hashing (HiGH) by some polynomially bounded algorithms.

Definition 7 (Hidden group with hashing). *A hidden group with hashing (HiGH) in dimension d consists of the following algorithms:*

- $\mathsf{Gen}(1^\lambda) \to \mathsf{pgp}, \mathsf{tgp}$: *A probabilistic polynomial-time algorithm which generates at random some public group parameters pgp and some trapdoor group parameters tgp.*
- $\mathsf{Hom}(\mathsf{tgp}, x) \to y$: *A deterministic polynomial-time algorithm which maps $x \in \mathbb{Z}^d$ to y. We denote by G_{tgp} the set of all $\mathsf{Hom}(\mathsf{tgp}, x)$, for $x \in \mathbb{Z}^d$. When it is clear from context, we omit tgp and write $\mathsf{Hom}(x)$ and G. Hence, $y \in G$.*
- $\mathsf{Mul}(\mathsf{pgp}, y, y') \to z$: *A deterministic polynomial-time algorithm which maps a pair (y, y') to a new element z. We denote by $S_{\mathsf{pgp},\mathsf{tgp}}$ the smallest superset of G_{tgp} which is stable by this operation. When it is clear from context, we omit pgp and write $\mathsf{Mul}(y, y')$ and S. Hence, $y, y', z \in S$ and $G \subseteq S$.*
- $\mathsf{Prehash}(\mathsf{pgp}, y) \to h$: *A deterministic polynomial-time algorithm which maps an element $y \in S$ to a "pre-hash" h which belongs to another domain.[2] When it is clear from context, we omit pgp and write $\mathsf{Prehash}(y)$.*

We define by induction

$$\mathsf{Pow}(y_1, \ldots, y_t, 1^{a_1}, \ldots, 1^{a_t}) = \mathsf{Mul}(\mathsf{Pow}(y_1, \ldots, y_t, 1^{a_1}, \ldots, 1^{a_t-1}), y_t)$$

for $a_t > 0$ and

$$\mathsf{Pow}(y_1, \ldots, y_{t-1}, y_t, 1^{a_1}, \ldots, 1^{a_{t-1}}, 1^0) = \mathsf{Pow}(y_1, \ldots, y_{t-1}, 1^{a_1}, \ldots, 1^{a_{t-1}})$$

with $\mathsf{Pow}(y_1, \ldots, y_t, 1^0, \ldots, 1^0, 1^1) = y_t$.

We write the a_i inputs to Pow in unary to stress that the complexity is polynomial in terms of $\sum_i a_i$.

For HiGH to be correct, these algorithms must be such that

- *they are all polynomially bounded;*
- *for all $\mathsf{Gen}(1^\lambda) \to (\mathsf{pgp}, \mathsf{tgp})$ and $y, y' \in G$, if $\mathsf{Prehash}(y) = \mathsf{Prehash}(y')$ then $y = y'$;*
- *for all $\mathsf{Gen}(1^\lambda) \to (\mathsf{pgp}, \mathsf{tgp})$, $x, x' \in \mathbb{Z}^d$, and $y, y' \in S$ if $\mathsf{Prehash}(y) = \mathsf{Prehash}(\mathsf{Hom}(x))$ and $\mathsf{Prehash}(y') = \mathsf{Prehash}(\mathsf{Hom}(x'))$, then*

$$\mathsf{Prehash}(\mathsf{Mul}(y, y')) = \mathsf{Prehash}(\mathsf{Hom}(x + x')) \tag{1}$$

---

[2] We call h a *pre-hash* because our construction for a WKEM is extractable one-way and we need the additional construction of Theorem 6 to hash h after pre-hash and get the key K.

The idea of the HiGH is that there is a hidden group in which elements have multiple representations but a unique pre-hash. We can use Mul to find a representation of the product of two represented factors. The computation is somewhat blind. The interface to Mul and Prehash is public. The interface also comes with a hidden group homomorphism Hom from $\mathbb{Z}^d$ which requires a trapdoor tgp. The additional property of HiGH which will play a role is that Mul can make representations grow so that computing an exponential of a large integer is not possible. Note that there is no interface to compute inverses. Our proposed instance based on RSA will also make it hard. It will consist of integers modulo a hidden number.

Lemma 8. *Given a* HiGH, *we have the following properties.*

1. *For all* $\mathsf{Gen}(1^\lambda) \to (\mathsf{pgp}, \mathsf{tgp})$, *for all* t, $(x_1, \dots, x_t) \in (\mathbb{Z}^d)^t$, *and non-negative integers* $a_1, \dots, a_t$, *if* $y_i = \mathsf{Hom}(x_i)$, $i = 1, \dots, t$, *we have*

$$\mathsf{Prehash}\left(\mathsf{Pow}\left(y_1, \dots, y_t, 1^{a_1}, \dots, 1^{a_t}\right)\right) = \mathsf{Prehash}(\mathsf{Hom}(a_1 x_1 + \cdots + a_t x_t))$$

2. $\mathsf{Prehash}(S) = \mathsf{Prehash}(G)$
3. *For any* $y \in S$, *there exists a unique* $z \in G$ *such that* $\mathsf{Prehash}(y) = \mathsf{Prehash}(z)$. *We call* z *reduced and we denote it by*

$$\mathsf{Red}(y) = G \cap \mathsf{Prehash}^{-1}(\mathsf{Prehash}(y))$$

4. *The* $*$ *operation on* G *defined by* $y * y' = \mathsf{Red}(\mathsf{Mul}(y, y'))$ *makes* G *an Abelian group and* Hom *a surjective group homomorphism from* $\mathbb{Z}^d$ *to* G. *We denote by* Ker *the kernel of* Hom.

The proof is given in the full version of this paper.

For instance (with $d = 1$), for $x \in \mathbb{Z}$, we can define $\mathsf{tgp} = (\ell, k)$, $\mathsf{Hom}(x) = k^x \bmod \ell$, $\mathsf{Mul}(y, y') = y \times y'$ in $\mathbb{Z}$, $\mathsf{pgp} = (n, g)$, and $\mathsf{Prehash}(y) = g^y \bmod n$, where g has order ℓ in $\mathbb{Z}_n^*$ and n is an RSA modulus. We obtain $G = \langle k \rangle \subset \mathbb{Z}_\ell^*$ and S is the set of integers which factor in G. We have $\mathsf{Red}(y) = y \bmod \ell$. Here, Hom is from $\mathbb{Z}$ to $\mathbb{Z}$ and the hidden group is a cyclic subgroup of $\mathbb{Z}_\ell^*$.

Actually, we focus on cases where G is cyclic. As we will need representation of group elements to be hard to forge except by making generic use of Mul on known group elements, we will make G as a sparse subgroup of a supergroup $\bar{G}$.

For instance, for $x \in \mathbb{Z}$, we can define $\mathsf{tgp} = (\ell, k, k^\theta)$ for some invertible θ and $\mathsf{Hom}(x) = (k^x \bmod \ell, k^{\theta x} \bmod \ell)$ with the regular Mul in $\mathbb{Z}^2$. We obtain Hom from $\mathbb{Z}$ to $\mathbb{Z}^2$ and the hidden group is a cyclic subgroup of $(\mathbb{Z}_\ell^*)^2$. Our construction from Sect. 6 is based on this, with higher dimension.

4.2 HiGH Knowledge Exponent Assumption (HiGH-KE)

In the following definition, X denotes a set of tuples $(x_1, \dots, x_t, \mathsf{aux})$ where aux could be anything, which could potentially give a clue to the adversary about the instance $(x_1, \dots, x_t)$.

Definition 9. *A* HiGH *of dimension d satisfies the* HiGH *Knowledge Exponent Assumption for a set X if for any PPT algorithm $\mathcal{A}'$, there exists a PPT algorithm $\mathcal{E}'$ such that for all $x \in X$, the probability that the following game returns 1 is negligible:*

Game HiGH-KE$(1^\lambda, x)$:

1: *parse* $x = (x_1, \ldots, x_t, \mathsf{aux})$
2: $\mathsf{Gen}(1^\lambda) \to (\mathsf{pgp}, \mathsf{tgp})$ ▷ *this defines* $G = \mathsf{Hom}_{\mathsf{tgp}}(\mathbb{Z}^d)$
3: $y_i \leftarrow \mathsf{Hom}(\mathsf{tgp}, x_i)$, $i = 1, \ldots, t$
4: $\mathcal{A}'(x_1, \ldots, x_t, y_1, \ldots, y_t, \mathsf{pgp}, \mathsf{aux}) \to h$
5: *if* $h \notin \mathsf{Prehash}(\mathsf{pgp}, G)$ *then abort*[3]
6: *set* ρ *to the random coins used by* $\mathcal{A}'$
7: $\mathcal{E}'(x_1, \ldots, x_t, y_1, \ldots, y_t, \mathsf{pgp}, \mathsf{aux}, \rho) \to (1^{a_1}, \ldots, 1^{a_t})$ ▷ $a_i \in \mathbb{N}$
8: *if* $\mathsf{Prehash}(\mathsf{pgp}, \mathsf{Hom}(\mathsf{tgp}, a_1 x_1 + \cdots + a_t x_t)) = h$ *then return 0*
9: *return 1*

The point is that whenever the adversary succeeds to forge an element h of $\mathsf{Prehash}(G)$, the extractor, who has the same view (including ρ), should almost always manage to express it as the $\mathsf{Prehash}$ of a combination of the known pairs (x_i, y_i), with small coefficients a_i.[4] It means that only algorithms $\mathcal{A}'$ making Mul operations can forge valid prehashes h. The nice thing about this assumption is that it allows to get similar results as in the generic group model (i.e., to extract the combination) by remaining in the standard model.

This assumption combines the preimage awareness of $\mathsf{Prehash}$ and the knowledge-of-exponent assumption in G. By $\mathsf{Prehash}$ being *preimage aware*, we mean that whenever $\mathcal{A}$ succeeds to forge an element of $\mathsf{Prehash}(S)$ (which is also $\mathsf{Prehash}(G)$), then he must know some preimage in S.

4.3 HiGH Kernel Assumption (HiGH-Ker)

In the following definition, X denotes a set of tuples $(x_1, \ldots, x_t, \mathsf{aux})$ like in the previous definition.

Definition 10. *A* HiGH *satisfies the* HiGH *Kernel assumption for a set X of instances $x = (x_1, \ldots, x_t, \mathsf{aux})$ if for any PPT algorithm $\mathcal{A}''$, for any $x \in X$, the probability that the following game returns 1 is negligible.*

Game HiGH-Ker$(1^\lambda, x)$:

1: *parse* $x = (x_1, \ldots, x_t, \mathsf{aux})$
2: $\mathsf{Gen}(1^\lambda) \to (\mathsf{pgp}, \mathsf{tgp})$
3: $y_i \leftarrow \mathsf{Hom}(\mathsf{tgp}, x_i)$, $i = 1, \ldots, t$
4: *run* $\mathcal{A}''(x_1, \ldots, x_t, y_1, \ldots, y_t, \mathsf{pgp}) \to z$
5: *if* $z = 0$ *then abort*
6: *if* $\mathsf{Prehash}(\mathsf{pgp}, \mathsf{Hom}(\mathsf{tgp}, z)) \neq \mathsf{Prehash}(\mathsf{pgp}, \mathsf{Hom}(\mathsf{tgp}, 0))$ *then abort*
7: *return 1*

---

[3] We stress that this step may not be simulatable by a PPT algorithm.
[4] a_i is small because it is retrieved in unary by a polynomially bounded algorithm $\mathcal{E}'$.

This means that even with a few (x_i, y_i) pairs for Hom, it is hard to find a kernel element.

5   WKEM from HiGH

We now construct a WKEM based on a HiGH and prove its security.

We abstract our WKEM scheme with HiGH for the Multi-SS language on Fig. 1. Essentially, to encrypt with $x = (x_1, \ldots, x_t, s)$, we generate a HiGH, we put all $y_i = \mathsf{Hom}(x_i)$ in the ciphertext, and the plaintext is

$$h = \mathsf{Prehash}(\mathsf{Hom}(s))$$

To decrypt with $\omega = (1^{a_1}, \ldots, 1^{a_t})$, we compute

$$h' = \mathsf{Prehash}(\mathsf{Pow}(y_1, \ldots, y_t, \omega)).$$

To present our construction in the frame of Barta et al. [2], we have a 2-message predictable argument for x in which the verifier generates from x a query $q = \mathsf{ct}$ and an expected response $\mathsf{st} = h$: $\mathcal{Q}(x) \to (q, \mathsf{st})$. The prover computes $\mathcal{P}(q, x, \omega) \to \pi$ the proof π which is accepted if $\pi = h$.

We first show that our construction is correct. Due to the correctness property (1) of HiGH, we have

$$\mathsf{Prehash}(\mathsf{Pow}(y_1, \ldots, y_t, \omega)) = \mathsf{Prehash}(\mathsf{Hom}(a_1 x_1 + \cdots + a_t x_t)).$$

If $R(x, \omega)$ holds, we have $a_1 x_1 + \cdots + a_t x_t = s$. We can then deduce that $h = h'$.

$\mathsf{Enc}(1^\lambda, x)$:
1: parse $x = (x_1, \ldots, x_t, s)$
2: $\mathsf{Gen}(1^\lambda) \to (\mathsf{pgp}, \mathsf{tgp})$
3: $y_i \leftarrow \mathsf{Hom}(\mathsf{tgp}, x_i)$, $i = 1, \ldots, t$
4: $z \leftarrow \mathsf{Hom}(\mathsf{tgp}, s)$
5: $h \leftarrow \mathsf{Prehash}(\mathsf{pgp}, z)$
6: set $\mathsf{ct} = (y_1, \ldots, y_t, \mathsf{pgp})$
7: **return** h, ct

$\mathsf{Dec}(\omega, \mathsf{ct})$:
8: parse $\mathsf{ct} = (y_1, \ldots, y_t, \mathsf{pgp})$
9: parse $\omega = (1^{a_1}, \ldots, 1^{a_t})$
10: $z' \leftarrow \mathsf{Pow}(\mathsf{pgp}, y_1, \ldots, y_t, \omega)$
11: $h' \leftarrow \mathsf{Prehash}(\mathsf{pgp}, z')$
12: **return** h'

Fig. 1. WKEM construction

We show that WKEM is an extractable one-way witness key encapsulation mechanism for instances of Multi-SS.

Theorem 11. *The* WKEM *construction for* Multi-SS *on Fig. 1 is extractable one-way for a set X of instances $x = (x_1, \ldots, x_t, s)$ if the underlying* HiGH *satisfies the* HiGH-KE *and the* HiGH-Ker *assumptions for X.*

Proof. Let $\mathcal{A}$ be an OW-EWE adversary. We first construct an algorithm $\mathcal{A}'$ for the HiGH-KE game in Sect. 4.1 as follows which receives a target s as an auxiliary input aux:

$\mathcal{A}'(x_1, \ldots, x_t, y_1, \ldots, y_t, \mathsf{pgp}, \mathsf{aux}; \rho)$:
1: parse s from aux
2: $x \leftarrow (x_1, \ldots, x_t, s)$
3: $\mathsf{ct} \leftarrow (y_1, \ldots, y_t, \mathsf{pgp})$
4: $\mathcal{A}(x, \mathsf{ct}; \rho) \rightarrow h$
5: **return** h

Thanks to the HiGH-KE assumption, there exists an extractor $\mathcal{E}'$ making the HiGH-KE game return 1 with negligible probability for every $x \in X$. We then construct the OW-EWE extractor $\mathcal{E}$ as follows:

$\mathcal{E}(1^\lambda, x, \mathsf{ct}, \rho)$:
1: parse $x = (x_1, \ldots, x_t, s)$
2: parse $\mathsf{ct} = (y_1, \ldots, y_t, \mathsf{pgp})$
3: set aux to s
4: $\mathcal{E}'(x_1, \ldots, x_t, y_1, \ldots, y_t, \mathsf{pgp}, \mathsf{aux}, \rho) \rightarrow \omega$
5: **return** ω

Next, we will prove that $\mathcal{E}$ extracts well with nearly the same probability as $\mathcal{A}'$ wins in OW-EWE.

Below, we detail the OW-EWE game (on the left) and the HiGH-KE game (on the right). To make the comparison easier, we expanded Enc and $\mathcal{A}'$ in gray in a line starting with a dot.

OW-EWE$(1^\lambda, x)$:
1: . parse $x = (x_1, \ldots, x_t, s)$
2: . $\mathsf{Gen}(1^\lambda) \rightarrow (\mathsf{pgp}, \mathsf{tgp})$
3: . $y_i \leftarrow \mathsf{Hom}(x_i)$, $i = 1, \ldots, t$
4: . $z \leftarrow \mathsf{Hom}(s)$
5: . $K \leftarrow \mathsf{Prehash}(z)$
6: . $\mathsf{ct} \leftarrow (y_1, \ldots, y_t, \mathsf{pgp})$
7: $\mathcal{A}(x, \mathsf{ct}) \rightarrow h$
8: **return** $\mathbb{1}_{h=K}$

HiGH-KE$(1^\lambda, x)$:
1: parse $x = (x_1, \ldots, x_t, s)$
2: $\mathsf{Gen}(1^\lambda) \rightarrow (\mathsf{pgp}, \mathsf{tgp})$
3: $y_i \leftarrow \mathsf{Hom}(x_i)$, $i = 1, \ldots, t$
4: . $\mathsf{ct} \leftarrow (y_1, \ldots, y_t, \mathsf{pgp})$
5: . $\mathcal{A}(x, \mathsf{ct}; \rho) \rightarrow h$
6: **if** $h \notin \mathsf{Prehash}(G)$ **then** abort
7: set ρ to the random coins used by $\mathcal{A}$
8: $\mathcal{E}'(x_1, \ldots, x_t, y_1, \ldots, y_t, \mathsf{pgp}, s, \rho) \rightarrow (1^{a_1}, \ldots, 1^{a_t})$
9: **if** $\mathsf{Prehash}(\mathsf{Hom}(a_1 x_1 + \cdots + a_t x_t)) = h$ **then return** 0
10: **return** 1

Clearly, everything until Step 6 is equivalent, with the same random coins. When OW-EWE returns 1, h is in $\mathsf{Prehash}(G)$ so HiGH-KE does not abort. Instead, HiGH-KE returns 0 or 1. We know by assumption that HiGH-KE returns 1 with negligible probability. Hence,

$$\Pr[\mathsf{HiGH\text{-}KE} \rightarrow 0] \geq \Pr[\mathsf{OW\text{-}EWE} \rightarrow 1] - \mathsf{negl}$$

Cases when HiGH-KE returns 0 are the one when $\mathcal{E}'$ extracts successfully. Therefore, $\mathcal{E}'$ extracts $(1^{a_1}, \ldots, 1^{a_t})$ satisfying $\mathsf{Prehash}(\mathsf{Hom}(a_1 x_1 + \cdots + a_t x_t)) = h$ with probability at least $\Pr[\mathsf{OW\text{-}EWE} \rightarrow 1] - \mathsf{negl}$. Due to the properties of HiGH, this implies that $a_1 x_1 + \cdots + a_t x_t - s \in \mathsf{Ker}$.

We construct the following algorithm playing the HiGH-Ker game:

$\mathcal{A}''(x_1, \ldots, x_t, s, y_1, \ldots, y_t, z, \mathsf{pgp})$:

1: set $x = (x_1, \ldots, x_t, s)$
2: $\mathsf{ct} \leftarrow (y_1, \ldots, y_t, \mathsf{pgp})$
3: $\mathcal{A}(x, \mathsf{ct}) \rightarrow h$
4: set ρ to the random coins used by $\mathcal{A}$
5: $\mathcal{E}'(x_1, \ldots, x_t, y_1, \ldots, y_t, \mathsf{pgp}, s, \rho) \rightarrow (1^{a_1}, \ldots, 1^{a_t})$
6: **return** $a_1 x_1 + \cdots + a_t x_t - s$

Note that (s, z) plays the role of a new pair (x_{t+1}, y_{t+1}) here.

We now expand $\mathcal{A}''$ in the $HiGHKer$ game and we compare it to the HiGH-KE game:

HiGH-Ker$(1^\lambda, x)$:
1:   parse $x = (x_1, \ldots, x_t, s)$
2:   $\mathsf{Gen}(1^\lambda) \rightarrow (\mathsf{pgp}, \mathsf{tgp})$
3:   $y_i \leftarrow \mathsf{Hom}(x_i)$, $i = 1, \ldots, t$
4:   . $\mathsf{ct} \leftarrow (y_1, \ldots, y_t, \mathsf{pgp})$
5:   . $\mathcal{A}(x, \mathsf{ct}) \rightarrow h$
6:   . set ρ to the random coins used by $\mathcal{A}$
7:   . $\mathcal{E}'(x_1, \ldots, x_t, y_1, \ldots, y_t, \mathsf{pgp}, s, \rho) \rightarrow$ $(1^{a_1}, \ldots, 1^{a_t})$
8:   . $z \leftarrow a_1 x_1 + \cdots + a_t x_t - s$
9:   **if** $z = 0$ **then** abort
10:     **if** $\mathsf{Prehash}(\mathsf{pgp}, \mathsf{Hom}(\mathsf{tgp}, z)) \neq$ $\mathsf{Prehash}(\mathsf{pgp}, \mathsf{Hom}(\mathsf{tgp}, 0))$ **then** abort
11: **return** 1

HiGH-KE$(1^\lambda, x)$:
1:   parse $x = (x_1, \ldots, x_t, s)$
2:   $\mathsf{Gen}(1^\lambda) \rightarrow (\mathsf{pgp}, \mathsf{tgp})$
3:   $y_i \leftarrow \mathsf{Hom}(x_i)$, $i = 1, \ldots, t$
4:   . $\mathsf{ct} \leftarrow (y_1, \ldots, y_t, \mathsf{pgp})$
5:   . $\mathcal{A}(x, \mathsf{ct}; \rho) \rightarrow h$
6:   **if** $h \notin \mathsf{Prehash}(G)$ **then** abort
7:   set ρ to the random coins used by $\mathcal{A}$
8:   $\mathcal{E}'(x_1, \ldots, x_t, y_1, \ldots, y_t, \mathsf{pgp}, s, \rho) \rightarrow$ $(1^{a_1}, \ldots, 1^{a_t})$
9:   **if** $\mathsf{Prehash}(\mathsf{Hom}(a_1 x_1 + \cdots + a_t x_t)) = h$ **then return** 0
10: **return** 1

If HiGH-KE returns 0, then HiGH-Ker with the same coins either returns 1 (which happens with negligible probability) or $z = 0$. Hence, $\Pr[\text{HiGH-Ker} \rightarrow z = 0] \geq \Pr[\text{OW-EWE} \rightarrow 1] - \mathsf{negl}$. We deduce $\Pr[\mathcal{E} \text{ extracts}] \geq \Pr[\text{OW-EWE} \rightarrow 1] - \mathsf{negl}$. □

Reusability of the Parameters. The generated HiGH parameters $(\mathsf{pgp}, \mathsf{tgp})$ may require some computational effort in each encryption. This could be amortized by reusing some of the values. Namely, in our proposed HiGH, the parameters ℓ, n, g could be reused. Since generating the parameters $(k, \alpha_1, \ldots, \alpha_d, \theta)$ requires no effort, it is advised not to reuse them. Indeed, reusing them would help an adversary to pool many (x_i, y_i) pairs in the very same structure. It is also nice not to store them as the dimension d can be very large. Then, finding a linear relation with small coefficients would become easier and easier with the number of pairs.

However, using a long term ℓ is harming *forward secrecy* because disclosing it allows to decrypt all encryptions.

6   Our Instantiation of HiGH

6.1   Construction

We propose an instantiation of HiGH from the hardness of factorization of RSA modulus. Let $\mathsf{GenRSA}(1^\lambda)$ be an algorithm which outputs a tuple (n, ℓ, g) where

n is an RSA modulus and g is an element of order ℓ in $\mathbb{Z}_n^*$. Our proposed instance is given in Fig. 2. Gen runs GenRSA and generates $k \in \mathbb{Z}_\ell^*$ so that g^k has order ℓ in $\mathbb{Z}_n^*$. The values k and ℓ are not revealed. They are to derive a sequence $(k_1, k_1', \ldots, k_d, k_d')$ of elements of $\mathbb{Z}_\ell^*$ such that there is a hidden relation $k_i' = k_i^\theta$ (mod ℓ) with $k_i = k^{\alpha_i}$ (mod ℓ) for $i = 1, \ldots, d$.

The hidden group is $\bar{G} = (\mathbb{Z}_\ell^*)^2$ which has representation in $\mathbb{Z}^2$. Our homomorphism Hom goes from $\mathbb{Z}^d$ to $\bar{G} = (\mathbb{Z}_\ell^*)^2$ by $(\xi_1, \ldots, \xi_d) \mapsto (k_1^{\xi_1} \cdots k_d^{\xi_d}, k_1'^{\xi_1} \cdots k_d'^{\xi_d})$ mod ℓ, but Mul treats $\bar{G}$ elements as belonging to $\mathbb{Z}^2$ and does the multiplication therein. When reduced modulo ℓ, we fall back to the hidden group. Hence, we use as Prehash the basis-g exponential modulo n because g has order ℓ. The exponential is made on the two components of the input from $\mathbb{Z}^2$.

G is the subgroup of $\bar{G}$ generated by (k, k^θ). We have $\mathsf{Red}(\nu_1, \nu_2) = (\nu_1 \bmod \ell, \nu_2 \bmod \ell)$. The kernel is a subgroup Ker of $\mathbb{Z}^d$ of all $(\xi_1, \ldots, \xi_d)$ such that $\alpha_1 \xi_1 + \cdots + \alpha_d \xi_d = 0$ modulo the order of k. Prehash is injective when restricted on $\mathbb{Z}_\ell^2$, so it is injective when restricted on G. G is the hidden group of the super-structure $S \subseteq \mathbb{Z}^2$. We stress that Mul makes operations in the super-structure S of the hidden group G, and that Pow needs the a_i to be small because elements of $\mathbb{Z}^2$ can become huge when raised to the power a_i.

In our construction, the input of Hom is in $\mathbb{Z}^d$ as it comes from a vector in a Multi-SS instance. Contrarily, the output of Hom is in $\mathbb{Z}^2$. Having two components allows to make it part of a sparse subset in which it is hard to forge elements without knowing a relation with known elements.

$\underline{\mathsf{Gen}(1^\lambda):}$
1: $\mathsf{GenRSA}(1^\lambda) \rightarrow (n, \ell, g)$ ▷ g of order ℓ in $\mathbb{Z}_n^*$

                           1. pick an RSA modulus ℓ of length λ
                           2. pick a random p' such that $p = p'\ell + 1$ is prime
      example   3. pick a random q' such that $q = q'\ell + 1$ is prime
                           4. set $n = pq$
                           5. pick g as a random number power $p'q'$ modulo n until it has order ℓ

2: pick $k \in \mathbb{Z}_\ell^*$ at random
3: pick $\alpha_1, \ldots, \alpha_d, \theta \in \mathbb{Z}_{\varphi(\ell)}^*$ at random
4: $k_i \leftarrow k^{\alpha_i} \bmod \ell, \ i = 1, \ldots, d$
5: $k_i' \leftarrow k^{\theta \alpha_i} \bmod \ell, \ i = 1, \ldots, d$
6: $\mathsf{pgp} \leftarrow (n, g)$ ▷ public group parameters
7: $\mathsf{tgp} \leftarrow (\ell, (k_i, k_i')_{i=1,\ldots,d})$ ▷ trapdoor group parameters
8: **return** $(\mathsf{pgp}, \mathsf{tgp})$

$\underline{\mathsf{Hom}(\mathsf{tgp}, \xi):}$
9: $\mathsf{tgp} \rightarrow (\ell, (k_i, k_i')_{i=1,\ldots,d})$
10: $\xi \rightarrow (\xi_1, \ldots, \xi_d)$
11: $\nu_1 \leftarrow k_1^{\xi_1} \cdots k_d^{\xi_d} \bmod \ell$
12: $\nu_2 \leftarrow k_1'^{\xi_1} \cdots k_d'^{\xi_d} \bmod \ell$
13: **return** (ν_1, ν_2)

$\underline{\mathsf{Mul}(\mathsf{pgp}, \nu, \nu'):}$
14: $\nu \rightarrow (\nu_1, \nu_2)$
15: $\nu' \rightarrow (\nu_1', \nu_2')$
16: $z_i \leftarrow \nu_i \nu_i', \ i = 1, 2$
17: **return** (z_1, z_2)

$\underline{\mathsf{Prehash}(\mathsf{pgp}, \nu):}$
18: $\mathsf{pgp} \rightarrow (n, g)$
19: $\nu \rightarrow (\nu_1, \nu_2)$
20: $h_i \leftarrow g^{\nu_i} \bmod n, \ i = 1, 2$
21: **return** (h_1, h_2)

Fig. 2. Our HiGH construction

Efficient Implementation. To reduce the size of tgp, we can replace the $(k_i, k'_i)_i$ family by a seed which generates $k, \alpha_1, \ldots, \alpha_d, \theta$.

6.2   Possible Attacks

Finding a multiple ℓ' of ℓ allows an adversary to do multiplications in $\mathbb{Z}^2_{\ell'}$ which is a supergroup of G and to keep the size of numbers bounded by ℓ'. Hence, the adversary can implement some Mul' and Pow' algorithms which match to Mul and Pow when reduced modulo ℓ. Given enough known pairs $(x_i, \text{Hom}(x_i))$, the adversary can find some integers a_i such that $a_1 x_1 + \cdots + a_t x_t = (0, \ldots, 0, 1, 0, \ldots, 0)$ over $\mathbb{Z}$. Using Pow' allows to recover a pair equal to (k_j, k'_j) modulo ℓ'. Next, the adversary can implement an $\xi \mapsto \text{Hom}'(\xi)$ algorithm which matches Hom when reduced modulo ℓ.

We can then make a HiGH-KE adversary who picks some random (large enough, with polynomial length) ξ, then $h = \text{Prehash}(\text{Hom}'(\xi))$. Either it breaks the HiGH-KE assumption, or there exists an extractor who extracts some (polynomially bounded) $a_1, \ldots, a_t$ such that $h = \text{Prehash}(\text{Hom}'(\xi'))$ with $\xi' = a_1 x_1 + \cdots + a_t x_t$. In the latter case, we let $z = \xi - \xi'$. Since the set of all possible ξ' is polynomially bounded while the set of all possible ξ has exponential size, $z = 0$ happens with negligible probability. Hence, the adversary producing z breaks the HiGH-Ker assumption. Therefore, either HiGH-KE or HiGH-Ker is broken.

Essentially, the adversary recovers some tgp' which is functionally equivalent to tgp and allows to break the scheme. For this reason, it is essential that the adversary cannot find a relation which is true modulo ℓ but not in $\mathbb{Z}$, as it would reveal a multiple of ℓ. We give an example below.

Small Solutions to the Homogeneous Problem. Given some (x_i, y_i) pairs with $y_i = \text{Hom}(x_i)$, if an adversary finds some small[5] a'_i (positive or negative) such that $\sum_i a'_i x_i = 0$, then he can compute

$$\ell'_j = \prod_i y_{i,j}^{\max(0, a'_i)} - \prod_i y_{i,j}^{\max(0, -a'_i)}$$

for $j = 1, 2$, which are multiples of ℓ. Their gcd ℓ' is a multiple of ℓ which can be used in its place. Then, the adversary can break the HiGH.

This means that for the HiGH-Ker to hold on X, there should be no $x \in X$ with a small relation $\sum_i a'_i x_i = 0$. This is why we must consider a subset X of all instances of Multi-SS.

6.3   Security Results

Knowledge-of-Exponent Assumption. Wu and Stinson define the generalized knowledge-of-exponent assumption (GKEA) [16] over a group G. It says that

---

[5] By "small", we mean that computing $y_i^{|a'_i|}$ over $\mathbb{Z}$ is doable.

for an adversary who gets $y_1, \ldots, y_t \in G$ and succeeds to produce $z \in G$, there must be an extractor who would, with the same view, make $a_1, \ldots, a_t \in \mathbb{Z}$ such that $z = y_1^{a_1} \times \cdots \times y_t^{a_t}$. In our group $G = \langle (k, k^\theta) \rangle \subset (\mathbb{Z}_\ell^*)^2$, this assumption is usual, even when ℓ is known. In our settings, ℓ is not known but a preimage x_i by Hom for each y_i is known.

We conjecture that the HiGH-KE assumption holds in our construction for every $(x_1, \ldots, x_t, s)$ such that there is no relation $a_1 x_1 + \cdots + a_t x_t = 0$ with small a_i.

Kernel Assumption. The *RSA order assumption* says that given an RSA modulus ℓ and a random $k \in \mathbb{Z}_\ell^*$, it is hard to find a positive integer z' such that $k^{z'} \bmod \ell = 1$. The game is defined relative to the distribution P of ℓ as follows:

1: pick a random ℓ following P
2: pick a random $k \in \mathbb{Z}_\ell^*$ uniformly
3: run $\mathcal{B}(\ell, k) \to z'$
4: **if** $z' = 0$ or $k^{z'} \bmod \ell \neq 1$ **then** abort
5: **return** 1

For our construction, we can prove that the HiGH-Ker problem is at least as hard as the RSA order problem when ℓ is a strong RSA modulus. However, the HiGH-Ker problem is likely to be hard even when ℓ is not a strong RSA modulus.

Theorem 12. *We assume that* GenRSA *generates only strong RSA moduli ℓ and we let P be their distribution. Given an adversary $\mathcal{A}$ with advantage $\mathsf{Adv}_\mathcal{A}^{\mathsf{HiGH\text{-}Ker}}$ in the* HiGH-Ker$(1^\lambda, x)$ *game for a given x, we can construct an adversary $\mathcal{B}$ with same advantage (up to a negligible term) in the order problem with this modulus distribution, and similar complexity.*

Proof. We consider an adversary $\mathcal{A}$ playing the HiGH-Ker game with input x. We define an adversary $\mathcal{B}(\ell, k)$ playing the order game. The adversary $\mathcal{B}$ receives (ℓ, k) from the order game then simulates the rest of the HiGH-Ker game with $\mathcal{A}$. This simulator must generate n. There is a little problem to select $\alpha_1, \ldots, \alpha_d, \theta$ because $\mathcal{B}$ does not know $\varphi(\ell)$. However, if ℓ is a strong RSA modulus, by sampling in a domain which is large enough and with only odd integers, the statistical distance Δ between the real and simulated distributions of $(\mathsf{pgp}, \mathsf{tgp})$ is negligible. $\mathcal{A}$ may give some kernel elements $z = (z_1, \ldots, z_d)$ from which $\mathcal{B}$ can compute $\alpha_1 z_1 + \cdots + \alpha_d z_d$.

More precisely, $\mathcal{B}(\ell, k)$ works as follows:

$\mathcal{B}(\ell, k)$:
1: pick a random p' such that $p = p'\ell + 1$ is prime
2: pick a random q' such that $q = q'\ell + 1$ is prime
3: set $n = pq$
4: pick g as a random number power $p'q'$ modulo n until $g \neq 1$
   ▷ g has order ℓ except with negligible probability

5: pick $\alpha_1, \ldots, \alpha_d, \theta$ odd in $\{0, \ldots, B-1\}$, $B = \ell^2$
                   ▷ statistical distance with correct $(\alpha_1, \ldots, \alpha_d, \theta)$ is $\Delta = \mathsf{negl}(\lambda)$
6: $k_1 \leftarrow k^{\alpha_i} \bmod \ell$, $i = 1, \ldots, d$
7: $k_1' \leftarrow k^{\theta \alpha_i} \bmod \ell$, $i = 1, \ldots, d$
8: $\mathsf{pgp} \leftarrow (n, g)$
9: $\mathsf{tgp} \leftarrow (\ell, (k_i, k_i')_{i=1,\ldots,d})$
10: $y_i \leftarrow \mathsf{Hom}(\mathsf{tgp}, x_i)$, $i = 1, \ldots, d$
11: run $\mathcal{A}(x_1, \ldots, x_t, y_1, \ldots, y_t, \mathsf{pgp}) \to z$
12: **return** z

The two steps which deviate from the HiGH-Ker game played by $\mathcal{A}$ introduce no noticeable difference. Namely, it is rare that g does not have order g (it is similar than finding factors of ℓ by chance). The statistical distance Δ is negligible, as estimated by the lemma below. Hence, $\mathcal{B}$ succeeds in his game with (nearly) the same probability as $\mathcal{A}$ succeeds in the HiGH-Ker game.   □

Lemma 13. *If $\ell = \ell_p \times \ell_q$ is a strong RSA modulus, then the statistical distance Δ between the modulo $\varphi(\ell)$ reduction of the two following generators*

1. *pick $(\alpha_1, \ldots, \alpha_d, \theta) \in \left(\mathbf{Z}^*_{\varphi(\ell)} \right)^{d+1}$ uniformly at random*
2. *pick $(\alpha_1, \ldots, \alpha_d, \theta) \in \{1, 3, 5, \ldots, B-2\}^{d+1}$ uniformly at random*

where $B = \ell^2$ is such that

$$\Delta \leq (d+1) \left(\frac{2}{\ell_p - 1} + \frac{2}{\ell_q - 1} + \frac{\ell}{B-1} \right)$$

Note that the second generator simply picks odd elements in $\{0, \ldots, B-1\}$.

Proof. The two generators take independent $d+1$ samples from two distributions. Hence, Δ is bounded by $d+1$ times the statistical distance between these two distributions.

The first distribution is uniform in $\mathbf{Z}^*_{\varphi(\ell)}$.

The second distribution selects an element in $\{1, 3, \ldots, B-1\}$ then reduces it modulo $\varphi(\ell)$.

We define an intermediate distribution which uniform in $\{1, 3, \ldots, \varphi(\ell) - 1\}$, which is a superset of $\mathbf{Z}^*_{\varphi(\ell)}$.

Clearly, the statistical distance between the first distribution and the intermediate distribution is bounded by the probability to take a multiple of $\ell_{p'}$ or a multiple of $\ell_{q'}$, which is bounded by the sum $\frac{2}{\ell_p - 1} + \frac{2}{\ell_q - 1}$.

The statistical distance between the intermediate distribution and the second distribution is bounded by the cardinality $\varphi(\varphi(\ell))$ times the gap between the largest and the lowest probabilities in the distribution, which is $\frac{2}{B-1}$. This is

$$2 \frac{\varphi(\varphi(\ell))}{B-1} \leq \frac{\ell}{B-1}$$

    □

7   Conclusion

We have shown how to construct a WKEM for a variant of the subset sum problem, based on HiGH. This is secure in the generic HiGH model. We proposed an HiGH construction based on RSA which has a restriction on the subset sum instances. One open question is to make it work even for instances having a small linear combination which vanishes.

Another interesting challenge is to build a post-quantum HiGH.

Acknowledgement. Gwangbae Choi is supported by the Swiss National Science Foundation (SNSF) Project funding no. 169110.

References

1. Abe, M., Fehr, S.: Perfect NIZK with adaptive soundness. In: Vadhan, S.P. (ed.) TCC 2007. LNCS, vol. 4392, pp. 118–136. Springer, Heidelberg (2007). https://doi.org/10.1007/978-3-540-70936-7_7
2. Barta, O., Ishai, Y., Ostrovsky, R., Wu, D.J.: On succinct arguments and witness encryption from groups. In: Micciancio, D., Ristenpart, T. (eds.) CRYPTO 2020. LNCS, vol. 12170, pp. 776–806. Springer, Cham (2020). https://doi.org/10.1007/978-3-030-56784-2_26
3. Chvojka, P., Jager, T., Kakvi, S.A.: Offline witness encryption with semi-adaptive security. In: Conti, M., Zhou, J., Casalicchio, E., Spognardi, A. (eds.) ACNS 2020. LNCS, vol. 12146, pp. 231–250. Springer, Cham (2020). https://doi.org/10.1007/978-3-030-57808-4_12
4. Cramer, R., Shoup, V.: A practical public key cryptosystem provably secure against adaptive chosen ciphertext attack. In: Krawczyk, H. (ed.) CRYPTO 1998. LNCS, vol. 1462, pp. 13–25. Springer, Heidelberg (1998). https://doi.org/10.1007/BFb0055717
5. Cramer, R., Shoup, V.: Universal hash proofs and a paradigm for adaptive chosen ciphertext secure public-key encryption. In: Knudsen, L.R. (ed.) EUROCRYPT 2002. LNCS, vol. 2332, pp. 45–64. Springer, Heidelberg (2002). https://doi.org/10.1007/3-540-46035-7_4
6. Cramer, R., Shoup, V.: Design and analysis of practical public-key encryption schemes secure against adaptive chosen ciphertext attack. SIAM J. Comput. **33**(1), 167–226 (2003)
7. Damgård, I.: Towards practical public key systems secure against chosen ciphertext attacks. In: Feigenbaum, J. (ed.) CRYPTO 1991. LNCS, vol. 576, pp. 445–456. Springer, Heidelberg (1992). https://doi.org/10.1007/3-540-46766-1_36
8. Dent, A.W.: The hardness of the DHK problem in the generic group model. IACR Cryptology ePrint Archive **2006**, 156 (2006)
9. Faonio, A., Nielsen, J.B., Venturi, D.: Predictable arguments of knowledge. In: Fehr, S. (ed.) PKC 2017. LNCS, vol. 10174, pp. 121–150. Springer, Heidelberg (2017). https://doi.org/10.1007/978-3-662-54365-8_6
10. Garg, S., Gentry, C., Sahai, A., Waters, B.: Witness encryption and its applications. In: Proceedings of the Forty-Fifth Annual ACM Symposium on Theory of Computing, pp. 467–476. ACM (2013)

11. Goldwasser, S., Kalai, Y.T., Popa, R.A., Vaikuntanathan, V., Zeldovich, N.:
    How to run Turing machines on encrypted data. In: Canetti, R., Garay, J.A.
    (eds.) CRYPTO 2013. LNCS, vol. 8043, pp. 536–553. Springer, Heidelberg (2013).
    https://doi.org/10.1007/978-3-642-40084-1_30
12. Groth, J., Ostrovsky, R., Sahai, A.: Perfect non-interactive zero knowledge for NP.
    In: Vaudenay, S. (ed.) EUROCRYPT 2006. LNCS, vol. 4004, pp. 339–358. Springer,
    Heidelberg (2006). https://doi.org/10.1007/11761679_21
13. Karp, R.M.: Reducibility among Combinatorial Problems. In: Miller, R.E.,
    Thatcher, J.W., Bohlinger, J.D. (eds.) Complexity of Computer Computations.
    IRSS, pp. 85–103. Springer, Boston (1972). https://doi.org/10.1007/978-1-4684-
    2001-2_9
14. Liu, J., Jager, T., Kakvi, S.A., Warinschi, B.: How to build time-lock encryption.
    Des. Codes Crypt. 86(11), 2549–2586 (2018). https://doi.org/10.1007/s10623-018-
    0461-x
15. Naor, M.: On cryptographic assumptions and challenges. In: Boneh, D. (ed.)
    CRYPTO 2003. LNCS, vol. 2729, pp. 96–109. Springer, Heidelberg (2003). https://
    doi.org/10.1007/978-3-540-45146-4_6
16. Wu, J., Stinson, D.R.: An efficient identification protocol and the knowledge-of-
    exponent assumption. IACR Cryptology ePrint Archive 2007, 479 (2007)

Cryptographic Protocol II

Designated-Verifier Linkable Ring Signatures

Pourandokht Behrouz$^{(\boxtimes)}$ ⓘ, Panagiotis Grontas ⓘ, Vangelis Konstantakatos ⓘ, Aris Pagourtzis ⓘ, and Marianna Spyrakou ⓘ

School of Electrical and Computer Engineering, National Technical University of Athens, 9, Iroon Polytechniou Street, 157 80 Athens, Greece
{pbehrouz,mspyrakou}@mail.ntua.gr, pgrontas@corelab.ntua.gr,
pagour@cs.ntua.gr

Abstract. We introduce *Designated-Verifier Linkable Ring Signatures (DVLRS)*, a novel cryptographic primitive which combines designated-verifier and linkable ring signatures. Our goal is to guarantee signer ambiguity and provide the capability to the designated verifier to add 'noise' using simulated signatures that are publicly verifiable, thus increasing overall privacy. More formally, we model unforgeability, anonymity, linkability and non-transferability for DVLRS and provide a secure construction in the Random Oracle model. Finally, we explore applications for our primitive, that revolve around the use case of an anonymous assessment system that also protects the subject of the evaluation, even if the private key is compromised.

Keywords: Ring signatures · Designated verifier · Non-transferability · Linkability · Anonymity

1 Introduction

We present *Designated-Verifier Linkable Ring Signatures (DVLRS)*, a new type of privacy-oriented digital signature. Our primitive is a linkable ring signature [15], i.e. it protects the anonymity of the signers by 'hiding' their identity among a set of peers. Signed messages appear to be coming from the set as a whole, without the ability to exactly pinpoint the sender. Moreover, messages are publicly linkable, i.e. messages coming from the same sender can be identified and grouped together, without disclosing the sender's identity. At the same time our primitive is a designated-verifier signature [7], as it is simulatable by an entity designated during signing, while maintaining public verifiability. As a result, only this designated verifier can be convinced of which messages actually originate from signers in the ring. This option, however, is not available to the public, as all signatures are indistinguishable to them. Consequently, our scheme enhances the privacy of ring members, as no entity apart from the designated verifier can be convinced of the actual sender. At the same time, DVLRS provide more control to the designated verifier, as they can be used to inject 'noise' - fake messages with simulated signatures - thus altering the public view of the adversary. More importantly, it provides protection to the designated verifier against an adversary who tries to extort or otherwise gain hold of their private key, as even if they succeed, they can gain no valuable information on which messages come from real ring members and which are 'noise'. This makes our scheme useful to a number of privacy-focused scenarios such as evaluation systems and surveys for sensitive data.

1.1   Related Work

Since our primitive combines the notions of *Designated-Verifier Signatures (DVS)* and *Linkable Ring Signatures (LRS)*, we review the evolution of these primitives by focusing on their semantics and their security properties.

DVS were proposed in [7] as a way to restrict the entities that can be convinced by a proof. The relevant property, *non-transferability*, states that the verifier cannot use the resulting signatures to convince other parties. Their construction utilizes an OR proof, stating in effect that the signer knows their secret signing key or the secret key of the verifier. Verification uses both public keys. As a result, the designated verifier can be sure that the signer created a signature they did not create themselves. However, the public, while being able to check if the signature is valid, cannot distinguish between a signer-generated and a *simulated* signature, i.e. one created with the secret key of the verifier. A variation, *strong* DVS, also proposed in [7], are not publicly verifiable as the secret key of the designated verifier is a required input of the verification algorithm. The simplest way to create strong DVS is to encrypt (part of) the signature with the public key of the designated verifier, but other constructions are possible [21]. The applications of DVS range from copyright management to receipt-free and coercion-resistance electronic voting [8].

Subsequent works refined the construction and security properties of DVS. In [22] *non-transferability* was formally defined in the context of *universal designated-verifier* signatures, where the designation functionality is not restricted to the signer. In [12], it was noted that in some previous schemes the signer or the designated verifier could delegate their signing rights, by giving away a function of their respective secret keys and not fully revealing them. As this capability could have negative effects in some applications, a new property *non-delegatability* was defined. It essentially states that a non-delegatable DVS is a proof of knowledge of the signer or designated verifier secret key. They also note that the original DVS scheme of [7] was non-delegatable. In [11] a generic definition of DVS and their related security notions is presented.

Ring signatures were originally proposed in [20] as a method to *anonymize* the signer of a message, by hiding their identity inside a group of possible signers-peers. The signature was verified by the ring public key, without anyone being able to pinpoint the exact signer. Unlike previous schemes, e.g. [3], rings can be formed spontaneously and there is no group manager that may revoke the anonymity of the members. [15] proposed a ring signature as an OR proof by using the classic technique of [5] and added the feature of linkability, where signatures coming from the same signer were linked together using *pseudoidentities* or *tags*. The pseudoidentities were 'alternate' public keys - group elements computed using the private key of the signer - embedded in the signature that enabled the signer to remain anonymous. Their construction could be used to prevent double-voting in anonymous electronic elections. Linkable ring signatures have also been used in anonymous cryptocurrencies like Monero [18]. While in [15] the linkability tag results in computational anonymity, other constructions provided for perfect anonymity [13] and improved security models [16]. *Non-slanderability* [13] ensures that no signer can generate a signature that is determined to be linked to another one not generated by the same signer. Another variation, ring signatures with *designated linkability* [14] restrict who can link signatures. We stress that these signatures are in essence designated linker as the designation is applicable only to linking. Our primitive is entirely different as it considers designation for the verifier, specifying who can be certain that a signature is real and therefore be convinced by it. One drawback of ring signatures, is that while the cryptographic construction might hide the signer, its identity could be revealed from the contents of the message. DVLRS bypasses this problem with the capacity for simulated messages created by the designated verifier.

The notions of designated verifier and ring signatures have been combined in [10], where any holder of a ring signature can designate it to a verifier, and [9] which provides a *strong* DV ring signature for whistle blowing. However, these works do not consider the property of linkability, which makes our scheme more versatile. A first attempt to add linkability to designated verifier ring signatures was made in [4] for use in receipt free e-voting. The resulting signatures, however, are only strongly designated, since part of the signature is encrypted with the public key of the verifier. In addition they are not publicly linkable as the pseudoidentities are encrypted as well. So both verification and linking require the secret key. Our approach, DVLRS, are both publicly verifiable and publicly linkable. Furthermore, in [4], they only achieve non-transferability against a computationally bounded adversary[1]. A big advantage of our work is that we accomplish perfect non-transferability, i.e. even an unbounded attacker cannot distinguish signatures from simulations.

1.2 Contribution

To the best of our knowledge, Designated-Verifier Linkable Ring Signatures are the first attempt to combine *plain* designated-verifier signatures and *publicly* linkable ring signatures. We provide a generic security model and formally define all the relevant security properties that we think should be satisfied: unforgeability, anonymity, linkability and non-transferability. The definition of linkability is extended to include non-slanderability. Our definition for non-transferability is also novel since it adapts the one in [11] for linkability. This is of particular interest, since one has to make sure that the linkability tag does not allow an

---

[1] There is no security model or security analysis provided in [4] for their signature scheme, however it is straightforward to see that a computationally unbounded attacker can distinguish simulations. We omit the proof due to space limitations.

attacker to distinguish simulations. Our security model is a novel contribution on its own, as it can be used to evaluate future DVLRS instantiations.

We also provide a concrete construction for DVLRS and proofs for all its claimed security properties in the random oracle model. The proposed scheme builds upon the work of [15] and adds a designated verifier capable of simulating signatures and linking them to arbitrary ring members. We achieve *perfect* non-transferability, by making these simulations information theoretically indistinguishable. By construction, in our scheme, unforgeability amounts to a proof of knowledge for the secret key of the signer or the designated verifier. Thus DVLRS cannot be delegated and our proof of unforgeability directly implies a proof of non-delegatability [7,12]. Finally, we discuss applications of DVLRS by generalizing the case of an anonymous evaluation system that also protects the subject of the evaluation, even if the private key is compromised, by allowing the insertion of simulated signatures.

2   DVLRS Model

2.1   Notation and Assumptions

The security parameter is denoted by λ. We let n denote the size of the universe $\mathcal{U}$ of possible public keys and $n_L = |L|$ for a subset (ring) $L \subseteq \mathcal{U}$. We denote equality with $=$ and assignment with $\leftarrow$. All our security definitions are in the form of games which take as input the security parameter and return 1 for *True* and 0 for *False*. For conciseness, we return the condition and not its result. An algorithm that terminates unsuccessfully is denoted as returning $\bot$. A uniformly at random selection is denoted with $\leftarrow_s$. We assume the adversary $\mathcal{A}$ has state which is maintained throughout successive calls. In the games it is always omitted for brevity. We collectively refer to the cryptographic parameters of our scheme (groups, generators etc.) as params. They are an input to all our algorithms, but are also omitted. We denote a public key as pk and a secret key as sk. A pseudoidentity is denoted as pid. Typically it is computed as a function of the sk that is believed to be difficult to invert. Other parameters can also take part in its computation like the public keys of L like in [15], possibly combined with some event description from $\{0,1\}^*$ as in [13]. Its actual form depends on the application. We denote by $\mathcal{PID}$ the set of pid's. The designated verifier is denoted as D, while the index of the signer in the ring is π. The security of our scheme rests on standard cryptographic assumptions like the hardness of the discrete logarithm problem (DLP) and the decisional Diffie-Hellman assumption (DDH), which are omitted for brevity.

2.2   DVLRS Definition and Basic Properties

We begin by defining DVLRS and their basic security properties.

Definition 1. *A Designated-Verifier Linkable Ring Signature Π is a tuple of PPT algorithms (*Setup, KGen, Sign, Extract, Sim, Vrfy, Link*) with the following syntax:*

- params ← Setup(λ) *generates the parameters of DVLRS. These include cryptographic groups, the message space $\mathcal{MSG}$, and the set of possible pseudoidentities $\mathcal{PID}$.*
- (sk, pk) ← KGen() *is the key generation algorithm which allows keys to be created in an ad-hoc manner. This algorithm is used by all players including the designated verifier.*
- σ ← Sign(L, m, pk$_D$, sk$_\pi$) *is used to sign a message m by some $\pi \in [n_L]$.*
- pid ← Extract(σ) *is an algorithm that can obtain the pseudoidentity pid from a signature.*
- σ ← Sim(L, m, pk$_D$, sk$_D$, pid) *is the signature simulation algorithm that allows the designated verifier D to produce indistinguishable signatures for pseudoidentity pid.*
- $\{0, 1\}$ ← Vrfy(σ, L, m, pk$_D$) *is the verification algorithm which outputs 1 if the signature is valid and 0 otherwise.*
- $\{0, 1\}$ ← Link(σ, L, σ', L) *is the linking algorithm which outputs 1 if σ and σ' originate from the same signer or if they are simulated to look like they originate from the same signer.*

In Definition 1, the pseudoidentity pid must be given as input to the simulator to allow linking. This means that to link a simulated signature to a ring member, the designated verifier must first see a single signature from them. This might seem as a drawback of our definition, but in a practical application it is of no importance as its protocol could force all participants to post a single signed registration message for each pseudoidentity they assume. Such a message would not carry sensitive content. Then the designated verifier could use the Extract functionality to create a registry of pseudoidentities to simulate signatures. Furthermore, the designated verifier can create simulations taking random pid ←$_\$$ $\mathcal{PID}$. These won't be linked to the signatures of a real signer and can be generated before the verifier sees any signatures.

The completeness of our scheme is obtained from the following correctness properties that guarantee that honestly generated signatures are usable.

Verification Correctness states that honestly user-generated or simulated signatures are valid. More formally: If σ ← Sign(L, m, pk$_D$, sk) for sk $\in L$ or σ ← Sim(L, m, pk$_D$, sk$_D$, pid) for (pk$_D$, sk$_D$) ← KGen(), then Vrfy(σ, L, m, pk$_D$) = 1 with overwhelming probability. Otherwise Vrfy(σ, L, m, pk$_D$) = 0.

Linking Correctness states the conditions for linking. Two signatures over the same ring L, should always be linked if they are honestly generated by the same signer, if one is an honestly generated signature and a verifier created a simulation with the particular pseudoidentity or if they are simulations using the same pseudoidentity. Note that the inputs of the linking algorithm have to be valid signatures. If they are not, the output of this algorithm is irrelevant. Formally: Link(σ, L, σ', L) = 1 if and only if one of the following holds:

i σ ← Sign(L, m, pk$_D$, sk$_\pi$) and σ' ← Sign(L, m$'$, pk$'_D$, sk$_\pi$)
ii σ ← Sign(L, m, pk$_D$, sk$_\pi$) and σ' ← Sim(L, m$'$, pk$'_D$, sk$'_D$, Extract(σ))
iii σ ← Sim(L, m, pk$_D$, sk$_D$, pid) and σ' ← Sim(L, m$'$, pk$'_D$, sk$'_D$, pid)

Note here that we have limited linking to signatures formed over the same ring L. This is simply a choice made for ease of exposition. Modifying the definitions for linking over event tags [13] or even with no restrictions [1] is straightforward.

2.3 Adversarial Capabilities

We will consider a strong adaptive adversary that has the ability to add more users to the system, take control of users of its choice, collect all signatures ever exchanged and request signatures and simulations at will on behalf of any of the users of any ring. To model these capabilities of $\mathcal{A}$ we utilize the following oracles[2], similar to [12,13,17]:

- pk ← $\mathcal{JO}()$. The *Joining Oracle*, upon request adds a public key to the list of public keys $\mathcal{U}$, and returns it.
- sk ← $\mathcal{CO}(\mathsf{pk})$. The *Corruption Oracle*, on input a public key pk that is an output of $\mathcal{JO}$ returns the secret key sk such that $(\mathsf{pk}, \mathsf{sk}) \leftarrow \mathsf{KGen}()$.
- $\sigma \leftarrow \mathcal{SO}(L, \mathtt{m}, \mathsf{pk}_D, \mathsf{pk}_\pi)$. The *Signing Oracle*, on input a list of public keys L a message $\mathtt{m}$, a public key pk_D and a public key $\mathsf{pk}_\pi \in L$, outputs a signature σ such that $\sigma \leftarrow \mathsf{Sign}(L, \mathtt{m}, \mathsf{pk}_D, \mathsf{sk}_\pi)$ and $(\mathsf{pk}_\pi, \mathsf{sk}_\pi) \leftarrow \mathsf{KGen}()$.
- $\sigma \leftarrow \mathcal{MO}(L, \mathtt{m}, \mathsf{pk}_D, \mathsf{pid})$. The *Simulation Oracle*, on input a list of public keys L a message $\mathtt{m}$, a public key pk_D, a pseudoidentity pid, outputs a signature σ such that $\sigma \leftarrow \mathsf{Sim}(L, \mathtt{m}, \mathsf{pk}_D, \mathsf{sk}_D, \mathsf{pid})$ and $(\mathsf{pk}_D, \mathsf{sk}_D) \leftarrow \mathsf{KGen}()$.

These oracles capture the adaptive nature of $\mathcal{A}$. For example, as part of a potential attack, he can after receiving signatures of his choice from $\mathcal{SO}$, request that more users are added to the system from $\mathcal{JO}$, then request even more signatures potentially even from the newly added users, and so forth.

We must point out that while the adversary can collect all messages and signatures, it does not monitor communication addresses, timing information and related metadata, as such information would trivially enable them to distinguish between simulated and real signatures. In essence, we can assume that all signed messages are publicly available as standalone items. Additionally, we expect the designated verifier to adopt an obfuscation strategy when posting fake signatures.

2.4 Unforgeability

Unforgeability intuitively implies the inability of a party that is not a member of a ring to produce a valid signature for that ring, without designating themselves as the Designated-Verifier. To formally define unforgeability for a DVLRS scheme Π, we consider the experiment $\mathsf{Exp}^{\mathrm{unf}}_{\mathcal{A},\Pi,n}$ in Game 1.1.

The adversary queries all the oracles $(\mathcal{RO}, \mathcal{JO}, \mathcal{CO}, \mathcal{SO}, \mathcal{MO})$ according to any adaptive strategy. The corruption oracle $\mathcal{CO}$ models the ability of $\mathcal{A}$ to control any number of members of $\mathcal{U}$. With D_t we denote the set of indices of the keys that have been corrupted. $\mathcal{A}$ chooses the list of public keys L, a

---

[2] For convenience, we use the same symbol to denote both an oracle and its set of outputs.

Game 1.1: Unforgeability experiment $\mathsf{Exp}^{\mathrm{unf}}_{\mathcal{A},\Pi,n}$

Input : λ
Output: $\{0,1\}$

params $\leftarrow \Pi.\mathsf{Setup}(1^\lambda)$
$\mathcal{U} \leftarrow \left\{(\mathsf{pk}_i,\mathsf{sk}_i) \leftarrow \Pi.\mathsf{KGen}()\right\}_{i=1}^n$
$(\sigma, L = \{\mathsf{pk}_i\}_{i=1}^{n_L}, \mathtt{m}, \mathsf{pk}_D, D_t) \leftarrow \mathcal{A}^{\mathcal{RO},\mathcal{JO},\mathcal{CO},\mathcal{SO},\mathcal{MO}}(\mathcal{U})$
return $\mathsf{Vrfy}(\sigma, L, \mathtt{m}, \mathsf{pk}_D) = 1$ AND $\forall i \in D_t\ \mathsf{pk}_i \notin L$ AND $D \notin D_t$ AND
$\sigma \notin \mathcal{SO}$ AND $\sigma \notin \mathcal{MO}$

---

designated verifier D with corresponding public key pk_D, a message $\mathtt{m}$ and creates a forged signature σ. The adversary succeeds if the signature verifies, (i.e. $\mathsf{Vrfy}(\sigma, L, \mathtt{m}, \mathsf{pk}_D) = 1$) and if none of the keys contained in L, nor pk_D, have been queried to $\mathcal{CO}$ and if the signature is not the query output of $\mathcal{SO}$ or $\mathcal{MO}$.

Note that this corresponds to the strong security notion of *Unforgeability w.r.t insider corruption* of [2], adapted for the existence of a Designated-Verifier.

Definition 2. *Unforgeability*
A DVLRS scheme Π is unforgeable if for any PPT *adversary $\mathcal{A}$:*

$$\mathsf{Adv}^{\mathrm{unf}}_{\mathcal{A}}(\lambda) = \Pr\left[\mathsf{Exp}^{\mathrm{unf}}_{\mathcal{A},\Pi,n}(\lambda) = 1\right] \leq \mathsf{negl}(\lambda)$$

2.5   Anonymity

Anonymity, also referred to as *signer ambiguity* in [15], intuitively implies the inability of any party, including the designated verifier, to identify the private key used to create a signature. Formally, we consider the experiment $\mathsf{Exp}^{\mathrm{anon}}_{\mathcal{A},\Pi,n,t}$.

Game 1.2: Anonymity experiment $\mathsf{Exp}^{\mathrm{anon}}_{\mathcal{A},\Pi,n,t}$

Input : λ
Output: $\{0,1\}$

params $\leftarrow \Pi.\mathsf{Setup}(1^\lambda)$
$\mathcal{U} \leftarrow \left\{(\mathsf{pk}_i,\mathsf{sk}_i) \leftarrow \Pi.\mathsf{KGen}()\right\}_{i=1}^n$
$\mathsf{pk}_D \leftarrow \mathcal{A}(\mathbf{choose}, \mathcal{U})$
$(n_L, L = \{\mathsf{pk}_i\}_{i=1}^{n_L}, \mathtt{m}, D_t) \leftarrow \mathcal{A}^{\mathcal{RO},\mathcal{JO},\mathcal{CO},\mathcal{SO},\mathcal{MO}}(\mathcal{U})$
$\pi \leftarrow_\$ [n_L]$
$\sigma \leftarrow \Pi.\mathsf{Sign}(L, \mathtt{m}, \mathsf{pk}_D, \mathsf{sk}_\pi)$
$\xi \leftarrow \mathcal{A}^{\mathcal{RO},\mathcal{SO},\mathcal{CO},\mathcal{MO}}(\mathbf{guess}, L, \mathtt{m}, \sigma, D_t)$
if $\mathcal{SO}$ has not been invoked for (pk_π, L) AND $\pi \notin D_t$ AND $\xi \neq \bot$ **then**
| return $\xi = \pi$ AND $0 \leq t < n_L - 1$
else
| return $\bot$
end

The adversary selects a designated verifier and samples public keys in order to be able to request signatures for messages of their choice. $\mathcal{A}$ can also utilise existing signatures or simulations by respectively querying the oracles $\mathcal{RO}, \mathcal{SO}, \mathcal{MO}$. In order to perform the attack, it selects a ring L of n_L public keys and a message $\mathbf{m}$ to its benefit. $\mathcal{A}$ has also the power to control up to t members of the ring L, modelled by calls to the oracle $\mathcal{CO}$. The set of indices of corrupted members is again denoted by D_t and is dynamically updated each time $\mathcal{CO}$ is used. The challenger randomly selects a ring member (indexed by π) and creates a signature on its behalf. $\mathcal{A}$ must guess which member of the ring has signed the signature. Clearly, if $\mathcal{A}$ controls all members of L except π it can trivially win. As a result, we require that there are at least two members that are not controlled by $\mathcal{A}$ and that the oracle $\mathcal{CO}$ has not been queried for π.

Also, recall that our definition of linking correctness, does not allow linking signatures on different rings. As a result, $\mathcal{A}$ cannot link σ with signatures originating from singleton subrings of L.

Definition 3. *Anonymity*
A DVLRS scheme Π is t-anonymous if for any PPT *adversary $\mathcal{A}$:*

$$\mathsf{Adv}_{\mathcal{A}}^{\mathsf{anon}}(\lambda) = \Pr\left[\mathsf{Exp}_{\mathcal{A},\Pi,n,t}^{\mathsf{anon}}(\lambda) = 1\right] - \frac{1}{n_L - t} \leq \mathsf{negl}(\lambda)$$

2.6   Linkability

Linkability intuitively means that if two signatures come from the same signer over the same ring L, they have to be linked. Our notion is even stronger, we require that a signer that controls $k-1$ private keys cannot produce k valid pairwise unlinkable signatures. To formally define linkability for a DVLRS scheme Π, we use the experiment $\mathsf{Exp}_{\mathcal{A},\Pi,n}^{\mathsf{link}}$ in Game 1.3.

Game 1.3: Linkability experiment $\mathsf{Exp}_{\mathcal{A},\Pi,n}^{\mathsf{link}}$

Input : λ
Output: $\{0,1\}$

params $\leftarrow \Pi.\mathsf{Setup}(1^\lambda)$
$\mathcal{U} \leftarrow \left\{(\mathsf{pk}_i, \mathsf{sk}_i) \leftarrow \Pi.\mathsf{KGen}()\right\}_{i=1}^{n}$
$(\{\sigma_i\}_{i=1}^{k}, L = \{\mathsf{pk}_i\}_{i=1}^{n_L}, \{\mathbf{m}_i\}_{i=1}^{k}, \{\mathsf{pk}_{D_i}\}_{i=1}^{k}, D_t) \leftarrow \mathcal{A}^{\mathcal{RO},\mathcal{JO},\mathcal{CO},\mathcal{SO},\mathcal{MO}}(\mathcal{U})$

return $\mathsf{Vrfy}(\sigma_i, L, \mathbf{m}_i, \mathsf{pk}_{D_i}) = 1 \, \forall i \in [k]$ AND
$\mathsf{Link}(\sigma_i, L, \sigma_j, L) = 0 \, \forall i,j \in [k], \, i \neq j$ AND
$|\{pk_i : i \in D_t\} \cap L| < k$ AND $D_i \not\subseteq D_t \, \forall i \in [k]$ AND
$\sigma_i \notin \mathcal{SO} \, \forall i \in [k]$ AND
$\sigma_i \notin \mathcal{MO} \, \forall i \in [k]$

The adversary $\mathcal{A}$ queries all the oracles $(\mathcal{RO}, \mathcal{JO}, \mathcal{CO}, \mathcal{SO}, \mathcal{MO})$ according to any adaptive strategy. We denote by D_t the set of indices of ring members $\mathcal{A}$ has taken control of. This is modeled by calls to the corruption oracle $\mathcal{CO}$. $\mathcal{A}$ chooses the list of public keys L, k messages $\{\mathtt{m}_i\}_{i=1}^k$, k designated verifiers $\{\mathsf{pk}_{D_i}\}_{i=1}^k$ and creates k signatures $\{\sigma_i\}_{i=1}^k$. The adversary succeeds if all k signatures verify, (i.e. $\mathsf{Vrfy}(\sigma_i, L, \mathtt{m}_i, \mathsf{pk}_{D_i}) = 1$, $\forall i \in [k]$), if the signatures are pairwise unlinkable (i.e. $\mathsf{Link}(\sigma_i, L, \sigma_j, L) = 0$, $\forall i,j \in [k]$, $i \neq j$), if strictly less than k keys that are contained in L have been queried to $\mathcal{CO}$, if none of the signatures have a corrupted key as designated verifier and finally if the signatures $\{\sigma_i\}_{i=1}^k$ are not query outputs of $\mathcal{SO}$ or $\mathcal{MO}$. It should be noted, that designated verifiers are allowed to create signatures that are linked or unlinked with any given signature that is designated to them. This is by design, to ensure non-transferability.

Definition 4. *Linkability*
    A DVLRS scheme Π is linkable if for any PPT *adversary $\mathcal{A}$:*

$$\mathsf{Adv}_{\mathcal{A}}^{\mathrm{link}}(\lambda) = \Pr\left[\mathsf{Exp}_{\mathcal{A},\Pi,n}^{\mathrm{link}}(\lambda) = 1\right] \leq \mathsf{negl}(\lambda)$$

In the literature for linkable ring signatures, a weaker definition of linkability is often used [1,13]. This definition requires that a signer who controls a single private key, should not be able to produce two unlinkable signatures, but it allows, for example, a signer who knows two secret keys to produce three pairwise unlinkable signatures. This allows the adversary to circumvent linkability with a very realistic attack [16]; two colluding ring members who share their secret keys with each other can create signatures that are not linked to either of them. Therefore we opted for the stronger definition.

Finally, there is another notion closely related to linkability, called *non-slanderability* in [23]. Intuitively this ensures that given a signature generated by a member of a ring, even a collusion by all the rest, cannot produce a valid signature that is linked to it. However, this is a property that is implied by our stronger notion of linkability, together with unforgeability.

2.7   Non-transferability

Non-Transferability means that given a valid signature that is linked to signatures that are the output of the Sign algorithm, an adversary cannot distinguish whether it is the output of the Sign or Sim algorithm. Intuitively this ensures that signatures are only useful to the designated verifier, since a third party can never know whether a signature is real or a simulation. To formally define Non-Transferability for a DVLRS scheme Π, we use $\mathsf{Exp}_{\mathcal{A},\Pi,n}^{\mathrm{trans}}$ in Game 1.4.

The adversary in this experiment can be computationally unbounded. Consequently, it is not given access to the oracles $\mathcal{CO}, \mathcal{SO}, \mathcal{MO}$ since it can just compute their outputs. $\mathcal{A}$ chooses the ring L, a message $\mathtt{m}$, a designated verifier pk_D and a target ring member $\mathsf{pk}_\pi \in L$. The system produces a signature σ_0 and a simulation σ_1 with the same pseudoidentity pid, and randomly chooses to give one of them to $\mathcal{A}$. Note that for σ_1 to be created, σ_0 has to be generated first, so that the pid can be extracted. $\mathcal{A}$ then must guess if they received the signature or the simulation. Thus:

Game 1.4: Non-Transferability experiment $\mathsf{Exp}^{\text{trans}}_{\mathcal{A},\Pi,n}$

Input : λ
Output: $\{0,1\}$

params $\leftarrow \Pi.\mathsf{Setup}(1^{\lambda})$
$\mathcal{U} \leftarrow \left\{ (\mathsf{pk}_i, \mathsf{sk}_i) \leftarrow \Pi.\mathsf{KGen}() \right\}_{i=1}^{n}$
$(L = \{\mathsf{pk}_i\}_{i=1}^{n_L}, \mathtt{m}, \mathsf{pk}_D, \mathsf{pk}_\pi) \leftarrow \mathcal{A}^{\mathcal{RO},\mathcal{JO}}(\mathbf{choose}, \mathcal{U})$
$\sigma_0 \leftarrow \Pi.\mathsf{Sign}(L, \mathtt{m}, \mathsf{pk}_D, \mathsf{sk}_\pi)$
$\mathsf{pid}_0 \leftarrow \Pi.\mathsf{Extract}(\sigma_0)$
$\sigma_1 \leftarrow \Pi.\mathsf{Sim}(L, \mathtt{m}, \mathsf{pk}_D, \mathsf{sk}_D, \mathsf{pid}_0)$
$b \leftarrow_\$ \{0,1\}$
$b' \leftarrow \mathcal{A}^{\mathcal{RO},\mathcal{JO}}(\mathbf{guess}, L, \mathtt{m}, \sigma_b)$
return $b = b'$

Definition 5. *Non-Transferability*

A DVLRS scheme Π is perfectly non-transferable if for any unbounded adversary $\mathcal{A}$:

$$\mathsf{Adv}^{\text{trans}}_{\mathcal{A}}(\lambda) = \Pr\left[\mathsf{Exp}^{\text{trans}}_{\mathcal{A},\Pi,n}(\lambda) = 1 \right] - \frac{1}{2} = 0$$

It is worth noting that in $\mathsf{Exp}^{\text{trans}}_{\mathcal{A},\Pi,n}$, $\mathcal{A}$ has to distinguish between a signature and a simulation for the same pid. A more general security experiment would be for the system to randomly select a signer index $\pi \leftarrow_\$ [n_L]$ to generate $\sigma_0 \leftarrow \Pi.\mathsf{Sign}(L, \mathtt{m}, \mathsf{pk}_D, \mathsf{sk}_\pi)$ and randomly select a pid to generate $\sigma_1 \leftarrow \Pi.\mathsf{Sim}(L, \mathtt{m}, \mathsf{pk}_D, \mathsf{sk}_D, \mathsf{pid})$. $\mathcal{A}$ would again have to guess if they received the signature or the simulation. This stronger requirement however, is not needed to capture the intuitive notion of non-tranferability.

3   A DVLRS Construction

Our construction builds upon the signatures of [15], by adding a designated verifier capable of simulating signatures. Intuitively, the signature generation algorithm takes as input the public key of the designated verifier, apart from the public keys of the ring members. In effect, this means that a signature is a proof of knowledge of *either* a secret signing key *or* the secret designated verifier key. A 'real' signature is obtained from knowing the former, while a simulated signature from knowing the latter.

3.1   Setup

Our scheme operates in a group $\mathbb{G}$ of prime order q, where the DDH assumption holds. Messages are binary strings i.e. $\mathcal{MSG} = \{0,1\}^*$. The pseudoidentities are computed in $\mathbb{G}$, that is, $\mathcal{PID} = \mathbb{G}$. We assume that each signer has a credential consisting of a private part and its public counterpart. In particular, we consider n_L signers with private keys $\{\mathsf{sk}_i = x_i\}_{i=1}^{n_L} \in \mathbb{Z}_q$ and corresponding public keys

$\{\mathsf{pk}_i = y_i = g^{x_i}\}_{i=1}^{n_L} \in \mathbb{G}$. Messages are encoded as group elements $\mathbf{m} \in \mathbb{G}$. We assume two random oracles $\mathsf{H}_G, \mathsf{H}_q$ that map binary strings to $\mathbb{G}, \mathbb{Z}_q$ respectively.

3.2   Signature

The signer decides on a message $\mathbf{m}$ and signs it using DVLRS. Signature verification is public, but tied to a specific verifier identified by a key. The ring L consists of n_L public keys, namely $L = \{y_i\}_{i=1}^{n_L}$. The signer's index is π. We denote the designated verifier's private key by x_D and public key by $y_D = g^{x_D}$.

Signing. In order to generate the signature for message $\mathbf{m}$, the signer invokes the $\mathsf{Sign}(L, \mathbf{m}, \mathsf{pk}_D, \mathsf{sk}_\pi)$ algorithm:

- The signer computes $h \leftarrow \mathsf{H}_\mathbb{G}(L)$ and $\hat{y} \leftarrow h^{x_\pi}$ as the pseudoidentity.
- The signer picks $u, w_\pi, r_\pi \leftarrow_\$ \mathbb{Z}_q$ uniformly at random and computes:

$$c_{\pi+1} \leftarrow \mathsf{H}_q(L, \hat{y}, y_D, g^u, h^u, g^{w_\pi} y_D^{r_\pi}, \mathbf{m})$$

- For $i \in \{\pi+1, ..., n_L, 1, ..., \pi-1\}$, the signer picks $s_i, w_i, r_i \leftarrow_\$ \mathbb{Z}_q$ and computes:

$$c_{i+1} \leftarrow \mathsf{H}_q(L, \hat{y}, y_D, g^{s_i} y_i^{c_i+w_i}, h^{s_i} \hat{y}^{c_i+w_i}, g^{w_i} y_D^{r_i}, \mathbf{m})$$

- Finally, the signer sets $s_\pi \leftarrow u - (c_\pi + w_\pi) x_\pi$.
- The signature is $\sigma = (c_1, \{s_i\}_{i=1}^{n_L}, \{w_i\}_{i=1}^{n_L}, \{r_i\}_{i=1}^{n_L}, \hat{y})$

It is obvious from the form of the signature that $\mathsf{Extract}(\sigma) = \hat{y}$.

Verification. To verify the signature $\sigma = (c_1, \{s_i\}_{i=1}^{n_L}, \{w_i\}_{i=1}^{n_L}, \{r_i\}_{i=1}^{n_L}, \hat{y})$ a public verifier invokes the $\mathsf{Vrfy}(\sigma, L, \mathbf{m}, y_D)$ algorithm which:

- Recomputes $h \leftarrow \mathsf{H}_\mathbb{G}(L)$.
- For all ring members indexed by $i \in [n_L]$ it computes:

$$z_i' \leftarrow g^{s_i} y_i^{c_i+w_i}, \quad z_i'' \leftarrow h^{s_i} \hat{y}^{c_i+w_i}, \quad z_i''' \leftarrow g^{w_i} y_D^{r_i},$$
$$c_{i+1} \leftarrow \mathsf{H}_q(L, \hat{y}, y_D, z_i', z_i'', z_i''', \mathbf{m})$$

- The signature verifies if and only if:

$$c_1 = \mathsf{H}_q(L, \hat{y}, y_D, z_n', z_n'', z_n''', \mathbf{m})$$

Simulation. In order to generate a simulated signature on message $\mathbf{m}$, the designated verifier invokes the $\mathsf{Sim}(L, \mathbf{m}, y_D, x_D, \hat{y})$ algorithm, for some pseudoidentity $\hat{y} \in \mathbb{G}$:

- Compute $h \leftarrow \mathsf{H}_\mathbb{G}(L)$.
- Pick $\alpha, \beta, s_1 \leftarrow_\$ \mathbb{Z}_q$ and compute:

$$c_2 \leftarrow \mathsf{H}_q(L, \hat{y}, y_D, g^{s_1} y_1^{\beta}, h^{s_1} \hat{y}^{\beta}, g^{\alpha}, \mathbf{m})$$

- For $i \in \{2, ..., n_L\}$ wrapping-up to 1, select $s_i, w_i, r_i \leftarrow_\$ \mathbb{Z}_q$ and compute:

$$c_{i+1} \leftarrow \mathsf{H}_q(L, \hat{y}, y_D, g^{s_i} y_i^{c_i+w_i}, h^{s_i} \hat{y}^{c_i+w_i}, g^{w_i} y_D^{r_i}, \mathbf{m})$$

- Set $w_1 \leftarrow \beta - c_1$ and $r_1 \leftarrow (\alpha - w_1) \cdot x_D^{-1}$.
- The simulated signature is $\sigma = (c_1, \{s_i\}_{i=1}^{n_L}, \{w_i\}_{i=1}^{n_L}, \{r_i\}_{i=1}^{n_L}, \hat{y})$

Linking. The linking algorithm $\mathsf{Link}(\sigma, L, \sigma', L)$ outputs 1 if and only if $\mathsf{Extract}(\sigma) = \mathsf{Extract}(\sigma')$.

4 Security Analysis of Our Construction

We now analyse the security of our construction for completeness, unforgeability (Definition 2), anonymity (Definition 3), linkability (Definition 4) and nontranferability (Definition 5).

4.1 Completeness

Lemma 1. *An honestly generated DVLRS σ verifies correctly.*

Proof. It suffices to show that $z'_\pi = g^u$ and $z''_\pi = h^u$. Indeed:

$$z_\pi = g^{s_\pi} y_i^{c_\pi + w_\pi} = g^{u - x_\pi(c_\pi + w_\pi)} y_\pi^{c_\pi + w_\pi} = g^u$$
$$z''_\pi = h^{s_\pi} \hat{y}^{c_\pi + w_\pi} = h^{u - x_\pi(c_\pi + w_\pi)} \hat{y}^{c_\pi + w_\pi} = h^u$$

$\square$

Lemma 2. *A simulated DVLRS σ verifies correctly.*

Proof. It suffices to show that $z'_1 = g^{s_1} y_1{}^\beta$ and $z''_1 = h^{s_1} \hat{y}^\beta$ and $z'''_1 = g^a$. Indeed:

$$z'_1 = g^{s_1} y_1^{c_1 + w_1} = g^{s_1} y_1^{c_1 + \beta - c_1} = g^{s_1} y_1^\beta$$
$$z''_1 = h^{s_1} \hat{y}^{c_1 + w_1} = h^{s_1} \hat{y}^{c_1 + \beta - c_1} = h^{s_1} \hat{y}^\beta$$
$$z'''_1 = g^{w_1} y_D^{r_1} = g^{w_1} g^{x_D(a - w_1) x_D^{-1}} = g^a$$

$\square$

Lemma 3. *Our DVLRS scheme has linking correctness.*

Proof. Assume two signatures σ, σ' created on the same ring L. If they are honestly generated from the same signer π then $\mathsf{Extract}(\sigma) = \mathsf{Extract}(\sigma') = \hat{y} = h^{x_\pi}$ which means that $\mathsf{Link}(\sigma, L, \sigma', L) = 1$. If σ is honestly generated from signer π and σ' is a simulation for $\hat{y} = h^{x_\pi}$ then by construction $\mathsf{Link}(\sigma, L, \sigma', L) = 1$. The same applies to the case of two honest simulations. $\square$

Theorem 1. *Our DVLRS scheme has verification and linking correctness.*

Proof. A direct consequence of Lemma 1, Lemma 2, Lemma 3. $\square$

4.2   Unforgeability

Theorem 2 (Unforgeability). *Our DVLRS scheme is unforgeable in the $\mathcal{RO}$ model if DLP is hard in $\mathbb{G}$.*

The proof for Theorem 2 employs techniques from [6,13,15,19].

Proof. Assume a PPT adversary $\mathcal{A}$ which makes at most q_H queries to H_q and $\mathsf{H}_{\mathbb{G}}$ combined, and at most q_O queries to $\mathcal{JO}$, $\mathcal{CO}$, $\mathcal{SO}$ and $\mathcal{MO}$ combined and $\mathrm{Adv}_{\mathcal{A}}^{\mathrm{unf}}(\lambda) > \mathsf{negl}(\lambda)$. We will create an algorithm $\mathcal{M}$, that given as an input a generator $g \in \mathbb{G}$ and n_0 DLP instances $\{y_i\}_{i=1}^{n_0}$, outputs the discrete logarithm of at least one of them, i.e. a x_j such that $g^{x_j} = y_j$ for some $j \in [n_0]$ by using $\mathcal{A}$ as a subroutine, and therefore providing us with the desired contradiction. $\mathcal{M}$ sets as params $\mathbb{G}, g, q$ and $\mathcal{U} = \{y_i\}_{i=1}^{n_0}$ as the initial set of public keys, and gives them to $\mathcal{A}$. Whenever $\mathcal{A}$ queries one of the oracles, $\mathcal{M}$ will answer as below:

- H_q: $\mathcal{M}$ outputs $r \leftarrow_\$ \mathbb{Z}_q$.
- $\mathsf{H}_{\mathbb{G}}$: $\mathcal{M}$ calculates $r \leftarrow_\$ \mathbb{Z}_q$ and outputs g^r.
- $\mathcal{JO}$: $\mathcal{M}$ calculates $r \leftarrow_\$ \mathbb{Z}_q$ and adds g^r to $\mathcal{U}$.
- $\mathcal{CO}$: $\mathcal{M}$ on a query for a $y_j \notin \{y_i\}_{i=1}^{n_0}$ outputs the corresponding secret key r_j such as $g^{r_j} = y_j$. Otherwise halts for queries of $y_j \in \{y_i\}_{i=1}^{n_0}$.
- $\mathcal{SO}$: $\mathcal{A}$ gives $\mathcal{M}$, $L \subset \mathcal{U}$, a message $\mathbf{m} \in \mathbb{G}$, $y_\pi \in L$ and $y_D \in \mathcal{U}$. Let $g^r = h = \mathsf{H}_{\mathbb{G}}(L)$. If $y_\pi \notin \{y_i\}_{i=1}^{n_0}$ $\mathcal{M}$ knows r_π such that $g^{r_\pi} = y_\pi$ and computes $\sigma \leftarrow \mathsf{Sign}(L, \mathbf{m}, y_D, r_\pi)$, while maintaining consistencies for H_q and $\mathsf{H}_{\mathbb{G}}$. It outputs σ. Otherwise it chooses randomly $\{c_i\}_{i=1}^{n_L}, \{w_i\}_{i=1}^{n_L}, \{r_i\}_{i=1}^{n_L}, \{s_i\}_{i=1}^{n_L} \leftarrow_\$ \mathbb{Z}_q$ and computes $\hat{y} \leftarrow y_\pi^r$. For each $i \in [n_L]$ back patch to:

$$c_{i+1} \leftarrow \mathsf{H}_q(L, \hat{y}, y_D, g^{s_i} y_i^{c_i + w_i}, h^{s_i} \hat{y}^{c_i + w_i}, g^{w_i} y_D^{r_i}, \mathbf{m})$$

and output $\sigma = (c_1, \{s_i\}_{i=1}^{n_L}, \{w_i\}_{i=1}^{n_L}, \{r_i\}_{i=1}^{n_L}, \hat{y})$. Note that this looks just like a signature generated by ring member with public key y_π.
- $\mathcal{MO}$: $\mathcal{A}$ gives $\mathcal{M}$, $L \subseteq \mathcal{U}$, message $\mathbf{m} \in \mathbb{G}$, $y_D \in \mathcal{U}$ and $\hat{y} \in \mathbb{G}$. Let $g^r = h = \mathsf{H}_{\mathbb{G}}(L)$. If $y_D \notin \{y_i\}_{i=1}^{n_0}$ $\mathcal{M}$ knows r_D such that $g^{r_D} = y_D$ and computes $\sigma \leftarrow \mathsf{Sim}(L, \mathbf{m}, y_D, r_D, \hat{y})$, while keeping consistencies for H_q and $\mathsf{H}_{\mathbb{G}}$. It outputs σ. Otherwise it chooses randomly $\{c_i\}_{i=1}^{n_L}, \{w_i\}_{i=1}^{n_L}, \{r_i\}_{i=1}^{n_L}, \{s_i\}_{i=1}^{n_L} \leftarrow_\$ \mathbb{Z}_q$. For each $i \in [n_L]$ back patch to:

$$c_{i+1} \leftarrow \mathsf{H}_q(L, \hat{y}, y_D, g^{s_i} y_i^{c_i + w_i}, h^{s_i} \hat{y}^{c_i + w_i}, g^{w_i} y_D^{r_i}, \mathbf{m})$$

and output $\sigma = (c_1, \{s_i\}_{i=1}^{n_L}, \{w_i\}_{i=1}^{n_L}, \{r_i\}_{i=1}^{n_L}, \hat{y})$. Note that this looks just like a simulation generated by designated verifier with public key y_D and pseudoidentity $\hat{y}$.

We can assume that whenever $\mathcal{A}$ outputs a successful forgery, it has queried to the random oracles all of the n_L queries used in the Vrfy algorithm. It is trivial to show that if it had not, it would have only $\mathsf{negl}(\lambda)$ probability of success.

Also without loss of generality we can assume that successful forgeries will have $L \subseteq \{y_i\}_{i=1}^{n_0}$ and $y_D \in \{y_i\}_{i=1}^{n_0}$. Let $\{X_i\}_{i=i_1}^{i_{n_L}}$ denote the first time each of the queries used in Vrfy appear in the transcript of $\mathcal{A}$. We call a successful forgery σ an (l, π)-forgery if $i_1 = l$ and

$$X_{i_{n_L}} = \mathsf{H}_q(L, \hat{y}, y_D, g^{s_\pi - 1} y_{\pi - 1}^{c_\pi - 1 + w_{\pi - 1}}, h^{s_\pi - 1} \hat{y}^{c_\pi - 1 + w_{\pi - 1}}, g^{w_\pi - 1} y_D^{r_\pi - 1}, \mathsf{m})$$

Since $1 \leq l \leq q_H + n_L q_O$ and $1 \leq \pi \leq n_L$, there exist some l, π such that the probability that $\mathcal{A}$ produces a successful (l, π)-forgery is non negligible.

$\mathcal{M}$ will do a rewind simulation for each value of l and π. From the Rewind on Success Lemma [15] it will obtain with non negligible probability two successful (l, π)-forgeries σ, σ' with:

$$g^u = g^{s_\pi} y_\pi^{c_\pi + w_\pi} = g^{s_\pi + x_\pi (c_\pi + w_\pi)} \tag{1}$$

$$h^v = h^{s_\pi} \hat{y}^{c_\pi + w_\pi} = h^{s_\pi + x(c_\pi + w_\pi)} \tag{2}$$

$$g^\nu = g^{w_\pi} y_D^{r_\pi} = g^{w_\pi + x_D \cdot r_\pi} \tag{3}$$

$$g^u = g^{s_\pi'} y_\pi^{c_\pi' + w_\pi'} = g^{s_\pi' + x_\pi (c_\pi' + w_\pi')} \tag{4}$$

$$h^v = h^{s_\pi'} \hat{y}^{c_\pi' + w_\pi'} = h^{s_\pi' + x(c_\pi' + w_\pi')} \tag{5}$$

$$g^\nu = g^{w_\pi'} y_D^{r_\pi'} = g^{w_\pi' + x_D \cdot r_\pi'} \tag{6}$$

Since $c_\pi \neq c_\pi'$ it holds that $s_\pi \neq s_\pi'$ or $w_\pi \neq w_\pi' \wedge r_\pi \neq r_\pi'$.

- If $s_\pi \neq s_\pi'$: solving 1, 4 yields:

$$x_\pi = \frac{s_\pi' - s_\pi}{c_\pi - c_\pi' + w_\pi - w_\pi'} \mod q$$

- If $w_\pi \neq w_\pi' \wedge r_\pi \neq r_\pi'$: solving 3, 6 yields:

$$x_D = \frac{w_\pi' - w_\pi}{r_\pi - r_\pi'} \mod q$$

$\mathcal{M}$ has solved at least one hard DLP instance, a contradiction.   □

4.3   Anonymity

Theorem 3 (Anonymity).   *Our DVLRS scheme is anonymous (signer ambiguous) in the $\mathcal{RO}$ model if the DDH assumption holds in $\mathbb{G}$.*

To prove Theorem 3 we adapt the proofs of [15,16] for our scheme. In particular, assume a PPT adversary $\mathcal{A}$ which succeeds in the experiment $\mathsf{Exp}_{\mathcal{A}, \Pi, n, t}^{\mathrm{Anon}}$ with $\mathsf{Adv}_{\mathcal{A}}^{\mathrm{Anon}}(\lambda)$ at least ϵ after at most n queries to $\mathcal{JO}$, $q_{\mathsf{H_G}}$ queries to $\mathsf{H_G}$ and running time T. Then there exists an algorithm $\mathcal{M}$ that breaks the DDH assumption for $\mathbb{G}$ in time at most $n q_{\mathsf{H_G}} T$ with probability at least $\frac{1}{2} + \frac{\epsilon}{4}$.

Proof. We construct $\mathcal{M}$. Its input will be the group $\mathbb{G}$ (of order q) and a tuple of elements $A_\beta, B_\beta, C_\beta \in \mathbb{G}$. Assume that $A_\beta = g^a, B_\beta = g^b$ for $a, b \in \mathbb{Z}_q$ unknown to $\mathcal{M}$. Its output will be a bit β indicating if $C_\beta = g^{ab}$, $(\beta = 1)$ or not $(\beta = 0)$.

$\mathcal{M}$ begins by simulating $\mathcal{JO}$. For $y_\pi \in L$ to hold, it follows that $\mathcal{A}$ has queried $\mathcal{JO}$ for it. $\mathcal{M}$ selects a random $\mathcal{A}$ query and substitutes $y_\pi = A_\beta$. All other such queries are answered with a random $y \leftarrow_\$ \mathbb{G}$. In the same manner $\mathcal{M}$ randomly selects one of the queries to $\mathsf{H_G}$ and returns $h = B_\beta$. All other queries to $\mathsf{H_G}$ are simulated by returning $h = g^k, k \leftarrow_\$ \mathbb{Z}_q$. The answer to an $\mathcal{SO}(L', \mathsf{m}', y_D, y)$ query for some $L' = \{y_i\}_{i=1}^{n'_L}$ is simulated as:

- Select $\pi' \leftarrow_\$ [n_{L'}]$
- If $h \neq B_\beta$ then set $\hat{y} = y_{\pi'}^k$,
- If $h = B_\beta$ and $y_\pi = A_\beta$ then set $\hat{y} = C_\beta$
- If $h = B_\beta$ and $y_\pi \neq A_\beta$ then set $\hat{y} = B_\beta^{x_{\pi'}}$
- Select $c_{\pi'}, \{s_i, w_i, r_i\}_{i=1}^{n_{L'}} \leftarrow_\$ \mathbb{Z}_q$ and for $i \in \{\pi', \cdots, n_{L'}, 1, \cdots, \pi'-1\}$ compute $\{c_{i+1} \leftarrow \mathsf{H}_q(L', \hat{y}, y_D, g^{s_i} y_i^{c_i+w_i}, h^{s_i} \hat{y}^{c_i+w_i}, g^{w_i} y_D^{r_i}, \mathsf{m}')\}$
- Set $c_{\pi'} \leftarrow \mathsf{H}_q(L', \hat{y}, y_D, g^{s_{\pi'-1}} y_{\pi'-1}^{c_{\pi'-1}+w_{\pi'-1}}, h^{s_{\pi'-1}} \hat{y}^{c_{\pi'-1}+w_{\pi'-1}}, g^{w_{\pi'-1}} y_D^{r_{\pi'-1}}, \mathsf{m}')$.

When $\mathcal{M}$ receives (L, m, D_t) it checks if $y_\pi \in L$ and $\pi \notin D_t$, which occurs with probability $\frac{n_L - t}{n}$ and that there exists a query for L in $\mathsf{H_G}$, which is true with probability $\frac{1}{q_H}$. Otherwise it halts. If $\mathsf{H_G}(L)$ has not been queried with L, then it sets $B_\beta = \mathsf{H_G}(L)$. Then $\mathcal{M}$ generates the challenge signature σ. The $\mathcal{CO}$ calls are answered faithfully, except if x_π is requested. Then $\mathcal{M}$ returns $\perp$. If the **guess** stage is successfully completed, $\mathcal{A}$ returns $\xi \in [n_L]$. If $\xi = \pi$ then $\mathcal{M}$ returns 1. Otherwise $\mathcal{M}$ selects uniformly at random from $\{0, 1\}$.

In the case of a DDH tuple $(\beta = 1)$, $\mathcal{A}$ succeeds in $\mathsf{Exp}_{\mathcal{A}, \Pi, n, t}^{\mathrm{Anon}}$ with probability at least $\frac{1}{n_L - t} + \epsilon$. This means:

$$\Pr[\mathcal{M}(A_\beta, B_\beta, C_\beta) = 1 | \beta = 1] \geq (\frac{1}{n_L - t} + \epsilon) + \frac{1}{2}(1 - \frac{1}{n_L - t} - \epsilon) \geq \frac{1}{2} + \frac{1}{2(n_L - t)} + \frac{\epsilon}{2}$$

In the case of a non-DDH tuple $(\beta = 0)$, if $\xi = \pi$ then $\mathcal{M}$ cannot return 0. Otherwise, it selects its output uniformly at random:

$$\Pr[\mathcal{M}(A_\beta, B_\beta, C_\beta) = 0 | \beta = 0] = (\frac{1}{n_L - t}) \cdot 0 + (1 - \frac{1}{n_L - t}) \cdot \frac{1}{2} = \frac{1}{2} - \frac{1}{2(n_L - t)}$$

As a result: $\Pr[\mathcal{M}(A_\beta, B_\beta, C_\beta) = \beta] \geq \frac{1}{2} + \frac{\epsilon}{4}$, a contradiction.

Regarding the running time $\mathcal{M}$ halts with probability $\frac{n_L - t}{n} \cdot \frac{1}{q_H}$. Thus after at most $\frac{n q_H}{n_L - t}$ executions $\mathcal{A}$ will have succeed once. If the running time of $\mathcal{A}$ is at most T on success, $\mathcal{M}$ requires at most $n q_h T$ steps. $\square$

4.4   Linkability

Theorem 4 (Linkability). *Our DVLRS scheme is linkable in the $\mathcal{RO}$ model if DLP is hard in $\mathbb{G}$.*

Proof. We adapt the techniques of [6,15,19] for our stronger definition. Assume a PPT adversary $\mathcal{A}$ which makes at most q_H queries to H_q and $H_{\mathbb{G}}$ combined, and at most q_O queries to $\mathcal{JO}, \mathcal{CO}, \mathcal{SO}$ and $\mathcal{MO}$ combined, with $\mathsf{Adv}_{\mathcal{A}}^{\mathrm{link}}(\lambda) > \mathsf{negl}(\lambda)$. We will create an algorithm $\mathcal{M}$ that given as input a group $\mathbb{G}$ of order q, and n_0 DLP instances $\{y_i\}_{i=1}^{n_0}$ outputs the discrete logarithm of at least one of them, i.e. a x_j such that $g^{x_j} = y_j$ for some $j \in [n_0]$ by using $\mathcal{A}$, and therefore providing us with the desired contradiction on the assumption that DLP is hard. $\mathcal{M}$ sets as params $\mathbb{G}, g, q$ and $\mathcal{U} = \{y_i\}_{i=1}^{n_0}$ as the initial set of public keys, and gives them to $\mathcal{A}$. $\mathcal{M}$ simulates the oracle calls of $\mathcal{A}$ as in the proof of Theorem 2.

After a successful run, $\mathcal{A}$ will have output k signatures $\{\sigma_i\}_{i=1}^{k}$ that are pairwise unlinkable, for a ring $L \subseteq \mathcal{U}$ of its choice, for which it has corrupted less than k keys and has not corrupted any of the designated verifier keys $\{y_{D_i}\}_{i=1}^{k}$. W.l.o.g $\{y_{D_i}\}_{i=1}^{k} \subset \{y_i\}_{i=1}^{n_0}$ and at least one of the $y_i \in L$ for $i \in [n_0]$. The adversary must have, with negligible exception, queried to the random oracles all of the queries used in the Vrfy algorithm. So following the notation of the unforgeability proof in Subsect. 4.2, these will be (l_i, π_i)-forgeries for some values of $0 < l_i < q_H + n_L q_O$ and $1 < \pi_i < n_L$ for all $i \in [k]$.

We can distinguish 2 cases:

Case 1: $\mathcal{A}$ produces, with negligible exception, signature tuples with less than k distinct π_i. Therefore there will be at least one pair of signatures that are (l_a, π)-forgery and (l_b, π)-forgery for the same value π and w.l.o.g $l_a < l_b$. $\mathcal{M}$ will do a rewind simulation to the l_a'th query, and by the Rewind on Success Lemma [15], will get with non negligible probability $\{\sigma_i'\}_{i=a}^{k}$ with σ_a' being an (l_a, π)-forgery.

As in the proof of Theorem 2, we can derive from Eqs. 1, 2, 3, 4, 5, 6 that:

- If $s_\pi \neq s_\pi'$: solving 1, 2, 4, 5 yields:

$$x_\pi = x = \frac{s_\pi' - s_\pi}{c_\pi - c_\pi' + w_\pi - w_\pi'} \mod q$$

- If $w_\pi \neq w_\pi' \wedge r_\pi \neq r_\pi'$: solving 3, 6 yields:

$$x_D = \frac{w_\pi' - w_\pi}{r_\pi - r_\pi'} \mod q$$

This means that either the pseudoidentity of σ_a is $\hat{y}_a = h^{x_\pi}$ or the discrete logarithm of y_{D_a} is solved.

Now $\mathcal{M}$ does a rewind of the first transcript of $\mathcal{A}$ to the l_b'th query, and similarly ether solves the discrete logarithm of y_{D_b} or the pseudoidentity of σ_b is $\hat{y}_b = h^{x_\pi}$. However that means that $\mathsf{Link}(\sigma_a, L, \sigma_b, L) = 1$ which contradicts our assumption that the signatures $\mathcal{A}$ outputs are pairwise unlinkable.

Case 2: $\mathcal{A}$ produces signatures with k distinct π_i. $\mathcal{M}$ will do k rewind simulations, to the l_i'th query for every $i \in [k]$ and similarly to the unforgeability proof in Subsect. 4.2 will each time solve the discrete logarithm of y_{D_i} or y_{π_i}. Solving even one of the y_{D_i} is enough, since we assumed that $\{y_{D_i}\}_{i=1}^{k} \subset \{y_i\}_{i=1}^{n_0}$. Otherwise the discrete logarithm of every $y \in L$ is found, and since we assumed that at least one of the $y_i \in L$ for $i \in [n_0]$, again $\mathcal{M}$ has won. $\qquad\square$

4.5 Non-transferability

Theorem 5 (Non-Transferability). *Our DVLRS scheme is perfectly non-transferable in the $\mathcal{RO}$ model.*

Proof. We argue that the distributions of Sign and Sim for the same message m, ring L, designated verifier public key y_D and pseudoidentity $\hat{y}$ are the same.

We can look at each part of the signature σ_0 and simulation σ_1 separately: c_1 for both is the output of the random oracle H_q with at least one part of it's input chosen at random. Thus, c_1 is distributed uniformly at random in $\mathbb{Z}_q$.

All of the s_i are chosen at random for σ_1. For σ_0 all but s_π are also chosen at random. However $s_\pi \leftarrow u - (c_\pi + w_\pi)x_\pi$ with u being a random value, therefore s_π is also a uniformly random value in $\mathbb{Z}_q$. With a similar argument it can be shown that the values r_i and w_i are also distributed uniformly at random in $\mathbb{Z}_q$ for both the signature and the simulation.

The only remaining part of the signature is the pseudoidentity $\hat{y}$ and this will be the exact same group element for both σ_0 and σ_1. Note that the verifier can only produce such a simulation after first having seen a real signature from a ring member with that given pseudoidentity. This however gives no advantage to an adversary who tries to distinguish a signature from a simulation.

It is clear that $\mathcal{A}$ in $\mathsf{Exp}^{\mathrm{trans}}_{\mathcal{A},\Pi,n}$ is given at random one of two valid σ_0, σ_1 which follow the same distribution. Thus $\mathcal{A}$ cannot do better than a random guess. $\square$

Another property that we can prove for our scheme, is that an adversary that is given a simulation or a signature that have a random pseudoidentity, cannot distinguish them with non-negligible advantage. This additional property can be useful in some applications to give the designated verifier more freedom on creating 'noise'. Our scheme has this property, albeit only against a computationally bounded adversary. We omit the details.

5 Applications

DVLRS schemes have a number of useful applications which benefit from the novel combination of anonymity, linkability and non-transferability. Concretely, anonymous surveys or feedback systems satisfy the need for quality improvement by involving anonymous opinions of reviewers. Such systems are used, for instance, in educational institutions for instructor evaluation. However, the possibility of negative reviews, exacerbated by the anonymity of the reviewers, might hinder adoption. DVLRS allow for the evaluation to keep only its intrinsic value for the instructors by enabling them, as designated verifiers, to add 'noise' to the reviews using messages with simulated signatures. Thus the reviewees will be able to improve themselves and at the same time avoid repercussions for negative reviews. This feature will make adoption of such systems easier.

In particular, by using DVLRS, reviewers can form rings according to organizational characteristics (e.g. a course) and anonymously submit authentic feedback using the Sign algorithm. The reviewees, on the other hand, will be able to group feedback signed by the same reviewer, using the Link algorithm. The linkability property, will allow the formation of a consistent view of individual opinions and their evolution through the course of time. Thus, instructors, as the designated verifiers, will be able to adapt their techniques and monitor the results. At the same time, they will be able to simulate signatures using the Sim algorithm and link them to the pseudoidentity of a reviewer, or to a random one. By the non-transferability property of the designated verifier signature, only the reviewee is aware which of the feedback were signed by the reviewers, and the results of the feedback are not transferable to a third party - i.e. a higher authority. Even if the private key of the designated verifier or any of the signers is compromised, it would still be impossible to distinguish which messages were generated by the designated verifier and which by the ring members. So, as we discussed in Subsect. 1.1, removing public verifiability cannot provide any help in this scenario.

Another use case of the DVLRS scheme is for enhanced privacy for leaking secrets, an application that served as the original motivation for ring signatures in [20]. As an example, assume that a member of a corrupted organisation wants to leak information to the authorities without revealing his identity. Using a plain ring signature as in [20], could result in the corrupted leadership punishing all the ring members indiscriminately. With DVLRS the information can be safely leaked by setting the authorities as the designated verifier so that there can be no proof of any leak. Now the signature cannot be used to convince the public, but the law enforcement can still use the information to initiate an investigation. Additionally, linkability helps the informant give updates on his information.

Similar applications, that benefit from the non-transferability property of the designated verifier apart from anonymity and linkability, can be found in protecting databases that contain sensitive data (such as medical or financial records). In many such cases, anonymity in the identities of the participants is not enough, since such data is extremely valuable or the subjects can be identified from the content of the messages. For instance, in financial surveys the participating companies usually submit fiscal data, which can be collected and correlated to other public sources. DVLRS schemes defend against such attacks, as the simulated signatures cast doubt on the authenticity of such data to everyone except the designated verifier. For the same reason, they add another layer of protection for the survey participants, as the ability to simulate signatures indistinguishable to the original makes buyers unsure of whether they are paying for authentic data. Furthermore, using the linkability property all the data belonging to a single entity could be linked, speeding up data retrieval and change tracking in the survey data for any participant.

6   Conclusion and Future Work

In further work, we plan to implement DVLRS and integrate it with an anonymous evaluation system, as described in Sect. 5. We also intend to explore different constructions of DVLRS that improve their security, functionality and efficiency. Concretely, our instantiation has signatures with size that scales linearly to that of the ring. We plan to make a construction with constant size signatures as in [1,23], while retaining all the desired security properties. Another direction we aim to explore, is an alternative construction that achieves unconditional anonymity in a manner similar to [13].

Finally, we plan to consider the possibility of modifying the semantics of nontransferability so that it treats ring members in a privileged manner, by allowing them to distinguish which signatures actually come from other ring members and which are simulations. This will open up new applications for DVLRS.

References

1. Au, M.H., Chow, S.S.M., Susilo, W., Tsang, P.P.: Short linkable ring signatures revisited. In: Atzeni, A.S., Lioy, A. (eds.) EuroPKI 2006. LNCS, vol. 4043, pp. 101–115. Springer, Heidelberg (2006). https://doi.org/10.1007/11774716_9
2. Bender, A., Katz, J., Morselli, R.: Ring signatures: stronger definitions, and constructions without random oracles. J. Cryptol. 22(1), 114–138 (2007). https://doi.org/10.1007/s00145-007-9011-9
3. Chaum, D., van Heyst, E.: Group signatures. In: Davies, D.W. (ed.) EUROCRYPT 1991. LNCS, vol. 547, pp. 257–265. Springer, Heidelberg (1991). https://doi.org/10.1007/3-540-46416-6_22
4. Chen, G., Wu, C., Han, W., Chen, X., Lee, H., Kim, K.: A new receipt-free voting scheme based on linkable ring signature for designated verifiers. In: 2008 International Conference on Embedded Software and Systems Symposia, pp. 18–23 (2008). https://doi.org/10.1109/ICESS.Symposia.2008.54
5. Cramer, R., Damgård, I., Schoenmakers, B.: Proofs of partial knowledge and simplified design of witness hiding protocols. In: Desmedt, Y.G. (ed.) CRYPTO 1994. LNCS, vol. 839, pp. 174–187. Springer, Heidelberg (1994). https://doi.org/10.1007/3-540-48658-5_19
6. Herranz, J., Sáez, G.: Forking lemmas for ring signature schemes. In: Johansson, T., Maitra, S. (eds.) INDOCRYPT 2003. LNCS, vol. 2904, pp. 266–279. Springer, Heidelberg (2003). https://doi.org/10.1007/978-3-540-24582-7_20
7. Jakobsson, M., Sako, K., Impagliazzo, R.: Designated verifier proofs and their applications. In: Maurer, U. (ed.) EUROCRYPT 1996. LNCS, vol. 1070, pp. 143–154. Springer, Heidelberg (1996). https://doi.org/10.1007/3-540-68339-9_13
8. Juels, A., Catalano, D., Jakobsson, M.: Coercion-resistant electronic elections. In: WPES 2005, pp. 61–70. ACM (2005). https://doi.org/10.1145/1102199.1102213
9. Lee, J.S., Chang, J.H.: Strong designated verifier ring signature scheme. In: Sobh, T. (ed.) Innovations and Advanced Techniques in Computer and Information Sciences and Engineering, pp. 543–547. Springer, Dordrecht (2007). https://doi.org/10.1007/978-1-4020-6268-1_95. ISBN 978-1-4020-6268-1
10. Li, J., Wang, Y.: Universal designated verifier ring signature (proof) without random oracles. In: Zhou, X., et al. (eds.) EUC 2006. LNCS, vol. 4097, pp. 332–341. Springer, Heidelberg (2006). https://doi.org/10.1007/11807964_34. ISBN 978-3-540-36851-9
11. Li, Y., Susilo, W., Mu, Y., Pei, D.: Designated verifier signature: definition, framework and new constructions. In: Indulska, J., Ma, J., Yang, L.T., Ungerer, T., Cao, J. (eds.) UIC 2007. LNCS, vol. 4611, pp. 1191–1200. Springer, Heidelberg (2007). https://doi.org/10.1007/978-3-540-73549-6_116

12. Lipmaa, H., Wang, G., Bao, F.: Designated verifier signature schemes: attacks, new security notions and a new construction. In: Caires, L., Italiano, G.F., Monteiro, L., Palamidessi, C., Yung, M. (eds.) ICALP 2005. LNCS, vol. 3580, pp. 459–471. Springer, Heidelberg (2005). https://doi.org/10.1007/11523468_38

13. Liu, J.K., Au, M.H., Susilo, W., Zhou, J.: Linkable ring signature with unconditional anonymity. IEEE Trans. Knowl. Data Eng. 26(1), 157–165 (2014)

14. Liu, J.K., Susilo, W., Wong, D.S.: Ring signature with designated linkability. In: Yoshiura, H., Sakurai, K., Rannenberg, K., Murayama, Y., Kawamura, S. (eds.) IWSEC 2006. LNCS, vol. 4266, pp. 104–119. Springer, Heidelberg (2006). https://doi.org/10.1007/11908739_8

15. Liu, J.K., Wei, V.K., Wong, D.S.: Linkable spontaneous anonymous group signature for ad hoc groups. In: Wang, H., Pieprzyk, J., Varadharajan, V. (eds.) ACISP 2004. LNCS, vol. 3108, pp. 325–335. Springer, Heidelberg (2004). https://doi.org/10.1007/978-3-540-27800-9_28

16. Liu, J.K., Wong, D.S.: Enhanced security models and a generic construction approach for linkable ring signature. Int. J. Found. Comput. Sci. 17(06), 1403–1422 (2006)

17. Liu, J.K., Wong, D.S.: Solutions to key exposure problem in ring signature. Int. J. Netw. Secur. 6(2), 170–180 (2008)

18. Noether, S.: Ring Signature Confidential Transactions for Monero. Cryptology ePrint Archive, Report 2015/1098

19. Pointcheval, D., Stern, J.: Security proofs for signature schemes. In: Maurer, U. (ed.) EUROCRYPT 1996. LNCS, vol. 1070, pp. 387–398. Springer, Heidelberg (1996). https://doi.org/10.1007/3-540-68339-9_33

20. Rivest, R.L., Shamir, A., Tauman, Y.: How to leak a secret. In: Boyd, C. (ed.) ASIACRYPT 2001. LNCS, vol. 2248, pp. 552–565. Springer, Heidelberg (2001). https://doi.org/10.1007/3-540-45682-1_32

21. Saeednia, S., Kremer, S., Markowitch, O.: An efficient strong designated verifier signature scheme. In: Lim, J.-I., Lee, D.-H. (eds.) ICISC 2003. LNCS, vol. 2971, pp. 40–54. Springer, Heidelberg (2004). https://doi.org/10.1007/978-3-540-24691-6_4. ISBN 978-3-540-21376-5

22. Steinfeld, R., Bull, L., Wang, H., Pieprzyk, J.: Universal designated-verifier signatures. In: Laih, C.-S. (ed.) ASIACRYPT 2003. LNCS, vol. 2894, pp. 523–542. Springer, Heidelberg (2003). https://doi.org/10.1007/978-3-540-40061-5_33

23. Tsang, P.P., Wei, V.K.: Short linkable ring signatures for e-voting, e-cash and attestation. In: Deng, R.H., Bao, F., Pang, H.H., Zhou, J. (eds.) ISPEC 2005. LNCS, vol. 3439, pp. 48–60. Springer, Heidelberg (2005). https://doi.org/10.1007/978-3-540-31979-5_5

ATSSIA: Asynchronous Truly-Threshold Schnorr Signing for Inconsistent Availability

Snehil Joshi$^{(\boxtimes)}$, Durgesh Pandey, and Kannan Srinathan

International Institute of Information Technology, Hyderabad,
Hyderabad, Telangana, India
{snehil.joshi,durgesh.pandey}@research.iiit.ac.in, srinathan@iiit.ac.in

Abstract. Threshold signature schemes allow any qualified subset of participants (*t-out-of-n*) to combine its shares and generate a signature that can be verified using a single threshold public key. While there are several existing threshold signature schemes, most are either *n-out-of-n* and/or require *consistent availability* of the exact same set of participants through several rounds. This can result in signer availability becoming a bottleneck in the signing process. Our threshold signature scheme removes this dependence by introducing truly threshold asynchronous signatures, i.e., once the message to be signed has been revealed, the signers simply sign and broadcast their signature. Our scheme also uses misbehaviour detection to impose accountability for invalid signing. We prove that our scheme is safe against known distributed attacks and is $EUF - CMA$ secure in the Random Oracle Model for up to $t - 1$ malicious participants.

Keywords: Digital signature · Threshold signatures · Secret sharing · Blockchain · Distributed protocols

1 Introduction

Currently, multi-signatures [12,20], aggregate signatures [13] and threshold signatures [12] are relevant approaches that are aiming to solve the problem of distributed signing. The *t-out-of-n* (t, n) threshold signature is a protocol which allows a subset S of the players to combine their shares and reconstruct the private key to sign a message if, $S, \geq t$, but disallows generating a valid signature if, $S, < t$. This property holds even in the presence of colluding, malicious participants as long as they number less than the threshold t.

Threshold signatures have seen an increased interest since the advent of blockchain technology after Nakamoto's white-paper on Bitcoin [1] as these signatures can be used by participants for signing transactions in blockchains. However, with a *dynamic and distributed* system spanning the world, the problem of latency due to communication overhead or unavailability of participating nodes arises. Any improvement in this regard is very useful in not just blockchains, but any application requiring distributed permissions.

J. H. Park and S.-H. Seo (Eds.): ICISC 2021, LNCS 13218, pp. 71–91, 2022.
https://doi.org/10.1007/978-3-031-08896-4_4

1.1   Related Work and Motivation

Several distributed signature schemes exist for DSA (and ECDSA), Schnorr and BLS signatures. One of the first ideas came from the paper by Micali et al. [22] on accountable subgroup multi-signatures. Their protocol uses Schnorr signatures and takes three rounds to sign. First the validity of the individual signatures is checked and then they are counted to see if they reach the threshold value. Other multi-signature schemes use similar methods where each signature needs to be verified separately. Similarly for simple aggregate signatures, a *t-out-of-n* multi-signature would result in $^{n}C_t$ possible key pairs for the group signature. A neater solution would have a single public key that the aggregated threshold signature can be verified with.

In this direction, Shoup [5] developed a threshold scheme based on RSA signatures. Boneh et al. [13,14] created the BLS signature scheme that uses pairing based cryptography to provide a more efficient signing. Similarly, Maxwell et al. [12] used Schnorr aggregate signatures for signing blockchain transactions, Lindell et al. [9,10] presented a result for threshold ECDSA signatures using multiplicative-to-additive technique while Gennaro et al. [7,8] created a scheme for ECDSA signatures.

While current threshold signature work well in specific scenarios, they suffer from one or more of the following issues:

- For truly-threshold (t, n) non-interactive protocols, only pairing-based solutions [13] exist. Pairing-based protocols while being excellent, may be difficult to adopt in some systems due to compatibility issue with already deployed signing protocols as well as reliance on a different security assumption, namely pairings, which is an additional security assumption which everyone may not be willing to incorporate in their systems right away.
- For non-pairing based protocols, most protocols focus on the all-or-nothing case of $t = n$ [8,12,16] but ignore an efficient implementation of the same in *truly* threshold protocols where $t \leq n$.
- Even with the case of $t = n$, multiple interactive rounds are required in the signing phase (at least 2 for Schnorr signatures) [12,16] in most cases to generate the group's threshold signature.
- A signer that opts to participate in the a Schnorr-based multi-party signing protocol has to be available in *every* round till the aggregation of the protocol. Even with more efficient approaches like Komolo and Goldberg [15], the signers once fixed in the nonce-determining round can not be substituted during the signing phase without invalidating the threshold signature.

Our work looks at all these issues and aims to improve upon them.

We take time here to compare our scheme with that of Komlo and Goldberg [15] since ours is most similar to it. There are two main advantages of our scheme over [15]:

- In [15], signature scheme a signature aggregator selects the participants for nonce-generation. Once this selection has been made, the exact same group of

signers need to sign the message in the singing round. This effectively makes the signing round all-or-nothing, where if a participant from the previous round is missing, it will result in an incomplete signature. In our scheme, the signing is truly independent in terms for choice of participants. When any $\geq t$ signers sign the message, it will always result in the correct threshold signature.
- The second advantage is in terms of rounds used. Our protocol does not require the signers to be online together at all in the signing phase. In [15], there are one round (with pre-processing) and two rounds (without pre-processing).

To obtain these advantages, we have to bear a overhead of communication complexity in our pre-processing round (an extra overhead of 2π distributed nonce-generations) as compared to simple commitments used in [15]. However, we consider it a fair trade-off in return of an asynchronous and robust signing round.

1.2 Contributions

We present an efficient threshold signing scheme based on Schnorr signature, ATSSIA, with a non-interactive signing phase allowing for players to asynchronously participate without requiring to be online simultaneously. It achieves the same level of security as single-Schnorr signatures while having all the following desirable properties:

- Truly (t, n) threshold
- Based on widely-used cryptographic assumptions (DLOG)
- Asynchronous non-interactive signing phase
- No presumption on choice of t participants that will sign
- No wait-latency for unavailable participants because of 4 above
- Secure against ROS Solver and Drijvers' attacks during concurrent signing
- Provides in-built misbehaviour detection

Table 1 illustrates these properties

Table 1. Comparison with other Threshold schemes

Scheme	Musig	Musig2	BLS	FROST (1R)	FROST (2R)	ATSSIA
Truly (t, n)	No	No	Yes	Yes	Yes	Yes
Dynamic participants	No	No	Yes	No	No	Yes
Non-interactive	No (3)	No (2)	Yes	No (1)	No (2)	Yes
Base scheme	**Schnorr**	**Schnorr**	Pairings	**Schnorr**	**Schnorr**	**Schnorr**
Without pre-processing	Yes	No	Yes	No	Yes	No
Robust	Yes	Yes	Yes	No	No	Yes

In addition, our scheme retains all the important properties of threshold signatures while having a single public key for the threshold signature [12].

All the computations are distributed and the secret values are never directly reconstructed to avoid a single point of failure. Unlike Stinson and Strobl [30], our scheme supports asynchronous signing and is also secure against the ROS Solver [17] and Drijvers' attacks [29] under the Random Oracle Model. Additionally, we provide for misbehaviour detection for robustness. A faulty signature will be verified for misbehaviour and removed (and economically penalised in a blockchain setting) and the threshold signature can then be calculated as long as honest partial-signatures meet the threshold criteria.

1.3   Organization of the Paper

Our paper is divided into six sections. Section 1 introduces our main idea and underlines the motivation for our work. Section 2 consists of the preliminaries and definitions we will be using for the rest of the paper. Section 3 and 4 describe the protocol and the security proof for it respectively. The last section underlines the importance of the usage of our protocol in blockchain and upcoming directions in the research.

2   Preliminaries

2.1   Communication and Adversary Model

Our communication model has a reliable broadcast channel as well as *peer-to-peer* channels between all participating nodes. We assume a probabilistic polynomial time malicious adversary who can statically corrupt up to $t - 1$ participating nodes. The key and nonce generation phases require *all* participants to be present. However, the signing phase doesn't require all the signing parties to be present at the same time. We also assume possibility of a rushing adversary.

2.2   Message Indexing

Since our protocol uses batch processing for generating pre-nonce values, we need a method for keeping track of the message to be signed in any signing round so signers can provide the correct partial-signature for that message. A reliable message indexing system will make it possible for any available signer i to sign multiple messages without risk of wasting its nonce on an out-of-queue message. This can be achieved using a message server which indexes the messages in a queue: $m_1....m_j...m_\pi$. Any signer i can check the message index j to be signed and match it against the appropriate pre-nonce values.

Please note that this does not affect the security of our protocol. Since our protocol is secure in concurrent signing, even a malicious adversary controlling the message server and $t - 1$ signers will not be able to forge the threshold signature. At its best, a malicious message server can generate invalid threshold signatures using different messages for the same round. Faulty threshold signatures thus generated will be promptly invalidated and removed during signature aggregation.

2.3   Cryptographic Assumptions

The DLOG assumption: Let p be a prime whose size is linear in k. Given a generator g of a multiplicative group G of order p and $a \in Z_p^*$, the discrete logarithm or $DLog$ assumption suggests that $Pr[A_{DLog}(g, g^x) = x] \in (\kappa)$ for every polynomial-time adversary A_{DLog}.

Now we will define the concepts of VSS, Threshold signatures and Schnorr signature scheme that we will use to build our protocol.

2.4   Threshold (t, n) Secret Sharing

Given integers t, n where $t \leq n$, a (t, n) threshold secret sharing scheme is a protocol used by a dealer to share a secret s among a set of n nodes in such a way that any subset of $\geq t$ can efficiently construct the secret, while any subset of size $\leq t - 1$ can not [23].

To distribute the secret, the dealer first randomly selects $t - 1$ values $a_1, ..., a_{t-1}$, and then uses them as coefficients of polynomial $f(x) = \Sigma a_i \cdot x_i$. The secret is defined as $f(0) = s$.

The dealer then assigns indices i to each of the n nodes and gives them their secret share as $(i, f(i))$. The secret can then be reconstructed using Lagrange interpolation with any subset of size $\geq t$. Since a minimum of t points are needed to represent the polynomial, no subset of size less than t can find the secret [23].

2.5   Verifiable Threshold (t, n) Secret Sharing

To prevent malicious dealing by the trusted dealer, we utilize verifiable secret sharing (VSS) [24]. The (t, n) VSS scheme consists of a sharing and a reconstruction phase.

In the sharing phase, the dealer distributes the secret $s \in G$ among n nodes. At the end of this, each honest node holds a share s_i of the secret. In the reconstruction phase, each node broadcasts its secret share and a reconstruction function is applied in order to compute the secret $s = Reconstruct(s_0, ...s_n)$ or to output $\perp$ indicating that the dealer is malicious.

2.6   The Schnorr Signature Scheme

Let $\mathbb{G}$ be the elliptic curve group of prime order q with generator G. Let H be a cryptographic hash function mapping to Z_q^*. For a message m the Schnorr signature is calculated as follows:

- *Key Generation*
  Generate public-private key pair: $(x, P = x \cdot G)$ where x is a random point in Z_q and G is a generator in $\mathbb{G}$ be the elliptic curve group of prime order q with generator G
- *Signing*
  Choose random nonce $k \in Z_q$; Compute public commitment $r = k \cdot G$
  Compute: $e = H(P, r, m)$;
  Compute: $s = k + e \cdot x$
  The signature is $\sigma = (r, s)$
- *Verification*:
  Given values m, P, σ
  extract r and s from σ and compute $e_v = H(P, r, m)$
  compute $r_v = s \cdot G - e_v \cdot P$
  if $r_v = r$ then verified successfully

While we are specifically using Schnorr signature scheme over elliptic curves in our paper, our protocol can directly translate to the discrete logarithm problem as we are following standard group operations.

2.7   Threshold Signatures Schemes

Threshold signature schemes utilize the (t, n) security property of threshold protocols in aggregate signature schemes. This allows signers to produce a group signature over a message m using their secret key shares such that the final signature is identical to a single party one. This allows signing without knowing the secret and also verification of the threshold aggregate signature is as simple as that of a regular signature. In threshold signature schemes, the secret key s is distributed among the n participants, while a single key P is used to represent the group's public key.

To avoid point of single failure, most threshold schemes also need to generate their shares distributively instead of relying on a trusted dealer [26].

3   ATSSIA: Asynchronous Truly Threshold Schnorr Signatures for Inconsistent Availability

3.1   Overview

A signature scheme has three stages: *KeyGen*, *Sign* and *Verify*. We modify it by adding a pre-processing phase for nonce-generation *PreNonceGen* and replace the *Sign* phase with two separate phases of *PartSign* and *Aggregate*. We also provide the optional phase for misbehaviour detection in case of faulty partial signatures being generated.

To keep our signing phase non-interactive, we generate pre-nonce values for all participants in the interactive *PreNonceGen* phase. All the n participants are indexed using numbers $\{1, ...n\}$ both for clarity as well as ease of calculating Lagrange coefficients and other values. The participant index values are made publicly available. Additionally, we have a message indexing system that maintains an index table for each message being broadcast for signing. This index is also publicly available. This is a necessity for coordination for concurrent message signing in a non-interactive signing phase as signers need to match the values produced in *PreNonceGen* phase with the corresponding message.

Our signature scheme is denoted by $(\mathbb{G}, q, g)$, where q is a k-bit prime, $\mathbb{G}$ is a cyclic group of order q and G is the generator of $\mathbb{G}$. The correctness for group parameter generation follow standard procedures that can be verified.

We provide an overview of our scheme next.

Overview of ATSSIA

- **KeyGen** : All n-participants generate their key pairs (x_i, p_i) using a DKG

- **PreNonceGen**: All n-participants generate π pairs of pre-nonce pairs $k_{ij}{}^a$ and $k_{ij}{}^b$ using π parallel DKGs. They broadcast the corresponding commitment values of $r_{ij}{}^a = k_{ij}{}^a \cdot G$ and $r_{ij}{}^b = k_{ij}{}^b \cdot G$

- **PartSign**: When an individual signer receives a message m_j for it confirms the message index j and signs the message using the corresponding nonce value:
  $\sigma_{ij} = (s_{ij}, R_j, r_{ij})$ where:
  $s_{ij} = (k_{ij}{}^a + h_j \cdot k_{ij}{}^b) + H_m(m_j, R_j, P) \cdot x_i + \rho \cdot H_m(m_j, r_{ij}, p_i) \cdot x_i$
  (we will explain in Section 3.3 how the values h_j, R_j and ρ are calculated)
  This value is then broadcast for aggregation.
- **Aggregate**: Once at least t valid partial-signatures have been broadcast for a given message, they can be aggregated publicly by anyone using Lagrange interpolation
  $S_j = \sum_i \lambda_i \cdot s_{ij}$

- **Verify**: The final signature can be verified as:
  $(S_j \cdot G) \bmod \rho =? R_j + H_m(m_j, R_j, P) \cdot P$
  (mod by ρ removes the misbehaviour detection portion of the signature)

- *Misbehaviour Detection (Optional)*: A misbehaving signer can be detected by verifying the individual signer's signature using:
  $S_j \cdot G -? R_j + H_m(m_j, R_j, P) \cdot P + \rho \cdot H_m(m_j, r_{ij}, p_i)) \cdot p_i$

3.2 KeyGen

We use a variation of Pedersen's DKG scheme [18] by Komlo and Goldberg [15] to generate our threshold keys. It differs from Pedersen's scheme by providing security against a rogue-key attack for a dishonest majority setting by demanding a ZKPoK from each participant w.r.t their secret. Note that Pedersen's DKG is simply where each participant executes Feldman's VSS as the dealer in parallel, and derives their secret share as the sum of the shares received from each of the n VSS executions. So we get n eligible nodes running n VSS protocols in parallel to distributively generate the shares for the secret key X for the threshold signature. The 2-round KeyGen phase is as follows:

KeyGen

We assume $WLOG$ the n participants are indexed as i where $i \in 1, 2...n$. This improves reading the text of the protocol and makes it easier to calculate their Lagrange coefficients in the aggregate phase.

1. Each participant i generates t random values $(a_{i_0}, ..., a_{i_{t-1}})$ in Z_q and uses these values as coefficients to define a polynomial $f_i(x) = \Sigma_{l=0}^{t-1}(a_{i_l} \cdot y^l)$ of degree $t - 1$ in Z_q

2. Each i also computes a proof of knowledge for each secret a_{i_0} by calculating $\sigma = (w_i, c_i)$ where a_{i_0} is the secret key, such that $k \in Z_q, R_i = k \cdot G, h_i = H(i, S, a_{i_0} \cdot G, R_i), c_i = k + a_{i_0} \cdot h_i$, where S is the context string to prevent replay attacks.

3. Each i then computes its public commitment $C_i = < A_{i_0}, ..., A_{i_{t-1}} >$, where $A_{i_j} = a_{i_j} \cdot G$, and broadcasts (C_i, σ_i) to all other participants.

4. After participant i receives (C_j, σ_j), $j \neq i$, from all other participants $j \neq i$ it verifies $\sigma_j = (w_j, c_j)$ by computing $h_j = H(j, S, A_{j_0}, w_j \cdot G)$ and then checking for $w_j = c_j \cdot G - A_{j_0} \cdot h_j$ with $\perp$ (abort) on failure.

5. Next each i sends the secret share $(i, f_i(j))$, to every other participant P_j while keeping $(i, f_i(i))$ for itself.

6. Now each i verifies its shares by checking if $f_j(i) \cdot G = \Sigma(A_{j_k} \cdot (i^k mod q)), k = 0...t - 1$, with $\perp$ on failure.

7. Each i finally calculates its individual private key share by computing $x_i = \Sigma_j f_j(i), j = 1...n$, and stores $x(i)$ securely.

---

8. Additionally, each i also calculates its public share for verification $p_i = x_{(i)} \cdot G$, and the group's public key $P = \Sigma_j^n A_{j_0}, j = 1...n$. The participants can then compute the public share for verification for all the other participants by calculating $p_j = \Sigma_j^n \Sigma_k^{t-1} (A_{j_k} \cdot (i^k mod q)), j = 1...n, k = 0...t-1)$. These p_i values also act as the individual public key for the corresponding i participant.

At the end of the KeyGen phase we get:

partial private key shares: $x_1 ... x_n$ partial public key shares: $p_1 ... p_n$

group public key: P where $P = X \cdot G$

Each participant has the value (i, x_i). Any $\geq t$ such values can combine to give the secret X.

We point here that there might be more scalable protocols available with similar level of security. For example, Canny and Sorkin [27] can provide more efficient (poly-logarithmic) DKGs. However, all such protocols currently require special use-cases of low tolerance and a trusted dealer in the pre-processing phase which makes them impractical for our specific case of truly distributed threshold signing.

3.3   PreNonceGen

Before signing a message m for a round j, at least t nodes need to collaborate to generate a unique group nonce R_j. Since this can not be achieved using deterministic nonce generation in our case, we opt to generate and store nonces in a batch of pre-determined size ϕ in a pre-processing phase.

Gennaro [28] presented a threshold Schnorr signature protocol that uses DKG to generate multiple nonce values in a pre-processing stage independently of performing signing operations. We use the same approach to our problem but use the modified DKG as used in KeyGen. This leads to a communication overhead, but is still the most secure method to achieve a non-interactive signing phase.

In the **PreNonceGen** phase we do not use the DKG directly to generate individual nonces and commitments. This step is crucial to prevent two specific attacks used to forge signatures in a concurrent signing protocol.

In order to make our signing phase completely non-interactive, we need to ensure that no extra interaction rounds are needed while calculating the threshold nonce commitment values. However, as shown by Maxwell et al. [12], this opens the possibility of the ROS Solver [17] and Drijvers' attacks [29]. These attacks rely on the attacker's ability to control the signature hash by controlling the threshold nonce value R_j, by either adaptively selecting their own commitment after victim's nonce commitment values are known, or by adaptively choosing the message to be signed to manipulate the resulting challenge for the set of participants performing the signing operation. The obvious way to avoid this, is by committing the $r_i j$ values before the message is revealed so it can not be adaptively changed later.

However, since we want to prevent these attacks *without* introducing an extra round of interaction or sacrificing concurrency, we instead use a modification of the work by Nick et al. [16]. Their approach essentially binds each participant's nonce commitment to a specific message as well as the commitments of the other participants involved in that particular signing operation.

To achieve this, our scheme replaces the single nonce commitment r_{ij} with a pair (r_{ij}^a, r_{ij}^b). Each prospective signer then commits r_{ij}^a and r_{ij}^b in the pre-processing phase and given h_j is the output of a hash function $H_r()$ applied to all committed pre-nonces in the previous phase, the threshold public key, and the message m_j, the nonce commitment for any signer i will now be:

$$r_{ij} = r_{ij}^a + h_j.r_{ij}^b.$$

To initiate an attack, when any corrupt signer changes either its nonce values or the message, it will result in changing the value of h_j, thereby changing the nonce-commitment of honest signers as well. Without a constant nonce-commitment value, the attacks in [17] and [29] can't be applied. We can therefore overcome these two attacks without needed an extra commitment round.

So the **PreNonceGen** phase will use $2 * \phi$ parallel DKGs to generate batch of ϕ pre-nonce pairs per participant for a total of π prospective messages.

PreNonceGen

1. Each participant needs to conduct 2π parallel nonce-generation protocols to generate two shares (k_{ij}^a, k_{ij}^b) per nonce for the prospective j^{th} message. *WLOG* we will show how to distributively generate k_{ij}^a for all participants. The same procedure will apply to k_{ij}^b.
2. For every k_{ij}^a value, each participant i generates t random values $(a_{i_0}, ..., a_{i_{t-1}})$ in Z_q and uses these values as coefficients to define a polynomial $f_i(x) = \Sigma_{l=0}^{t-1}(a_{i_l} \cdot y^l)$ of degree $t-1$ in Z_q
3. Each i also computes a proof of knowledge for each secret a_{i_0} by calculating $\sigma = (w_i, c_i)$ where a_{i_0} is the secret key, such that $k \in Z_q, R_i = k \cdot G, h_i = H(i, S, a_{i_0} \cdot G, R_i), c_i = k + a_{i_0} \cdot h_i$, where S is the context string to prevent replay attacks.
4. Each i then computes its public commitment $C_i = < A_{i_0}, ..., A_{i_{t-1}} >$, where $A_{i_j} = a_{i_j} \cdot G$, and broadcasts (C_i, σ_i) to all other participants.
5. After participant i receives (C_j, σ_j), $j \neq i$, from all other participants $j \neq i$ it verifies $\sigma_j = (w_j, c_j)$ by computing $h_j = H(j, S, A_{j_0}, w_j \cdot G)$ and then checking for $w_j = c_j \cdot G - A_{j_0} \cdot h_j$ with $\perp$ (abort) on failure.
6. Each i next sends the secret share $(i, f_i(j))$, to every other participant P_j while keeping $(i, f_i(i))$ for itself.
7. Each i now verifies its shares by checking if $f_j(i) \cdot G = \Sigma(A_{j_k} \cdot (i^k mod q)), k = 0...t-1$, with $\perp$ on failure.
8. Each i finally calculates its individual pre-nonce share by computing $k_{ij}^a = \Sigma_j f_j(i), j = 1...n$, and stores k_{ij}^a securely.
9. Additionally, each i also calculates the corresponding public share for nonce verification $r_{ij}^a = k_{ij}^a \cdot G$

10. The participants can also compute the public share for verification for all the other participants by calculating $r_{ij}^a = \Sigma_j^n \Sigma_k^{t-1}(A_{j_k} \cdot (i^k mod q)), j = 1...n, k = 0...t-1)$

As is evident from above, the **PreNonceGen** phase of our protocol is the main bottleneck in terms of efficiency. All n participants are required to be present in this phase and each one will have to do 2π nonce-generations to prepare nonces for up to π prospective signatures. Unfortunately, so far, there has been no other way to remove or reduce this overhead and this is an unavoidable trade-off if we want to prevent the availability bottleneck in the signing round.

At the end of the **PreNonceGen** stage, every eligible signer i ends with a private nonce share of (k_{ij}^a, k_{ij}^b) to sign the prospective j^{th} message as well as the nonce commitment pairs of all other signers (r_{ij}^a, r_{ij}^b).

The values of private nonce shares and commitments are not yet determined. They will be generated when the message is known as we will explain in the **PartSign** stage.

3.4   PartSign

The signing phase of our protocol commences once the message to be signed is revealed. Before signing, the signer needs to determine the value of threshold nonce-commitment. Doing this *without* an extra round of commitment would normally make the scheme prone to the ROS Solver [17] and Drijvers' attacks [29] but we take care of that through the **PreNonceGen** phase.

Now we account for the values each participant i has received so far at the beginning of the **PartSign** phase. We denote the individual signer with its participant-index i and others with index o in order to avoid any confusion with the message index denoted by j.

private group key: X (VSS distributed) public group key: P
private key share: x_i public key shares: $p_o = x_o \cdot G$
Tuples of π individual pre-nonce commitment pairs: (r_{oj}^a, r_{oj}^b) for each participant i and prospective message m_j
From the values of (r_{oj}^a, r_{oj}^b) the signers can calculate the π threshold pre-nonce commitment pairs (R_j^a, R_j^b)

The VSS distributed values are not yet constructed and can only be calculated by Lagrange interpolation of at least t corresponding shares. Optionally, all the public/commitment values can be broadcast publicly or stored on a trusted server for use by an outside party for signature aggregation and verification.

In our scheme, the partial-signature also contains an additional portion with the signer's individual nonce-commitment as a challenge. This is done in order to make individual misbehaviour detection possible in case an invalid partial-signature is sent. This is explained in detail in Sect. 3.7. It doesn't affect the functionality or security of the rest of the protocol.

PartSign

For the j_{th} message $m_j \in Z_q$ and available hash functions $H_r(.)$ and $H_m(.)$ mapping $\{0,1\}^*$ to $\{0,1\}^l$ in Z_q^*, each individual signer calculates its partial-signature:

1. Each signer i for the message m_j sums the pre-nonce commitment pairs of all the eligible participants from *PreNonceGen* for the message m_j, (r_{oj}^a, r_{oj}^b) and individually calculates the value:
   $h_j = H_r(m_j, \sum_{o=1}^n r_{oj}^a, \sum_{o=1}^n r_{oj}^b, P)$

2. Each signer i calculates its own nonce value for m_j and the value of at least t (including self) nonce-commitments using:
   $k_{ij} = k_{ij}^a + h_j.k_{ij}^b$ *(for own nonce)*
   $r_{ij} = k_{ij} \cdot G$ *(for own nonce-commitment)*
   $r_{oj} = r_{oj}^a + h_j.r_{oj}^b$ *(for nonce-commits of other signers)*

3. Next the signer i uses any t values of r_{oj} calculated in step 2 and reconstructs the group nonce-commitment value by Lagrange interpolation as:
   $R_j = \sum_i \lambda_i.r_{oj}$ *(λ_i are the corresponding Lagrange coefficients)*

4. Now signer i can sign the message m_j as:
   $s_{ij} = k_{ij} + H(m_j, R_j, P) \cdot x_i + \rho \cdot H_m(m_j, r_{ij}, p_i) \cdot x_i$

The signer i broadcasts $\sigma_{ij} = (s_{ij}, R_j, r_{ij})$

3.5 Aggregate

Aggregation of the threshold signature is rather simple and straightforward. For a given message m_j, once at least t partial-signatures have been broadcast, they can be aggregated using simple Lagrange interpolation.

We can use a designated signature aggregator like Komlo and Goldberg [15], to improve efficiency of our **Verify** stage: signer sending single message to an aggregator vs broadcasting messages to everyone. As long as the aggregation is done by anyone in at least a semi-honest way, the threshold signature will be correctly constructed. The duty of the aggregator can be undertaken by one or more of the signers themselves, in which case, the signer that decides to be the aggregator will have to be present throughout the partial signing phase until the threshold qualifying number of honest partial-signatures is not met.

Along with aggregating the threshold signature, an additional role of the aggregator is to ensure that the threshold signature is formed correctly by verifying it using the group public key. In case of a discrepancy, the aggregator should be able to detect the misbehaving signature shares from the signature, upon which it can remove those and use other available honest partial-signature(s) to re-aggregate the threshold signature. As long as t honest partial-signatures are available, the correct signature can be reconstructed.

Even a malicious aggregator can not forge the threshold signature or learn anything about the signing parties thereby maintaining EUF-CMA security. If it falsely accuses honest signers of misbehaviour or constructs an incorrect signature using fake shares, both those results can be later verified independently. A malicious aggregator can also deny constructing the correct signature. However in case of blockchains, semi-honest behaviour can be imposed on the aggregator via the incentive of a financial payment per honest aggregation and/or a deterrent in form of a financial penalty per wrongfully submitted signature since the final signature is publicly verifiable.

WLOG, for the rest of this paper, we will assume an external party as the aggregator.

Aggregate

1. The aggregator waits for the partial-signatures to be broadcast. As each $\sigma_{ij} = (s_{ij}, R_j, r_{ij})$ is received for some message m_j the aggregator checks it for validity using misbehaviour detection steps from *Section* 3.7.
   The partial-signatures that fail verification are discarded.
2. Once at least t correct partial-signatures are received, the aggregator generates Lagrange coefficients λ_i for each partial-signature using index values i of the corresponding signers.
3. The threshold signature can now be aggregated as:
   $S_j = \Sigma \lambda_{ij} \cdot s_{ij}$
   The aggregator broadcasts the threshold signature as $\sigma_j = (S_j, R_j)$

While this approach is sufficient in itself, in a special setup like a blockchain, we can leverage the environment to our advantage. In such a scenario, we can take a more optimistic approach by assuming that malicious behaviour is rare and instead of checking for partial-signature validity for each σ_{ij}, we can allow for misbehaviour to take place, as long as it can be detected and the faulty signer economically penalised. Misbehaviour will be easy to prove publicly later since all required values are public. If sufficient correct partial-signatures ($\geq t$) are still available for a given message, the aggregator can replace erroneous partial-signatures with correct ones and re-aggregate the signature.

Assuming rational participants, the threat of a penalty should drastically reduce the probability of invalid partial-signatures. It will make this alternative approach more efficient as in most cases, only the threshold signature will be needed to be verified. We now illustrate this alternate approach.

Alternate Aggregate with Penalty

1. The aggregator waits for the partial-signatures to be broadcast. Once at least t correct partial-signatures $\sigma_{ij} = (s_{ij}, R_j, r_{ij}$ are received, the aggregator generates Lagrange coefficients λ_i for each partial-signature using index values i of the corresponding signers.
2. The threshold signature is aggregated as:
   $S_j = \Sigma\lambda_{ij} \cdot s_{ij}$
3. The aggregator now checks the validity of the threshold signature S_j as in *Section* 3.6:
   $(S_j \cdot G)mod\rho =?R_j + H_m(m_j, R_j, P) \cdot P$
4. If this verification succeeds, aggregator goes to step 6. If verification fails, the aggregator starts checking the individual partial-signatures σ_{ij} for misbehaviour using steps from *Section* 3.7 and removes them. IT additionally penalises the signers that sent an invalid signature.
5. After all misbehaving partial-signatures have been removed, the threshold signature value S_j will be re-aggergated if at least t valid signatures are available:
   $S_j = \Sigma\lambda_{ij} \cdot s_{ij}$
6. The aggregator broadcasts the threshold signature as:
   $\sigma_j = (S_j, R_j)$

3.6   Verify

Verification of the threshold signature is the same as the standard Schnorr signature verification with a small modification: we mod the LHS of the verification equation with ρ before checking it. This is done in order to remove the individual signer's misbehaviour detection portion from the signature.

The new verification phase looks like:

Verify

Given values m_j, P, σ_j and ρ, the threshold signature is verified as follows:

1. Verifier parses σ_j to get S_j and R_j
2. Verifier then removes the misbehaviour detection portion from the signature using:
   $S = S_j mod\rho$
3. Next it calculates:
   $e_v = H_m(m_j, R_j, P)$

---

4. From e_v it calculates the expected nonce-commitment value:
$R_v = S \cdot G - e_v \cdot P$
5. if $R_v = R_j$ then signature is valid, else invalid

3.7   Misbehaviour Detection

Among mutually distrusting, distributed parties, misbehaviour by one of the parties might warrant immediate detection and subsequent adjustment in the protocol. To achieve this, we generated an additional portion in our signature as the individual signers misbehaviour detection part. All the other phases of the signature scheme remained the same. The only change that occurred, was in the **PartSign** phase of the scheme. We elaborate on this.

Modified Partial-Signature. Misbehaviour detection required the addition of an individual identifier to the regular signature. Our scheme achieved this by adding a new portion to the partial-signature (see Sect. 3.4) that contains the nonce-commitment for the individual signer i as part of the challenge value in the hash. Given the regular signature as:

$s_{ij} = k_{ij} + H(m_j, R_j, P) \cdot x_i$

The new signature became:

$s_{ij} = k_{ij} + H(m_j, R_j, P) \cdot x_i + \rho \cdot H_m(m_j, r_{ij}, p_i) \cdot x_i$

The signature value was modified to:

$\sigma_{ij} = (s_{ij}, R_j, r_{ij})$

Choosing the ρ Value: The ρ value should have these features:

1. It should be sufficiently large so that modulus of the signature with ρ still preserves the rest of the signature as before, i.e., $\rho > (k_{ij} + H_m(.) \cdot x_i) \forall i, j$
2. It should be kept as small as possible to keep the signature footprint as close to the original partial-signature.

Combining these two properties we get ρ to be a prime number such that, $q + q^2 < \rho < q^3$ keeping it as close to $q^2 + q$ as possible. This makes our signature of a size around $2q$ to $3q$ which is similar to that of the original partial-signature.

As we see in the next step, this does not affect the size of the aggregate threshold signature since the individual component will be removed before aggregation.

Verification of the Threshold Signature. The new addition didn't change the way we aggregate the threshold signature. While aggregating we simply removed the individual identifier by taking the partial-signature modulus rho, i.e., $S = S_j mod \rho$ and followed regular verification from thereon (see Sect. 3.6 for details).

Checking for Misbehaviour. Of our two approaches to signature aggregation, the first one necessarily while the second one in rare cases, requires misbehaviour detection to remove invalid signatures from the aggregation pool. The aggregator, verifier or any interested party can now check a given partial-signature for misbehaviour as shown below:

Misbehaviour Detection

Given values m_j, P, σ_{ij}, p_i and ρ, misbehaviour detection is tested as follows:

1. Verifier parses σ_{ij} to extract s_{ij}, R_j and r_{ij}
2. Verifier next calculates:
   $$e_v = H_m(m_j, R_j, P) + \rho \cdot H_m(m_j, r_{ij}, p_i)$$
3. From this e_v it calculates the expected nonce-commitment value:
   $$r_v = s_{ij} \cdot G - e_v \cdot P$$
4. if $r_v = r_{ij}$ then its a valid partial-signature, else misbehaviour has been detected

---

Cost Analysis. In this section, we provide the total cost in terms of round communication and exponentiation (the $\cdot G$) computation for participants in various phases of the protocol.

For **KeyGen** phase, a participant requires two round of communication: one broadcast round and another P2P communication round. A participant need to broadcast the proof of knowledge of a secret a_{i_0} along with commitment of t coefficient A_{i_j}. After each participant verify the correctness of broadcast data of other participants, a party need to send the polynomial f_i's evaluation for player j along with his own id. In complete key generation phase, a player need to compute a total of $(3n + t) \cdot G$ computation: 2 computations in step 2 for calculating R_i and h_i, t computations for calculating commitment C_i in step 3, $2 \times (n - 1)$ for calculating w_j and h_j in step 4, $(n - 1)$ for calculating $f_j(i) \cdot G$ in step 6 and one computation in step 8 for calculating p_i.

The cost of generating pre-nonce values for a batch size of π by following is $2\pi \times$ that of the **KeyGen** phase as we need to run two DKG protocol for per participant to generate the two pre-nonces that will be used to calculate the nonce value later.

The **PartSign** doesn't involve any round of communication and is completely non interactive. The partial signature just need to be broadcast or sent to aggregator once it is generated. It requires just one exponentiation computation for calculating r_{i_j} in step 2.

The simple **Aggregate** phase just waits for all the partial signatures to arrive and doesn't require any communication round or exponentiation computation. The **Aggregate with Penalty** phase requires one computation in step 2, a variable number of misbehaviour detection cost and communication, spanning from 0 to $n - t$ depending on the number of misbehaving parties present.

The **Verify** phase just requires one exponentiation computation. The additional misbehaviour detection phase for detecting misbehaviour in one partial signature also requires only one such computation.

4   Proof of Security for ATSSIA

4.1   Proof of Correctness

The various portions of the signature satisfy the properties of digital signatures. The key and nonce are distributively generated using existed secure methods from Gennaro's DKG [28] combined with a **PreNonceGen** phase to keep it safe even with concurrency.

We prove correctness by demonstrating how our scheme is equivalent to a single signer Schnorr scheme.

Theorem 1. *For some message m, given a public-private key pair (X, P), pre-nonce and pre-nonce commit values pairs (K^a, R^a) and (K^b, R^b) and H_r and H_m, the threshold signature generated using ATSSIA is equivalent to the single signer Schnorr signature:*

$S = K + e.X$

where $K = (K^a + H_r(m, K^a, K^b, P).K^b)$, $R = K \cdot G$ and $e = H_m(m, R, P)$

Proof. For our signature scheme, let there be some polynomials $f(.)$ and $(g_a(.), g_b(.))$ that are used to distribute the group key and pre-nonce values respectively, i.e., $f(.)$ distributes the private key X and $(g_a(.), g_b(.))$ distribute the pre-nonce pairs (K^a, K^b).

Therefore for a signer i we will get the signature value as $h(i)$:

$h(i) = (g_a(i) + c_r \cdot g_b(i)) + c_{m_R} \cdot f(i) + c_{m_{r_i}} \cdot f(i)$

where $c_r = H_r(m, \sum r_i^a, \sum r_i^b, P)$, $c_{m_R} = H_m(m, R, P)$ and $c_{m_{r_i}} = H_m(m, r_i, p_i)$

Lagrange interpolation on this results in:

$S = \sum(\lambda_i(g_a(i) + c_r \cdot g_b(i))) + (c_{m_R} + c_{m_{r_i}}) \cdot \sum(\lambda_i \cdot f(i))$
$S = K^a + c_r \cdot K^b + (c_{m_R} + c_{m_{r_i}}) \cdot X$

substituting notations by $K = K^a + c_r \cdot K^b$ and $e = (c_{m_R} + c_{m_{r_i}})$, we get:
$S = K + e \cdot X$, which is equivalent to the single signer Schnorr signature with key X, nonce K and challenge e.

Since our scheme replicates a single-party Schnorr proof substituting the threshold key and nonce values for individual ones, it provides correctness at the same level as the single signer protocol.

4.2   Proof of EUF-CMA Security

We will prove security against existential unforgeability in chosen message attacks $(EUF - CMA)$ by demonstrating that the difficulty to forge our threshold signature by performing an adaptively chosen message attack in the Random Oracle (RO) model reduces to the difficulty of computing the discrete logarithm of an arbitrary challenge value ω in the same underlying group, so long as the adversary controls only up to $t - 1$ participants.

Our proof uses these main algorithms:

- The Forger $\mathcal{F}$ which is the undermost-lying algorithm. We assume that $\mathcal{F}$ has the property of forging a signature in our threshold signature scheme with probability ϵ in time t. WLOG we assume that $\mathcal{F}$ also controls $t - 1$ signers in our protocol and plays the role of the signature aggregator.
- A simulator $\mathcal{A}$ which manages the input and outputs for $\mathcal{F}$ and also simulates the honest participants and the RO queries.
- The Generalised Forking Algorithm $GF_{\mathcal{A}}$ which provides $\mathcal{A}$ with a random tape for its inputs and also provides outputs to its RO queries. It then utilises these to "fork" $\mathcal{A}$ to produce two forgeries (σ, σ') for the same RO query index.
- The Extractor algorithm $\mathcal{E}$ which takes the challenge value ω as input, embeds it into our scheme and then obtains the forgeries (σ, σ'). It then uses these to extract the discrete logarithm of ω.

Our security proof utilizes the General Forking Lemma by Bellare and Neven [2] to reduce the security of our signature to the security of the Discrete Logarithm Problem (DLP) in $\mathbb{G}$. We end up proving that if F can forge the signature with probability acc, then DLOG problem can definitely be solved with a probability ϵ. However, since solving the DLOG is hard, this result implies that forging a signature in our scheme will be hard as well. We provide a quick understanding of our proof here:

Theorem 2. *If the discrete logarithm problem in G is (τ', ϵ')-hard, then our signature scheme over G with n signing participants, a threshold of t, and a pre-processing batch size of π is $(\tau, n_h, n_s, \epsilon)$-secure whenever:*

$$\epsilon' \leq (\epsilon^2)/((2\pi + 1)n_h + 1)$$

$$and \ \tau' \geq 4\tau + 2(n_s + 2\pi n_h + 1)t_{exp} + \mathcal{O}(\pi n_h + n_s + 1)$$

Proof. First we embed the challenge value ω into the group public key P. Our extractor algorithm $\mathcal{E}$ then uses the generalized forking algorithm to initialize our simulator $\mathcal{A}$ as $\mathcal{A}(P, h_1, ..., h_{n_r}; \beta)$, providing the group public key P, outputs for $n_r = (2\pi + 1)n_h + 1$ random oracle queries $h_1, ..., h_{n_r}$ and the random tape β. $\mathcal{A}$ then invokes the forger $\mathcal{F}$, simulating the responses to forger's random oracle queries by providing values selected from $h_1, ..., h_{n_r}$ and also acting as the honest party i_t in the *KeyGen*, *PreNonceGen* and *PartSign* phases.

$\mathcal{A}$ needs to trick forger by simulating signing of i_t without knowing its secret share of the key. For this, $\mathcal{A}$ generates a commitment and signature for participant i_t. To guess the challenge to return for a particular commitment when simulating a signing operation, $\mathcal{A}$ forks $\mathcal{F}$ to extract for each participant controlled by F, and consequently can directly compute its corresponding nonce. This is achieved by using the signers' commit of their pre-nonces. $\mathcal{A}$ who sees all random oracle queries, can therefore look up the commits before $\mathcal{F}$ can, and can thus correctly program the RO.

Once $\mathcal{A}$ has returned a valid forgery ($\sigma = (S, R)$) and the associated random oracle query index J, $GF_{\mathcal{A}}$ re-executes $\mathcal{A}$ with the same random tape and public key, but with fresh responses to random oracle queries $h_1, \cdots h_{J-1}, h'_J., h'_{n_r}$ where $h'_J, ..., h'_{n_r}$ are different from previous inputs.

This effectively forks the execution of $\mathcal{A}$ from the J_{th} RO query. Given a forger $\mathcal{F}$ that with probability ϵ produces a valid forgery, the probability that $\mathcal{A}$ returns a valid forgery for our signature is ϵ, and the probability of $GF_{\mathcal{A}}$ returning two valid forgeries using the same commitments after forking $\mathcal{A}$ is roughly ϵ^2/n_r (ignoring the negligible portion).

The time taken to compute this comes out to be:

$$4\tau + 2(n_s + 2\pi n_h + 1)t_{exp} + \mathcal{O}(\pi n_h + n_s + 1).$$

The running time for extractor E to compute the discrete logarithm by procuring two forgeries is 4τ (four times that for F because of the forking of $\mathcal{A}$, which itself forks F) plus the time taken by $\mathcal{A}$ for computing the signature and RO queries with additional operations $2(n_s + 2\pi n_h + 1)t_{exp} + \mathcal{O}(\pi n_h + n_s + 1)$.

5 Conclusion

Current blockchain transaction consist of the spending amount, hash of all transactions of previous block and the approving party's digital signature to allow spending. For increased security, Bitcoin-based chains allow for multi-signatures for spending. Any subgroup of participants can validate the transaction. In a practical network as dynamic as a blockchain network, where participant availability can not be guaranteed, an asynchronous, concurrent threshold signing protocol fulfils a very crucial need.

Our work improves upon these specific aspects and provides an alternative approach to existing protocols while being $EUF - CMA$ secure even with $t - 1$ corrupt signers as long as solving DLOG is hard.

We are presently working on reducing the communication required in **PreNonceGen** phase, while still maintaining secure asynchronous concurrent signing.

References

1. Nakamoto, S.: Bitcoin: a peer-to-peer electronic cash system. Manubot (2019)
2. Bellare, M., Neven, G.: Multi-signatures in the plain public-key model and a general forking lemma. In: Proceedings of the 13th ACM SIGSAC Conference on Computer and Communications Security (CCS) (2006)

3. Tomescu, A., et al.: Towards scalable threshold cryptosystems. In: 2020 IEEE Symposium on Security and Privacy (SP). IEEE (2020)
4. Seurin, Y.: On the exact security of Schnorr-type signatures in the random oracle model. In: Pointcheval, D., Johansson, T. (eds.) EUROCRYPT 2012. LNCS, vol. 7237, pp. 554–571. Springer, Heidelberg (2012). https://doi.org/10.1007/978-3-642-29011-4_33
5. Shoup, V.: Practical threshold signatures. In: Preneel, B. (ed.) EUROCRYPT 2000. LNCS, vol. 1807, pp. 207–220. Springer, Heidelberg (2000). https://doi.org/10.1007/3-540-45539-6_15
6. Doerner, J., et al.: Secure two-party threshold ECDSA from ECDSA assumptions. In: 2018 IEEE Symposium on Security and Privacy (SP). IEEE (2018)
7. Gennaro, R., Goldfeder, S., Narayanan, A.: Threshold-optimal DSA/ECDSA signatures and an application to bitcoin wallet security. In: Manulis, M., Sadeghi, A.-R., Schneider, S. (eds.) ACNS 2016. LNCS, vol. 9696, pp. 156–174. Springer, Cham (2016). https://doi.org/10.1007/978-3-319-39555-5_9
8. Gennaro, R., Goldfeder, S.: Fast multiparty threshold ECDSA with fast trustless setup. In: Proceedings of the 2018 ACM SIGSAC Conference on Computer and Communications Security (CCS) (2018)
9. Lindell, Y.: Fast secure two-party ECDSA signing. In: Katz, J., Shacham, H. (eds.) CRYPTO 2017. LNCS, vol. 10402, pp. 613–644. Springer, Cham (2017). https://doi.org/10.1007/978-3-319-63715-0_21
10. Lindell, Y., Nof, A.: Fast secure multiparty ECDSA with practical distributed key generation and applications to cryptocurrency custody. In: Proceedings of the 2018 ACM SIGSAC Conference on Computer and Communications Security (CCS) (2018)
11. Bünz, B., et al.: Bulletproofs: short proofs for confidential transactions and more. In: 2018 IEEE Symposium on Security and Privacy (SP). IEEE (2018)
12. Maxwell, G., Poelstra, A., Seurin, Y., Wuille, P.: Simple Schnorr multi-signatures with applications to Bitcoin. Des. Codes Cryptogr. **87**(9), 2139–2164 (2019). https://doi.org/10.1007/s10623-019-00608-x
13. Boneh, D., Gentry, C., Lynn, B., Shacham, H.: Aggregate and verifiably encrypted signatures from bilinear maps. In: Biham, E. (ed.) EUROCRYPT 2003. LNCS, vol. 2656, pp. 416–432. Springer, Heidelberg (2003). https://doi.org/10.1007/3-540-39200-9_26
14. Boneh, D., Boyen, X., Shacham, H.: Short group signatures. In: Franklin, M. (ed.) CRYPTO 2004. LNCS, vol. 3152, pp. 41–55. Springer, Heidelberg (2004). https://doi.org/10.1007/978-3-540-28628-8_3
15. Komlo, C., Goldberg, I.: FROST: flexible round-optimized Schnorr threshold signatures. In: Dunkelman, O., Jacobson, Jr., M.J., O'Flynn, C. (eds.) SAC 2020. LNCS, vol. 12804, pp. 34–65. Springer, Cham (2021). https://doi.org/10.1007/978-3-030-81652-0_2
16. Nick, J., Ruffing, T., Seurin, Y.: MuSig2: simple two-round Schnorr multi-signatures. In: Malkin, T., Peikert, C. (eds.) CRYPTO 2021. LNCS, vol. 12825, pp. 189–221. Springer, Cham (2021). https://doi.org/10.1007/978-3-030-84242-0_8
17. Benhamouda, F., Lepoint, T., Loss, J., Orrù, M., Raykova, M.: On the (in)security of ROS. In: Canteaut, A., Standaert, F.-X. (eds.) EUROCRYPT 2021. LNCS, vol. 12696, pp. 33–53. Springer, Cham (2021). https://doi.org/10.1007/978-3-030-77870-5_2
18. Pedersen, T.P.: A threshold cryptosystem without a trusted party. In: Davies, D.W. (ed.) EUROCRYPT 1991. LNCS, vol. 547, pp. 522–526. Springer, Heidelberg (1991). https://doi.org/10.1007/3-540-46416-6_47

19. Kate, A.P.: Distributed Key Generation and Its Applications. Dissertation. University of Waterloo (2010)

20. Boneh, D., Drijvers, M., Neven, G.: Compact multi-signatures for smaller blockchains. In: Peyrin, T., Galbraith, S. (eds.) ASIACRYPT 2018. LNCS, vol. 11273, pp. 435–464. Springer, Cham (2018). https://doi.org/10.1007/978-3-030-03329-3_15

21. Chiesa, A., Green, M., Liu, J., Miao, P., Miers, I., Mishra, P.: Decentralized anonymous micropayments. In: Coron, J.-S., Nielsen, J.B. (eds.) EUROCRYPT 2017. LNCS, vol. 10211, pp. 609–642. Springer, Cham (2017). https://doi.org/10.1007/978-3-319-56614-6_21

22. Micali, S., Ohta, K., Reyzin, L.: Accountable-subgroup multisignatures. In: Proceedings of the 8th ACM Conference on Computer and Communications Security (CCS) (2001)

23. Shamir, A.: How to share a secret. Commun. ACM **22**(11), 612–613 (1979)

24. Schnorr, C.P.: Efficient identification and signatures for smart cards. In: Brassard, G. (ed.) CRYPTO 1989. LNCS, vol. 435, pp. 239–252. Springer, New York (1990). https://doi.org/10.1007/0-387-34805-0_22

25. Chor, B., et al.: Verifiable secret sharing and achieving simultaneity in the presence of faults. In: 26th Annual Symposium on Foundations of Computer Science (SFCS 1985). IEEE (1985)

26. Feldman, P.: A practical scheme for non-interactive verifiable secret sharing. In: 28th Annual Symposium on Foundations of Computer Science (SFCS 1987). IEEE (1987)

27. Canny, J., Sorkin, S.: Practical large-scale distributed key generation. In: Cachin, C., Camenisch, J.L. (eds.) EUROCRYPT 2004. LNCS, vol. 3027, pp. 138–152. Springer, Heidelberg (2004). https://doi.org/10.1007/978-3-540-24676-3_9

28. Gennaro, R., Jarecki, S., Krawczyk, H., Rabin, T.: Secure applications of Pedersen's distributed key generation protocol. In: Joye, M. (ed.) CT-RSA 2003. LNCS, vol. 2612, pp. 373–390. Springer, Heidelberg (2003). https://doi.org/10.1007/3-540-36563-X_26

29. Drijvers, M., et al.: On the security of two-round multi-signatures. In: 2019 IEEE Symposium on Security and Privacy (SP). IEEE (2019)

30. Stinson, D.R., Strobl, R.: Provably secure distributed Schnorr signatures and a (t, n) threshold scheme for implicit certificates. In: Varadharajan, V., Mu, Y. (eds.) ACISP 2001. LNCS, vol. 2119, pp. 417–434. Springer, Heidelberg (2001). https://doi.org/10.1007/3-540-47719-5_33

Cryptographic Protocol in Quantum Computer Age

Delegating Supersingular Isogenies over $\mathbb{F}_{p^2}$ with Cryptographic Applications

Robi Pedersen[1]([✉])([ID]) and Osmanbey Uzunkol[2]([ID])

[1] imec-COSIC KU Leuven, Kasteelpark Arenberg 10 Bus 2452, 3001 Leuven, Belgium
robi.pedersen@esat.kuleuven.be
[2] Information und Kommunikation, Flensburg University of Applied Sciences, Flensburg, Germany

Abstract. Although isogeny-based cryptographic schemes enjoy the smallest key sizes amongst current post-quantum cryptographic candidates, they come at a high computational cost, making their deployment on the ever-growing number of resource-constrained devices difficult. Speeding up the expensive post-quantum cryptographic operations by delegating these computations from a weaker client to untrusted powerful external servers is a promising approach. Following this, we present in this work mechanisms allowing computationally restricted devices to securely and verifiably delegate isogeny computations to potentially untrusted third parties. In particular, we propose two algorithms that can be integrated into existing isogeny-based protocols and which lead to a much lower cost for the delegator than the full, local computation. For example, compared to the local computation cost, we reduce the public-key computation step of SIDH/SIKE by a factor 5 and zero-knowledge proofs of identity by a factor 16 for the prover, while it becomes almost free for the verifier, respectively, at the NIST security level 1.

Keywords: Isogeny-based cryptography · Post-quantum cryptography · Secure computation outsourcing · Lightweight cryptography

1 Introduction

Delegation of Cryptographic Primitives. In recent years, the number of interconnected devices using new computational paradigms such as cloud, edge and mobile computing, and their interactions with the industrial internet of things, big data and artificial intelligence, are steadily increasing in numbers. As a result, delegating expensive computations from clients such as RFID-cards and low power sensors with constrained resources or capabilities to powerful external resources has become a highly active and an indispensable research and development area for researchers and industry alike. Delegation of sensitive computation to *potentially malicious* external devices and services, however, comes with some additional challenges, such as requiring security of the clients' inputs/outputs

J. H. Park and S.-H. Seo (Eds.): ICISC 2021, LNCS 13218, pp. 95–118, 2022.
https://doi.org/10.1007/978-3-031-08896-4_5

as well as verifiability of the outputs coming from these external devices and services. A particular case of interest is the delegation of cryptographic algorithms and protocols. The security and verifiability properties of cryptographic delegations were first formalized in a security model introduced by Hohenberger and Lysyanskaya [25], introduced in the context of modular exponentiations. In this model, a weak, trusted client T makes queries to a set of untrusted external servers U in such a way that their interaction T^U realizes a computational task Alg in a joint manner. The goal is to reduce the computational cost of T while guaranteeing the security of its inputs and outputs, and the possibility of verifying the correctness of the outputs of U.

Isogenies and Cryptography. Many currently deployed public-key cryptographic primitives are based on the infeasibility of either the factorization or discrete logarithm problems. Possible efficient implementations of Shor's algorithm [38] on large scale quantum computers could render these schemes insecure against such quantum adversaries. This threat resulted in the United States' National Institute of Standards and Technology (NIST) launching a post-quantum cryptography standardization process at the end of 2017. Of the 69 initially proposed key-establishment and signature protocols, a list of 15 main and alternate candidates (9 encryption and KEMs, 6 digital signature schemes) have progressed to the third round of scrutiny, announced in July 2020 [33].

One of these alternate candidates is the key encapsulation scheme SIKE [39] which is based on the Supersingular Isogeny Diffie-Hellman (SIDH) key exchange protocol, originally proposed by Jao and De Feo [27]. SIDH is a quantum resistant key agreement scheme, which uses isogenies between supersingular elliptic curves over finite fields $\mathbb{F}_{p^2}$. Besides the key agreement scheme in [27] and SIKE [39], several other cryptographic schemes based on the supersingular elliptic curves have been recently proposed in the literature ranging from group key agreement schemes [3,22], zero-knowledge proofs of identity [17,27], identification and signature schemes [23] and hash functions [10,21] to verifiable delay functions [20].

Motivation. A significant advantage of isogeny-based cryptographic schemes are the small key sizes when compared to their lattice- or code-based post-quantum counterparts. However, the main drawback is performance: SIKE is about an order of magnitude slower than its NIST competitors [1,7]. Furthermore, as pointed out in [32], post-quantum cryptographic schemes are especially required to also work efficiently on resource-constrained devices with highly limited processing storage, power and battery life to be able to utilize them in lightweight environments, which is highly desired for various applications requiring certain interoperability properties. We address this problem and study the secure and verifiable delegation of isogeny computations between supersingular elliptic curves over $\mathbb{F}_{p^2}$ in order to reduce the computational cost of resource-constrained clients requiring to utilize different isogeny-based cryptographic schemes.

Previous Work. In [34], two isogeny delegation algorithms in the *honest-but-curious* (HBC) and *one-malicious version of a two-untrusted program* (OMTUP) assumptions were proposed using the security model of Hohenberger and Lysyanskaya [25]. The first, ScIso, allowed to delegate the computation of any isogeny with revealed kernel, while allowing to push through hidden elliptic curve points or multiply unprotected points with hidden scalars. Random torsion point generation was done using lookup-tables of the form $\{(i, \ell^i P)\}_{i \in \{1,\dots,e-1\}}$, $\{(i, \ell^i Q)\}_{i \in \{1,\dots,e-1\}}$ for generators $\langle P, Q \rangle \in E[\ell^e]$. The second algorithm, HIso, used ScIso as a subroutine and allowed to hide the kernel and the codomain of the delegated isogeny. The work of [34] did not propose a protocol to delegate public-key computations.

Our Contributions. The main contribution of this paper is to propose two new delegation algorithms for isogeny computations using the security model of Hohenberger and Lysyanskaya [25] in the HBC and OMTUP models, and to show how to apply these to different isogeny-based cryptographic protocols and computing the respective gains for the delegator. In particular,

1. We show how to break the HIso subroutine of [34] using pairings, and discuss some new approaches to hide the codomain curve in delegation algorithms.
2. We introduce the delegation algorithm Iso, which allows to delegate isogeny computations with unprotected kernel and to push through public and hidden points. Iso does not require lookup-tables, eliminating the large local memory requirement of the ScIso-algorithm from [34] on the delegator's side, while also speeding up the delegation algorithms.
3. The second algorithm, IsoDetour, uses Iso as a subroutine and allows to delegate the computation of an isogeny without revealing the kernel. This allows the computation of public keys, a question left open in [34]. The security of IsoDetour is based on a difficulty assumption implicitly used in the identification protocol of [27], which we introduce as the *decisional point preimage problem* (DPP). We show that this problem reduces to the decisional supersingular product problem (DSSP) introduced in [27].
4. We discuss applications of algorithms to the protocols introduced in [3,10,17,20–23,27] and benchmark our delegation algorithms for various standardized SIKE primes ($p434, p503, p610, p751$) corresponding to NIST's security levels 1, 2, 3 and 5. We also indicate the necessary communication costs between the delegator and the servers. Iso allows to reduce the delegator's cost in the identification protocols of [17,27] to about 6% of the local computation cost in the OMTUP and 11% in the HBC assumption for $p503$. On the other hand, IsoDetour allows to reduce the cost of SIDH-type public-key generation to about 20% and 35% for OMTUP and HBC, respectively.

2 Background

2.1 Elliptic Curves and Isogenies

We work with supersingular elliptic curves over the field $\mathbb{F}_{p^2}$ with p prime and with Frobenius trace $t_\pi = \mp 2p$. The group of points on elliptic curves of this type is given as $E(\mathbb{F}_{p^2}) \simeq (\mathbb{Z}/(p \pm 1)\mathbb{Z})^2$ [40], so that the choice of p allows full control of the subgroup structure. Like most isogeny-based schemes, e.g. [27,39], we use $t_\pi = -2p$. The elliptic curves with $t_\pi = 2p$ correspond to the quadratic twists of these curves, i.e. curves having the same j-invariant which become first isomorphic over $\mathbb{F}_{p^4}$. We slightly abuse notation and write e.g. $P \in E$ for $P \in E(\mathbb{F}_{p^2})$. We indicate by $E[\tau]$ the τ-torsion group on $E(\mathbb{F}_{p^2})$ for $\tau \in \mathbb{Z}$ non-zero. Torsion groups of specific points and the generators of these groups are written with the specific point as index, e.g. we write $A \in E[\tau_A]$ and $\langle P_A, Q_A \rangle = E[\tau_A]$, where we assume A to have full order, i.e. $|\langle A \rangle| = \tau_A$. We further use the shorthand $\mathbb{Z}_\tau = \mathbb{Z}/\tau\mathbb{Z}$. We assume that different torsion groups are always coprime.

Isogenies. Isogenies are homomorphisms between two elliptic curves, that are also algebraic maps [16,40]. Separable isogenies are uniquely defined by their kernel. In the cryptographic schemes treated in this work, these kernels are subgroups of torsion groups, generated by a primitive point. For example, the group generated by $A \in E[\tau_A]$, i.e. $\langle A \rangle = \{\lambda A | \lambda \in \mathbb{Z}_{\tau_A}\} \subset E[\tau_A]$, defines the isogeny $\alpha : E \to E/\langle A \rangle$ with $\ker \alpha = \langle A \rangle$. Any other primitive point within $\langle A \rangle$ generates the same isogeny, so we can define the equivalence class $[A]$ of points generating $\langle A \rangle$. One can efficiently verify if two points in $E[\tau_A]$ belong to the same equivalence class by checking if they define the same isogeny or by using pairings. In order to allow efficient isogeny computations between elliptic curves, torsion groups $E[\tau]$ need τ to be smooth [27]. For most cryptographic applications, we require several smooth torsion groups of approximately the same size. This can be guaranteed by choosing $p + 1 = \prod_{i=1}^{n} \tau_i$, where $\tau_i \approx \tau_j$ for all i, j and all smooth. By this choice, supersingular elliptic curves consist of the smooth torsion groups $E[\tau_i]$ for $i = 1, \ldots, n$. Each of these torsion groups is generated by two elements, $\langle P_i, Q_i \rangle = E[\tau_i]$, so any point can be written as a linear combination of these two generators.

Notation. We write isogeny codomains in index notation, e.g. $E_A = E/\langle A \rangle$, $E_{AB} = E/\langle A, B \rangle$, where the index represents (the equivalence class of) the isogeny kernel generator. We represent points on elliptic curves with a superscript corresponding to the index of the elliptic curve they are defined on, e.g. if $P \in E$, then $P^A \in E_A$ and $P^{AB} \in E_{AB}$, where we assume the used map to be clear from context. The same holds for point sets, e.g. $\{P, Q\}^A = \{P^A, Q^A\} \subset E_A$.

2.2 Elliptic Curve Arithmetic

Computational Costs. We denote by A and D the theoretical cost estimates of point addition and point doubling on E, respectively, by $S(\tau)$ the cost estimate of a (large) scalar multiplication of a point by a scalar in $\mathbb{Z}_\tau$ and by $I(\tau, \mu)$ the cost estimate of computing a (large) τ-isogeny, and pushing μ points through this isogeny. Each of these operations can be expressed in terms of the cost of multiplications m of elements over $\mathbb{F}_{p^2}$. To this end, we assume that squaring on $\mathbb{F}_{p^2}$ costs 0.8 m, while addition on $\mathbb{F}_{p^2}$ and comparisons are negligible. Expensive inversions are circumvented by using projective coordinates. Large scalar multiplications are typically done using a double-and-add approach, so that we can express the cost of scalar multiplication by an element τ as [34]

$$\mathsf{S}(\tau) = \mathsf{M}\lceil \log_2 \tau \rceil - \mathsf{A}, \quad \text{where} \quad \mathsf{M} = \mathsf{A} + \mathsf{D}. \tag{1}$$

Scalar multiplications by a small prime ℓ_i are written as S_{ℓ_i}. We further define C_{ℓ_i} and P_{ℓ_i} as the cost of a computing the codomain of an ℓ_i-isogeny and evaluating an ℓ_i-isogeny respectively. In the full version of the paper, we establish the following cost of a τ-isogeny with $\tau = \prod_{i=1}^n \ell_i^{e_i}$:

$$\mathsf{I}(\tau, \mu) = \sum_{i=1}^n \left[(\mathsf{P}_{\ell_i} + \mathsf{S}_{\ell_i}) \frac{e_i}{2} \log_2 e_i + (\mathsf{C}_i + \mu \mathsf{P}_i) e_i \right] + \sum_{i=1}^{n-1} \mathsf{P}_{\ell_i} e_i (n - i). \tag{2}$$

Elliptic Curve Models. We will work with elliptic curves in Montgomery [31] and in twisted Edwards form with extended coordinates [4,24]. For lack of space, we refrain from fully defining them here, and refer the reader to the original sources for more information. Montgomery curves are used in most deployed isogeny-based protocol, as they are particularly efficient if they are reduced to the Kummer line. However, points on the Kummer line form no longer a group, and addition operations have to be substituted by differential additions. Optimized arithmetic on twisted Edwards curves is a bit slower, but points still form a group, which will prove necessary for some of our applications. Note that there is a one-to-one correspondence between Montgomery and twisted Edwards curves, and switching between equivalent curves can be done very efficiently [4,8,30]. As estimates for the cost of point addition and doubling on Montgomery curves over $\mathbb{F}_{p^2}$, we use [5,15]

$$\mathsf{A} = 5.6\,\mathrm{m}, \quad \mathsf{D} = 3.6\,\mathrm{m} \quad \text{and} \quad \mathsf{M} = 9.2\,\mathrm{m},$$

where M represents a step in the Montgomery ladder algorithm [31]. For twisted Edwards curves with extended coordinates, we find [24]

$$\mathsf{A} = 9\,\mathrm{m}, \quad \mathsf{D} = 7.2\,\mathrm{m} \quad \text{and} \quad \mathsf{M} = 16.2\,\mathrm{m},$$

where M represents a step in the typical double-and-add scheme.

Isogeny computations will always be performed on Montgomery curves, for which we can use the optimized results from [14]:

$$\mathsf{C}_3 = 4.4\,\mathrm{m}, \quad \mathsf{S}_3 = 9.2\,\mathrm{m}, \quad \mathsf{P}_3 = 5.6\,\mathrm{m},$$
$$\mathsf{C}_4 = 3.2\,\mathrm{m}, \quad \mathsf{S}_4 = 7.2\,\mathrm{m}, \quad \mathsf{P}_4 = 7.6\,\mathrm{m},$$

2.3   Security Model

The security model for delegating cryptographic computations used throughout this paper was originally proposed by Hohenberger and Lysyanskaya [25]. In this model, delegation algorithms are split into a trusted component $\mathcal{T}$ and a set of untrusted servers $\mathcal{U}$. The delegator makes oracle queries to the servers such that their interaction $T^{\mathcal{U}}$ results in the correct execution of an algorithm Alg with the goal of reducing the computational cost of T when compared to the local execution of Alg. Since $\mathcal{U}$ might potentially be malicious, the delegator needs to both ensure that $\mathcal{U}$ is not able to extract any sensitive data from the interaction, and be able to verify that the results returned by $\mathcal{U}$ are computed correctly. The full adversary in this model $\mathcal{A} = (\mathcal{E}, \mathcal{U})$ further includes the environment $\mathcal{E}$, representing any third party, that should also not be able to extract sensitive data, while having a different view of the inputs and output of Alg as $\mathcal{U}$ does.

The *outsource input/output specification* (or *outsource-IO*) distinguishes *secret* (only T has access), *protected* (T and $\mathcal{E}$ have access) and *unprotected* (everyone has access) inputs and outputs, while non-secret inputs are further subdivided into *honest* and *adversarial*, depending on whether they originate from a trusted source or not. An important assumption of this model is that, while the servers in $\mathcal{U}$ and the environment $\mathcal{E}$ might initially devise a joint strategy, there is no direct communication channel between the different servers within $\mathcal{U}$ or between $\mathcal{U}$ and the environment $\mathcal{E}$ after T starts using them ($\mathcal{U}$ can be seen to be installed behind T's firewall). However, they could try to establish an indirect communication channel via the unprotected inputs and un/protected outputs of Alg. To mitigate this threat, T should ensure that the adversarial, unprotected input stays empty (see also Remark 2.4 in [25]), while the non-secret outputs do not contain any sensitive data. The security of delegation schemes is formalized in the following definition, which also formalizes T's efficiency gain due to the delegation, as well as its ability to verify correctness of $\mathcal{U}$'s outputs.

Definition 1 ((α, β)-outsource-security [25]). *Let* Alg *be an algorithm with outsource-IO. The pair $(T, \mathcal{U})$ constitutes an* outsource-secure *implementation of* Alg *if:*

- **Correctness:** $T^{\mathcal{U}}$ *is a correct implementation of* Alg.
- **Security:** *For all PPT adversaries* $\mathcal{A} = (\mathcal{E}, \mathcal{U})$, *there exist PPT simulators* $(\mathcal{S}_1, \mathcal{S}_2)$ *that can simulate the views of* $\mathcal{E}$ *and* $\mathcal{U}$ *indistinguishable from the real process. We write* $\mathcal{E}VIEW_{real} \sim \mathcal{E}VIEW_{ideal}$ *($\mathcal{E}$ learns nothing) and* $UVIEW_{real} \sim UVIEW_{ideal}$ *($\mathcal{U}$ learns nothing). The details of these experiments can be found in Definition 2.2 of [25]. If $\mathcal{U}$ consists of multiple servers, then there is a PPT-simulator $\mathcal{S}_{2,i}$ for each of their views.*
- **Cost reduction:** *for all inputs x, the running time of T is at most an α-multiplicative factor of the running time of* Alg(x),
- **Verifiability:** *for all inputs x, if $\mathcal{U}$ deviates from its advertised functionality during the execution $T^{\mathcal{U}}(x)$, then T will detect the error with probability $\geq \beta$.*

Adversarial models differ along the number and intent of servers. The models we will analyze in this work are the following.

Definition 2 (Honest-but-curious [11]). *The* one honest-but-curious program model *defines the adversary as* $\mathcal{A} = (\mathcal{E}, \mathcal{U})$, *where* $\mathcal{U}$ *consists of a single server that always returns correct results, but may try to extract sensitive data.*

Definition 3 (OMTUP [25]). *The one-malicious version of a two untrusted program model defines the adversary as $\mathcal{A} = (\mathcal{E}, (\mathcal{U}_1, \mathcal{U}_2))$ and assumes that at most one of the two servers $\mathcal{U}_1$ or $\mathcal{U}_2$ deviates from its advertised functionality (for a non-negligible fraction of the inputs), while $\mathcal{T}$ does not know which one.*

We refer to the paper of Hohenberger and Lysyanskaya [25] for other security models without any honest party, namely the *two untrusted program model* (TUP) and the *one untrusted program model* (OUP). Models without honest entity are further discussed in the full version of this paper [35].

2.4 Cryptographic Protocols and Difficulty Assumptions

Let $E/\mathbb{F}_{p^2}$ be a publicly known supersingular elliptic curve with at least two coprime torsion groups $\langle P_A, Q_A \rangle = E[\tau_A]$ and $\langle P_B, Q_B \rangle = E[\tau_B]$, whose generators are also publicly known. Cryptographic protocols in the SIDH setting are generally based on the following commutative diagram:

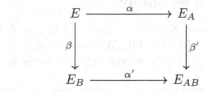

Let $\langle A \rangle = \ker \alpha$ and $\langle B \rangle = \ker \beta$, then the commutativity of the upper diagram is given by choosing $\ker \alpha' = \langle A^B \rangle$ and $\ker \beta' = \langle B^A \rangle$.

We revisit some of the security assumptions upon which isogeny-based cryptographic protocols are based. Note that we only show the ones that are explicitly used in this work. For other hard problems, we refer for example to [27].

Problem 1 (Computational Supersingular Isogeny Problem (CSSI) [27]). Given the triplet (E_B, P_A^B, Q_A^B), find an element in $[B] \subset E[\tau_B]$.

Problem 2 (Decisional Supersingular Product Problem (DSSP) [27]). Let $\alpha : E \rightarrow E_A$. Given a tuple $(E, E_A, E_1, E_2, \alpha, \alpha')$, determine from which of the following distributions it is sampled

- E_1 is random with $|E_1| = |E|$ and $\alpha' : E_1 \rightarrow E_2$ is a random τ_A-isogeny,
- $E_1 \times E_2$ is chosen at random among those isogenous to $E \times E_A$ and where $\alpha' : E_1 \rightarrow E_2$ is a τ_A-isogeny.

We further define the following difficulty assumption and show that it is at least as hard as DSSP.

Problem 3 (Decisional Point Preimage Problem (DPP)). Given (E, E_B, A, Λ'^B), where $A \in E[\tau_A]$, and $A'^B \in E_B[\tau_A]$, decide whether $[A] = [A']$.

Let $\mathcal{A}_{\text{DPP}}$ be an adversary to the DPP problem which, upon receiving the tuple (E, E_B, A, A'^B), returns $b = 1$ if $[A^B] = [A'^B]$, otherwise $b = 0$. Then, we can construct an adversary $\mathcal{B}_{\text{DSSP}}^{\mathcal{A}_{\text{DPP}}}$ against DSSP, which returns $b = 0$ in the first and $b = 1$ in the second case of Problem 2. Upon receiving $(E, E_A, E_B, E_C, \alpha, \alpha')$, $\mathcal{B}_{\text{DSSP}}^{\mathcal{A}_{\text{DPP}}}$ extracts kernel generators $\langle S \rangle = \ker \alpha$ and $\langle S'^B \rangle = \ker \alpha'$, then sends the query (E, E_B, S, S'^B) to $\mathcal{A}_{\text{DPP}}$. $\mathcal{B}_{\text{DSSP}}^{\mathcal{A}_{\text{DPP}}}$ returns what $\mathcal{A}_{\text{DPP}}$ returns: if $[S] = [S']$, then $E_B \times E_C$ is isogenous to $E \times E_A$ and we have $b = 1$, otherwise $b = 0$.

3 Delegating Isogenies

Throughout this section, we assume that the delegator $\mathcal{T}$ is able to generate elements in $\mathbb{Z}$ uniformly at random in an efficient manner. We further assume that $\mathcal{T}$ knows a representation of any of its secret and protected points in terms of the public torsion group generators.

3.1 Advertised Server Functionality

Let $E/\mathbb{F}_{p^2}$ be an elliptic curve, $\mathcal{K} \subset \mathbb{Z}_\tau \times E[\tau]$, $\mathcal{M} \subset \mathbb{Z} \times E$ two distinct sets of scalar-point pairs and $b \in \{0, 1\}$ a bit. We assume that the delegator gives inputs of the form $(E, \mathcal{K}; \mathcal{M}; b)$ to the server, who proceeds as follows.

- $\mathcal{K}$ encodes the kernel of the isogeny to compute, thus the server computes $K = \sum_{(a,P) \in \mathcal{K}} aP$, which it uses to compute the isogeny $\phi : E \to E_K$. Throughout this work, we are only interested in sets of the form $\mathcal{K} = \{(1, P), (k, Q)\}$ for generators $\langle P, Q \rangle = E[\tau]$.
- $\mathcal{M}$ contains points to push through and multiply with the associated scalar, i.e. the server computes $\mathcal{M}^K := \{aX^K \mid (a, X) \in \mathcal{M}\}$, where $X^K = \phi(X)$.
- If $b = 1$, the server generates a deterministic *return basis* $\mathcal{B}^K = \{R^K, S^K\} \subset E_K[\tau]$, such that $R^K + kS^K = P^K$.[1] If $b = 0$, then $\mathcal{B}^K = \emptyset$.

The server then returns $(E_K; \mathcal{M}^K; \mathcal{B}^K)$. We write the delegation step as follows

$$(E_K; \mathcal{M}^K; \mathcal{B}^K) \leftarrow \mathcal{U}(E, \mathcal{K}; \mathcal{M}; b).$$

The points in $\mathcal{M}$ are always submitted in a random order in order to avoid distinguishability. Further, to reduce the communication cost we assume that servers return all points scaled with $Z = 1$.

Notation. For a scalar-point pair (a, P) in $\mathcal{K}$ or $\mathcal{M}$, we simply write P if $a = 1$. If a set contains multiple pairs of the same point, e.g. $\{(a_1, P), (a_2, P), (a_3, P)\}$, we condense them as $\{(\{a_1, a_2, a_3\}, P)\}$.

---

[1] This can simply be achieved by first generating $S^K \in E_K[\tau]$ deterministically (e.g. by hashing into the elliptic curve using a procedure such as the one described in [26], and map out the unwanted torsion), then computing $R^K = P^K - kS^K$.

3.2   The Iso-Algorithm

Definition 4 (The Iso-algorithm). *The* isogeny delegation algorithm Iso *takes as inputs a supersingular elliptic curve $E/\mathbb{F}_{p^2}$, a kernel set $\mathcal{K} \subset \mathbb{Z} \times E(\mathbb{F}_{p^2})$, two scalar-point pair sets $\mathcal{H}_0, \mathcal{H} \subset \mathbb{Z} \times E(\mathbb{F}_{p^2})$ and a bit $b \in \{0,1\}$, then computes the isogeny $\phi : E \to E_K$ and produces the output $(E_K; \mathcal{H}_0^K, \mathcal{H}^K; \mathcal{B}^K)$, where $K = \sum_{(a,P) \in \mathcal{K}} aP$, $\mathcal{H}_{(0)}^K = \{aP^K \mid (a,P) \in \mathcal{H}_{(0)}\}$ and $\mathcal{B}^K$ is a return basis as described in Sect. 3.1, if $b = 1$ and $\emptyset$ otherwise. The inputs $E, \mathcal{K}, \mathcal{H}_0, b$ are all honest, unprotected parameters, while $\mathcal{H}$ contains secret or (honest/adversarial) protected scalars and honest, unprotected points. The outputs E_K, $\mathcal{H}_0^K$ and $\mathcal{B}^K$ are unprotected while $\mathcal{H}^K$ is secret or protected. We write*

$$(E_K; \mathcal{H}_0^K, \mathcal{H}^K; \mathcal{B}^K) \leftarrow \mathsf{Iso}(E, \mathcal{K}; \mathcal{H}_0, \mathcal{H}; b).$$

If $b = 0$ and thus $\mathcal{B}^K = \emptyset$, we shorten this as $(E_K; \mathcal{H}_0^K, \mathcal{H}^K) \leftarrow \mathsf{Iso}(E, \mathcal{K}; \mathcal{H}_0, \mathcal{H})$.

In Figs. 1 and 2, we show how a delegator $\mathcal{T}$ can use the advertised server functionality from Sect. 3.1 in order to implement Iso in an outsource-secure way under the HBC and OMTUP assumptions. The delegation subroutines are organized according to 5 main steps: First, auxiliary elements are generated (Gen), which are used to shroud protected elements (Shr), before being delegated to the server (Del). After the delegation, the server outputs are verified (Ver) and finally the results are recovered and output (Out).

Note that the HBC case does not need a verification step by assumption. The idea behind Fig. 1 is relatively trivial but effective: the delegator hides the secret/protected scalars simply by not disclosing them to the server and computing the scalar multiplication on the codomain point itself. The OMTUP case of Fig. 2 is a bit more complex, but will result in a lower cost for the delegator when compared to the HBC case. The underlying idea (for $N = 1$) is that the delegator shrouds the secret/protected scalars as a linear combination of small and large random scalars. The large scalars are distributed between the two servers in order to prevent reconstruction of the secrets, while the small scalars are kept secret by the delegator and used to ultimately verify correctness of the returned points. The size of the small scalars influences the cost for the delegator and the verifiability of the protocol. To further increase verifiability, the delegator can add more random scalars to the mix by increasing N, which leads to multiple, interconnected verification conditions, and results in an even higher verifiability, albeit at a higher cost for the delegator. There is an optimal trade-off between these two parameters, depending on the desired verifiability. We will discuss this trade-off further in Sect. 3.2. In the full version of this paper [35], we establish the protocol execution costs for the delegator

$$T_{\mathrm{HBC}}(\mu, \tau_A) = \mu \mathsf{S}(\tau_A), \tag{3}$$

$$T_{\mathrm{OMTUP}}(\mu, t) = \mu \left[(4N + 3)\mathsf{m} + 2M t + (2^{N+1} - N - 3)\mathsf{A} \right], \tag{4}$$

of Figs. 1 and 2 and further prove the following theorems.

Theorem 1. *Under the honest-but-curious assumption, the outsourcing algorithm $(\mathcal{T}, \mathcal{U})$ given in Fig. 1 is a $\left(O\left(\frac{1}{\log\log\tau} \right), 1 \right)$-outsource secure implementation of Iso, where τ is the smooth degree of the delegated isogeny.*

Theorem 2. *Under the OMTUP assumption, the outsourcing algorithm $(\mathcal{T}, (\mathcal{U}_1, \mathcal{U}_2))$ given in Fig. 2 is an $\left(O\left(\frac{t}{\log\tau\log\log\tau} \right), 1 - \frac{1}{(N+1)2^{Nt}} \right)$-outsource secure implementation of Iso, where τ is the smooth degree of the delegated isogeny. If $\mathcal{H} = \emptyset$, then it is fully verifiable.*

Hiding a Point. If the delegator wants to push through a secret or (honest/adversarial) protected elliptic curve point $A = P + aQ \in E[\tau_A]$, then $\mathcal{T}$ simply has to delegate

$$(E_K; \mathcal{H}_0^K \cup \{P\}, \mathcal{H}^K \cup \{aQ^K\}; \mathcal{B}^K) \leftarrow \mathsf{Iso}(E, \mathcal{K}; \mathcal{H}_0 \cup \{P\}, \mathcal{H} \cup \{(a, Q)\}; b),$$

and compute $A^K = P^K + aQ^K$. We assume that a representation of A in the normal form is always known, as will always be the case in the cryptographic protocols that we discuss in this paper.

Honest-but-curious approach.

Gen: No auxiliary elements are needed.

Shr: Set $\mathcal{H}' = \{Q \mid (a, Q) \in \mathcal{H}\}$.

Del: Delegate $(E_K; \mathcal{H}_0^K \cup \mathcal{H}'^K; \mathcal{B}^K) \leftarrow \mathcal{U}(E, \mathcal{K}; \mathcal{H}_0 \cup \mathcal{H}'; b)$.

Out: Compute $\mathcal{H}^K = \{aQ^K \mid (a, Q) \in \mathcal{H}, Q^K \in \mathcal{H}'^K\}$, then return $(E_K; \mathcal{H}_0^K, \mathcal{H}^K; \mathcal{B}^K)$.

Fig. 1. Implementation of Iso in the HBC assumption

OMTUP approach.

Gen: For each $(a, Q) \in \mathcal{H}$, choose $N \in \mathbb{N}$, then (assuming $Q \in E[\tau]$) generate
- small non-zero scalars $c_1, \ldots, c_N, d_1, \ldots, d_N \in \{-2^{t-1}, \ldots, 2^{t-1}\}$, and
- random scalars $r_0, s_0, s_1, \ldots, s_{N-1} \in \mathbb{Z}_\tau$.

Shr: For each $(a, Q) \in \mathcal{H}$, compute $r_i = -s_i + c_i s_0 + d_i r_0$ for $i = 1, \ldots, N - 1$. Define $\sigma = \sum_{i=1}^{N-1}(s_i + r_i)$ and let γ be the smallest integer > 1 coprime to τ, then compute $s_N = \gamma^{-1}(d_N r_0 + c_N s_0 + \sigma - a)$ and $r_N = -s_N + c_N s_0 + d_N r_0$. Set

$$\mathcal{H}'_1 = \{(\{s_0, \ldots, s_N\}, Q) \mid (a, Q) \in \mathcal{H}\}, \quad \mathcal{H}'_2 = \{(\{r_0, \ldots, r_N\}, Q) \mid (a, Q) \in \mathcal{H}\}.$$

Del: Delegate $(E_K; \mathcal{H}_0^K \cup \mathcal{H}_1'^K; \mathcal{B}^K) \leftarrow \mathcal{U}_1(E, \mathcal{K}; \mathcal{H}_0 \cup \mathcal{H}'_1; b)$ and $(E'_K; \mathcal{H}_0'^K \cup \mathcal{H}_2'^K; \mathcal{B}'^K) \leftarrow \mathcal{U}_2(E, \mathcal{K}; \mathcal{H}_0 \cup \mathcal{H}'_2; b)$.

Ver: Verify, if $E_K \overset{?}{=} E'_K$, $\mathcal{H}_0^K \overset{?}{=} \mathcal{H}_0'^K$, $\mathcal{B}^K \overset{?}{=} \mathcal{B}'^K$, and if $(s_i Q)^K + (r_i Q)^K \overset{?}{=} c_i(s_0 Q)^K + d_i(r_0 Q)^K$, for $i = 1, \ldots, N$.

Out: If any of the verifications fail, return $\perp$, otherwise return $(E_K; \mathcal{H}_0^K, \mathcal{H}^K; \mathcal{B}^K)$, where

$$\mathcal{H}^K = \left\{ r_N Q^K - (\gamma - 1)s_N Q^K + \sum_{i=1}^{N-1}(s_i Q^K + r_i Q^K) \Big| (a, Q) \in \mathcal{H} \right\}.$$

Fig. 2. Implementation of Iso in the OMTUP assumption

The Parameter t. In some cases, the parameter t does not only influence the verifiability and cost of the underlying system, but also its security. Related attacks become unfeasible, if the size of t reflects the security of the underlying cryptosystem against both classical and quantum attackers, i.e. in general we need to ensure that guessing all $c_1, \ldots, c_N$ correctly is at least as hard as some targeted security level 2^λ, i.e. $(N + 1)2^{Nt} \approx 2^\lambda$ or $t \approx \frac{\lambda}{N}$. In this case, using Eq. (4), the protocol cost per hidden point becomes

$$\mu^{-1}T_{\mathrm{OMTUP}}(\mu, \lambda/N) = (4N + 3)\mathsf{m} + \frac{2\lambda}{N}(\mathsf{D} + \mathsf{A}) + \left(2^{N+1} - N - 3\right)\mathsf{A}.$$

In Sect. 5, we minimize this cost with respect to N for specific choices of λ. Note that choosing $tN = \lambda$ further implies a verifiability of $1 - O(2^{-\lambda})$, which is very close to 1 for a cryptographically sized λ.

Difference to Delegation of Mudular Exponentiation. We want to point out a few key differences of isogeny delegation schemes to those of modular exponentiation as in [11,25,29]. First of all, in contrast to modular exponentiations, the domain and codomain of isogenies are different (except in the trivial case where $\mathcal{K} = \emptyset$), and more importantly, these are a priori unknown to the delegator. This means that the delegator not only has to verify if the codomain is correct, but also can not generate points on the codomain before the delegation step is completed. This also means that lookup-tables with points in the domain and codomain curves are not possible, hence the delegator can compute the final result only from linear combinations of elements the server(s) returned. Another circumstance of isogenies is that elliptic curves can not be combined in an easy way without computing isogenies, which means that combinations, such as $(A, E_A) \circ (B, E_B) = ((A, B), E_{AB})$ are not available to the delegator.

Now we turn our attention to what the delegator actually can do. One of the most important properties of isogenies in this context is that they are group homomorphisms. This means that linear combinations of points on the domain curve still hold on the codomain curve and can therefore be used to shroud and verify points, as Iso does. In order to verify the codomain curve, there seems to be no efficient way except for including at least one honest server, which will consistently return the correct curve and verify the malicious servers' results against it. The honest server is also necessary to verify if mapped points are correct. If none of the servers were honest, all points could be scaled by some previously determined factors, returning wrong results, which would still satisfy the verification conditions.

4 Shrouding Isogenies

We aim to hide the kernel generator $A \in E[\tau_A]$ via the isogenies generated by a coprime torsion group $E[\tau_I]$ with $\tau_I \approx \tau_A$. The idea is to go from E to E_A via the path $E \xrightarrow{\kappa} E_K \xrightarrow{\alpha} E_{AK} \xrightarrow{\hat{\kappa}'} E_A$, where $\hat{\kappa}'$ is the dual of κ pushed through α. The path is depicted in Fig. 3. The point A (or the isogeny α) is hidden via the isogeny $A^K = \kappa(A)$, since the knowledge of $[A^K]$ does not give any information about $[A]$ by the DPP-assumption (Problem 3). Note that our approach necessarily has to take at least three steps, since any linear combination of A with elements from $E[\tau_I]$ (i.e. any "shortcut") would always reveal information about A by mapping out the τ_I-torsion elements. Similarly, any shorter isogeny, smaller than the length of $\tau_A \approx \tau_I$, would reduce the security of the system.

$$
\begin{array}{ccc}
E & \underset{\hat{\kappa}}{\overset{\kappa}{\rightleftarrows}} & E_K \\
\alpha \downarrow & & \downarrow \alpha' \\
E_A & \underset{\hat{\kappa}'}{\overset{\kappa'}{\rightleftarrows}} & E_{AK}
\end{array}
\qquad
\begin{array}{ll}
\ker \alpha = \langle A \rangle & \ker \alpha' = \langle A^K \rangle \\
\ker \kappa = \langle K \rangle & \ker \kappa' = \langle K^A \rangle \\
\ker \hat{\kappa} = \langle \hat{K}^K \rangle & \ker \hat{\kappa}' = \langle \hat{K}^{AK} \rangle
\end{array}
$$

Fig. 3. Detour from $E \to E_A$ via E_K and E_{AK} and the associated kernel generators. The point $\hat{K}$ is any point of full order in $E[\tau_I]\backslash\langle K \rangle$.

Another important aspect is that any server that has computed the delegation in Step 2 should not see any information of the delegation performed in Steps 1 or 3 (and vice versa), since the knowledge of K (or $\hat{K}^{AK}$) and A^K can be used to recover A. We therefore in general need to work with multiple sets of servers, each being composed of one or more servers according to the underlying server assumptions (e.g. HBC, OMTUP). We denote these sets as $\mathbf{U}_1, \mathbf{U}_2, \mathbf{U}_3$, for delegation steps 1, 2 and 3. Under certain conditions, we can choose $\mathbf{U}_1 = \mathbf{U}_3$, which we will discuss further below. We also note, that in the OMTUP case, the malicious servers within these sets could exchange their knowledge about the kernel generators indirectly, which also needs to be addressed in our algorithm.

Definition 5 (The IsoDetour-algorithm). *The isogeny detour delegation algorithm* IsoDetour *takes as inputs a supersingular elliptic curve $E/\mathbb{F}_{p^2}$, a kernel generator $A = P_A + aQ_A$ where $\langle P_A, Q_A \rangle = E[\tau_A]$, two scalar-point pair sets $\mathcal{H}_0, \mathcal{H} \subset \mathbb{Z} \times E\backslash(E[\tau_A] \cup E[\tau_I])$, and a torsion-group indicator I. It then computes the isogeny $\phi : E \to E_A$ as $\phi = \kappa' \circ \alpha' \circ \kappa$ via the kernels $\ker \kappa = \langle K \rangle$, $\ker \alpha' = \langle A^K \rangle$ and $\ker \kappa' = \langle \hat{K}^{AK} \rangle$, where $K, \hat{K} \in E[\tau_I]$, both of full order and such that $\langle \hat{K} \rangle \neq \langle K \rangle$.* IsoDetour *then produces the output $(E_A; \mathcal{H}_0^A, \mathcal{H}^A)$. The inputs $E, \mathcal{H}_0$ are honest, unprotected parameters. $\mathcal{A}$ is secret, or (honest/adversarial) protected and $\mathcal{H}$ contains honest, unprotected points and secret or (honest/adversarial) protected scalars. The outputs E_A and $\mathcal{H}_0^A$ are unprotected while $\mathcal{H}^A$ is secret or protected. We write*

$$(E_A; \mathcal{H}_0^A, \mathcal{H}^A) \leftarrow \mathsf{IsoDetour}(E, A, I; \mathcal{H}_0, \mathcal{H}).$$

In Fig. 4, we present the IsoDetour-Algorithm, that uses the commutative diagram from Fig. 3 in order to delegate α via a detour over the curves E_K and E_{AK}. We assume that the generators $\langle P_I, Q_I \rangle = E[\tau_I]$ are known.

IsoDetour proceeds as follows: First, the isogeny κ is delegated to $\mathbf{U}_1$ and the point A is pushed through, hidden from the servers. The servers are also prompted to return a basis $R^K, S^K \in E_K$, such that $R^K + kS^K = P^K \in \ker \hat{\kappa}$. These points will later be used to compute the "return" isogeny $\hat{\kappa}'$. The point A^K is then used as the kernel generator for α', computed by $\mathbf{U}_2$, with R^K, S^K are pushed through. Finally, the delegator constructs the kernel generator $R^{AK} + kS^{AK}$ of $\hat{\kappa}'$ for the third delegation by $\mathbf{U}_3$. For any other scalar-point pair, that we want to push through, the general idea is to extract the (unprotected) points in $\mathcal{H}_0$ and $\mathcal{H}$ and simply push them through the first two rounds of delegation; the desired multiplication with hidden scalars needs to be done in the third round only. Note that since these points are pushed through κ and later through $\hat{\kappa}'$, the result will be multiplied by a factor $\deg \kappa = \deg \hat{\kappa}' = \tau_I$. Thus, we need to multiply the related scalars with τ_I^{-1}, in order to compensate for this.

IsoDetour$(E, A, I; \mathcal{H}_0, \mathcal{H})$

1. Generate random $k \in \mathbb{Z}_{\tau_I}^*$ and let $\mathcal{H}_0' = \{Q \mid (a, Q) \in \mathcal{H}_0 \cup \mathcal{H}\}$.
2. Delegate to server (group) $\mathbf{U}_1$ (in the OMTUP case, choose $tN \geq \lambda$)

$$(E_K; \mathcal{H}_0'^K \cup \{P_A^K\}, \{aQ_A^K\}; \{R^K, S^K\}) \leftarrow \mathsf{Iso}(E, \{P_I, (k, Q_I)\}; \mathcal{H}_0' \cup \{P_A\}, \{(a, Q_A)\}; 1).$$

and compute $A^K = P_A^K + aQ_A^K$.
3. Delegate to server (group) $\mathbf{U}_2$ (in the OMTUP case, choose $tN \geq \lambda$)

$$(E_{AK}; \{R^{AK}\} \cup \mathcal{H}_0'^{AK}, \{kS^{AK}\}; \emptyset) \leftarrow \mathsf{Iso}(E_K, \{A^K\}; \{R^K\} \cup \mathcal{H}_0'^K, \{(k, S^K)\}; 0).$$

4. From $\mathcal{H}_0'^{AK}$, build $\mathcal{H}_{(0)}''^{AK} = \{(a\tau_I^{-1}, Q^{AK}) \mid (a, Q) \in \mathcal{H}_{(0)}\}$. Then, compute the kernel $\hat{K}^{AK} = R^{AK} + kS^{AK}$.
5. Delegate $(E_A; \mathcal{H}_0^A, \mathcal{H}^A; \emptyset) \leftarrow \mathsf{Iso}(E_{AK}, \{\hat{K}^{AK}\}; \mathcal{H}_0''^{AK}, \mathcal{H}''^{AK}; 0)$ to server (group) $\mathbf{U}_1$.
6. Return $(E_A; \mathcal{H}_0^A, \mathcal{H}^A)$.

Fig. 4. Implementation of the IsoDetour algorithm given in Definition 5 using the Iso algorithm from Definition 4 as a subroutine.

Mapping Points. Note that since $\hat{\kappa}'$ is represents the dual isogeny of κ pushed through α', any points mapped via the detour path will necessarily by multiplied by τ_I. This is corrected in step 4 by multiplying these points with the inverse of τ_I. Note that this multiplication is only defined for points in torsion groups of order coprime to τ_I,[2] thus not for points in $E[\tau_I]$. An important aspect of SIDH and related protocols (such as SIKE [2,39] and the PKE from [27]) is that there are two large torsion groups $E[\tau_A]$, $E[\tau_B]$ with generators P_A, Q_A and P_B, Q_B, respectively. Each party chooses a torsion group, in which it computes its isogeny. Then it transports the generators of the other torsion group via its isogeny to the codomain curve in order to create their public key, e.g. the public key of Alice is (E_A, P_B^A, Q_B^A). These point maps turn out to be a problem for the IsoDetour-algorithm, since any point in $E[\tau_B]$ will map to $\mathcal{O}$ on E_A, and we are not able to map P_B, Q_B along this path. We present two ways to circumvent this problem below. We also note that due to the security constraints of IsoDetour,

---

[2] We assume τ_I^{-1} to be known with respect any other torsion group.

we also cannot map points in $E[\tau_A]$ to E_A. Fortunately, this is not necessary for the cryptographic protocols analyzed in this work.

More Torsion Groups. Assuming the protocol has more torsion groups than two, we can easily transport Bob's kernel generators $P_B, Q_B \in E[\tau_B]$ by doing a detour via isogenies defined over a third torsion group $I \neq A, B$. More generally, let $p = \prod_{i=1}^{n} \tau_i \mp 1$ with $n > 2$, then Alice can delegate the computation of her public key (E_A, P_B^A, Q_B^A) as

$$(E_A; \{P_B, Q_B\}^A, \emptyset) \leftarrow \mathsf{IsoDetour}(E, A, I; \{P_B, Q_B\}, \emptyset).$$

Working with Twists. If we are working with a prime of the form $p \pm 1 = f\tau_A\tau_B$, i.e. we only have two torsion groups at our disposal on E, we can use twists to generate "new" torsion groups [13] on E^t. Assuming the prime decomposition $p \mp 1 = D\tau_S$, with $\tau_S \approx \tau_A$ smooth and D a co-factor, we have another torsion group on the "backside" of our elliptic curve, $E^t[\tau_S]$. We can simply delegate the public key computation via

$$(E_A; \{P_B, Q_B\}^A, \emptyset) \leftarrow \mathsf{IsoDetour}(E, A, S; \{P_B, Q_B\}, \emptyset),$$

by running over the twists $E \simeq E^t \rightarrow E_K^t \rightarrow E_{AK}^t \rightarrow E_A^t \simeq E_A$. For efficiency reasons, τ_S has to be smooth. There are not many primes p such that $p \pm 1$ and $\tau_S \mid p \mp 1$ are smooth. We call primes of this type *delegation-friendly primes* and generalize them in the following definition. We present an approach to generate such primes in the full version of the paper [35].

Definition 6 (Delegation-friendly primes). *An n-delegation-friendly prime (DFP) is a prime p with n smooth factors $\prod_{i=1}^{n} \tau_i \mid p \pm 1$ and at least one smooth factor $\tau_S \mid p \mp 1$, such that $\tau_i \approx \tau_S$ for all i.*

We discuss under which conditions we can choose $\mathbf{U}_1 = \mathbf{U}_3$. An important consequence of using multiple torsion groups or delegation-friendly primes are the susceptibility to torsion-attacks as described in [36,37]. The security of such a delegation depends strongly on the points revealed on E_K and E_{AK}, which in turn reveal the action of α' on these subgroups. As an example, consider standard SIDH with a DFP, i.e. where we have $p \pm 1 = f\tau_A\tau_B$ and $p \mp 1 = \tau_S D$. Using $\mathsf{IsoDetour}$ in order to compute a public key reveals the action of α' on $E[\tau_B]$ and $E[\tau_S]$, which would allow a quadratic speedup of the isogeny recovery attack by [37, Prop. 25 and Prop.27]. In this case, we would need three sets of servers in order to not allow this attack. Taking the non-DFP $p \pm 1 = f\tau_A\tau_B\tau_I$ instead, results in a slightly less than quadratic speedup, but in more expensive arithmetic. While small speedups might in some situations not pose a problem, we will discuss under which conditions these occur in Sect. 5 as well as in the proofs of Theorems 3 and 4, found in the full version of this paper [35]. Note that this does not make our schemes insecure, as we simply point out, under which conditions two server groups can be used instead of three. In the case of three different server sets, these attacks do not apply.

Choosing t. We point out the issues outlined in Remark 2.4 of [25], which in short states that *"the adversarial, unprotected input must be empty"*. In Fig. 4, the kernel generators A^K and $\hat{K}^{AK}$ actually do constitute adversarial unprotected inputs, and might allow the malicious server in $\mathbf{U}_1$ to communicate information about K to $\mathbf{U}_2$, revealing information about A. To mitigate this threat, $\mathcal{T}$ can increase the parameter t so far to make this attack at least as hard as breaking the underlying cryptosystem. As discussed in Sect. 3.2, choosing $tN \geq \lambda$ guarantees that the unprotected inputs are actually honest up to a negligible probability. Note that if such points do not constitute adversarial unprotected inputs, t and N will only influence the cost and verifiability of the protocol. There is no advantage in choosing N different from 1 in this case.

Outsource-Security of IsoDetour. In the full version of the paper [35], we derive the following costs

$$T_{\mathsf{IsoDet}}^{\mathrm{HBC}}(\mu, \tau_A) = (\mu + 2)\mathsf{S}(\tau_A) + 2\mathsf{A},$$

$$T_{\mathsf{IsoDet}}^{\mathrm{OMTUP}}(\mu, t) = (8N + 6 + 5\mu)\mathsf{m} + \left(\frac{4\lambda}{N} + 2t\mu\right)\mathsf{M} + \left(2^{N+2} - 2N - 3 + \mu\right)\mathsf{A}.$$

for the delegator and prove the following theorems.

Theorem 3. *Under the honest-but-curious assumption, the outsourcing algorithm $(\mathcal{T}, \mathcal{U})$ given in Fig. 4 is an $\left(O\left(\frac{1}{\log\log\tau}\right), 1\right)$-outsource secure implementation of IsoDetour, where τ is the smooth degree of the delegated isogeny.*

Theorem 4. *Under the OMTUP assumption, the outsourcing algorithm $(\mathcal{T}, (\mathcal{U}_1, \mathcal{U}_2))$ given in Fig. 4 is an $\left(O\left(\frac{\lambda}{\log\tau\log\log\tau}\right), 1 - \frac{1}{2^{t+1}}\right)$-outsource secure implementation of IsoDetour, where τ is the smooth degree of the delegated isogeny and λ a security parameter. If $\mathcal{H} = \emptyset$, then IsoDetour is fully verifiable.*

Hiding the Kernel Generator. A first attempt of hiding the kernel generator of a delegated isogeny was presented with the HIso algorithm of [34]. In the full version of this paper, we show that this scheme is not secure and that the secret can be recovered using pairings. We then discuss how this would be possible using the approach presented in this section. Unfortunately, it turns out to be too expensive for realistic scenarios. In protocols that need a hidden codomain, we therefore assume that the delegator computes them locally.

5   Delegation of Isogeny-Based Protocols

We apply our proposed delegation subroutines to some of the cryptographic protocols based on supersingular isogenies over $\mathbb{F}_{p^2}$. In order to assess the computational and communication costs, we will use the 2^{e_2}-torsion groups of the standardized SIKE primes from [28].[3] To maximize efficiency, we implement the HBC case on Montgomery curves on the Kummer line, while we need a group structure to implement point hiding under the OMTUP-assumption, hence we will use twisted Edwards curves in this case. The efficient transformations between these curves allow seamless integration of our delegation schemes into typically Montgomery-curve based protocols. We assume local computations to always be performed in optimized Montgomery arithmetic.

In the following subsections, we compare the delegated runtimes to the local (non-delegated) cost of some cryptographic protocols. We express our results in terms of the cost reduction function α introduced in Definition 1. To avoid adversarial inputs in the OMTUP-assumption, we use $\lambda = e_2/2$, which reflects the classical security of the underlying protocols. The optimal value of N for all SIKE primes is $N = 4$ (also considering communication costs).

We present our results using the theoretical runtimes established throughout this work and compare them to benchmarks illustrating the runtimes of the delegator under both the HBC- and OMTUP-assumptions.[4] The benchmarks were implemented using Magma v2.25-6 on an Intel(R) Xeon(R) CPU E5-2630 v2 @ 2.60 GHz with 128 GB memory. Our implementation uses parts of the Microsoft(R) vOW4SIKE implementation from [12].[5]

Communication costs between delegator and server are expressed in bits. Let $b(p) = \lceil \log_2 p \rceil$, then elements in $\mathbb{F}_{p^2}$ then contain $2b(p)$ bits of information. We note that Montgomery curves and points on their Kummer line can be expressed by a single $\mathbb{F}_{p^2}$-element, while twisted Edwards curves and their points are expressed using two such elements. Note that we assume $Z = 1$, which can always be achieved by an inversion and that the T-coordinate in the latter case can be recovered by a simple multiplication. In the case $p \approx \prod_{i=1}^{n} \tau_i$ with $\forall i, j : \tau_i \approx \tau_j$, elements in $\mathbb{Z}_{\tau_i}$ can be expressed using approximately $b(p)/n$ bits.

For the sake of conciseness, we assume that the protocols in this section are known. While we briefly review the protocol steps in order to assess the local computation cost, we refer the reader to the original sources for more details.

Remark 1 (Free Delegation). Note that we can freely delegate any protocol that does not need hiding, i.e. where the kernel is unprotected and $\mu = 0$. Verification of the server outputs then reduce to simple comparison operations under the OMTUP-assumption. Some examples of such schemes are isogeny-based hash functions [10,21] with unprotected messages or verifiable delay functions [20].

5.1   Key-Agreement Protocols

We consider the key agreement protocols from [3,22], which are n-party extensions to SIDH [18]. In this scenario, we have $p + 1 = \prod_{i=1}^{n} \ell_i^{e_i}$ for n parties.

---

[3] $p434 = 2^{216}3^{137} - 1$, $p503 = 2^{250}3^{159} - 1$, $p610 = 2^{305}3^{192} - 1$, $p751 = 2^{372}3^{239} - 1$.

[4]   Our implementation can be found at https://github.com/gemeis/SIDHdelegation and includes representative benchmarks for the delegator's operations as well as a proof-of-concept implementation for the correctness of our algorithms.

[5]   https://github.com/microsoft/vOW4SIKE.

Each party $\mathcal{P}_i$ is assigned a subgroup $\langle P_i, Q_i \rangle = E[\ell_i^{e_i}]$ and has a secret key $a_i \in \mathbb{Z}_{\ell_i^{e_i}}$, defining $A_i = P_i + a_i Q_i$ as the kernel of $\phi_i : E \to E_i = E/\langle A_i \rangle$, while the corresponding public key is $(E_i, P_1^i, Q_1^i, \ldots, P_n^i, Q_n^i)$ for party i. While we consider the n-party case in order to stay general, we point out that n-party key agreement protocols have to be used with caution, as torsion point attacks can be quite effective in these settings. In particular, [37] presents improved attacks for $n > 2$ and a polynomial-time break for $n \geq 6$.

Public Key Generation Step. Let Alice be $\mathcal{P}_1$. If $n > 2$, Alice can delegate her public key computation using IsoDetour twice, along two paths $I_1 \neq I_2$:

$$(E_{A_1}; \mathcal{N}_1^{A_1}, \emptyset) \leftarrow \text{IsoDetour}(E, A_1, I_1; \mathcal{N}_1, \emptyset),$$

$$(E_{A_1}; \mathcal{N}_2^{A_1}, \emptyset) \leftarrow \text{IsoDetour}(E, A_1, I_2; \mathcal{N}_2, \emptyset),$$

Where $\mathcal{N}_1 \cup \mathcal{N}_2 = \{(P_i, Q_i)\}_{i \in \{2,\ldots,n\}}$, the set of all other torsion group generators on E, such that $\mathcal{N}_1 \cap \mathcal{N}_2 = \emptyset$ and $(P_{I_1}, Q_{I_1}) \in \mathcal{N}_2$ and $(P_{I_2}, Q_{I_2}) \in \mathcal{N}_1$. By using alternating server groups $\mathbf{U}_1$ and $\mathbf{U}_2$ as indicated in Fig. 5, and by carefully choosing $\mathcal{N}_1$ and $\mathcal{N}_2$, we can assure that the servers get as little information as possible about the action of the isogenies α_1' and α_2' on the torsion groups, so that we only need two server groups for delegation.[6]

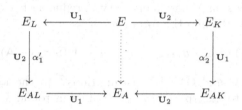

Fig. 5. Alice's concept of delegating the computation of her public key via two detours using two server groups $\mathbf{U}_1$ and $\mathbf{U}_2$. L and K are from different torsion groups.

With an n-DFP, this step can be delegated with a single instance of IsoDetour using the smooth torsion group on the twist side. This case needs three server groups. Let $d \in \{0, 1\}$ distinguish, if we have an n-DFP ($d = 1$) or not ($d = 0$) at our disposal. The cost reduction for public-key delegation can then be expressed as

$$\alpha_{\text{PubKey},n}(d, \tau_A) = \frac{(2-d)T_{\text{IsoDet}}(0, \tau_A)}{\mathsf{I}(\tau_A, 3(n-1)) + \mathsf{S}(\tau_A) + \mathsf{A}}.$$

Figure 6 compares our theoretical estimates with the benchmarked results for $n = 2$, used in most cryptographic protocols. In this case, a delegation-friendly prime is necessary. The communication costs are summarized in Table 1.

---

[6] For example, we could simply split up generators P_i, Q_i into both sets for all i.

Intermediate Steps. If $n > 2$, Alice performs $n - 2$ intermediate steps $k \in \{2, \ldots, n - 1\}$, in which she has to compute $(E_{k'}, \mathcal{N}^{k'})$ from $(E_k, \mathcal{N}^k \cup \{(P_A^k, Q_A^k)\})$, where $E_{k'} = E_k/\langle P_A^k + a_1 Q_A^k \rangle$ and $\mathcal{N}^{k^{(')}} = \{(P_i^{k^{(')}}, Q_i^{k^{(')}})\}_{i \in \{k+1, \ldots, n\}}$. Note that in this scenario, it is cheaper to compute A_1^k locally and delegate

$$(E_{k'}; \mathcal{N}^{k'}, \emptyset) \leftarrow \mathsf{Iso}(E_k, \{A_1^k\}; \mathcal{N}^k, \emptyset),$$

than using IsoDetour. Note again that A_1^k does not reveal any information about A_1 because of the difficulty of solving the Decisional Point Preimage Problem 3.

Final Step. Alice's final step is the computation of the shared secret. As discussed in Sect. 4, this step needs to be computed locally. It involves the computation of the kernel generator and then of the final isogeny.

Cost. We establish the total cost of an n-party key agreement protocol. Let $d \in \{0, 1\}$ again distinguish if we have a delegation-friendly prime ($d = 1$) or not ($d = 0$) at our disposal. The public-key is computed using $2 - d$ invocations of IsoDetour with $\mu = 0$. The $n - 2$ intermediate computations can then each be delegated using Iso with $\mu = 0$. The final step is then computed locally at the cost of $\mathsf{S}(\tau_A) + \mathsf{A} + \mathsf{I}(\tau_A, 0)$. Since after the public-key computation, Alice does not need to hide any points in either of the steps, she can simply perform all of these computations on Montgomery curves, reducing her computational and communication cost. We find the total cost of

$$T_{n\mathrm{PDH}}(d, \tau_A) = (2 - d)T_{\mathsf{IsoDet}}(0) + (n - 1)(\mathsf{S}(\tau_A) + \mathsf{A}) + \mathsf{I}(\tau_A, 0),$$

under both the HBC and OMTUP assumptions.[7] In the local version of the protocol, Alice has to transport $2(n - k)$ points in round k, and compute the map of A given her generators on each curve except the first. We find

$$\alpha_{n\mathrm{PDH}}(d, \tau_A) = \frac{(2 - d)T_{\mathsf{IsoDetour}}(0) + (n - 1)(\mathsf{S}(\tau_A) + \mathsf{A}) + \mathsf{I}(\tau_A, 0)}{n(\mathsf{I}(\tau_A, n - 1) + \mathsf{S}(\tau_A) + \mathsf{A})}.$$

Figure 6 shows the evolution of the cost reduction for $p434$ in terms of n for the cases with and without delegation-friendly primes and compares our theoretical estimates and benchmarks for the 2-party case ($d = 1$). Table 1 summarizes the communication costs for different n.

Remark 2. Note that the computational and communication cost established throughout this section also apply to the delegation of isogeny-based public-key encryption [18] and key encapsulation [39] as the steps of these protocols are the same (up to some negligible computations) as (2-party) SIDH.

---

[7] $T_{\mathsf{IsoDet}}(0)$ denotes a placeholder for either $T_{\mathsf{IsoDet}}^{\mathrm{HBC}}(\mu = 0, \tau_A)$ or $T_{\mathsf{IsoDet}}^{\mathrm{OMTUP}}(\mu = 0, t)$ of Sect. 4 depending on the underlying assumption.

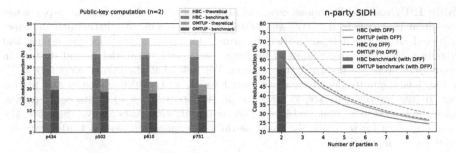

Fig. 6. Cost reduction functions in the HBC and OMTUP assumptions. The left figure compares theoretical costs and benchmarks for delegating 2-party public-key computations for different security levels. The discrepancy between these costs is mainly due to the computational overhead of local isogeny computations, which becomes less important for higher degree isogenies, since the cost of isogeny computation itself increases. The figure on the right shows the theoretical cost of n-party key agreement protocols for different n with and without a delegation-friendly prime in the case of $p434$. The case $n = 2$ further includes benchmarks. We see that the gain for the delegator increases with the security level and with the number of parties n.

5.2   Identification Protocols and Signatures

In this section, we establish the costs of identification protocols and signature schemes. We assume the public key (E_A, P_B^A, Q_B^A) to be precomputed as it is directly related to the identity of the prover.

Zero-Knowledge Proof of Identity. We show how the ZKPI-protocol from [18] can be delegated. In every round of the protocol, the prover needs to compute the isogenies $\beta : E \to E_B$, $\beta' : E_A \to E_{AB}$ and the map A^B of the prover's secret. This can be done by delegating

$$(E_B; P_A^B, aQ_A^B) \leftarrow \mathsf{Iso}(E, \{P_B, (b, Q_B)\}; \{P_A\}, \{(a, Q_A)\}),$$
$$(E_{AB}; \emptyset, \emptyset) \leftarrow \mathsf{Iso}(E_A, \{P_B^A, (b, Q_B^A)\}; \emptyset, \emptyset).$$

Depending on the challenge, the response is either b or $A^B = P_A^B + aQ_A^B$ for $c = 0, 1$, respectively. If $c = 0$, the verifier delegates

$$(E_B; \emptyset, \emptyset) \leftarrow \mathsf{Iso}(E; \{P_B, (b, Q_B)\}; \emptyset, \emptyset), \quad (E_{AB}; \emptyset, \emptyset) \leftarrow \mathsf{Iso}(E_A; \{P_B^A, (b, Q_B^A)\}; \emptyset, \emptyset),$$

otherwise $(E_{AB}; \emptyset, \emptyset) \leftarrow \mathsf{Iso}(E_B, \{A^B\}; \emptyset, \emptyset)$.

Signature Schemes. The delegation procedure of the signature schemes in [23] based on this identification scheme is completely analogous, i.e. for each of the commitments, the prover and/or verifier proceed exactly as in the identification protocol. The delegator further needs to compute hash-functions, but we assume that these have negligible cost (or are delegated with other schemes).

Table 1. Upload and Download costs (in kB per server) of delegating the n-party key agreement protocols in the HBC and OMTUP assumptions. We distinguish the cases with and without a delegation-friendly prime. The cost is given by the inputs and outputs within the three rounds of IsoDetour, assuming the initial E and its torsion group generators are known by the servers. We note that the kernel generator $\hat{K}^{AK}$ in Fig. 4 is computed locally and we thus have $Z \neq 1$, which increases the upload cost. In the intermediate steps, Alice has to transport $2(n - k)$ unprotected points. Since the final step is computed locally, no communication costs apply. Therefore, the communication for $n = 2$ is the same as the communication needed to delegate the public key computation.

| | | no DFP | | | | DFP | | | |
| | | p434 | | p751 | | p434 | | p751 | |
		HBC	OMT	HBC	OMT	HBC	OMT	HBC	OMT
$n = 2$	Upload	–	–	–	–	1.30	2.83	2.25	4.90
	Download	–	–	–	–	1.80	4.86	3.12	8.43
$n = 3$	Upload	3.95	7.68	6.84	13.32	2.24	4.11	3.88	7.12
	Download	5.18	12.58	8.98	21.81	2.75	6.45	4.77	11.18
$n = 4$	Upload	5.53	10.02	9.58	17.37	3.40	5.64	5.89	9.78
	Download	6.98	15.65	12.1	27.13	3.91	8.25	6.78	14.3

Remark 3. We note that an alternative ID protocol to [18] has recently been proposed in [17]. This scheme is quite similar, except that an $E_B[\tau_A]$ basis needs to be deterministically generated using an algorithm called CanonicalBasis. We can delegate this newer scheme in exactly the same fashion as the one presented here, except that we have to add the execution of CanonicalBasis to the advertised server functionality. Since the algorithm is deterministic, we only have to compare the output of both servers in the OMTUP assumption, in order to verify that the output is correct. Note that the download communication cost is increased by these extra points.

Cost. Following the discussion from Sect. 3.2, since A^B might be used as an unprotected input by the verifier, we have to choose $tN \geq \lambda$, so the cost for the prover becomes $T_{\text{OMTUP}}(1, N/\lambda)$ in the OMTUP and $T_{\text{HBC}}(1, \tau_A)$ in the HBC assumption. For both cases, we get the cost reduction functions

$$\alpha_{\text{ZKPI.P}}(\tau_B) = \frac{T(1)}{2(\mathsf{S}(\tau_B) + \mathsf{A}) + \mathsf{I}(\tau_B, 1) + \mathsf{I}(\tau_B, 0)}, \quad \alpha_{\text{ZKPI.V}} = O(1).$$

Figure 7 shows theoretical estimates and benchmarked results for ZKPI-delegation by the prover. We summarize the communication costs in Table 2.

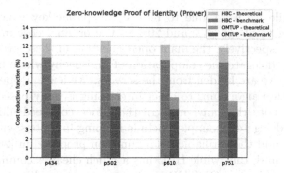

Fig. 7. Theoretical and benchmarked cost reduction function of the prover delegating zero-knowledge proofs of identity in the HBC and OMTUP assumptions. The theoretical predictions again underestimate the cost reduction via delegation, due to the overhead in isogeny computations. The discrepancy is higher this time higher than in Fig. 6 due to the much lower cost for the delegator. Again, the gain increases with higher security.

Table 2. Upload and Download costs (in B per server) of delegating the zero-knowledge proof of identity in the HBC and OMTUP assumptions, as well as for the verifier. The cost for the verifier is averaged over both challenge scenarios. We assume that the starting curve E and the associated generators are known by the servers. In the case of the prover, we further assume that its public key E_A and associated generators are also known to the servers. We also assume that the ephemeral parameter b has to be transmitted only once. Since the OMTUP case reduces to simple comparison operations for the verifier, these can also be done on Montgomery curves, saving some of the communication.

	$p434$			$p751$		
	HBC	OMTUP	Ver.	HBC	OMTUP	Ver.
Upload	54	189	298	94	328	516
Download	433	1516	162	751	2628	282

6 Conclusion and Future Work

In this work, we presented two outsource-secure delegation schemes, Iso and IsoDetour, under the *one honest-but-curious* (HBC) and *one-malicious version of a two untrusted program* (OMTUP) models of [25]. Our delegation algorithms can be used as a toolbox to delegate common isogeny-based cryptographic protocols in a secure and verifiable manner. Our approach reduces the cost of the zero-knowledge proof of identity from [27] as well as the related signature schemes from [23] to about 11% of the original cost in the HBC case and 6% in the OMTUP case. While the cost of n-party key-exchange delegation strongly decreases with increasing n, the case $n = 2$ only reaches a reduction to about 65% of the original cost. It is of substantial interest to further reduce this number in order to make e.g. the standardization candidate SIKE efficiently delegatable. While we were able to reduce the public-key generation step in the SIDH setting to about 35% and 20% of the original cost in the HBC and OMTUP cases, respectively, the main open question in these protocols remains how to efficiently delegate the computation of an isogeny where both the kernel and codomain curve are hidden from the servers. We leave it open to apply the proposed delegation algorithms to other interesting isogeny-based schemes over $\mathbb{F}_{p^2}$. We further note that any protocol that does not need hiding of data is virtually free to delegate. Examples include hashing functions with unprotected messages [10,21] and the verifiable delay function proposed in [20].

We generally find, that while HBC has a much cheaper communication cost and is fully verifiable, our OMTUP implementations result in lower computational cost for the delegator. Further, in all the schemes of Sect. 5, OMTUP has a very high verifiability, close to 1. It would be interesting to see, if other server assumptions are possible in the isogeny framework, especially using only malicious servers, such as the *two-untrusted program* (TUP) or *one-untrusted program* (OUP) models introduced in [25].

For future work, it is also of interest to construct delegation algorithms for other isogeny-based schemes, such as CSIDH [9] and CSI-FiSh [6] over $\mathbb{F}_p$, or the endomorphism ring based signature protocol of [23] as well as SQI-Sign [19].

Acknowledgments. The authors would like to thank Frederik Vercauteren for discussions and valuable feedback during this work. We would also like Jason LeGrow for valuable discussions concerning the isogeny cost function. This work was supported in part by the European Research Council (ERC) under the European Union's Horizon 2020 research and innovation programme (Grant agreement No. 101020788 - Adv-ERC-ISOCRYPT), the Research Council KU Leuven grant C14/18/067, and by CyberSecurity Research Flanders with reference number VR20192203.

References

1. Alagic, G., et al.: Status report on the second round of the NIST post-quantum cryptography standardization process. NISTIR 8309, July 2020. https://doi.org/10.6028/NIST.IR.8309
2. Azarderakhsh, R., et al.: Supersingular isogeny key encapsulation. Submission to the NIST Post-Quantum Standardization project (2017)
3. Azarderakhsh, R., Jalali, A., Jao, D., Soukharev, V.: Practical supersingular isogeny group key agreement. IACR Cryptol. ePrint Arch. **2019**, 330 (2019)
4. Bernstein, D.J., Birkner, P., Joye, M., Lange, T., Peters, C.: Twisted edwards curves. In: Vaudenay, S. (ed.) AFRICACRYPT 2008. LNCS, vol. 5023, pp. 389–405. Springer, Heidelberg (2008). https://doi.org/10.1007/978-3-540-68164-9_26
5. Bernstein, D., Lange, T.: Explicit-formulas database. https://www.hyperelliptic.org/EFD. Accessed 5 May 2021
6. Beullens, W., Kleinjung, T., Vercauteren, F.: CSI-FiSh: efficient isogeny based signatures through class group computations. In: Galbraith, S.D., Moriai, S. (eds.) ASIACRYPT 2019. LNCS, vol. 11921, pp. 227–247. Springer, Cham (2019). https://doi.org/10.1007/978-3-030-34578-5_9
7. Bouvier, C., Imbert, L.: An alternative approach for SIDH arithmetic. IACR Cryptol. ePrint Arch. **2020** (2020)

8. Castryck, W., Galbraith, S.D., Farashahi, R.R.: Efficient arithmetic on elliptic curves using a mixed Edwards-Montgomery representation. IACR Cryptol. ePrint Arch. **2008**, 218 (2008)
9. Castryck, W., Lange, T., Martindale, C., Panny, L., Renes, J.: CSIDH: an efficient post-quantum commutative group action. In: Peyrin, T., Galbraith, S. (eds.) ASIACRYPT 2018. LNCS, vol. 11274, pp. 395–427. Springer, Cham (2018). https://doi.org/10.1007/978-3-030-03332-3_15
10. Charles, D.X., Lauter, K.E., Goren, E.Z.: Cryptographic hash functions from expander graphs. J. Cryptol. **22**(1), 93–113 (2009). https://doi.org/10.1007/s00145-007-9002-x
11. Chevalier, C., Laguillaumie, F., Vergnaud, D.: Privately outsourcing exponentiation to a single server: cryptanalysis and optimal constructions. In: Askoxylakis, I., Ioannidis, S., Katsikas, S., Meadows, C. (eds.) ESORICS 2016. LNCS, vol. 9878, pp. 261–278. Springer, Cham (2016). https://doi.org/10.1007/978-3-319-45744-4_13
12. Costello, C., Longa, P., Naehrig, M., Renes, J., Virdia, F.: Improved classical cryptanalysis of SIKE in practice. In: Kiayias, A., Kohlweiss, M., Wallden, P., Zikas, V. (eds.) PKC 2020, Part II. LNCS, vol. 12111, pp. 505–534. Springer, Cham (2020). https://doi.org/10.1007/978-3-030-45388-6_18
13. Costello, C.: B-SIDH: Supersingular isogeny diffie-hellman using twisted torsion. In: Moriai, S., Wang, H. (eds.) ASIACRYPT 2020. LNCS, vol. 12492, pp. 440–463. Springer, Cham (2020). https://doi.org/10.1007/978-3-030-64834-3_15
14. Costello, C., Hisil, H.: A simple and compact algorithm for SIDH with arbitrary degree isogenies. In: Takagi, T., Peyrin, T. (eds.) ASIACRYPT 2017. LNCS, vol. 10625, pp. 303–329. Springer, Cham (2017). https://doi.org/10.1007/978-3-319-70697-9_11
15. Costello, C., Smith, B.: Montgomery curves and their arithmetic. J. Cryptogr. Eng. **8**(3), 227–240 (2017). https://doi.org/10.1007/s13389-017-0157-6
16. De Feo, L.: Mathematics of isogeny based cryptography. arXiv preprint arXiv:1711.04062 (2017)
17. De Feo, L., Dobson, S., Galbraith, S., Zobernig, L.: SIDH proof of knowledge. IACR Cryptol. ePrint Arch. **2021**, 1023 (2021)
18. De Feo, L., Jao, D., Plût, J.: Towards quantum-resistant cryptosystems from supersingular elliptic curve isogenies. J. Math. Cryptol. **8**(3), 209–247 (2014)
19. De Feo, L., Kohel, D., Leroux, A., Petit, C., Wesolowski, B.: SQISign: compact post-quantum signatures from quaternions and isogenies. In: Moriai, S., Wang, H. (eds.) ASIACRYPT 2020. LNCS, vol. 12491, pp. 64–93. Springer, Cham (2020). https://doi.org/10.1007/978-3-030-64837-4_3
20. De Feo, L., Masson, S., Petit, C., Sanso, A.: Verifiable delay functions from Supersingular isogenies and pairings. In: Galbraith, S.D., Moriai, S. (eds.) ASIACRYPT 2019. LNCS, vol. 11921, pp. 248–277. Springer, Cham (2019). https://doi.org/10.1007/978-3-030-34578-5_10
21. Doliskani, J., Pereira, G.C., Barreto, P.S.: Faster cryptographic hash function from supersingular isogeny graphs. IACR Cryptol. ePrint Arch. **2017**, 1202 (2017)
22. Furukawa, S., Kunihiro, N., Takashima, K.: Multi-party key exchange protocols from supersingular isogenies. In: 2018 International Symposium on Information Theory and Its Applications (ISITA), pp. 208–212. IEEE (2018)
23. Galbraith, S.D., Petit, C., Silva, J.: Identification protocols and signature schemes based on supersingular isogeny problems. J. Cryptol. **33**(1), 130–175 (2020)
24. Hisil, H., Wong, K.K.-H., Carter, G., Dawson, E.: Twisted Edwards curves revisited. In: Pieprzyk, J. (ed.) ASIACRYPT 2008. LNCS, vol. 5350, pp. 326–343. Springer, Heidelberg (2008). https://doi.org/10.1007/978-3-540-89255-7_20

25. Hohenberger, S., Lysyanskaya, A.: How to securely outsource cryptographic computations. In: Kilian, J. (ed.) TCC 2005. LNCS, vol. 3378, pp. 264–282. Springer, Heidelberg (2005). https://doi.org/10.1007/978-3-540-30576-7_15
26. Icart, T.: How to hash into elliptic curves. In: Halevi, S. (ed.) CRYPTO 2009. LNCS, vol. 5677, pp. 303–316. Springer, Heidelberg (2009). https://doi.org/10.1007/978-3-642-03356-8_18
27. Jao, D., De Feo, L.: Towards quantum-resistant cryptosystems from supersingular elliptic curve isogenies. In: Yang, B.-Y. (ed.) PQCrypto 2011. LNCS, vol. 7071, pp. 19–34. Springer, Heidelberg (2011). https://doi.org/10.1007/978-3-642-25405-5_2
28. Jaques, S., Schanck, J.M.: Quantum cryptanalysis in the RAM model: claw-finding attacks on SIKE. In: Boldyreva, A., Micciancio, D. (eds.) CRYPTO 2019. LNCS, vol. 11692, pp. 32–61. Springer, Cham (2019). https://doi.org/10.1007/978-3-030-26948-7_2
29. Kiraz, M.S., Uzunkol, O.: Efficient and verifiable algorithms for secure outsourcing of cryptographic computations. Int. J. Inf. Secur. **15**(5), 519–537 (2015). https://doi.org/10.1007/s10207-015-0308-7
30. Meyer, M., Reith, S., Campos, F.: On hybrid SIDH schemes using Edwards and Montgomery curve arithmetic. IACR Cryptol. ePrint Arch. **2017**, 1213 (2017)
31. Montgomery, P.L.: Speeding the Pollard and elliptic curve methods of factorization. Math. Comput. **48**(177), 243–264 (1987)
32. NIST: NIST reveals 26 algorithms advancing to the post-quantum crypto 'semifinals' (2019). https://www.nist.gov/news-events/news/2019/01/nist-reveals-26-algorithms-advancing-post-quantum-crypto-semifinals
33. NIST: NIST post-quantum cryptography PQC (2020). https://csrc.nist.gov/projects/post-quantum-cryptography/round-3-submissions
34. Pedersen, R., Uzunkol, O.: Secure delegation of isogeny computations and cryptographic applications. In: Proceedings of the 2019 ACM SIGSAC Conference on Cloud Computing Security Workshop, pp. 29–42 (2019)
35. Pedersen, R., Uzunkol, O.: Delegating supersingular isogenies over $\mathbb{F}_{p^2}$ with cryptographic applications. IACR Cryptol. ePrint Arch. **2021**, 506 (2021)
36. Petit, C.: Faster algorithms for isogeny problems using torsion point images. In: Takagi, T., Peyrin, T. (eds.) ASIACRYPT 2017. LNCS, vol. 10625, pp. 330–353. Springer, Cham (2017). https://doi.org/10.1007/978-3-319-70697-9_12
37. de Quehen, V., et al.: Improved torsion point attacks on sidh variants. arXiv preprint arXiv:2005.14681 (2020)
38. Shor, P.W.: Algorithms for quantum computation: Discrete logarithms and factoring. In: Proceedings of the 35th Annual Symposium on Foundations of Computer Science, pp. 124–134 (1994)
39. SIKE: Supersingular Isogeny Key Encapsulation (2018). https://sike.org
40. Silverman, J.H.: The Arithmetic of Elliptic Curves, vol. 106. Springer, Heidelberg (2009). https://doi.org/10.1007/978-0-387-09494-6

Improved Lattice-Based Mix-Nets
for Electronic Voting

Valeh Farzaliyev[1,2,3], Jan Willemson[1(✉)] [iD], and Jaan Kristjan Kaasik[1,3]

[1] Cybernetica AS, Narva mnt 20, 51009 Tartu, Estonia
jan.willemson@cyber.ee
[2] STACC OÜ, Narva mnt 20, 51009 Tartu, Estonia
[3] Tartu University, Narva mnt 18, 51009 Tartu, Estonia

Abstract. Mix-networks were first proposed by Chaum in the late 1970s – early 1980s [10] as a general tool for building anonymous communication systems. Classical mix-net implementations rely on standard public key primitives (e.g. ElGamal encryption) that will become vulnerable when a sufficiently powerful quantum computer will be built. Thus, there is a need to develop quantum-resistant mix-nets. This paper focuses on the application case of electronic voting where the number of votes to be mixed may reach hundreds of thousands or even millions. We propose an improved architecture for lattice-based post-quantum mix-nets featuring more efficient zero-knowledge proofs while maintaining established security assumptions. Our current implementation scales up to 100000 votes, still leaving a lot of room for future optimisation.

Keywords: Lattice-based post-quantum cryptography · Mix-nets · Zero-knowledge proofs · Electronic voting · Implementation

1 Introduction

Voting is the main mechanism of public opinion polling utilised e.g. in the context of general elections. Traditionally, voting has happened in a controlled location (polling station) to ease electoral management and reduce potential fraud.

However, by the beginning of the 21st century, people have become more mobile than ever before, so taking all the electorate into one place for a short period of time has become increasingly challenging. This challenge has been amplified by the recent COVID-19 outburst that has brought along the need to avoid gathering people in small spaces.

Thus, the need for the methods of remote voting has increased significantly. E.g. during the 2020 U.S. presidential elections, more than 65 million votes were sent in by post. Even though there seems to be little evidence of direct fraud, the extent of postal voting still caused a lot of controversy and discussion.

Indeed, the unreliability of postal services may raise questions about what to do with late votes, voter identification of postal votes is not particularly strong, and due to voting in an uncontrolled environment, it is hard to guarantee voting privacy and coercion-resistance.

© The Author(s), under exclusive license to Springer Nature Switzerland AG 2022
J. H. Park and S.-H. Seo (Eds.): ICISC 2021, LNCS 13218, pp. 119–136, 2022.
https://doi.org/10.1007/978-3-031-08896-4_6

Such problems motivate a search for alternatives, with remote electronic (Internet) voting being one of the prime candidates.

The votes stored on and transmitted via digital media are, contrary to paper votes, not directly perceivable by humans. Thus, the central problem of remote electronic voting is the independent verifiability of all the actions. In this paper, we are going to focus on a particular method of ensuring verifiability of the central voting system, since this is potentially the most critical point of failure.

What makes central server-side verification challenging is the need to also maintain the privacy of the votes. There are two main approaches used to implement privacy-preserving verifiable electronic voting systems – homomorphic tallying and mixing the votes before decryption [7]. There are a number of implementations known for both of these approaches, typically relying on some form of homomorphic encryption, e.g. Paillier or ElGamal scheme [24].

However, the classical asymmetric algorithms used in these implementations are known to become weak due to Shor's algorithm once a sufficiently capable quantum computer will be built [26]. Thus, looking for post-quantum alternatives is a necessity.

In recent years, both post-quantum homomorphic tallying [11,25] and mixing [12,13,27] have been studied. In this paper, we will concentrate on quantum-resistant mix-nets, aiming at improving their efficiency in terms of the number of votes they are able to shuffle in a given time period.

As the most expensive part of a cryptographic mix-net is the generation and verification of zero-knowledge proofs of correct operation, we concentrate on improving these proofs. Technically, we build upon the recently proposed protocol by Costa et al. [13], implementing amortization techniques described by Attema et al. [4] and using a commitment scheme by Baum et al. [5].

As a result, we design a purely lattice-based zero-knowledge proof of a shuffle for lattice-based mixing scheme that can be scaled up to about 100000 votes. We instantiate the protocol with specific parameters such that the protocol achieves 128-bit soundness and 180-bit post-quantum encryption security level. Finally, we provide a proof-of-concept implementation of the proposed scheme and benchmark its practical performance.

The structure of this paper is as follows. In Sect. 2 we specify notation and Preliminaries used in the construction of the protocol and its security proof. The protocol itself is presented in Sect. 3. Implementation and experimental results are presented in Sect. 4. Finally, Sect. 5 draws some conclusions and sets directions for future work. Details of the proofs can be found in the Appendices.

2   Preliminaries

2.1   Notation

For a prime q, let $\mathbb{Z}_q$ be the ring of integers modulo q, with its elements considered in the interval $\left[-\frac{q-1}{2}, \frac{q-1}{2}\right]$, and let $\mathbb{Z}_n^\times$ denote the group of invertible elements modulo n. $\lfloor x \rceil$ represents the closest integer to x in $\mathbb{Z}_q$. Vectors over

$\mathbb{Z}_q$ are denoted as $\vec{v} \in \mathbb{Z}_q^m$ and matrices over $\mathbb{Z}_q$ are denoted by regular capital letters (e.g. A) unless explicitly stated otherwise. Letting d be a power of two, we consider the rings $\mathcal{R} = \mathbb{Z}[X]/(X^d + 1)$ and $\mathcal{R}_q = \mathbb{Z}_q[X]/(X^d + 1)$. Elements of these rings are written in bold lower-case letters (e.g. $\boldsymbol{p}$), and vectors with elements from these rings will naturally be denoted as $\vec{\boldsymbol{b}}$. Matrices over $\mathcal{R}$ or $\mathcal{R}_q$ are bold upper-case letters, e.g. $\boldsymbol{B}$. By default, all vectors and their concatenations are column vectors. More precisely, an element $\boldsymbol{a} \in \mathcal{R}_q$ can be written as column vector $\mathcal{V}_{\boldsymbol{a}} = |a_0, a_1, \ldots, a_{d-1}|^T$ where $\boldsymbol{a} = \sum_{i=0}^{d-1} a_i X^i$ and $a_i \in \mathbb{Z}_q$. Especially for ring $\mathcal{R}_q$, the same element can be represented as a matrix in $\mathbb{Z}_q$ when it is a multiplicand:

$$\mathcal{M}_{\boldsymbol{a}} = \begin{vmatrix} a_0 & -a_{d-1} & -a_{d-2} & \cdots & -a_1 \\ a_1 & a_0 & -a_{d-1} & \cdots & -a_2 \\ \vdots & \ddots & \ddots & \ddots & \vdots \\ a_{d-1} & a_{d-2} & a_{d-3} & \cdots & a_0 \end{vmatrix}.$$

l_2 and l_∞ norms are defined as usual:

$$\|\boldsymbol{a}\|_\infty = \max_i |a_i| \text{ and } \|\boldsymbol{a}\|_2 = \sqrt{|a_0|^2 + \cdots + |a_{d-1}|^2}.$$

These norms can naturally be extended to vectors over $\mathcal{R}_q$. For $\vec{\boldsymbol{w}} = \{\boldsymbol{w}_1, \ldots, \boldsymbol{w}_k\} \in \mathcal{R}_q^k$, we have

$$\|\vec{\boldsymbol{w}}\|_\infty = \max_i \|\boldsymbol{w}_i\| \text{ and } \|\vec{\boldsymbol{w}}\|_2 = \sqrt{\|\boldsymbol{w}_1\|_2^2 + \cdots + \|\boldsymbol{w}_k\|_2^2}.$$

Polynomials and vectors with short norms will simply be referred to as short.

2.2 Splitting Rings

In this work, we set $q - 1 \equiv 2l \bmod 4l$, so that $X^d + 1$ splits into l irreducible polynomials of degree d/l, i.e.

$$X^d + 1 = \prod_{i \in \mathbb{Z}_{2l}^\times} (X^{d/l} - \zeta^i) \bmod q = \prod_{i=1}^l \varphi_i \bmod q,$$

where ζ is primitive $2l$-th root of unity in $\mathbb{Z}_q$ and $\varphi_i = X^{d/l} - \zeta^{2i-1}$. Thus, the ring $\mathcal{R}_q$ is isomorphic to the product of the corresponding residue fields:

$$\mathcal{R}_q \cong \mathbb{Z}_q[X]/(\varphi_1) \times \cdots \times \mathbb{Z}_q[X]/(\varphi_l).$$

We call a ring fully splitting when $l = d$.

The Number Theoretic Transform (NTT) of a polynomial $\boldsymbol{p} \in \mathcal{R}_q$ is defined as

$$\mathbf{NTT}(\boldsymbol{p}) = \begin{bmatrix} \hat{\boldsymbol{p}}_0 \\ \vdots \\ \hat{\boldsymbol{p}}_{l-1} \end{bmatrix} \text{ where } \hat{\boldsymbol{p}}_{i-1} = \boldsymbol{p} \bmod \varphi_i.$$

By Chinese Remainder Theorem, there exists a unique inverse transformation – Inverse NTT – such that, $\mathbf{INTT}(\mathbf{NTT}(p)) = p$. Also, NTT allows the computing of the product of two polynomials faster and saves time in other operations.

$$ab = \mathbf{INTT}(\mathbf{NTT}(a) \circ \mathbf{NTT}(b))$$
$$\mathbf{NTT}(a + b) = \mathbf{NTT}(a) + \mathbf{NTT}(b)$$

Here $\circ$ is the component-wise multiplication operation.

2.3   Ring-LWE Encryption, Module SIS/LWE

In our constructions, we will rely on hardness of Ring-LWE (RLWE) [21] and Module-LWE (MLWE)/ Module-SIS (MSIS) [14,23] problems.

Definition 1 ($RLWE_\chi$). *In the decisional Ring-LWE problem with an error distribution χ over $\mathcal{R}$, the probabilistic polynomial time (PPT) adversary $\mathcal{A}$ is asked to distinguish $(a, b) \xleftarrow{\$} \mathcal{R}_q \times \mathcal{R}_q$ from $(a, a \cdot s + e)$ for $a \xleftarrow{\$} \mathcal{R}_q$ and $s, e \leftarrow \chi$.*

The corresponding *search*-RLWE problem asks to find s from several (a, b) RLWE samples. RLWE assumption is that *search*-RLWE and/or *decisional*-RLWE problem is hard for any PPT adversaries.

We implement the encryption scheme described in [21]. Let χ_1 be error distribution over $\mathcal{R}$ where each coefficient is sampled from $\{-1, 0, 1\}$.

- *KeyGen*: Given a uniformly sampled in $\mathcal{R}_q$, a secret $s \leftarrow \chi_1$ and an error $e \leftarrow \chi_1$, the public key is defined as $pk = (a, b) = (a, a \cdot s + e)$ and private key as s.
- *Encryption*: To encrypt a message $z \in \mathcal{R}_2$, sample new randomness r and error terms e_1, e_2 from error distribution χ_1. Then the ciphertext is a pair of polynomials (u, v) such that

$$u = a \cdot r + e_1,$$
$$v = b \cdot r + e_2 + \left\lfloor \frac{q}{2} \right\rceil z.$$

- *Decryption*: Given ciphertext (u, v), compute

$$v - u \cdot s = (r \cdot e - e_1 \cdot s + e_2) + \left\lfloor \frac{q}{2} \right\rceil z.$$

If each coefficient of the resulting polynomial is close to 0, set the respective coefficient of the decrypted message to 0. Otherwise, set the decrypted message as 1.

The RLWE encryption scheme defined as above is semantically secure under RLWE_{χ_1} assumption. To see this, just observe that the ciphertext consists of two RLWE samples, which by the RLWE_{χ_1} assumption are indistinguishable from uniformly random elements. Thus, unless one can solve the *decisional*-RLWE problem, all ciphertexts look uniform and no information can be extracted about the plaintext.

Definition 2 ($MLWE_{n,m,\chi}$). *In the Module-LWE problem with parameters $n, m > 0$ and an error distribution χ over $\mathcal{R}$, the PPT adversary $\mathcal{A}$ is asked to distinguish $(\boldsymbol{A}, \overrightarrow{\boldsymbol{t}}) \xleftarrow{\$} \mathcal{R}_q^{m \times n} \times \mathcal{R}_q^m$ from $(\boldsymbol{A}, \boldsymbol{A}\overrightarrow{\boldsymbol{s}} + \overrightarrow{\boldsymbol{e}})$ for $\boldsymbol{A} \xleftarrow{\$} \mathcal{R}_q^{m \times n}$, a secret vector $\overrightarrow{\boldsymbol{s}} \leftarrow \chi^n$, and an error vector $\overrightarrow{\boldsymbol{e}} \leftarrow \chi^m$.*

Definition 3 ($MSIS_{m,n,\beta}$). *The goal in the Module-SIS problem with parameters $n, m > 0$ and $0 < \beta < q$ is to find $\overrightarrow{\boldsymbol{x}} \in \mathcal{R}_q^m$ for a given matrix $\boldsymbol{A} \xleftarrow{\$} \mathcal{R}_q^{n \times m}$ such that $\boldsymbol{A}\overrightarrow{\boldsymbol{x}} = \overrightarrow{\boldsymbol{0}} \bmod q$ and $0 < \|\overrightarrow{\boldsymbol{x}}\|_\infty < \beta$.*

In practical security estimations, the parameter m in Definitions 2 and 3 does not play a crucial role, therefore we simply omit it and use the notations $\mathsf{MLWE}_{n,\chi}$ and $\mathsf{MSIS}_{n,\beta}$. Furthermore, we let the parameters μ and λ denote the module ranks for MSIS and MLWE, respectively.

2.4   Challenge Space

Elements of the ring $\mathcal{R}_q$ are not always invertible. In fact, Lyubashevsky *et al.* proved a relation between the probability of invertibility in this ring and the number of residue fields it splits into [22, Corollary 1.2]. Their claim is that generally short non-zero polynomials are invertible. In lattice-based zero-knowledge proofs, the verifier often samples from a challenge set such that the difference between any two elements in that set is invertible. However, constructing such a set and uniformly sampling from it is not a trivial task.

Therefore, Lyubashevsky *et al.* proposed another method where they relaxed the invertiblity requirement. They defined the challenge space as the set of ternary polynomials $\mathcal{C} = \{-1, 0, 1\}^d \subset \mathcal{R}$. Coefficients of a challenge $c \in \mathcal{C}$ are identically and independently distributed where 0 has probability $1/2$ and ± 1 both have probability $1/4$. In [4, Lemma 3.3], it is shown that if $c \leftarrow \mathcal{C}$, the distribution of coefficients of $c \bmod (X^{d/l} - \zeta)$ is almost uniform and the maximum probability of coefficients over $\mathbb{Z}_q$ is bounded. Denote this bound with p. For example, in [4] it is estimated that $p = 2^{-31.44}$ for $l = d = 128$, $q \approx 2^{32}$. An element c in splitting ring $\mathcal{R}_q$ is non-invertible when $c \bmod \varphi_i = 0$ for any $i = 1, \ldots, l$. Then the difference between any two challenges $\bar{c} = c - c'$ is non-invertible with probability at most $p^{d/l}$.

2.5   Error Distribution and Rejection Sampling

Security of RLWE and MLWE problems depends on the error distribution. The original security proofs [14, 21] assumed the errors from discrete spherical Gaussian distribution. However, in literature we can find different choices such as centered binomial distribution [1, 16] or uniform distribution in a small interval [9]. We use the former for sampling randomness in MLWE and the latter for randomness and error terms in RLWE.

Rejection Sampling. It is a common practice to hide secret commitment randomness $\vec{r} \in \mathcal{R}_q^\kappa$ in another vector $\vec{z}$ without leaking any information about $\vec{r}$. For this purpose, we use uniform rejection sampling technique from [16]. In the protocol the prover samples a "masking" vector $\vec{y}$ using uniform distribution in $[-\delta + 1, \delta]$. Upon receiving the challenge $c \xleftarrow{\$} C$ by the verifier, the prover responds with $\vec{z} = \vec{y} + c\vec{r}$. The dependency of $\vec{z}$ on $\vec{r}$ is removed if $\|\vec{z}\|_\infty < \delta - \beta$ where $\|c\vec{r}\|_\infty \leq \beta$. Otherwise, the prover rejects the masked vector and aborts the protocol to start over again.

The expected number of repetitions M required by rejection sampling can be estimated by

$$1/M = \left(\frac{2(\delta - \beta) - 1}{2\delta - 1}\right)^{\kappa d} \approx e^{-\kappa d\beta/\delta}.$$

For more details see [16]. The parameter δ is typically chosen so that the expected value of M is small (say, 2 or 3).

2.6   Commitment Scheme

In this work, we will be using a variant of BDLOP commitment scheme [5]. Let, $B_0 \in \mathcal{R}_q^{\mu \times (\mu+\lambda+1)}$, $\vec{b}_1 \in \mathcal{R}_q^{\mu+\lambda+1}$ and $\vec{r} \leftarrow \chi_2^{(\mu+\lambda+1)d}$. The commitment of a single message $m \in \mathcal{R}_q$ is a pair $(\vec{t}_0, t_1)$ where

$$\vec{t}_0 = B_0 \vec{r},$$
$$t_1 = \langle \vec{b}_1, \vec{r} \rangle + m.$$

It is easy to see that the commitment scheme is binding and hiding due to MSIS_μ and MLWE_λ assumptions, respectively.

Definition 4. *A weak opening for the commitment* $\vec{t} = \vec{t}_0 \| t_1$ *consists of l polynomials $\bar{c}_i \in \mathcal{R}_q$, randomness vector $\vec{r}^\star$ over $\mathcal{R}_q$ and a message $m^\star \in \mathcal{R}_q$ such that*

$$\|\bar{c}_i\|_1 \leq 2d \text{ and } \bar{c}_i \bmod \varphi_i \neq 0 \text{ for all } 1 \leq i \leq l,$$
$$\|\bar{c}_i \vec{r}^\star\|_\infty \leq 2\beta \text{ for all } 1 \leq i \leq l,$$
$$B_0 \vec{r}^\star = \vec{t}_0,$$
$$\langle \vec{b}_1, \vec{r}^\star \rangle + m^\star = t_1.$$

The BDLOP commitment scheme is proven to be binding also with respect to the weak opening in [4, Lemma 4.3].

2.7   Generalized Schwartz-Zippel Lemma

The generalized Schwartz-Zippel lemma is stated as follows [13, Appendix A].

Lemma 1. *Let $p \in R[x_1, x_2, \ldots, x_n]$ be a non-zero polynomial of total degree $d \geq 0$ over a commutative ring R. Let S be a finite subset of R such that none of the differences between two elements of S is a divisor of 0 and let $r_1, r_2, \ldots, r_n$ be selected at random independently and uniformly from S. Then $Pr[p(r_1, r_2, \ldots, r_n) = 0] \leq d/|S|$.*

In general, it is not trivial to construct the set S. A polynomial in $\mathcal{R}_q$ is a zero divisor when at least one of its NTT coefficients is zero. Thus, the difference between two elements is not a divisor of zero when they do not have a common NTT coefficient. There can be at most q pairwise different modulo degree 1 prime ideals for fully splitting rings. This strictly reduces soundness. However, for partially splitting rings, this number increases to $q^{d/l}$. For any random polynomial, one can find $q^{d/l} - 1$ other polynomials which do not have common NTT coefficients and construct the set S. We fix this set to be $\mathcal{S} = \{ f \in \mathcal{R}_q \mid \deg f < d/l \}$.

2.8   Mix-Node Security

Costa *et al.* [13] proposed a stronger security definition for a mix-node. Assume that **MixVotes** is a generic mixing algorithm such that, given input ciphertexts and a permutation vector, produces shuffled and re-encrypted ciphertexts. Moreover, let $z^{(i_A)}$ and $z^{\pi(j_A)}$ be the message before and after running the algorithm.

Definition 5. *Let J be a uniform random variable taking values in $[1, \ldots, N]$. A mix-node given by algorithm **MixVotes** is said to be secure if the advantage of any PPT adversary $\mathcal{A}$ over random guess is negligible in the security parameter. That is, $\forall c, \exists \kappa_0 \ s.t \ if \ \kappa > \kappa_0$:*

$$Adv_{\mathcal{A}}^{sec} = \left| \Pr\left[z^{(i_A)} = z^{\pi(j_A)} \right] - \Pr\left[z^{(i_A)} = z^{\pi(J)} \right] \right| < \frac{1}{\kappa^c}.$$

3   Improved Mix-Node

Our proof of shuffle protocol is based on Costa *et al.*'s work [13]. Assume that there are N RLWE ciphertexts (u_i, v_i) encrypted with public key $(pk.a, pk.b)$ to be shuffled. A mixing node will generate secret random zero encryption ciphertexts $(u_{i,0}, v_{i,0})$ and permutation π, and output (u_i', v_i') such that

$$(u_{i,0}, v_{i,0}) = (pk.a \cdot r_{E,i} + e_{u,i}, pk.b \cdot r_{E,i} + e_{v,i} + 0)$$
$$(u_i', v_i') = (u_{\pi(i)} + u_{i,0}, v_{\pi(i)} + v_{i,0})$$

where $r_{E,i}, e_{u,i}, e_{v,i} \leftarrow \chi_1$ for all $i = 1, \ldots, N$. We extend the proof in [13] for any splitting rings in the full version of the paper [17] to show that if π is a valid permutation, then for any $\alpha, \beta, \gamma \in \mathcal{S}$ the equation

$$\prod_{i=1}^{N} (\beta i + \alpha^i - \gamma) = \prod_{i=1}^{N} (\beta \pi(i) + \alpha^{\pi(i)} - \gamma) \tag{1}$$

holds due to generalized Schwartz-Zippel lemma with small cheating probability. Furthermore,

$$\sum_{i=1}^{N} \boldsymbol{\alpha}^i \boldsymbol{u}_i = \sum_{i=1}^{N} \boldsymbol{\alpha}^{\pi(i)} (\boldsymbol{u}'_i - \boldsymbol{u}_{i,0}), \tag{2}$$

$$\sum_{i=1}^{N} \boldsymbol{\alpha}^i \boldsymbol{v}_i = \sum_{i=1}^{N} \boldsymbol{\alpha}^{\pi(i)} (\boldsymbol{v}'_i - \boldsymbol{v}_{i,0}). \tag{3}$$

One can think of (2) and (3) as two polynomials with coefficients in $\mathcal{R}_q$ evaluated at the same point $\boldsymbol{\alpha}$. Again, due to generalized Schwartz-Zippel lemma, if equality holds, then both polynomials are equal to each other, thus their coefficients are the same. Moreover, the relations (1), (2) and (3) along with proof of correct encryption are shown in [13] to be enough to argue for the correctness of shuffle.

The protocol in [13] uses a commitment scheme from [6] to prove the aforementioned arguments mainly due to the existence of zero-knowledge proofs for linear and multiplicative relations for the commitment scheme. We recap the protocol briefly below.

First, the prover $\mathcal{P}$ commits to zero encryption ciphertexts $(\boldsymbol{u}_{i,0}, \boldsymbol{v}_{i,0})$, sends them to the verifier $\mathcal{V}$ and runs amortized zero-knowledge proof of knowledge of small secret elements that those commitments are indeed commitments to encryptions of zero with valid error parameters. Next, $\mathcal{P}$ commits to the permutation vector π and sends the commitment to the verifier again. Committing to permutation vector means committing to $\pi(1), \ldots, \pi(N)$. Then, $\mathcal{V}$ samples a polynomial $\boldsymbol{\alpha}$ from the challenge set and sends it back to the prover. Following to that, $\mathcal{P}$ calculates commitments to $\boldsymbol{\alpha}^{\pi(1)}, \ldots, \boldsymbol{\alpha}^{\pi(N)}$. To show that the permutation vector is chosen before challenges and is a valid permutation, the prover runs linear and multiplicative relation proofs several times and calculates the product in (1) using the committed values. Next, again by the relation proofs, it proves the remaining two equalities to show shuffling is correct. During the verification phase, the verifier has to verify zero-knowledge proofs of knowledge of small secret elements and relations (1), (2) and (3).

Costa *et al.* [13] mention that it is possible to use amortization techniques described in [25] to reduce the complexity and total cost of the protocol. Unfortunately, they have not explicitly shown how to do that, nor have they instantiated the parameters to evaluate the performance and concrete security level of the protocol.

We solve both issues by replacing the commitment scheme with a variant of the Module SIS/LWE based commitment scheme from [5]. This allows us to use more efficient zero-knowledge arguments for proving linear and product relations between committed messages [4,20]. Those protocols are short, efficient, and have no extra cost when amortized over many relations. Besides, there is no need to repeat the protocol several times to get desired soundness properties. Nevertheless, as we change the mathematical setting, there is a need for additional careful analysis of security.

For example, another change we introduce is regarding challenge sets. Previously, prime modulus q was required to satisfy $q \equiv 3 \mod 8$, which implies that the ring $\mathcal{R}_q$ splits only into two residue fields. This condition is required to define a concrete sufficiently large set of challenge polynomials of which any of the differences between two elements in this set is invertible. Now, we relax this restriction and allow q to split into more than 2 residue fields.

Now we proceed to describe our protocol.

First, let μ and λ be rank of secure MSIS and MLWE instances, respectively, $q - 1 \equiv 2l \mod 4l$ be such that $\mathcal{R}_q$ is a partially splitting ring and $\boldsymbol{B}_0 \in \mathcal{R}_q^{\mu \times (\mu + \lambda + 9N + 1)}$, $\overrightarrow{\boldsymbol{b}}_1, \overrightarrow{\boldsymbol{b}}_2, \dots \overrightarrow{\boldsymbol{b}}_{9N+1} \in \mathcal{R}_q^{\mu + \lambda + 9N + 1}$. Furthermore, set $q^{d/l} \approx 2^{256}$ and $\beta'_i = \delta_i - \beta_i - 1$ for $i = 1, 2$.

Theorem 1. *The protocol in Fig. 1 is statistically complete, computationally honest verifier zero-knowledge under the Module-LWE assumption, computationally special-sound under the Module-SIS assumption, and is a computationally secure mix-node under* RLWE_{χ_1} *and* $\mathrm{MSIS}_{\mu, 8d\beta'_2}$ *assumptions. That is, if p is the maximum probability over* $\mathbb{Z}_q$ *of the coefficients of* $\boldsymbol{c} \mod X^{d/l} - \zeta$, *then*

- *for completeness, in case of non-aborting transcript due to rejection sampling, the honest verifier* $\mathcal{V}$ *is always convinced.*
- *For zero-knowledge, there exists a simulator* Sim *that, without access to secret information, outputs a simulation of accepting the transcript of the protocol. Any adversary capable of distinguishing an actual transcript from a simulated one with an advantage* ϵ *also has an advantage* ϵ *in distinguishing* $\mathrm{MLWE}_{\lambda, \chi_2}$ *within the same running time.*
- *For soundness, there is an extractor* $\mathcal{E}$ *with rewindable black-box access to a deterministic prover* $\mathcal{P}^*$ *that convinces* $\mathcal{V}$ *with probability* $\epsilon \geq (3p)^k$, *either outputting a weak opening for commitment*

$$\overrightarrow{\boldsymbol{t}} = \overrightarrow{\boldsymbol{t}}_0 \| \boldsymbol{t}_{u_0^{(i)}} \| \boldsymbol{t}_{v_0^{(i)}} \| \boldsymbol{t}_{\pi(i)} \| \boldsymbol{t}_{\boldsymbol{\alpha}^{\pi(i)}} \| \boldsymbol{t}_{4N+1} \| \dots \| \boldsymbol{t}_{9N+1}$$

such that extracted messages satisfy Eqs. (1), (2) and (3), or being able to solve $\mathrm{MSIS}_{\mu, 8d\beta'_1}$.
- *And finally, an adversary with advantage* ϵ *over random guessing has also advantage over* $\mathrm{MSIS}_{\mu, 8d\beta'_2}$ *and/or* RLWE_{χ_1} *problems with probability at least* ϵ.

Prover $\mathcal{P}$ 　　　　　　　　　　　　　　　　　　　　Verifier $\mathcal{V}$

$u_i, u_{i,0}, u_i' \in \mathcal{R}_q$ 　　　　　　　　　　　　　　　　　u_i, u_i'
$v_i, v_{i,0}, v_i' \in \mathcal{R}_q$ 　　　　　　　　　　　　　　　　v_i, v_i'
$\kappa = \mu + \lambda + 9N + 1$
$B_0 \in \mathcal{R}_q^{\mu \times \kappa}; \ \vec{b}_0, \vec{b}_1, \ldots, \vec{b}_{9N+1} \in \mathcal{R}_q^\kappa$ 　　　　$B_0, \vec{b}_1, \ldots, \vec{b}_{9N+1}$
$\pi = \mathrm{Perm}(N)$

$\vec{r} \in \chi_2^{\kappa d};$
$\vec{t}_0 = B_0 \vec{r}$
For $i = 1, \ldots, N$
$t_{u_{i,0}} = \langle \vec{b}_i, \vec{r} \rangle + u_{i,0}$
$t_{v_{i,0}} = \langle \vec{b}_{N+i}, \vec{r} \rangle + v_{i,0}$
$t_{\pi(i)} = \langle \vec{b}_{2N+i}, \vec{r} \rangle + \pi(i)$
Shortness proof Σ_1

$\xrightarrow{\vec{t}_0, t_{\pi(i)}, t_{u_{i,0}}, t_{v_{i,0}}, \Sigma_1} \ \alpha \in \mathcal{S}$
$\xleftarrow{\quad \alpha \quad}$

for $i = 1, \ldots, N$:
$t_{\alpha^{\pi(i)}} = \langle \vec{b}_{3N+i}, \vec{r} \rangle + \alpha^{\pi(i)}$
$t_{4N+i} = \langle \vec{b}_{4N+i}, \vec{r} \rangle + \alpha^{\pi(i)} u_{i,0}$
$t_{5N+i} = \langle \vec{b}_{5N+i}, \vec{r} \rangle + \alpha^{\pi(i)} v_{i,0}$

$\xrightarrow{t_{\alpha^{\pi(i)}}, t_{4N+i}, t_{5N+i}} \ \beta, \gamma \in \mathcal{S}$
$\xleftarrow{\quad \beta, \gamma \quad}$

$\Pi = 1$
for $i = 1, \ldots, N$:
$t_{6N+i} = \langle \vec{b}_{6N+i}, \vec{r} \rangle + \beta \pi(i) + \alpha^{\pi(i)} - \gamma$
$t_{7N+i} = \langle \vec{b}_{7N+i}, \vec{r} \rangle + \Pi$
$t_{8N+i} = \langle \vec{b}_{8N+i}, \vec{r} \rangle + \Pi(\beta \pi(i) + \alpha^{\pi(i)} - \gamma)$
$\Pi = \Pi \cdot (\beta \pi(i) + \alpha^{\pi(i)} - \gamma)$

$\xrightarrow{t_{6N+i}, t_{7N+i}, t_{8N+i}}$

$\vec{y} \xleftarrow{\$} [-\delta_1 + 1, \delta_1]^{\kappa d}$
$\vec{w} = B_0 \vec{y}$

$\xrightarrow{\quad \vec{w} \quad}$
$\xleftarrow{\quad \epsilon \quad} \ \epsilon_1, \epsilon_2, \ldots, \epsilon_{(4N+4)} \in \mathcal{R}_q$

$v_1 = \sum_{j=1}^N \epsilon_j \left(\beta \langle \vec{b}_{2N+j}, \vec{y} \rangle + \langle \vec{b}_{3N+j}, \vec{y} \rangle - \langle \vec{b}_{6N+j}, \vec{y} \rangle \right)$
$v_2 = \langle \vec{b}_{9N+1}, \vec{y}_0 \rangle + \sum_{j=1}^N \epsilon_{N+j} (\langle \vec{b}_{6N+j}, \vec{y} \rangle \langle \vec{b}_{7N+j}, \vec{y} \rangle) +$
$\quad + \sum_{i=0}^{k-1} \sum_{j=1}^N \epsilon_{2N+j} (\langle \vec{b}_{3N+j}, \vec{y} \rangle \langle \vec{b}_j, \vec{y} \rangle) +$
$\quad + \sum_{j=1}^N \epsilon_{3N+j} (\langle \vec{b}_{3N+j}, \vec{y} \rangle \langle \vec{b}_{N+j}, \vec{y} \rangle)$

$t_{9N+1} = \langle \vec{b}_{9N+1}, \vec{r} \rangle + \sum_{j=1}^N \epsilon_{N+j} (\langle \vec{b}_{8N+j}, \vec{y} \rangle -$
$\quad - \Pi \langle \vec{b}_{6N+j}, \vec{y} \rangle - (\beta \pi(j) + \alpha^{\pi(j)} - \gamma) \langle \vec{b}_{7N+j}, \vec{y} \rangle) +$
$\quad + \sum_{j=1}^N \epsilon_{2N+j} (\langle \vec{b}_{4N+j}, \vec{y} \rangle - \alpha^{\pi(j)} \langle \vec{b}_j, \vec{y} \rangle - u_{j,0} \langle \vec{b}_{3N+j}, \vec{y}_i \rangle) +$
$\quad + \sum_{j=1}^N \epsilon_{3N+j} (\langle \vec{b}_{5N+j}, \vec{y} \rangle - \alpha^{\pi(j)} \langle \vec{b}_{N+j}, \vec{y} \rangle - v_{j,0} \langle \vec{b}_{3N+j}, \vec{y} \rangle)$

$v_3 = \epsilon_{4N+1} \left(\sum_{j=1}^N u_j' \langle \vec{b}_{3N+j}, \vec{y} \rangle - \sum_{j=1}^N \langle \vec{b}_{4N+j}, \vec{y} \rangle \right) +$
$\quad\quad + \epsilon_{4Nk+2} \left(\sum_{j=1}^N v_j' \langle \vec{b}_{3N+j}, \vec{y} \rangle - \sum_{j=1}^N \langle \vec{b}_{5N+j}, \vec{y} \rangle \right)$
$v_4 = \epsilon_{4N+3} (\langle \vec{b}_{9N}, \vec{y} \rangle) + \epsilon_{4N+4} (\langle \vec{b}_{7N+1}, \vec{y} \rangle)$

$\xrightarrow{v_1, v_2, v_3, v_4, t_{9N+1}}$
$\xleftarrow{\quad c \quad} \ c \xleftarrow{\$} C$

$\vec{z} = \vec{y} + c \vec{r}$
If $\| \vec{z} \|_\infty \geq \delta_1 - \beta_1$, abort 　$\xrightarrow{\quad \vec{z} \quad}$ 　　　　　**Verify**

Fig. 1. ZK-proof of shuffle

Verify

Verify Shortness proof Σ_1

$$\|\overrightarrow{z}\|_\infty \overset{?}{<} \delta_1 - \beta_1$$
$$B_0 \overrightarrow{z} \overset{?}{=} \overrightarrow{w} + c\,\overrightarrow{t}_0$$

For $j = 1, \ldots N:$
$$f^{u_0^{(j)}} = \langle \overrightarrow{b}_j, \overrightarrow{z} \rangle - ct_{u_{j,0}}$$
$$f^{v_0^{(i)}} = \langle \overrightarrow{b}_{N+j}, \overrightarrow{z} \rangle - ct_{v_{j,0}}$$
$$f^{\pi(j)} = \langle \overrightarrow{b}_{2N+j}, \overrightarrow{z} \rangle - ct_{\pi(j)}$$
$$f^{\alpha^{\pi(j)}} = \langle \overrightarrow{b}_{3N+j}, \overrightarrow{z} \rangle - ct_{\alpha^{\pi(j)}}$$
$$f^{4N+j} = \langle \overrightarrow{b}_{4N+j}, \overrightarrow{z} \rangle - ct_{4N+j}$$
$$f^{5N+j} = \langle \overrightarrow{b}_{5N+j}, \overrightarrow{z} \rangle - ct_{5N+j}$$
$$f^{6N+j} = \langle \overrightarrow{b}_{6N+j}, \overrightarrow{z} \rangle - ct_{6N+j}$$
$$f^{7N+j} = \langle \overrightarrow{b}_{7N+j}, \overrightarrow{z} \rangle - ct_{7N+j}$$
$$f^{8N+j} = \langle \overrightarrow{b}_{8N+j}, \overrightarrow{z} \rangle - ct_{8N+j}$$
$$f_{9N+1} = \langle \overrightarrow{b}_{9N+1}, \overrightarrow{z} \rangle - ct_{9N+1}$$

$$\sum_{j=1}^N \epsilon_j \left(\beta f^{\pi(j)} + f^{\alpha^{\pi(j)}} - f^{6N+j} + c\gamma \right) \overset{?}{=} v_1$$

$$\sum_{j=1}^N \epsilon_{N+j}(f^{6N+j}f^{7N+j} + cf^{8N+j}) +$$
$$+ \sum_{j=1}^N \epsilon_{2N+j}(f^{\alpha^{\pi(j)}} f^{u_0^{(j)}} + cf^{4N+j}) +$$
$$+ \sum_{j=1}^N \epsilon_{3N+j}(f^{\alpha^{\pi(j)}} f^{v_0^{(j)}} + cf^{5N+j}) + f_{9N+1} \overset{?}{=} v_2$$

$$M_1 = \sum_{i=1}^N \alpha^i u_i \quad M_2 = \sum_{i=1}^N \alpha^i v_i$$
$$\epsilon_{4N+1}\left(\sum_{j=1}^N u'_j f^{\alpha^{\pi(j)}} - \sum_{j=1}^N f^{4N+j} + cM_1 \right) +$$
$$+ \epsilon_{4N+2}\left(\sum_{j=1}^N v'_j f^{\alpha^{\pi(j)}} - \sum_{j=1}^N f^{5N+j} + cM_2 \right) \overset{?}{=} v_3$$

$$\Pi = \prod_{j=1}^N (\beta j + \alpha^j - \gamma)$$
$$\epsilon_{4N+3}(f^{9N} + c\Pi) + \epsilon_{4N+4}(f^{7N+1} + c) \overset{?}{=} v_4$$

Fig. 2. Verification equations

Proof. Completeness. Observe that in a non-aborting transcript vector $\overrightarrow{z}$ is bounded by $\delta_1 - \beta_1$. The remaining four verification equations in Fig. 2 regarding v_1, v_2, v_3 and v_4 are straightforward to verify. Similarly, proof of shortness protocol is complete.

Zero-Knowledge. Zero-knowledge property of proof of shortness protocol is given in [20]. Indeed, following the same steps, it is possible to simulate this protocol as well. First, sample $\overrightarrow{z} \overset{\$}{\leftarrow} [-(\delta_1 - \beta_1) + 1, \delta_1 - \beta_1 - 1]^{\kappa d}$, which is the distribution of $\overrightarrow{z}$ in non-aborting transcript. Next, due to rejection sampling step, $c\overrightarrow{r}$ is independent of $\overrightarrow{z}$ and thus the simulator chooses $c \xleftarrow{\$} C$, $\overrightarrow{r} \in \chi_2^{ld}$ like an honest prover. Now, the simulator can calculate $\overrightarrow{w}$ which is uniquely determined by previous variables. Other challenges $\alpha, \beta, \gamma \in S$ are independent of each other, thus they can also be randomly chosen. Straightforwardly, the simulator computes $\overrightarrow{t}_0$. The rest of commitments can be uniformly sampled from $\mathcal{R}_q$ as by the MLWE assumption they will be indistinguishable from real MLWE samples. Finally, remaining equations of v_i are deterministic functions of $\overrightarrow{t}$, $\overrightarrow{z}$ and c.

Soundness. The soundness relation for proof of shortness protocol is described in detail in [20] and is similar to the proof for a protocol in Fig. 1. Consider the extractor given in [4] which can extract weak openings after rewinding the protocol l times and get $\overrightarrow{r}^\star$ and $\overrightarrow{y}^\star$, or finds $\mathsf{MSIS}_{8d\beta_1}$ solution for B_0. It can also extract messages simply from commitment relations.

$$t_{u_{i,0}} = \langle \overrightarrow{b}_i, \overrightarrow{r}^\star \rangle + m_0^{(i)\star}$$
$$t_{v_{i,0}} = \langle \overrightarrow{b}_{N+i}, \overrightarrow{r}^\star \rangle + m_1^{(i)\star}$$
$$t_{\pi(i)} = \langle \overrightarrow{b}_{2N+i}, \overrightarrow{r}^\star \rangle + m_2^{(i)\star}$$
$$t_{\alpha^{\pi(i)}} = \langle \overrightarrow{b}_{3N+i}, \overrightarrow{r}^\star \rangle + m_3^{(i)\star}$$
$$t_{4N+i} = \langle \overrightarrow{b}_{4N+i}, \overrightarrow{r}^\star \rangle + m_4^{(i)\star}$$
$$t_{5N+i} = \langle \overrightarrow{b}_{5N+i}, \overrightarrow{r}^\star \rangle + m_5^{(i)\star}$$
$$t_{6N+i} = \langle \overrightarrow{b}_{6N+i}, \overrightarrow{r}^\star \rangle + m_6^{(i)\star}$$
$$t_{7N+i} = \langle \overrightarrow{b}_{7N+i}, \overrightarrow{r}^\star \rangle + m_7^{(i)\star}$$
$$t_{8N+i} = \langle \overrightarrow{b}_{8N+i}, \overrightarrow{r}^\star \rangle + m_8^{(i)\star}$$
$$t_{9N+1} = \langle \overrightarrow{b}_{9N+1}, \overrightarrow{r}^\star \rangle + m_9^\star$$

Setting $\overrightarrow{z}^\star = \overrightarrow{y}^\star + c\overrightarrow{r}^\star$, masked openings are defined below.

$$f^{u_{j,0}} = \langle \overrightarrow{b}_j, \overrightarrow{y}^\star \rangle - cm_0^{(j)\star}$$
$$f^{v_{j,0}} = \langle \overrightarrow{b}_{N+j}, \overrightarrow{y}^\star \rangle - cm_1^{(j)\star}$$
$$f^{\pi(j)} = \langle \overrightarrow{b}_{2N+j}, \overrightarrow{y}^\star \rangle - cm_2^{(j)\star}$$
$$f^{\alpha_0^{\pi(j)}} = \langle \overrightarrow{b}_{3N+j}, \overrightarrow{y}^\star \rangle - cm_3^{(j)\star}$$
$$f^{4N+j} = \langle \overrightarrow{b}_{4N+j}, \overrightarrow{y}^\star \rangle - cm_4^{(j)\star}$$
$$f^{5N+j} = \langle \overrightarrow{b}_{5N+j}, \overrightarrow{y}^\star \rangle - cm_5^{(j)\star}$$
$$f^{6N+j} = \langle \overrightarrow{b}_{6N+j}, \overrightarrow{y}^\star \rangle - cm_6^{(j)\star}$$
$$f^{7N+j} = \langle \overrightarrow{b}_{7N+j}, \overrightarrow{y}^\star \rangle - cm_7^{(j)\star}$$
$$f^{8N+j} = \langle \overrightarrow{b}_{8N+j}, \overrightarrow{y}^\star \rangle - cm_8^{(j)\star}$$
$$f^{9N+1} = \langle \overrightarrow{b}_{9N+1}, \overrightarrow{y}^\star \rangle - cm_9^{(j)\star}$$

Now, let's substitute those terms to their respective places in verification equations. After simplifications (see the full version of the paper [17]) and following the argument in [4, Theorem 5.1], for some j, $\Pr[\beta m_2^{(j)\star} + m_3^{(j)\star} - m_6^{(j)\star} + \gamma \neq 0] = \epsilon < (3p)^k$. Similarly, with the same probability bound, we get $m_0^{(j)\star} m_3^{(j)\star} - m_4^{(j)\star} \neq 0$; $m_1^{(j)\star} m_3^{(j)\star} - m_5^{(j)\star} \neq 0$ and $m_6^{(j)\star} m_7^{(j)\star} - m_8^{(j)\star} \neq 0$ altogether, or $\sum_{j=1}^{N} u'_j m_3^{(j)\star} - \sum_{j=1}^{N} m_4^{(j)\star} - M_1 \neq 0$ and $\sum_{j=1}^{N} v'_j m_3^{(j)\star} - \sum_{j=1}^{N} m_5^{(j)\star} - M_2 \neq 0$; and $m_8^{(N)\star} - \Pi \neq 0$.

Combining all extracted relations we obtain

$$\prod_{j}^{N}(\beta m_2^{(j)\star} + m_3^{(j)\star} - \gamma) = \Pi = \prod_{j}^{N}(\beta j + \alpha^j - \gamma),$$

$$\sum_{j}^{N} m_3^{(j)\star}(u'_j - m_0^{(j)\star}) = M_1 = \sum_{i=1}^{N} \alpha^i u_i,$$

$$\sum_{j}^{N} m_3^{(j)\star}(v'_j - m_1^{(j)\star}) = M_2 = \sum_{i=1}^{N} \alpha^i v_i.$$

Mix-Node Security. Once more, we refer to [13] where mix-node security is proved using a game-based approach. By following exactly the same steps, and only replacing statistical closeness of Game 0 and Game 1 with computational closeness under $\mathsf{MLWE}_{8d\beta_2}$ assumption guaranteeing shortness error terms in RLWE encryptions, it is possible to show that the advantage of an adversary over random guessing is bounded by

$$\epsilon = \mathbf{Adv}_{\mathcal{A}}^{sec}(\kappa) \leq \epsilon_{MLWE} + \epsilon_{RLWE}.$$

3.1 Non-interactivity and Proof Size

The protocol in Fig. 1 can be made non-interactive with the help of Fiat-Shamir transformation. In other words, challenges are computed by the prover by hashing all previous messages and public information. Furthermore, instead of sending $\vec{w}, v_1, v_2, v_3, v_4$ which are used as inputs to the hash function to generate challenges, the standard technique is to send the hash output and let the verifier recompute those values from verification equations and check that the hashes of the computed input terms match with the prover's hash. Thus, it is enough to send the commitment $\vec{t}_0 \| t_1 \| \cdots \| t_{9N}$, garbage term t_{9N+1} and vector $\vec{z}$. A polynomial in $\mathcal{R}_q$ consists of d coefficients less than q, so it takes $d\lfloor \log q \rfloor$ bits at most. $\vec{t}_0$ and $\vec{z}$ consist of μ and $\lambda + \mu + 9N + 1$ polynomials, respectively. The full cost of shortness proof is analysed in the full version of the paper [17]. Combining all of these, the size of accepting transcript for our protocol is

$$(\mu + 9N + 1)d\lfloor \log q \rfloor + (\lambda + \mu + 9N + 1)d\lfloor \log q \rfloor + 256$$
$$+ (2\lambda + 10N)\frac{d^2}{l}\lfloor \log q \rfloor + (\lambda + 2\mu + 7)d\lfloor \log q \rfloor + 256$$
$$= \left(18 + \frac{10d}{l}\right)Nd\lfloor \log q \rfloor + (2\lambda(1 + d/l) + 4\mu + 9)d\lfloor \log q \rfloor + 512.$$

Overall, the size of the proof of shuffle protocol is linearly dependent on the number of ciphertexts (i.e. votes in the voting scenario). However, the number of public variables, such as commitment keys, is increasing quadratically. A possible optimization method is to choose a common shared seed and derive all the public polynomials using that seed.

Another possible place for optimization is to choose public variables in a specific format such as $\boldsymbol{B}_0 = [\mathbf{I}_\mu | \boldsymbol{B}_0']$ where $\boldsymbol{B}_0' \in \mathcal{R}_q^{\mu \times (\lambda + 9N + 1)}$ and vectors $\overrightarrow{\boldsymbol{b}}_i = \overrightarrow{\mathbf{0}}_\mu \| \overrightarrow{\boldsymbol{e}}_i \| \overrightarrow{\boldsymbol{b}}_i'$ where $\overrightarrow{\boldsymbol{e}}_i$ is the i-th standard basis vector of length $9N + 1$ and $\overrightarrow{\boldsymbol{b}}_i' \in \mathcal{R}_q^\lambda$ as suggested in [20], so that total number of uniform polynomials will be linear in N. (This optimization is already taken into account in the size of shortness proof transcript, see the full version of the paper [17]).

4   Implementation and Benchmarks

We want to instantiate the protocol parameters in a way that the protocol achieves 128 bit classical soundness, and post-quantum encryption security of RLWE is at least that much. For Module SIS security, $8d(\delta_1 - \beta_1 - 1) = 8d\beta_1' < q$ and $8d(\delta_2 - \beta_2 - 1) = 8d\beta_2' < q$. Coefficients of secret key and error terms used in RLWE encryption are sampled uniformly in $\{-1, 0, 1\}$, i.e. $\chi_1 = \mathcal{U}(\{-1, 0, 1\}^d)$. Similarly, distribution C and χ_2 are defined on the same set: $Pr(x = 1) = Pr(x = -1)$ and $Pr(x = 0) = 1/2$ in C and $Pr(x = 0) = 6/16$ in χ_2. We find that for $q \approx 2^{32}$, mixing node is secure up to 10 voters which is insufficient. For this reason and in order to easily represent coefficients with primary data types, we choose $q \approx 2^{63}$. Then, using LWE and SIS security estimator script[1] we get that for $\beta_1 = \beta_2 = d = 4096, \lambda = 1, \mu = 1$ and $\delta_1 = \delta_2 = 2^{45}$ ($M \leq 2$ for $N < 10^5$ voters) Hermite factor for $\mathsf{MLWE}_{\lambda, \chi_2}$ with ternary noise is 1.0029 and $\mathsf{MSIS}_{8d\beta_{1,2}'}$ has root Hermite factor 1.003. Finally, by Lemma 3 in [4], $p \approx 2^{-62}$, which implies that $d/l = 2$ is enough for the desired soundness level. However, following the analysis in the full version of the paper [17], we set $d/l = 4$.

We can estimate the performance of proof of shuffle protocol in terms of expensive operations. Sampling challenges uniformly random from $\mathcal{C}, \chi_1$ or in interval $[-\delta_1 + 1, \delta_1]$ is not complex. Thus, the only expensive operation is polynomial multiplication in $\mathcal{R}_q$. When the ring is fully splitting, multiplication can be handled in NTT domain in a linear number of steps. But, due to the large soundness error, we avoid using such rings. In [22], authors show the performance of NTT-based polynomial multiplication in partially splitting rings. We believe

---

[1] https://github.com/pq-crystals/security-estimates.

that their optimized implementation can further reduce overall protocol performance. In Fig. 1, we see that the protocol uses $O(N^2)$ multiplication operations due to $18N$ inner products between vectors of length $\lambda + \mu + 9N + 1$. However, applying the optimization trick in Sect. 3.1, this dependency becomes linear in N. Because the complexity of polynomial multiplication depends only on the ring structure, it can be assumed to be constant. Thus, the time complexity of the protocol becomes linear in the number of voters.

As a proof of concept, the proposed scheme is implemented in C language and made publicly available.[2] The polynomial operations are borrowed from Kyber/Dilithium reference implementations and modified afterward for chosen parameters. SHAKE128 is used as a hash function while generating challenges. In Table 1, the average runtime to generate and verify the proof of shuffle protocol is given. Tests are run on Intel Haswell CPUs with 2.2 GHz clock speed and 64 GB RAM.

Table 1. Performance table of our implementation of the protocol in Fig. 1.

	Shortness proof generation/verification	Shuffle proof generation/verification	Whole proof generation/verification	Proof size
Per voter	1.5 s/1.48 s	20 ms /13 ms	1.52 s/1.49 s	15 MB

Relying on the numbers shown in Table 1, in case the number of voters is 100000, we can expect the proofs to take about 150000 s (approximately 41.7 h) and the proof size to be about 1.4 TB, which is still manageable. We note that our implementation has not been heavily optimised. In order to go beyond the 100000 order of magnitude, further optimisations are needed.

In the existing literature, a few other lattice-based e-voting protocols are proposed aiming at practical performance. EVOLVE [25] performs about 10 times faster than our implementation using a highly optimized mathematical library. Correctness, privacy, and consistency of EVOLVE scheme are based on only hardness of MLWE and MSIS problems which is also the case for our protocol. However, EVOLVE is a homomorphic tally-based protocol, limiting its potential usage scenarios. The decryption mix-net-based voting solution by Boyen et al. [8] avoids using Non-Interactive Zero-knowledge proofs and bases security claims on trusted public audits. As a result, their proposed system achieves very fast results, but they need to trust the auditors is a significant restriction. To the best of our knowledge, the fastest fully lattice-based proof of correct shuffle is presented in [3] where the authors use the shuffle of known values technique. The problem here is that the shuffle server can break the privacy of voters if the ballot box, decrypted ballots, and shuffle proofs are made public. The proposed verifiable shuffle protocol is 5 times faster (33 ms per voter) than EVOLVE scheme benchmarked on an almost two times more powerful CPU. Our protocol, while being slower in the current

---

[2] https://github.com/Valeh2012/ilmx

implementation by about an order of magnitude, does not allow the shuffle server to break vote privacy.

Post-quantum security of Fiat-Shamir transform has not been fully proven in the quantum random oracle model (QROM) yet. Several works in this research area restricted definitions for security properties. For example, computationally binding commitment schemes can be insecure against quantum attacks, as shown in [2]. Collapse-binding is a stronger security property that allows to the construction of a quantum argument of knowledge [29]. The BDLOP commitment scheme used in our protocol has not been shown to satisfy the collapse-binding property. But because SIS hash functions are collapse-binding [19], hopefully one can prove for Module-SIS based BDLOP commitments as well. Another main challenge is to prove the security of mutli-round Fiat-Shamir[15] in QROM. Until these problems are solved, unfortunately, we cannot claim full post-quantum security of non-interactive protocol described in Sect. 3.1. An alternative solution is Unruh transform [28], but applying it will result in reduced performance.

However, the interactive protocol in Fig. 1 will be *potentially* post-quantum secure. In the online voting context, election auditors can be assumed to be honest verifiers. They can be restricted to have access to the powerful quantum device during the mixing procedure in order to prevent them obtain the secret permutation vector. After the successfully verified mixing phase is over, RLWE ciphertexts can be publicly shared at no risk due to the post-quantum security level of chosen parameters.

5   Conclusions and Further Work

In this work, we have presented an improved lattice-based proof of shuffle protocol for secure mix-nets. The resulting scheme has linear memory cost and time complexity. As a result, we can potentially handle mixing up to 100000 values. This is a significant landmark considering our motivating example case of mixing electronic votes.

The performance of the protocol can be improved even further with the help of parallel programming approaches. For example with OpenMP SIMD [18] computations can be distributed to multiple processors, and at each of them, 8 polynomial coefficients can be processed at a time on 512-bit wide registers using AVX512 instruction set. Another approach is to use GPUs as they are much faster than CPUs in matrix calculations [14]. We expect the effect of such optimisations to be approximately one or two orders of magnitude, but establishing the exact amount will remain the subject for future work.

Acknowledgements. This paper has been supported by the Estonian Research Council under the grant number PRG920 and European Regional Development Fund through the grant number EU48684.

References

1. Alkim, E., Ducas, L., Pöppelmann, T., Schwabe, P.: Post-quantum key exchange - a new hope. IACR Cryptol. ePrint Arch. **2015**, 1092 (2015)

2. Ambainis, A., Rosmanis, A., Unruh, D.: Quantum attacks on classical proof systems: the hardness of quantum rewinding. In: 55th IEEE Annual Symposium on Foundations of Computer Science, FOCS 2014, Philadelphia, PA, USA, 18–21 October 2014, pp. 474–483. IEEE Computer Society (2014). https://doi.org/10.1109/FOCS.2014.57

3. Aranha, D.F., Baum, C., Gjøsteen, K., Silde, T., Tunge, T.: Lattice-based proof of shuffle and applications to electronic voting. In: Paterson, K.G. (ed.) CT-RSA 2021. LNCS, vol. 12704, pp. 227–251. Springer, Cham (2021). https://doi.org/10.1007/978-3-030-75539-3_10

4. Attema, T., Lyubashevsky, V., Seiler, G.: Practical product proofs for lattice commitments. In: Micciancio, D., Ristenpart, T. (eds.) CRYPTO 2020, Part II. LNCS, vol. 12171, pp. 470–499. Springer, Cham (2020). https://doi.org/10.1007/978-3-030-56880-1_17

5. Baum, C., Damgård, I., Lyubashevsky, V., Oechsner, S., Peikert, C.: More efficient commitments from structured lattice assumptions. In: Catalano, D., De Prisco, R. (eds.) SCN 2018. LNCS, vol. 11035, pp. 368–385. Springer, Cham (2018). https://doi.org/10.1007/978-3-319-98113-0_20

6. Benhamouda, F., Krenn, S., Lyubashevsky, V., Pietrzak, K.: Efficient zero-knowledge proofs for commitments from learning with errors over rings. In: Pernul, G., Ryan, P.Y.A., Weippl, E. (eds.) ESORICS 2015, Part I. LNCS, vol. 9326, pp. 305–325. Springer, Cham (2015). https://doi.org/10.1007/978-3-319-24174-6_16

7. del Blanco, D.Y.M., Alonso, L.P., Alonso, J.A.H.: Review of cryptographic schemes applied to remote electronic voting systems: remaining challenges and the upcoming post-quantum paradigm. Open Math. 16(1), 95–112 (2018)

8. Boyen, X., Haines, T., Müller, J.: A verifiable and practical lattice-based decryption mix net with external auditing. In: Chen, L., Li, N., Liang, K., Schneider, S. (eds.) ESORICS 2020, Part II. LNCS, vol. 12309, pp. 336–356. Springer, Cham (2020). https://doi.org/10.1007/978-3-030-59013-0_17

9. Cabarcas, D., Göpfert, F., Weiden, P.: Provably secure LWE encryption with smallish uniform noise and secret. In: Emura, K., Hanaoka, G., Zhao, Y. (eds.) Proceedings of ASIAPKC 2014, pp. 33–42. ACM (2014)

10. Chaum, D.: Untraceable electronic mail, return addresses, and digital pseudonyms. Commun. ACM 24(2), 84–88 (1981)

11. Chillotti, I., Gama, N., Georgieva, M., Izabachène, M.: A homomorphic LWE based e-voting scheme. In: Takagi, T. (ed.) PQCrypto 2016. LNCS, vol. 9606, pp. 245–265. Springer, Cham (2016). https://doi.org/10.1007/978-3-319-29360-8_16

12. Costa, N., Martínez, R., Morillo, P.: Proof of a shuffle for lattice-based cryptography. In: Lipmaa, H., Mitrokotsa, A., Matulevičius, R. (eds.) NordSec 2017. LNCS, vol. 10674, pp. 280–296. Springer, Cham (2017). https://doi.org/10.1007/978-3-319-70290-2_17

13. Costa, N., Martínez, R., Morillo, P.: Lattice-based proof of a shuffle. In: Bracciali, A., Clark, J., Pintore, F., Rønne, P.B., Sala, M. (eds.) FC 2019. LNCS, vol. 11599, pp. 330–346. Springer, Cham (2020). https://doi.org/10.1007/978-3-030-43725-1_23

14. Dai, W., Sunar, B.: cuHE: a homomorphic encryption accelerator library. In: Pasalic, E., Knudsen, L.R. (eds.) BalkanCryptSec 2015. LNCS, vol. 9540, pp. 169–186. Springer, Cham (2016). https://doi.org/10.1007/978-3-319-29172-7_11

15. Don, J., Fehr, S., Majenz, C.: The measure-and-reprogram technique 2.0: multi-round Fiat-Shamir and more. In: Micciancio, D., Ristenpart, T. (eds.) CRYPTO 2020, Part III. LNCS, vol. 12172, pp. 602–631. Springer, Cham (2020). https://doi.org/10.1007/978-3-030-56877-1_21

16. Ducas, L., Lepoint, T., Lyubashevsky, V., Schwabe, P., Seiler, G., Stehlé, D.: CRYSTALS - dilithium: digital signatures from module lattices. IACR Cryptol. ePrint Arch. **2017**, 633 (2017)

17. Farzaliyev, V., Willemson, J., Kaasik, J.K.: Improved lattice-based mix-nets for electronic voting. Cryptology ePrint Archive, Report 2021/1499 (2021). https://ia.cr/2021/1499

18. Fortin, P., Fleury, A., Lemaire, F., Monagan, M.: High performance SIMD modular arithmetic for polynomial evaluation, April 2020. https://hal.archives-ouvertes.fr/hal-02552673. Working paper or preprint

19. Liu, Q., Zhandry, M.: Revisiting post-quantum Fiat-Shamir. In: Boldyreva, A., Micciancio, D. (eds.) CRYPTO 2019, Part II. LNCS, vol. 11693, pp. 326–355. Springer, Cham (2019). https://doi.org/10.1007/978-3-030-26951-7_12

20. Lyubashevsky, V., Nguyen, N.K., Seiler, G.: Practical lattice-based zero-knowledge proofs for integer relations. In: Ligatti, J., Ou, X., Katz, J., Vigna, G. (eds.) Proceedings of ACM CCS 2020, pp. 1051–1070. ACM (2020)

21. Lyubashevsky, V., Peikert, C., Regev, O.: On ideal lattices and learning with errors over rings. J. ACM **60**(6), 43:1–43:35 (2013)

22. Lyubashevsky, V., Seiler, G.: Short, invertible elements in partially splitting cyclotomic rings and applications to lattice-based zero-knowledge proofs. In: Nielsen, J.B., Rijmen, V. (eds.) EUROCRYPT 2018, Part I. LNCS, vol. 10820, pp. 204–224. Springer, Cham (2018). https://doi.org/10.1007/978-3-319-78381-9_8

23. Peikert, C., Rosen, A.: Efficient collision-resistant hashing from worst-case assumptions on cyclic lattices. In: Halevi, S., Rabin, T. (eds.) TCC 2006. LNCS, vol. 3876, pp. 145–166. Springer, Heidelberg (2006). https://doi.org/10.1007/11681878_8

24. Peng, K., Aditya, R., Boyd, C., Dawson, E., Lee, B.: Multiplicative homomorphic e-voting. In: Canteaut, A., Viswanathan, K. (eds.) INDOCRYPT 2004. LNCS, vol. 3348, pp. 61–72. Springer, Heidelberg (2004). https://doi.org/10.1007/978-3-540-30556-9_6

25. del Pino, R., Lyubashevsky, V., Neven, G., Seiler, G.: Practical quantum-safe voting from lattices. In: Thuraisingham, B.M., Evans, D., Malkin, T., Xu, D. (eds.) Proceedings of ACM CCS 2017, pp. 1565–1581. ACM (2017)

26. Shor, P.W.: Polynomial-time algorithms for prime factorization and discrete logarithms on a quantum computer. SIAM Rev. **41**(2), 303–332 (1999)

27. Strand, M.: A verifiable shuffle for the GSW cryptosystem. In: Zohar, A., et al. (eds.) FC 2018. LNCS, vol. 10958, pp. 165–180. Springer, Heidelberg (2019). https://doi.org/10.1007/978-3-662-58820-8_12

28. Unruh, D.: Non-interactive zero-knowledge proofs in the quantum random oracle model. In: Oswald, E., Fischlin, M. (eds.) EUROCRYPT 2015, Part II. LNCS, vol. 9057, pp. 755–784. Springer, Heidelberg (2015). https://doi.org/10.1007/978-3-662-46803-6_25

29. Unruh, D.: Computationally binding quantum commitments. In: Fischlin, M., Coron, J.-S. (eds.) EUROCRYPT 2016, Part II. LNCS, vol. 9666, pp. 497–527. Springer, Heidelberg (2016). https://doi.org/10.1007/978-3-662-49896-5_18

Practical Post-quantum Password-Authenticated Key Exchange Based-on Module-Lattice

Peixin Ren[1,2] and Xiaozhuo Gu[1,2(✉)]

[1] SKLOIS, Institute of Information Engineering, CAS, Beijing, China
[2] School of Cyber Security, University of Chinese Academy of Sciences, Beijing, China
{renpeixin,guxiaozhuo}@iie.ac.cn

Abstract. Password-authenticated key exchange (PAKE) is a neat technology that can establish secure remote communications between the client and the server, especially with the preponderance of amplifying a memorable password into a strong session key. However, the arrival of the quantum computing era has brought new challenges to traditional PAKE protocols. Thus, designing an efficient post-quantum PAKE scheme becomes an open research question. In this paper, we construct a quantum-safe PAKE protocol which is a horizontal extension of the PAK protocol [22] in the field of module lattice. Subsequently, we accompany our proposed protocol with a rigorous security proof in the Bellare-Pointcheval-Rogaway (BPR) model with two adaptions: applying the CDF-Zipf model to characterize the ability of the adversary and using the pairing with errors (PWE) assumption to simplify the proof. Taking the flexibility of the module learning with errors (MLWE) problem, we elaborately select 3 parameter sets to meet different application scenarios (e.g., classical/quantum-safe Transport Layer Security (TLS), resource-constrained Internet of Things (IoT) devices). Specifically, our Recommended implementation achieves 177-bit post-quantum security with a generous margin to cope with later improvement in cryptanalysis. The performance results indicate that our MLWE-PAKE is quite practical: compared with the latest Yang-PAK, our Recommended-PAK reduces the communication cost and the running time by 36.8% and 13.8%, respectively.

Keywords: Password-authenticated key exchange · Module learning with errors · Post-quantum · Lattice-based

1 Introduction

Passwords have several advantages of being human-memorable, avoiding expensive computation of public key infrastructure (PKI) to distribute client certificates, and preventing dedicated hardware for storing secret keys. Thus, passwords constitute the prevalent and irreplaceable authentication approach to identify human users [26,31], especially in the proliferation of mobile devices.

© The Author(s), under exclusive license to Springer Nature Switzerland AG 2022
J. H. Park and S.-H. Seo (Eds.): ICISC 2021, LNCS 13218, pp. 137–156, 2022.
https://doi.org/10.1007/978-3-031-08896-4_7

PAKE is an important cryptographic primitive that enables two parties (e.g., a client and a server) to utilize a simple password to negotiate a high-entropy session key in an insecure network. In 1992, Bellovin and Merritt [3] proposed a *symmetric*-PAKE protocol, encrypted key exchange (EKE), where two parties hold the same password and establish a shared session-key at the end. However, *symmetric*-PAKE protocols [2,14,18] only focus on the part of password-using and omit how to constrain the impact of password leakage.

In reality, *asymmetric*-PAKE protocols [4] are widely deployed and standardized in the domain of existing client-to-server Internet or IoT. In asymmetric-PAKE schemes, the server only gets the knowledge of the hashed password with a random salt, not the actual password. In this case, even if the server is compromised, the adversary cannot obtain the password directly. Therefore, many asymmetric-PAKE protocols have been proposed and analyzed, such as [5,15,19,32]. However, the hardness of these protocols depends on traditional number-theoretic problems (the integer factorization problem, the discrete logarithm problem etc.) that are vulnerable to quantum attacks [16,27].

With the advent of quantum computing, standards bodies and academia [23, 24] have triggered widespread interest in cryptographic algorithms believed to resist quantum computers. According to [23], lattice is one of the most promising and ideal competitive primitives for the construction of post-quantum schemes. However, the majority of lattice-based schemes focus on key exchange without authentication [1,7,11] and key encapsulation mechanisms [8,12].

Until 2017, Ding et al. [10] constructed a post-quantum asymmetric-PAKE protocol in the ideal lattice area and proved its security in the BPR model. The primary problem is that this protocol emphasizes the theoretical feasibility at the expense of efficient implementation in practice. Subsequently, following the work of [10], many literatures [13,21,30] proposed or implemented quantum-safe PAKE protocols. More specifically, Gao et al. [13] utilized the NFLlib library to accelerate the optimization of Ding's scheme [10], and gave a parameter set suitable for the use of the number theoretic transform (NTT) algorithm (for speeding up polynomial multiplication), but the proposed parameter set does not consider the communication burden. Yang et al. [30] further optimized Ding's solution, but only provided one lightweight parameter set without considering multiple security requirements. Moreover, inspired by the two-party, Liu et al. [21] presented a three-party RLWE-based PAKE protocol, where two clients aim to agree on a session key with the help of a trusted server. To our knowledge, as a compromise between learning with errors (LWE) and RLWE, MLWE [9] retains the matrix format, and concurrently introduces the ring polynomials. Therefore, when designing a lattice-based scheme in multiple security scenarios, MLWE is more flexible and straightforward than other primitives [8].

Given the above, we try to solve the following question: *Is it possible to construct an efficient and lightweight MLWE-based asymmetric PAKE protocol while resisting against quantum computer attacks?*

1.1 Contributions

In this work, we answer the above question in the affirmative. We construct a three-flow asymmetric PAKE protocol which is a parallel extension of the class of Random Oracle Model (ROM)-based PAK protocol [22] but in the module lattice setting. We prove its security under the BPR model and implement 3 deployment schemes that are tailored to the security level as well as the potential applications.

To construct the protocol efficiently, the majority of lattice-based schemes [1,10,13,30] are based on the RLWE problem. However, in the light of our observation, the MLWE problem [9] with the advantage of a compromise between LWE and RLWE is more suitable for the construction of practical PAKE. Using the feature of MLWE, by superimposing or reducing the number of ring polynomials, different deployment schemes can be realized. As a result, we propose the practical MLWE-based PAKE protocol in the random oracle model.

By constructing the PAKE as a self-contained system, we demonstrate that our protocol is directly dependent on the hardness of MLWE and PWE, which can be reduced to MLWE. The security of our proposed protocol is proved under the BPR model [2] with two adaptions: first, to simplify the proof, we introduce the PWE assumption; second, we use the CDF-Zipf model [29] to characterize the ability of the adversary to conduct an online dictionary attack. Finally, we establish a complete security proof of the protocol, reduce its security to online dictionary attacks, and demonstrate that it satisfies the forward security.

In terms of concrete implementation, we comprehensively consider indicators such as failure rate, post-quantum security, communication cost, and computational efficiency, and select 3 high-quality parameter sets. To evaluate the performance of our proposals, we summarize the key technologies and the security level of state-of-the-art lattice-based schemes and our schemes in Table 2, and compare the running time, the communication cost and the failure rate of these schemes in Table 3. Particularly, our Recommended-PAK offers 177-bit post-quantum security with a generous margin to cope with later improvement in cryptanalysis. Compared with the latest RLWE-based Yang-PAK, the communication cost and the running time are reduced by 36.8% and 13.8%, respectively. Finally, in conjunction with the performance results, we discuss two potential real-world applications for our MLWE-PAK protocol: resource-constrained IoT devices and classical/post-quantum TLS.

2 Preliminaries

In this section, we provide both the notations of the parameters used in our construction and the description of some basic knowledge.

2.1 Notations

If A is a probabilistic algorithm, $a \leftarrow A(b)$ represents the output of A assigned to a. If χ is a probability distribution, $a \leftarrow \chi$ denotes sampling a following

χ. We represent sampling a uniformly at random from a set S as $a \leftarrow S$. We denote $R_q = \mathbb{Z}_q[X]/(X^n + 1)$ as the ring of integer polynomials modulo $(X^n + 1)$ where each coefficient is reduced by modulus q. We define a centered binomial distribution with parameter $\eta \in \mathbb{Z}_+$ as β_η. Throughout this paper, a normal font letter such as p represents a ring element in R_q. For the vector $\mathbf{v}$ including d elements, we denote it as $\mathbf{v} \in R_q^d$ using the bold lower-case letter; for the matrix $\mathbf{A}$ consisting of $m \times n$ entities, we denote it as $\mathbf{A} \in R_q^{m \times n}$ using the bold upper-case letter. By default, all vectors are column vectors. For a vector $\mathbf{v}$ (or a matrix $\mathbf{A}$), $\mathbf{v}^T$ (or $\mathbf{A}^T$) is used as its transpose.

2.2   The Decision Module-LWE Problem

Here, we define the decision version of the MLWE problem as follows.

Definition 1 (The decision MLWE$_{n,d,q,\chi}$ problem). *Let n, d and $q \geq 2$ be the degree of a polynomial, the dimension of a vector, and the modulus, respectively. Let χ be an error distribution and $\mathbf{s} \leftarrow \chi^d$. Define $O_{\chi,\mathbf{s}}$ as the oracle which does the following:*

1. *Sample $\mathbf{A} \leftarrow R_q^{d \times d}$, $\mathbf{e} \leftarrow \chi^d$;*
2. *Return $(\mathbf{A}, \mathbf{As} + \mathbf{e}) \in R_q^{d \times d} \times R_q^d$.*

The decision MLWE problem for n, d, q, χ is to distinguish between polynomial independent samples from $O_{\chi,\mathbf{s}}$ and the same number of independent samples from an oracle $\mathcal{U}$ that returns uniform random samples from $(R_q^{d \times d}, R_q^d)$.

Remark 1. The secret $\mathbf{s}$ is chosen from the error distribution instead of the uniform distribution since the literature [9] has shown that this problem is as hard as the one in which $\mathbf{s}$ is chosen uniformly at random.

2.3   Bellare-Pointcheval-Rogaway Security Model

Here we review the BPR model [2] that will be used in our security analysis.

Participants, Passwords, and Execution of the Protocol. A client is denoted as $C \in \mathcal{C}$ and a server is denoted as $S \in \mathcal{S}$. Each client C holds a password pw_c, which is independently sampled from the password space $\mathcal{D}$ in accordance with Zipf's law [20], and each server S holds correlated hash value $H(pw_c)$. Moreover, in this model, each participant enables to execute the protocol with different partners multiple times. Thus, we denote instance i of participants $U \in \mathcal{U} = \mathcal{C} \cup \mathcal{S}$ as Π_U^i. Each Π_U^i can be used only once.

Adversarial Model. We assume that an adversary $\mathcal{A}$ completely controls the network and provides the input to the instance of principals. Formally, as a probabilistic algorithm with a distinguished query tape, $\mathcal{A}$ launches attacks utilizing random queries in the real world. Thus, we summarize the allowed queries defined in [2] here.

- Execute(C, i, S, j): causes protocol P between Π_C^i and Π_S^j to be executed and outputs the transcript to $\mathcal{A}$.
- Send(U, i, M): causes message M to be sent to instance Π_U^i. Π_U^i computes what the protocol says, and sends it back to $\mathcal{A}$.
- Reveal(U, i): If the instance Π_U^i has accepted and holds its session key sk, this query outputs sk to the adversary $\mathcal{A}$.
- Test(U, i): A coin b possessed by Π_U^i is tossed, then the following happens. If $b = 0$, Π_U^i returns sk to $\mathcal{A}$; otherwise, it returns a random string drawing from the space of session keys.
- Corrupt(U): If $U \in Client$, pw_c is output; otherwise, $H(pw_c)$ is output.

Partnering. An instance Π_C^i holding (pid, sid, sk) and an instance Π_S^j holding (pid', sid', sk') are *partnered*, if $pid = S, pid' = C, sid = sid', sk = sk'$, where pid, sid and sk denote the partner-id, the session-id and the session-key, respectively. In addition, no other instance accepts with its session-id equal to sid.

Freshness with Forward Secrecy. An instance Π_U^i is *fresh-fs* unless either 1) a Reveal(U, i) query occurs, or 2) a Reveal(U', j) query occurs, where Π_U^i has partnered with $\Pi_{U'}^j$, or 3) a Corrupt(U) query occurs before the Test(U, i) query and the Send(U, i, M)) query.

Advantage of the Adversary. We now define the advantage of the adversary against the authenticated key exchange protocol P. Let $\mathrm{Succ}_{\mathcal{A}}^P(\lambda)$ be the event that the adversary $\mathcal{A}$ makes a Test(U, i) query to some fresh instances Π_U^i, and outputs a single bit b', where $b' = b$ for the bit b which was chosen in the Test query. The advantage of $\mathcal{A}$ is defined as follows

$$\mathrm{Adv}_{\mathcal{A}}^P(\lambda) = 2\Pr[\mathrm{Succ}_{\mathcal{A}}^P(\lambda)] - 1.$$

Furthermore, if we have two protocols P and P' which satisfy the following relationship

$$\Pr[\mathrm{Succ}_{\mathcal{A}}^P(\lambda)] = \Pr[\mathrm{Succ}_{\mathcal{A}}^{P'}(\lambda)] + \epsilon,$$

then we have the fact that

$$\mathrm{Adv}_{\mathcal{A}}^P(\lambda) = \mathrm{Adv}_{\mathcal{A}}^{P'}(\lambda) + 2\epsilon.$$

2.4 Error Reconciliation Mechanism

In [17], Jin and Zhao formally formulated a universal and convenient error reconciliation mechanism referred to as optimally-balanced key consensus with noise (OKCN). The inherent upper-bound analyzed in Jin's paper guides the parameter selection and balances between the accuracy and the bandwidth. Especially, OKCN is more suitable for incorporating into the existing DH-based protocols like TLS, IKE. Thus, it shows more advantages in choosing OKCN as the error reconciliation mechanism of our scheme.

Before showing the description of the OKCN algorithm, we first give a function $|a - b|_q$ to represent the distance between two elements $a, b \in \mathbb{Z}_q$.

$$|a - b|_q = \min\{(a - b) \bmod q, (b - a) \bmod q\}.$$

Moreover, for two approximate polynomials $w = \sum_{i=0}^{n-1} w_i X^i, v = \sum_{i=0}^{n-1} v_i X^i$, we define the distance between them as

$$|w - v|_q = \max\{|w_1 - v_1|_q, |w_2 - v_2|_q, \cdots, |w_{n-1} - v_{n-1}|_q\}.$$

Algorithm 1. OKCN: Optimally-balanced Key Consensus with Noise

---

$\mathsf{params} = (q, m, g, l, aux), aux = \{q' = \mathsf{lcm}(q, m), \alpha = q'/q, \beta = q'/m\}$
procedure $\mathrm{CON}(\sigma_s, \mathsf{params})$ $\triangleright \sigma_s \in [0, q-1]$
   $e \leftarrow [-\lfloor (\alpha - 1)/2 \rfloor, \lfloor \alpha/2 \rfloor]$
   $\sigma_A = (\alpha \sigma_s + e) \bmod q'$
   $k_s = \lfloor \sigma_A / \beta \rfloor \in \mathbb{Z}_m$
   $v' = \sigma_A \bmod \beta$
   $v = \lfloor v'g/\beta \rfloor$
   return (k_s, v)
end procedure
procedure $\mathrm{REC}(\sigma_c, v, \mathsf{params})$ $\triangleright \sigma_c \in [0, q-1]$
   $k_c = \lfloor \alpha \sigma_c / \beta - (v + 1/2)/g \rceil \bmod m$
   return k_c
end procedure

Algorithm 1 describes the calculation process of the conciliate function Con and the reconcile function Rec. The error reconciliation can be extended to R_q by applying OKCN to each coefficient of the ring. For any ring polynomial $\sigma = \{\sigma_0, \cdots, \sigma_{n-1}\} \in R_q$, we set $\mathsf{Con}(\sigma) = \{\mathsf{Con}(\sigma_0), \cdots, \mathsf{Con}(\sigma_{n-1})\}$. Rec function does the same way.

Theorem 1 (Efficiency Upper Bound [17]). *OKCN = (params, Con, Rec) is a secure and correct mechanism, then*

$$(2l + 1)m < q(1 - \frac{1}{g})$$

with $\mathsf{params} = (q, m, g, l, aux)$, *where q is the modulus, m is the length of each negotiated value, g is the length of the hint signal, l represents the distance between two approximate polynomials σ_c and σ_s in R_q.*

3   MLWE-Based PWE Assumption and Security Reduction

To expediently prove the security of our construction, we proposed the PWE assumption with the different version of the MLWE problem. This assumption with the version of the RLWE problem first appeared in the literature [10] so as to provide the security proof of its RLWE-PAKE.

Definition 2 (Pairing with Errors). *We define a probabilistic, polynomial-time adversary $\mathcal{A}$ taking $(\mathbf{A}, \mathbf{x}, \mathbf{y}, v)$ as its input, where $\mathbf{A} \leftarrow R_q^{d \times d}$, $\mathbf{x} \leftarrow R_q^d$, $\mathbf{s}, \mathbf{e} \leftarrow \beta_\eta^d$, $e_\sigma \leftarrow \beta_\eta$, $\mathbf{y} = \mathbf{A}^T \mathbf{s} + \mathbf{e}$, $(v, k) = \text{Con}(\mathbf{x}^T \mathbf{s} + e_\sigma)$. The goal of $\mathcal{A}$ is to obtain the value of string k from its output. Therefore, we define the advantage of $\mathcal{A}$ as follows:*

$$Adv_{\mathcal{A}}^{PWE}(\lambda) = \Pr[k \in \mathcal{A}(\mathbf{A}, \mathbf{x}, \mathbf{y}, v)].$$

Let $Adv_{\mathcal{A}}^{PWE}(t, N) = \max_{\mathcal{A}}\{Adv_{\mathcal{A}}^{PWE}(\lambda)\}$, where the maximum is take over all adversaries in running time t that output a list containing at most N elements of $\{0,1\}^k$. The PWE assumption denotes that $Adv_{\mathcal{A}}^{PWE}(t, N)$ is negligible for t and N which are polynomial in security parameter λ.

Now, we describe a reduction from the PWE assumption to the decision MLWE problem. We consider the following sequence of reductions:

$$\text{PWE} \longrightarrow \text{DPWE} \xrightarrow{\text{Lemma 1}} \text{MLWE-DH} \xrightarrow{\text{Lemma 2}} \text{D-MLWE}$$

The decision version of the PWE problem can be defined as follows. Obviously, if DPWE is hard so is PWE.

Definition 3 (DPWE). *Given $(\mathbf{A}, \mathbf{x}, \mathbf{y}, v, k) \in R_q^{d \times d} \times R_q^d \times R_q^d \times \{0,1\}^n \times \{0,1\}^k$ where $(v, k) = \text{Con}(\sigma)$ for some $\sigma \in R_q$. The decision Pairing with Errors (DPWE) problem is to decide whether $\sigma = \mathbf{x}^T \mathbf{s} + e_\sigma$ and $\mathbf{y} = \mathbf{A}^T \mathbf{s} + \mathbf{e}$ for some $\mathbf{s}, \mathbf{e} \leftarrow \beta_\eta^d, e_\sigma \leftarrow \beta_\eta$, or $(\sigma, \mathbf{y})$ is uniformly random in $R_q \times R_q^d$.*

Definition 4 (MLWE-DH). *Given $(\mathbf{A}, \mathbf{x}, \mathbf{y}, \sigma)$, where $(\mathbf{A}, \mathbf{x})$ is uniformly random in $R_q^{d \times d} \times R_q^d$, the MLWE-DH problem is to figure out whether $\sigma = \mathbf{x}^T \mathbf{s} + e_\sigma$ and $\mathbf{y} = \mathbf{A}^T \mathbf{s} + \mathbf{e}$ for some $e_\sigma \leftarrow \beta_\eta$ and $\mathbf{e} \leftarrow \beta_\eta^d$, or $(\sigma, \mathbf{y})$ is uniformly random in $R_q \times R_q^{d \times d}$.*

Lemma 1. *The DPWE problem is hard if the MLWE-DH problem is hard.*

Proof. Suppose that the MLWE-DH problem is hard to solve, and there exists a polynomial-time algorithm D can solve the DPWE problem with non-negligible probability. Using algorithm D as a subroutine call, we build a distinguisher D' to solve the MLWE-DH problem.

1. Input $(\mathbf{A}, \mathbf{x}, \mathbf{y}, \sigma)$
2. Compute $(v, k) = \text{Con}(\sigma)$
3. Call D to solve DPWE problem using the input $(\mathbf{A}, \mathbf{x}, \mathbf{y}, v, k)$
4. If D outputs 1 then D' outputs 1, means that $\sigma = \mathbf{x}^T \mathbf{s} + e_\sigma$ and $\mathbf{y} = \mathbf{A}^T \mathbf{s} + \mathbf{e}$; otherwise, $(\sigma, \mathbf{y})$ is uniformly random in $R_q \times R_q^d$.

Since D solves the DPWE problem with a non-negligible advantage, D' solves the MLWE-DH problem with a non-negligible advantage as well, which contradicts the hardness assumption of the MLWE-DH problem. □

Lemma 2. *If the D-MLWE problem is hard, the MLWE-DH problem is hard as well.*

Proof. Suppose that there exists a probabilistic polynomial-time algorithm D can solve the MLWE-DH problem with non-negligible advantage. Given two samples of an MLWE challenge $(\mathbf{A}_1, \mathbf{b}_1)$ and $(\mathbf{a}_2, b_2)$, both share the same $\mathbf{s} \leftarrow \beta_\eta^d$. We call algorithm D to build a distinguisher D' to solve the MLWE problem as follows:

1. Set $(\mathbf{A}, \mathbf{x}, \mathbf{y}, \sigma) = (\mathbf{A}_1, \mathbf{a}_2, \mathbf{b}_1, b_2)$
2. Input $(\mathbf{A}, \mathbf{x}, \mathbf{y}, \sigma)$ to D
3. If D outputs 1, then D' outputs 1 which D' determines $b_2 = \mathbf{a}_2^T \mathbf{s} + e_\sigma$ and $\mathbf{b}_1 = \mathbf{A}_1^T \mathbf{s} + \mathbf{e}$ for some $e_\sigma \leftarrow \beta_\eta, \mathbf{e} \leftarrow \beta_\eta^d$; otherwise, D outputs 0, then D' outputs 0, means that $b_2, \mathbf{b}_1$ is uniformly random in $R_q \times R_q^d$.

Obviously, D' can solve the MLWE problem with non-negligible advantage as well, which contradicts the hardness of the MLWE problem. Hence, if the MLWE problem is hard to solve then the MLWE-DH problem is also hard to solve. □

4   Our MLWE-Based PAKE Scheme

Here we describe our MLWE-PAKE protocol in detail and show its correctness.

4.1   Protocol Description

Client C		Server S
Input S, pw_c		$\mathbf{\Gamma}' = -H_1(pw_c)$
$\rho \sim \{0,1\}^{256}$		
$\mathbf{A} \sim R_q^{d \times d} := Sam(\rho)$		Abort if $\mathbf{m} \notin R_q^d$
$(\mathbf{s}_c, \mathbf{e}_c) \leftarrow \beta_\eta^d \times \beta_\eta^d$	$\xrightarrow{\ C, \mathbf{m}, \rho\ }$	$\mathbf{A} \sim R_q^{d \times d} := Sam(\rho)$
$\mathbf{y}_c = \mathbf{A}\mathbf{s}_c + \mathbf{e}_c$		$(\mathbf{s}_s, \mathbf{e}_s) \leftarrow \beta_\eta^d \times \beta_\eta^d$
$\mathbf{\Gamma} = H_1(pw_c)$		$\mathbf{y}_s = \mathbf{A}^T \mathbf{s}_s + \mathbf{e}_s$
$\mathbf{m} = \mathbf{y}_c + \mathbf{\Gamma}$		$\mathbf{y}_c = \mathbf{m} + \mathbf{\Gamma}'$
		$e_\sigma \leftarrow \beta_\eta$
		$\sigma_s = \mathbf{y}_c^T \mathbf{s}_s + e_\sigma$
Abort if $\mathbf{y}_s \notin R_q^d$	$\xleftarrow{\ \mathbf{y}_s, v, k\ }$	$(k_\sigma, v) = \mathrm{Con}(\sigma_s)$
$\sigma_c = \mathbf{s}_c^T \mathbf{y}_s$		$k = H_2(C, S, \mathbf{m}, \mathbf{y}_s, k_\sigma, \mathbf{\Gamma}')$
$k_\sigma = \mathrm{Rec}(\sigma_c, v)$		$k'' = H_3(C, S, \mathbf{m}, \mathbf{y}_s, k_\sigma, \mathbf{\Gamma}')$
Abort if $k \neq H_2(C, S, \mathbf{m}, \mathbf{y}_s, k_\sigma, \mathbf{\Gamma}')$		
$k' = H_3(C, S, \mathbf{m}, \mathbf{y}_s, k_\sigma, \mathbf{\Gamma}')$	$\xrightarrow{\ k'\ }$	Abort if $k' \neq k''$
$sk_c = H_4(C, S, \mathbf{m}, \mathbf{y}_s, k_\sigma, \mathbf{\Gamma}')$		$sk_s = H_4(C, S, \mathbf{m}, \mathbf{y}_s, k_\sigma, \mathbf{\Gamma}')$

Fig. 1. The MLWE-based PAKE protocol

Figure 1 describes the complete protocol. Let the rank n of a ring be a power of 2. Let q be an odd prime such that $q \equiv 1 \bmod 2n$. Function $H_1 : \{0,1\}^* \to R_q^d$

hashes passwords into a vector in R_q^d; $H_i : \{0,1\}^* \to \{0,1\}^k$ $(i = 2,3)$ be hash functions for verification of communications; $H_4 : \{0,1\}^* \to \{0,1\}^k$, the Key Derivation Function (KDF), generates the session-key of length k-bit. The comprehensive protocol is described as follows:

- **Client Initiation.** A client C takes on the role of initiating the protocol by inputting its password and the server-id S. Then, C produces its ephemeral key pair $(\mathbf{y}_c, \mathbf{s}_c)$, and uses the password to encapsulate $\mathbf{y}_c$ as the message $\mathbf{m}$. Finally, C finishes the initiation process by sending initialized message $\langle C, \mathbf{m}, \rho \rangle$ to the server S, where ρ is a seed that generates the public matrix.
- **Server Response.** Upon receiving $\langle C, \mathbf{m}, \rho \rangle$, the server S checks the rationality of $\mathbf{m}$. If $\mathbf{m} \in R_q^d$, S first generates ephemeral public-key/secret-key pair $(\mathbf{y}_s, \mathbf{s}_s)$. Then, S recovers $\mathbf{y}_c$ from $\mathbf{m}$. In the next moment, S uses $\mathbf{s}_s$ and $\mathbf{y}_c$ to compute the coordination polynomial σ_s and the shared-key $(k_\sigma, v) = \mathsf{Con}(\sigma_s)$. Subsequently, S generates two hash values k, k'' for indicating its identity and verifying the identity of C, respectively. Finally, S sends its public-key $\mathbf{y}_s$, the signal hint v and the hash value k to C.
- **Client Finish.** After receiving $\langle \mathbf{y}_s, v, k \rangle$, C utilizes its secret-key $\mathbf{s}_c$ and the public-key $\mathbf{y}_c$ to generate its coordination polynomial σ_c (which is appropriately equal to σ_s) so that it can obtain the shared key through $k_\sigma = \mathsf{Rec}(\sigma_c, v)$. C verifies the identity of S and generates the hash value k' to indicate its identity. Finally, C sends out k' and derives the session-key sk_c.
- **Server Finish.** Server S verifies k' and k'' in the same way. If $k' = k''$, S computes its session-key sk_s; otherwise, S rejects to compute a session-key.

Remark 2 (Mutual authentication). The client hashes its password, appends it to the message, and sends it out. At this time, only the server storing the hash value of the password can correctly recover the message and use the hash function H_2 to generate its verification key k. When the client receives the verification key k from the server, the client uses reconcile function Rec to negotiate its shared key k_σ and verifies whether H_2 is equal to k, thereby achieving authentication of the server. Meanwhile, it uses H_3 to generate its verification key k' provided verification information to the server. Finally, mutual authentication finishes.

4.2   Correctness

Obviously, the protocol's correctness is revealed by the equality of the values negotiated by the participants. Therefore, the correctness depends on the distance between the two approximate elements used to derive the shared-key. If this distance is within the allowable range of OKCN, correctness can be guaranteed. We compare the two approximate polynomials in R_q:

$$
\begin{aligned}
|\sigma_s - \sigma_c|_q &= |\mathbf{y}_c^T \mathbf{s}_s + e_\sigma - \mathbf{s}_c^T \mathbf{y}_s|_q \\
&= |\mathbf{s}_c^T \mathbf{A}^T \mathbf{s}_s + \mathbf{e}_c^T \mathbf{s}_s + e_\sigma - \mathbf{s}_c^T \mathbf{A}^T \mathbf{s}_s + \mathbf{s}_c^T \mathbf{e}_s|_q \\
&= |\mathbf{e}_c^T \mathbf{s}_s + e_\sigma - \mathbf{s}_c^T \mathbf{e}_s|_q \\
&\leq l < \frac{q(1 - \frac{1}{g}) - m}{2m}.
\end{aligned}
$$

P_0	The original protocol P.
P_1	If the value of $\mathbf{m}$ or $\mathbf{y}_s$ randomly chosen by the honest participants has already appeared in the previous protocols, then the protocol halts and $\mathcal{A}$ fails.
P_2	The protocol answers Send and Execute queries without making any random oracle queries. Subsequently, random oracle queries are backpatched to be consistent with the responses to Send and Execute queries as much as possible.
P_3	If an $H_l(\cdot), l \in \{2,3,4\}$ query is made, it is not checked for consistency against Execute queries. The protocol responds with a random output instead of maintaining consistency with an Execute query.
P_4	If a correct password guess is made against an instance Π_C^i or Π_S^j before a Corrupt query, the protocol halts and the adversary automatically succeeds.
P_5	Once the adversary $\mathcal{A}$ makes a password guess against the client and the server instances that have partnered, the protocol halts and the adversary fails.
P_6	There is an internal password oracle that knows all passwords and tests the correctness of a given password for a specific client/server pair.

Fig. 2. Description of the protocol P_0 through P_6

By Theorem 1, if $|\sigma_s - \sigma_c| \leq l$ where $l < \frac{q(1-\frac{1}{g})-m}{2m}$, both sides can reconcile the same value in our MLWE-PAK scheme. We represent the failure rate δ of our scheme as

$$\delta = \Pr\left[|\sigma_s - \sigma_c|_q \geq \frac{q(1-\frac{1}{g})-m}{2m}\right].$$

In Sect. 6, we will select the parameter sets to make the failure rate δ negligible in the practical implementations.

5 Proof of Security

The security proof is to show that $\mathcal{A}$ attacking the protocol is unable to determine the fresh sk with greater advantage than that of an *online* dictionary attack.

Theorem 2 (Advantage of the adversary). *The PAKE protocol P is secure, if the advantage of the adversary $\mathcal{A}$ is*

$$Adv_{\mathcal{A}}^P(\lambda) \leq C'N^{s'}(\lambda) + O\big(n_{se}Adv_D^{PWE}(\lambda) + Adv_D^{PWE}(\lambda)\big) + negl(\lambda).$$

where $N(\lambda)$ is the number of online attacks, and the password dictionary follows the Zipf-like distribution with parameter $C' = 0.062239$ and $s' = 0.155478$ [20].

Remark 3. The majority of existing PAKE schemes (e.g. [10,19]) assumed that passwords adhere to a uniformly random distribution. Thus, the advantage of the adversary $\mathcal{A}$ was formulated as $N(\lambda)/\mathcal{D} + negl(\lambda)$. However, according to

[20], the traditional uniform-model based expression significantly underestimates the power of real adversary $\mathcal{A}$. Instead, we prefer to characterize the adversary $\mathcal{A}$ using the CDF-Zipf model [29].

Proof. Our proof will proceed by introducing a series of protocols $P_0, P_1, \cdots, P_6$ (can be seen in Fig. 2) related to P, with $P_0 = P$. In P_6, $\mathcal{A}$ will be reduced to an *online* guessing attack which will provide a straightforward analysis. The detail description of each P_i can be seen in Fig. 2. A fixed adversary $\mathcal{A}$ makes n_{se}, n_{ex}, n_{ro} queries of Send, Execute and random oracles, respectively.

Corollary 1. *For any adversary $\mathcal{A}$, we have that*

$$|\mathsf{Adv}_{\mathcal{A}}^{P_1}(\lambda) - \mathsf{Adv}_{\mathcal{A}}^{P_0}(\lambda)| \leq negl(\lambda).$$

Proof. By inspection, the probability that the $\mathbf{m}$ or $\mathbf{y}_s$ has appeared in previous Send, Execute, or random oracle query is $\frac{n_{se}+n_{ex}+n_{ro}}{q^{nd}}$. Consider the newly generated value $\mathbf{m}$ or $\mathbf{y}_s$, there are $(n_{se} + n_{ex})$ values to obtain from the Send and Execute query uniquely. Therefore, the probability of the $\mathbf{m}$ or $\mathbf{y}_s$ which has been generated previously is $\frac{O((n_{se}+n_{ex})(n_{se}+n_{ex}+n_{ro}))}{q^{nd}}$, where the space of R_q^d is q^{nd}. However, this probability is negligible.   □

Corollary 2. *For any adversary $\mathcal{A}$, we have that*

$$|\mathsf{Adv}_{\mathcal{A}}^{P_2}(\lambda) - \mathsf{Adv}_{\mathcal{A}}^{P_1}(\lambda)| \leq negl(\lambda).$$

Proof. This design of P_2 is a standard technique for security analysis of protocols involving random oracles. P_1 and P_2 are indistinguishable unless the adversary makes an $H_l(\cdot)$ query, for $l \in \{2, 3, 4\}$, but the adversary has not actually made the $H_1(pw_c)$ query, the total of probability for this case can be bounded by $O(\frac{n_{ro}}{q^{nd}})$. Or the adversary makes a Send(C, i, k) (resp. Send(S, j, k')) query that is not the output of an $H_2(\cdot)$ (resp. $H_3(\cdot)$) query which would be a correct password guess. It is easy to show that the probability of this case can be bound by $O(\frac{n_{se}}{2^k})$. The corollary follows.   □

Corollary 3. *For any adversary $\mathcal{A}$, we have that*

$$|\mathsf{Adv}_{\mathcal{A}}^{P_3}(\lambda) - \mathsf{Adv}_{\mathcal{A}}^{P_2}(\lambda)| \leq negl(\lambda).$$

Proof. This can be shown using a reduction from PWE. Given $(\mathbf{A}, \mathbf{x}, \mathbf{y}, v)$, we construct an algorithm D that attempts to solve PWE assumption by running $\mathcal{A}$ on a simulation of the protocol P_2 with these changes:

(1) In an Execute query, D set $\mathbf{m} = \mathbf{x} + (\mathbf{A}\mathbf{s}_f + \mathbf{e}_f)$, $\mathbf{y}_s = \mathbf{y} + (\mathbf{A}^T\mathbf{s}_{ff} + \mathbf{e}_{ff})$ where $\mathbf{s}_f, \mathbf{e}_f, \mathbf{s}_{ff}, \mathbf{e}_{ff} \leftarrow \beta_\eta^d$, and select $v \leftarrow \{0, 1\}^n$.
(2) When $\mathcal{A}$ finishes, for every $H_l(\cdot)$ query where $l \in \{2, 3, 4\}$, $\mathbf{m}$ and $\mathbf{y}_s$ were generated in an Execute query, and an $H_1(pw_c)$ query returned $-\mathbf{\Gamma}' = \mathbf{A}\mathbf{s}_h + \mathbf{e}_h \in R_q^d$, then the simulator can compute,

$$\sigma_s = \mathbf{y}_c{}^T \cdot (\mathbf{s}_s + \mathbf{s}_{ff}) + e_\sigma = (\mathbf{x} + \mathbf{A}(\mathbf{s}_f - \mathbf{s}_h) + (\mathbf{e}_f - \mathbf{e}_h))^T \cdot (\mathbf{s}_s + \mathbf{s}_{ff}) + e_\sigma$$
$$\approx \mathbf{x}^T \cdot \mathbf{s}_s + (\mathbf{s}_f - \mathbf{s}_h)^T \cdot \mathbf{y} + (\mathbf{x} + \mathbf{A}(\mathbf{s}_f - \mathbf{s}_h) + (\mathbf{e}_f - \mathbf{e}_h))^T \cdot \mathbf{s}_{ff}$$
$$= \mathbf{x}^T \cdot \mathbf{s}_s + (\mathbf{s}_f - \mathbf{s}_h)^T \cdot \mathbf{y} + (\mathbf{x} + \mathbf{\Gamma}' + (\mathbf{A}\mathbf{s}_f + \mathbf{e}_f))^T \cdot \mathbf{s}_{ff},$$
$$k_{\sigma'} = \mathsf{Rec}(\mathbf{x}^T \cdot \mathbf{s}_s, v) = \mathsf{Rec}(\sigma_s - (\mathbf{s}_f - \mathbf{s}_h)^T \cdot \mathbf{y} - (\mathbf{x} + \mathbf{\Gamma}' + (\mathbf{A}\mathbf{s}_f + \mathbf{e}_f))^T \cdot \mathbf{s}_{ff}, v).$$

Finally, add the value of $k_{\sigma'}$ to the list of possible values. Thus, $|\mathsf{Adv}_{\mathcal{A}}^{\mathsf{P}_2}(\lambda) - \mathsf{Adv}_{\mathcal{A}}^{\mathsf{P}_3}(\lambda)| \le 2\mathsf{Adv}_D^{\mathsf{PWE}}(\lambda)$ which is negligible. □

Corollary 4. *For any adversary $\mathcal{A}$, we have that*

$$\mathsf{Adv}_{\mathcal{A}}^{\mathsf{P}_3}(\lambda) \le \mathsf{Adv}_{\mathcal{A}}^{\mathsf{P}_4}(\lambda).$$

Proof. This change will only increase the probability of $\mathcal{A}$ winning the game. □

Corollary 5. *For any adversary $\mathcal{A}$, we have that*

$$|\mathsf{Adv}_{\mathcal{A}}^{\mathsf{P}_5}(\lambda) - \mathsf{Adv}_{\mathcal{A}}^{\mathsf{P}_4}(\lambda)| \le negl(\lambda).$$

Proof. We define the event pairedpwguess that $\mathcal{A}$ makes a password guess against partnered client and server. Obviously, if the pairedpwguess event does not occur, P_4 and P_5 are indistinguishable, thus, we define the event as E with probability ϵ. If $\mathcal{A}$ attacking P_4, we have that $\Pr\left[\mathsf{Succ}_{\mathcal{A}}^{\mathsf{P}_4}(\lambda)\right] \le \Pr\left[\mathsf{Succ}_{\mathcal{A}}^{\mathsf{P}_5}(\lambda)\right] + \epsilon$, and go further, $\mathsf{Adv}_{\mathcal{A}}^{\mathsf{P}_4}(\lambda) \le \mathsf{Adv}_{\mathcal{A}}^{\mathsf{P}_5}(\lambda) + 2\epsilon$.

Now we build an algorithm D by calling $\mathcal{A}$ on a simulation of the protocol to solve the PWE assumption. Give the sample $(\mathbf{A}, \mathbf{x}, \mathbf{y}, v)$, D choose a random $m \in \{1, 2, \cdots, n_{se}\}$ and simulates P_4 for $\mathcal{A}$ as follows:

(1) In the mth $\mathsf{Send}(C, i', S)$ query to the instance $\Pi_C^{i'}$, set $\mathbf{m} = \mathbf{x}$.
(2) In a $\mathsf{Send}(S, j, \langle C, \mathbf{m}, \rho \rangle)$ query, set $\mathbf{y}_s = \mathbf{y} + (\mathbf{A}\mathbf{s}_f + \mathbf{e}_f)$ where $\mathbf{s}_f, \mathbf{e}_f \leftarrow \beta_\eta^d$.
(3) In a $\mathsf{Send}(C, i', \langle \mathbf{y}_s, v, k \rangle)$ query, if $\Pi_C^{i'}$ is unpaired, D outputs 0 and halts.
(4) In a $\mathsf{Send}(S, j, k)$ query to Π_S^j, if Π_S^j has paired with $\Pi_C^{i'}$ after its $\mathsf{Send}(S, j, \langle C, \mathbf{m}, \rho \rangle)$ query, but is not now paired with $\Pi_C^{i'}$, no test for correctpw is made, and Π_S^j aborts.
(5) When $\mathcal{A}$ finishes, for every $H_l(\cdot)$ query for $l \in \{2, 3, 4\}$, where $\mathbf{m}$ and $\mathbf{y}_s$ were generated in an $\Pi_C^{i'}$ query, and an $H_1(pw_c)$ query return $-\mathbf{\Gamma}' = \mathbf{A}\mathbf{s}_h + \mathbf{e}_h \in R_q^d$, then the simulator computes:

$$\sigma_s = \mathbf{y}_c^T \cdot (\mathbf{s}_s + \mathbf{s}_f) + e_\sigma = (\mathbf{x} - (\mathbf{A}\mathbf{s}_h + \mathbf{e}_h))^T \cdot (\mathbf{s}_s + \mathbf{s}_f) + e_\sigma$$
$$\approx \mathbf{x}^T \cdot \mathbf{s}_s - \mathbf{s}_h{}^T \cdot \mathbf{y} + (\mathbf{x} - (\mathbf{A}\mathbf{s}_h + \mathbf{e}_h))^T \cdot \mathbf{s}_f$$
$$= \mathbf{x}^T \cdot \mathbf{s}_s - \mathbf{s}_h{}^T \cdot \mathbf{y} + (\mathbf{x} + \mathbf{\Gamma}')^T \cdot \mathbf{s}_f,$$

$$k_{\sigma'} = \mathsf{Rec}(\mathbf{x}^T \cdot \mathbf{s}_s, v) = \mathsf{Rec}(\sigma_s + \mathbf{s}_h{}^T \cdot \mathbf{y} - (\mathbf{x} + \mathbf{\Gamma}')^T \cdot \mathbf{s}_f, v).$$

Finally, add the value of $k_{\sigma'}$ to the list of possible values. Thus, $|\mathsf{Adv}_{\mathcal{A}}^{\mathsf{P}_4}(\lambda) - \mathsf{Adv}_{\mathcal{A}}^{\mathsf{P}_5}(\lambda)| \le 2n_{se}\mathsf{Adv}_D^{PWE}(\lambda)$ which is negligible. □

Corollary 6. *For any adversary $\mathcal{A}$, we have that*

$$\mathsf{Adv}_{\mathcal{A}}^{\mathsf{P}_5}(\lambda) = \mathsf{Adv}_{\mathcal{A}}^{\mathsf{P}_6}(\lambda).$$

Proof. It is visible that P_5 and P_6 are perfectly indistinguishable. $\square$

Now, we analyze the advantage of $\mathcal{A}$ against the protocol P_6. In the P_6, the adversary $\mathcal{A}$ has only two ways to succeed, making online guessing attacks or making a Test query, namely. We define the event correctpw as $\mathcal{A}$ successfully obtaining the password through online dictionary attacks. Thus, the probability of the event correctpw can be bounded by $C'n_{se}^{s'}$ following the CDF-Zipf model [29].

For the second case, $\mathcal{A}$ makes a Test query to a fresh instance Π_U^i, since the view of $\mathcal{A}$ is independent of sk_U^i, the probability of success is exactly $\frac{1}{2}$. Thus,

$$\Pr[\mathsf{Succ}_{\mathcal{A}}^{\mathsf{P}_6}(\lambda)] \leq \Pr[\mathsf{correctpw}] + \Pr[\mathsf{Succ}_{\mathcal{A}}^{\mathsf{P}_6}(\lambda)|\neg\mathsf{correctpw}]\Pr[\neg\mathsf{correctpw}]$$

$$\leq C'n_{se}^{s'} + \frac{1}{2}(1 - C'n_{se}^{s'})$$

$$\leq \frac{1}{2}(1 + C'n_{se}^{s'}).$$

Then, we conclude that $\mathsf{Adv}_{\mathcal{A}}^{\mathsf{P}_6}(\lambda) = 2\Pr[\mathsf{Succ}_{\mathcal{A}}^{\mathsf{P}_6}(\lambda)] - 1 \leq C'n_{se}^{s'}$. Finally, the Theorem 2 follows from the above conclusion and corollaries from 1 to 6. $\square$

6 Implementation

This section gives all details of our implementation of MLWE-PAK written in C and describes the encoding of messages.

6.1 Parameter Selection

Table 1 lists the concrete parameter sets. In the MLWE-based protocol, the most time-consuming operation is polynomial multiplication. An efficient parameter instantiation under the MLWE problem is such that the degree n of a polynomial is a power of 2 and the modulus q is a prime satisfying the congruence condition $q \equiv 1 \bmod 2n$. At this time, the underlying finite field exists primitive $2n$-th root of unity, so that the NTT algorithm can be used efficiently to perform polynomial multiplications. Consider that public-key protocols only need to transmit 256 bits of information, we decide to fix the degree $n = 256$. Increasing or decreasing the dimension d of the vector can change the security of the scheme. We choose the modulus $q = 7681$, as 7681 is the smallest prime that satisfies the aforementioned condition so that polynomials can be transferred in NTT encoding.

For the parameters of OKCN algorithm, we choose $(m, g, l) = (2, 2^6, 1895)$. $m = 2$ means that one-bit shared-key is negotiated by one coefficient of a polynomial. The size g of the hint value per coefficient is 6, which is a comprehensive consideration of the communication cost and the error tolerance distance.

Finally, we provide 3 parameter sets to deal with distinct security scenarios by changing the dimension d of the vector and the parameter η of the error distribution. The Lightweight-PAK can resist classical attacks and be deployed in the lightweight applications. The Recommended-PAK and the Paranoid-PAK with higher security are used to resist quantum attacks.

Table 1. Proposed parameter sets

Scheme	Parameters (n, q, d, η)	Failure rate	Com. cost $\mathcal{C} \to \mathcal{S}$	$\mathcal{S} \to \mathcal{C}$
Lightweight-PAK	$(256, 7681, 2, 13)$	$2^{-53.4}$	928	1056
Recommended-PAK	$(256, 7681, 3, 8)$	$2^{-97.4}$	1,344	1,472
Paranoid-PAK	$(256, 7681, 4, 6)$	$2^{-131.6}$	1,760	1,888

6.2   NTT Domain

A polynomial multiplication can be performed by computing

$$c = \mathsf{NTT}^{-1}(\mathsf{NTT}(a) \circ \mathsf{NTT}(b))$$

where $\circ$ denotes the point-wise multiplication.

For a polynomial $p = \sum_{i=0}^{n} p_i X^i \in R_q$, we define the polynomial $\hat{p}$ in NTT domain as

$$\hat{p} = \mathsf{NTT}(p) = \sum_{i=0}^{n} \hat{p}_i X^i, \text{ where } \hat{p}_i = \sum_{j=0}^{n} \psi^j p_j \omega^{ij},$$

where we fix the primitive n-th root of unity $\omega = 3844 \in \mathbb{Z}_q$ and $\psi = \sqrt{\omega} = 62$.

As the inverse of function NTT, the computation of function NTT^{-1} uses $\omega^{-1} \bmod q = 6584$, after the summation, multiplies by powers of $\psi^{-1} \bmod q = 1115$ and multiplies each coefficient by the scalar $n^{-1} \bmod q = 7651$, so that

$$p = \mathsf{NTT}^{-1}(\hat{p}) = \sum_{i=0}^{n} p_i X^i, \text{ where } p_i = n^{-1}\psi^{-i} \sum_{j=0}^{n} \hat{p}_j \omega^{-ij}.$$

6.3   Hash Functions

In our protocol, we use 4 hash functions. Let $H_1(\cdot)$ be an extendable-output function (XOF), it extends a password pw into a polynomial vector Γ. Let $H_l(\cdot)$, $l \in \{2, 3\}$ be hash functions for verification of communications. And let $H_4(\cdot)$ be a key derivation function (KDF). We choose SHAKE-128 and SHA3-256 as our hash functions, both of them are provided by FIPS-202 [6]. We have $H_1(\cdot) = $ SHAKE-128, and $H_l(\cdot) = $ SHA3-256 where $l \in \{2, 3, 4\}$.

6.4   Generation of A

We use a 256-bit random seed ρ as the input for the generation of $\mathbf{A} = (a_{i,j}) \in R_q^{d \times d}$. For each entry $a_{i,j} \in R_q$, we expand ρ through SHAKE-128 into a stream of 16-bit little-endian integers. On the sequence of 16-bit integers, we adopt the following strategy: If an integer belongs to $\{0, 1, \ldots, q - 1\}$, we accept it as the coefficient of $a_{i,j}$; otherwise, reject it. Finally, $\mathbf{A}$ including $d \times d$ polynomials is considered to be in NTT domain, since NTT transforms uniform noise to uniform noise.

6.5   Generation of Noise Polynomials

For each noise polynomial e, we sample it from β_η. First, we extend a uniformly random seed into an array of $n = 256$ with each element of 2η-bit, and then generate the coefficient of the noise polynomial by subtracting the Hamming weight of the most significant η-bit of r_i from the Hamming weight of the least significant η-bit of r_i. Finally, the aforementioned procedure is iterated d times to generate the polynomial vector $\mathbf{e} = \{e_1, \cdots, e_d\}^T \in \beta_\eta^d$.

6.6   Encoding of Messages

An initialized message is a 3-tuple $\langle \mathcal{C}, \mathbf{m}, \rho \rangle$, where $\mathcal{C}$ denotes the client ID with $256/8 = 32$ bytes, $\mathbf{m}$ is a vector of d polynomials with 256 13-bit coefficients each, and ρ is a 32-byte seed. We compress the polynomial by the little-endian format to $(256 \times 13)/8 = 416$ bytes. Eventually, we obtain the initialized message of $(416d + 64)$ bytes by concatenating $\mathcal{C}$, compressed polynomials and the seed ρ. The response message is also a 3-tuple $\langle \mathbf{y}_s, v, k \rangle$, where $\mathbf{y}_s$ is a vector of d polynomials with 256 13-bit coefficients as well, the hint signal v is a polynomial with 256 6-bit coefficients each and the verification key k is 32-byte. We compress $\mathbf{y}_s$ by the little-endian format to $((13 \times 256)/8) \times d = 416d$ bytes, then concatenate the encoded hint signal $\mathbf{v}$ of $(256 \times 6)/8 = 192$ bytes followed the little-endian format and the verification key k, in a total of $(416d + 224)$ bytes.

7   Performance and Potential Applications

The benchmarked implementations are written in C. We compiled them with gcc-9.3.0 with optimization flags -O3 -formit-frame-pointer-march = nat ive -fPIC. Our implementations are executed on a 3.60 GHz Intel(R) Core(TM) i7-4790 CPU and 4 GB RAM computer with 64-bit system.

7.1   Comparison

Here we compare the proposed MLWE-PAKE scheme with several other competitive schemes. The comparative summary is presented in Table 2 and the performance difference is shown in Table 3.

Table 2. Properties comparison of lattice-based candidate schemes.

Scheme	Assumption	Auth. Material[a]	PQ. Security[b]	Mul.[c]	RO[d]	Flows	Error Rec.[e]
NewHope512 [1]	RLWE	×	101	NTT	-	2	D_4 [1]
NewHope1024 [1]	RLWE	×	233	NTT	-	2	D_4 [1]
Frodo [7]	LWE	×	78	FFT	-	2	Peikert [25]
Kyber-AKE-2 [8]	MLWE	Static keys	102	NTT	✓	2	-
Kyber-AKE-3 [8]	MLWE	Static keys	161	NTT	✓	2	-
Ding-PAK [10]	RLWE	Passwords	76	FFT	✓	3	Ding [11]
Ding-PPK [10]	RLWE	Passwords	76	FFT	✓	2	Ding [11]
Gao-PAK [13]	RLWE	Passwords	82	NTT	✓	3	Ding [11]
Gao-PPK [13]	RLWE	Passwords	82	NTT	✓	2	Ding [11]
Yang-PAK [30]	RLWE	Passwords	206	NTT	✓	3	AKCN [17]
Liu-3PAK [21]	RLWE	Passwords	84	NTT	✓	-	Peikert [25]
Our-LightWeight-PAK	MLWE	Passwords	116	NTT	✓	3	OKCN [17]
Our-Recommended-PAK	MLWE	Passwords	177	NTT	✓	3	OKCN [17]
Our-Paranoid-PAK	MLWE	Passwords	239	NTT	✓	3	OKCN [17]

[a] Auth. Material denotes authentication materials.
[b] PQ. Security denotes the post-quantum security level.
[c] Mul. denotes the algorithm of polynomial multiplication.
[d] RO denotes whether this protocol is constructed in the random oracle model.
[e] Error Rec. denotes the error reconciliation mechanism.

Table 2 summarizes protocols [1,7,8,10,13,21,30] and our proposals from different aspects. The majority of these lattice-based protocols are built on RLWE or MLWE, as LWE holds the unattractive feature of low performance and expensive communication cost due to the large matrix. Furthermore, to illustrate the post-quantum security level attained by various schemes, we include an estimation of core-SVP hardness using the approach described in [1]. The results show that NewHope1024, Kyber-AKE-3, Yang-PAK, Our-Recommended-PAK and Our-Paranoid-PAK achieve 128-bit post-quantum security.

Table 3 provides a comparison of our scheme with state-of-the-art lattice-based protocols [1,7,8,10,30] in the running time, the communication cost, and the failure rate. It is visible that the overall performance of our implementation outperforms other PAKE protocols. Compared with the latest Yang-PAK [30], Our-Recommended-PAK reduces the communication overhead and running time by 36.8% and 13.8%, respectively. The performance of Our-Lightweight-PAK is close to that of NewHope512, but NewHope512 does not achieve authentication. As a MLWE-based AKE scheme, the running time of Our-Recommended-PAK is 43.8% of Kyber-AKE-3's, and the communication cost is 60.7% of Kyber-AKE-3's.

7.2   Potential Applications

Resource-Constrained IoT Mobile Devices. At present, a variety of multi-factor authentication schemes [20,28] augment passwords with fingerprint or iris recognition in order to ensure the security of IoT devices. However, with the advent of quantum computing, conventional schemes based on the intractability of the integer factorization problem and the discrete logarithm problem will be insecure. As shown in Table 3, our **Lightweight-PAK** scheme with the advantage of lower communication cost and higher performance is more effectively that can be used to connect resource-constrained IoT devices to resource-rich servers.

Table 3. Performance comparison of lattice-based candidate schemes (us)

Scheme	Running time (us)				Message size ($bytes$)			Failure
	C_{init}	$S_{resp} + S_{fin}$	C_{fin}	Total	$Client$	$Server$	Total	Rate
NewHope512 [1]	46.089	55.630	60.639	162.358	928	960	1 888	$2^{-55.0}$
NewHope1024 [1]	77.778	108.325	122.772	308.875	1 824	2 048	3 872	$2^{-61.4}$
Frodo [7]	790.013	870.856	107.419	1 768.288	11 296	11 288	22 584	$2^{-38.9}$
Kyber-AKE-2 [8]	81.920	150.490	115.200	347.610	1 568	1 664	3 232	2^{-145}
Kyber-AKE-3 [8]	134.362	268.716	173.876	576.954	2 272	2 368	4 640	2^{-142}
Ding-PAK [10]	2 643.838	2 884.243	337.413	6 702.656	4 136	4 256	8 392	2^{-1023}
Gao-PAK [13]	–	–	–	–	3 904	4 000	7 904	2^{-1023}
Yang-PAK [30]	84.172	144.290	64.859	293.321	1 864	2 592	4 456	2^{-41}
Our-Lightweight-PAK	55.202	93.353	34.558	183.113	928	1 056	1 984	$2^{-53.4}$
Our-Recommended-PAK	79.141	126.048	47.565	252.754	1 344	1 472	2 816	$2^{-97.4}$
Our-Paranoid-PAK	113.891	169.524	61.082	344.497	1 760	1 888	3 648	$2^{-131.6}$

[a] C_{init} denotes the running time of the client initiation.
[b] $S_{resp} + S_{fin}$ denotes the running time of the server response and the server finish.
[c] C_{fin} denotes the running time of the client finish.

Classical/Quantum-Safe TLS. We consider that TLS should be combined with post-quantum cryptographic primitives since TLS has taken over more than half of web traffic and has been widely deployed with applications such as HTTPS, IMAPS, SMTPS in the real world. As a self-contained system, our MLWE-PAK is designed without additional primitives, which are typically prohibitively expensive in specific applications such as public-key encryption, signatures, or message authentication code. In Table 3, although our Lightweight-PAK has 116-bit post-quantum security, it has 128-bit security against the classical attacks according to the approach from [1]. Therefore, our **Lightweight-PAK** can be deployed in current TLS to resist classical attacks; our **Recommended-PAK** and **Paranoid-PAK** with higher security can be deployed in TLS to resist quantum attacks.

8   Conclusion

The advancement of quantum computing has sparked widely interest in the research of post-quantum cryptography. This paper designed an efficient post-quantum MLWE-based PAKE protocol whose security is demonstrated under the BPR framework. Moreover, benefiting from the flexibility of MLWE, we provided 3 parameter sets and discussed corresponding potential applications (e.g., classic/post-quantum TLS, resource-constrained IoT devices) in real life. Compared with the latest Yang-PAK [30], Our-Recommended-PAK reduces the communication overhead and running time by 36.8% and 13.8%, respectively.

One of our follow-up works will be aimed at integrating our MLWE-PAKE protocol into TLS. In addition, optimizing the implementation of our MLWE-PAKE protocol on embedded microcontrollers is especially useful for IoT applications once the quantum era comes.

References

1. Alkim, E., Ducas, L., Pöppelmann, T., Schwabe, P.: Post-quantum key exchange - a new hope. In: 25th USENIX Security Symposium (USENIX Security 16), pp. 327–343 (2016). https://www.usenix.org/conference/usenixsecurity16/technical-sessions/presentation/alkim
2. Bellare, M., Pointcheval, D., Rogaway, P.: Authenticated key exchange secure against dictionary attacks. In: Preneel, B. (ed.) EUROCRYPT 2000. LNCS, vol. 1807, pp. 139–155. Springer, Heidelberg (2000). https://doi.org/10.1007/3-540-45539-6_11
3. Bellovin, S.M., Merritt, M.: Encrypted key exchange: password-based protocols secure against dictionary attacks. In: Proceedings of the 1992 IEEE Symposium on Security and Privacy, p. 72 (1992). https://doi.org/10.1109/RISP.1992.213269
4. Bellovin, S.M., Merritt, M.: Augmented encrypted key exchange: a password-based protocol secure against dictionary attacks and password file compromise. In: Proceedings of the 1st ACM Conference on Computer and Communications Security, pp. 244–250 (1993). https://doi.org/10.1145/168588.168618
5. Benhamouda, F., Pointcheval, D.: Verifier-based password-authenticated key exchange: new models and constructions. IACR Cryptol. ePrint Arch. 2013, 833 (2013). https://eprint.iacr.org/2013/833.pdf
6. Bernstein, D.J., Schwabe, P., Assche, G.: Tweetable fips 202, 2015 (2015). http://keccak.noekeon.org/tweetfips202.html
7. Bos, J., et al.: Frodo: take off the ring! Practical, quantum-secure key exchange from LWE. In: Proceedings of the 2016 ACM SIGSAC Conference on Computer and Communications Security, pp. 1006–1018 (2016). https://dl.acm.org/doi/abs/10.1145/2976749.2978425
8. Bos, J., et al.: CRYSTALS-Kyber: a CCA-secure module-lattice-based KEM. In: 2018 IEEE European Symposium on Security and Privacy (EuroS&P), pp. 353–367. IEEE (2018). https://ieeexplore.ieee.org/abstract/document/8406610
9. Brakerski, Z., Gentry, C., Vaikuntanathan, V.: (Leveled) fully homomorphic encryption without bootstrapping. ACM Trans. Comput. Theory (TOCT) $\mathbf{6}(3)$, 1–36 (2014). https://dl.acm.org/doi/abs/10.1145/2633600
10. Ding, J., Alsayigh, S., Lancrenon, J., RV, S., Snook, M.: Provably secure password authenticated key exchange based on RLWE for the post-quantum world. In: Handschuh, H. (ed.) CT-RSA 2017. LNCS, vol. 10159, pp. 183–204. Springer, Cham (2017). https://doi.org/10.1007/978-3-319-52153-4_11
11. Ding, J., Xie, X., Lin, X.: A simple provably secure key exchange scheme based on the learning with errors problem. IACR Cryptol. ePrint Arch. 2012, 688 (2012). https://citeseerx.ist.psu.edu/viewdoc/download?doi=10.1.1.638.6793&rep=rep1&type=pdf
12. D'Anvers, J.-P., Karmakar, A., Sinha Roy, S., Vercauteren, F.: Saber: module-LWR based key exchange, CPA-secure encryption and CCA-secure KEM. In: Joux, A., Nitaj, A., Rachidi, T. (eds.) AFRICACRYPT 2018. LNCS, vol. 10831, pp. 282–305. Springer, Cham (2018). https://doi.org/10.1007/978-3-319-89339-6_16

13. Gao, X., Ding, J., Li, L., Saraswathy, R., Liu, J.: Efficient implementation of password-based authenticated key exchange from RLWE and post-quantum TLS. IACR Cryptol. ePrint Arch. 2017, 1192 (2017). https://eprint.iacr.org/2017/1192.pdf
14. Gennaro, R., Lindell, Y.: A framework for password-based authenticated key exchange. In: Biham, E. (ed.) EUROCRYPT 2003. LNCS, vol. 2656, pp. 524–543. Springer, Heidelberg (2003). https://doi.org/10.1007/3-540-39200-9_33
15. Groce, A., Katz, J.: A new framework for efficient password-based authenticated key exchange. In: Proceedings of the 17th ACM Conference on Computer and Communications Security, pp. 516–525 (2010). https://dl.acm.org/doi/abs/10.1145/1866307.1866365
16. Grover, L.K.: A fast quantum mechanical algorithm for database search. In: Proceedings of the Twenty-Eighth Annual ACM Symposium on Theory of Computing, pp. 212–219 (1996). https://dl.acm.org/doi/pdf/10.1145/237814.237866
17. Jin, Z., Zhao, Y.: Optimal key consensus in presence of noise. arXiv preprint arXiv:1611.06150 (2016). https://arxiv.org/abs/1611.06150
18. Katz, J., Ostrovsky, R., Yung, M.: Efficient password-authenticated key exchange using human-memorable passwords. In: Pfitzmann, B. (ed.) EUROCRYPT 2001. LNCS, vol. 2045, pp. 475–494. Springer, Heidelberg (2001). https://doi.org/10.1007/3-540-44987-6_29
19. Katz, J., Vaikuntanathan, V.: Round-optimal password-based authenticated key exchange. In: Ishai, Y. (ed.) TCC 2011. LNCS, vol. 6597, pp. 293–310. Springer, Heidelberg (2011). https://doi.org/10.1007/978-3-642-19571-6_18
20. Li, Z., Wang, D.: Achieving one-round password-based authenticated key exchange over lattices. IEEE Trans. Serv. Comput. (2019). https://ieeexplore.ieee.org/abstract/document/8826379
21. Liu, C., Zheng, Z., Jia, K., You, Q.: Provably secure three-party password-based authenticated key exchange from RLWE. In: Heng, S.-H., Lopez, J. (eds.) ISPEC 2019. LNCS, vol. 11879, pp. 56–72. Springer, Cham (2019). https://doi.org/10.1007/978-3-030-34339-2_4
22. MacKenzie, P.: The PAK suite: protocols for password-authenticated key exchange. In: IEEE P1363. 2. Citeseer (2002). https://citeseerx.ist.psu.edu/viewdoc/summary?doi=10.1.1.20.5299
23. NIST post-quantum cryptography round 3 submissions. https://csrc.nist.gov/projects/post-quantum-cryptography/round-3-submissions. Accessed 23 Dec 2020
24. NSA: NSA suite B cryptography. https://www.nsa.gov/ia/programs/suiteb_cryptography/. Accessed 19 Aug 2015
25. Peikert, C.: Lattice cryptography for the internet. In: Mosca, M. (ed.) PQCrypto 2014. LNCS, vol. 8772, pp. 197–219. Springer, Cham (2014). https://doi.org/10.1007/978-3-319-11659-4_12
26. Shirvanian, M., Saxena, N., Jarecki, S., Krawczyk, H.: Building and studying a password store that perfectly hides passwords from itself. IEEE Trans. Dependable Secure Comput. 16(5), 770–782 (2019). https://ieeexplore.ieee.org/abstract/document/8667308
27. Shor, P.W.: Algorithms for quantum computation: discrete logarithms and factoring. In: Proceedings 35th Annual Symposium on Foundations of Computer Science, pp. 124–134 (1994). https://ieeexplore.ieee.org/abstract/document/365700
28. Srinivas, J., Das, A.K., Wazid, M., Kumar, N.: Anonymous lightweight chaotic map-based authenticated key agreement protocol for industrial internet of things. IEEE Trans. Dependable Secure Comput. 17(6), 1133–1146 (2018). https://ieeexplore.ieee.org/abstract/document/8413130

156   P. Ren and X. Gu

29. Wang, D., Cheng, H., Wang, P., Huang, X., Jian, G.: Zipf's law in passwords. IEEE Trans. Inf. Forensics Secur. **12**(11), 2776–2791 (2017). https://ieeexplore.ieee.org/abstract/document/7961213
30. Yang, Y., Gu, X., Wang, B., Xu, T.: Efficient password-authenticated key exchange from RLWE based on asymmetric key consensus. In: Liu, Z., Yung, M. (eds.) Inscrypt 2019. LNCS, vol. 12020, pp. 31–49. Springer, Cham (2020). https://doi.org/10.1007/978-3-030-42921-8_2
31. Zhang, Y., Xu, C., Li, H., Yang, K., Cheng, N., Shen, X.S.: PROTECT: efficient password-based threshold single-sign-on authentication for mobile users against perpetual leakage. IEEE Trans. Mob. Comput. **20**, 2297–2312 (2020). https://ieeexplore.ieee.org/abstract/document/9007394
32. Zhang, Z., Yang, K., Hu, X., Wang, Y.: Practical anonymous password authentication and TLS with anonymous client authentication. In: Proceedings of the 2016 ACM SIGSAC Conference on Computer and Communications Security, pp. 1179–1191 (2016). https://dl.acm.org/doi/abs/10.1145/2976749.2978354

Security Analysis

Improved Lattice Enumeration Algorithms by Primal and Dual Reordering Methods

Kazuki Yamamura[1], Yuntao Wang[2(✉)] (iD), and Eiichiro Fujisaki[3]

[1] NTT Social Informatics Laboratories, Tokyo, Japan
kazuki.yamamura.by@iecl.ntt.co.jp
[2] Graduate School of Engineering, Osaka University, Osaka, Japan
wang@comm.eng.osaka-u.ac.jp
[3] School of Information Science, Japan Advanced Institute of Science
and Technology, Nomi, Japan
fujisaki@jaist.ac.jp

Abstract. The security of lattice-based cryptosystems is generally based on the hardness of the Shortest Vector Problem (SVP). There are two common categories of lattice algorithms to solve SVP: search algorithms and reduction algorithms. The original enumeration algorithm (ENUM) is one of the former algorithms which run in exponential time due to the exhaustive search. Further, ENUM is used as a subroutine for the BKZ algorithm, which is one of the most practical reduction algorithms. It is a critical issue to reduce the computational complexity of ENUM. In this paper, first, we improve the mechanism in the so-called reordering method proposed by Wang in ACISP 2018. We call this improvement Primal Projective Reordering (PPR) method which permutates the projected vectors by decreasing norms; therefore it performs better to reduce the number of search nodes in ENUM. Then, we propose a Dual Projective Reordering (DPR) method permutating the projected vectors in its dual lattice. In addition, we propose a condition to decide whether the reordering method should be adopted or not. Preliminary experimental results show that our proposed reordering methods can successfully reduce the number of ENUM search nodes comparing to the predecessor, e.g., PPR reduces around 9.6% on average in 30-dimensional random lattices, and DPR reduces around 32.8% on average in 45-dimensional random lattices. Moreover, our simulation shows that the higher the lattice dimension, the more the proposed reordering method can reduce ENUM search nodes.

Keywords: Lattice cryptography · Enumeration algorithm · Reordering method · Dual lattice

1 Intruduction

1.1 Background

Cryptosystems such as RSA [13] and ECC [9,11] are currently used to protect private information, relying on hard mathematical problems like integer factoring

© The Author(s), under exclusive license to Springer Nature Switzerland AG 2022
J. H. Park and S.-H. Seo (Eds.): ICISC 2021, LNCS 13218, pp. 159–174, 2022.
https://doi.org/10.1007/978-3-031-08896-4_8

problem (IFP) and discrete logarithm problem (DLP). However, if a quantum computer is developed in the near future, it can be compromised by quantum algorithms such as Shor's algorithm [16], which can solve IFP and DLP in polynomial time. Therefore, we need to move forward with post-quantum cryptography (PQC) as soon as possible. Hence NIST officially started PQC standardization project in 2016 and announced third round PQC candidates in 2020, including four public key cryptography (CRYSTALS-KYBER, NTRU, SABER, and Classic McEliece) and three digital signature schemes (CRYSTALS-DILITHIUM, FALCON, Rainbow). Among these candidates, around 70% are lattice-based cryptosystems [1]. At the evaluating stage, cryptanalysis is essential to work. Namely, it is necessary to decide on secure and practical parameters. The security of lattice-based cryptography such as NTRU [8] and LWE-based schemes [12] depend on the hardness of some lattice problems, such as SVP, CVP, and their variants. The analysis of the concrete hardness of these problems is essential to decide the proper parameter settings. In particular, TU Darmstadt published open problems called the lattice challenge [5] to analyze the practical hardness of lattice problems. In order to evaluate our proposed methods, We utilize a random lattice provided by the lattice challenge.

Various algorithms for SVP have been proposed, and they can be classified into two main categories. First, there are lattice basis reduction algorithms, which convert a bad basis of a lattice into a good one, such as LLL reduction (Lenstra-Lenstra-Lovász) reduction and BKZ (block Korkin-Zolotarev) reduction [3,4,15]. LLL reduction is a remarkable lattice reduction that runs in polynomial time; therefore, we often use the LLL reduction to get a good basis before using other algorithms to solve hard lattice problems. In our experiments, we use LLL reduction, which is implemented in the open-source library NTL [17].

BKZ reduction, proposed by Schnorr and Euchner, was a hybrid LLL reduction and ENUM algorithms that finds the shortest vector of a lattice. Given a lattice basis and a block size parameter β, BKZ reduction reduced the block size lattice basis by the LLL reduction before inputting them into ENUM iteratively. Since the complexity of ENUM is much larger than LLL reduction, the complexity of BKZ reduction depends on ENUM.

Second, lattice point search algorithms such as ENUM [15] and Sieve [2]. ENUM proposed in the same paper of BKZ reduction is an exhaustive search method that finds the shortest lattice vector by the depth-first search in a tree constructed with nodes labeled by coefficients. The complexity of ENUM is $2^{O(n^2)}$ for a given n-dimensional lattice basis. As mentioned above, the BKZ reduction depends on the complexity of ENUM; therefore, we can see that it is important to work to reduce the complexity of ENUM for BKZ reduction.

The sieve algorithm proposed by Ajtai is well-known lattice point search algorithms, which requires a runtime of $2^{0.292n+O(n)}$ and exponential memory of $2^{0.2n+(n)}$ in lattice dimension n.

Quick reordering technique (QRT) [18,19] is an initial reordering method applied in lattice reduction. QRT reorders the output reduced basis vectors by their decreasing norm, which is applied in BKZ reduction to reduce the number of search nodes in ENUM by a certain probability.

1.2 Our Contribution

The BKZ, one of the lattice basis reductions, is one of the most powerful algo-rithms known today. The runtime of the BKZ depends on the complexity of a subroutine called ENUM, an enumeration search algorithm. In other words, reducing the runtime of ENUM leads to reducing that of the BKZ, which is expected to bring us much closer to the SVP solution. In this paper, we examine how much the runtime of ENUM can be reduced by changing the order of the input basis into ENUM, using the properties of projective and dual lattices. Our contributions are as follows:

1. improving the previous reordering method using the property of projected lattice;
2. proposing a reordering method using the property of dual lattice;
3. proposing condition to decide whether the reordering method should be adopted or not.

Our experimental results show that the proposed improvement method for the previous method, named **PPR**, can reduce around 9.6% on average in 30-dimensional random lattices and that the proposed reordering method using the property of dual lattice, named **DPR**, can successfully reduce the large number of ENUM search nodes, e.g., reducing around 32.8% on average in 45-dimensional random lattices. Moreover, we experimentally show that DPR overcomes the QRT weakness that the reduction of the search node number decreases as the dimension increase and can increase the reduction as the dimension increase.

1.3 Organization

We introduce mathematical backgrounds in Sect. 2 and the details of some clas-sic lattice algorithms and the quick reordering technique (QRT), which is invited to improve ENUM in Sect. 3. In Sect. 4, we propose our new reordering methods, which are called PPR and DPR, and condition t_R to decide whether the reorder-ing method should be adopted or not. We then present the experimental results on our proposed method in Sect. 5. Finally, the conclusion is given in Sect. 6.

2 Preliminaries

Given n linearly independent vectors $\mathbf{B} := (\mathbf{b}_1, \cdots, \mathbf{b}_n) \in \mathbb{R}^m$, the lattice gen-erated by them is defined as $L(\mathbf{b}_1, \ldots, \mathbf{b}_n) := \{\sum_{i=1}^n v_i \mathbf{b}_i \mid v_i \in \mathbb{Z}\}$. Here, n is the rank of L, and m is the dimension of L. If n=m, L is called a full-rank lattice. The fundamental domain of L corresponding to this basis $\mathbf{B}$ is the set $P(L) := \{\sum_{i=1}^n x_i \mathbf{b}_i \mid 0 \leq x_i < 1\}$ called the fundamental parallelepiped of L. $vol(P(L))$ is called the volume of a lattice L which depends on the basis $\mathbf{B}$.

Shortest Vector Problem (SVP). A lattice L has at least nonzero shortest vectors. The Shortest Vector Problem (SVP) is to find one shortest nonzero vector of L given the basis B of lattice L, which is expected to be very difficult to solve in polynomial time.

Gram-Schmidt Orthogonalization (GSO). Gram-Schmidt Orthogonalization (GSO) is a classic procedure in linear algebra that creates a set of orthogonal vectors given a set of linearly independent vectors. It works by projecting each vector on the space orthogonal to the span of the previous vectors in order from front to front of linearly independent vectors. Note that on changing the order of the inputs of linearly independent vectors, Gram-Schmidt Orthogonalization outputs different orthogonal vectors. We denote by $\mathbf{B}^* = (\mathbf{b}_1^*, \cdots, \mathbf{b}_n^*)$ Gram-Schmidt orthogonal vector (GSO vectors) of the given lattice basis $\mathbf{B} = (\mathbf{b}_1, \cdots \mathbf{b}_n)$. The GSO vectors of a linearly independent vectors $\mathbf{B}$ in order from front to front can be computed as follows:

$$
\begin{cases}
\mathbf{b}_1^* := \mathbf{b}_1 \\
\mathbf{b}_i^* := \mathbf{b}_i - \displaystyle\sum_{j=1}^{i-1} \mu_{i,j} \mathbf{b}_j^* \ (2 \leq i \leq n)
\end{cases}
$$

where

$$
\mu_{i,j} := \frac{\langle \mathbf{b}_i, \mathbf{b}_j^* \rangle}{\|\mathbf{b}_j^*\|^2} \ (1 \leq j < i \leq n)
$$

and let $\langle \cdot, \cdot \rangle : \mathbb{R}^m \times \mathbb{R}^m \to \mathbb{R}$ to be inner product.

The GSO vector of a linearly independent vectors $\mathbf{B}$ in order from back to front can be computed as follows

$$
\begin{cases}
\mathbf{b}_n^\dagger := \mathbf{b}_n \\
\mathbf{b}_i^\dagger := \mathbf{b}_i - \displaystyle\sum_{j=n}^{i+1} \nu_{i,j} \mathbf{b}_j^\dagger \ (1 \leq i \leq n-1)
\end{cases}
$$

where

$$
\nu_{i,j} := \frac{\langle \mathbf{b}_i, \mathbf{b}_j^\dagger \rangle}{\|\mathbf{b}_j^\dagger\|^2} \ (1 \leq i < j \leq n)
$$

Note that the volume of $L(\mathbf{B})$ can also be computed by $vol(L(\mathbf{B})) = \prod_{i=1}^n \|\mathbf{b}_i^*\|$. For any $1 \leq i \leq n$, let $\pi_i : \mathbb{R}^n \to span_{\mathbb{R}}(\mathbf{b}_1, \cdots, \mathbf{b}_{i-1})^\perp$ be an orthogonal projection of a vector onto $span_{\mathbb{R}}(\mathbf{b}_1, \cdots, \mathbf{b}_{i-1})^\perp$. We also denote by $\pi_i(L)$ a projective sublattice with basis vectors of $(\pi_i(\mathbf{b}_i), \ldots, \pi_i(\mathbf{b}_n))$.

Dual Lattice. We define the notation of the dual of a lattice and see its applications. We denote the dual lattice of L by $\hat{L} := \{\mathbf{x} \in span_{\mathbb{R}}(L) \mid \langle \mathbf{x}, \mathbf{y} \rangle \in \mathbb{Z} \ (\forall \mathbf{y} \in L)\}$, where let $\langle \cdot, \cdot \rangle : \mathbb{R}^m \times \mathbb{R}^m \to \mathbb{R}$ to be inner product. If $\mathbf{D} := (\mathbf{d}_1, \cdots, \mathbf{d}_n)$ is the basis of a dual lattice $\hat{L}(\mathbf{B})$ then $\mathbf{D} = (\mathbf{B}\mathbf{B}^T)^{-1}\mathbf{B}$. A dual lattice has good properties: let $\{\mathbf{b}_1^*, \cdots, \mathbf{b}_n^*\}$ be GSO vectors of lattice basis $\mathbf{B}$ and let

$\{\mathbf{d}_1^\dagger, \cdots, \mathbf{d}_n^\dagger\}$ be GSO vectors of dual lattice basis $\mathbf{D}$ in reverse order, then for all i,

$$\|\mathbf{b}_i^*\| \cdot \|\mathbf{d}_i^\dagger\| = 1.$$

The properties of the dual lattice have been applied to attacks to lattice cryptography [6,10]. Our proposed algorithm also uses the properties of a dual lattice.

Gaussian Heuristic. Given a lattice L and a continuous subset C of $\mathbb{R}$, we can estimate the number of points in $C \cap L$ approximately $vol(C)/vol(L)$, which is called the Gaussian heuristic. Using Gaussian heuristic, We can estimate the shortest lattice vector norm approximately, denoted by $GH(L) := \sqrt{\frac{n}{2\pi e}} vol(L)^{\frac{1}{n}}$.

Geometric Series Assumption (GSA). The geometric assumption (GSA) [14] says that the norms of GSO vectors $\|\mathbf{b}_i^*\|$ in the LLL-reduced basis decline geometrically with quotient q such as $\|\mathbf{b}_i^*\|^2/\|\mathbf{b}_{i-1}^*\|^2 = q$ for $i = 1, \cdots, n$ and $q \in [3/4, 1)$ Here, q is called the GSA constant, whose size depends on the reduction algorithm and the corresponding parameter setting.

3 Lattice Algorithms

This section introduces some classic lattice algorithms, such as the LLL basis reduction algorithm, the enumeration search algorithm (ENUM), and the BKZ algorithm [15]. Furthermore, we recall the quick reordering technique (QRT), which is invited to improve the previous algorithms.

3.1 LLL Reduction

The LLL reduction, an approximation algorithm to SVP, was developed in 1982 by A.K.Lenstra, J.W.Lenstra, Jr., and L.Lovasz. Given a lattice basis and a parameter $3/4 < \delta_{LLL} < 1$, LLL reduction repeats size reduction and the swap of basis neighbors until the basis is a good one which means nearly orthogonal. Note that the closer δ_{LLL} is to one, the better the LLL-reduced basis is. Since LLL reduction terminates in the polynomial time, it is applied to many attacks on cryptosystems.

3.2 ENUM

We describe Schnorr-Euchner's enumeration algorithm (**ENUM**) [15] associated with our proposal algorithms. Given a lattice basis $\mathbf{B} = (\mathbf{b}_1, \cdots, \mathbf{b}_n)$, the inputs of the ENUM are GSO coefficients $(\mu_{i,j})_{1 \le j \le i \le n}$, the square norms $\{\|\mathbf{b}_1^*\|, \cdots, \|\mathbf{b}_n^*\|\}$ of $\mathbf{B}^*$ and search bound R which is usually $GH(L) \times 1.05$. The output is one shortest vector $\mathbf{v} = \sum_{i=1}^n u_i \mathbf{b}_i$, where $\{u_i\}_{i=1}^n$ is the set of integer coefficients that ENUM searches.

ENUM performs the depth-first search of the ENUM tree formed by half vectors in the projected lattice $\pi_n(L), \pi_{n-1}(L), \cdots, \pi_1(L)$ within the norm bound R. The depth of the ENUM tree is equal to the lattice dimension n. For $0 \le k \le n$,

Algorithm 1. Quick Reordering Technique (QRT)

Input: A basis $\{\mathbf{b}_1, \cdots, \mathbf{b}_n\}$, index q'_n
Output: A basis $\{\mathbf{b}_1, \cdots, \mathbf{b}_n\}$
1: **if** $n \geq 10$ **then**
2:    *Compute the slope q_{curr} of current GSO vector lengths by LSF.*
3:    **if** $q_{curr} < q'_n$ **then**
4:        $\{\mathbf{b}'_1, \cdots, \mathbf{b}'_n\} \leftarrow Normal\ Reordering(\{\mathbf{b}_1, \cdots, \mathbf{b}_n\})$
5:        *Compute AveGSO and AveGSO'*
6:        **if** $AveGSO \leq AveGSO'$ **then**
7:            $\{\mathbf{b}_1, \cdots, \mathbf{b}_n\} \leftarrow \{\mathbf{b}'_1, \cdots, \mathbf{b}'_n\}$
8:            *Compute GSO information.*
9:        **end if**
10:   **end if**
11: **end if**

---

the nodes at depth k are half of the number of the vectors in the rank-k projected lattice $\pi_{n+1-k}(L)$ with norm $\leq R$. Therefore The Gaussian heuristic estimates of the number of nodes at depth k as:

$$H_k(R) := \frac{1}{2} \cdot \frac{vol(B_k(R))}{vol(\pi_{n+1-k}(L))} = \frac{1}{2} \cdot \frac{vol(B_k(R))}{\prod_{i=n+1-k}^{n} \|\mathbf{b}_i^*\|}$$

where $B_k(R)$ is the k-dimensional Euclidean ball of radius R centered around 0. Then the total number of search nodes in ENUM is approximately $N = \sum_{k=1}^{n} H_k(R) = \frac{1}{2} \cdot \sum_{k=1}^{n} \frac{vol(B_k(R))}{\prod_{i=n+1-k}^{n} \|\mathbf{b}_i^*\|}$. From [7], $H_k(R)$ is maximal around the middle depth $k \simeq n/2$ (see an example of 30-dimension in Fig. 2).

3.3 BKZ Reduction

The BKZ reduction is a powerful lattice reduction algorithm [3,4,15]. Given a lattice basis, one sets a proper blocksize $\beta \geq 2$ on which both the runtime and the output quality depend. Assuming that j is the first index of each local block $B_{j,min(j+\beta-1,n)}$, BKZ reduction iteratively performs the LLL reduction and the ENUM on each local block for j from 1 to $n-1$. Note that the ENUM subroutine is the most expensive part of the BKZ reduction. Therefore it is important to decrease the total number of search nodes in ENUM in order to reduce the runtime of BKZ reduction.

3.4 Quick Reordering Technique

The Quick Reordering Technique (QRT) [18,19] is a reordering method to reduce the runtime of the BKZ using ENUM as subroutines. Using a quick sort to reorder the input basis vectors by their decreasing norms (in this paper, we call this operation **Normal Reordering (NR)**. QRT can decrease the number of search nodes in ENUM with high probability both when the GSA assumption [14] does not hold and when the average of $\|\mathbf{b}^*_{\lfloor n/2 \rfloor - 1}\|$, $\|\mathbf{b}^*_{\lfloor n/2 \rfloor}\|$, $\|\mathbf{b}^*_{\lfloor n/2 \rfloor + 1}\|$ is bent larger after reordering the basis.

We show the QRT algorithm in Algorithm 1. The first step is to decide whether the basis is a good basis, i.e., nearly orthogonal. To do this, we calculate the constant q under the GSA assumption in the input basis using the least-squares method (LSF). LSF is a method frequently used in regression analysis. Given n points $\{(x_i, y_i) \mid 1 \le i \le n\}$, find the line $y = ax + b$ that minimizes the distance between these points. Specifically, it can be obtained by $a = \frac{\sum_{i=1}^{n} x_i\, y_i - n \cdot \bar{x}\, \bar{y}}{\sum_{i=1}^{n} n x_i^2 - n \cdot (\bar{x})^2}$ and $b = \bar{y} - a$. If $q_{curr} = a$ and $q_{curr} < q'_n$, i.e., the basis is judged to be bad, It calculates the GSO of $\{\mathbf{b}'_1, \cdots, \mathbf{b}'_n\}$ that is Normal Reordered and obtains vectors $\{\mathbf{b}'^*_1, \cdots, \mathbf{b}'^*_n\}$ before getting $AveGSO$ such that

$$AveGSO := \frac{\|\mathbf{b}^*_{\lfloor n/2 \rfloor - 1}\| + \|\mathbf{b}^*_{\lfloor n/2 \rfloor}\| + \|\mathbf{b}^*_{\lfloor n/2 \rfloor + 1}\|}{3}$$

If $AveGSO < AveGSO'$ holds, we decide that the number of search nodes in ENUM is less for $\{\mathbf{b}'_1, \cdots, \mathbf{b}'_n\}$ than for $\{\mathbf{b}_1, \cdots, \mathbf{b}_n\}$ and thus we set $\{\mathbf{b}'_1, \cdots, \mathbf{b}'_n\}$ to be ENUM input. The reason why we consider the ENUM to be less computationally intensive when $AveGSO < AveGSO'$ is that the number of search nodes in ENUM is highest around $\lfloor \frac{n}{2} \rfloor$ and the surrounding GSO vector norm is large, the number of search nodes can decrease.

It has been pointed out that QRT can efficiently reduce the total ENUM runtime up to about 30 dimensions of the lattice, but the reduction decreases as the dimensionality increases.

4 Our Proposals

In this section, we propose two methods to decrease the number of search nodes N in ENUM. Recall that $N \approx \sum_{k=1}^{n} \frac{vol(B_k(R))}{\prod_{i=n-k+1}^{n} \|\mathbf{b}^*_i\|}$, which depends on the input basis. By enlarging the back half of the GSO vectors' norm, it is possible to decrease the number of search nodes in the ENUM process. Note that because the lattice volume is invariant, the shorter the front half of the GSO vectors' norm, the longer the back half of the GSO vectors' norm. In this paper, we propose two lattice basis reordering methods with the following strategies.

1. Shorten the former half of the GSO vectors' norm, which correspondingly lengthens the latter half of the GSO vectors' norm;
2. Directly lengthen the back half of the GSO vectors' norm.

Primal Projective Reordering (PPR) introduced in Sect. 4.1 is based on the former strategy, while **Dual Projective Reordering (DPR)** introduced in Sect. 4.2 is based on the latter strategy.

4.1 Primal Projective Reordring

First, we describe the Primal Projective Reordering (PPR) method to decrease the number of search nodes in ENUM by shortening the former half of the input

Algorithm 2. Primal Projective Reordering (PPR)

Input: A basis $\{\mathbf{b}_1, \ldots, \mathbf{b}_n\} \in \mathbb{R}^m$

Output: A basis $\{\mathbf{b}_1, \cdots, \mathbf{b}_n\} \in \mathbb{R}^m$ such that $\forall i \in \{1, \cdots, n\}$, $\|\mathbf{b}_i^*\| = \min_{i \leq j \leq n} \|\pi_i(\mathbf{b}_j)\|$

1: $(\mathbf{b}_0^*, \mathbf{b}_1^*, \cdots, \mathbf{b}_n^*) \leftarrow (\mathbf{0}, \mathbf{b}_1, \cdots, \mathbf{b}_n)$;
2: $(B_{-1}, B_0, B_1, \cdots, B_n) \leftarrow (\infty, 1, \|\mathbf{b}_1\|^2, \cdots, \|\mathbf{b}_n\|^2)$;
3: **for** $i = 1$ to $n - 1$ **do**
4:     $k \leftarrow -1$
5:     **for** $j = i$ to n **do**
6:         $t \leftarrow \langle \mathbf{b}_j, \mathbf{b}_{i-1}^* \rangle$;
7:         $\mathbf{b}_j^* \leftarrow \mathbf{b}_j^* - \frac{t}{B_{i-1}} \mathbf{b}_{i-1}^*$;
8:         $B_j \leftarrow B_j - \frac{t^2}{B_{i-1}}$;
9:         **if** $B_k > B_j$ **then**
10:             $k \leftarrow j$;
11:         **end if**
12:     **end for**
13:     Swap$(\mathbf{b}_i, \mathbf{b}_k)$;
14: **end for**

GSO vectors' norm. As a result, the latter half of the GSO vectors' norm become larger. This strategy is similar to the previous study [18, 19], Normal Reordering (NR) method, which directly reorders the input basis vectors by decreasing norm. Specifically, in PPR method, we move the shortest basis vector to ahead, and move the vector whose projective norm onto $\mathbf{b}_1$ is the shortest in the projected sublattice $\pi_1(L)$. Then we repeat this procedure and get a reordered basis. PPR can be regarded as an improved version of NR method.

We denote by $\mathbf{B} := \{\mathbf{b}_1, \cdots, \mathbf{b}_n\}$ the lattice basis and by $\{\mathbf{b}_1^*, \cdots, \mathbf{b}_n^*\}$ the GSO vectors of $\mathbf{B}$. Then the PPR changes the lattice basis order such that

$$\|\mathbf{b}_1^*\| = \min\{\|\mathbf{b}_1\|, \cdots, \|\mathbf{b}_n\|\}$$
$$\|\mathbf{b}_2^*\| = \min\{\|\pi_2(\mathbf{b}_2)\|, \cdots, \|\pi_2(\mathbf{b}_n)\|\}$$
$$\vdots$$
$$\|\mathbf{b}_{n-1}^*\| = \min\{\|\pi_{n-1}(\mathbf{b}_{n-1})\|, \|\pi_{n-1}(\mathbf{b}_n)\|\}$$
$$\|\mathbf{b}_n^*\| = \|\pi_n(\mathbf{b}_n)\|$$

which is equivalent to

$$\forall i \in \{1, \cdots, n\}, \quad \|\mathbf{b}_i^*\| = \min_{i \leq j \leq n} \|\pi_i(\mathbf{b}_j)\|$$

We show the PPR in Algorithm 2. Note that for all $1 \leq i \leq n$

$$\pi_i(\mathbf{b}_j) = \mathbf{b}_j - \sum_{k=1}^{i-1} \frac{\langle \mathbf{b}_j, \mathbf{b}_k^* \rangle}{\|\mathbf{b}_k^*\|^2} \mathbf{b}_k^*.$$

Algorithm 3. Dual Projective Reordering (DPR)

Input: A basis $\{\mathbf{b}_1, \ldots, \mathbf{b}_n\} \in \mathbb{R}^m$,
Output: $\{\mathbf{b}_1, \cdots, \mathbf{b}_n\} \in \mathbb{R}^m$ such that $\forall i \in \{1, \cdots, n\}$, $\|\mathbf{d}_i^\dagger\| = \min_{1 \leq j \leq i} \|\tau_i(\mathbf{d}_j)\|$
1: $\mathbf{D} \leftarrow (\mathbf{BB}^\mathrm{T})^{-1}\mathbf{B}$;
2: $(\mathbf{d}_1, \cdots, \mathbf{d}_n) \leftarrow (\mathbf{d}_n, \cdots, \mathbf{d}_1)$,;
3: $\mathrm{PPR}((\mathbf{d}_1, \cdots, \mathbf{d}_n))$;
4: $(\mathbf{d}_1, \cdots, \mathbf{d}_n) \leftarrow (\mathbf{d}_n, \cdots, \mathbf{d}_1)$;
5: $\mathbf{B} \leftarrow (\mathbf{DD}^\mathrm{T})^{-1}\mathbf{D}$;

Therefore,

$$\pi_i(\mathbf{b}_j) = \pi_{i-1}(\mathbf{b}_j) - \frac{\langle \mathbf{b}_j, \mathbf{b}_{i-1}^* \rangle}{\|\mathbf{b}_{i-1}^*\|^2} \mathbf{b}_{i-1}^*$$

and

$$\|\pi_i(\mathbf{b}_j)\|^2 = \|\pi_{i-1}(\mathbf{b}_j)\|^2 - \frac{\langle \mathbf{b}_j, \mathbf{b}_{i-1}^* \rangle^2}{\|\mathbf{b}_{i-1}^*\|^2}$$

Note that the complexity of PPR is at most $O(n^3)$ for a given n-dimensional lattice, which is negligible compared to the complexity of ENUM.

4.2 Dual Projective Reordering

We further introduce another reordering method to decrease the number of search nodes in ENUM by directly lengthening the back half of the GSO vectors' norm. Here we use the property of a dual lattice. Let $\{\mathbf{d}_n^\dagger, \cdots, \mathbf{d}_1^\dagger\}$ be the dual lattice basis $\{\mathbf{d}_1, \cdots, \mathbf{d}_n\}$ in reverse order. Since $\|\mathbf{b}_i^*\| \cdot \|\mathbf{d}_i^\dagger\| = 1$ holds, reducing the norm of each GSO vector $\mathbf{d}_i^\dagger$ incurs enlarging the norm of $\mathbf{b}_i^*$ correspondingly. Based on this idea, we propose the Dual Projective Reordering (DPR) method which applies the PPR method to the reversed dual basis $\{\mathbf{d}_n^\dagger, \cdots, \mathbf{d}_1^\dagger\}$. Then DPR changes the lattice basis order such that

$$\|\mathbf{d}_n^\dagger\| = \min\{\|\mathbf{d}_1\|, \cdots, \|\mathbf{d}_n\|\}$$
$$\|\mathbf{d}_{n-1}^\dagger\| = \min\{\|\tau_{n-1}(\mathbf{d}_1)\|, \cdots, \|\tau_{n-1}(\mathbf{d}_{n-1})\|\}$$
$$\vdots$$
$$\|\mathbf{d}_2^\dagger\| = \min\{\|\tau_2(\mathbf{d}_1)\|, \|\tau_2(\mathbf{d}_2)\|\}$$
$$\|\mathbf{d}_1^\dagger\| = \|\tau_1(\mathbf{d}_1)\|$$

which is equivalent to

$$\forall i \in \{1, \cdots, n\}, \quad \|\mathbf{d}_i^\dagger\| = \min_{1 \leq j \leq i} \|\tau_i(\mathbf{d}_j)\|.$$

We show the DPR in Algorithm 3. Note that the DPR method also cost at most $O(n^3)$ for a given n-dimensional lattice, which is negligible compared to the ENUM complexity.

Algorithm 4. Reordering with t_R

Input: A basis $\{\mathbf{b}_1, \ldots, \mathbf{b}_n\} \in \mathbb{R}^m$, its GSO vectors $\{\mathbf{b}_1^*, \cdots, \mathbf{b}_n^*\}$ and a parameter $t_{succ} \geq 1$.

Output: A reordered basis $\{\mathbf{b}_1', \cdot, \mathbf{b}_n'\}$ or a input basis $\{\mathbf{b}_1, \ldots, \mathbf{b}_n\}$.

1: $\{\mathbf{b}_1^*, \cdots, \mathbf{b}_n^*\} \leftarrow$ computeGSO($\{\mathbf{b}_1, \cdots, \mathbf{b}_n\}$);
2: $\{\mathbf{b}_1', \cdots, \mathbf{b}_n'\} \leftarrow$ Reordering($\{\mathbf{b}_1, \cdots, \mathbf{b}_n\}$);
3: $\{\mathbf{b}_1'^*, \cdots, \mathbf{b}_n'^*\} \leftarrow$ computeGSO($\{\mathbf{b}_1', \cdots, \mathbf{b}_n'\}$);
4: $t_R \leftarrow 1$;
5: **for** $i = \lfloor n/2 \rceil$ to n **do**
6:     $t_R \leftarrow t_R \cdot \frac{\|\mathbf{b}_i'^*\|}{\|\mathbf{b}_i^*\|}$;
7: **end for**
8: **if** $t_{succ} < t_R$ **then**
9:     output $\{\mathbf{b}_1', \cdots, \mathbf{b}_n'\}$;
10: **end if**
11: output $\{\mathbf{b}_1, \cdots, \mathbf{b}_n\}$;

4.3 Observation

Because of the possibility that reordering basis vectors may incur an increase of search nodes in ENUM, it is necessary to observe and set an threshold to enhance the effect of the reordering methods. Let the GSO vectors of the lattice basis be $\{\mathbf{b}_1^*, \cdots, \mathbf{b}_n^*\}$, and let the GSO vector of the DPR-reordered basis be $\{\mathbf{b}_1'^*, \cdots, \mathbf{b}_n'^*\}$. Here we define a parameter t_R as

$$t_R := \prod_{i=\lfloor n/2 \rceil}^{n} \frac{\|\mathbf{b}_i'^*\|}{\|\mathbf{b}_i^*\|}.$$

A larger t_R indicates a larger GSO vectors of the latter reordered basis vectors, and a potentially better performance of the reordering method. We can apply this idea to PPR, DPR, and NR, too.

We show the algorithm of reordering with t_R in Algorithm 4. An input parameter $t_{succ} \geq 1$ is a threshold, where the larger t_R is than t_{succ}, the more search nodes will be reduced by the reordering method.

5 Experimental Results

In this section, we show the experimental results of the PPR method and the DPR method. The implementation was done in C++ language using the number theory library NTL [17]. For the random lattice, we generate the random lattice bases from the SVP Challenge [5]. The upper bound R input into ENUM is fixed at $1.05 \times GH(L)$.

5.1 Experimental Result for 30-Dimensional Random Lattice

We performed the following experiment. We have prepared 1000 cases of 30-dimensional random lattice bases LLL-reduced with $\delta_{LLL} = 0.8$ and applied

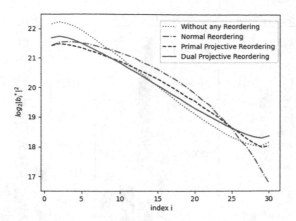

Fig. 1. The distribution of $\|\mathbf{b}_i^*\|$. (average value of 1000 cases of 30-dimensional random lattice LLL-reduced with $\delta_{LLL} = 0.8$)

NR, PPR and DPR to them before inputting that basis into ENUM, respectively. Figure 1 shows the distribution of the GSO vectors' norm respectively, which is the average value of 1000 cases of 30-dimensional random lattice LLL-reduced with $\delta_{LLL} = 0.8$.

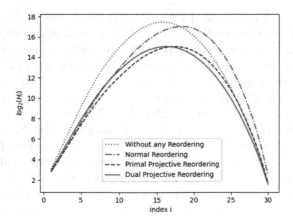

Fig. 2. Total number of search nodes at each level in ENUM (average value of 1000 cases of 30-dimensional random lattice LLL-reduced with $\delta = 0.8$)

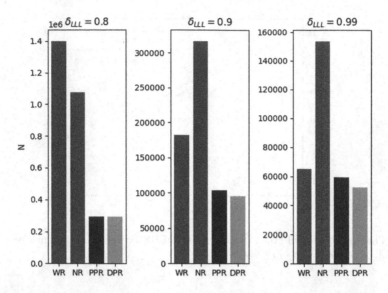

Fig. 3. The number of search nodes in ENUM (average value of 1000 cases of 30-dimensional random lattice LLL-reduced with $\delta = 0.8, 0.9, 0.99$). WR: Without any Reordering, NR: Normal Reordering, PPR: Primal Projective Reordering, DPR: Dual Projective Reordering.

From Fig. 1, we can see that PPR and DPR satisfy the condition to lengthen the back half of the GSO vectors' norm, while Normal Reordering (NR), unfortunately, shortens the back half of the GSO vectors' compared to PPR, DPR. Therefore we can see that PPR and DPR are an improvement on N. Next, Fig. 2 shows the number of search nodes at each level in the ENUM tree (the average value of 1000 cases of 30-dimensional random lattices). From Fig. 2, we can see that the number of search node in ENUM is the largest around $\frac{n}{2}$ as pointed out in [7]. Moreover, the numbers of search nodes in ENUM using PPR and DPR are respectively much smaller than that of the case with NR or without Reordering. The large-small relationship of the experimental results on the total search node number $(= \sum_{i=1}^{n} H_i)$ for each method was DPR < PPR < NR < Without any Reordering. (i.e., The number of ENUM search node with DPR was the lowest of four). When we usually use LLL reduction, we set δ_{LLL} as close to 1 as possible, e.g., $\delta_{LLL} = 0.99$. Figure 3 shows the search node number in ENUM when lattice basis LLL-reduced with $\delta = 0.8, 0.9, 0.99$ in the four cases: without reordering, using NR, PPR and DPR.

From Fig. 3, we can see that every three reordering methods reduce the number of search nodes compared to the case without reordering for $\delta_{LLL} = 0.8$. However, when $\delta_{LLL} = 0.9$ and 0.99, the total number of search nodes increases. The reason is that the norm in the middle of the GSO vectors NR-reordered becomes large, while the back half of the GSO vectors' norm becomes extremely small. Although previous studies claim that the larger the norm in the middle of the GSO vector is, the more the total number of search nodes can be reduced,

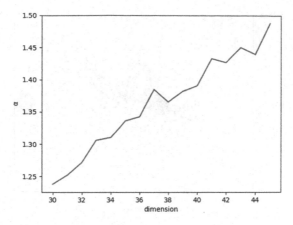

Fig. 4. $\alpha := \bar{N}_{WR}/\bar{N}_{DPR}$ at each dimensional lattices. (average value of 1000 cases of 30 to 45 dimensional random lattices LLL-reduced with $\delta_{LLL} = 0.99$)

we claim that it is necessary to lengthen the back half of the GSO vectors' norm in order to decrease the number of search nodes. We can see that both PPR and DPR can reduce the number of search nodes compared to the case without reordering with $\delta_{LLL} = 0.9$ or 0.99.

Moreover, the experimental result shows that DPR decreases the number of search nodes more than PPR. i.e., Directly lengthening the back half of the GSO vectors' norm decreases the number of search nodes more than shortening the front half. Therefore in the following subsection, we will focus on our discussion on the case with DPR.

5.2 Experimental Results on a High-Dimensional Lattice

Next, to see the performance of DPR in more than 30-dimensional lattice, we performed the same experiment about DPR, not only 30 dimensions but also 30–45 dimensions. (The same Experiments in more than 46-dimensional lattice were impossible due to the exponential computation time of ENUM). Figure 4 shows that experimental result. $\bar{N}_{DPR}$ is the number of search nodes when the basis without reordering is input to ENUM, while $\bar{N}_{DPR}$ is the number of search nodes when DPR.

Figure 4 shows that the more the dimension increases, the more DPR decreases the average number of search nodes, although it has been pointed out that NR decreases as the dimension increases. Therefore we overcome the QRT weakness that the reduction of the number of search nodes decreases as the dimension increase, and obtained the result that the reduction can increase as the dimension increase. Furthermore, from experimental results, DPR decreased the number of search nodes by 32.8% on average on 45-dimensional lattices.

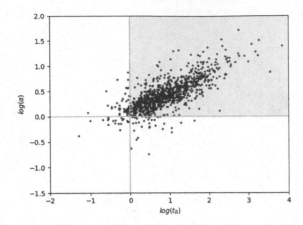

Fig. 5. The scatter plot of t_R and $\alpha := N_{WR}/N_{DPR}$. (1000 cases of 40-dimensional random lattices LLL-reduced with $\delta_{LLL} = 0.99$) (Color figure online)

5.3 Experimental Results on t_R

To observe the lattice basis condition on which DPR can decrease the number of search nodes in ENUM, we have confirmed the usefulness of DPR's t_R through experiments by 40-dimensional random lattices. Figure 5 shows the experimental results of the relation between t_R and $\alpha := N_{WR}/N_{DPR}$. N_{WR} is the number of search nodes in ENUM without reordering, while N_{DPR} is the number of search nodes when using DPR.

From Fig. 5, we can see that the larger α, the larger t_R. In other words, the larger t_R, the larger the number of search nodes. Moreover, we can see that the events often happen that t_R exceeds one and α exceeds one. (i.e., when the back half of the GSO vectors' norm becomes large, the number of search nodes successfully decreases). The experimental result shows that when the t_R is greater than one, the DPR-reordered basis can efficiently decrease the number of search nodes in ENUM and that events often happen. (See the green area in Fig. 5) Therefore we can see that if t_{succ} in Algorithm 4 is larger than one, the number of search nodes decreases with high probabilities.

6 Conclusion and Future Work

In this paper, we observed whether the number of search nodes in ENUM decreases by changing the order of the inputted into ENUM, using the properties of projective and dual lattices. Our contributions are as follows.

1. A proposal of a basis reordering method, **PPR**, that extends the methods of previous studies;
2. A proposal of a basis reordering method **DPR** using the properties of a dual lattice;

3. A proposal of t_R to decide how much the reordered basis reduces the computational complexity of ENUM compared to the original basis.

The experimental results show that PPR can decrease the number of search nodes in ENUM by decreasing the projection length orders, which improves the QRT in the previous study. Moreover, they show that DPR has better performance than PPR and decreases the number of search nodes by 32.8% on average on 45-dimensional lattices. Furthermore, we experimentally show that DPR can increase the quantities to decrease the number of search nodes as dimensions increase: i.e., DPR overcomes the QRT weakness that the quantities to decrease the number of search nodes decreases as the dimension increase.

The reordered basis cannot always decrease the number of search nodes in ENUM compared to the original basis. Therefore, based on the idea that the larger the norm of the latter GSO vector of DPR-reordered basis, the more the reordered basis can decrease the number of search nodes in ENUM, we proposed t_R to decide how much the reordered basis reduces the computational complexity of ENUM compared to the original basis. We experimentally showed that the larger the t_R, the more the number of search node in ENUM decreases.

Future work includes the application of DPR to the BKZ and Extreme Pruning [7]. If we can efficiently decide whether the number of search nodes can decrease by using t_R, we can reduce the complexity of these algorithms by using DPR.

Acknowledgments. This work was supported by JSPS KAKENHI Grant Number JP20K23322, JP21K11751 and JP19K11960, Japan.

References

1. PQC Standardization Process: Third Round Candidate Announcement (2020). https://csrc.nist.gov/News/2020/pqc-third-round-candidate-announcement
2. Ajtai, M., Kumar, R., Sivakumar, D.: A sieve algorithm for the shortest lattice vector problem. In: Proceedings of the Thirty-Third Annual ACM Symposium on Theory of Computing, pp. 601–610 (2001)
3. Aono, Y., Wang, Y., Hayashi, T., Takagi, T.: Improved progressive BKZ algorithms and their precise cost estimation by sharp simulator. In: Fischlin, M., Coron, J.-S. (eds.) EUROCRYPT 2016, Part I. LNCS, vol. 9665, pp. 789–819. Springer, Heidelberg (2016). https://doi.org/10.1007/978-3-662-49890-3_30
4. Chen, Y., Nguyen, P.Q.: BKZ 2.0: better lattice security estimates. In: Lee, D.H., Wang, X. (eds.) ASIACRYPT 2011. LNCS, vol. 7073, pp. 1–20. Springer, Heidelberg (2011). https://doi.org/10.1007/978-3-642-25385-0_1
5. Darmstadt, T.: SVP challenge (2019). https://www.latticechallenge.org/svp-challenge
6. Gama, N., Nguyen, P.Q.: Finding short lattice vectors within Mordell's inequality. In: Dwork, C. (ed.) Proceedings of the 40th Annual ACM Symposium on Theory of Computing, Victoria, British Columbia, Canada, 17–20 May 2008, pp. 207–216. ACM (2008)

7. Gama, N., Nguyen, P.Q., Regev, O.: Lattice enumeration using extreme pruning. In: Gilbert, H. (ed.) EUROCRYPT 2010. LNCS, vol. 6110, pp. 257–278. Springer, Heidelberg (2010). https://doi.org/10.1007/978-3-642-13190-5_13

8. Hoffstein, J., Pipher, J., Silverman, J.H.: NTRU: a ring-based public key cryptosystem. In: Buhler, J.P. (ed.) ANTS 1998. LNCS, vol. 1423, pp. 267–288. Springer, Heidelberg (1998). https://doi.org/10.1007/BFb0054868

9. Koblitz, N.: Constructing elliptic curve cryptosystems in characteristic 2. In: Menezes, A.J., Vanstone, S.A. (eds.) CRYPTO 1990. LNCS, vol. 537, pp. 156–167. Springer, Heidelberg (1991). https://doi.org/10.1007/3-540-38424-3_11

10. Micciancio, D., Walter, M.: Practical, predictable lattice basis reduction. In: Fischlin, M., Coron, J.-S. (eds.) EUROCRYPT 2016, Part I. LNCS, vol. 9665, pp. 820–849. Springer, Heidelberg (2016). https://doi.org/10.1007/978-3-662-49890-3_31

11. Miller, V.S.: Use of elliptic curves in cryptography. In: Williams, H.C. (ed.) CRYPTO 1985. LNCS, vol. 218, pp. 417–426. Springer, Heidelberg (1986). https://doi.org/10.1007/3-540-39799-X_31

12. Regev, O.: On lattices, learning with errors, random linear codes, and cryptography. J. ACM **56**(6), 34:1–34:40 (2009)

13. Rivest, R.L., Shamir, A., Adleman, L.M.: A method for obtaining digital signatures and public-key cryptosystems. Commun. ACM **21**(2), 120–126 (1978)

14. Schnorr, C.P.: Lattice reduction by random sampling and birthday methods. In: Alt, H., Habib, M. (eds.) STACS 2003. LNCS, vol. 2607, pp. 145–156. Springer, Heidelberg (2003). https://doi.org/10.1007/3-540-36494-3_14

15. Schnorr, C., Euchner, M.: Lattice basis reduction: improved practical algorithms and solving subset sum problems. Math. Program. **66**, 181–199 (1994)

16. Shor, P.W.: Algorithms for quantum computation: discrete logarithms and factoring. In: 35th Annual Symposium on Foundations of Computer Science, Santa Fe, New Mexico, USA, 20–22 November 1994, pp. 124–134. IEEE Computer Society (1994)

17. Shoup, V.: NTL, a library for doing number theory (2017). http://www.shoup.net/ntl/

18. Wang, Y., Takagi, T.: Improving the BKZ reduction algorithm by quick reordering technique. In: Susilo, W., Yang, G. (eds.) ACISP 2018. LNCS, vol. 10946, pp. 787–795. Springer, Cham (2018). https://doi.org/10.1007/978-3-319-93638-3_47

19. Wang, Y., Takagi, T.: Studying lattice reduction algorithms improved by quick reordering technique. Int. J. Inf. Secur. **20**(2), 257–268 (2020). https://doi.org/10.1007/s10207-020-00501-y

Compiler-based Attack Origin Tracking with Dynamic Taint Analysis

Oliver Braunsdorf(✉)[ID], Stefan Sessinghaus, and Julian Horsch[ID]

Fraunhofer AISEC, Lichtenbergstr. 11, 85748 Garching near Munich, Germany
{oliver.braunsdorf,stefan.sessinghaus,julian.horsch}@aisec.fraunhofer.de
https://www.aisec.fraunhofer.de/

Abstract. Over the last decade, many exploit mitigations based on Control Flow Integrity (CFI) have been developed to secure programs from being hijacked by attackers. However, most of them only abort the protected application after attack detection, producing no further information for attack analysis. Solely restarting the application leaves it open for repeated attack attempts. We propose *Resilient CFI*, a compiler-based CFI approach that utilizes dynamic taint analysis to detect code pointer overwrites and trace attacks back to their origin. Gained insights can be used to identify attackers and exclude them from further communication with the application. We implemented our approach as extension to LLVM's Dataflow Sanitizer, an actively maintained data-flow tracking engine. Our results show that control-flow hijacking attempts can be reliably detected. Compared to previous approaches based on Dynamic Binary Instrumentation, our compiler-based static instrumentation introduces less run-time overhead: on average 3.52x for SPEC CPU2017 benchmarks and 1.56x for the real-world web server NginX.

Keywords: Software security · Control Flow Integrity · Resiliency · Taint analysis · Dynamic information flow tracking · LLVM

1 Introduction

Control-flow hijacking attacks are one of the most harmful threats for today's software landscape. They enable attackers to execute malicious code inside a victim program to gain complete control over its execution context and eventually further infiltrate whole IT systems. Depending on purpose and leverage of IT systems, attackers could misuse them to extract confidential information, manipulate sensitive data or control physical operations.

Because of the severe consequences, motivation for academia and industry is high to create new approaches to effectively mitigate control-flow hijacking attacks of programs written in low-level programming languages like C and C++. Developed countermeasures like Data Execution Prevention (DEP), Stack

J. H. Park and S.-H. Seo (Eds.): ICISC 2021, LNCS 13218, pp. 175–191, 2022.
https://doi.org/10.1007/978-3-031-08896-4_9

Canaries and Address Space Layout Randomization (ASLR) proved to be practical and are now used by default in many runtime environments. They successfully protect against code injection attacks but are only partially effective against advanced exploit techniques such as *return-to-libc* or *Return-Oriented Programming (ROP)*. Therefore, within the past 15 years, academia developed a countermeasure called *Control Flow Integrity (CFI)*. Abadi et al. originally introduced CFI [1] as a technique which statically instruments binaries to secure *forward-edge* (indirect jumps, indirect function calls) and *backward-edge* (function returns) control-flow instructions with additional run-time checks. Within the last years, this technique has been taken up by many publications which improved concepts for backward-edge CFI and forward-edge CFI. As CFI has proven an efficient and mostly effective countermeasure, it nowadays becomes more and more adopted in industry standard compilers [16].

Unfortunately, most (if not all) existing CFI approaches only consider detection of control-flow hijacking attacks. Their default behavior upon attack detection is to abort the program to prevent further exploitation. While "Detect and Abort" might be a reasonable strategy to prevent extraction of confidential information or manipulation of sensitive data, it can result in loss or damage of data and affects the availability of provided services. Service providers are well prepared for occasional restart and recovery procedures after program abort but in case of a targeted attack, the attacker can start the exploit over and over again. If no appropriate countermeasures are taken between aborting and restarting, subsequent exploitation attempts can cause non-negligible downtimes. For providers of critical services, this can be serious threat to availability.

In this paper, we present *Resilient CFI (ReCFI)*, an approach for control-flow integrity which enables advanced attack reaction strategies to counter repeated control-flow hijacking attempts via similar attack vectors. ReCFI is able to determine the source of attacks at program level and extract information about attackers which can be used to exclude them from further communication with the program. ReCFI is designed as a compiler plug-in, providing both forward- and backward-edge CFI. It aims for small run-time overhead as well as zero false negatives and false positives in order to be a solution for attack mitigation and not only being used as a tool for testing or debugging. As a basis for our work, we employ *dynamic taint analysis* to detect malicious overwrites of code pointers, track back the attack to its originating interface and generate useful information for identifying the attacker.

The idea of utilizing dynamic taint analysis for detecting code pointer overwrites is not completely new. In the past, approaches have been proposed to use specialized hardware in order to track data-flow and check the integrity of code pointers efficiently while the program is executed [5,8,10,15]. Unfortunately, specialized hardware is too expensive to deploy those solutions widely. Newsome and Song [14], followed by other authors [6,7,11], proposed software-implemented taint-tracking engines based on Dynamic Binary Instrumentation (DBI) to ensure control-flow integrity on commodity systems. However, dynamic instrumentation causes unacceptable run-time delays, hindering practical usability of those approaches.

With ReCFI, we propose a compiler-based approach that statically inserts additional instructions to a program at compile-time, thus eliminating the runtime overhead for dynamic instrumentation. Our contributions are summarized in the following:

- We provide a concept for utilizing dynamic taint analysis to detect malicious overwrites of code pointers which additionally provides the ability to generate information to identify the attack origin.
- We implement[1] our concept as an extension to LLVM's *Dataflow Sanitizer*, an actively maintained data-flow tracking framework.
- We implement security measures necessary for static instrumentation solutions to protect against attackers modeled with *contiguous write* capabilities.
- We evaluate the performance using SPEC CPU2017 benchmarks and conduct a case study with the popular NginX web server to exemplify how ReCFI can be applied to complex real-world programs and protect them from repeated exploitation attempts.

We present our design goals and the attacker model under which we developed ReCFI in Sect. 2. We explain the concept of ReCFI in Sect. 3 before describing details of its implementation in Sect. 4. In Sect. 5, we show how ReCFI can be applied to the NginX web server as a case study. We discuss the security properties of ReCFI in Sect. 6 and evaluate its performance in Sect. 7. In Sect. 8, we summarize related work before concluding the paper in Sect. 9.

2   Design Goals and Attacker Model

ReCFI aims to prevent repeated attacks on the control-flow integrity of a program. It is a security mechanism designed to (1) detect manipulation of code pointers resulting from memory corruption-based attacks like heap or stack-based buffer-overflows, (2) identify the origin of an attack, i.e., the interface used by the attacker to inject malicious input, (3) provide detailed information about the origin of an attack gained directly from the running program, and (4) support programs which need to run natively without an interpreter or virtual machine environment.

We assume that the program protected by ReCFI contains memory-corruption errors. An attacker is able to (remotely) send malicious input data to exploit those errors and thereby gain the following capabilities:

Arbitrary read: The attacker can read from arbitrary memory locations of the target program's address space.
Contiguous write: Starting from the memory location of a vulnerable buffer or array variable, the attacker can overwrite adjacent memory locations (that are not write-protected by the operating system).

---

[1] ReCFI source code published here: https://github.com/Fraunhofer-AISEC/ReCFI.

This is a realistic attacker model which, in practice, means we assume that all attacks utilize buffer over- and underflows on the stack or heap. ReCFI is implemented to also detect more powerful attackers which are able to overwrite code pointers *not* adjacent to the vulnerable buffer but at arbitrary locations. However, we rely on the integrity of taint tracking metadata as ground truth for our attack detection algorithm and therefore cannot assume an attacker with *arbitrary write* capabilities because that would include the ability to maliciously overwrite the metadata.

3   Resilient CFI

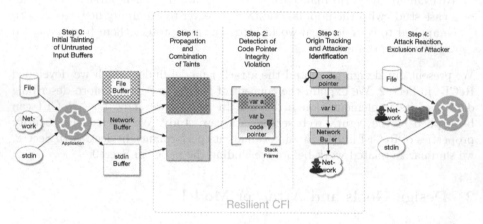

Fig. 1. Overview of ReCFI's steps to protect an application with input from standard input stream (trusted), and network and filesystem (untrusted).

ReCFI is a compiler-based approach for Control Flow Integrity (CFI), driven by dynamic taint analysis. It protects both, forward and backward control-flow edges and provides information about the origin of the attack. ReCFI works by assigning taint labels to untrusted program input data, propagating these taint labels in memory throughout program execution and verifying the absence of taint of code pointers before execution of control-flow instructions. We designed ReCFI as a compiler-based security mechanism and implemented it on top of the LLVM[2] compiler infrastructure. At compile-time, ReCFI instruments the program at LLVM IR level to insert additional instructions. At run-time, original and instrumented instructions are executed together natively to perform taint propagation simultaneously and to detect attacks as they happen. The LLVM developer community maintains a framework for dynamic taint analysis called *Dataflow Sanitizer (DFSan)*[3], which we extended to implement our

---

[2] https://llvm.org/.
[3] https://clang.llvm.org/docs/DataFlowSanitizer.html.

CFI approach. Figure 1 illustrates ReCFI's methodology, which we divided into sequential steps that are described in the following.

Step 0: Initial Input Tainting. ReCFI requires an initial tainting of untrusted program input. For most applications, network or file I/O is untrusted. Depending on the application domain, other buffer variables containing program input from, e.g., command-line arguments, environment variables, or memory-mapped peripherals could also be untrusted. In the example shown in Fig. 1, file and network interfaces are untrusted and their respected buffers get tainted while the standard input stream is considered trustworthy. Finding the complete and sound set of untrusted input buffers for a given program is a highly application-dependent task. Our approach does not aim to provide a general solution to this task. Instead, ReCFI provides a simple API that can be used by application developers to set the initial taint label of variables in the program's source code.

Step 1: Taint Propagation. To model the program's taint state at run-time, we utilize DFSan to split up the program's memory space and set up a shadow memory area as shown in Fig. 2. For every byte of application memory, the shadow memory contains the corresponding taint label. To keep track of the program's taint state, DFSan instruments every data-flow instruction with additional instructions to propagate taint labels. Before an instruction is executed, the taint labels of every instruction operand are loaded from shadow memory and propagated according to the semantics of the instruction. For binary operations, e.g., an arithmetic instructions, DFSan combines the taint of both operands, generating a new *union taint label*. As an example, in Fig. 1, the taints of the file and network buffers are combined, e.g., because of an XOR operation within a cryptographic function decrypting a network packet with a key read from a file. Hence a new *union taint label* is created and assigned to the decryption result buffer. DFSan provides the ability to regain the original taint labels from the union taint label they have been combined to. This is essential to ReCFI's *Attack Origin Tracking* step.

Step 2: Attack Detection. In addition to DFSan's instrumentation of data-flow instructions, ReCFI also instruments control-flow instructions. Our approach provides both, forward- and backward-edge control-flow integrity by instrumenting every indirect jump, call and return instruction. In front of any of those instructions, ReCFI inserts additional instructions to check the taint label of the target address. If the taint label indicates that the target address is tainted, then the current program execution is considered to be under attack because a tainted target address implies that the control flow is directly controlled by input from untrusted sources. In the exemplary program execution illustrated in Step 2 of in Fig. 1, a code pointer (e.g. the return address) is overwritten with data from variable b as part of an attack that exploits a buffer-overflow vulnerability. In this case, ReCFI detects the tainted return address and prevents the program from executing the control flow instruction with the corrupted code pointer. Instead invokes an attack reaction routine which acts as the entry point to Step 3.

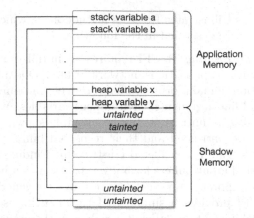

Fig. 2. Memory layout of an application protected by ReCFI.

Step 3: Attack Origin Tracking. After an attack has been detected, ReCFI analyzes the taint label of the corrupted code pointer. Thereby, it recursively resolves union taint labels to their original taint labels to eventually identify from which particular program input source the code pointer has been derived from. ReCFI supports 2^{16} different taint labels and therefore can distinguish between many different input sources, respectively different potential attackers. In the example in Fig. 1, ReCFI is able to resolve the taint label of the corrupted code pointer and trace the attack back to an attacker who used the network interface. The quality of identification of a particular attacker strongly depends on the granularity of input tainting, as shown in the following three examples:

1. If the same taint label is assigned to every data packet read from the network interface, ReCFI is only able to identify that the attacker is coming from the network.
2. If a new taint label is generated per communication peer, then ReCFI can narrow down the attacker's identity, e.g., to an IP or MAC address, a username, or a TLS certificate—depending on how communication peers are distinguished when generating the new taint label in the first place.
3. If a new taint label is generated per incoming network packet, ReCFI can deduce the actual network packet that triggered the vulnerability. Hence, it is possible to conduct advanced analyses of the packet's payload to identify the attacker.

The more fine-grained the input tainting, the more precise an attacker can be identified, which can be highly valuable for Step 4.

Step 4: Attack Reaction. After an attack has been detected, an appropriate reaction has to be conducted to mitigate subsequent similar attacks. Those reactions are highly application dependent. Nevertheless, we want to briefly point out two common patterns for attack reactions enabled by ReCFI in the following:

Attack reactions can utilize filtering mechanisms to blacklist communication with peers identified as attackers. In networked applications, a firewall can be configured based on the network address (IP, MAC, etc.) of a malicious packet which can be identified by ReCFI. Consequently, after restarting the application, the attacker will not be able to conduct the exploit again from the same network address. In applications authenticating their users using username-password combinations or X.509 certificates, ReCFI can be also used to create a new taint label for every user and deny access to the service by blacklisting usernames or revoking certificates.

Another possible attack reaction could be to *selectively* apply memory-safety techniques to the program under attack, e.g. adding bounds checks to overflown buffers or move them into guarded memory locations[4]. Provided with detailed information about the attack origin generated by ReCFI, those memory-safety techniques can be selectively applied only to data structures on the attack path, thus minimizing the performance and memory overheads.

Besides reactions that aim to protect a single program, with ReCFI it is also possible to forward attack information via network sockets or IPC mechanisms to a monitoring component in order to contribute in assessing the overall security status of a system and select appropriate actions to protect the system.

4   Implementation Details

The implementation of ReCFI is based on *Dataflow Sanitizer (DFSan)*, a framework for dynamic taint analysis which is actively maintained as part of LLVM. Since DFSan is not designed as a CFI mechanism, we had to implement additional security measures to protect programs according to our attacker model. In this section, we summarize relevant implementation internals of DFSan and describe the modifications we conducted in order to implement ReCFI.

Memory Layout and Taint Representation. DFSan divides the process' virtual memory into application memory and shadow memory, as schematically depicted in Fig. 2. Every byte of application memory is associated with two bytes (16 bit) of shadow memory representing its corresponding taint label. The mapping between application memory and shadow memory is calculated via a bitmask.

With DFSan's taint labels being two bytes (16 bit) in size, ReCFI can differentiate between $2^{16} - 1$ potential attackers (excluding the "untainted" label). By default, DFSan aborts the application if more than 2^{16} taint labels are created. To support use cases where more taint labels are needed, we modified DFSan to wrap around instead of aborting, and reuse taint label identifiers. ReCFI emits a warning every time the number of taint labels wraps around. Security implications of this wrap-around strategy are further discussed in Sect. 6.

---

[4] As realized by Electric Fence (https://linux.die.net/man/3/efence) or LLVM's Address Sanitizer (https://clang.llvm.org/docs/AddressSanitizer.html).

Checking the Integrity of Code Pointers. For the implementation of Step 2 of ReCFI, we additionally instrument control-flow instructions. Implementing CFI checks for indirect jumps and function calls in LLVM is straight-forward because the target address pointer is an argument of the call/jump instruction. Therefore, ReCFI just has to calculate the shadow memory location corresponding to the pointer's location which is represented in LLVM IR.

For return instructions, the location of the return address is architecture-specific and therefore only known by the machine code generation backend of LLVM. On x86 and aarch64 processor architectures the LLVM intrinsic function llvm.addressofreturnaddress[5] can be utilized to obtain the location of the return address on the current stack frame. ReCFI inserts this intrinsic to locate the return address and check its corresponding taint label before every return instruction. Moreover, ReCFI extends DFSan to properly initialize the taint label of the return address to *untainted* on creation of new stack frames, i.e. in every function prologue.

Although ReCFI instruments function prologue and epilogue, it does not rely on correct stack unwinding. This is because it only inserts taint checking instructions to the epilogue which are read-only. No cleanup instructions are required. Therefore, there are no compatibility issues when the applications use setjmp/longjmp or other related functions for exception handling.

Avoiding Taint Labels on the Stack. DFSan implements an optimization strategy to minimize its performance overhead, which introduces a weakness that could be utilized by an attacker to circumvent our control-flow integrity checks: for each local variable, DFSan allocates space for a taint label on the stack. Every time the variable's taint label needs to be checked or updated, DFSan accesses the taint label allocated on the stack instead of accessing the shadow memory region. This optimization saves a few instructions to calculate the shadow address. However, if attackers manage to overflow a stack variable, they might be able to overwrite the value of the taint label and reset it to *untainted*. In this case, our CFI checks could miss the integrity violation and the attack would not be detected. To avoid this potential security breach we removed this optimization.

A second optimization strategy of DFSan concerns propagation of taint labels through function calls. By default, taint labels of arguments and return values are passed through Thread-Local Storage (TLS). To reduce the number of memory accesses, DFSan provides an option to pass taint labels as additional function call arguments alongside their corresponding original arguments in CPU registers. However, for more than 3 parameters (more than 6 in total with taint labels), taint labels would be passed by pushing them to the stack, leading to the same potential security weakness as the first optimization strategy described above. Therefore, we disabled this optimization for ReCFI.

Input Tainting and Collection of Attacker Information. DFSan provides the basic API for input tainting. Application developers can use it to create new

---

[5] https://llvm.org/docs/LangRef.html#llvm-addressofreturnaddress-intrinsic.

taint labels and assign them to buffer variables that are considered entry points for attacker-controlled input data. Additionally, DFSan maintains a global map structure `dfsan_label_info` which maps each 16-bit taint label identifier to a pointer of arbitrary application-specific data. With ReCFI, this application-specific data can be used to provide detailed information about the source of the tainted input data, e.g. the source address of a received network packet or the fingerprint of a TLS certificate associated with the current communication session. The more detailed those information, the more precise an attacker can be identified. In case ReCFI detects a CFI violation, it invokes an attack reaction routine and passes taint label information and the associated application-specific data as arguments. We implemented this attack reaction routine in ReCFI's runtime library as a function with **weak** linkage. In this way, application developers can redefine the function symbol to implement their custom attack reaction routine and perform application-specific reactions based on the provided information that ReCFI extracts from the taint labels.

5   Case Study: NginX Web Server

To confirm ReCFI's ability to detect control-flow hijacking attacks on complex programs, we conducted a case study with the popular web server NginX. Versions 1.3.9 and 1.4.0 of NginX contain a stack buffer overflow vulnerability (CVE-2013-2028), which can be exploited to gain remote code execution (RCE). The exploit can be triggered by sending specifically crafted HTTP requests. The vulnerability is caused by an unsound cast from signed to unsigned integer, misinterpreting the size of the network buffer as overly large. Thus, too much bytes are written to the buffer, leading to an overwrite of the return address.

According to ReCFI's Step 0, we first classified the network interface as non-trustworthy and searched for input buffers into which data is read from the network socket. We assigned the initial taint label to network input buffers as shown in Listing 1. We added a call to `dfsan_set_label` to taint the bytes starting at the address of **buf** up to **buf + n**, which equals the number of bytes read from the network socket. The taint label is represented by `c->recfi_label`. It is initialized during connection establishment with the HTTP client and associated to the object **c**, representing the connection. As shown in Listing 2, we modified the function `ngx_event_accept` to insert taint label initialization after NginX accepts the connection request.

With these few manual modifications to NginX, we compiled it with ReCFI which automatically inserts additional code for Steps 1–3. Running the exploit[6], ReCFI successfully detects the corruption of the return address and is able to track the origin of the attack back to the IP address of the client who started the exploit.

For Step 4, we defined a custom attack reaction function directly in the NginX source code, overwriting ReCFI's default attack handler with an applica-

---

[6] https://dl.packetstormsecurity.net/papers/general/nginx_exploit_documentation.pdf.

Listing 1. Instrumentation of NginX's function `ngx_unix_recv()`. Additional instructions for initial input tainting are highlighted.

```
1  ssize_t
2  ngx_unix_recv(ngx_connection_t *c, u_char *buf, size_t size)
3  {
4    [...]
5    do {
6      ssize_t n = recv(c->fd, buf, size, 0);
7      dfsan_set_label(c->recfi_label, buf, n);
8      [...]
9    }
10 }
```

Listing 2. Instrumentation of NginX's function `ngx_event_accept()`. Additional instructions for initial input tainting are highlighted.

```
1  void ngx_event_accept(ngx_event_t *ev) {
2    [...]
3    s = accept(lc->fd, (struct sockaddr *) sa, &socklen);
4    struct sockaddr_in *sa_in = (struct sockaddr_in*) sa;
5    char *ip = inet_ntoa(sa_in->sin_addr);
6    c->recfi_label = dfsan_create_label("accept", ip);
7    [...]
8  }
```

tion specific reaction as described in Sect. 4. We implemented a custom attack handler to which ReCFI passes the attacker's IP address. The attackers IP is then blacklisted by adding a new *Linux iptables* rule. This is only an example for attack reactions possible with NginX. If NginX is configured for client authentication via username & password or X.509 certificates, ReCFI could also associate taint labels with the username or the client certificate's fingerprint and blacklist them.

To measure the performance overhead of ReCFI in NginX we used the WRK benchmark[7]. In server software, compute time only makes up a fraction of the overall performance because I/O operations are much more time-consuming. To account for this, we measured the throughput of served HTTP requests within 30 s for different file sizes. Results are shown in Table 1. Averaging over all file sizes (geometric mean), ReCFI introduces a slowdown of 1.56x.

---

[7] https://github.com/wg/wrk.

Table 1. Slowdown of ReCFI in NginX.

File size	1 KB	10 KB	100 KB	1 MB
Slowdown	2.10x	1.88x	1.34x	1.11x

6 Security Discussion

In this section, we discuss security guarantees and limitations of ReCFI.

Accuracy in Attack Detection. ReCFI uses dynamic analysis to track the data-flow along actual execution paths. In contrast to CFI approaches solely based on static analysis, there is no over- or under-approximation of the control-flow graph. Hence, there are no false positives when detecting an overwrite of a jump or return address. Therefore, all potential attacks detected by ReCFI are indeed overwrites of code pointers with attacker-supplied input. Assuming every attacker-controllable interface is correctly tainted in Step 0, ReCFI also does not have false negatives, i.e., it is able to detect every overwrite of code pointers with attacker-controlled input data. Accidental overwrites from benign interfaces are not detected because these interfaces are not marked as taint source in Step 0. This is acceptable, because we can assume that they are very unlikely and happen accidentally and thus are a one-time event as opposed a targeted, repeated attack with the intention to exploit the program.

Bounded Number of Taint Labels. As described in Sect. 4, our implementation of ReCFI can create up to $2^{16} - 1$ distinct taint labels. If applications generate new taint labels very frequently, this can eventually cause a wrap-around of the 16-bit taint label identifier. This could lead to confusion in associating taint labels with their corresponding taint source (potential attack origin). However, ReCFI still prevents the application from exploitation.

Protection of Taint Metadata. With ReCFI, we adapted DFSan to avoid storing taint labels on the stack as described in Sect. 4. Therefore, attackers with *contiguous write* capabilities cannot overwrite the security-critical taint metadata. Hence, ReCFI successfully protects programs against attackers complying to our attacker model.

Protection of Programs with External Libraries. Because ReCFI is a compiler-based approach, it can only protect those parts of a program which have been compiled with it. It cannot detect overwrites of code pointers if they happen in external libraries, which *have not been* compiled with ReCFI. In order to effectively protect those parts of the program which *have been* compiled with ReCFI, we have to ensure correct propagation of taint labels even through calls to functions of external libraries. This issue is solved by DFSan which automatically generates a wrapper function for each external library function. Within each wrapper function, the actual external function is called and the taint labels of arguments and return values are propagated according to the data-flow semantic of the external function. DFSan provides a so called *ABI list*[8] which can be used by developers to conveniently specify the data-flow semantic for each external library function.

7   Performance Evaluation

We measured the performance impact of ReCFI using the CPU-bound SPEC CPU2017 benchmark suite[9]. Since we implemented ReCFI primarily for the C programming language, we tested all SPEC CPU2017 benchmarks written in C, omitting those written in C++ and Fortran. All measurements were taken on an Intel Xeon E7-4850 v3 CPU with 2.20 GHz.

Run-Time Overhead. To understand the performance overhead of ReCFI and separately DFSan, we measured both versions and compared their overheads to the baseline compiled with default compiler flags. We ran each benchmark 3 times and used their medians to calculate the overhead relative to the baseline. The resulting run-time overheads are shown in Fig. 3. The slowdown caused by ReCFI ranges from 1.99x for the nab benchmark to 7.30x for the perlbench benchmark, averaging at 3.52x (geometric mean). For comparison with other published approaches and related work, we list their run-time overheads in Sect. 8.

As depicted in Fig. 3, enabling DFSan introduces most of the performance overhead. There are several factors that cause its decrease in run-time performance: (1) An additional memory access to read or write the corresponding taint label for every memory load or store operation, (2) two additional memory accesses to write and read function arguments passed through TLS, (3) taint label union operations for arithmetic instructions, (4) register spills due to additional operations on taint labels, (5) displacement of application memory/code from cache lines in favor of taint label handling. On top of that, ReCFI's additional control-flow integrity checks add (1) an additional memory access to initialize the taint label of the return address to *untainted*, (2) an additional memory access to load the taint label of code pointers before return- and indirect call/jump instructions, and (3) the related instruction to check this label for taintedness. The measurement results show that the overhead introduced by ReCFI on top of DFSan is comparatively small, which endorses our approach for software projects where DFSan is already used.

For the benchmarks perlbench and gcc, ReCFI and DFSan introduce larger overheads, presumably because both benchmarks test program compilation workloads which execute many memory load and store operations while the other benchmarks are more bound to integer and floating point arithmetic. For some benchmarks, e.g., lbm or nab, the measurement results suggest that

---

[8] https://clang.llvm.org/docs/DataFlowSanitizer.html.
[9] https://www.spec.org/cpu2017/.

ReCFI has smaller overhead than DFSan. We assume that for those benchmarks, ReCFI does not have a significant impact on performance compared to DFSan, and that ReCFI's additional memory access instructions have a positive effect on internal caching structures of the CPU, leading to minor improvements in the overall run-time compared to DFSan.

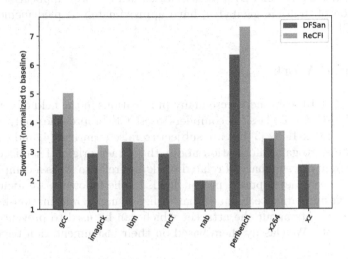

Fig. 3. Normalized run-time overhead for SPEC CPU2017.

Memory Overhead. During our run-time benchmarks, we also measured the peak memory usage of every benchmark program by monitoring their maximum resident set size. The average memory overhead measured for ReCFI is 3.07x. As ReCFI does not allocate any memory on top of DFSan, there is no significant difference from DFSan's memory overhead. It is caused by the following factors: (1) two additional bytes shadow memory for every byte of application memory, (2) the DFSan union table, and (3) the `dfsan_label_info` map as described in Sect. 4. The `dfsan_label_info` structure is a map that associates 20 byte of additional data and pointers per taint label identifier and thus uses $2^{16} \times 20\,\mathrm{B} \approx 1.3\,\mathrm{MB}$ of memory. DFSan's union table UT is a two-dimensional array implementing a strictly triangular matrix which tracks whether two taint labels i and j have been combined to a new union taint label k as result of an arithmetic instruction with two tainted operands.

$$UT[i][j] \mapsto k, \text{ with } i < j \quad \text{(strictly triangular)}$$

With taint labels being 16 bit in size, a full union table would consume approximately 4.2 GB of memory.

$$\sum_{k=1}^{2^{16}-1} (k) \times 16bit \approx 2.1 \times 10^9 \times 2\,\mathrm{B} \approx 4.2\,\mathrm{GB}$$

However, in practice only few distinct taint label combinations exist in the union table. Therefore, only few of the virtual memory pages containing the union labels are actually mapped to physical RAM. Thus, the physical memory usage for the `dfsan_label_info` map and the union table is constant while shadow memory additionally consumes 2x application memory. Hence, programs like the SPEC CPU2017 benchmarks, which have application memory consumption[10] of multiple gigabytes, have approximately tripled memory usage with ReCFI.

8   Related Work

Within the last 10 years there were many publications in the field of control-flow integrity. Most of the classical compiler-based CFI approaches only introduce overheads of 1.01x-1.45x [3] but are subject to false negatives [4] and completely lack the ability to gain information about the attack origin. Therefore, we will omit them from our summary of related work and refer to [3] as a comprehensive overview of recent development in that field. In the following, we focus on proposed exploit mitigation techniques that utilize dynamic information-flow tracking to gain insights about the attacker which can be used to prevent repeated attack attempts. We classify them based on their instrumentation techniques.

Hardware-Based. Early approaches were based on architectural modifications (e.g. to CPU or MMU) to track data-flow and check for tainted return/jump addresses in hardware [5,8,10,15]. Dedicated hardware clearly brings the advantage of low run-time overhead. Reported slowdowns range between <1.01x to 1.17x for compute-bound benchmarks. However, implementations are based on non-commodity hardware prototypes that are not widely available, greatly inhibiting their adoption. They do not need access to applications' source code but often require modifications to the operating system, further decreasing practicability. ReCFI is a compiler-based approach which can run on commodity CPUs and only requires minimal changes to the application code to mark potentially attacker-controlled interfaces as taint source.

Dynamic Binary Instrumentation. Chronologically, hardware-based approaches have been superseded by approaches based on Dynamic Binary Instrumentation (DBI). With DBI, an application's binary code is loaded and executed by a binary interpreter. During execution, it can analyze and modify program code on-the-fly to add instructions for taint propagation and monitoring of code pointers. This technique is very flexible and does not require recompilation. However, analysis and instrumentation during run-time introduce more overhead than ReCFI in most cases. The authors of TaintCheck [14] (based on the *Valgrind* framework[10] reported a slowdown of up to 40x. *Dytan* [7] and *libdft* [11] both

---

[10] https://valgrind.org/.

utilize the Intel PIN framework [12]. Their respective authors reported 50x slowdown and 7-11x slowdown. TaintTrace [6] (based on DynamoRIO[11]) proposes multiple performance optimizations, the most impactful of which is using a direct shadow mapping between application memory and taint metadata similar to our approach. The authors measured a slowdown of 5.5x on SPEC2000 INT benchmarks.

Static Instrumentation. Static instrumentation techniques have been proposed to eliminate overheads of DBI for inserting additional instructions at run-time. Instead, they insert all additional instructions before the program is executed. Xu et al. [17] accomplish this by utilizing the CIL framework [13] for *Source-to-Source Transformation* of C code to insert additional instructions. They report a slowdown of 1.76x on average for compute-bound benchmarks. However, for performance optimization they use stack variables to store the taint metadata of the protected application's stack variables. This introduces new security vulnerabilities in cases of stack buffer overflow attacks. ReCFI actively avoids that as we described in Sect. 4. Moreover, building on source-to-source transformation, Xu et al. only protect applications written in C while ReCFI is a compiler-based approach and therefore is able to protect programs of all languages that compile to LLVM IR.

The most recent work related to ReCFI is *Iodine* [2]. It is also a compiler-based static instrumentation approach and is built on top of DFSan. Iodine reduces run-time overhead by applying *Optimistic Hybrid Analysis (OHA)* [9] to taint tracking. They use a profile-guided static analysis to eliminate some of the additional taint checking instructions on the fast-path and fall back to conservative dynamic taint checking on the slow-path. Banerjee et al. report an average slowdown of 1.41x for SPECint C benchmarks. While they focus mainly on performance optimizations for generic information-flow tracking problems, ReCFI specializes on detection of code pointer overwrites and generating information about the attack origin. Hence, they are complementary approaches.

9   Conclusion

In this paper, we presented ReCFI, a compiler-based security mechanism to detect control-flow hijacking attacks and gain information about the attack origin by utilizing dynamic taint analysis. Our system statically instruments applications at compile-time to insert additional instructions for taint propagation and integrity-checking of return addresses, function pointers and indirect jump targets. Our implementation is based on LLVM's Dataflow Sanitizer (DFSan), an actively maintained framework for dynamic data-flow analysis. ReCFI can be used by enabling compiler-flags of the clang C compiler and only requires minimal modifications to the source code by developers to identify potentially attacker-controlled interfaces as taint source. We extended DFSan with security measures to protect against attackers with contiguous write capabilities.

---

[11] https://dynamorio.org/.

Utilizing dynamic analysis, ReCFI precisely tracks the data-flow of the program without over- or under-approximation and therefore does not yield false positives nor false negatives as opposed to classical compiler-based CFI approaches [4]. We outlined how ReCFI can be used in server software to track an attack back to the attackers' IP addresses and exclude them from further communication. ReCFI introduces a slowdown of 3.52x on average for SPEC CPU2017 benchmarks and only 1.56x on average for the real-world web server NginX. Thus, ReCFI advances the state of the art for control-flow integrity solutions with attack origin identification.

Acknowledgments. This work is partially funded by the Bavarian Ministry of Economic Affairs, Regional Development and Energy.

References

1. Abadi, M., Budiu, M., Erlingsson, Ú., Ligatti, J.: Control-flow integrity. In: Proceedings of the 12th ACM Conference on Computer and Communications Security, pp. 340–353. CCS 2005, Association for Computing Machinery, NY (2005)
2. Banerjee, S., Devecsery, D., Chen, P.M., Narayanasamy, S.: Iodine: fast dynamic taint tracking using rollback-free optimistic hybrid analysis. In: 2019 IEEE Symposium on Security and Privacy (SP), pp. 490–504. IEEE, San Francisco, CA (2019)
3. Burow, N., et al.: Control-flow integrity: precision, security, and performance. ACM Comput. Surv. **50**(1), 16:1–16:33 (2017)
4. Carlini, N., Barresi, A., Payer, M., Wagner, D., Gross, T.R.: Control-flow bending: on the effectiveness of control-flow integrity. In: 24th USENIX Security Symposium, pp. 161–176 (2015)
5. Chen, S., Xu, J., Nakka, N., Kalbarczyk, Z., Iyer, R.K.: Defeating memory corruption attacks via pointer taintedness detection. In: 2005 International Conference on Dependable Systems and Networks (DSN 2005), pp. 378–387 (2005)
6. Cheng, W., Zhao, Q., Yu, B., Hiroshige, S.: TaintTrace: efficient flow tracing with dynamic binary rewriting. In: 11th IEEE Symposium on Computers and Communications (ISCC 2006), pp. 749–754 (2006)
7. Clause, J., Li, W., Orso, A.: Dytan: a generic dynamic taint analysis framework. In: Proceedings of the 2007 International Symposium on Software Testing and Analysis, pp. 196–206. ISSTA 2007, Association for Computing Machinery, NY (2007)
8. Dalton, M., Kannan, H., Kozyrakis, C.: Raksha: a flexible information flow architecture for software security. In: Proceedings of the 34th Annual International Symposium on Computer Architecture, pp. 482–493. ISCA 2007, Association for Computing Machinery, NY (2007)
9. Devecsery, D., Chen, P.M., Flinn, J., Narayanasamy, S.: Optimistic hybrid analysis: accelerating dynamic analysis through predicated static analysis. ACM SIGPLAN Not. **53**(2), 348–362 (2018)
10. Katsunuma, S., et al.: Base address recognition with data flow tracking for injection attack detection. In: 2006 12th Pacific Rim International Symposium on Dependable Computing (PRDC 2006), pp. 165–172 (2006)
11. Kemerlis, V.P., Portokalidis, G., Jee, K., Keromytis, A.D.: libdft: practical dynamic data flow tracking for commodity systems. ACM SIGPLAN Not. **47**(7), 121–132 (2012)

12. Luk, C.K., et al.: Pin: building customized program analysis tools with dynamic instrumentation. ACM SIGPLAN Not. **40**(6), 190–200 (2005)
13. Necula, G.C., McPeak, S., Rahul, S.P., Weimer, W.: CIL: intermediate language and tools for analysis and transformation of C programs. In: Horspool, R.N. (ed.) CC 2002. LNCS, vol. 2304, pp. 213–228. Springer, Heidelberg (2002). https://doi.org/10.1007/3-540-45937-5_16
14. Newsome, J., Song, D.: Dynamic taint analysis: automatic detection, analysis, and signature generation of exploit attacks on commodity software. In: Proceedings of the 12th Network and Distributed Systems Security Symposium (2005)
15. Suh, G.E., Lee, J.W., Zhang, D., Devadas, S.: Secure program execution via dynamic information flow tracking. In: Proceedings of the 11th International Conference on Architectural Support for Programming Languages and Operating Systems, pp. 85–96. ASPLOS XI, Association for Computing Machinery, Boston, MA (2004)
16. Tice, C., et al.: Enforcing forward-edge control-flow integrity in GCC & LLVM. In: 23rd USENIX Security Symposium, pp. 941–955 (2014)
17. Xu, W., Bhatkar, S., Sekar, R.: Taint-enhanced policy enforcement: a practical approach to defeat a wide range of attacks. In: 15th USENIX Security Symposium (2006)

Security Analysis of Hash Algorithm

Preimage Attacks on 4-Round Keccak by Solving Multivariate Quadratic Systems

Congming Wei[1], Chenhao Wu[2], Ximing Fu[3(✉)], Xiaoyang Dong[1], Kai He[4], Jue Hong[4], and Xiaoyun Wang[1]

[1] Institute for Advanced Study, BNRist, Tsinghua University, Beijing, China
[2] The Chinese University of Hong Kong, Shenzhen, Shenzhen, China
[3] Harbin Institute of Technology, Shenzhen, Shenzhen, China
fuximing@hit.edu.cn
[4] Baidu Inc., Beijing, China

Abstract. In this paper, we present preimage attacks on 4-round Keccak-224/256 as well as 4-round Keccak$[r = 640, c = 160, l = 80]$ in the preimage challenges. We revisit the Crossbred algorithm for solving the Boolean multivariate quadratic (MQ) system and elaborate the computational complexity for the case $D = 2$. The result shows that the Crossbred algorithm has advantages when n is small and m outperforms n with feasible memory costs. In our attacks, we construct Boolean MQ systems in order to make full use of variables. With the help of solving MQ systems, we successfully improve preimage attacks on Keccak-224/256 reduced to 4 rounds. Moreover, we implement the preimage attack on 4-round Keccak$[r = 640, c = 160, l = 80]$, an instance in the Keccak preimage challenges, and find 78-bit matched *near preimages*.

Keywords: Keccak · Preimage attack · Multivariate quadratic systems

1 Introduction

Due to the breakthrough attacks on hash functions [17–20], the National Institute of Standards and Technology (NIST) started new standardization of hash functions. The Keccak sponge function [2] won the competition and became the new generation of Secure Hash Algorithm, known as SHA-3. Since its publication in 2008, both the keyed modes and the unkeyed modes of Keccak have been widely studied.

This paper is focused on the preimage attack. Morawiecki et al. [15] gave the experiment of preimage attack with SAT solver, illustrating that using SAT solver outperforms exhaustive search when Keccak is reduced to 3 rounds. Then in 2013, rotational cryptanalysis [14] was applied to the preimage attack on 4-round Keccak$[r = 1024, c = 576]$ with complexity 2^{506}. Then a breakthrough in the preimage attack occurred in 2016. Guo et al. proposed a new linear structure

© The Author(s), under exclusive license to Springer Nature Switzerland AG 2022
J. H. Park and S.-H. Seo (Eds.): ICISC 2021, LNCS 13218, pp. 195–216, 2022.
https://doi.org/10.1007/978-3-031-08896-4_10

of Keccak [7] and gave 3/4-round preimage attacks based on the linear structure. After that, some improved attack methods have been proposed. Li et al. [11] constructed a new structure called cross-linear structure, and improved preimage attacks on several 3-round Keccak instances. A two-block method [10] was proposed to attack 3/4-round Keccak-224/256, such that the constraints could be allocated to two blocks and the complexity was lowered. Besides, Rajasree [16] proposed a nonlinear structure, focusing on Keccak-384/512 reduced to 2, 3 and 4 rounds. Later, He et al. [8] developed the linearization method of [10] to save degrees of freedom and improved the preimage attacks on 4-round Keccak-224/256.

Apart from solving linear systems, methods for solving nonlinear systems have been applied such that more degrees of freedom could be saved. Liu et al. [12] made full use of equations derived from the hash value by constructing Boolean quadratic systems. They used relinearization techniques to solve quadratic systems and improved the attacks on Keccak-384/512. After that, Dinur [5] gave an efficient polynomial method-based algorithm [13] for solving multivariate equation systems and applied it in cryptanalysis including preimage attacks on Keccak. The method solved equations of degree 4 and successfully improved preimage attacks on Keccak-384/512 but did not outperform attacks on Keccak-224/256 in [8].

Our Contributions. In this paper, we draw our attention to preimage attacks and present several results of attacks on 4-round Keccak-224/256 as well as 4-round Keccak$[r = 640, c = 160, l = 80]$.

One key technique in our attacks is to solve multivariate quadratic (MQ) polynomial systems. We present a new observation on MQ polynomials and elaborate the complexity of the Crossbred algorithm with $D = 2$. Our elaboration shows that the Crossbred algorithm outperforms the brute force even in the worst case, improving the complexity analysis in [6]. More impressively, although our algorithm is no better than Dinur's [5] in terms of time complexity asymptotically, our algorithm uses feasible memory in a wide range of parameters and is easy to implement. Especially in our attack, the derived MQ systems have small number of variables and larger number of equations, our method needs lower computational costs.

For preimage attacks on Keccak, we exploit the output of the inverse χ^{-1} and carefully select constant values to linearize one round backward and one round forward. Compared with the structure in [8,10], our structure has more arbitrary constants. Guessing values of arbitrary constants helps to get messages later. Based on our structure, all input bits of χ in the 4th round are quadratic, and then we construct MQ systems in order to fully utilize degrees of freedom and derived equations. Using the Crossbred algorithm, we give a preimage attack on 4-round Keccak$[r = 640, c = 160, l = 80]$ using one message block and preimage attacks on 4-round Keccak-224/256 using two message blocks.

To the best of our knowledge, we propose the first analysis of 4-round Keccak $[r = 640, c = 160, l = 80]$ in the Keccak preimage challenges and give several 78-bit matched preimages. Besides, we improve complexities of preimage attacks on 4-round Keccak-224/256. Table 1 lists the results of this paper compared with the previous ones. The complexity in list is the times of 4-round Keccak permutation.

The rest of this paper is organized as follows. Section 2 shows notations and preliminaries of Keccak as well as the properties of the nonlinear layer χ, followed by the complexity elaboration of solving MQ systems. Preimage attacks on 4-round Keccak-224/256 are present in Sect. 3. And the preimage attack on the challenge with implementation details is shown in Sect. 4. Finally, Sect. 5 concludes this paper.

2 Preliminaries and Main Techniques

In this section, we will give the notation and the introduction to Keccak with some properties of the nonlinear layer χ. Then we elaborate the complexity of solving a MQ system.

2.1 Notation

r Rate of a sponge function

c Capacity of a sponge function

b Bit width of a permutation, $b = r + c$

R The round function of Keccak permutation

$\theta, \rho, \pi, \chi, \iota$ The five mapping steps of R. A subscript i denotes the mapping step in the i-th round, e.g., χ_i denotes χ in the i-th round for $i = 0, 1, 2, \ldots$.

L Composition of θ, ρ and π and its inverse denoted by L^{-1}

M Input message

A_i Input of the i-th round function, $A_{i+1} = \chi(B_i)$, $i = 0, 1, 2, \ldots$

A'_i Input of ρ in the i-th round, $A'_i = \theta(A_i)$, $i = 0, 1, 2, \ldots$

B_i Input of χ in the i-th round, $B_i = L(A_i)$, $i = 0, 1, 2, \ldots$

2.2 Keccak-f Permutation

In the Keccak hash function, the Keccak-f permutation with width b is denoted by Keccak-$f[b]$, where $b \in \{25, 50, 100, 200, 400, 800, 1600\}$. The state for Keccak-$f[b]$ can be represented as a $5 \times 5 \times w$-bit state as depicted in Fig. 1. $A[x, y]$ denotes a lane in the state, where x, y are in $\{0, 1, 2, 3, 4\}$. Each bit in $A[x, y]$ is denoted as $A[x, y, z]$ with $0 \leq z < w$.

Keccak-$f[b]$ consists of $12 + 2log_2(b/25)$ rounds of permutation R. Each round R consists of five steps, denoted by θ, ρ, π, χ and ι. $R = \iota \circ \chi \circ \pi \circ \rho \circ \theta$.

$$\theta : A[x, y, z] = A[x, y, z] \oplus \sum_{y=0}^{4} A[x - 1, y, z] \oplus \sum_{y=0}^{4} A[x + 1, y, z - 1],$$

$$\rho : A[x, y, z] = A[x, y, z] \lll T[x, y],$$

$$\pi : A[y, 2x + 3y, z] = A[x, y, z],$$

$$\chi : A[x, y, z] = A[x, y, z] \oplus (A[x + 1, y, z] \oplus 1) \cdot A[x + 2, y, z],$$

$$\iota : A[0, 0, z] = A[0, 0, z] \oplus RC_i[z].$$

Table 1. Comparison of preimage attacks on 4-round Keccak.

Digest length	Instances	Guessing times	Solving complexity	Total complexity	Ref
224	Keccak-224	2^{213}	2^6	2^{219}	[7]
		2^{207}	2^8	2^{215}	[10]
		–	–	[a]2^{202}	[5]
		2^{192}	2^8	2^{200}	[8]
		2^{164}	2^{18}	[b]2^{182}	Sect. 3.1
256	Keccak-256	2^{251}	2^3	2^{254}	[7]
		2^{239}	2^8	2^{247}	[10]
		–	–	[c]2^{231}	[5]
		2^{218}	2^8	2^{226}	[8]
		2^{196}	2^{18}	[d]2^{214}	Sect. 3.2
80	Keccak[$r = 1440$, $c = 160, l = 80$]	2^{54}	–	Solved	[3]
	Keccak[$r = 640$, $c = 160, l = 80$]	2^{39}	2^{19}	2^{58}	Sect. 4.1

[a]The complexity is equal to 2^{217} bit operations.
[b]The complexity is equal to 2^{197} bit operations.
[c]The complexity is equal to 2^{246} bit operations.
[d]The complexity is equal to 2^{229} bit operations.

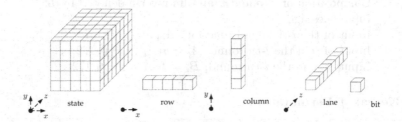

Fig. 1. State of Keccak

Here "$\oplus$" and "$\cdot$" are additions and multiplications over $\mathbb{F}_2$. $T[x, y]$ are offsets and RC_i are constants for round i. Since ι has no influence on our attacks, we ignore it in the rest of the paper.

2.3 The Keccak Hash Function

The Keccak hash function is the family of sponge functions [1] with Keccak-$f[b]$ permutation. The function is parameterized by the rate r, capacity c, and output length l which satisfies $r + c = b$, and denoted as Keccak[r,c,l]. The standardized Keccak functions restricted to Keccak[1152,448,224], Keccak[1088,512,256],

Keccak[832,768,384], and Keccak[576,1024,512] are called Keccak-224, Keccak-256, Keccak-384 and Keccak-512 respectively.

As illustrated in Fig. 2, the sponge function has two phases, absorbing phase and squeezing phase. The b-bit initial state (IV) is set to be all 0's. At the beginning, padded message is divided into blocks with length of r. The first r-bits of IV is XORed with the first block and then is sent to f. Again, the first r-bits of output is XORed with the second block and computed in f. This procedure is repeated until all the blocks are absorbed. After that, if l is smaller than r, the first l-bit output of the absorbing phase is the output string. Otherwise, if l is greater than r, another function f is applied to produce r more bits. This procedure is repeated until we obtain enough output strings. Then the output strings are truncated to a l-bit digest.

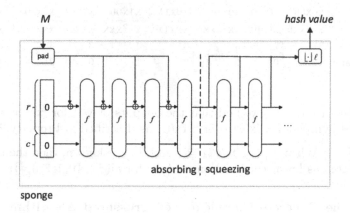

Fig. 2. Sponge construction

The padding rule for Keccak, named multi-rate padding, extends a message M to be a message of the form $M10^*1$. That is, M is first padded with a single bit "1" and then with a smallest non-negative number of "0" and finally with a single bit "1" in order to produce a padded message whose bit length becomes multiple of r. The SHA-3 family adopts standardized Keccak functions except that it applies a different padding rule of the form $M0110^*1$. We refer the readers to [2] for more details.

2.4   Properties of Step χ

Before introducing attacks on Keccak functions, we first show some properties of the nonlinear step χ and its inverse χ^{-1}.

For the 5-bit input $a = a_0a_1a_2a_3a_4$ of χ, the output $b = b_0b_1b_2b_3b_4$ can be expressed as $b_i = a_i \oplus (a_{i+1} \oplus 1)a_{i+2}$.

Property 1. [7] Given two consecutive bits b_i, b_{i+1} of the output of χ, a linear equation can be set up on the input bits as $b_i = a_i \oplus (b_{i+1} \oplus 1) \cdot a_{i+2}$. Specifically, the equation turns to be $a_i = b_i$ in the case of $b_{i+1} = 1$.

The inverse operation χ^{-1} has algebraic degree 3, and its algebraic normal form can be written as

$$a_i = b_i \oplus (b_{i+1} \oplus 1) \cdot (b_{i+2} \oplus (b_{i+3} \oplus 1) \cdot b_{i+4}). \tag{1}$$

To reduce algebraic degrees of the output, the input has at most two variables and these variables should not be consecutive. Let x and c stand for the variable and constant, respectively. Each constant c could be 1 or 0. Since variables are not consecutive, the inputs are in the form of 'xcxcc'. Table 2 lists the inputs and their corresponding outputs of χ^{-1}.

Table 2. Inputs and their corresponding outputs of χ^{-1} for the 'xcxcc' input pattern

Inputs	x0x00	x0x01	x0x10	x0x11	x1x00	x1x01	x1x10	x1x11
Outputs	xx^2xx0	x0x01	xx^2xxx^2	$xxx1x^2$	xx^2xxx	x1x0x	xx^2xxx^2	$xxx1x^2$
#Linear	3	2	3	3	4	3	3	3
#Quadratic	1	0	2	1	1	0	2	1

According to Table 2, we find that the outputs of χ^{-1} for 'xcxcc' are linear only when the inputs are 'x0x01' or 'x1x01' as described in Property 2.

Property 2. [7] When $b_{i+3} = 0$, $b_{i+4} = 1$ and b_{i+1} is known, then the input a_j's can be written as linear combinations of b_j's, for all $i \in \{0, 1, 2, 3, 4\}$.

2.5   On the Concrete Complexity of Crossbred Algorithm with $D = 2$

In this section, we introduce an algorithm, the Crossbred algorithm [9] with $D = 2$ case, and elaborate the concrete complexity for solving MQ systems. The subsequent attacks on 4-round Keccak are based on this algorithm.

An MQ polynomial of n Boolean variables $x_1, x_2, \ldots, x_n$ over binary field $\mathbb{F}_2$ is defined as

$$z(x_1, \ldots x_n) = \sum_{1 \leq i < j \leq n} a_{i,j} x_i x_j + \sum_{1 \leq i \leq n} b_i x_i + c, \tag{2}$$

where $a_{i,j} \in \mathbb{F}_2$, $b_i \in \mathbb{F}_2$ and $c \in \mathbb{F}_2$. Then an MQ system of m equations and n variables, called an (m, n) MQ system, is given by

$$\begin{cases} z_1(x_1, \ldots, x_n) = 0, \\ z_2(x_1, \ldots, x_n) = 0, \\ \quad \vdots \\ z_m(x_1, \ldots, x_n) = 0. \end{cases}$$

where $z_i(x_1, \ldots, x_n)$ are MQ polynomials for $i = 1, 2, \ldots, m$.

The MQ polynomial z in (2) can be written in the residual form

$$z(x_1, \ldots x_n) = x_1 f_1 + \cdots + x_{n-1} f_{n-1} + L + c \tag{3}$$

where f_i is a linear functions from variables $x_{i+1}, \ldots, x_n$ and L is a linear combination of $x_1, \ldots, x_n$. According to (3), an (m, n) MQ system can be transformed to the following form

$$\begin{cases} z_1 = x_1 f_1^1 + x_2 f_2^1 + \cdots + x_{n-1} f_{n-1}^1 + L_1 + c_1 & = 0, \\ z_2 = x_1 f_1^2 + x_2 f_2^2 + \cdots + x_{n-1} f_{n-1}^2 + L_2 + c_2 & = 0, \\ \vdots \\ z_m = x_1 f_1^m + x_2 f_2^m + \cdots + x_{n-1} f_{n-1}^m + L_m + c_m & = 0 \end{cases} \tag{4}$$

Our next step is to derive polynomials such that more coefficients of x_i are constants based on the residual form (4). Taking f_{n-1}^j as instance, all possibilities of f_{n-1}^j are 0, x_n, which means that there exists a linear combination $(\alpha_1, \alpha_2, \ldots, \alpha_m)$ such that $\sum_{j=1}^m \alpha_j f_{n-1}^j = 0$. We use a vector v_{n-1}^j of dimension 1 to illustrate f_{n-1}^j. If $f_{n-1}^j = x_n$, set $v_{n-1}^j = (1)$; otherwise, set $v_{n-1}^j = (0)$. The problem of finding α_j can be reduced to solving the linear system as follows

$$\left(v_{n-1}^1, v_{n-1}^2, \ldots, v_{n-1}^m\right) \begin{pmatrix} \alpha_1 \\ \alpha_2 \\ \vdots \\ \alpha_m \end{pmatrix} = 0.$$

There are at least $m - 1$ linearly independent solutions and each solution corresponds to a combination of $z_1, z_2, \ldots, z_m$ which derives a polynomial

$$\sum_{j=1}^m \alpha_j z_j = x_1 \sum_{j=1}^m \alpha_j f_1^j + \cdots + x_{n-2} \sum_{j=1}^m \alpha_j f_{n-2}^j + \sum_{j=1}^m \alpha_j L_j + \sum_{j=1}^m \alpha_j c_j.$$

The same execution can be performed on other coefficients. In general, we aim to find linear combinations $\alpha = (\alpha_1, \ldots, \alpha_m)$ such that $\sum_{j=1}^m \alpha_j f_i^j = 0$ for each $i = n - t, n - t + 1, \ldots, n - 1$ with a given $1 < t < n$. Then we obtain the following *remainder equation*

$$\sum_{j=1}^m \alpha_j z_j = \sum_{i=1}^{n-t-1} x_i \sum_{j=1}^m \alpha_j f_i^j + \sum_{j=1}^m \alpha_j L_j + \sum_{j=1}^m \alpha_j c_j = 0. \tag{5}$$

Now we discuss the number of solutions of α, which determines the number of remainder equations we have. Let $f_i^j = v_i^j (x_{i+1}, \ldots, x_n)^\top$, where v_i^j is an $(n - i)$ dimensional binary row vector. Then α satisfies the condition $\alpha M = 0$, where

$$M = \begin{pmatrix} v_{n-t}^1 & v_{n-t+1}^1 & \cdots & v_{n-1}^1 \\ v_{n-t}^2 & v_{n-t+1}^2 & \cdots & v_{n-1}^2 \\ \vdots & \vdots & \ddots & \vdots \\ v_{n-t}^m & v_{n-t+1}^1 & \cdots & v_{n-1}^m \end{pmatrix}$$

and is of dimension $m \times \frac{t(t+1)}{2}$. There are at least $m - \frac{t(t+1)}{2}$ independent solutions of α, and hence $m - \frac{t(t+1)}{2}$ remainder equations can be derived.

We use guess-and-determine techniques to solve remainder equations. It is obvious that for any fixed values of $x_1, \ldots, x_{n-t-1}$, each remainder Eq. (5) is reduced to a linear equation. Then a linear system of $m - \frac{t(t+1)}{2}$ equations over $t + 1$ variables can be derived for each guess of variables and can be solved by Gaussian elimination. If the system is solvable, a solution can be verified by substituting it into the MQ system of equations. If the solution is verified correctly, we find the solution for the MQ equations, otherwise, the corresponding guess is wrong. In order to guarantee that there is no more than one solution on average for each guess, choose t such that $m - \frac{t(t+1)}{2} \geq t + 1$.

Complexity Analysis: The computational complexity involves three parts, of which the first is for computing the remainder equations, the second is for solving the remainder equations and the third is for verifying the survived solutions.

The remainder equations can be obtained by Gaussian elimination on an $m \times \frac{t(t+1)}{2}$ binary matrix with the complexity of $m^2 \cdot \frac{t(t+1)}{2}$ bit operations. The memory cost is $m \times \frac{t(t+1)}{2} < m^2$ bits.

For solving the remainder equations, guess $n - t - 1$ bits and solve a derived linear system of $m - \frac{t(t+1)}{2}$ equations over $t + 1$ variables. With the help of Gray code, each equation update needs only n bit operations and totally $(m - \frac{t(t+1)}{2})n$ bit operations are needed to update a linear system. Then the linear system can be solved by Gaussian elimination with $(m - \frac{t(t+1)}{2})^2(t + 1)$ bit operations. On average, there are $2^{t+1-(m-\frac{t(t+1)}{2})} = 2^{\frac{(t+1)(t+2)}{2}-m}$ solutions for each linear system. Here, we use two binary matrices of size $(m - \frac{t(t+1)}{2}) \times (t + 1)$ in the memory, one for storing the iterated system and the other for solving the linear system. This memory cost can be shared by all guesses.

In order to verify the solutions, a solution is substituted into the MQ equations. Assume that each solution is verified correct for each equation with the probability $1/2$, then verifying a solution needs to compute $\sum_{i=1}^{m} i (1/2)^i \approx 2$ equations. Computing each equation needs at most $\binom{n}{2}$ AND operations and $\binom{n}{2} + n$ XOR operations. And hence, verifying a solution needs about $2n(n+1) \approx 2n^2$ bit operations. In order to store the (m, n) MQ equations, the memory cost is at most $m(\binom{n}{2} + n + 1) = m\left(\frac{n(n+1)}{2} + 1\right)$ bits.

Let T and M denote the computational cost in terms of bit operations and memory cost in terms of bits for solving an (m, n) MQ system, then we have

$$
T = m^2 \cdot \frac{t(t+1)}{2} + 2^{n-t-1}\left((m - \frac{t(t+1)}{2}) \cdot n + (m - \frac{t(t+1)}{2})^2(t+1)\right)
$$

$$
+ 2^{n-t-1} \cdot 2^{\frac{(t+1)(t+2)}{2}-m} \cdot 2n^2
$$

$$
\approx 2^{n-t-1}(t+1)\left(m - \frac{t(t+1)}{2}\right)^2 + 2^{n-m+\frac{t(t+1)}{2}+1} \cdot n^2
$$

and

$$M = m \cdot \frac{t(t+1)}{2} + 2 \left(m - \frac{t(t+1)}{2} \right) (t+1) + m \left(\frac{n(n+1)}{2} + 1 \right)$$
$$< \left(\frac{(t+1)(t+5)}{2} + \frac{n(n+1)}{2} \right) m.$$

For the worst case $m = n$,

$$T \approx 2^{n-t-1} \left(n - \frac{t(t+1)}{2} \right)^2 (t+1) + 2^{\frac{t(t+1)}{2}+1} \cdot n^2.$$

Choose t such that $n - \frac{t(t+1)}{2} \geq t+1$ and $n - \frac{(t+1)(t+2)}{2} < t+2$, i.e., $\sqrt{2n} - 3 < t < \sqrt{2n} - 1$. Then we have $n - \frac{t(t+1)}{2} = n - \frac{(t+1)(t+2)}{2} + t < 2t + 3$ and $\frac{t(t+1)}{2} \leq n-t-1$. Consequently, $T < 2^{n-t-1} \cdot (2t+3)^2 (t+1) + 2^{n-t-1} \cdot 2n^2 < 2^{n+2-\sqrt{2n}} \cdot \left(2n^2 + 8n\sqrt{2n} + 8n + \sqrt{2n} \right)$.

It is noted that our algorithm is suitable to any parameter (m, n). Generally, the number of equations is larger than that of equations, i.e., $m \geq n$. $m < n$ corresponds to the case with more than 1 solutions on average. $n - m$ variables can be set to constant and the case is reduced to the $m = n$ case.

Comparison. In this section, we compare our method with the fast exhaustive search [4] and polynomial method [5].

In [4], the brute force can be sped up by enumeration in the standard Gray code. The fast exhaustive search (FES) needs $2d \cdot \log n \cdot 2^n$ bit operations. When $m = n$, in order to compare the complexity with that of the FES, which is $2^{n+2} \log n$ bit operations, we just need to compare $C(n) = 2^{-\sqrt{2n}} \cdot \left(2n^2 + 8n\sqrt{2n} + 8n + \sqrt{2n} \right)$ with $\log n$. When $n \geq 64$, $C(n) < \log n$, Crossbred algorithm has lower complexity than FES in terms of bit operations.

The polynomial method [5] includes two procedures, of which the first is enumerating the isolated solutions to the polynomial system and the second is testing the solutions. In the first procedure, to achieve lower complexity, the algorithm enumerates solutions to probabilistic polynomials that are of lower degree, and hence the algorithm is probabilistic, though the probability may be high and close to 1. In this algorithm, exponential potential solutions are obtained, stored and handled in the memory with extensive use of Möbius transformations, giving rise to heavy memory cost.

By contrast, our method is a deterministic algorithm. Our algorithm avoids storing many candidate solutions and high degree polynomials. In our algorithm, the memory is used to store linear systems and the original quadratic systems, where the updated linear systems can share the same memory, such that the memory cost in our method is feasible. When used in security analysis of cryptosystems, the memory cost is within the ability of a single PC.

Here, we list the comparison of our algorithm with fast exhaustive search [4] and memory-optimized variant of polynomial method [5] in Table 3 for some practical parameters.

Table 3. Comparison of concrete complexities in terms of bit operations and memory costs in terms of bits. The memory cost of exhaustive search is small and omitted here.

Variables n	Complexity (bit operations)	Memory (bits)	Algorithm
80	2^{84}	–	Exhaustive search [4]
	2^{77}	2^{60}	Polynomial method [5]
	2^{80}	2^{18}	Ours($m = n, t = 11$)
	2^{76}	2^{19}	Ours($m = 2n, t = 16$)
128	2^{133}	–	Exhaustive search [4]
	2^{117}	2^{91}	Polynomial method [5]
	2^{126}	2^{20}	Ours($m = n, t = 14$)
	2^{120}	2^{21}	Ours($m = 2n, t = 21$)
192	2^{197}	–	Exhaustive search [4]
	2^{170}	2^{132}	Polynomial method [5]
	2^{188}	2^{22}	Ours($m = n, t = 18$)
	2^{180}	2^{23}	Ours($m = 2n, t = 26$)
256	2^{261}	–	Exhaustive search [4]
	2^{223}	2^{173}	Polynomial method [5]
	2^{249}	2^{23}	Ours($m = n, t = 21$)
	2^{241}	2^{24}	Ours($m = 2n, t = 30$)

The results in Table 3 show that the Crossbred algorithm requires lower computational costs than polynomial method when n is small and m outperforms n. When n becomes larger and m is close to n, our method needs more bit operations. Hence our method is more suitable for the subsequent attacks on 4-round Keccak which yield MQ problems with small n and large m. By this algorithm, solving an MQ problem can be reduced to calls to solving linear systems, which are easy to parallelize using single instruction multiple data (SIMD) speedup. More details about implementation are discussed in Sect. 4.2. Take an example to show the efficiency of this method. For example, an ($m = 4n, n = 80$) MQ instance can be solved by solving 2^{45} linear systems of 45 equations over 35 variables with memory cost 2^{20} bits, which are feasible on modern microprocessors.

3   Preimage Attacks on 4-Round Keccak

In this section, we introduce preimage attacks on 4-round Keccak via solving systems of quadratic Boolean equations. Based on a 2-round linear structure, we derive an algebraic system such that the output after 3 rounds of degree at most 2, and then we solve this algebraic system using the algorithm in Sect. 2.5.

3.1 Preimage Attack on 4-Round Keccak-224

In the following, we extend the linear structure in [7] and improve the preimage attack on 4-round Keccak-224, where two message blocks are used.

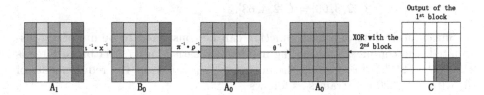

Fig. 3. The one backward round of Keccak-224

Our structure, applied on the second block, consists of one backward round $A_0 = R^{-1}(A_1)$ and two forward rounds $A_2 = R(A_1), A_3 = R(A_2)$. Here, A_0 is the XOR of the output of the first message block with the second message block. Figure 3 shows one backward round for 4-round Keccak-224. The bits of lanes in green boxes are of degree 1. The lanes in light gray(resp. dark gray) boxes are set to constants 0's(resp. 1's). And those in white boxes represent arbitrary constants. We set 10 lanes of state $A_1[0, y]$ and $A_1[2, y], y \in \{0, \ldots, 4\}$ as variables, i.e., there are totally $10 \times 64 = 640$ variables, while the other lanes are set to constants. According to Property 2, we have

$$A_1[3, y] = 0, y \in \{0, \ldots, 4\},$$
$$A_1[4, y] = \text{0xFFFF FFFF FFFF FFFF}, y \in \{0, \ldots, 4\},$$

then the output in B_0 are linear. Instead of directly setting all 5 lanes of $A_1[1, y]$ to zero like [8,10], we only set

$$A_1[1, y] = 0, y \in \{0, 1, 3\},$$

and $A_1[1, 2]$ and $A_1[1, 4]$ are arbitrary constants which helps to find different messages by setting all possible values. Furthermore, after ρ^{-1} and π^{-1} we have $A_0'[x, 3] \oplus A_0'[x, 4] = \text{0xFFFF FFFF FFFF FFFF}, x \in \{2, 3, 4\}$. When using only one message block, the last 449 bits of A_0 are set to 0 or 1 as the capacity or padding bits. Here we use two message blocks to reduce the number of constraints on A_0. Denote the output state of the first block as C, the constraints resulting from capacity and padding rules become

$$\begin{aligned}
A_0[x, 3] &= C[x, 3], x = 3, 4, \\
A_0[x, 4] &= C[x, 4], x \in \{0, 1, \cdots, 4\}, \\
A_0[2, 3, 63] &= C[2, 3, 63] \oplus 1.
\end{aligned} \tag{6}$$

Due to step θ, $A_0[x,3,z] \oplus A_0[x,4,z] = A_0'[x,3,z] \oplus A_0'[x,4,z] = 1, x \in \{2,3,4\}, z \in \{0,1,\cdots,63\}$. Hence, C should satisfy

$$C[3,3] \oplus C[3,4] = \text{0xFFFF FFFF FFFF FFFF},$$
$$C[4,3] \oplus C[4,4] = \text{0xFFFF FFFF FFFF FFFF}, \tag{7}$$
$$C[2,3,63] = C[2,4,63].$$

Since output bits of a hash function can be considered to be uniformly distributed, the complexity of finding a preimage satisfying (7) via brute force is $2^{64+64+1} = 2^{129}$. Once getting the output C, A_0 can meet the requirements of (6) with only 320 constraints as follows

$$A_0[x,4] = C[x,4], x \in \{0,1,\cdots,4\}. \tag{8}$$

Then we linearize bits in A_2 as illustrated in Fig. 4. To avoid the propagation by θ, the following $2 \times 64 = 128$ constraints are added

$$\sum_{y=0}^{4} A_1[0,y] = \alpha, \sum_{y=0}^{4} A_1[2,y] = \beta, \tag{9}$$

where α, β are 64-bit constants. In this way, the outputs in A_2 are linear on the variables. After a round of R, the outputs in A_3 are of degree 2, which are indicated in orange in Fig. 4. Since L is a linear operation, we can set up series of quadratic polynomials of B_3.

Due to Property 1, we obtain $2 \times 64 + 32 = 160$ quadratic equations from 224-bit hash value, i.e.,

$$B_3[0,0,z] \oplus (A_4[1,0,z] \oplus 1) \cdot B_3[2,0,z] = A_4[0,0,z], z = 0,1,\cdots,63,$$
$$B_3[1,0,z] \oplus (A_4[2,0,z] \oplus 1) \cdot B_3[3,0,z] = A_4[1,0,z], z = 0,1,\cdots,63, \tag{10}$$
$$B_3[2,0,z] \oplus (A_4[3,0,z] \oplus 1) \cdot B_3[4,0,z] = A_4[2,0,z], z = 0,1,\cdots,31.$$

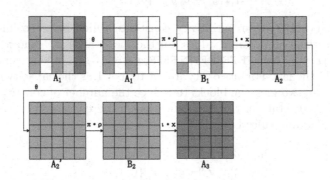

Fig. 4. The 2 forward rounds of Keccak-224

Assuming that 0s and 1s appear equally in A_4, about half of equations can be written as $B_3[x, y, z] = A_4[x, y, z]$. By Guo et al.'s study [7], quadratic bits in B_3 can be linearized by guessing values of linear polynomials. Appendix A shows how to linearize a bit in B_3. Here we give 2-bit linearization by guessing 11 values of linear polynomials. For $B_3[0, 0, z]$ and $B_3[1, 0, z + 44]$, since both ρ and π are permutation steps, we can get the corresponding bits $A'_3[0, 0, z]$ and $A'_3[1, 1, z]$. According to

$$A'_3[x, y, z] = A_3[x, y, z] \oplus \sum_{y=0}^{4} A_3[x - 1, y, z] \oplus \sum_{y=0}^{4} A_3[x + 1, y, z - 1],$$

as shown in Fig. 5, linearizing two bits requires 21 linearized bits in A_3, i.e.,

$$A_3[4, y, z], A_3[0, y, z], A_3[1, 1, z], A_3[1, y, z - 1], A_3[2, y, z - 1], y \in \{0, \cdots, 4\}. \tag{11}$$

According to the equation

$$A_3[x, y, z] = B_2[x, y, z] \oplus (B_2[x + 1, y, z] \oplus 1) \cdot B_2[x + 2, y, z],$$

it is obvious that the only quadratic term in $A_3[x, y, z]$ is generated by $B_2[x + 1, y, z]$ and $B_2[x + 2, y, z]$. Hence we can linearize $A_3[x, y, z]$ by guessing values of $B_2[x + 1, y, z]$ or $B_2[x + 2, y, z]$. Note that $A_3[x, y, z]$ and $A_3[x - 1, y, z]$ share a common operand $B_2[x + 1, y, z]$ in their quadratic terms. By fixing the value of $B_2[x + 1, y, z]$, $A_3[x, y, z]$ and $A_3[x - 1, y, z]$ are linearized as well. Thus by guessing 11 bits

$$B_2[3, 1, z], B_2[3, y, z - 1], B_2[1, y, z], y \in \{0, \cdots, 4\}, \tag{12}$$

$B_3[0, 0, z]$ and $B_3[1, 0, z + 44]$ are linearized. Similarly, two equations $B_3[1, 0, z + 1] = A_4[1, 0, z + 1]$ and $B_3[2, 0, z] = A_4[2, 0, z]$ can also be linearized at the same time by guessing 11 values of linear polynomials.

According to (8), (9), (10), we have 160 quadratic equations over $640 - 320 - 128 = 192$ variables. Since the hash value can be regarded as random values, about 24 pairs from 160 quadratic equations can be used during 2-bit linearization. When $m = 12$, $n = 0$[1], an MQ problem with 136 equations over 36 variables is constructed.

Complexity Analysis: The MQ system has a solution with the probability 2^{-100}. Let t be 15, according to Sect. 2.5, the computing complexity is $2^{32} + 2^{31.3} \approx 2^{33}$ bit operations, which is equivalent to 2^{18} calls to the 4-round Keccak permutation. The memory complexity for solving the MQ system is 2^{17} bits. Compared with solving the MQ system, the computational cost of performing Gaussian Elimination on linear constraints can be omitted while the memory cost is 2^{19} bits for storing the linear system. In this case, the time complexity of this attack

---

[1] When $m > 12$, computing the remainder equations and verifying solutions cost more time than solving the remainder equations during the MQ system solving process, which increases the whole computing complexity.

is $2^{129} + 2^{64+100+18} = 2^{182}$ and the memory complexity is 2^{19} bits, which are shared by different MQ systems. By guessing $A[1,2], A[1,4], \alpha, \beta$ and guessing bits in B_2, we can get $2^{64+100} = 2^{164}$ messages that satisfy the conditions and thus our attack is feasible. For SHA3-224, the time complexity of the preimage attack is 2^{182} while the padding rule changes.

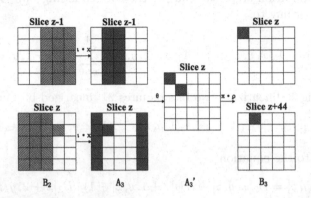

Fig. 5. Linearization of two quadratic bits in B_3. In the figure, bits related to the first bit are indicated by up diagonal slash and those related to the second bit are indicated by down diagonal slash. Besides, bits in green boxes are linear and bits in orange boxes are quadratic. (Color figure online)

3.2   Preimage Attack on 4-Round Keccak-256

The attack on 4-round Keccak-256 works similarly, where two message blocks are applied. Figure 6 shows one backward round for 4-round Keccak-256. We set 10 lanes of state $A_1[0,y]$ and $A_1[2,y], y \in \{0,\dots,4\}$ as variables. For constant bits in A_1, we have

$$A_1[1,y] = 0, y \in \{0,1,3,4\},$$
$$A_1[3,y] = 0, y \in \{0,\dots,4\},$$
$$A_1[4,y] = \texttt{0xFFFF FFFF FFFF FFFF}, y \in \{0,\dots,4\}.$$

The outputs of χ^{-1} are linear according to Property 2. Further, we have $A_0'[x,3] \oplus A_0'[x,4] = \texttt{0xFFFF FFFF FFFF FFFF}, x \in \{1,2,3,4\}$. According to the capacity and the padding rule, the output C of the first block and A_0 should satisfy

$$A_0[x,3] = C[x,3], x = 2,3,4,$$
$$A_0[x,4] = C[x,4], x \in \{0,1,\cdots,4\},$$
$$A_0[1,3,63] = C[1,3,63] \oplus 1.$$

Due to step θ, $A_0[x, 3, z] = A_0[x, 4, z] \oplus 1, x \in \{1, 2, 3, 4\}, z \in \{0, 1, \cdots, 63\}$. Hence C should satisfy

$$
\begin{aligned}
C[2, 3] \oplus C[2, 4] &= \text{0xFFFF FFFF FFFF FFFF}, \\
C[3, 3] \oplus C[3, 4] &= \text{0xFFFF FFFF FFFF FFFF}, \\
C[4, 3] \oplus C[4, 4] &= \text{0xFFFF FFFF FFFF FFFF}, \\
C[1, 3, 63] &= C[1, 4, 63].
\end{aligned}
\tag{13}
$$

The complexity of finding a preimage whose 4-round output satisfy (13) by brute force is $2^{3 \times 64 + 1} = 2^{193}$. Once obtaining the first message block, we set $5 \times 64 = 320$ constraints on A_0 as follows

$$
A_0[x, 4] = C[x, 4], x \in \{0, 1, \cdots, 4\}.
\tag{14}
$$

Thus A_0 meets the requirement of the capacity and the padding rule.

The two rounds forward for Keccak-256 is similar with Keccak-224 except that $A[1, 4, z] = 0, z = 0, 1, \ldots, 63$. To avoid the propagation by θ, we add $2 \times 64 = 128$ constraints

$$
\sum_{y=0}^{4} A_1[0, y] = \alpha, \sum_{y=0}^{4} A_1[2, y] = \beta,
\tag{15}
$$

where α and β are 64-bit constants. Totally, there are $(5 + 2) \times 64 = 448$ constraints on 640 variables. Similar to Keccak-224, we have $3 \times 64 = 192$ quadratic equations from 256-bit hash value. Assuming that 0s and 1s appear equally in the states, half of equations are in the form of $B_3[x, y, z] = A_4[x, y, z]$ on average. Similar to the preimage attack on 4-round Keccak-224, quadratic bits can be linearized by guessing values of linear polynomials.

We have 192 quadratic equations and $640 - 448 = 192$ variables. Among 192 quadratic Eqs. 32 pairs meet the requirement for the 2-bit linearization on average. When using $m = 12$ pairs of equations[2], an MQ problem with 168 equations over 36 variables is constructed and has a solution with the probability 2^{-132}. Let $t = 16$, the computing complexity is $2^{33.1} + 2^{15.3} \approx 2^{33}$ which is equivalent to 2^{18} calls to the 4-round Keccak permutation. The memory complexity for solving the MQ system and the constraint system are 2^{17} and 2^{19} bits. Totally, the time complexity of this attack is $2^{193} + 2^{64+132+18} = 2^{214}$ and the memory cost is 2^{19} bits. We can get 2^{196} two-block messages which satisfy the conditions by guessing the value of constants $A[1, 2], \alpha, \beta$ as well as bits in B_2 and thus our attack is feasible. For SHA3-256 and SHAKE256, in despite of different padding rules, the time complexities are also 2^{214}.

---

[2] When $m > 12$, computing the remainder equations and verifying solutions cost more time than solving the remainder equations during the MQ system solving process, which increases the whole computation costs.

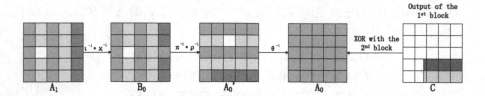

Fig. 6. The one backward round of Keccak-256

4 Application to Keccak Challenge

In this section, we implement the preimage attack on Keccak$[r = 640, c = 160, l = 80]$ in the Keccak challenges.

4.1 Preimage Attack on 4 Round Keccak$[r = 640, c = 160, l = 80]$

4-round Keccak$[r = 640, c = 160, l = 80]$ is an instance of Keccak with the width 800 in the Keccak Crunchy Crypto Collision and Preimage Contest [3]. In this section, we apply our structure to the preimage attack on 4 round Keccak$[r = 640, c = 160, l = 80]$ with only one message block.

The structure consists of one backward round $A_0 = R^{-1}(A_1)$ and two forward rounds $A_2 = R(A_1), A_3 = R(A_2)$, as illustrated in Fig. 7. We set 10 lanes of state $A_1[0, y]$ and $A_1[2, y], y \in \{0, \ldots, 4\}$ as variables, i.e., there are totally $10 \times 32 = 320$ variables. The other lanes are set as 448 constants, and we have

$$A_1[3, y] = 0, y \in \{0, \ldots, 4\},$$
$$A_1[4, y] = \texttt{0xFFFF FFFF}, y \in \{0, \ldots, 4\}.$$

Thus A_0 are all linear due to Property 2. According to capacity and padding rules, the last 162 bits satisfy the following constraints

$$A_0[3, 4, 30] = 1, A_0[3, 4, 31] = 1,$$
$$A_0[x, 4, z] = 0, x \in \{0, \ldots, 4\}, z \in \{0, \ldots, 31\}. \tag{16}$$

To avoid the propagation by θ, we add extra 64 constraints

$$\sum_{y=0}^{4} A_1[0, y] = \alpha, \sum_{y=0}^{4} A_1[2, y] = \beta, \tag{17}$$

where α, β are 32-bit constants. Totally, we have $320 - 162 - 64 = 94$ variables. Figure 7 presents how variables propagate in 2 forward rounds.

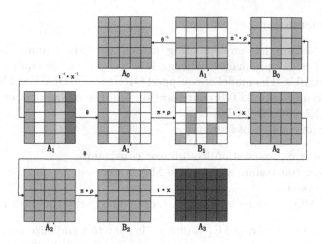

Fig. 7. The linear structure of Keccak$[r = 640, c = 160, n = 4]$

Similar to the preimage attack on 4-round Keccak-224, two equations satisfying $B_3[0, 0, z] = A_4[0, 0, z]$ and $B_3[1, 0, z + 12] = A_4[1, 0, z + 12]$ can be linearized by adding 11 equations. After linearizing some equations we use the method of solving MQ systems in Sect. 2.5 to deal with the rest ones.

In the Keccak preimage challenge, the given hash value of 4-round Keccak$[r = 640, c = 160, l = 80]$ is

75 1a 16 e5 e4 95 e1 e2 ff 22

and its bit representation is shown below.

$$H[0] = 10101110 \ 01011000 \ 01101000 \ 10100111$$
$$H[1] = 00100111 \ 10101001 \ 10000111 \ 01000111$$
$$H[2] = 11111111 \ 01000100$$

Due to Property 1, we obtained 48 quadratic equations from $H[i]$ and 26 equations are of the form of $B_3[x, y, z] = A_4[x, y, z]$ as underlined. We found that there are totally 5 pairs of bits satisfying the 2-bit linearization which is indicated in red. When linearizing these bits, note that there are 2 repetitive conditions so the number of extra equations is 53 rather than 55. After that, there remain 38 quadratic equations over 31 variables. The MQ system has a solution with the probability 2^{-7}. Let $t = 7$, according to Sect. 2.5, solving this MQ system needs to solve 2^{23} linear systems of 10 equations over 8 variables. The computing complexity is $2^{32.6} + 2^{31.9} \approx 2^{33}$ bit operations if the system is solvable, which is equivalent to 2^{19} calls to the 4-round Keccak permutation. And the memory complexity is 2^{14} bits. The memory cost of performing Gaussian Elimination on linear constraints is 2^{17} bits while the time cost can be omitted. Our attack obtains a preimage with the computing complexity $2^{32+7+19} = 2^{58}$ and the memory complexity 2^{17}. We give 78-bit matched preimages of 4-round Keccak$[r = 640, c = 160, l = 80]$ in Sect. 4.3.

4.2 Implementation

Our target platform for implementing attack towards 4-round Keccak[$r = 640, c = 160, l = 80$] preimage challenge is a hybrid cluster equipped with 50 GPUs and 20 CPUs. The model of equipped GPUs is NVIDIA Tesla V100 (Volta micro-architecture) with 32 GB configuration and the model of equipped CPUs is Intel Xeon E5-2699@2.2 GHz.

Our program consists of four steps:

1. Extract linear representation from linear constraints.
2. Iterate linear constraints and update MQ systems.
3. Solve MQ systems.
4. Substitute MQ solutions into original input and verify the hash result.

Since the program of solving MQ problems is easy to parallelize and suitable to GPU, we program the MQ solving routine on GPU and deploy the remaining subroutines on CPU.

As described in Sect. 4.1, the original Keccak system consists of 800 variables. In the preprocessing, the $480 + 162 + 64 = 706$ constraints could be imposed in advance so that the entire Keccak system can be represented by the remaining 94 variables and the computing complexity in further steps can be therefore reduced. In the main iteration, the program sets all the possible values of 53 extra equations and extracts the linear representation. These constraints, as well as 10 quadratic constraints which have been linearized by extra equations, are substituted into the 94-variables MQ system, resulting in a 31-variable MQ system of 38 equations. Subsequently, these MQ problems are copied to GPUs for the next solving process.

For each time a new constraint system is imposed, we apply Gaussian Elimination to extract the linear representations of variables. The yielded row echelon form matrix is stored in memory, thereby reproducing the complete message in the verification step.

To solve MQ systems, we employ the method in Sect. 2.5. A solution candidate can be obtained if the MQ problem is solvable. Using the solution and all the matrices stored in the previous steps, a message candidate can be reproduced. We verify a message candidate by comparing its 4-round hash with the target one. In practice, the execution time of the verification process is negligible.

Benchmarks. To inspect the practical performance of each subroutine in terms of the execution time, we present a benchmark on our implementation. All the subroutines are implemented using CUDA and C++. The computation time of each subroutine is shown in Table 4.

The subroutine to preprocess on 706 constraints will be executed only once. Need to mention that, the subroutine to iterate linear constraints, update MQ systems, and verify produced hashes are multithreaded and the program would process on a batch (2^{14}) of candidates, thus for these subroutines the execution time is measured as the elapsed time to process one batch. Also note that, the above-mentioned subroutines are executed on CPU. When a new batch of MQ systems is updated, it is copied to the off-chip memory of GPU for solving process. In practice, the GPU program to solve MQ systems can be pipelined with the subroutine to update MQ systems.

The result in Table 4 shows that setting $D = 2$ has the best practical performance for the Crossbred algorithm. According to Table 4, the entire search space is 2^{39} and the program takes 209.53 s to process on 2^{14} guess candidates. We estimate one preimage can be found in 223 GPU years.

Table 4. Preimage attack on 4-round Keccak$[r = 640, c = 160, l = 80]$ with 4 CPU cores and a single Tesla V100 GPU card.

MQ solving method	D	Runtime of preprocessing constant linear constraints (s)	Runtime of setting iterating constraints and updating MQ systems (s)	Runtime of solving MQ systems (s)	Runtime of verification (s)	Estimate runtime to obtain a preimage (GPU year)
Crossbred	2	7.76	21.21	183.89	4.43	223
Crossbred	3			263.94		308
Fast exhaustive search	N/A			212.13		253

4.3 Results

We executed our program on the GPU cluster consisting of 50 NVIDIA Tesla V100 GPUs for a total of 45 d and 7 h. Our program had traversed about $2^{33.84}$ guessing times, namely, $2^{33.84+19} = 2^{52.84}$ time complexity, which is equivalent to $2^{52.84}/2^{58} = 2.8\%$ of traversal space and obtained 2 message candidates which could produce hashes with 2 bit differentials.

The message and corresponding result hash of the first candidate are:
$A = $ d7 c4 77 ec   e8 22 18 ca   80 90 8a 29   7d 39 78 fc   10 93 1c 97
2e 42 88 81   f8 21 45 4e   04 8f d8 cd   74 27 c9 67   00 00 00 00
e2 7d d6 d0   c4 26 8d c2   19 23 07 6f   16 03 21 61   99 26 41 f8
d1 bd 77 7e   07 de ba b1   fb 70 27 32   8b d8 36 98   01 48 1a e4
00 00 00 00   00 00 00 00   00 00 00 00   00 00 00 00   00 00 00 00,
$H = $ 75 1a 16 e5   e4 95 c1 e2   f7 22,
where the differences are highlighted red.

The message and result hash of the second candidate are:
$A = $ 61 47 20 d5   57 c0 64 06   62 ef 6d 7c   f1 b3 38 2a   cb 8c 48 b6
ff 01 e4 e4   9f 09 9b 05   92 76 dd 25   d5 5e 82 61   11 c7 78 1a
f8 9d 2c b7   82 52 7b 9f   1e f9 59 b0   2d 3e a6 0b   60 57 6c 9f
00 fe 1b 1b   60 f6 64 fa   6d 89 22 da   2a a1 7d 9e   ee 38 87 e5
00 00 00 00   00 00 00 00   00 00 00 00   00 00 00 00   00 00 00 00,
$H = $ 75 1a 16 e5   e4 95 e1 e2   f7 32.

Along with the obtained 2-bit differential candidates, the frequencies of hamming distance between candidates' hash and target hash are counted in Table 5.

Table 5. Number of candidates with respect to the hamming distance from the target hash.

Hamming distance	Number	Hamming distance	Number
2	2	13	78146
3	7	14	97193
4	28	15	95992
5	115	16	69338
6	389	17	33109
7	1136	18	10398
8	2883	19	1866
9	7223	20	175
10	15155	21	11
11	30203	22	1
12	52239		
Total			425279

5   Conclusion

In this paper, improved preimage attacks are proposed on 4-round Keccak-224/256. We extend the attacks to the Keccak preimage challenge, implemented on a GPU cluster. Preimages of two-bit differentials with the target hashing value are found. Specifically, our attacks are based on the complexity elaboration of solving Boolean MQ systems, which is a fundamental tool in solving cryptographic problems and hence of independent interest.

Acknowledgment. This work was funded by The National Key Research and Development Program of China (Grant No. 2018YFA0704701), The Major Program of Guangdong Basic and Applied Research (Grant No. 2019B030302008) and Major Scientific and Techological Innovation Project of Shandong Province, China (Grant No. 2019JZZY010133).

A   Linearization of A Bit in B_3

By Guo et al.'s study [7], a quadratic bit in B_3 can be linearized by guessing 10 values of linear polynomials, which is called the *first linearization* method. Figure 8 illustrates how to linearize a bit in B_3. Since both ρ and π are permutation steps, we can get the corresponding bit in A_3'. According to

$$A_3'[x, y, z] = A_3[x, y, z] \oplus \sum_{y=0}^{4} A_3[x - 1, y, z] \oplus \sum_{y=0}^{4} A_3[x + 1, y, z - 1],$$

the corresponding bit is the *XOR*ed sum of 11 bits in A_3, as shown in Fig. 8. According to the equation

$$A_3[x, y, z] = B_2[x, y, z] \oplus (B_2[x + 1, y, z] \oplus 1) \cdot B_2[x + 2, y, z],$$

it is obvious that the only quadratic term in $A_3[x, y, z]$ is generated by $B_2[x + 1, y, z]$ and $B_2[x + 2, y, z]$. Hence we can linearize $A_3[x, y, z]$ by guessing values of $B_2[x + 1, y, z]$ or $B_2[x + 2, y, z]$. Note that $A_3[x, y, z]$ and $A_3[x - 1, y, z]$ share a common operand $B_2[x + 1, y, z]$ in their quadratic terms. By fixing the value of $B_2[x + 1, y, z]$, $A_3[x, y, z]$ and $A_3[x - 1, y, z]$ are linearized as well. Thus the 11 bits in A_3 can be linearized by guessing only 10 bits, i.e.,

$$B_2[x + 1, y, z], B_2[x + 3, y, z - 1], y \in \{0, \cdots, 4\}. \tag{18}$$

Equivalently, the bit in A_3' is linearized and the corresponding equation $B_3[x, y, z] = A_4[x, y, z]$ turns to be linear one.

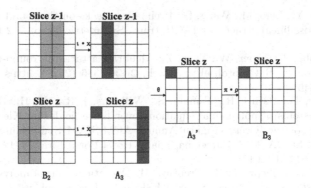

Fig. 8. The first quadratic bit linearization. We illustrate how to linearize a quadratic bit in B_3. In the figure, bits in green boxes are linear and bits in orange boxes are quadratic.

References

1. Bertoni, G., Daemen, J., Peeters, M., Assche, G.V.: Cryptographic sponge functions. Submission to NIST (Round 3) (2011). http://sponge.noekeon.org/CSF-0.1.pdf
2. Bertoni, G., Daemen, J., Peeters, M., Assche, G.V.: The Keccak reference, version 3.0. Submission to NIST (Round 3) (2011). http://keccak.noekeon.org/Keccak-reference-3.0.pdf
3. Bertoni, G., Daemen, J., Peeters, M., Asscher, G.V.: The Keccak crunchy crypto collision and preimage contest. https://keccak.team/crunchy_contest.html
4. Bouillaguet, C., et al.: Fast exhaustive search for polynomial systems in $\mathbb{F}_2$. In: Mangard, S., Standaert, F.-X. (eds.) CHES 2010. LNCS, vol. 6225, pp. 203–218. Springer, Heidelberg (2010). https://doi.org/10.1007/978-3-642-15031-9_14

5. Dinur, I.: Cryptanalytic applications of the polynomial method for solving multivariate equation systems over GF(2). Cryptology ePrint Archive, Report 2021/578 (2021). https://eprint.iacr.org/2021/578
6. Duarte, J.D.: On the complexity of the crossbred algorithm. IACR Cryptol. ePrint Arch. **2020**, 1058 (2020)
7. Guo, J., Liu, M., Song, L.: Linear structures: applications to cryptanalysis of round-reduced KECCAK. In: Cheon, J.H., Takagi, T. (eds.) ASIACRYPT 2016. LNCS, vol. 10031, pp. 249–274. Springer, Heidelberg (2016). https://doi.org/10.1007/978-3-662-53887-6_9
8. He, L., Lin, X., Yu, H.: Improved preimage attacks on 4-round Keccak-224/256. IACR Trans. Symmetric Cryptol. **2021**(1), 217–238 (2021)
9. Joux, A., Vitse, V.: A crossbred algorithm for solving Boolean polynomial systems. In: Kaczorowski, J., Pieprzyk, J., Pomykała, J. (eds.) NuTMiC 2017. LNCS, vol. 10737, pp. 3–21. Springer, Cham (2018). https://doi.org/10.1007/978-3-319-76620-1_1
10. Li, T., Sun, Y.: Preimage attacks on round-reduced KECCAK-224/256 via an allocating approach. In: Ishai, Y., Rijmen, V. (eds.) EUROCRYPT 2019. LNCS, vol. 11478, pp. 556–584. Springer, Cham (2019). https://doi.org/10.1007/978-3-030-17659-4_19
11. Li, T., Sun, Y., Liao, M., Wang, D.: Preimage attacks on the round-reduced Keccak with cross-linear structures. IACR Trans. Symmetric Cryptol. **2017**(4), 39–57 (2017)
12. Liu, F., Isobe, T., Meier, W., Yang, Z.: Algebraic attacks on round-reduced Keccak/Xoodoo. IACR Cryptol. ePrint Arch. **2020**, 346 (2020). https://eprint.iacr.org/2020/346
13. Lokshtanov, D., Paturi, R., Tamaki, S., Williams, R.R., Yu, H.: Beating brute force for systems of polynomial equations over finite fields. In: Klein, P.N. (ed.) Proceedings of the Twenty-Eighth Annual ACM-SIAM Symposium on Discrete Algorithms, SODA 2017, Barcelona, Spain, Hotel Porta Fira, 16–19 January, pp. 2190–2202. SIAM (2017)
14. Morawiecki, P., Pieprzyk, J., Srebrny, M.: Rotational cryptanalysis of round-reduced KECCAK. In: Moriai, S. (ed.) FSE 2013. LNCS, vol. 8424, pp. 241–262. Springer, Heidelberg (2014). https://doi.org/10.1007/978-3-662-43933-3_13
15. Morawiecki, P., Srebrny, M.: A SAT-based preimage analysis of reduced Keccak hash functions. Inf. Process. Lett. **113**(10–11), 392–397 (2013)
16. Rajasree, M.S.: Cryptanalysis of round-reduced KECCAK using non-linear structures. In: Hao, F., Ruj, S., Sen Gupta, S. (eds.) INDOCRYPT 2019. LNCS, vol. 11898, pp. 175–192. Springer, Cham (2019). https://doi.org/10.1007/978-3-030-35423-7_9
17. Wang, X., Lai, X., Feng, D., Chen, H., Yu, X.: Cryptanalysis of the hash functions MD4 and RIPEMD. In: Cramer, R. (ed.) EUROCRYPT 2005. LNCS, vol. 3494, pp. 1–18. Springer, Heidelberg (2005). https://doi.org/10.1007/11426639_1
18. Wang, X., Yin, Y.L., Yu, H.: Finding collisions in the full SHA-1. In: Shoup, V. (ed.) CRYPTO 2005. LNCS, vol. 3621, pp. 17–36. Springer, Heidelberg (2005). https://doi.org/10.1007/11535218_2
19. Wang, X., Yu, H.: How to break MD5 and other hash functions. In: Cramer, R. (ed.) EUROCRYPT 2005. LNCS, vol. 3494, pp. 19–35. Springer, Heidelberg (2005). https://doi.org/10.1007/11426639_2
20. Wang, X., Yu, H., Yin, Y.L.: Efficient collision search attacks on SHA-0. In: Shoup, V. (ed.) CRYPTO 2005. LNCS, vol. 3621, pp. 1–16. Springer, Heidelberg (2005). https://doi.org/10.1007/11535218_1

A Preimage Attack on Reduced
GIMLI-HASH

Yongseong Lee[1], Jinkeon Kang[2], Donghoon Chang[2,3], and Seokhie Hong[1(✉)]

[1] Institute of Cyber Security and Privacy (ICSP), Korea University,
Seoul, Republic of Korea
{yslee0804,shhong}@korea.ac.kr
[2] National Istitute of Standards and Technology (NIST), Gaithersburg, MD, USA
[3] Department of Computer Science, Indraprastha Institute of Information
Technology Delhi (IIIT-Delhi), Delhi, India
donghoon@iiitd.ac.in

Abstract. In CHES 2017, Bernstein et al. proposed GIMLI, a 384-bit permutation with 24 rounds, which aims to provide high performance on various platforms. In 2019, the full-round (24 rounds) GIMLI permutation was used as an underlying primitive for building AEAD GIMLI-CIPHER and hash function GIMLI-HASH. They were submitted to the NIST Lightweight Cryptography Standardization process and selected as one of the second-round candidates. In ToSC 2021, Liu et al. presented a preimage attack with a divide-and-conquer method on round-reduced GIMLI-HASH, which uses 5-round GIMLI. In this paper, we present preimage attacks on a round-reduced variant of GIMLI-HASH, in which the message absorbing phase uses 5-round GIMLI and the squeezing phase uses 9-round GIMLI. We call this variant as 5-9-round GIMLI-HASH. Our first preimage attack on 5-9-round GIMLI-HASH requires $2^{96.44}$ time complexity and 2^{97} memory complexity. This attack requires the memory for storing several precomputation tables in GIMLI SP-box operations. In our second preimage attack, we take a time-memory trade-off approach, reducing memory requirements for precomputation tables but increasing computing time for solving SP-box equations by SAT solver. This attack requires $2^{66.17}$ memory complexity and $2^{96+\epsilon}$ time complexity, where ϵ is a time complexity for solving SP-box equations. Our experiments using CryptoMiniSat SAT solver show that the maximum time complexity for ϵ is about $2^{20.57}$ 9-round GIMLI.

Keywords: Hash function · Preimage attack · GIMLI, GIMLI-HASH

1 Introduction

GIMLI [3] is a 384-bit permutation proposed at CHES 2017 by Bernstein et al. The number of rounds in GIMLI permutation is 24. GIMLI was designed for high performance in a broad range of platforms from 8-bit AVR microcontrollers to 64-bit Intel/AMD server CPUs. In 2019, AEAD GIMLI-CIPHER and hash function GIMLI-HASH were developed using GIMLI with 24 rounds as an underlying

© The Author(s), under exclusive license to Springer Nature Switzerland AG 2022
J. H. Park and S.-H. Seo (Eds.): ICISC 2021, LNCS 13218, pp. 217–237, 2022.
https://doi.org/10.1007/978-3-031-08896-4_11

primitive and submitted to the NIST Lightweight Cryptography Standardization process and selected as one of the second-round candidates [2]. GIMLI-HASH produces 256-bit fixed-length output but can be used as an extendable one-way function (XOF). GIMLI-CIPHER is based on a duplex mode of operation, and GIMLI-HASH uses the sponge mode with a rate of 128 bits and a capacity of 256 bits.

Since the GIMLI was proposed in 2017, it has been investigated by a number of analyses. Hamburg [6] analyzed 22.5-round GIMLI with meet-in-the-middle attack and pointed out the weak diffusion of GIMLI. However, this attack is not applicable to AEAD or hashing scheme. In ToSC 2021, Liu et al. [9] performed the full-round (24 rounds) distinguishing attack with 2^{52} time complexity using zero-internal-differential method. In Asiacrypt 2020, Flórez-Gutiérrez et al. [5] performed 24-round and 28-round distinguishing attacks against round-shifted GIMLI with time complexities of 2^{32} and 2^{64}, respectively. Although many rounds of round-shifted GIMLI were analyzed by the distinguishing attacks, there is no relation to the security of GIMLI-CIPHER or GIMLI-HASH.

Zong et al. [14] proposed the collision attack on 6-round GIMLI-HASH using differential characteristics with 2^{113} time complexity. In Crypto 2020, Liu et al. [8] performed the collision attack on 6-round GIMLI-HASH with a time complexity of 2^{64}. They also presented the semi-free-start collision with a time complexity of 2^{64} for a round-shifted 8-round GIMLI-HASH. In Asiacrypt 2020, Flórez-Gutiérrez et al. [5] performed the collision and semi-free-start collision attacks on round-shifted GIMLI-HASH, reaching up to 12 and 18 rounds, respectively. Both require $2^{96+\epsilon}$ time complexity, where ϵ is about 2^{10} GIMLI operations, experimentally obtained from the SAT solver.

As we can see in analyzing collision attacks on GIMLI-HASH by Flórez-Gutiérrez et al. [5], SAT solver is actively used for cryptanalysis. The SAT solver can determine whether a given boolean satisfiability problem (SAT problem) is satisfiable or unsatisfiable. Some cryptographic problems, such as finding differential trails or linear trails with minimal probability, are difficult to solve. To solve the complex cryptographic problems, these problems are transformed into SAT problems. For example, [11] made use of SAT solver to find differential trails on ARX cipher Salsa20. Using this method, differential cryptanalysis of the block cipher SIMON was performed [7]. Moreover, [10] was applied SAT solver to find linear trails on SPECK and Chaskey. Additionally, [13] analyzed integral cryptanalysis for ARX ciphers using SAT-solver of division property.

In ToSC 2021, Liu et al. [9] proposed preimage attacks on GIMLI-HASH and GIMLI-XOF-128 with divide-and-conquer method. Due to the weak diffusion of GIMLI, the preimage attack on reduced GIMLI-HASH can reach up to 5 rounds. It utilizes five message blocks that produce a specific 256-bit hash value of GIMLI-HASH.

Because of the weak diffusion of GIMLI, the divide-and-conquer method of dividing manipulable space into smaller spaces was effective on 5-round GIMLI-HASH. However, as the number of rounds increases, the effect of diffusion increases. Hence, the preimage attacks on GIMLI using the divide-and-conquer method do not apply more than 5-round. Instead, a preimage attack on 9-round GIMLI-XOF-128 was possible. Since the output size of GIMLI-XOF-128 is 128bit, the preimage attack on GIMLI-XOF-128 has fewer constraints than GIMLI-HASH which has the 256-bit output size. Moreover, because some results of SP function could be known under certain conditions, the effect of the first Small-swap operation disappeared. Therefore, the preimage attack on 9-round GIMLI-XOF performed with 2^{104} time complexity and 2^{70} memory complexity.

Our Contributions. In this paper, we present preimage attacks on 5-9-round GIMLI-HASH. GIMLI-HASH uses 24-round GIMLI, and Liu et al. proposed preimages attacks on 5-round GIMLI-HASH with the round-reduced GIMLI of 5 rounds (out of 24). As shown in Fig. 5, the 5-9-round GIMLI-HASH uses 5-round GIMLI in the message absorbing phase and 9-round GIMLI in the squeezing phase under the sponge construction. GIMLI-HASH has absorbed all message blocks into the state with 5-round GIMLI. In the squeezing phase of GIMLI-HASH, the first 128 bits of the state are returned as output blocks, interleaved with applications of 9-round GIMLI.

Given a 256-bit hash value of GIMLI-HASH, half of the hash value can make the other half with some appropriate 256-bit value and GIMLI. In the preimage attack on 5-round GIMLI-HASH [9], the divide-and-conquer method made the halves of the hash values overlap by weak diffusion of GIMLI. However, when the number of rounds increases, additional connections are needed to find the relation in the hash value, so the idea of Liu et al. no longer works. In this paper, we propose a new collision-finding trail to overcome the limitation of Liu et al.'s approach, and show that the preimage attack on 5-9-round GIMLI-HASH is possible with $2^{96.44}$ time complexity and 2^{97} memory complexity by using precomputation tables.

In addition, to reduce memory complexity, we propose equations that can be used instead of the precomputation tables. During the preimage attack, we find solutions on the fly by solving the equations instead of the precomputation tables. Using this method, the time complexity increases to $2^{96+\epsilon}$, but the memory complexity decreases to $2^{66.17}$, where ϵ is the time complexity of solving equations. To solve equations, we use CryptoMiniSat [12], one of the SAT solvers. Because our equations can be transformed to conjunctive normal form(CNF), we introduce how to transform given equations to CNF. Hence, the problem of finding solutions to the given our equations change to a SAT problem. Moreover, we conduct an experiment to measure the average time required to solve equations[1]. As the result of the experiments, the average time to find the solution of the most complex equation was $2^{19.15}$ times that of the full-round GIMLI($\approx 2^{20.57}$ 9-round GIMLI). Since the $\epsilon \approx 20.57$, the time complexity of solving equation method does not exceed 2^{128}. A summary of our results can be seen in Table 1.

Organization. This paper is organized as follows. In Sect. 2, we describe GIMLI and GIMLI-HASH with notations. In Sect. 3, we describe the general approach of preimage attack on GIMLI-HASH introduced in [9]. Our improved preimage

---

[1] The test code is on https://github.com/yslee0804/Gimli_hash_9r_test.

Table 1. Summary of attacks on GIMLI

Attack	Round	Technique	Time[a]	Memory[a],[b]	Reference
Preimage on GIMLI-HASH(256-bit output)	2	Divide-and-Conquer	42.4	32	[9]
	5		93.68	66	[9]
	5-9[c]		96.44	97	Sect. 4.2
			96+ϵ_1[e]	66.17	Sect. 4.3
Preimage on GIMLI-XOF-128(128-bit output)	9	Divide-and-Conquer	104	70	[9]
Distinguisher on GIMLI	24	Zero-Internal-Differential	52	Negligible	[9]
	24[d]	Symmetry	32	Negligible	[5]
	28[d]		64	Negligible	[5]
Collision on GIMLI-HASH (256-bit output)	6	Divide-and-Conquer	64	64	[8]
	12[d]	Symmetry	96+ϵ_2[e]	Negligible	[5]
	14[d]	Quantum	64+ϵ_2[e]	Negligible	[5]
Semi-free start Collision on GIMLI-HASH (256-bit output)	8[d]	Symmetry	64	Negligible	[8]
	18[d]		96+ϵ_2[e]	64	[5]
	20[d]	Quantum	64+ϵ_2[e]	64	[5]

(a) The time and memory complexity is expressed in log scale.
(b) The memory complexity measured base on 128-bit blocks.
(c) The last two permutations of GIMLI-HASH use 9-round GIMLI. The remaining permutations of GIMLI-HASH use 5-round GIMLI.
(d) This attack is on the round shifted GIMLI : starting from third round.
(e) ϵ_1 and ϵ_2 are the experimentally measured complexity($\epsilon_1 \approx 20.57$ and $\epsilon_2 \approx 10$). ϵ_1 is in Sect. 4.3 and ϵ_2 is in [5].

attack on GIMLI-HASH is in Sect. 4. The method using precomputation tables is in Sect. 4.2 and using equations with SAT-solver is in Sect. 4.3. The conclusion of this paper is in Sect. 5. Additionally, Liu et al.'s preimage attack on 5-round GIMLI-HASH, which motivated this paper, is included in Appendix A.

2   Preliminaries

In this section, we describe the GIMLI and GIMLI-HASH. We describe the structure and notation of GIMLI in Sect. 2.1, and GIMLI-HASH in Sect. 2.2.

2.1   Description of GIMLI

The permutation GIMLI consists of non-linear layer SP-box, linear layer Small-swap(S_SW) and Big-swap(B_SW), and constant addition. SP-box operation is performed preferentially every round, whereas other operations are applied a particular round of GIMLI. For $0 \leq i \leq 6$, Small-swap and constant addition occurs every $(4i + 1)$-th round, and Big-swap operation occur every $(4i + 3)$-th round. In other words, the GIMLI repeats the following 4 round process six times.

$$\underbrace{(SP \to S\_SW \to AC)}_{(4i+1)\text{-th round}} \to \underbrace{(SP)}_{(4i+2)\text{-th round}} \to \underbrace{(SP \to B\_SW)}_{(4i+3)\text{-th round}} \to \underbrace{(SP)}_{(4i+4)\text{-th round}}$$

The whole process of GIMLI can be seen in Algorithm 1.

GIMLI State. The GIMLI state S can be seen as a two-dimensional array with 3 rows and 4 columns, where each element is a 32-bit word as shown in Fig. 1. The notation $S[i][j]$ refers the 32-bit word in i-th row and j-th column where $0 \leq i \leq 2$ and $0 \leq j \leq 3$. In addition, the representation $S[i,k][j,l]$ means 4 words $S[i][j]$, $S[i][l]$, $S[k][j]$, and $S[k][l]$. For example, $S[1,2][0,2]$ indicate the words $S[1][0]$, $S[1][2]$, $S[2][0]$, and $S[2][2]$. Additionally, the representation $S[*][j]$ means the whole word in j-th column and $S[i][*]$ means the whole word in i-th row. In other words, $S[*][j]$ means $S[0,1,2][j]$ and $S[i][*]$ means $S[i][0,1,2,3]$.

To distinguish the state after each round, the notation S^i indicates the state after i-th round. In particular, S^0 indicates the state before the first round. Moreover, the notation $S^{i.5}$ means the state after the SP operation and before Small-swap or Big-swap. For example, $S^{0.5}$ indicates the state in the first round after SP operation but before Small-swap and constant addition.

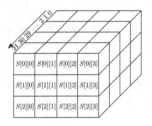

Fig. 1. The state of GIMLI

Non-linear Layer: SP-Box. The non-linear layer is the SP-Box on 96 bits, which is applied column-wise. The SP-Box is often treated as a function such that $SP : \mathbb{F}_2^{32 \times 3} \to \mathbb{F}_2^{32 \times 3}$. On three 32-bit input x, y, and z, SP updates them as follows:

$$
\begin{aligned}
x &\leftarrow x \lll 24 \\
y &\leftarrow y \lll 9
\end{aligned} \quad \Big\} \text{Compute in parallel}
$$

$$
\begin{aligned}
x &\leftarrow x \oplus (z \ll 1) \oplus ((y \wedge z) \ll 2) \\
y &\leftarrow y \oplus x \oplus ((x \vee z) \ll 1) \\
z &\leftarrow z \oplus y \oplus ((x \wedge y) \ll 3)
\end{aligned} \quad \Big\} \text{Compute in parallel}
$$

$$
\begin{aligned}
x &\leftarrow z \\
z &\leftarrow x
\end{aligned} \quad \Big\} \text{Compute in parallel}
$$

Linear Layers: Small-Swap, Big-Swap. The GIMLI consists of two linear operations; Small-swap(S_SW) and Big-swap (B_SW). These operations do not occur every round. S_SW is executed on the $(4i + 1)$ round, and B_SW is executed on the $(4i + 3)$ round, where $0 \leq i \leq 5$.

S_SW and B_SW affect only the first row of GIMLI state. S_SW operation swap the values $S[0][0]$ and $S[0][1]$, and swap the values $S[0][2]$ and $S[0][3]$. Similarly, B_SW operation swap the values $S[0][0]$ and $S[0][2]$, and swap the values $S[0][1]$ and $S[0][3]$. Figure 2 illustrates the S_SW and B_SW operations.

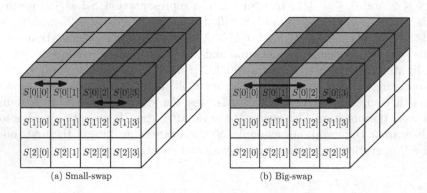

Fig. 2. GIMLI Small-swap (a) and Big-swap (b) operations

Constant Addition: AC. In constant addition, 32-bit round constant $rc_i = 0x9e377900 \oplus (24 - 4i)$ is xored to the state $S[0][0]$ in every fourth round where $0 \leq i \leq 5$.

2.2 GIMLI-HASH

GIMLI-HASH was built using the sponge construction framework. Sponge construction framework is a way to make a function with arbitrary input/output length from a permutation with fixed input/output length [4] (Fig. 3).

Algorithm 1. The permutation GIMLI

Input: A 384-bit state S. $S[i][j]$ is 32-bit word, where $0 \leq i \leq 2$ and $0 \leq j \leq 3$
Output: Gimli(S)

1: **for** $r = 0$ to 23 **do**
2:     **for** $j = 0$ to 3 **do**
3:         $S[*][j] \leftarrow SP(S[*][j])$
4:     **end for**
5:     **if** $r \bmod 4 = 0$ **then**
6:         Swap $S[0][0]$ and $S[0][1]$, swap $S[0][2]$ and $S[0][3]$
7:         $S[0][0] \leftarrow S[0][0] \oplus (0\text{x}9e377900 \oplus (24 - r))$
8:     **else if** $r \bmod 4 = 2$ **then**
9:         Swap $S[0][0]$ and $S[0][2]$, swap $S[0][1]$ and $S[0][3]$
10:    **end if**
11: **end for**
12: **return** S

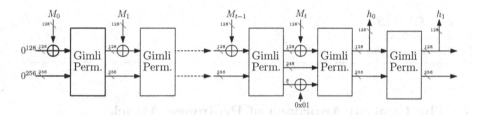

Fig. 3. The illustration of GIMLI-HASH

Algorithm 2 describes the GIMLI-HASH process. The GIMLI-HASH initializes the GIMLI state to 0. Then the input message of arbitrary length is read by dividing it into 16-byte blocks. Before reading the message, XOR 1 next to the last byte of input message. Then the input message is read by dividing it into 16-byte blocks. The remaining bytes in the last block are set to 0. This message modifying process is **pad**(M) in Algorithm 2.

The 16-byte blocks are sequentially XOR to the 0-th row of GIMLI state (which is $S[0][*]$) and perform GIMLI. When the last block is XORed to the first row of the state, 1 is also XORed to the last byte of the state which the byte position is 47 (line 5 in Algorithm 2). After the last message block is absorbed, perform the GIMLI and squeeze out the first 16-byte of the state (which is $h_0 = S[0][*]$). This value is the first 16-byte of the hash value. To get the remaining 16-byte of the hash value, perform the GIMLI again and then squeeze out the first 16-byte of the state (which is $h_1 = S[0][*]$). The final hash value is $h = (h_0, h_1)$ (line 10-13 in Algorithm 2).

In this paper, we consider the separated state in the GIMLI-HASH. That means the state after M_0 absorbed and the state after M_1 absorbed should be distinguishable. To distinguish these states, S_i indicates the state after M_i is absorbed. For example, if the message has $t + 1$ length$((M_0, M_1, \cdots, M_t))$, S_2 indicates the state $\mathbf{Gimli}(\mathbf{Gimli}(0^{384} \oplus (M_0\|0^{256})) \oplus (M_1\|0^{256})) \oplus (M_2\|0^{256})$ where the notation $\|$ is concatenation. Moreover, S_{h_0} and S_{h_1} indicate the states where h_0 and h_1 are squeezed, respectively. Note that $\mathbf{Gimli}(S_{h_0}) = S_{h_1}$.

Algorithm 2. The GIMLI-HASH function

Input: $M \in \{0, 1\}^*$
Output: 256-bit hash value $h = (h_0, h_1)$
1: The state S set to 0
2: $(M_0, M_1, \cdots, M_t) \leftarrow \mathbf{pad}(M)$
3: **for** $i = 0$ to t **do**
4:    **if** $i = t$ **then**
5:       $S[2][3] \leftarrow S[2][3] \oplus \text{0x01000000}$
6:    **end if**
7:    $S[0][*] \leftarrow S[0][*] \oplus M_i$
8:    $S \leftarrow \mathbf{Gimli}(S)$
9: **end for**
10: $h_0 \leftarrow S[0][*]$
11: $S \leftarrow \mathbf{Gimli}(S)$
12: $h_1 \leftarrow S[0][*]$
13: **return** $h = (h_0, h_1)$

---

3   The General Approach of Preimage Attack

In this section, we summarized the general approach of preimage attack on GIMLI-HASH, which Liu et al. performed in [9]. The overall preimage attack uses the meet-in-the-middle method and consists of four phases. It is also assumed to recover five message blocks $(M_0, M_1, M_2, M_3, M_4)$ for a given 256-bit hash value as shown in Fig. 4. A brief description of each phase is as follows.

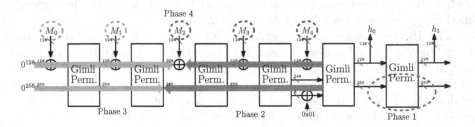

Fig. 4. The framework of preimage attack of GIMLI-HASH

Phase 1. From given hash values, find a 256-bit valid capacity part such that **Gimli**$(S_{h_0}) = S_{h_1}$. The 256-bit hash value can be seen as (h_0, h_1) which h_0 and h_1 are 128-bit length, respectively. Moreover, h_0 and h_1 are rate part of GIMLI. Therefore, if the valid capacity part of S_{h_1} or S_{h_0} is known, the whole state data is revealed and can be computed in the backward direction of GIMLI-HASH.

Phase 2. Choose M_3 and M_4, and compute backward direction. Since S_{h_0} was known, S_4 can be computed. Moreover, S_3 and S_2 can be known because M_4 and M_3 are chosen.

Phase 3. Choose M_0 and M_1 such that the capacity part of S_2 collides. The attacker can only control the rate part of S_0, S_1, and S_2 by M_0, M_1, and M_2, respectively. Moreover, the capacity parts of S_2 and S_0 are fixed. The strategy of this phase is making collisions in the capacity part of S_1 by the rate parts of S_0 and S_2. If the capacity part of S_1 is collide, M_1 can be obtain from $M_1 = $ **Gimli**$(S_0)[0][*] \oplus S_1[0][*]$. Since the size of the controllable variable is 256-bit, one value is matched in the capacity part of S_1 as expected.

Phase 4. From the found values in phase2 and phase3, M_2 can be obtain from $M_2 = $ **Gimli**$(S_1)[0][*] \oplus S_2[0][*]$.

Phase 1 and **Phase 3** have most of the complexity for this preimage attack, while **Phase 2** and **Phase 4** are simple.

Liu et al. performed a preimage attack on 5-round GIMLI-HASH based on a general approach with $2^{93.68}$ time complexity and 2^{66} memory complexity [9]. The 5-round attack by Liu et al. can be seen in Appendix A.

4   Preimage Attack on 5-9-Round GIMLI-HASH

The Liu et al.'s preimage attack on 5-round GIMLI-HASH has a big difference in complexity between **phase 1** and **phase 3**. The time complexity of **phase 1** is 2^{64}. On the other side, the time complexity of **phase 3** is $2^{93.68}$. Therefore, **phase 1** of the preimage attack on GIMLI-HASH seems to be able to analyze more rounds. However, extending the round in **phase 1** is not easy in a direct way. This is because when the round is extended, it does not overlap in the intermediate state. In Appendix A, the *step 2* of **phase 1** checks whether the calculated values collide with the T_8 created in *step 1*. Hence, it cannot be extended by approaching [9] method. On the other hand, we extend the rounds by making precomputation tables and solving equations.

We describe the 5-9-round GIMLI-HASH in Sect. 4.1. Then, we will show finding a valid inner part (**phase 1**) by making precomputation tables in Sect. 4.2. Moreover, Sect. 4.3 describes how to reduce memory by solving equations with SAT-solver instead of using precomputation tables.

4.1   Description 5-9-Round GIMLI-HASH

The 5-9-round GIMLI-HASH is a reduced GIMLI-HASH that uses two types of permutations. One of the permutations consists of a 5-round GIMLI, and the other consists of a 9-round GIMLI. The 5-round GIMLI is used in the message absorbing stage. On the other hand, the 9-round GIMLI is used in the hash squeezing stage after the message absorbing stage. Figure 5 shows the 5-9-round GIMLI-HASH.

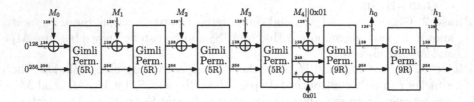

Fig. 5. The illustration 5-9-Round GIMLI-HASH with 5 message blocks

The strategy of using two kinds of permutations within an algorithm is not unique. This strategy can take advantage of message processing speed, or it can provide additional security when transitioning from the absorbing phase to the squeezing phase. For example, the hash scheme of SPARKLE [1], one of the NIST lightweight cryptography competition finalists, has two kinds of permutations. One is the 11-round permutation located after message absorbing, and the other is 7-round permutation consisting of the remaining permutation.

4.2   Finding Valid Inner Part on 9-Round GIMLI (Phase 1)

To find valid capacity part, we make precomputation table T_1, T_2, T_3, T_4, and T_5 preferentially.

Precomputation. Given a 256-bit hash output $h = (h_0 \| h_1)$, let $h_0 = (h_{0,0} \| h_{0,1} \| h_{0,2} \| h_{0,3})$ and $h_1 = (h_{1,0} \| h_{1,1} \| h_{1,2} \| h_{1,3})$ where h_0 and h_1 are 128-bit values and $h_{i,j}(0 \le i \le 1, 0 \le j \le 3)$ is a 32-bit value. For all (a, b, x), we compute SP-box operation as follows.

$$SP(h_{0,3}, a, b) = (c, d, e)$$
$$SP(SP(x, d, e)) = (f, g, h)$$

In the calculation, store (a, b) in table $T_1[(c \| x \| f)]$. It requires 2^{96} 64-bit memory complexity. For all (a, b), compute $(c, d, e) = SP(h_{0,2}, a, b)$ and store (a, b, c) in table $T_2[(d \| e)]$. Consider the $h_{1,0}$, for all (a, b), compute $(c, d, e) = SP^{-1}(SP^{-1}(h_{1,0}, a, b))$ and store (a, b, c) in table $T_3[(d \| e)]$. The tables T_2 and T_3 require 2^{64} 64-bit memory complexity, respectively. For all (a, b, c), compute $(d, e, f) = SP(SP(a, b, c))$. Then (a, e, f) are stored in $T_4[(b \| c \| d)]$ and (b, c, d) are stored in $T_5[(a \| e \| f)]$. Each table has 2^{96} 96-bit memory complexity. The Algorithm 3 shows a description of generating precomputation tables.

Algorithm 3. Generating precomputation tables for finding the valid inner part

Input: Hash values h_0 and h_1
Output: Precomputation table T_1, T_2, T_3, T_4, and T_5

  for all a and b **do**
    $(c, d, e) \leftarrow SP(h_{0,3}, a, b)$
    for all x **do**
      $(f, g, h) \leftarrow SP(SP(x, d, e))$
      $T_1[(c\|x\|f)] \leftarrow (a, b)$
    end for
    $(c, d, e) \leftarrow SP(h_{0,2}, a, b)$
    $T_2[(d\|e)] \leftarrow (a, b, c)$
    $(c, d, e) \leftarrow SP^{-1}(SP^{-1}(h_{1,0}, a, b))$
    $T_3[(d\|e)] \leftarrow (a, b, c)$
    for all c **do**
      $(d, e, f) \leftarrow SP(SP(a, b, c))$
      $T_4[(b\|c\|d)] \leftarrow (a, e, f)$
      $T_5[(a\|e\|f)] \leftarrow (b, c, d)$
    end for
  end for

Finding the Valid Inner Part. The 9-round preimage attack starts from the guess 128-bit capacity part of S^0 and S^9. It is a meet-in-the-middle attack, but it does not overlap in the GIMLI state. The precomputation table is helpful to fill the gap in the middle. After making the connection, we guess the left of the inner part and find the valid values (Figs. 6, 7, 8 and 9).

Step 1 (line 1–8 in Algorithm 4): Choose random values for $S^0[1, 2][0, 1]$ and compute $(S^3[1, 2][0, 1], S^3[0][2, 3])$. Store $(S^0[1, 2][0, 1], S^3[1, 2][0, 1], S^3[0][2, 3])$ in the table T_6 and repeat 2^{64}. Then choose random values for $(S^9[1, 2][0, 2])$ and compute $(S^{4.5}[1, 2][0, 2], S^{4.5}[0][1, 3])$. Store $(S^9[1, 2][0, 2], S^{4.5}[1, 2][2], S^{4.5}[0][1, 3])$ in the table $T_7[(S^{4.5}[1][0])\| (S^{4.5}[2][0])]$ and repeat 2^{64}.

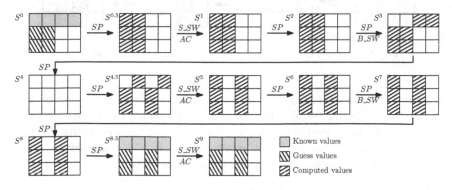

Fig. 6. Finding the valid inner part of 9-round GIMLI (*step 1*)

Step 2 (line 9–15 in Algorithm 4): Given the values ($S^0[1,2][0,1]$, $S^3[1,2][0,1]$, $S^3[0][2,3]$) from T_6, choose 2^{32} values for $S^3[0][0]$ and find the values ($S^9[1,2][0,2]$, $S^{4.5}[1,2][2]$, $S^{4.5}[0][1,3]$) in $T_7[(S^{4.5}[1][0])\|(S^{4.5}[2][0])]$. For each matched value, determine the value of ($S^3[0][1]$, $S^{4.5}[1,2][1]$) in $T_4[(S^3[1][1])\|(S^3[1][1])\|(S^{4.5}[0][1])]$. Similarly, determine the value of ($S^3[1,2][2]$, $S^{4.5}[0][2]$) in $T_5[(S^3[0][2])\|(S^{4.5}[1][2])\|(S^{4.5}[2][2])]$.

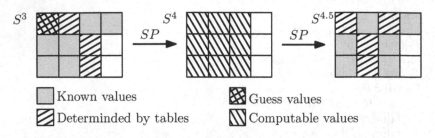

Known values   Guess values
Determinded by tables   Computable values

Fig. 7. Finding the valid inner part of 9-round GIMLI (*step 2*)

Step 3 (line 16–18 in Algorithm 4): From the found values, compute the forward and backward direction as possible rounds. Then $S^{0.5}[1,2][2]$, $S^{0.5}[0][3]$, $S^7[1,2][1]$, and $S^7[0][3]$ can be computed from the state S^3 and $S^{4.5}$ respectively. Determine the $S^0[1,2][2]$, and $S^{0.5}[0][2]$ in the table $T_2[(S^{0.5}[1][2])\|(S^{0.5}[2][2])]$. Moreover, determine the $S^7[0][1]$, and $S^{8.5}[1,2][1]$ in the table $T_3[(S^7[1][1])\|(S^7[2][1])]$.

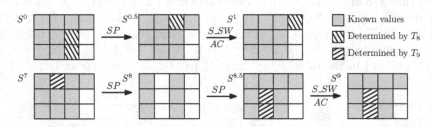

Known values
Determined by T_8
Determined by T_9

Fig. 8. Finding the valid inner part of 9-round GIMLI (*step 3*)

Step 4 (line 19–23 in Algorithm 4): Let the values $c = S^{0.5}[0][3]$, $x = S^1[0][3]$, and $f = S^3[0][1]$ Then determine the value $S^0[1,2][3]$ using the table $T_1[(c\|x\|f)]$. To verify the capacity part, compute from S^0 to S^9 and checking the values $S^{4.5}[0][3]$, $S^7[0][3]$, and $S^{8.5}[0][3]$ are matched. If it is matched, return the $S^9[1,2][*]$. If not, go to *step 2* and try the other values in T_6.

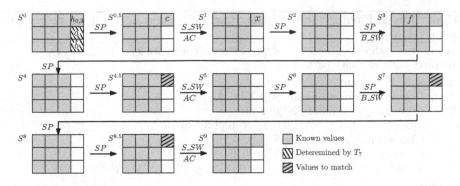

Fig. 9. Finding the valid inner part of 9-round GIMLI (*step 4*)

Complexity. In the precomputation, five precomputation tables were created. Table T_1 can be made with all a, b, and x. Therefore, T_1 has 2^{96} 64-bit memory complexity and 3×2^{96} SP operations. Similar way, the memory complexity of T_2, T_3, T_4, and T_5 is 2^{64} 64-bit, 2^{64} 64-bit, 2^{96} 96-bit, and 2^{96} 96-bit, respectively. To create the tables, T_2 and T_3 needs 2^{64} and 2×2^{64} SP operation, respectively. When creating tables T_4 and T_5, the equation $(d, e, f) = SP(SP(a, b, c))$ can fill the tables T_4 and T_5 with one operation. Therefore, making T_4 and T_5 requires only 2×2^{96} SP operations in total. Overall, precomputation has 2^{97} 128-bit memory complexity and $(5 \times 2^{96}$ SP operation) $\approx (2^{93.152}$ 9-round GIMLI) time complexity.

In the Step 1, T_6 can be made by 2^{64} random variables for $S^0[1, 2][0, 1]$, and each variable performs 6 SP operations. T_7 is similar except that each random variable performs 8 SP operations. Therefore, the time complexity is 14×2^{64} SP operations in Step 1. In terms of memory complexity, T_6 has 2^{64} 320-bit memory complexity and T_7 has 2^{64} 256-bit memory complexity. At Step 2, each value in T_6 need 2^{32} random variables, 2 SP operations, 2 table lookup. If one table lookup is considered as one SP operation, the time complexity of each value in T_6 is $2^{32} \times 4$ SP operations. At Step 3, it is 6 SP operations that fill some unknown values from the found values in Step 2. Then 2 table lookup need to find $(S^0[1, 2][2], S^{0.5}[0][2])$ and $(S^7[0][1], S^{8.5}[1, 2][1])$. Step 4 only has 1 table lookup and 36 SP operations. Therefore, the time complexity of the main computation is $2^{64} \times 14 + 2^{64} \times 2^{32} \times (4 + 8 + 37) \approx 2^{96.44}$ 9-round GIMLI. The memory complexity of the main computation is $(2^{64} \times 576\text{-bit}) \approx (2^{66.17}$ 128-bit).

Overall, the time complexity is $2^{96.44}$ 9-round GIMLI, and the memory complexity is 2^{97} 128-bit block.

4.3   Reducing Precomputation Memory Using SAT Solver

To find the valid capacity part of 9-round GIMLI, Algorithm 4 uses five sorted precomputation tables, T_1, T_2, T_3, T_4, and T_5. These tables are used to find unknown values from the given values. If we find unknown values another way, we should

Algorithm 4. Finding the valid inner part of 9-round GIMLI using precomputation tables

Input: Hash value $h = (h_0, h_1)$ and precomputation tables T_1, T_2, T_3, T_4, T_5
Output: Valid capacity part of S_{h_1}

1: **for** 0 to $2^{64} - 1$ **do**
2:     Choose random values for $S^0[1,2][0,1]$
3:     Compute $(S^3[1,2][0,1], S^3[0][2,3])$
4:     Store $(S^0[1,2][0,1], S^3[1,2][0,1], S^3[0][2,3])$ in T_6
5:     Choose random values for $S^9[1,2][0,2]$
6:     Compute $(S^{4.5}[1,2][0,2], S^{4.5}[0][1,3])$
7:     $T_7[(S^{4.5}[1][0])\|(S^{4.5}[2][0])] \leftarrow (S^9[1,2][0,2], S^{4.5}[1,2][2], S^{4.5}[0][1,3])$
8: **end for**
9: **for** 0 to $2^{64} - 1$ **do**
10:     Get $(S^0[1,2][0,1], S^3[1,2][0,1], S^3[0][2,3])$ from T_6
11:     **for all** $S^3[0][0]$ **do**
12:         Compute $S^{4.5}[*][0] = SP(S^3[*][0])$
13:         Get $(S^9[1,2][0,2], S^{4.5}[1,2][2], S^{4.5}[0][1,3])$ from $T_7[(S^{4.5}[1][0])\|(S^{4.5}[2][0])]$
14:         Get $(S^3[0][1], S^{4.5}[1,2][1])$ from $T_4[(S^3[1][1])\|(S^3[2][1])\|(S^{4.5}[0][1])]$
15:         Get $(S^3[1,2][2], S^{4.5}[0][2])$ from $T_5[(S^3[0][2])\|(S^{4.5}[1][2])\|((S^{4.5}[2][2]))]$
16:         Compute $(S^{0.5}[1,2][2], S^{0.5}[0][3])$ and $(S^7[1,2][1], S^7[0][3])$ from $S^3, S^{4.5}$
17:         Get $(S^0[1,2][2], S^{0.5}[0][2])$ from $T_2[(S^{0.5}[1][2])\|(S^{0.5}[2][2])]$
18:         Get $(S^7[0][1], S^{8.5}[1,2][1])$ from $T_3[(S^7[1][1])\|(S^7[2][1])]$
19:         Get $S^0[1,2][3]$ from $T_1[(S^{0.5}[0][3])\|(S^1[0][3])\|(S^3[0][1])]$
20:         Recover the state S^0 and compute all states to S^9
21:         **if** $S^{4.5}[0][3], S^7[0][3]$, and $S^{8.5}[0][3]$ are collide **then**
22:             **return** $S^9[1,2][*]$
23:         **end if**
24:     **end for**
25: **end for**

reduce the memory complexity for precomputation tables. The solutions of the following equations replace the precomputation table.

Given $h_{0,3}, c, f$, and x, find a, b such that
$$SP(h_{0,3}, a, b) = (c, d, e) \text{ and } SP^2(x, d, e)_x = f. \tag{1}$$

Given $h_{0,2}, d, e$, find c such that $SP(h_{0,2}, a, b) = (c, d, e)$. $\tag{2}$

Given b, c, d, find a, e, f such that $SP^2(a, b, c) = (d, e, f)$. $\tag{3}$

Given a, e, f, find b, c, d such that $SP^2(a, b, c) = (d, e, f)$. $\tag{4}$

The Eq. (1), (2), (3), and (4) replace precomputation table T_1, T_2, T_4, and T_5 in 4.2 respectively. T_3 can be replaced by Eq. (3) because T_3 is specific case of T_4. The Eq. (1), (2), (3), and (4) are expected to have 1 solution. For the case of Eq. (2), $h_{0,2}, d, e$ are fixed variables and the cardinal number of range of variable c is 2^{32}. Since the SP-box operation is a permutation, we can expect that there is 1 solution in the range of variable c. Similarly since SP^2 is also a permutation,

Eq. (3) and (4) are expected to have 1 solution. For the case Eq. (1), $h_{0,3}, a, b, x$ are fixed variables and the number of candidate of a, b is 2^{64}. Because c is a fixed 32-bit variable, there are 2^{32} candidates of a, b, d, e. In addition, f is also fixed 32-bit variable, so Eq. (1) can be expected to have 1 solution.

There are a lot of ways to solve the Eq. (1), (2), (3), and (4). One of the fast ways is transforming the equations to SAT problems and using SAT solver. Some of the cryptographic equations are too complex to transform into SAT problems. For example, the S-boxes with a high algebraic degree are hard to convert to CNF, so sometimes it is easier to use the truth table. However, CNF of GIMLI SP function is not complex because the SP-box of GIMLI has a low algebraic degree.

The SP-box of the GIMLI consists of bitwise AND($\wedge$), OR($\vee$), XOR($\oplus$) operations. When converting the SP operation to CNF, the AND and OR operations should be considered as basic operations first. For example, the equation in which the intermediate variable x_3 is calculated by AND operation of x_1 and x_2 is as follows.

$$x_1 \wedge x_2 = x_3$$

This equation can be treated as a logical expression such that x_1 is **true** if x_1 is '1' and x_1 is **false** if x_1 is '0'. Then the equation can be transformed to CNF equation as follow.

$$(\neg x_1 \vee \neg x_2 \vee x_3) \wedge (x_1 \vee \neg x_3) \wedge (x_2 \vee \neg x_3) = \textbf{true}$$

Similarly, the equation $x_1 \vee x_2 = x_3$ can be transformed to CNF equation as follow.

$$(x_1 \vee x_2 \vee \neg x_3) \wedge (\neg x_1 \vee x_3) \wedge (\neg x_2 \vee x_3) = \textbf{true}$$

To complete the SP-box, 3 variables must be XORed to the output variable. In other words,

$$x_1 \oplus x_2 \oplus x_3 = x_4.$$

This XOR equation can be transformed to CNF equation with 8 clauses.

$$(x_1 \vee x_2 \vee x_3 \vee \neg x_4) \wedge (x_1 \vee x_2 \vee \neg x_3 \vee x_4) \wedge$$
$$(x_1 \vee \neg x_2 \vee x_3 \vee x_4) \wedge (\neg x_1 \vee x_2 \vee x_3 \vee x_4) \wedge$$
$$(\neg x_1 \vee \neg x_2 \vee \neg x_3 \vee x_4) \wedge (\neg x_1 \vee \neg x_2 \vee x_3 \vee \neg x_4) \wedge$$
$$(\neg x_1 \vee x_2 \vee \neg x_3 \vee \neg x_4) \wedge (x_1 \vee \neg x_2 \vee \neg x_3 \vee \neg x_4) = \textbf{true}$$

Rotation and bit shift operations can be treated by changing the variable index. The SP-box operation can be transformed to CNF combining the above equations.

To solve Eqs. (1), (2), (3), and (4), we use CryptoMiniSat library [12] (https://github.com/msoos/cryptominisat). We construct a test to measure the average number of solutions and the operation time in the **Ubuntu 16.04.4 LTS** with g++ **5.5.0** compiler using **C++** code. Our test code is on https://github.com/yslee0804/Gimli_hash_9r_test.

When the input variables are uniformly random, Eq. (1), (2), (3), (4) have on average 1 solution as expected. Table 2 shows the result of the average solving time for equations. Based on full round GIMLI, the solving time ranged from $2^{7.74}$ to $2^{19.15}$. Equation (2) finds the solution the fastest because it has simpler operations and fewer intermediate variables than other equations (only 1 SP-box operation). On the other hand, Eq. (1) has complex operations and many intermediate variables, so the solution is found the slowest. Equation (3) and (4) are very similar, but there is difference in solving speed. This is presumed to be due to the structure of SP-box. The forward direction of SP-box can be treat variables independently. That means any intermediate variable can be calculated with only input variables in the forward direction. However, when calculated in the backward direction, intermediate variables must be calculated sequentially. Since Eq. (4) is restricted by the given output variables, the intermediate variables were woven as if they were operating in the backward direction. On the other hand, Eq. (3) has more free output variables.

Table 2. Time complexity to solve equations

	GIMLI (full round)	Eq. (1)	Eq. (2)	Eq. (3)	Eq. (4)
Time complexity	1	$2^{19.15}$	$2^{7.74}$	$2^{10.34}$	$2^{18.15}$

The Algorithm 5 shows the process of finding the valid inner part of 9-round GIMLI using equations instead of precomputation tables. Except for the line 14 to 19 of Algorithm 5, the rest are the same as Algorithm 4.

Complexity. In 4.2, time and memory complexity is $2^{96.44}$ and 2^{97} respectively. Because of T_6 and T_7, The memory complexity of 4.3 is equal to $2^{66.17}$. However, 5 table lookups in 4.2 change to Eq. (1) (4). Hence, the time complexity of 4.3 is $2^{96.29+\epsilon}$ where 2^{ϵ} is the complexity of solving equations. Referring to the Table 2, the worst case time complexity of solving the equation(which is Eq. (1)) is about $2^{20.57}$ 9-round GIMLI. The memory complexity decreased from 2^{97} to $2^{66.17}$ compared to Sect. 4.2.

5   Conclusion

In this paper, we analyzed preimage attack on 5-9-round GIMLI-HASH, which extends the last two permutations of GIMLI-HASH to 9-round. In the structure which the last two permutations extended to 9-round, it is difficult to apply the Liu et al.'s preimage attack. This is because there is a gap between the states S^3 and $S^{4.5}$ in the process of finding the valid inner part of 9-round GIMLI. We bridge this gap using precomputation tables. As a result, finding the valid inner part has $2^{96.44}$ time-complexity and 2^{97} memory complexity. Moreover, equations that can replace the precomputation tables are presented to lower the high memory

Algorithm 5. Finding the valid inner part of 9-round GIMLI using equations

Input: Hash values h_0 and h_1
Output: Valid capacity part

Find a valid capacity part
1: **for** 0 to $2^{64} - 1$ **do**
2:     Choose random values for $S^0[1,2][0,1]$
3:     Compute $(S^3[1,2][0,1], S^3[0][2,3])$
4:     Store $(S^0[1,2][0,1], S^3[1,2][0,1], S^3[0][2,3])$ in T_6
5:     Choose random values for $S^9[1,2][0,2]$
6:     Compute $(S^{4.5}[1,2][0,2], S^{4.5}[0][1,3])$
7:     $T_7[(S^{4.5}[1][0])\|(S^{4.5}[2][0])] \leftarrow (S^9[1,2][0,2], S^{4.5}[1,2][2], S^{4.5}[0][1,3])$
8: **end for**
9: **for** 0 to $2^{64} - 1$ **do**
10:     Get $(S^0[1,2][0,1], S^3[1,2][0,1], S^3[0][2,3])$ from T_6
11:     **for all** $S^3[0][0]$ **do**
12:         Compute $S^{4.5}[*][0] = SP(S^3[*][0])$
13:         Get $(S^9[1,2][0,2], S^{4.5}[1,2][2], S^{4.5}[0][1,3])$ from
                 $T_7[(S^{4.5}[1][0])\|(S^{4.5}[2][0])]$
14:         Solve the equation (3) from $(S^3[1,2][1], S^{4.5}[0][1])$
            From the solution of equation (3), determine $(S^3[0][1], S^{4.5}[1,2][1])$
15:         Solve the equation (4) from $(S^3[0][2], S^{4.5}[1,2][2])$
            From the solution of equation (4), determine $(S^3[1,2][2], S^{4.5}[0][2])$
16:         Compute $(S^1[*][2]), (S^7[1,2][1], S^7[0][3])$ start from $S^3, S^{4.5}$
17:         Solve the equation (2) from $(S^{0.5}[1,2][2])$
            From the solution of equation (2), determine $(S^0[1,2][2], S^{0.5}[0][2])$
18:         Solve the equation (3) from $(S^7[1,2][1], S^{8.5}[0][1])$
            From the solution of equation (3), determine $(S^7[0][1], S^{8.5}[1,2][1])$
19:         Solve the equation (1) from $(h_{0,3}, S^{0.5}[0][3], S^1[0][3], S^3[0][1])$
            From the solution of equation (1), determine $S^0[1,2][3]$
20:         Recover the state S^0 and compute all states to S^9
21:         **if** $S^{4.5}[0][3], S^7[0][3]$, and $S^{8.5}[0][3]$ are collide **then**
22:             **return** $S^9[1,2][*]$
23:         **end if**
24:     **end for**
25: **end for**

complexity. We proposed a method of transforming the equations to CNF that can be solved with SAT-solver. The solutions were found experimentally with the time complexity up to $2^{20.57}$ 9-round GIMLI. If we use these equations instead of precomputation tables, the memory complexity is reduced to $2^{66.17}$ instead of $2^{96+\epsilon}$ time complexity, where ϵ is the time complexity of finding solutions of equations. A future work is preimage attack to 9-round GIMLI-HASH. If two states S_0 and S_1 can be connected effectively, the preimage attack of 9-round GIMLI-HASH may be possible.

Acknowledgments. This work was supported as part of Military Crypto Research Center(UD210027 XD) funded by Defense Acquisition Program Administration(DAPA) and Agency for Defense Development(ADD).

A   The Preimage Attack of Liu et al.'s on 5-Round GIMLI-HASH

The 5-round GIMLI-HASH is a modification of the internal GIMLI of GIMLI-HASH to 5 rounds. The preimage attack on 5-round GIMLI-HASH was analyzed in [9]. The aim of this attack is to find five 128-bit message blocks for a given 256-bit hash value. The attack process follows the general approach in Sect. 3.

Phase 1: Finding a Valid Inner Part. For the given hash value $h = (h_0, h_1)$, h_0 and h_1 are the 128-bit values of the rate part of state S_{h_0} and S_{h_1}. Thus, the states $S^0[0][*] = h_0$ and $S^5[0][*] = h_1$ are set. Then, the following steps can be found an appropriate capacity part that $\text{Gimli}(S^0) = S^5$.

Step 1: Choose 2^{64} random values for $S^0[1, 2][0, 1]$. Since $S^0[0][*]$ was known by h_0, two columns $S^0[*][0, 1]$ can compute the values of $S^3[1, 2][0, 1]$ and $S^3[0][2, 3]$. Store the $S^3[1, 2][0, 1]$ and $S^3[0][2, 3]$ in the table T_8.

Step 2: Similar to step 1, choose a random value for $S^5[1, 2][0, 1]$. Then the value $S^3[*][0, 1]$ can be obtained from two columns $S^5[*][0, 1]$ with backward direction computation. Check whether the values $S^3[1, 2][0, 1]$ are in the table T_8. If the values are in the table T_8, hold all selected values and go to the next step. Otherwise, repeat this step. This step may be repeated 2^{64} times.

Step 3: Note that $S^3[0][*]$, $S^3[1, 2][0, 1]$ and $S^5[1, 2][0, 1]$ are fixed in Step 2. For all values of $S^5[1, 2][2]$, $S^3[*][2]$ can be obtained with backward direction computation. Check that computed $S^3[0][1]$ matches the fixed $S^3[0][1]$. If it matched, then store the values $(S^5[1, 2][2], S^3[1, 2][2])$ in the table T_9. The expected number of stored values is about 2^{32}. Similar to the previous process, for all values of $S^5[1, 2][3]$, $S^3[*][3]$ can be obtained. Check if it matches the fixed $S^3[0][3]$ and store $(S^5[1, 2][3], S^3[1, 2][3])$ in the table T_{10}

Step 4: Select each value in T_9 and T_{10} and then compute $S^0[*][2, 3]$ in backward direction. Then check the values $S^0[0][2, 3]$ matches the given $S^0[0][2, 3]$ which is the part of hash value h_0. If it is matched, return $S^5[1, 2][*]$ which is capacity part of S_{h_1}. Else, repeat this step. Because all possible number of combinations is about 2^{64}, we can expect the one will be matched.

Complexity. The time complexity of Step 1 is $2^{64} \times 6$ SP operations and the memory complexity is $2^{64} \times 192$ bits $\approx 2^{64.58}$ 128-bit block. Since Step 2 may be repeat 2^{64} times, the time complexity is $2^{64} \times 4$ SP operations. In the Step 3, all $S^5[1, 2][2]$ values and all $S^5[1, 2][3]$ are searched. Also, in each search, the time complexity is $2^{64} \times 2$ SP operations and the memory complexity is 2^{32}. In the Step 4, 2^{64} T_9, T_{10} combination are possible, and each pair need

6 SP operation. Since 5-round GIMLI consist of 20 SP operations, total time complexity is $(2^{64} \times (6 + 4 + 2 + 2 + 6)$ SP operations$) \approx (2^{64}$ 5-round GIMLI$)$, and total memory complexity is about $2^{64.58}$.

Phase 2: Choosing M_3 and M_4. The capacity part of S_{h_1} was found by **phase 1**, the full state of S_{h_1} and S_{h_0} can be recovered. Thus, the state S_2 can be obtained by selecting any M_3 and M_4. Therefore, choose random values for M_3 and M_4 and compute backward direction to get S_2.

Phase 3: Matching the Inner Part. In this phase, select the appropriate M_0 and M_1 connecting the capacity part of S_0 and S_2. The capacity part of S_0 was set to 0 and the rate part of S_0 can be controlled by M_0. Additionally, capacity part of S_1^5 can be known because S_2 was known and the rate part of S_1^5 can be controlled by M_2. Since the capacity part of S_0 is 0, the precomputation tables can be created. After creating precomputation tables, the part of S_1^5 would be guessed and connected it with the precomputation tables. In this process, the following property is used for checking validation.

Property 1 ([8]). Suppose $(OX, OY, OZ) = SP(IX, IY, IZ)$. Given a random triple (IY, IZ, OZ), (IX, OX, OY) can be uniquely determined. In addition, a random tuple (IY, IZ, OY, OZ) is valid with probability 2^{-32}.

The following steps show the way to find M_0 and M_1 which capacity part of states are connected.

Step 0 (precomputation step): Since $S_0^0[1, 2][*]$ is all zero, $S_0^{0.5}[0][*]$ is also zero. Therefore, for all values of $S_0^0[0][0, 2]$, the values $S_1^0[1, 2][0, 2]$ can be computed. $(S_0^0[0][0, 2], S_1^0[1, 2][2])$ is stored in the table $T_{10}[(S_1^0[1][0] \| S_1^0[2][0])]$. Similar to before process, for all values of $S_0^0[0][1, 3]$, calculate $S_1^0[1, 2][1, 3]$. $(S_0^0[0][1, 3], S_1^0[1, 2][3])$ is stored in the table $T_{11}[(S_1^0[1][1] \| S_1^0[2][1])]$.

Step 1: For a guessed value $S_1^5[0][1, 3]$, the values $(S_1^{0.5}[0][1, 3],\ S_1^{0.5}[1, 2][0, 2])$ can be calculated in the backward direction. Then, guess all values for $S_1^{0.5}[0][0]$, and calculate $S_1^0[1, 2][0]$. From $T_{10}[(S_1^0[1][0] \| S_1^0[2][0])]$, get the values for $(S_0^0[0][0, 2], S_1^0[1, 2][2])$. The value $S_1^0[1, 2][2]$ in the T_{10} and calculated value $S_1^{0.5}[1, 2][2]$ are valid with probability 2^{32} by Property 1. Hence, there is one valid pair $(S_1^0[1, 2][2], S_1^{0.5}[1, 2][2])$ for all $S_1^{0.5}[0][0]$ as expected. Moreover, if $(S_1^0[1, 2][2], S_1^{0.5}[1, 2][2])$ is valid, it can determine $S_1^{0.5}[0][2]$ by Property 1. From the valid $S_1^{0.5}[0][0]$, store $(S_0^0[0][0, 2], S_1^5[0][1, 3], S_1^{0.5}[0][*])$ in the table T_{12}. Repeat this step for all $S_1^5[0][1, 3]$.

Step 2: Similar to Step 1, for all values $S_1^5[0][0, 2]$, calculate the values $(S_1^{0.5}[0][0, 2],\ S_1^{0.5}[1, 2][1, 3])$. Then guess $S_1^{0.5}[0][1]$ for all possible value and calculate $S_1^0[1, 2][1]$. From $T_{11}[(S_1^0[1][1] \| S_1^0[2][1])]$, get the values for $(S_0^0[0][1, 3], S_1^0[1, 2][3])$. By Property 1, verify $(S_1^0[1, 2][3], S_1^{0.5}[1, 2][3])$ and recover valid $S_1^{0.5}[0][3]$. Check the values $S_1^{0.5}[0][*]$ are in the table T_{12}. If it in, move to step 3, else repeat this step.

Step 3: At the step 2, $S_0^0[0][1, 3]$ was guessed and $S_0^0[0][0, 2]$ was found in the table T_{12}. Therefore, the message $M_0 = S_0^0[0][*]$ can be recovered, and then the values $S_0^5[0][*]$ can be calculated. Moreover, $S_1^0[0][*]$ can be calculated because $S_1^5[0][0,2]$ and $S_1^5[0][1,3]$ were also known at the step 2. As a result, the message M_1 can be obtained by $S_0^5[0][*] \oplus S_1^0[0][*]$.

Complexity. In the precomputation, the time complexity is $2 \times 2^{64} \times 10$ SP operation and the memory complexity is 2×2^{64}. At the step 1, there are 2^{64} $S_1^5[0][0,2]$. Each $S_1^5[0][0,2]$ performs $8 + 2^{32} + 2^{32}$ SP operations and store one $(S_0^0[0][0,2], S_1^5[0][1,3], S_1^{0.5}[0][*])$ in T_{12} as an expected value. Thus, the time and memory complexity of step 1 is 2^{96} SP operations and 2^{64} 256-bit blocks, respectively. Similarly, the time complexity of step 2 is 2^{96} SP operations. The time complexity of step 3 is just 2 GIMLI. Therefore, total time complexity is $(2 \times 2^{97}$ SP operations$) \approx (2^{93.68}$ 5-round GIMLI$)$, and total memory complexity is 2^{66} 128-bit blocks.

Phase 4: Finding the Valid M_2. At the **phase 2**, the state S_2^0 was recovered. Additionally, at the **phase 3**, the state S_1^5 was also recovered. Therefore, the message M_2 can be obtained by $S_2^0[0][*] \oplus S_1^5[0][*]$.

References

1. Beierle, C., et al.: Lightweight AEAD and hashing using the sparkle permutation family. IACR Trans. Symm. Cryptol. **2020**(S1), 208–261 (2020). https://doi.org/10.13154/tosc.v2020.iS1.208-261

2. Bernstein, D.J., et al.: Gimli. Submission to the NIST Lightweight Cryptography Standardization Process (2019). https://csrc.nist.gov/Projects/lightweight-cryptography/round-2-candidates

3. Bernstein, D.J., et al.: GIMLI?: a cross-platform permutation. In: Fischer, W., Homma, N. (eds.) CHES 2017. LNCS, vol. 10529, pp. 299–320. Springer, Cham (2017). https://doi.org/10.1007/978-3-319-66787-4_15

4. Bertoni, G., Daemen, J., Peeters, M., Van Assche, G.: Sponge functions. In: ECRYPT Hash Workshop, vol. 2007 (2007)

5. Flórez Gutiérrez, A., Leurent, G., Naya-Plasencia, M., Perrin, L., Schrottenloher, A., Sibleyras, F.: New results on Gimli: full-permutation distinguishers and improved collisions. In: Moriai, S., Wang, H. (eds.) ASIACRYPT 2020. LNCS, vol. 12491, pp. 33–63. Springer, Cham (2020). https://doi.org/10.1007/978-3-030-64837-4_2

6. Hamburg, M.: Cryptanalysis of 22 1/2 rounds of gimli. Cryptology ePrint Archive, Report 2017/743 (2017). https://eprint.iacr.org/2017/743

7. Kölbl, S., Leander, G., Tiessen, T.: Observations on the SIMON block cipher family. In: Gennaro, R., Robshaw, M. (eds.) CRYPTO 2015. LNCS, vol. 9215, pp. 161–185. Springer, Heidelberg (2015). https://doi.org/10.1007/978-3-662-47989-6_8

8. Liu, F., Isobe, T., Meier, W.: Automatic verification of differential characteristics: application to reduced gimli. In: Micciancio, D., Ristenpart, T. (eds.) CRYPTO 2020. LNCS, vol. 12172, pp. 219–248. Springer, Cham (2020). https://doi.org/10.1007/978-3-030-56877-1_8

9. Liu, F., Isobe, T., Meier, W.: Exploiting weak diffusion of Gimli: improved distinguishers and preimage attacks. IACR Trans. Symm. Cryptol. **2021**(1), 185–216 (2021). https://doi.org/10.46586/tosc.v2021.i1.185-216

10. Liu, Y., Wang, Q., Rijmen, V.: Automatic search of linear trails in ARX with applications to SPECK and chaskey. In: Manulis, M., Sadeghi, A.-R., Schneider, S. (eds.) ACNS 2016. LNCS, vol. 9696, pp. 485–499. Springer, Cham (2016). https://doi.org/10.1007/978-3-319-39555-5_26

11. Mouha, N., Preneel, B.: Towards finding optimal differential characteristics for arx: application to salsa20. Cryptology ePrint Archive, Report 2013/328 (2013). https://eprint.iacr.org/2013/328

12. Soos, M.: Cryptominisat 5.8.0. https://github.com/msoos/cryptominisat/

13. Sun, L., Wang, W., Wang, M.: Automatic search of bit-based division property for ARX ciphers and word-based division property. In: Takagi, T., Peyrin, T. (eds.) ASIACRYPT 2017. LNCS, vol. 10624, pp. 128–157. Springer, Cham (2017). https://doi.org/10.1007/978-3-319-70694-8_5

14. Zong, R., Dong, X., Wang, X.: Collision attacks on round-reduced Gimli-hash/ascon-xof/ascon-hash. Cryptology ePrint Archive, Report 2019/1115 (2019). https://eprint.iacr.org/2019/1115

Security analysis of Symmetric Key Encryption Algorithm

Algebraic Attacks on Grain-Like Keystream Generators

Matthew Beighton$^{(\boxtimes)}$ (ID), Harry Bartlett (ID), Leonie Simpson (ID),
and Kenneth Koon-Ho Wong (ID)

Queensland University of Technology, Brisbane, QLD, Australia
matthew.beighton@hdr.qut.edu.au

Abstract. This paper analyses the resistance of certain keystream generators against algebraic attacks, namely generators consisting of a nonlinear feedback shift register, a linear feedback shift register and a filter function. We show that poorly chosen filter functions make such designs vulnerable to new algebraic attacks, using a divide and conquer approach that targets the LFSR first. This approach provides efficient LFSR initial state recovery followed by partial NFSR initial state recovery.

We apply our algebraic attacks to modified versions of the Grain family of stream ciphers. Our analysis shows that, despite the highly nonlinear filter functions used in these variants, the LFSR state can be recovered using our algebraic attack much faster than exhaustive search. Following this, the NFSR initial state can be partially recovered, leaving a smaller subset of NFSR stages to be exhaustively searched. This investigation highlights the importance of the filter function in keystream generators with a "Grain-like" structure, and demonstrates that many functions previously considered secure are vulnerable to this attack.

Keywords: Algebraic attack · Fast algebraic attack · Divide and conquer · Nonlinear feedback shift register · Linear feedback shift register · Filter generator · Grain

1 Introduction

Symmetric stream ciphers are used to provide confidentiality for a range of real-time applications. The most common type of stream cipher is the binary additive stream cipher, where encryption and decryption are performed by XORing a binary keystream with the plaintext or ciphertext bitstream, respectively. The reciprocal nature of the XOR operation provides high speed encryption and decryption processes. However, the security provided depends on the properties of the keystream. The security of the keystream generator is therefore crucial.

Many keystream generators are based on shift registers. In 2003, algebraic attacks on keystream generators based on linear feedback shift registers (LFSRs) were proposed [6]. A series of equations relating the keystream bits to underlying state bits can be solved, given known keystream outputs. The nonlinear

J. H. Park and S.-H. Seo (Eds.): ICISC 2021, LNCS 13218, pp. 241–270, 2022.
https://doi.org/10.1007/978-3-031-08896-4_12

filter generator was shown to be vulnerable to both algebraic attacks [6] and fast algebraic attacks [5]. The design of keystream generators has subsequently evolved to provide increased resistance to these and other known attacks.

One alternative approach is to use nonlinear feedback shift registers (NFSRs) in the design of keystream generators. The nonlinearity of the shift register update results in a system of equations that increases in degree over time. Solving such a system of nonlinear equations has extreme computational complexity and is often impractical. However, in 2008, Berbain et al. [2] showed that keystream generators consisting of a NFSR with a linear filter function (known as linearly filtered nonlinear feedback shift registers (LF-NFSR)), are also vulnerable to algebraic attacks.

Some contemporary keystream generators use a combination of a NFSR and a LFSR, together with a nonlinear filter function taking inputs from both registers. We refer to these generators as "Grain-like structures", as the well known Grain family of stream ciphers is designed in this way. There are five variants of Grain: the original proposal Grain-V0 [16], updated versions Grain-V1 [14], Grain-128 [15], Grain-128a [17], and the most recent variant Grain-128AEAD [18]; proposed in 2005, 2006, 2006, 2011 and 2019, respectively.

Berbain et al. [2] showed that a modified version of Grain-128 is vulnerable to algebraic attacks if the filter function takes only linear terms from the NFSR. Despite extensive analysis of the Grain family [3,7,8,20–22,29,30], since the work of Berbain et al. [2] little progress has been made in applying traditional algebraic attacks to Grain-like structures. In this paper, we investigate relationships between the properties of Grain-like structures and their resistance to algebraic attacks.

Motivated by the work of Berbain et al. [2] and Courtois [5], we identify cases where the filter function to a Grain-like structure can be algebraically manipulated to eliminate the involvement of the NFSR. This allows us to apply a divide and conquer approach, targeting the LFSR. We show that poorly chosen filter functions and sets of input positions to the filter functions allow Grain-like structures to be represented as systems of equations containing only LFSR initial state bits. Such a system can then be solved efficiently to recover the initial state of the LFSR. Following this, the NFSR may be partially recovered. This reduces the overall complexity of the exhaustive search required to recover the remaining bits of the NFSR.

We perform simulations to verify the effectiveness of our attack on Grain-like structures with internal states sizes of 40, 60, 80 and 100 bits, as well as on a modified version of Grain-V0. We also demonstrate that minor variations to the current variants of the Grain family render them vulnerable to our attack. Although the proposed attack is not applicable to the current variants of the Grain family, our results clearly show that care must be taken when choosing the filter function of a Grain-like structure. In particular, these structures may still be vulnerable to algebraic attacks, even when the output function incorporates bits form the LFSR and the NFSR both linearly and nonlinearly.

This paper is organised as follows: Sect. 2 provides background information on shift register based designs. Section 3 discusses current algebraic attack techniques. Section 4 presents our algebraic attack technique for application to Grain-like structures. We introduce the Grain family of stream ciphers in Sect. 5 and highlight why Grain currently resists algebraic attacks. We then apply our attack technique to modified Grain variants in Sect. 6. Experimental simulations for proof of concept are reported in Sect. 7 and discussed in Sect. 8. Conclusions are drawn in Sect. 9.

2   Preliminaries

2.1   Feedback Shift Registers

A binary feedback shift register (FSR) of length n is a set of n storage devices called *stages* $(r_0, r_1, ..., r_{n-1})$, each containing one bit, together with a Boolean update function g. We denote the initial state of the register as S_0, consisting of initial state bits $s_0, s_1, ..., s_{n-1}$. The state at any time t is defined to be S_t, where $S_t = s_t, s_{t+1}, ..., s_{t+(n-1)}$. The sequence of state bits that passes through register R over time is denoted S; that is $S = s_0, s_1, .., s_{n-1}, s_n, ...$. All bits s_{n+t}, $t \geq 0$ are referred to as update bits.

The registers investigated in this paper are regularly clocked Fibonacci style, as shown in Fig. 1. At time $t + 1$, the content of stage r_i is shifted to stage r_{i-1} for $1 \leq i \leq n - 1$, and the content of stage r_0 is lost from the register. The new content of stage r_{n-1} (referred to as the feedback) is computed by applying the Boolean feedback function $g(r_0, r_1, .., r_{n-1})$ to S^t. If g is linear, then the register is said to be a linear feedback shift register (LFSR) and if g is nonlinear, then the register is said to be a nonlinear feedback shift register (NFSR).

A binary sequence can be generated from a FSR by applying a Boolean function f to the state S_t, as shown in Fig. 1. A simple way to produce output from a FSR is to choose $f = r_0$, so the output sequence is just the sequence of bits shifted out of the register at each state update. Alternatively, the output can be a function of multiple register stages. In general, $y_t = f(s_t, ..., s_{t+n-1})$.

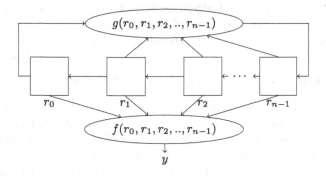

Fig. 1. An n-stage FSR with update function g and filter function f.

2.2   Filter Generators

Keystream generators where f is a function of the contents of multiple stages in R are called *filter generators*. Traditionally, keystream generators for stream ciphers used a LFSR together with a nonlinear filter function f [19]. If f is linear, the filter generator is equivalent to another LFSR. LFSRs, when used by themselves as keystream generators, provide very little security to the plaintext [23]. For this reason, LFSRs were traditionally filtered using a nonlinear Boolean function.

Nonlinear Filter Generators. A keystream generator consisting of a LFSR and a nonlinear filter function f is known as a *nonlinear filter generator* (NLFG) [27]. The security of nonlinear filter generators has been extensively analysed. These designs have been shown to be susceptible to numerous attacks, including correlation attacks [11,13,24,27], algebraic attacks [5,6,10] and distinguishing attacks [9]. The properties of the nonlinear filter function are important in determining the resistance of the NLFG to cryptanalysis. The underlying LFSR provides only desirable statistical properties for the binary sequence. As a single nonlinear Boolean function cannot display high levels of all the desirable cryptographic properties, such as high nonlinearity, correlation immunity, algebraic degree and algebraic immunity, choosing a filter function that resists one form of attack may leave the keystream generator vulnerable to other attacks [26].

Linearly Filtered Nonlinear Feedback Shift Registers. In response to the cryptanalysis of NLFGs, designs using NFSRs were proposed. One proposal is the dual construction of the nonlinear filter generator; where the update function g to the register is nonlinear and the filter function f is linear [12]. This is known as a linearly filtered nonlinear feedback shift register (LF-NFSR). Berbain et al. showed that LF-NFSRs are also susceptible to algebraic attacks, resulting in initial state (and possibly secret key) recovery [2]. We provide an overview of this attack in Sect. 3.3. From the work of Berbain et al. [2] it is obvious that the properties of the filter function used in a LF-NFSR are critical in providing resistance to a traditional algebraic attack. In this paper, we explore the relationship between the properties of the filter function and the resistance to algebraic attacks for a more recent class of keystream generators.

2.3   Composite Combiners and 'Grain-Like' Structures

Effective algebraic attacks have been proposed on both NLFG and LF-NFSR keystream generators. A more complex design incorporates both a LFSR and a NFSR, together with a nonlinear filter function taking inputs from both registers, as shown in Fig. 2. Keystream generators using this structure include Grain [16] and subsequent variants of Grain [14,15,17,18]. We denote this general design as a "Grain-like" structure. Other ciphers such as Sprout [1] and Plantlet [25] have adopted this structure. For simplicity, in this paper we consider the lengths of the NFSR and LFSR to be the same (n). However, the approach outlined also applies in the case where register lengths differ.

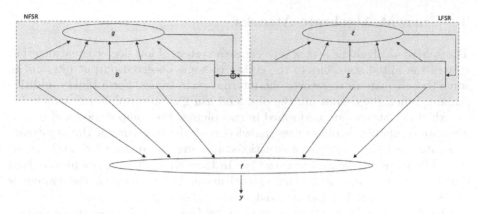

Fig. 2. Grain-like structure.

We denote the initial states of the NFSR and the LFSR as B_0 and S_0, respectively, and the initial state bits $b_0, b_1, ..., b_{n-1}$ and $s_0, s_1, ..., s_{n-1}$, respectively. The states of the registers at any time t are defined to be B_t and S_t. The sequences of state bits that pass through the registers over time are denoted B and S; that is $B = b_0, b_1, .., b_{n-1}, b_n, ...$ and $S = s_0, s_1, .., s_{n-1}, s_n, ...$ All bits b_{n+t} and s_{n+t}, $t \geq 0$ are referred to as update bits for either the NFSR or the LFSR. In the case of Grain-like structures, we denote the nonlinear update function as g, the linear update function as ℓ and the filter function as f. For a Grain-like structure, the LFSR is autonomous when producing output as all of the inputs to ℓ are from the LFSR. The NFSR is not autonomous, as the nonlinear update function g contains one input from the LFSR.

The filter function f can be considered as the XOR sum (here denoted '+') of several different types of monomials. That is, we consider sub-functions of f. We define the following sub-functions, each as a sum of the terms indicated:

- L_B - monomials with linear inputs from NFSR.
- L_S - monomials with linear inputs from LFSR.
- f_S - nonlinear monomials with inputs from LFSR only.
- f_B - nonlinear monomials with inputs from NFSR only.
- f_{BS} - nonlinear monomials with inputs from both NFSR and LFSR.

Thus, any filter function f in a Grain-like structure can be expressed as follows:

$$f(B, S) = L_B + L_S + f_B + f_S + f_{BS}. \tag{1}$$

For example, the output function for the keystream generator of Grain-128AEAD is as follows:

$$y = b_2 + b_{15} + b_{36} + b_{45} + b_{64} + b_{73} + b_{89} + s_{93} + b_{12}s_8 + s_{13}s_{20} + b_{95}s_{42} + b_{95}b_{12}s_{94} + s_{60}s_{79}.$$

This has the form $f(B, S) = L_B + L_S + f_S + f_{BS}$, where $L_B = b_2 + b_{15} + b_{36} + b_{45} + b_{64} + b_{73} + b_{89}$, $L_S = s_{93}$, $f_S = s_{13}s_{20} + s_{60}s_{79}$, $f_{BS} = s_8b_{12} + b_{95}s_{42} + b_{95}b_{12}s_{94}$ (and $f_B = 0$).

3   Current Algebraic Attacks

The goal of an algebraic attack is to create a system of low degree equations that relates the initial state bits of the cipher to some observed output bits and to solve these equations to recover the internal state values. For a binary additive stream cipher, the output may be obtained using a known-plaintext attack.

Algebraic attacks are performed in two phases: pre-computation and online. The pre-computation phase uses knowledge of the structure of the keystream generator to build a system of equations, relating initial state bits and output bits. These are represented as variables. In the online phase, given an observed output sequence, the appropriate substitutions are performed, the system is solved and the initial state recovered.

Algebraic attacks were first introduced by Courtois and Meier [6] on ciphers with linear feedback. An algebraic attack will be successful if the algebraic degree of the equations is low, and enough output can be observed to produce a meaningful solution.

3.1   Algebraic Attacks on NLFGs

Courtois and Meier [6] built a system of equations to represent a NLFG using a simple approach: at time $t = 0$ the output bit y_0 is produced by applying f to the state S_0:

$$y_0 = f(S_0) = f(s_0, \ldots, s_{n-1})$$

Similarly, for every subsequent time step an equation can be formed.

$$y_t = f(S_t) = f(s_t, \ldots, s_{t+n-1}) \tag{2}$$

As the NLFG is built on a LFSR, the linear update function g is used to replace state bits s_{t+n-1} with the corresponding linear combination of initial state bits keeping the equation system of a constant degree $(deg(f))$, while maintaining the number of unknown variables in the system.

Courtois and Meier noted that, in many cases, each equation in the system may be multiplied through by a low degree multivariate function h (of degree e) to reduce the overall degree of the system of equations [6]. We refer to h as a reduction function, and using the terminology from [5] note that if $fh = 0$, then h is defined as an annihilator of f. Each equation in the resulting system has the following form:

$$f(S_t)h(S_t) = y_t h(S_t).$$

The degree of this system will be equal to $deg(fh) = d$, where $d < deg(f)$, with n independent variables, where n is the length of the underlying LFSR.

In the online phase, a known output sequence $\{y_t\}_{t=0}^{\infty}$ provides values for y_t to be substituted into the equations and the system is solved using linearisation. For a more detailed explanation, the reader is referred to Courtois and Meier's paper [6].

The above considerations lead to the algorithms presented in Appendix A.1. In the online phase of the attack, the initial state of the LFSR can be recovered if approximately $\binom{n}{d}$ bits of output are known. This attack has a computational complexity of $\mathcal{O}(n\binom{n}{d} + \binom{n}{d}^{\omega})$, where d is the degree of the system and ω is the Guassian elimination exponent $\omega \approx 2.8$ [6]. If this output requirement cannot be met, it may be possible to solve the system by applying other methods for solving simultaneous equations, such as Gröbner bases or the XL algorithm [4].

3.2 Fast Algebraic Attacks on NLFGs

Following algebraic attacks on NLFGs, Courtois [5] showed that the attack could be improved if the overall degree of the system of equations could be reduced further, below the degree of fh. This increases the complexity of the precomputation phase, but greatly reduces the complexity of the online phase. However, precomputation only needs to be performed once for a particular cipher. This equation system may then be reused in multiple online phases to recover the states of the cipher corresponding to multiple different keystreams. These attacks are known as fast algebraic attacks.

Fast algebraic attacks make use of a concept Courtois [5] described as "double-decker equations". These equations allow an attacker to equate an expression in terms of initial state bits only to an expression in terms of initial state bits and observed output bits. The existence of "double-decker equations" in a system produced using Eq. 2 permits all of the monomials in initial state bits only of degree from $e = deg(h)$ to $d = deg(fh)$ to be separated from the other monomials. Given approximately $\binom{n}{d}$ equations, the monomials of degree e to d will occur in multiple equations. Consequently, linear combinations of the equations in the system can be identified that cancel these monomials. These linear combinations define a new system in n unknowns, of degree $e < d$. This new system can be solved by linearisation, with less computational complexity than for traditional algebraic attacks. For a detailed explanation, the reader is referred to Courtois' paper [5]. The above considerations lead to the algorithm presented in Appendix A.2. Note that the online phase of the attack is the same as for regular algebraic attacks.

When the Berlekamp-Massey algorithm is used to find the linear dependency, the pre-computation phase of the attack has a computational complexity of $\mathcal{O}(\binom{n}{d}log(\binom{n}{d}))$ [5]. The initial state of the LFSR can be recovered in the online phase of the attack by observing approximately $\binom{n}{d}$ bits of output with a computational complexity of $\mathcal{O}(\binom{n}{d}\binom{n}{e} + \binom{n}{e}^{\omega})$, where d is the degree of fh, e is the degree of h and $\omega \approx 2.8$ [5]. Note that at first glance the online complexities for an algebraic attack and a fast algebraic attack look similar. However, when n is much larger than d, as is the case with registers used in practice, $\binom{n}{d}^{\omega}$ is much larger than $\binom{n}{d}\binom{n}{e}$ and $\binom{n}{e}^{\omega}$. Thus, by reducing the degree from d to e, the complexity of the online phase is drastically reduced for registers of practical size.

3.3   Algebraic Attacks on LF-NFSRs

Initially, LF-NFSRs were considered resistant to algebraic attacks, due to the use of a nonlinear state update function. Using the nonlinear feedback function to derive equations for the update bits in terms of initial state bits causes the degree of the system of equations to increase over time. However, Berbain et al. [2] showed that it is possible to keep the degree of the system of equations constant by rearranging the linear output function to represent an initial state bit as a linear combination of other initial state bits and an output bit. Thus, an algebraic attack can be performed. Using this approach, the initial state of the underlying NFSR (and possibly the secret key) can be recovered. We provide an overview of Berbain's attack below.

Berbain's Preliminary Observation: Consider y_0, the output at time $t = 0$ produced by applying of the linear filter function to the LF-NFSR contents:

$$y_0 = \ell(s_0, ..., s_{n-1}) = \sum_{k=0}^{n-1} a_k s_k,$$

where a_k are coefficients from the set $\{0,1\}$.

There will exist a highest indexed term in this sum, s_j, such that $a_j = 1$. Thus, we can write y_0 as

$$y_0 = s_j + \sum_{k=0}^{j-1} a_k s_k.$$

We can rearrange this equation to represent s_j as a sum of an output bit and initial state bits,

$$s_j = \sum_{k=0}^{j-1} a_k s_k + y_0.$$

Repeating this process for all subsequent time steps allows us to express every bit, s_{j+t} for $t \geq 0$, in terms of output bits and initial state bits. This produces a set of equations of the form:

$$s_{j+t} = \sum_{k=0}^{j-1} a_{k+t} s_{k+t} + y_t,$$

for $t \geq 0$. Note that if the latter summations contain any term for which an equation already exists, the term can be replaced by the corresponding linear combination of initial state bits and output bits.

The above considerations lead to the algorithm presented in Appendix A.3. For certain update functions a reduction function of g, say h, may be used to reduce the overall degree of the system. If the degree of gh is d, then the overall system will be of degree at most d. The initial state of the LF-NFSR can be recovered in the online phase of the attack by observing approximately $\binom{n}{d}$ bits of output with a computational complexity of $\mathcal{O}(n\binom{n}{d} + \binom{n}{d}^{\omega})$, where d is the degree of the system and $\omega \approx 2.8$ [2]. Note that fast algebraic techniques are not applicable to LF-NFSRs.

3.4   Algebraic Attacks on Grain-Like Structures

After successfully applying algebraic attacks to LF-NFSRs, Berbain et al. proposed an algebraic attack on Grain-like structures where the output function f is the XOR combination of a LF-NFSR and a NLFG. That is, adopting the notation from Sect. 2.3, $f(B, S) = L_B + L_S + f_S$.

In this case the output of the keystream generator can be expressed as

$$y_0 = L_B + L_S + f_S = \sum_{k=0}^{n-1} a_k b_k + L_S + f_S. \tag{3}$$

As discussed in Sect. 3.3, there exists a highest indexed term in L_B (which we denote as b_j). Thus,

$$y_0 = b_j + \sum_{k=0}^{j-1} a_k b_k + L_S + f_S,$$

$$b_j = \sum_{k=0}^{j-1} a_k b_k + L_S + f_S + y_0.$$

Repeating this for $t > 0$ allows for NFSR state bits of index j or higher to be represented as the XOR sum of:

- a linear combination of NFSR initial state bits
- a linear and nonlinear combination of LFSR initial state bits
- a linear combination of observed output bits.

A second system of equations can then be built using the nonlinear update function to the NFSR, making substitutions from the system generated by Eq. 3 where applicable. This system will be of degree at most $deg(g)deg(f_S)$. Combining the two systems results in a system of equations of degree $deg(g)deg(f_S)$ in $n + j$ unknown initial state bits, where n is the size of LFSR and j is the index of the highest indexed term in L_B.

The success of this attack in recovering the LFSR and NFSR initial states demonstrated that using the contents of stages in the NFSR linearly in the output function is not sufficient to provide resistance to algebraic attacks; the NFSR contents must also be filtered nonlinearly in some way.

4   Our Algebraic Attacks on Grain-Like Structures

Currently, Grain-like structures are considered resistant to algebraic attacks if the filter function is chosen to incorporate inputs from both the LFSR and NFSR, and includes these both linearly and nonlinearly. In this paper, we show that this is insufficient. The filter function must be chosen more carefully than previously considered. We show that Grain-like structures designed with filter functions that use inputs from the LFSR and NFSR both linearly and nonlinearly may

still be susceptible to algebraic attacks. We consider the filter functions used
in Grain-like structures and identify possible combinations of the sub-functions,
each containing some (or all) of the monomials shown in Eq. 1. For each case we
examine the applicability of algebraic attacks.

4.1   Vulnerable Filter Functions

The algebraic attack presented by Berbain et al. [2] applies to the case where
$f(B, S) = L_B + L_S + f_S$. As the success of this case is already documented, we
omit this from our paper and investigate four additional cases as follows.

Case 1: $f(B,S) = L_S + f_S + f_{BS}$. Consider a keystream generator that produces
an output bit at each time step by:

$$z = L_S + f_S + f_{BS}. \tag{4}$$

That is, NFSR state bits are only used nonlinearly and only in f_{BS}. Every
monomial in f_{BS} will contain both NFSR bits and LFSR bits. Thus, using the
idea of annihilators presented by Courtois and Meier [6], we may multiply Eq. 4
by a low degree function containing only LFSR bits that will eliminate f_{BS}.
We denote this function as A_{BS}, and consider it to be a "partial annihilator"
in as much as A_{BS} only annihilates certain monomials. Note that the degree of
the NFSR bits in f_{BS} does not affect the ability to annihilate the monomials
containing bits from the NFSR.

Therefore Eq. 4 can be rewritten as

$$z A_{BS} = A_{BS}(L_S + f_S), \tag{5}$$

which is an equation containing only LFSR initial state bits. The degree of the
system of equations built using Eq. 5 will be at most $deg(A_{BS}) + deg(f_S)$. Note,
however, that the right hand side of Eq. 5 contains only initial state bits from the
LFSR. This means that fast algebraic attack methods can be performed in the
precomputation phase of the attack to reduce the degree of unknown variables
in the system from $deg(A_{BS}) + deg(f_S)$ to $deg(A_{BS})$.

To illustrate this point, consider the filter function

$$z = x_1 + x_0 x_3 + x_3 x_4 + x_0 x_1 x_2 + x_2 x_3 x_4, \tag{6}$$

where x_0, x_1, x_2, x_3 are inputs from the LFSR and x_4 is taken from the NFSR.
Equation 6 may be rewritten as

$$z = x_1 + x_0 x_3 + x_0 x_1 x_2 + x_3 x_4 (1 + x_2).$$

Multiplying through by x_2 gives:

$$x_2 z = x_1 x_2 + x_0 x_1 x_2 + x_0 x_2 x_3,$$

since $x_2(1 + x_2) = 0$.

The right hand side of this equation now contains only inputs from the LFSR and can therefore be used to mount an algebraic attack on the LFSR. Further processing (clocking the equation forward and taking suitable linear combinations of the resulting equations to eliminate all right hand side terms of degree higher than $deg(A_{BS}) = 1$) would then allow a fast algebraic attack on the LFSR, with much lower online complexity than the original algebraic attack.

Case 2: $f(B,S) = L_B + L_S + f_S + f_{BS}$. The simple idea presented for Case 1 can be extended to the case where $f(B,S) = L_B + L_S + f_S + f_{BS}$, under certain conditions. If the filter function is chosen such that each monomial in L_B uniquely divides a monomial in f_{BS} of degree at most 1 in NFSR bits, then a common factor containing only LFSR bits may be found. It follows that we can annihilate every monomial containing inputs from the NFSR by multiplying through by a low degree function of LFSR initial state bits.

For example, consider a keystream bit produced by

$$z = x_1 + x_4 + x_0x_3 + x_3x_4 + x_0x_1x_2 + x_2x_3x_4, \tag{7}$$

where x_0, x_1, x_2, x_3 are inputs from the LFSR and x_4 is input from the NFSR. This is the function used in the previous example, with the inclusion of x_4 used linearly. We now have:

$$z = x_1 + x_0x_3 + x_0x_1x_2 + x_4(1 + x_3 + x_2x_3).$$

Multiplying through by $x_3 + x_2x_3$ gives:

$$(x_3 + x_2x_3)z = (x_3 + x_2x_3)(x_1 + x_0x_3 + x_0x_1x_2).$$

As before, the right hand side of this equation now contains only inputs from the LFSR.

Case 3: $f(B,S) = L_S + f_S + f_B + f_{BS}$. Case 3 is a simple extension of Case 2. That is, if each of the monomials used in f_B is a factor of some monomial used in f_{BS} then a common factor containing only LFSR bits may again be found and a partial annihilator obtained.

For example, consider a keystream bit produced by

$$z = x_1 + x_4x_5 + x_0x_3 + x_0x_1x_2 + x_2x_3x_4x_5, \tag{8}$$

where x_0, x_1, x_2, x_3 are inputs from the LFSR and x_4, x_5 are inputs from the NFSR. We now have:

$$z = x_1 + x_0x_3 + x_0x_1x_2 + x_4x_5(1 + x_2x_3).$$

Multiplying through by x_2x_3 gives:

$$(x_2x_3)z = (x_2x_3)(x_1 + x_0x_3 + x_0x_1x_2).$$

As before, the right hand side of this equation now contains only inputs from the LFSR.

Case 4: $f(B,S) = L_B + L_S + f_S + f_B + f_{BS}$. Case 4 is a filter function that contains all possible monomial types (monomials that are linear and nonlinear in both the LFSR and the NFSR bits). If the filter function is chosen such that each monomial in L_B and f_B uniquely divides a monomial in f_{BS}, then there exists a partial annihilator that will eliminate L_B, f_B and f_{BS}.

For example, consider a keystream bit produced by

$$z = x_1 + x_4 + x_5 + x_0x_3 + x_0x_1x_2 + x_2x_4 + x_3x_5 + x_6x_7 + x_1x_2x_6x_7, \qquad (9)$$

where x_0, x_1, x_2, x_3 are inputs from the LFSR and x_4, x_5, x_6, x_7 are inputs from the NFSR. We now have:

$$z = x_1 + x_4 + x_5 + x_0x_3 + x_0x_1x_2 + x_2x_4 + x_3x_5 + x_6x_7 + x_1x_2x_6x_7$$
$$z = x_1 + x_4(1 + x_2) + x_5(1 + x_3) + x_0x_3 + x_0x_1x_2 + x_2x_4 + x_3x_5 + (1 + x_1x_2)x_6x_7.$$

Multiplying through by $x_1x_2x_3$ gives:

$$(x_1x_2x_3)z = (x_1x_2x_3)(x_1 + x_0x_3 + x_0x_1x_2 + x_2x_4 + x_3x_5).$$

As before, the right hand side of this equation now contains only inputs from the LFSR.

4.2   Generalised Algebraic Attack Algorithm

We present here an attack algorithm based on the analysis above. This attack uses a divide and conquer strategy. We first target the LFSR and recover the LFSR initial state. The NFSR is then targeted, with partial NFSR intitial state recovery possible.

Recovering the LFSR. We show that if an output function to a Grain-like structure fits any of the cases discussed in Sect. 4.1, then a system of equations can be developed that relates observable output bits to just LFSR initial state bits, and does not increase in algebraic degree over time.

The structure of a system of equations built in this way allows for the fast algebraic attack techniques highlighted in Sect. 3.2 to be applied. That is, given access to approximately $\binom{n}{d}$ bits of output (where n is the size of the LFSR and d is the algebraic degree of the system relating LFSR initial state bits to observable output bits), a precomputation phase can be performed that allows a new system of equations to be built of degree $e < d$, where e is the degree of A_{BS}. This precomputation phase has a complexity of $\mathcal{O}(\binom{n}{d}log\binom{n}{d} + n\binom{n}{d})$. The initial state of the LFSR can then be recovered in the online phase of the attack by observing approximately $\binom{n}{d}$ bits of output with complexity $\mathcal{O}(\binom{n}{d}\binom{n}{e}) + \binom{n}{e}^{\omega}$, where ω is the Guassian elimination exponent $\omega \approx 2.8$.

Recovering the NFSR. Once the LFSR initial state is recovered, every future LFSR state bit will be known, as the LFSR is autonomous. The next stage is to recover the NFSR initial state.

If the output function satisfies Cases 2 or 4 from Sect. 4.1, then it may be possible to build a system of equations where each equation is linear in NFSR initial state bits. It is likely, however, that for the cases covered in this paper this approach is not applicable. That is, the structure of the functions that allow us to target the LFSR inhibits the ability to build such a system for the NFSR state bits. In these cases, a different approach may be applied to recover the NFSR contents. The idea is best illustrated through an example.

Consider the example filter function used in Case 3 of Sect. 4.1. That is, at each time step a keystream bit is produced by

$$z = x_1 + x_4x_5 + x_0x_3 + x_0x_1x_2 + x_2x_3x_4x_5, \tag{10}$$

where x_0, x_1, x_2, x_3 are from the LFSR and x_4, x_5 are from the NFSR. Since the LFSR is known, each output bit will have the form

$$z = \alpha x_4x_5 + \beta,$$

where α and β may be 0 or 1, respectively.

Clearly, when $\alpha = 0$ no information about the initial state of the NFSR is leaked. We must therefore utilise the case where $\alpha = 1$. If $z = x_4x_5$ and $z = 1$, then we know $x_4 = x_5 = 1$. Likewise if $z = x_4x_5 + 1$ and $z = 0$, then we know $x_4 = x_5 = 1$. Once we have recovered these state bits, we may then look to equations where $z = x_4x_5$ and $z = 0$, but for which we know either x_4 or x_5 equals 1. We would then know that the unknown state bit is equal to zero. Similarly for the case where $z = x_4x_5 + 1$ and $z = 1$. Continuing in this way, we may be able to recover n consecutive bits of the NFSR. It may then be possible to reverse the NFSR update and therefore recover the NFSR initial state.

For certain filter functions it may not be possible to recover n consecutive state bits. In this case, the partially recovered initial state reduces the exhaustive search required to recover the correct initial state of the NFSR. For instance, suppose m bits of the NFSR can be recovered. This leaves 2^{n-m} possible candidates for the correct NFSR initial state which, for $m > 0$, is better than exhaustively searching the entire register. Each candidate can be used (together with the known LFSR initial state) to produce output. The candidate which produces the correct output sequence can be assumed to be the correct initial state.

Once the correct LFSR and NFSR initial states are recovered, it may be possible to reverse the initialisation process and reveal the secret key.

5 The Grain Family of Stream Ciphers

We now focus on the well known Grain family of stream ciphers. In the following sections we provide an overview of the functions used in the family and highlight why the variants currently resist traditional algebraic attacks. We then demonstrate how an algebraic attack is possible on modified versions of each of the Grain variants.

5.1   Description of the Grain

Grain is a well known family of stream ciphers that has been extensively analysed. There are five main variants: Grain-V0 [16], its revised specification Grain-V1 [14], Grain-128 [15], Grain-128a [17] and Grain-128AEAD [18]. Grain-V0, Grain-V1 and Grain-128 provide only confidentiality to a plaintext message. Grain-128a provides confidentiality, or confidentiality and integrity assurance. Grain-128AEAD provides confidentiality and integrity assurance to every plaintext message.

Keystream generators in the Grain family are based on three main building blocks: a nonlinear feedback shift register (NFSR), a linear feedback shift register (LFSR) and a nonlinear filter function. The length of the registers changes depending on key and initialisation vector (IV) size. Table 1 provides the sizes of the key, IV and component registers for each variant.

Table 1. Inputs, register lengths and internal state sizes of Grain variants.

Variant	Key (bits)	IV (bits)	NFSR length (bits)	LFSR length (bits)	Internal state (bits)
Grain-V0	80	64	80	80	160
Grain-V1	80	64	80	80	160
Grain-128	128	96	128	128	256
Grain-128a	128	96	128	128	256
Grain-128AEAD	128	96	128	128	256

5.2   Phases of Operation

Grain variants can be partitioned into two classes: those that are capable of authentication and those that are not. The phases of operation among the Grain variants are all similar. Each variant produces an initial state by loading a secret key and public IV, and then clocking the cipher a certain number of times. For Grain-128AEAD, this initialisation process uses the secret key to make reversing the initialisation process difficult.

Processing the Plaintext. Once the initialisation phase is complete, the output from the Grain keystream generator is used to encrypt plaintext to form ciphertext. When processing the plaintext, Grain-V0, Grain-V1, Grain-128 and Grain-128a (not in authentication mode) produce keystream z, which is XORed with the plaintext p to produce ciphertext c, where $c = z + p$. For Grain-128a (with authentication) and Grain-128AEAD, if the index of the output bit is even, then it is used as keystream and XORed with the plaintext to produce ciphertext. If the index of the output bit is odd, then the output is used to help generate the tag. We omit the process by which the tag is generated in this paper as it does not directly affect our findings.

5.3 Resistance Against Algebraic Attacks

All of the Grain variants use filter functions of the same form. In particular, all of the variants have filter functions of the form $f(B, S) = L_B + L_S + f_S + f_{BS}$. Recall from Sect. 4.1 that a Grain-like structure that uses a filter function of this form will be susceptible to an algebraic attack if each of the monomials in L_B is a factor of some monomial used in f_{BS}. Each Grain variant, however, uses terms in L_B that do not appear in any other monomial. This eliminates the ability to annihilate these terms from the NFSR and thus defeats our attack.

6   Algebraic Attack on Modified Versions of the Grain Family

We now mount an algebraic attack on adapted versions of the Grain family of stream ciphers with modified filter functions. We show that even with bits from the NFSR used nonlinearly in f, a system of equations that does not increase in degree over time can be constructed, enabling successful fast algebraic attacks on the modified variants of V0, V1, 128 and also 128a (without the authentication). We also mount algebraic attacks on the variants with authentication (128a and 128AEAD). We note that recovering the LFSR initial state is the same for all variants, but on average less of the NFSR initial state will be recovered for variants with authentication due to the decimation used on the output when generating keystream.

6.1   Modified Version of Grain

We introduce a modified version of the Grain family, where we replace any independent linear term taken from the NFSR by the corresponding term in the LFSR. That is, all filter functions $f(B, S)$ remain the same, except that monomials appearing only in L_B are replaced by monomials in L_S with the same indices. Note that we denote a modified version of Grain by appending the suffix $-m$.

Table 2 highlights the differences between original and modified versions of each Grain variant. To save space, we present the modifications for Grain-V0 in detail here and refer the interested reader to Appendix B for details of the other variants.

Table 2. Modifications to linear combinations in different Grain variants.

Variant	Original linear combination	Modified linear combination
V0	b_0	s_1
V1	$b_1 + b_2 + b_4 + b_{10} + b_{31} + b_{43} + b_{56}$	$s_1 + s_2 + s_4 + s_{10} + s_{31} + s_{43} + s_{56}$
128	$b_2 + b_{15} + b_{36} + b_{45} + b_{64} + b_{73} + b_{89} + b_{93}$	$s_2 + s_{15} + s_{36} + s_{45} + s_{64} + s_{73} + s_{89} + s_{93}$
128a	$b_2 + b_{15} + b_{36} + b_{45} + b_{64} + b_{73} + b_{89} + s_{93}$	$s_2 + s_{15} + s_{36} + s_{45} + s_{64} + s_{73} + s_{89} + s_{93}$
128AEAD	$b_2 + b_{15} + b_{36} + b_{45} + b_{64} + b_{73} + b_{89} + s_{93}$	$s_2 + s_{15} + s_{36} + s_{45} + s_{64} + s_{73} + s_{89} + s_{93}$

Grain-V0-m. In the case of Grain-V0-m, the bit b_0 was replaced by s_1 so as to not use the same bit used in the linear update of the LFSR.

For Grain-V0-m, the output function is as follows:

$$z = h(B, S) = s_1 + s_3 + s_{25} + b_{63} + s_3 s_{64} + s_{46} s_{64} + s_{64} b_{63} + s_3 s_{25} s_{46} + s_3 s_{46} s_{64}$$
$$+ s_3 s_{46} b_{63} + s_{25} s_{46} b_{63} + s_{46} s_{64} b_{63}.$$

Note that b_{63} was left as a linear term in f of Grain-V0-m as f satisfies the conditions of Case 2 covered in Sect. 4.1.

We show that for each variant, it is possible to build systems of equations that are independent of the NFSR. This means that the degree of the system of equations will not vary over time, despite the presence of NFSR bits in the filter function of each variant.

6.2   Stage 1: LFSR Recovery

In this section we apply the algorithm from Sect. 4. We provide the details for Grain-V0 and Grain-128a-m/128AEAD-m. The details for the other variants can be found in Appendix C. The theoretical data and computational complexity requirements to recover the LFSR initial state for each variant are summarised in Table 3. In Sect. 7, we provide experimental results for the modified version of Grain-V0.

Grain-V0-m

At time $t = 0$ an output bit in Grain-V0-m is produced as follows:

$$z_0 = s_1 + s_3 + s_{25} + s_3 s_{64} + s_{46} s_{64} + s_3 s_{25} s_{46} + s_3 s_{46} s_{64} + b_{63}(1 + s_{64} + s_3 s_{46} + s_{25} s_{46} + s_{46} s_{64})$$

Multiplying this equation by $(s_{64} + s_3 s_{46} + s_{25} s_{46} + s_{46} s_{64})$ gives

$$(s_{64} + s_3 s_{46} + s_{25} s_{46} + s_{46} s_{64})z_0 = s_1 s_3 s_{46} + s_1 s_{25} s_{46} + s_1 s_{46} s_{64} + s_3 s_{46} s_{64} + s_1 s_{64} + s_3 s_{46}$$
$$+ s_{25} s_{46} + s_{25} s_{64}$$

where the right hand side of the equation contains only LFSR initial state bits and is of degree 3. Thus, by observing at least $\binom{80}{3}$ keystream bits, fast algebraic techniques may be applied in the precomputation phase of the attack to reduce the overall degree of the system to the degree of the left hand side (which is of degree 2 in the unknown LFSR initial state bits) [5].

Grain-128a-m (with authentication)/Grain-128AEAD-m

The process for recovering the LFSR initial state in Grain-128a-m (with authentication) and Grain128AEAD-m is very similar to Grain-128a-m (without authentication). In keystream generation, Grain-128a-m (with authentication) and Grain-128AEAD-m use a decimated version of the output sequence as keystream. Therefore, every second equation produced using the output function will contain an unknown output bit (used for authentication and so not visible in a known plaintext scenario). To avoid this problem, an attacker simply builds the system following the process for Grain-128a-m (without authentication), and then builds a new system by taking all the even indexed equations. Note that this requires the attacker to produce twice as many equations as they would for Grain-128a-m (without authentication), but still only requires the same amount of keystream output.

The highest degree monomial is of order 5 (see Appendix C). Thus, by observing at least $\binom{80}{5}$ keystream bits, fast algebraic techniques may be applied in the precomputation phase of the attack to reduce the overall degree of the system to the degree of the left hand side (which is of degree 3 in the unknown LFSR initial state bits) [5]. Note that due to the keystream decimation used in these variants, the precomputation phase requires a higher complexity (as discussed by Courtois [5]).

6.3 Stage 2: NFSR Recovery

Once the LFSR initial state is recovered, the output function will contain only unknown initial state bits from the NFSR. Due to the structure of the output function for the Grain variants, we adopt the second approach described in Sect. 4.2. We provide details for Grain-V0-m in this section. Details for the other variants can be found in Appendix D.

The data requirement for this stage will utilise the data collected for LFSR state recovery. The computational complexity is considered to be negligible [3]. The number of NFSR initial state bits recovered through application of this method is hard to estimate and will vary depending on the particular initial state. However, some guidance based on experimental results is provided in Sect. 7.4. Moreover, if at least one bit of the NFSR can be recovered, the remaining exhaustive search is better than exhaustively searching the key space. Due to the low computational complexity of partial NFSR recovery we provide experimental results for this in the following section.

Grain-V0-m

At time $t = 0$ an output bit in Grain-V0 is produced as follows:

$$z_0 = s_1 + s_3 + s_{25} + s_3 s_{64} + s_{46} s_{64} + s_3 s_{25} s_{46} + s_3 s_{46} s_{64}$$
$$+ b_{63}(1 + s_{64} + s_3 s_{46} + s_{25} s_{46} + s_{46} s_{64})$$

This function is linear in the single NFSR bit b_{63}. At each time step we have:

$$z = \alpha b_{63+t} + \beta,$$

where α and β can be 0 or 1, respectively.

Table 3. Resource requirements for recovering the LFSR of the modified Grain variants.

Variant	Grain-V0-m	Grain-V1-m	Grain-128-m	Grain-128a-m(no authentication)	Grain-128a-m(authentication)/128AEAD
Precomputation phase					
Degree of system before applying fast algebraic techniques	3	3	5	5	5
Complexity	$\mathcal{O}(2^{19})$	$\mathcal{O}(2^{19})$	$\mathcal{O}(2^{31})$	$\mathcal{O}(2^{31})$	$\mathcal{O}(2^{78})$
Degree of system after applying fast algebraic techniques	2	2	3	3	3
Online phase					
Data	2^{17}	2^{17}	2^{28}	2^{28}	2^{28}
Complexity	$\mathcal{O}(2^{33})$	$\mathcal{O}(2^{33})$	$\mathcal{O}(2^{52})$	$\mathcal{O}(2^{52})$	$\mathcal{O}(2^{52})$

When $\alpha = 1$, an NFSR initial state bit will be recovered. This can be used for simple partial state recovery of the NFSR. The remaining stages of the NFSR initial state can then be found through exhaustive search. An estimate of the average exhaustive search requirement for each modified Grain variant is provided in Table 5 of Sect. 7.4.

7   Experimental Simulations

We have performed computer simulations of our algebraic attack, applying it to toy versions of Grain-like structures with total internal states of 40, 60, 80 and 100 bits, to demonstrate proof of concept. We have also performed simulations of the full modified version of Grain-V0. The details of these versions, the simulation setup and results are provided in the following sections. We also provide experimental results in Sect. 7.4 for the partial NFSR recovery of each of the full modified versions of Grain; this is possible because of the low time complexity required to partially recover these states.

7.1   Specifications

The toy Grain-like structures used in our simulations were formed using registers each of length 20, 30, 40 and 50 respectively. The details for the structures are as follows. Note that we use subscripts on the functions to distinguish between the registers of the different sizes. The modified version of Grain-V0 is denoted using the subscript 80.

The LFSR update functions correspond to primitive polynomials of the relevant order and are as follows:

$$\ell_{20} = s_0 + s_{11} + s_{15} + s_{17}$$
$$\ell_{30} = s_0 + s_7 + s_{28} + s_{29}$$
$$\ell_{40} = s_0 + s_{35} + s_{36} + s_{37}$$
$$\ell_{50} = s_0 + s_{46} + s_{47} + s_{48}$$
$$\ell_{80} = s_0 + s_{13} + s_{23} + s_{38} + s_{51} + s_{62}$$

The NFSR update functions $g_{20}, g_{30}, g_{40}, g_{50}$ are modified versions of the nonlinear update used in Sprout [1]. The modified functions use the same number of inputs and have the same algebraic degree of 4. The update function g_{80} is the same function used in Grain-V0. The nonlinear update functions are as follows:

$g_{20} = s_0 + b_0 + b_{13} + b_{19} + b_{15} + b_2 b_{15} + b_3 b_5 + b_7 b_8 + b_{14} b_{19} + b_{10} b_{11} b_{12} + b_6 b_{13} b_{17} b_{18}$

$g_{30} = s_0 + b_0 + b_{19} + b_{28} + b_{22} + b_4 b_{22} + b_5 b_7 + b_{11} b_{12} + b_{21} b_{28} + b_{15} b_{17} b_{19} + b_9 b_{19} b_{25} b_{27}$

$g_{40} = s_0 + b_0 + b_{27} + b_{38} + b_{28} + b_5 b_{28} + b_6 b_9 + b_{15} b_{14} + b_{31} b_{38} + b_{23} b_{25} b_{27} + b_{15} b_{27} b_{33} b_{37}$

$g_{50} = s_0 + b_0 + b_{33} + b_{47} + b_{38} + b_6 b_{38} + b_8 b_{13} + b_{17} b_{20} + b_{35} b_{47} + b_{25} b_{28} b_{30} + b_{15} b_{33} b_{42} b_{45}$

$g_{80} = s_0 + b_0 + b_9 + b_{15} + b_{21} + b_{28} + b_{33} + b_{37} + b_{45} + b_{52} + b_{60} + b_{63} + b_9) b_{15} + b_{33} b_{37} +$
$\quad + b_{60} b_{63} + b_{21} b_{28} b_{33} + b_{45} b_{52} b_{60} + b_9 b_{28} b_{45} b_{63} + b_{15} b_{21} b_{60} b_{63} + b_{33} b_{37} b_{52} b_{60} + b_9 b_{15} b_{21} b_{28} b_{33} +$
$\quad + b_{37} b_{45} b_{52} b_{60} b_{63} + b_{21} b_{28} b_{33} b_{37} b_{45} b_{52}$

The output functions used in the simulations are modified versions of the one used in Grain-V0 [16] with the same number of taps and algebraic degree. The output functions are as follows:

$f_{20} = s_1 + s_2 + s_6 + s_2 s_{16} + s_{12} s_{16} + s_2 s_6 s_{12} + s_2 s_{12} s_{16} + b_{15}(s_{16} + s_2 s_{12} + s_6 s_{12} + s_{12} s_{16} + 1)$

$f_{30} = s_1 + s_2 + s_9 + s_2 s_{24} + s_{17} s_{24} + s_2 s_9 s_{17} + s_2 s_{17} s_{24} + b_{23}(s_{24} + s_2 s_{17} + s_9 s_{17} + s_{17} s_{24} + 1)$

$f_{40} = s_1 + s_2 + s_{13} + s_2 s_{32} + s_{23} s_{32} + s_2 s_{13} s_{23} + s_2 s_{23} s_{32} + b_{31}(s_{32} + s_2 s_{23} + s_{13} s_{23} + s_{23} s_{32} + 1)$

$f_{50} = s_1 + s_2 + s_{16} + s_2 s_{40} + s_{29} s_{40} + s_2 s_{16} s_{29} + s_2 s_{29} s_{40} + b_{39}(s_{40} + s_2 s_{29} + s_{16} s_{29} + s_{29} s_{40} + 1)$

$f_{80} = s_1 + s_3 + s_{25} + s_3 s_{64} + s_{46} s_{64} + s_3 s_{25} s_{46} + s_3 s_{46} s_{64} + b_{63}(s_{64} + s_3 s_{46} + s_{25} s_{46} + s_{46} s_{64} + 1)$

7.2 Experimental Approach

For each simulation, random NFSR and LFSR states were produced. Output from the Grain-like structure was then produced. The attack from Sect. 4 was then applied to fully recover the LFSR initial state and partially recover the NFSR initial state. The remaining NFSR bits were then exhaustively searched. Each initial state candidate was used to produce output, which was checked against the correct output sequence. A candidate that produced the correct output was considered the correct initial state. The computed initial state was then checked against the correct initial state.

The code used for the simulations was written using the SageMath software package [28] and all calculations were performed using QUT's High Performance Computing facility. We used a single node from the cluster with an Intel Xeon core capable of 271 TeraFlops.

7.3   Results on Toy Grain-Like Structure

In precomputation, the initial system of equations was built, the linear dependency was found and the reduced system of equations was built. For $n = 20$, approximately 2^{11} bits of output were used in the precomputation phase of the attack. For $n = 30$, approximately 2^{13} bits of output were used, approximately 2^{14} bits of output were used for $n = 40$ and approximately 2^{15} bits of output were used for $n = 50$. For the modified version of Grain-V0, approximately 2^{17} bits of output were used. The majority of the computational complexity required for the precomputation comes from applying the linear dependency to produce the reduced system of equations. On average, precomputation was completed in 3 s, 37 s, 8 min and 1 h, respectively for the toy versions of Grain. The precomputation phase of the attack for the modified version of Grain-V0 took 24 h on average.

A total of 100 simulations were performed for each structure. In every simulation the full LFSR initial state was recovered. Each simulation for the toy version required on average 10 s to recover the LFSR initial state, regardless of the register size. For the modified version of Grain-V0, 30 s were required on average to recover the LFSR state in the online phase.

For each simulation, partially recovering the NFSR took less than a second. Table 4 provides a tally (across the 100 simulations) of how many times a certain number of state bits were recovered from the NFSR. For each simulation, the full available keystream was used. That is, the NFSR state was partially recovered using 2^{11}, 2^{13}, 2^{14}, and 2^{15} bits of keystream for registers of length 20, 30, 40 and 50 respectively. Note that the results for NFSR recovery of the modified version of Grain-V0 can be found in Sect. 7.4.

We see from Table 4 that the number of NFSR initial state bits that were recovered varied. On average, 18, 25, 34 and 45 bits were recovered for the respective NFSR initial states of size 20, 30, 40 and 50. The remaining 2, 3, 5 and 8 bits were recovered by exhaustive search and used to produce output. The output was then compared against the correct output. This process took a maximum of a few seconds in each case.

Table 4. Distribution table for NFSR bits recovered over 100 simulations for Grain-like structures of length $n = 20, n = 30, n = 40$ and $n = 50$.

$n = 20$										
No. bits recovered	0	...	13	14	15	16	17	18	19	20
Frequency	0	...	0	0	0	0	34	59	7	0

$n = 30$										
No. bits recovered	0	...	22	23	24	25	26	27	...	30
Frequency	0	...	0	3	9	72	16	0	...	0

$n = 40$										
No. bits recovered	0	...	32	33	34	35	36	37	...	40
Frequency	0	...	0	21	50	18	11	0	...	0

$n = 50$										
No. bits recovered	0	...	43	44	45	46	47	48	...	50
Frequency	0	...	0	10	53	33	4	0	...	0

7.4 NFSR Recovery on Full Modified Grain Family

Due to the low computational complexity of partially recovering the NFSR, we have performed simulations for the full modified versions of the Grain family. A total of 1000 simulations were performed for each variant. For each simulation, 2^{17} bits of output were produced and used to partially recover the NFSR initial state. Each simulation required less than a second to partially recover the NFSR state. Figure 3 and Fig. 4 provide tallies (across the 1000 simulations) of how many times a certain number of state bits were recovered for the NFSR of each variant, respectively. Grain-V0 and Grain-V1 have been graphed as a single data set due to the extreme similarity between the results for each variant. Similarly for Grain-128 and Grain-128a (without authentication), and Grain-128a (with authentication) and Grain-128AEAD. Table 5 provides an estimate for the exhaustive search requirements for each modified Grain variant, based on Figs. 3 and 4.

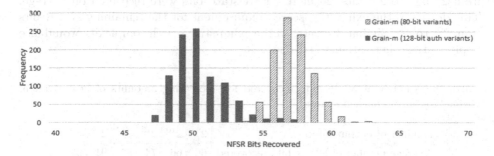

Fig. 3. Histogram for NFSR bits recovered over 1000 simulations for each modified Grain variant, using 2^{17} bits of output.

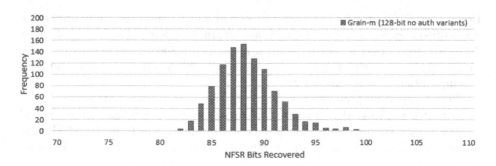

Fig. 4. Histogram for NFSR bits recovered over 1000 simulations for each modified Grain variant, using 2^{17} bits of output.

Table 5. Average exhaustive search requirement for the NFSR of each modified Grain variant using 2^{17} bits of output.

Variant	Grain-V0-m	Grain-V1-m	Grain-128-m	Grain-128a-m (no auth.)	Grain-128a-m (auth.)	Grain-128AEAD-m
Average NFSR exhaustive search complexity	2^{23}	2^{23}	2^{41}	2^{41}	2^{78}	2^{78}

It is worth noting that for the simulations presented in this paper, a limited number of output bits were used for the partial recovery of the NFSR. In practice, the NFSR only needs to be recovered once and so, an attacker may use all the available keystream for NFSR recovery. Using more keystream will increase the number of state bits recovered by an attacker, in general, but will take longer. For instance, Table 6 shows the average number of NFSR state bits recovered in Grain-128a-m, across 10 trials, when using 2^9, 2^{10}, 2^{13}, 2^{17}, 2^{19} and 2^{20} bits of keystream. By increasing the amount of keystream used for NFSR recovery from 2^9 bits to 2^{20} bits, 26 more NFSR state bits were recovered on average. This decreases the exhaustive search requirement for the remaining NFSR bits from 2^{62} to 2^{36}. Similar decreases in the exhaustive search complexity would also apply to the other variants in Table 5.

Table 6. Number of NFSR bits recovered for increasing amounts of keystream in Grain-128a-m (no authentication).

Number of output bits	2^9	2^{10}	2^{13}	2^{17}	2^{19}	2^{20}
Average number of NFSR bits recovered	66	66	74	87	91	92
Average exhaustive search complexity	2^{62}	2^{62}	2^{54}	2^{41}	2^{37}	2^{36}

8   Discussion/Observations

Berbain et al. [2] proposed two attacks, one of which was successfully applied to a modified version of Grain-128, with an output function of the form $f(B, S) = L_B + L_S + f_S$. This attack required a system of equations of degree 6 in 256 unknowns to be solved, requiring approximately 2^{39} bits of keystream and with a computational complexity of 2^{105}.

In this paper, we present a new divide and conquer algebraic attack on Grain-like structures. Unlike the attack of Berbain et al. [2], our method can be applied to Grain-like structures with filter functions containing taps from the NFSR that are used nonlinearly. We show that Grain-like structures with an output function of the form

$$f(B, S) = L_S + f_S + f_{BS}$$

are always susceptible to our attack. It is therefore not sufficient to include NFSR bits nonlinearly as components of f_{BS} alone. Furthermore, we showed that output functions satisfying any of the forms:

- $f(B,S) = L_B + L_S + f_S + f_{BS}$
- $f(B,S) = L_S + f_S + f_B + f_{BS}$
- $f(B,S) = L_B + L_S + f_S + f_B + f_{BS}$

are all susceptible to a divide and conquer attack, if the filter function is chosen poorly. We showed in Sect. 6 that this is the case for a modified version of each Grain variant.

For example, Grain-128-m with output function of the form $f(B,S) = L_S + f_S + f_{BS}$ is susceptible to attack. First, the LFSR initial state is recovered via a fast algebraic attack requiring approximately 2^{28} bits of keystream and complexity of $2^{51.51}$. Then the NFSR initial state is partially recovered using the keystream produced for the LFSR recovery. Partial recovery of the NFSR takes about a second. From Table 6 we see that, if 2^{20} bits of output are used an average of 92 bits from the NFSR are recovered. The remainder of the state can be recovered in 2^{36} operations. Thus the entire initial state can be recovered with a complexity of about $2^{51.51}$, by observing approximately 2^{28} bits of keystream.

The results of Berbain et al. [2] provide full initial state recovery, whereas our approach provides full recovery of the LFSR and partial recovery of the NFSR state, with the remaining state bits of the NFSR being recovered by exhaustive search. We see, however, that in all cases without authentication, the exhaustive search of the NFSR does not significantly add to the complexity of the attack. Furthermore, our attack approach applies to a much larger set of filter functions. We identified an additional four cases of such functions that are vulnerable to algebraic attacks providing efficient partial state recovery. Moreover, these attacks are, in general, much more efficient than the attack proposed by Berbain et al. [2], and require less keystream.

This analysis highlights that it is not only the choice of a filter function that includes the NFSR contents nonlinearly and linearly in the output function that currently provides resistance against algebraic attacks in the Grain variants. Rather, it is both the use of the NFSR bits linearly and nonlinearly, together with the careful choice of input stages that provides the resistance. The authors of Grain-128a state "Grain-128a does use an NFSR, which introduces much more nonlinearity together with the nonlinear filter function. Solving equations for the initial 256 bit state is not possible due to the nonlinear update of the NFSR and the NFSR state bits used nonlinearly in the nonlinear filter function [17]." We have shown that although Grain itself is currently resistant to algebraic attacks, the statement made by the authors is over simplified, and not always accurate. We have provided examples where functions satisfy this criterion, but the keystream generators are still susceptible to algebraic attacks.

9   Conclusion

This paper investigated the security of a certain type of contemporary keystream generator design against algebraic attacks. These keystream generators use a nonlinear feedback shift register, a linear feedback shift register and a nonlinear output function taking inputs from both registers. We refer to these designs as

"Grain-like" structures, as the well known Grain family of stream ciphers has this structure.

Motivated by the work of Berbain et al. [2] we looked for approaches that eliminate nonlinear contributions from the NFSR to the filter function. Courtois' method in [5] shows how to reduce the degree of a function by multiplying through by a "annihilator". We took a similar approach, but used it to annihilate the nonlinear monomials in the filter function that take inputs from the NFSR. This allowed us to build a system of algebraic equations taking inputs from LFSR bits only, permitting a divide and conquer approach, first targeting the LFSR in an algebraic attack. Following this, NFSR recovery is possible. Note that our attack is applicable to a much larger set of filter functions than the attack presented by Berbain et al. [2], since we are not constrained to filter functions in which NFSR bits are only present linearly.

To illustrate the effectiveness of the attack, we applied our attack method to modified versions of the Grain family of stream ciphers. We performed simulations of our attack on Grain-like structures with internal state sizes of 40, 60, 80 and 100 bits, as well as on a modified version of Grain-V0. In our experiments, the full LFSR initial state was always correctly recovered. The NFSR initial state was partially recovered, dramatically reducing the exhaustive search requirement to obtain the remaining NFSR bits. Having recovered the initial state, it may then be possible to recover the secret key.

These results are relevant to designers of keystream generators as they clearly demonstrate that even when the output function incorporates bits from the LFSR and the NFSR both linearly and nonlinearly, the keystream generator may still be susceptible to attack, resulting in state recovery faster than brute force. We emphasise that our attack method is not applicable to the original Grain family as the filter functions included in those designs do not meet the conditions that permit this attack. However, this paper clearly demonstrates that some output functions previously thought to be secure against algebraic attacks are, in fact, insecure. Designers should carefully assess their chosen functions with this in mind.

A   Algorithms

A.1   Algorithm for NLFG algebraic attack

Precomputation phase:

Step 1 Use $f(S_0) = y_0$ to relate initial state bits $(s_0, s_1, \ldots, s_{n-1})$ to observed output bit y_0.

Step 2 Multiply f by a function h (if applicable) to reduce overall degree to d.

Step 3 Clock forward using $f(S_t) = y_t$ to build a system of equations of constant algebraic degree, applying the linear update as required.

Online phase:

Step 4 Substitute observed output bits $\{y_t\}_{t=0}^{\infty}$ into the system of equations.
Step 5 Solve the system of equations by linearisation, to recover $S_0 = s_0, s_1, \ldots, s_{n-1}$.

A.2   Algorithm for Fast Algebraic Attack

The precomputation phase is similar to a regular algebraic attack, with Step 3 replaced by three steps (3a, 3b and 3c) as follows.

Step 3a Identify the combination of equations that will eliminate monomials of degree e to d in the initial state bits.
Step 3b Use this linear dependency to build a new general equation.
Step 3c Use this general equation to build a system of equations of degree e in the initial state bits.

A.3   Algorithm for LF-NFSR Algebraic Attack

Precomputation phase:

Step 1 A system of equations is developed using the linear filter function to represent every state bit as a linear combination of a subset of the initial state bits and some output bits. We denote this system of equation by system $\mathcal{L}$.
Step 2 A second system of equations is developed using the nonlinear update function g to represent update bits as a nonlinear combination of a subset of initial state bits. We denote this system by system $\mathcal{G}$. Substitutions are made for state bits in system $\mathcal{G}$ using system $\mathcal{L}$ where applicable to reduce the number of unknown state variables while keeping the degree of system $\mathcal{G}$ constant.
Step 3 The two systems are combined by aligning the equations from each system that represent the same state bit. The resulting system contains only initial state bits and observed output bits. We denote this system as system $\mathcal{L} + \mathcal{G}$.

Online phase:

Step 4 Substitute observed output bits $\{y_t\}_{t=0}^{\infty}$ into the system of equations
Step 5 Solve the system of equations by linearisation.

B   Modified Version of Grain

Grain-V1-*m*

$$z - h(B, S) = s_1 + s_2 + s_4 + s_{10} + s_{31} + s_{43} + s_{56} + s_{25} + b_{63} +$$
$$+ s_3 s_{64} + s_{46} s_{64} + s_{46} s_{64} + s_3 s_{25} s_{46} + s_3 s_{46} s_{64} + s_3 s_{46} b_{63} + s_{25} s_{46} b_{63} + s_{46} s_{64} b_{63}$$

As with Grain-V0$-m$, f of Grain-V1$-m$ satisfies Case 2 and so b_{63} was left in the function.

Grain-128-m

$$z = h(B, S) = s_2 + s_{15} + s_{36} + s_{45} + s_{64} + s_{73} + s_{89} + s_{93} + \\ s_8 b_{12} + s_{13} s_{20} + b_{95} s_{42} + s_{60} s_{79} + b_{12} b_{95} s_{95}$$

Grain-128a-m/Grain-128AEAD-m

$$z = h(B, S) = s_2 + s_{15} + s_{36} + s_{45} + s_{64} + s_{73} + s_{89} + s_{93} + \\ s_8 b_{12} + s_{13} s_{20} + b_{95} s_{42} + s_{60} s_{79} + b_{12} b_{95} s_{94}$$

Note that the structure of the filter function used Grain-128 is identical to the structure of the filter functions in Grain-128a, except that s_{95} in the final term for Grain-128 was changed to s_{94} in Grain-128a. This change is reflected in the modified versions shown here.

C   Recovering the LFSR Initial State of Grain

Grain-V1-m

At time $t = 0$ an output bit in Grain-V1 is produced as follows:

$$z_0 = s_1 + s_2 + s_3 + s_4 + s_{10} + s_{31} + s_{43} + s_{56} + s_{25} + \\ s_3 s_{64} + s_{46} s_{64} + s_3 s_{25} s_{46} + s_3 s_{46} s_{64} + b_{63}(1 + s_{64} + s_3 s_{46} + s_{25} s_{46} + s_{46} s_{64})$$

Multiplying this equation by $(s_{64} + s_3 s_{46} + s_{25} s_{46} + s_{46} s_{64})$ gives

$$(s_{64} + s_3 s_{46} + s_{25} s_{46} + s_{46} s_{64}) z_0 = (s_1 + s_2 + s_4 + s_{10} + s_{31} + s_{43} + s_{56} + s_{25} + \\ s_3 s_{64} + s_{46} s_{64} + s_3 s_{25} s_{46} + s_3 s_{46} s_{64}) \\ (s_{64} + s_3 s_{46} + s_{25} s_{46} + s_{46} s_{64}),$$

where the right hand side of the equation contains only LFSR initial state bits. When the right hand side is expanded, the highest degree monomial is of order 3. Thus, by observing at least $\binom{80}{3}$ keystream bits, fast algebraic techniques may be applied in the precomputation phase of the attack to reduce the overall degree of the system to the degree of the left hand side (which is of degree 2 in the unknown LFSR initial state bits) [5].

Grain-128-m

At time $t = 0$ an output bit in Grain-128 is produced as follows:

$$z_0 = s_2 + s_{15} + s_{36} + s_{45} + s_{64} + s_{73} + s_{89} + s_{93} + s_8 b_{12} + s_{13} s_{20} + b_{95} s_{42} + s_{60} s_{79} + b_{12} b_{95} s_{95}$$

Multiplying this equation by $(s_8 + 1)(s_{42} + 1)(s_{95} + 1)$ gives

$$(s_8 + 1)(s_{42} + 1)(s_{95} + 1)z_0 = (s_8 + 1)(s_{42} + 1)(s_{95} + 1)(s_2 + s_{15} + s_{36} + s_{45} + s_{64} + s_{73} + s_{89} + s_{93} + s_{13}s_{20} + s_{60}s_{79}),$$

where the right hand side of the equation contains only LFSR initial state bits. When the right hand side is expanded, the highest degree monomial is of order 5. Thus, by observing at least $\binom{80}{5}$ keystream bits, fast algebraic techniques may be applied in the precomputation phase of the attack to reduce the overall degree of the system to the degree of the left hand side (which is of degree 3 in the unknown LFSR initial state bits) [5].

Grain-128a-m (without authentication)

At time $t = 0$ an output bit in Grain-128a is produced as follows:

$$z_0 = s_2 + s_{15} + s_{36} + s_{45} + s_{64} + s_{73} + s_{89} + s_{93} + s_8 b_{12} + s_{13}s_{20} + b_{95}s_{42} + s_{60}s_{79} + b_{12}b_{95}s_{94}$$

Multiplying this equation by $(s_8 + 1)(s_{42} + 1)(s_{94} + 1)$ gives

$$(s_8 + 1)(s_{42} + 1)(s_{94} + 1)z_0 = (s_8 + 1)(s_{42} + 1)(s_{94} + 1)(s_2 + s_{15} + s_{36} + s_{45} + s_{64} + s_{73} + s_{89} + s_{93} + s_{13}s_{20} + s_{60}s_{79}),$$

where the right hand side of the equation contains only LFSR initial state bits. When the right hand side is expanded, the highest degree monomial is of order 5. Thus, by observing at least $\binom{80}{5}$ keystream bits, fast algebraic techniques may be applied in the precomputation phase of the attack to reduce the overall degree of the system to the degree of the left hand side (which is of degree 3 in the unknown LFSR initial state bits) [5].

D   Recovering the NFSR Initial State of Grain

Grain-V1-m

At time $t = 0$ an output bit in Grain-V1 is produced as follows:

$$z_0 = s_1 + s_2 + s_4 + s_{10} + s_{31} + s_{43} + s_{56} + s_{25} + s_3 s_{46} + s_{25}s_{46} + s_3 s_{25}s_{46} + s_3 s_{46}s_{64} + b_{63}(1 + s_{64} + s_3 s_{46} + s_{25}s_{46} + s_{46}s_{64})$$

Similarly to Grain-V0-m, this output function is already linear in b_{63} and the state can be partially recovered in a similar way.

Grain-128-m

At time $t = 0$ an output bit in Grain-128 is produced as follows:

$$z_0 = s_2 + s_{15} + s_{36} + s_{45} + s_{64} + s_{73} + s_{89} + s_{93} + s_8 b_{12} + s_{13}s_{20} + b_{95}s_{42} + s_{60}s_{79} + b_{12}b_{95}s_{95}$$

There is one monomial ($b_{12}b_{95}s_{95}$) that is of degree 2 in NFSR initial state bits. At each time step we have:

$$z_t = \alpha b_{12} + \beta b_{95} + \gamma b_{12}b_{95} + \zeta$$

As described in Sect. 4.2, these equations can be used to gain information about individual NFSR state bits when not all of α, β and γ are 0. This information can in turn be used to partially recover the NFSR initial state.

Grain-128a-m (without authentication)

At time $t = 0$ an output bit in Grain-128a is produced as follows:

$$z_0 = s_2 + s_{15} + s_{36} + s_{45} + s_{64} + s_{73} + s_{89} + s_{93} + s_8 b_{12} + s_{13}s_{20} + b_{95}s_{42} + s_{60}s_{79} + b_{12}b_{95}s_{94}$$

There is one monomial ($b_{12}b_{95}s_{94}$) that is of degree 2 in NFSR initial state bits. The possible output equations will be the same for Grain-128a$-m$ (without authentication) as it is for Grain-128-m. The state can then be partially recovered in the same way as Grain-128-m.

Grain-128a-m (with authentication)/Grain-128AEAD-m

The possible output equations will be the same for Grain-128a$-m$ (with authentication) as it is for Grain-128-m. In the case of Grain-128a$-m$ (with authentication)/Grain-128AEAD-m, we may only utilise even index output bits to recover NFSR initial state bits. This will result in less of the state being recovered overall.

References

1. Armknecht, F., Mikhalev, V.: On lightweight stream ciphers with shorter internal states. In: Leander, G. (ed.) FSE 2015. LNCS, vol. 9054, pp. 451–470. Springer, Heidelberg (2015). https://doi.org/10.1007/978-3-662-48116-5_22
2. Berbain, C., Gilbert, H., Joux, A.: Algebraic and correlation attacks against linearly filtered non linear feedback shift registers. In: Avanzi, R.M., Keliher, L., Sica, F. (eds.) SAC 2008. LNCS, vol. 5381, pp. 184–198. Springer, Heidelberg (2009). https://doi.org/10.1007/978-3-642-04159-4_12
3. Berbain, C., Gilbert, H., Maximov, A.: Cryptanalysis of grain. In: Robshaw, M. (ed.) FSE 2006. LNCS, vol. 4047, pp. 15–29. Springer, Heidelberg (2006). https://doi.org/10.1007/11799313_2
4. Courtois, N.T.: Higher order correlation attacks, XL algorithm and cryptanalysis of toyocrypt. In: Lee, P.J., Lim, C.H. (eds.) ICISC 2002. LNCS, vol. 2587, pp. 182–199. Springer, Heidelberg (2003). https://doi.org/10.1007/3-540-36552-4_13
5. Courtois, N.T.: Fast algebraic attacks on stream ciphers with linear feedback. In: Boneh, D. (ed.) CRYPTO 2003. LNCS, vol. 2729, pp. 176–194. Springer, Heidelberg (2003). https://doi.org/10.1007/978-3-540-45146-4_11
6. Courtois, N.T., Meier, W.: Algebraic attacks on stream ciphers with linear feedback. In: Biham, E. (ed.) EUROCRYPT 2003. LNCS, vol. 2656, pp. 345–359. Springer, Heidelberg (2003). https://doi.org/10.1007/3-540-39200-9_21

7. De Cannière, C., Küçük, Ö., Preneel, B.: Analysis of grain's initialization algorithm. In: Vaudenay, S. (ed.) AFRICACRYPT 2008. LNCS, vol. 5023, pp. 276–289. Springer, Heidelberg (2008). https://doi.org/10.1007/978-3-540-68164-9_19
8. Dinur, I., Shamir, A.: Breaking grain-128 with dynamic cube attacks. In: Joux, A. (ed.) FSE 2011. LNCS, vol. 6733, pp. 167–187. Springer, Heidelberg (2011). https://doi.org/10.1007/978-3-642-21702-9_10
9. Englund, H., Johansson, T.: A new simple technique to attack filter generators and related ciphers. In: Handschuh, H., Hasan, M.A. (eds.) SAC 2004. LNCS, vol. 3357, pp. 39–53. Springer, Heidelberg (2004). https://doi.org/10.1007/978-3-540-30564-4_3
10. Faugere, J.-C., Ars, G.: An algebraic cryptanalysis of nonlinear filter generators using Gröbner bases. Report, INRIA (2003)
11. Forré, R.: A fast correlation attack on nonlinearly feedforward filtered shift-register sequences. In: Quisquater, J.-J., Vandewalle, J. (eds.) EUROCRYPT 1989. LNCS, vol. 434, pp. 586–595. Springer, Heidelberg (1990). https://doi.org/10.1007/3-540-46885-4_56
12. Gammel, B.M., Göttfert, R.: Linear filtering of nonlinear shift-register sequences. In: Ytrehus, Ø. (ed.) WCC 2005. LNCS, vol. 3969, pp. 354–370. Springer, Heidelberg (2006). https://doi.org/10.1007/11779360_28
13. Golić, J.D., Salmasizadeh, M., Simpson, L., Dawson, E.: Fast correlation attacks on nonlinear filter generators. Inf. Process. Lett. **64**(1), 37–42 (1997)
14. Hell, M., Johansson, T., Maximov, A., Meier, W.: The grain family of stream ciphers. In: Robshaw, M., Billet, O. (eds.) New Stream Cipher Designs. LNCS, vol. 4986, pp. 179–190. Springer, Heidelberg (2008). https://doi.org/10.1007/978-3-540-68351-3_14
15. Hell, M., Johansson, T., Maximov, A., Meier, W.: A stream cipher proposal: grain-128. In: 2006 IEEE International Symposium on Information Theory, pp. 1614–1618. IEEE (2006)
16. Hell, M., Johansson, T., Meier, W.: Grain: a stream cipher for constrained environments. Int. J. Wirel. Mob. Comput. **2**(1), 86–93 (2007)
17. Hell, M., Johansson, T., Meier, W.: Grain-128a: a new version of Grain-128 with optional authentication. Int. J. Wirel. Mob. Comput. **5**, 48–59 (2011)
18. Hell, M., Johansson, T., Meier, W., Sönnerup, J., Yoshida, H.: Grain-128AEAD - a lightweight AEAD stream cipher. NIST Lightweight Cryptography Competition (2019)
19. Katz, J., Menezes, A.J., Van Oorschot, P.C., Vanstone, S.A.: Handbook of Applied Cryptography. CRC Press, Boca Raton (1996)
20. Khazaei, S., Hassanzadeh, M., Kiaei, M.: Distinguishing attack on Grain. ECRYPT Stream Cipher Proj. Rep. **71**, 2005 (2005)
21. Küçük, Ö: Slide resynchronization attack on the initialization of Grain 1.0. eSTREAM ECRYPT Stream Cipher Proj. Rep. **44**, 2006 (2006)
22. Lee, Y., Jeong, K., Sung, J., Hong, S.: Related-key chosen IV attacks on grain-v1 and grain-128. In: Mu, Y., Susilo, W., Seberry, J. (eds.) ACISP 2008. LNCS, vol. 5107, pp. 321–335. Springer, Heidelberg (2008). https://doi.org/10.1007/978-3-540-70500-0_24
23. Massey, J.: Shift-register synthesis and BCH decoding. IEEE Trans. Inf. Theory **15**(1), 122–127 (1969)
24. Meier, W., Staffelbach, O.: Fast correlation attacks on certain stream ciphers. J. Cryptol. **1**(3), 159–176 (1988). https://doi.org/10.1007/BF02252874
25. Mikhalev, V., Armknecht, F., Müller, C.: On ciphers that continuously access the non-volatile key. IACR Trans. Symm. Cryptol., 52–79 (2016)

26. Millan, W.: Analysis and Design of Boolean Functions for Cryptographic Applications. PhD Thesis, Queensland University of Technology (1997)
27. Siegenthaler, T.: Cryptanalysts representation of nonlinearly filtered ML-sequences. In: Pichler, F. (ed.) EUROCRYPT 1985. LNCS, vol. 219, pp. 103–110. Springer, Heidelberg (1986). https://doi.org/10.1007/3-540-39805-8_12
28. Stein, W., Joyner, D.: Sage: system for algebra and geometry experimentation. ACM Bull. **39**(2), 61–64 (2005)
29. Todo, Y., Isobe, T., Meier, W., Aoki, K., Zhang, B.: Fast correlation attack revisited. In: Shacham, H., Boldyreva, A. (eds.) CRYPTO 2018. LNCS, vol. 10992, pp. 129–159. Springer, Cham (2018). https://doi.org/10.1007/978-3-319-96881-0_5
30. Zhang, H., Wang, X.: Cryptanalysis of stream cipher Grain family. IACR Cryptol. ePrint Arch. **2009**, 109 (2009)

Improved See-In-The-Middle Attacks on AES

Jonghyun Park[1]([✉]), Hangi Kim[1], and Jongsung Kim[1,2]

[1] Department of Financial Information Security, Kookmin University,
Seoul, Republic of Korea
{mmo330,tiontta,jskim}@kookmin.ac.kr
[2] Department of Information Security, Cryptology, and Mathematics,
Kookmin University, Seoul, Republic of Korea

Abstract. The See-In-The-Middle attack is designed to work effectively even with a low signal to noise ratio; hence, it can be performed even with poor side-channel analysis tools. Because it exploits the side-channel leakage of the middle round of the block cipher implementations, it is effective for implementations with reduced masking. In this study, we propose attacks to improve the See-In-The-Middle attack against the 4-round masked implemented AES introduced in the previous work. In addition, we present an attack against AES-256 implemented with 12-round reduced masking to recover 2-byte of the master key using the related-key differential trail, showing that the See-In-The-Middle attack is only thwarted by masking the whole rounds of AES-256 in the related-key model.

Keywords: AES · Side-channel analysis · SITM · Middle rounds attack · Differential cryptanalysis

1 Introduction

The side-channel analysis (SCA) proposed in 1996 is currently the most powerful attack technique among the attacks on cryptographic implementations [7]. Many methods that utilize various side-channel information, such as power consumption and electromagnetic emanation of the device for attack, have been proposed [2,8].

Applying masking to the whole round of the block cipher can be a general countermeasure for all SCAs. However, in practice, it is often applied only to the first and last few rounds of the block cipher because the masking implementation causes a large overhead [10]. The side-channel assisted differential cryptanalyses have been recently proposed [3,4,6]. Among them, S. Bhasin et al. [3] presented

This work was supported by Institute for Information & communications Technology Promotion (IITP) grant funded by the Korea government (MSIT) (No. 2017-0-00520, Development of SCR-Friendly Symmetric Key Cryptosystem and Its Application Modes).

J. H. Park and S.-H. Seo (Eds.): ICISC 2021, LNCS 13218, pp. 271–279, 2022.
https://doi.org/10.1007/978-3-031-08896-4_13

the See-In-The-Middle (SITM) that attack targets the reduced masked implementations of block ciphers such as AES, SKINNY and PRESENT. They showed that SITM attack is possible even in harsh experimental environments with a low signal to noise ratio (SNR).

Contributions

In this study, we improve the SITM attacks against AES with a 4-round masked implementation. In addition, we show that SITM attacks against AES-256 are also possible in the related-key model. Our attack in the related-key model works on 12-round masked AES-256 and can recover 2-byte of a secret master key. Therefore, full-round masking should be applied to the AES-256 implementation to guarantee security against SCA in the related-key model. The attack complexities are summerized in Table 1. Target depth refers to the number of rounds for measuring power traces through side-channel observation.

Table 1. Comparison of the SITM attack complexities on AES

Distinguisher	Key size	Target depth	Data (chosen PTs)	Memory (bytes)	Time	Ref
Single-key characteristics	128	3	$2^{13.73}$	2^{10}	$\mathcal{O}(2^{11.5})$	[3]
		3	$2^{7.32}$	2^{11}	$2^{7.32}$	Sect. 3
	192	3, 4	$2^{14.73}$	2^{10}	$\mathcal{O}(2^{11.5})$	[3]
		3, 4	$2^{8.32}$	2^{11}	$2^{8.32}$	Sect. 3
	256	3, 4	$2^{14.73}$	2^{10}	$\mathcal{O}(2^{11.5})$	[3]
		3, 4	$2^{8.32}$	2^{11}	$2^{8.32}$	Sect. 3
Related-key characteristics	256	7	2^{31}	2^{5}	2^{32}	Sect. 4*

* 2-byte master key recovery, PT: PlainText

2 Attack Methodology

2.1 The Block Cipher AES

The block cipher AES encrypts a 16-byte plaintext using a 128-, 192- and 256-bit master key (MK) and processes 10, 12, and 14 rounds, respectively [9]. For convenience, we labeled the bytes in the cipher state column-wise from left to right:

$$\begin{bmatrix} s_0 & s_4 & s_8 & s_{12} \\ s_1 & s_5 & s_9 & s_{13} \\ s_2 & s_6 & s_{10} & s_{14} \\ s_3 & s_7 & s_{11} & s_{15} \end{bmatrix}.$$

The round function of AES is composed of SubBytes (SB), ShiftRows (SR), MixColumns (MC) and AddRoundKey (AK). SB applies an 8-bit S-box to each byte of the state. SR cyclic left rotates the ith row of the state by i-byte. MC applies a diffusion matrix to each column of the state. AK XORs the rth round key RK_r to the state.

AES-128 uses the master key as the first round key, while AES-192 and AES-256 also use the master key in the first and the second rounds without modification. To help understand the related-key differential trail in Sect. 4, we will describe the round key generation process of AES-256 below.

MK is divided by 16-byte and used as RK_0 and RK_1. We denote the ith cell of RK_r as $RK_r[i]$. $RK_2 - RK_{14}$ are generated by the following process:

For $r = 1, 2, \cdots, 7$,

$$RK_{2r}[i] \leftarrow S(RK_{r+1}[i+13]) \oplus RK_r[i] \oplus Rcon_r, \qquad 0 \le i \le 2;$$

$$RK_{2r}[i] \leftarrow S(RK_{r+1}[12]) \oplus RK_r[3] \oplus Rcon_r, \qquad i = 3;$$

$$RK_{2r}[i] \leftarrow RK_{2r}[i-4] \oplus RK_r[i], \qquad 4 \le i \le 15;$$

$$RK_{2r+1}[i-16] \leftarrow S(RK_{2r}[i-4]) \oplus RK_{r+1}[i-16], \qquad 16 \le i \le 19;$$

$$RK_{2r+1}[i-16] \leftarrow RK_{2r+1}[i-20] \oplus RK_{r+1}[i-16], \qquad 20 \le i < 32,$$

where $S()$ stands for the 8-bit S-box, and $Rcon_r$ is a round dependent constant. Please refer to [9] for more details.

2.2   SITM Overview

The SITM attack is a side-channel assisted differential cryptanalysis that targets reduced masked implementations of a block cipher. Differential cryptanalysis analyzes the difference that changes as the state with difference progresses to the next state. The sequence of the connected states is referred as the differential trail and if the difference is not a specific value other than zero, then it is referred as the differential pattern.

The difference between the side-channel traces occurring during the encryption processes is used for the attack. Suppose that we observe the side-channel leakage occurring in the encryption processes of two different plaintexts. If the S-box is applied to the same values, the two power traces will be similar. However, if the values are different, a recognizable difference will exist between the two power traces. We call the difference between the two power traces as the difference trace. Using this, we can determine whether a pair of encryption processes satisfies the target differential pattern (or differential trail) in the middle round. After finding such encryption pairs, the attacker can deduce the key candidates that can make a valid differential transition. We used the ChipWhisperer-Lite tool for the side-channel observation and implemented AES in C code on ATXMEGA128D4 8-bit RISC [1].

3   Improved SITM Attacks on AES Using Single-Key Differential Patterns

3.1   The Differential Patterns

Our SITM attack uses AES differential patterns other than the ones used in the attack proposed in [3]. We used 32 differential patterns for the attack. Figure 1 presents one of the cases among them.

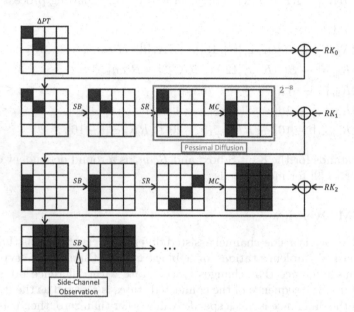

Fig. 1. AES differential pattern (Active cells are colored in red). (Color figure online)

In MC, the MDS matrix is applied to each column, such that at least five cells among the input and output cells of the matrix are active.[1] To follow our differential pattern, pessimal diffusion must occur in the first round MC. The number of differential trails, in which pessimal diffusion occurs such that the s_0 cell after the first round is inactive, is $2^8 - 1$; thus, a differential pattern in Fig. 1 occurs with a probability of approximately 2^{-8}.

An inactive column is guaranteed in the third round if only one cell among $s_0 - s_3$ is inactive after the first round. We call the group of these four differential patterns as a "type". We then define and use the following eight types of differential patterns:

type 1: s_0 and s_5 cells are active in PT.

type 2: s_1 and s_6 cells are active in PT.

---

[1] A cell with a non-zero difference is called "active".

type 3: s_2 and s_7 cells are active in PT.

type 4: s_3 and s_{14} cells are active in PT.

type 5: s_4 and s_9 cells are active in PT.

type 6: s_8 and s_{13} cells are active in PT.

type 7: s_{10} and s_{15} cells are active in PT.

type 8: s_{11} and s_{12} cells are active in PT.

3.2 Application of SITM

Our SITM attack process is divided into two processes: 1) finding plaintext pairs satisfying the differential pattern; and 2) key-recovery. These processes are independently performed for each type, so that the 2-byte key candidates can be recovered at each execution. This section describes the attack on type 1 as an example, which can be easily transformed into attacks on other types.

Finding Plaintext Pairs Satisfying the Differential Pattern. This process requires the following steps:

1. Randomly generate $2^{4.32}$ plaintexts satisfying the input differential pattern.
2. Encrypt each plaintext and collect the power traces of the third round SB operation.
3. Calculate the difference trace for one of the power trace pairs.
4. Check whether the difference trace has an inactive column in the third round SB operation. Collect the plaintext pair if there is any.
5. Repeat steps 3 and 4 for all difference traces.

A type has four differential patterns; therefore, the probability that a plaintext pair is collected in the abovementioned process is approximately 2^{-6}. We expect at least three plaintext pairs to be filtered because there are $2^{7.57}$ of difference traces.

We can classify the differential pattern of each filtered plaintext pair by analyzing their difference trace. For example, if the first column is inactive in the third round SB operation, the plaintext pair will have a differential pattern in which the s_0 of the first round output is inactive. Figure 2 shows the difference between the power traces of the plaintext pair following Fig. 1. It is easy to see that s_0-s_3 cells are inactive and s_4-s_{15} cells are active.

Key-Recovery. Each differential pattern has $2^8 - 1$ differential trails capable of pessimal diffusion. Among these differential trails, we exclude trails that do not occur through a valid differential transition from the plaintext pair. Since there are 32,385 differential transitions of the AES S-box, it is valid with a probability of $32385/2^{16} \approx 2^{-1}$; thus, the number of differential trails can be reduced to approximately $(2^8 - 1) \times 2^{-1-1} \approx 2^6$ according to the difference between plaintext pairs. For each valid differential trails, we can determine two or four 1-byte key candidates. Consequently, we obtain at most $2^6 \times 4 \times 4 = 2^{10}$ 2-byte key candidates.

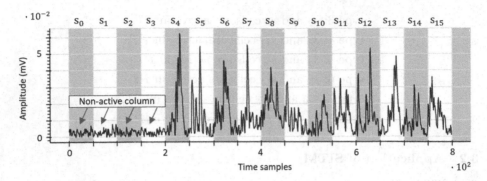

Fig. 2. Difference trace at the third round SB operation (The highlighted parts show that the first column is inactive).

By repeating this process for three plaintext pairs, the expected number of 2-byte key candidates is $2^{16-6-6-6} = 2^{-2}$. Therefore, we can recover the right 2-byte key of the master key.

Attack Complexity. For AES-128, we can recover the entire master key by performing the same attack on each of the eight types. Accordingly, $2^{4.32}$ encryptions and side-channel observations at the third round are needed to perform an attack on a single type. Thus, the attack requires $8 \times 2^{4.32} = 2^{7.32}$ chosen plaintexts and a time complexity of $2^{7.32}$. We need 2^{11} bytes of memory space because it stores up to 2^{10} of 2-byte key candidates.

This attack can easily be applied to AES-192 and AES-256. After the recovery of the first round key, we can now apply the types beginning from the second round and observe the difference traces at the fourth round. The second round key can be recovered by repeating the same attack. Thus, the attack requires $16 \times 2^{4.32} = 2^{8.32}$ chosen plaintexts, a time complexity of $2^{8.32}$, and 2^{11} bytes of memory space.

We tested this attack 10,000 times and found that we can collect 3 pairs of plaintext pairs when using 15 $(2^{3.9})$ plaintexts on average. From the three pairs of plaintexts belonging to a type, we could reduce the number of 2-byte master key candidates to an average 1.08.

4   SITM Attack on AES-256 Using Related-Key Differential Trail

This section presents a method of recovering a 2-byte master key of AES-256 using side-channel observation and related-key differential trail.

4.1   The Related-Key Differential Trail

The related-key differential trail of AES we use is shown in Fig. 3, which is a part of the multicollision trail proposed in [5]. In this related-key differential trail, there is difference only in the master key, not in the plaintext. Therefore, we search for a plaintext that satisfies the related-key differential trail existing with a probability of 2^{-30}. We can determine whether or not the related-key differential trail is satisfied by observing the difference trace of the seventh round SB operation.

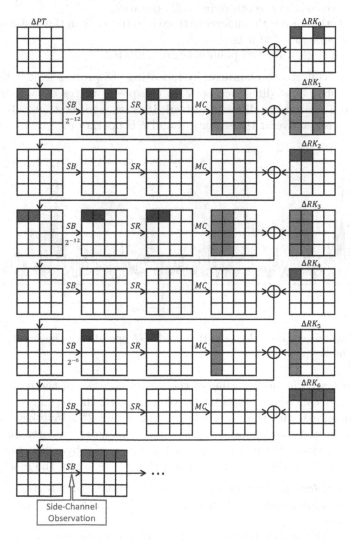

Fig. 3. The related-key differential trail of AES-256 with probability 2^{-30}. (The same colored cells have the same difference, except for the green and grey. Gray columns are the diffusion results of blue cells. Green denotes arbitrary difference.) (Color figure online)

4.2   Application of SITM

Our SITM attack process is divided into two processes: 1) finding a plaintext satisfying the related-key differential trail; and 2) key-recovery.

Finding a Plaintext Satisfying the Related-Key Differential Trail

1. Generate a random plaintext.
2. Encrypt the plaintext using the master key and collect the power traces of the seventh round SB operation.
3. Encrypt the plaintext using the master key with difference and collect the power traces of the seventh round SB operation.
4. Check whether or not the difference trace is active only in the first row (Fig. 4). Collect the plaintext if it is.
5. Repeat all steps until two plaintexts are collected.

We expect to collect two plaintexts by repeating the process for 2^{31} times.

Figure 4 shows the difference between the power traces of two encryptions satisfying the related-key differential trail. It is easy to see that only s_0, s_4, s_8, and s_{12} cells are active at the seventh round SB operation.

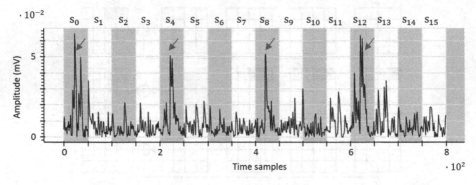

Fig. 4. Difference trace at the seventh round SB operation (The highlighted parts show that the first row is active).

Key-Recovery. The actual value of the s_0 and s_8 cells of the first round SB input has four candidate, respectively. We can XOR the s_0 and s_8 cells of the collected plaintext with those candidates, and obtain 2^4 2-byte key candidates. We have collected two plaintexts; hence, we can independently obtain 2^4 2-byte key candidates twice. The expected number of 2-byte key candidates is $2^{16-12-12} = 2^{-8}$, therefore, we can recover the 2-byte key of the master key.

Attack Complexity. The attack requires 2^{31} chosen plaintexts, 2^{32} times of encryptions and side-channel observations at the seventh round, and 2^5 bytes of memory space.

We tested this attack 100 times and found that we need an average of $2^{30.96}$ plaintexts to collect two plaintexts. From 2 plaintexts satisfying the related-key differential trail, we could reduce the number of 2-byte master key candidates to an average 1.

5   Conclusion

Our study shows that the SITM attack with the third round side-channel observation proposed in [3] can be improved. Our attack reduced the data and time complexities compared to the previous work.

We have shown that the SITM attack is possible in the related-key model and can be conducted with practical complexity. Shivam Bhasin et al. recommended a 12-round masking for AES-256 to mitigate SITM [3]. However, AES-256 requires full round masking to mitigate the SITM attacks in the related-key model because our attack uses power traces from the seventh round.

References

1. ChipWhisperer-Lite XMEGA. https://www.newae.com/products/NAE-CW1173. Accessed 14 Aug 2021
2. Agrawal, D., Archambeault, B., Rao, J.R., Rohatgi, P.: The EM side—channel(s). In: Kaliski, B.S., Koç, çK., Paar, C. (eds.) CHES 2002. LNCS, vol. 2523, pp. 29–45. Springer, Heidelberg (2003). https://doi.org/10.1007/3-540-36400-5_4
3. Bhasin, S., Breier, J., Hou, X., Jap, D., Poussier, R., Sim, S.M.: SITM: see-in-the-middle side-channel assisted middle round differential cryptanalysis on SPN block ciphers. CHES **2020**, 95–122 (2020)
4. Biham, E., Shamir, A.: Differential Cryptanalysis of the Data Encryption Standard. Springer Science & Business Media (2012). https://doi.org/10.1007/978-1-4613-9314-6
5. Biryukov, A., Khovratovich, D., Nikolić, I.: Distinguisher and related-key attack on the full AES-256. In: Halevi, S. (ed.) CRYPTO 2009. LNCS, vol. 5677, pp. 231–249. Springer, Heidelberg (2009). https://doi.org/10.1007/978-3-642-03356-8_14
6. Breier, J., Jap, D., Bhasin, S.: SCADPA: side-channel assisted differential-plaintext attack on bit permutation based ciphers. In: 2018 Design, Automation and Test in Europe Conference and Exhibition, DATE 2018, Dresden, Germany, 19–23 March 2018, pp. 1129–1134. IEEE (2018)
7. Kocher, P.C.: Timing attacks on implementations of Diffie-Hellman, RSA, DSS, and other systems. In: Koblitz, N. (ed.) CRYPTO 1996. LNCS, vol. 1109, pp. 104–113. Springer, Heidelberg (1996). https://doi.org/10.1007/3-540-68697-5_9
8. Kocher, P., Jaffe, J., Jun, B.: Differential power analysis. In: Wiener, M. (ed.) CRYPTO 1999. LNCS, vol. 1666, pp. 388–397. Springer, Heidelberg (1999). https://doi.org/10.1007/3-540-48405-1_25
9. Rijmen, V., Daemen, J.: Nist fips pub. 197: Advanced encryption standard (aes). Federal Information Processing Standards Publications (2001)
10. Tillich, S., Herbst, C., Mangard, S.: Protecting AES software implementations on 32-Bit processors against power analysis. In: Katz, J., Yung, M. (eds.) ACNS 2007. LNCS, vol. 4521, pp. 141–157. Springer, Heidelberg (2007). https://doi.org/10.1007/978-3-540-72738-5_10

Fault and Side-Channel Attack

Differential Fault Attack on Rocca

Ravi Anand[1][(✉)] and Takanori Isobe[1,2,3]

[1] University of Hyogo, Kobe, Japan
ravianandsps@gmail.com, takanori.isobe@ai.u-hyogo.ac.jp
[2] National Institute of Information and Communications Technology (NICT),
Tokyo, Japan
[3] PRESTO, Japan Science and Technology Agency, Tokyo, Japan

Abstract. Rocca is the first dedicated cipher for 6G systems accepted in ToSC 2021 and will be presented at *FSE* 2022. In this paper we show that Rocca is susceptible to differential fault attack under the nonce reuse scenario. The attack outcome results in a complete internal state recovery by injecting 4×48 faults in three out of eight internal state registers. Since the round update function of Rocca is reversible it also allows for key recovery. To the best of our knowledge this is the first third party analysis of Rocca.

Keywords: Fault attack · Differential fault attack · Random faults · Rocca · Side channel attack · AES SBox

1 Introduction

When it comes to implementing any cryptosystem on hardware, security of the cipher becomes a primary concern. The adversary can always take advantage of the cipher implementation by disturbing the normal operation mode of the cipher, and then trying to find the secrets of the cipher by restricting its computationally expensive search space to a smaller domain. By disturbing normal modes of operation of a cipher we mean causing glitches in the clock input, using focused laser beams to introduce bit flips, exposing the hardware to severe environments like high temperatures, over-voltage or anything that can change the internal state of the cipher. Once the changes are incorporated into the cipher and faulty ciphertexts are produced, the differences between fault-free and faulty ciphertexts are noted and we try to deduce the internal state of the cipher, and if possible, the secret key too. Since Boneh et al. [2] used fault attacks against an implementation of RSA. Since then, fault attacks have been widely used against many encryption algorithms, including DES [4] and AES [5].

Rocca [12] is the first dedicated cipher for 6G systems which was accepted in ToSC-2021 Issue 2 and will be presented at *FSE* 2022. Rocca [12] is an AES-based encryption scheme with a 256-bit key and 128-bit tag, which provides both a raw encryption scheme and an AEAD scheme. The design of this cipher is inspired by the work of Jean and Nikolic[8], in which the authors have described several constructions based on the AES round function which can be

© The Author(s), under exclusive license to Springer Nature Switzerland AG 2022
J. H. Park and S.-H. Seo (Eds.): ICISC 2021, LNCS 13218, pp. 283–295, 2022.
https://doi.org/10.1007/978-3-031-08896-4_14

used as building blocks for message authentication code (MAC) and authenticated encryption with associated data (AEAD). The AEGIS family [16] and Tiaoxin-346 [11] are some of the ciphers which are also inspired by these constructions. These two ciphers were submitted to the CAESAR competition and AEGIS-128 has been selected in the final portfolio for high-performance applications. The round functions of the AEGIS family and Tiaoxin-346 are quite similar. Both these ciphers have been found vulnerable to differential faults attacks [1,6,15].

Our Contribution. In this paper we describe a fault attack on Rocca. To the best of our knowledge this is the first third party analysis of Rocca. The fault attack described here is a differential fault attack targeted on one byte at a time. We provide a theoretical analysis of the feasibility of this attack.

We show that the complete internal state of Rocca can be recovered by injecting faults in all the 48 bytes of 3 internal state registers out of the total 8 registers. The recovery of the values of these 48 bytes using differential fault attack reduces to differential fault attack of AES S-box due to the design of the cipher. The complete attack strategy is described in Sect. 3.

The fact that we could extend the recovery of these 3 internal state registers to complete internal state recovery shows certain flaws in the design of the cipher. In comparision, the recovery of complete internal state requires the fault to be injected in all the 8 state registers of AEGIS-128L and in all 13 state registers of Tiaoxin-346 in the random fault model [15]. However, the number of faults required in Rocca is more than that of AEGIS-128L due to the strong cryptographic properties of AES Sbox. The comparision between our attack on Rocca and fault attacks on similarly designed ciphers in terms of the fault model, number of faults required, and the number of state registers in which fault is injected is described in Table 1.

We also discuss the possible strategies to reduce the threat the our differential fault attack in Sect. 4.2. We believe that the threat of a differential fault attack cannot be completely abated, but these strategies can help make the attack computationally hard or impractical.

The attack presented in this paper assumes that the adversary can induce faults at precise location and timing. When we assume that an adversary can inject faults into the cipher, it is a strong assumption. Similarly, if the fault attack model assumes that the adversary can inject faults with precise location and timing, it is an another strong assumption. Thus, the assumption in this paper is very strong. It should also be noted that this attack requires the assumption of nonce-misuse.

Motivation. As stated above the attack on Rocca described in this paper assumes the nonce misuse settings. The authors of Rocca does not claim any security of the cipher in nonce-misuse setting.

However, the security evaluation of ciphers in the nonce misuse setting is very important. It is considered near-impossible to prevent nonce misuse in the presence of physical attacks [3]. In the practical applications, the case of nonce misuse might exist due to the poor implementations, misuse of cipher and technical flaw of nonce generation function etc. The impossibility of full robustness against nonce-misuse settings in practical applications of a cryptographic algorithm is considered a reality. There has been a lot of study regarding the security of cryptographic systems in the nonce misuse settings, such as in [4,9,10,14] to cite a few. The differential fault attacks on AEGIS and Tiaoxin family of ciphers [1,6,15] also have the requirement of nonce-reuse.

Hence, cryptanalyzing Rocca in the nonce-misuse setting is very important for complete understanding of its security and this analysis should be done before the ciphers' wide commercial deployments.

Organization. In this work we have presented a differential fault attack on Rocca under the nonce reuse scenario. In Sect. 2, we describe the basics of DFA and the specification of Rocca. In Sect. 3, we describe our attack on Rocca for complete internal state and key recovery. In Sect. 4 we present a comparision of Rocca with other ciphers from the point of view of DFA, and present possible countermeasures. We conclude our work in Sect. 5.

2 Preliminaries

2.1 Differential Fault Attack

Differential fault attacks can be thought of as a combination of the classical differential attack and the side channel attacks (SCAs). While the procedure to retrieve the secret state (key or the internal state) in DFA is similar to the classical differential cryptanalysis, the DFA also belongs to the set of very powerful SCAs. The injected faults can be specified as positively observable leaked information by capable attackers [13]. These attacks injects a well-timed and well-aimed faults which exploits the confusion and diffusion property of a cryptographic algorithm and this allows the attacker to obtain a desired difference distribution in the ciphertext.

The first fault attack was presented by Boneh, DeMillo and Lipton [2] when they published an attack on RSA signature scheme. Inspired by this attack, Biham and Shamir [4] described such attacks on symmetric ciphers and called these attacks Differential Fault Attack (DFA). DFA are the most commonly used fault technique. In these attacks the attacker induces faults in the cryptographic primitive, then obtains at least one correct ciphertext and one faulty ciphertext and uses this information to obtain some knowledge of the secret state. These faults induced can be described using the fault models, which includes the timing, location of the fault and the number of bits or bytes affected in the register in which the fault is induced. The fault model provides the attacker some information about the difference between certain states of the computation of the cipher.

For a general idea of DFA one can take the following example: for a function S, a attacker injects a fault ϵ and obtains a relation of the type: $S(x) \oplus S(x \oplus \epsilon) = \delta$; where the difference δ is known to the attacker, x is the unknown value that she wants to retrieve and the fault ϵ is either known (deterministic model) or unknown (random model) to the attacker.

For the attack in this work, the attacker is assumed to have full control on the timing and the location of the fault. She should also be able to induce not permanent, but transient faults in the random model.

2.2 Specification of Encryption Phase of Rocca

We here describe only the encryption phase, which is where we intend to inject the faults. For details of other phases, such as initialization, associated data processing, finalization and tag generations, the readers are requested to refer to the cipher specification description [12].

Rocca has an internal state with eight 128-bit registers $S[0], S[1], \ldots, S[7]$ and thus has a total state size of $8 \times 128 = 1024$ bits. The internal state is updated using a nonlinear state update function defined below:

$$
\begin{aligned}
S_{i+1}[0] &= S_i[7] \oplus X_0 & S_{i+1}[4] &= S_i[3] \oplus X_1 \\
S_{i+1}[1] &= R(S_i[0], S_i[7]) & S_{i+1}[5] &= R(S_i[4], S_i[3]) \\
S_{i+1}[2] &= S_i[1] \oplus S_i[6] & S_{i+1}[6] &= R(S_i[5], S_i[4]) \\
S_{i+1}[3] &= R(S_i[2], S_i[1]) & S_{i+1}[7] &= S_i[0] \oplus S_i[6]
\end{aligned}
\tag{1}
$$

where $R(X)$ is defined as:

$$
R(X) = \text{MixColumns} \circ \text{ShiftRows} \circ \text{SubBytes}(X)
\tag{2}
$$

Note that the transformation R is invertible. We denote the reverse of R by R^{-1}. This is an important property for state recovery, and also in the case of key recovery, as it allows the internal state to be clocked backwards.

This update function has two external outputs X_0 and X_1 and the non-linearity is provided by the transformation R, which is applied to four out of the total eight registers. During the encryption phase, a block of $256-$bit plaintext $P_i = P_i^0 || P_i^1$ is encrypted to produce a 256-bit ciphertext $C_i = C_i^0 || C_i^1$ as defined below:

$$
\begin{aligned}
C_i^0 &= P_i^0 \oplus R(S_i[1]) \oplus S_i[5] \\
C_i^1 &= P_i^1 \oplus R(S_i[0] \oplus S_i[4]) \oplus S_i[2]
\end{aligned}
\tag{3}
$$

After this step the internal state is updated using the update function described in Eq. 1 and the next 256-bits of plaintext is encrypted as in Eq. 3, i.e.

$$
\begin{aligned}
C_{i+1}^0 &= P_{i+1}^0 \oplus R(S_{i+1}[1]) \oplus S_{i+1}[5] \\
C_{i+1}^1 &= P_{i+1}^1 \oplus R(S_{i+1}[0] \oplus S_{i+1}[4]) \oplus S_{i+1}[2]
\end{aligned}
\tag{4}
$$

For simplicity we assume the following in the rest of this section:

- $S_i[0] = [a_{i_0}, a_{i_1}, \ldots, a_{i_{15}}]$, where each $a_{i_l}^j$ is a byte.
- $S_i[1] = [b_{i_0}, b_{i_1}, \ldots, b_{i_{15}}]$, where each $b_{i_l}^j$ is a byte.
- $S_i[2] = [c_{i_0}, c_{i_1}, \ldots, c_{i_{15}}]$, where each $c_{i_l}^j$ is a byte.
- $S_i[3] = [d_{i_0}, d_{i_1}, \ldots, d_{i_{15}}]$, where each $d_{i_l}^j$ is a byte.
- $S_i[4] = [e_{i_0}, e_{i_1}, \ldots, e_{i_{15}}]$, where each $e_{i_l}^j$ is a byte.
- $S_i[5] = [f_{i_0}, f_{i_1}, \ldots, f_{i_{15}}]$, where each $f_{i_l}^j$ is a byte.
- $S_i[6] = [g_{i_0}, g_{i_1}, \ldots, g_{i_{15}}]$, where each $g_{i_l}^j$ is a byte.
- $S_i[7] = [h_{i_0}, h_{i_1}, \ldots, h_{i_{15}}]$, where each $h_{i_l}^j$ is a byte.

Also all the S_i's, can be represented as a 4×4 matrices. In our attack below we use this representation.

3   Key and Internal State Recovery of Rocca

In this section, we describe full state recovery attack on a block cipher Rocca using fault injections.

3.1   Attack Procedure

We describe here the process to recover the internal states $S_i[1]$, and $S_i[5]$. A similar procedure can be applied to recover the rest of the states. Let us assume that the adversary first encrypts a plaintext P_i^0 and obtains the corresponding ciphertext $C_{i,}^0$. Then the adversary repeats the encryption of the same plaintext after injecting a fault into b_{i_1}, such that this byte becomes faulty. Let ϵ is the fault injected and let the faulty state be denoted by $\tilde{S}_i[1]$. Thus the faulty state $\tilde{S}_i[1]$ differs from $S_i[1]$ only at the first byte, i.e. the first byte of $\tilde{S}_i[1]$ has the entry $b_{i_0} \oplus \epsilon$. This encryption with injection of the fault generates a faulty ciphertext, say $\tilde{C}_i^0$.

Without loss of generality, for the rest of the attack, we assume that the plaintext is all zeroes. The attack can easily be generalized for a randomly chosen plaintext. Now the difference between the fault-free ciphertext and faulty ciphertext is:

$$
\begin{aligned}
C_i^0 \oplus \tilde{C}_i^0 &= R(S_i[1]) \oplus S_i[5] \oplus R(\tilde{S}_i[1]) \oplus S_i[5] \\
&= R(S_i[1]) \oplus R(\tilde{S}_i[1])
\end{aligned}
\tag{5}
$$

The matrix representation of the above difference is:

$$
\begin{bmatrix}
\delta_0^0 & \delta_1^0 & \delta_2^0 & \delta_3^0 \\
\delta_4^0 & \delta_5^0 & \delta_6^0 & \delta_7^0 \\
\delta_8^0 & \delta_9^0 & \delta_{10}^0 & \delta_{11}^0 \\
\delta_{12}^0 & \delta_{13}^0 & \delta_{14}^0 & \delta_{15}^0
\end{bmatrix}
= R(
\begin{bmatrix}
b_{i_0} & b_{i_1} & b_{i_2} & b_{i_3} \\
b_{i_4} & b_{i_5} & b_{i_6} & b_{i_7} \\
b_{i_8} & b_{i_9} & b_{i_{10}} & b_{i_{11}} \\
b_{i_{12}} & b_{i_{13}} & b_{i_{14}} & b_{i_{15}}
\end{bmatrix}
) \oplus R(
\begin{bmatrix}
b_{i_0} \oplus \epsilon & b_{i_1} & b_{i_2} & b_{i_3} \\
b_{i_4} & b_{i_5} & b_{i_6} & b_{i_7} \\
b_{i_8} & b_{i_9} & b_{i_{10}} & b_{i_{11}} \\
b_{i_{12}} & b_{i_{13}} & b_{i_{14}} & b_{i_{15}}
\end{bmatrix}
)
\tag{6}
$$

where δ_j's denote the difference in the fault-free ciphertext and faulty ciphertext. Now using the definition of $R(X)$ from Eq. 2, we have:

1. Applying SubBytes we get

$$SubBytes(S_i[1]) = \begin{bmatrix} s(b_{i_0}) & s(b_{i_1}) & s(b_{i_2}) & s(b_{i_3}) \\ s(b_{i_4}) & s(b_{i_5}) & s(b_{i_6}) & s(b_{i_7}) \\ s(b_{i_8}) & s(b_{i_9}) & s(b_{i_{10}}) & s(b_{i_{11}}) \\ s(b_{i_{12}}) & s(b_{i_{13}}) & s(b_{i_{14}}) & s(b_{i_{15}}) \end{bmatrix} \text{ and }$$

$$SubBytes(\tilde{S}_i[1]) = \begin{bmatrix} s(b_{i_0} \oplus \epsilon) & s(b_{i_1}) & s(b_{i_2}) & s(b_{i_3}) \\ s(b_{i_4}) & s(b_{i_5}) & s(b_{i_6}) & s(b_{i_7}) \\ s(b_{i_8}) & s(b_{i_9}) & s(b_{i_{10}}) & s(b_{i_{11}}) \\ s(b_{i_{12}}) & s(b_{i_{13}}) & s(b_{i_{14}}) & s(b_{i_{15}}) \end{bmatrix}$$

where $s(x)$ is the S-box value of x.

2. Applying ShiftRows we get

$$ShiftRows \circ SB(S_i[1]) = \begin{bmatrix} s(b_{i_0}) & s(b_{i_1}) & s(b_{i_2}) & s(b_{i_3}) \\ s(b_{i_5}) & s(b_{i_6}) & s(b_{i_7}) & s(b_{i_4}) \\ s(b_{i_{10}}) & s(b_{i_{11}}) & s(b_{i_8}) & s(b_{i_9}) \\ s(b_{i_{15}}) & s(b_{i_{12}}) & s(b_{i_{13}}) & s(b_{i_{14}}) \end{bmatrix} \text{ and }$$

$$ShiftRows \circ SB(\tilde{S}_i[1]) = \begin{bmatrix} s(b_{i_0} \oplus \epsilon) & s(b_{i_1}) & s(b_{i_2}) & s(b_{i_3}) \\ s(b_{i_5}) & s(b_{i_6}) & s(b_{i_7}) & s(b_{i_4}) \\ s(b_{i_{10}}) & s(b_{i_{11}}) & s(b_{i_8}) & s(b_{i_9}) \\ s(b_{i_{15}}) & s(b_{i_{12}}) & s(b_{i_{13}}) & s(b_{i_{14}}) \end{bmatrix}$$

3. Applying MixColumns we get

$$R(S_i[1]) = \begin{bmatrix} 2 \cdot s(b_{i_0}) \oplus 3 \cdot s(b_{i_5}) \oplus 1 \cdot s(b_{i_{10}}) \oplus 1 \cdot s(b_{i_{15}}) & z_1 & z_2 & z_3 \\ 1 \cdot s(b_{i_0}) \oplus 2 \cdot s(b_{i_5}) \oplus 3 \cdot s(b_{i_{10}}) \oplus 1 \cdot s(b_{i_{15}}) & z_6 & z_7 & z_4 \\ 1 \cdot s(b_{i_0}) \oplus 1 \cdot s(b_{i_5}) \oplus 2 \cdot s(b_{i_{10}}) \oplus 3 \cdot s(b_{i_{15}}) & z_{11} & z_8 & z_9 \\ 3 \cdot s(b_{i_0}) \oplus 1 \cdot s(b_{i_5}) \oplus 1 \cdot s(b_{i_{10}}) \oplus 2 \cdot s(b_{i_{15}}) & z_{12} & z_{13} & z_{14} \end{bmatrix} \text{ and }$$

$$R(\tilde{S}_i[1]) = \begin{bmatrix} 2 \cdot s(b_{i_0} \oplus \epsilon) \oplus 3 \cdot s(b_{i_5}) \oplus 1 \cdot s(b_{i_{10}}) \oplus 1 \cdot s(b_{i_{15}}) & z_1 & z_2 & z_3 \\ 1 \cdot s(b_{i_0}) \oplus 2 \cdot s(b_{i_5}) \oplus 3 \cdot s(b_{i_{10}}) \oplus 1 \cdot s(b_{i_{15}}) & z_6 & z_7 & z_4 \\ 1 \cdot s(b_{i_0}) \oplus 1 \cdot s(b_{i_5}) \oplus 2 \cdot s(b_{i_{10}}) \oplus 3 \cdot s(b_{i_{15}}) & z_{11} & z_8 & z_9 \\ 3 \cdot s(b_{i_0}) \oplus 1 \cdot s(b_{i_5}) \oplus 1 \cdot s(b_{i_{10}}) \oplus 2 \cdot s(b_{i_{15}}) & z_{12} & z_{13} & z_{14} \end{bmatrix}$$

where each z_j's can be computed as the first column has been computed.

Replacing these values in Eq. 6, we get

$$\begin{bmatrix} \delta_0^0 & \delta_1^0 & \delta_2^0 & \delta_3^0 \\ \delta_4^0 & \delta_5^0 & \delta_6^0 & \delta_7^0 \\ \delta_8^0 & \delta_9^0 & \delta_{10}^0 & \delta_{11}^0 \\ \delta_{12}^0 & \delta_{13}^0 & \delta_{14}^0 & \delta_{15}^0 \end{bmatrix} = \begin{bmatrix} 2 \cdot (s(b_{i_0}) \oplus s(b_{i_0} \oplus \epsilon)) & 0 & 0 & 0 \\ 1 \cdot (s(b_{i_0}) \oplus s(b_{i_0} \oplus \epsilon)) & 0 & 0 & 0 \\ 1 \cdot (s(b_{i_0}) \oplus s(b_{i_0} \oplus \epsilon)) & 0 & 0 & 0 \\ 3 \cdot (s(b_{i_0}) \oplus s(b_{i_0} \oplus \epsilon)) & 0 & 0 & 0 \end{bmatrix}$$

Hence we have the following four equations

$$\begin{aligned} \delta_0^0 &= 2 \cdot (s(b_{i_0}) \oplus s(b_{i_0} \oplus \epsilon)) \\ \delta_4^0 &= (s(b_{i_0}) \oplus s(b_{i_0} \oplus \epsilon)) \\ \delta_8^0 &= (s(b_{i_0}) \oplus s(b_{i_0} \oplus \epsilon)) \\ \delta_{12}^0 &= 3 \cdot (s(b_{i_0}) \oplus s(b_{i_0} \oplus \epsilon)) \end{aligned} \tag{7}$$

where the value of δ_i^0 is known and b_{i_0} and ϵ are unknown. Analyzing the Eq. 7, we can recover the value of b_{i_0}. Similarly faults on other bytes will provide the information on other bytes of the state $S_i[1]$. Once $S_i[1]$ is recovered we can compute the value $S_i[5]$ as follows:

$$S_i[5] = R(S_i[1]) \oplus C_i^0$$

3.2 Analysis of Equation 7

Equation 7, can also be generalized as:

$$s(x) \oplus s(x + \epsilon) = c_i^{-1}\delta_i^0 \tag{8}$$

where $c_i = 1, 2$ or 3, (x and ϵ) are unknown variables, and δ_i^0 is a known constant. We know that the following two proposition holds for the AES S-box:

Proposition 1. *For any input difference ϵ of the AES S-box, a certain output difference δ always appears twice while the other output differences appear just once.*

Proposition 2. *For any input difference ϵ of the AES S-box, the number of possible output difference is always 127.*

Using Proposition 1, Proposition 2, and the analysis described in [7, Section 3.5] we can deduce that using four random S-box input differences i.e., four values of ϵ, and as the value of x remains the same, we can uniquely retrieve the value of x which satisfies the set of Eq. 8.

These faults are induced in the internal state and not the plaintext, i.e. the faults do not depend on the plaintext. However, inducing these faults will generate 4 faulty ciphertexts for the same plaintext. Thus using 4 pairs of faultfree and faulty ciphertexts we can retrieve the value of b_{i_0}. Similarly the complete value of $S_i[1]$, which contains 16 bytes $b_{i_0}, \cdots, b_{i_{15}}$, can be retrieved using 16×4 faults and four pairs of faultfree and faulty ciphertext.

3.3 Internal State Recovery

We now describe how to recover the remaining internal states using the process described above.

From Eq. 3 and the assumption that the plaintext is all zeroes we have

$$C_i^1 = R(S_i[0] \oplus S_i[4]) \oplus S_i[2] \tag{9}$$

If we inject a fault in the first byte of $S_i[4]$, then the faulty ciphertext generated would be

$$\tilde{C}_i^1 = R(S_i[0] \oplus \tilde{S}_i[4]) \oplus S_i[2] \tag{10}$$

From Eqs. 9 and 10 we get

$$C_i^1 \oplus \tilde{C}_i^1 = R(S_i[0] \oplus S_i[4]) \oplus R(S_i[0] \oplus \tilde{S}_i[4]) \tag{11}$$

Proceeding as the attack described above, we need to solve the following set of equations:

$$
\begin{aligned}
\delta_0^1 &= 2 \cdot (s(a_{i_0} \oplus e_{i_0}) \oplus s(a_{i_0} \oplus e_{i_0} \oplus \epsilon)) \\
\delta_4^1 &= (s(a_{i_0} \oplus e_{i_0}) \oplus s(a_{i_0} \oplus e_{i_0} \oplus \epsilon)) \\
\delta_8^1 &= (s(a_{i_0} \oplus e_{i_0}) \oplus s(a_{i_0} \oplus e_{i_0} \oplus \epsilon)) \\
\delta_{12}^1 &= 3 \cdot (s(a_{i_0} \oplus e_{i_0}) \oplus s(a_{i_0} \oplus e_{i_0} \oplus \epsilon))
\end{aligned} \tag{12}
$$

and we can recover the value of first byte of $S_i[0] \oplus S_i[4]$ using four faults and four pairs of faultfree and faulty ciphertext. Applying the same strategy to the remaining 15 bytes we can recover the complete values of $S_i[0] \oplus S_i[4]$ and $S_i[2]$.

We have recovered the registers $S_i[1]$, $S_i[5]$, $S_i[2]$ and the value of $S_i[0] \oplus S_i[4]$. Recovering $S_i[4]$ will give the value of $S_i[0]$. Thus now we try to obtain the value of $S_i[4]$.

Using Eq. 1, we can rewrite Eq. 4 as follows, along with the assumption that the plaintext is all zeroes:

$$C_{i+1}^0 = R(R(S_i[0]) \oplus S_i[7]) \oplus R(S_i[4]) \oplus S_i[3] \tag{13}$$

and

$$C_{i+1}^1 = R(S_i[7] \oplus S_i[3]) \oplus S_i[1] \oplus S_i[6] \tag{14}$$

Inducing a fault in the first byte of $S_i[3]$ will provide a faulty ciphertext corresponding to Eq. 14 and we have

$$\tilde{C}_{i+1}^1 = R(S_i[7] \oplus \tilde{S}_i[3]) \oplus S_i[1] \oplus S_i[6] \tag{15}$$

Thus we have

$$C_{i+1}^1 \oplus \tilde{C}_{i+1}^1 = R(S_i[7] \oplus S_i[3]) \oplus R(S_i[7] \oplus \tilde{S}_i[3]) \tag{16}$$

Using the same attack strategy we obtain the value of the first byte of $S_i[7] \oplus S_i[3]$ by solving the following equations:

$$
\begin{aligned}
\bar{\delta}_0^1 &= 2 \cdot (s(h_{i_0} \oplus d_{i_0}) \oplus s(h_{i_0} \oplus d_{i_0} \oplus \epsilon)) \\
\bar{\delta}_4^1 &= (s(h_{i_0} \oplus d_{i_0}) \oplus s(h_{i_0} \oplus d_{i_0} \oplus \epsilon)) \\
\bar{\delta}_8^1 &= (s(h_{i_0} \oplus d_{i_0}) \oplus s(h_{i_0} \oplus d_{i_0} \oplus \epsilon)) \\
\bar{\delta}_{12}^1 &= 3 \cdot (s(h_{i_0} \oplus d_{i_0}) \oplus s(h_{i_0} \oplus d_{i_0} \oplus \epsilon))
\end{aligned} \tag{17}
$$

Inducing 4 faults and using four pairs of faultfree and faulty ciphertext for each 16 bytes of $S_i[3]$, we recover the values of $S_i[7] \oplus S_i[3]$. Since the value of $S_i[1]$ is already known, from Eq. 14, we can recover the value of $S_i[6]$.

Since a fault was already induced in $S_i[4]$ and $S_i[3]$, thus from Eq. 13 we obtain the value of the faulty ciphertext as:

$$\tilde{C}^0_{i+1} = R(R(S_i[0], S_i[7])) \oplus R(\tilde{S}_i[4]) \oplus \tilde{S}_i[3] \tag{18}$$

Hence we have

$$C^0_{i+1} \oplus \tilde{C}^0_{i+1} = R(S_i[4]) \oplus R(\tilde{S}_i[4]) \oplus S_i[3] \oplus \tilde{S}_i[3] \tag{19}$$

Since the value of the fault induced in $S_i[3]$ is known, hence the value of $S_i[3] \oplus \tilde{S}_i[3]$ is also known. Using the same attack strategy we obtain the value of $S_i[4]$, which then allows us to determine the value of $S_i[0]$.

Let us assume that $R(S_i[4]) = \alpha_0$ and $R(S_i[0]) = \alpha_1$, where α_0, α_1 are known constants. Replacing these values in Eq. 13 we get

$$C^0_{i+1} = R(\alpha_1 \oplus S_i[7]) \oplus \alpha_0 \oplus S_i[3] \tag{20}$$

Since we already know the value of $S_i[7] \oplus S_i[3]$ and let $S_i[7] \oplus S_i[3] = \alpha_2$, Eq. 20 can be written as:

$$\begin{aligned} C^0_{i+1} &= R(\alpha_1 \oplus S_i[7]) \oplus \alpha_0 \oplus S_i[7] \oplus \alpha_2 \\ &= R(S_i[7] \oplus \alpha_1) \oplus S_i[7] \oplus \alpha_0 \oplus \alpha_2 \end{aligned} \tag{21}$$

We can obtain the value of $S[7]$ by solving Eq. 21.

Therefore we obtain the complete internal state. Once the entire internal state is known at a certain timestamp i, the cipher can be clocked forwards to recover all subsequent plaintext using known ciphertext and state contents.

3.4   Key Recovery

The round update function is reversible and thus the internal state can be clocked backwards to retrieve the value of the secret key. Consider that at any time stamp $i + 1$ the complete internal state is known, i.e. $S_{i+1}[0], S_{i+1}[1], S_{i+1}[2], S_{i+1}[3], S_{i+1}[4], S_{i+1}[5], S_{i+1}[6], S_{i+1}[7]$, is known. Now the internal state at the previous time stamp i can be retrieved by the following done in order:

1. $S_i[7] = S_{i+1}[0] \oplus X_0$, where X_0 is either the known plaintext or the constant $Z_0 = 428a2f98d728ae227137449123ef65cd$
2. $S_i[0] = R^{-1}(S_{i+1}[1] \oplus S_i[7])$
3. $S_i[3] = S_{i+1}[4] \oplus X_1$, where X_1 is either the known plaintext or the constant $Z_1 = b5c0fbcfec4d3b2fe9b5dba58189dbbc$
4. $S_i[4] = R^{-1}(S_{i+1}[5] \oplus S_i[3])$
5. $S_i[5] = R^{-1}(S_{i+1}[6] \oplus S_i[4])$
6. $S_i[6] = S_{i+1}[7] \oplus S_i[0]$
7. $S_i[1] = S_{i+1}[2] \oplus S_i[6]$
8. $S_i[2] = R^{-1}(S_{i+1}[3] \oplus S_i[1])$

We can reverse clock the internal state until we reach the initial state and recover the secret key.

4 Discussion

This paper shows that a differential fault attack is possible in the nonce-reuse scenario on Rocca. When implementing Rocca care must be taken to avoid nonce reuse so that any attacker cannot obtain plaintext-ciphertext pairs using the same parameters. In this section we compare the security of Rocca with some other ciphers against DFA and present some countermeasures to protect Rocca against DFA.

4.1 Comparison

We compare the fault attack presented in this paper with that of the fault attacks on the other two ciphers, the Aegis family and Tiaoxin which was described in [15]and [6]. All these ciphers are AES based encryption scheme inspired by the work of Jean and Nikolic [8]. The comparision is described in Table 1.

The security any cipher against DFA is generally measured by the fault model used in the attacks and the number of faults required to implement the attack. It is also assumed that the location and timing of the faults are known to the attacker (however in some cases the attacker does not need to know about the location and timing of the attack, depending on the construction of the cipher). In our work as well as the work of [15], the fault model used is a *single fault* model, i.e. the fault injected has a width of $\leq b$, where b is the input size of the Sbox used in the cipher, AES Sbox in this case. However, the difference is the nature of this fault injected.

- *Random fault*: a fault which can have any value between 1 and $2^b - 1$ and all these values are equally possible. This model is considered to be the most practical fault model. The DFA described in [15] uses this model.
- *Known fault*: in this case the fault has a specific value as defined by the attacker. This paper uses this model of fault. This fault model requires a stronger adversary. However, it has been shown that such fault model is achievable.

The fault model used in [6] is:

- *Bit Flipping*: A specific internal bit of the cipher is flipped. In practice, it is more complex than the random fault, but it has been shown to be practical in several papers/attacks.

From Table 1, we cannot make a fair comparison of the security of the ciphers against DFA, still the following conclusions would be fair:

- For a state size of 1024, the requirement 4×48 faults is more than AEGIS-128L in random byte model. Thus we could say it is slightly more resistant towards DFA.
- Since the key recovery for Tiaoxin-346 requires only 48 faults and only 1 known plaintext, it can be considered slightly weak against DFA. However, with regards to state recovery Tiaoxin-346 is the most secure against DFA among the ciphers described in Table 1.

We describe below some countermeasure strategies for Rocca.

Table 1. Comparision of security against DFA of AES based ciphers. Target* implies the number of registers in which the faults were injected out of the total registers the complete internal state is divided into.

Cipher	Recovery	State size	Fault model	No. of faults	Target*
AEGIS-128 [15]	State	540	Random	64	4/5
AEGIS-128 [6]	State	540	Bit Flipping	3×128	3/5
AEGIS-256 [15]	State	768	Random	80	5/6
AEGIS-256 [6]	State	768	Bit Flipping	4×128	4/6
AEGIS-128L [15]	State	1024	Random	128	8/8
AEGIS-128L [6]	State	1024	Bit Flipping	4×128	4/8
Rocca (Section 3)	State and Key	1024	Random	4×48	3/8
Tiaoxin-346 [15]	State	1664	Random	208	13/13
Tiaoxin-346 [15]	Key	1664	Random	48	3/13

4.2 Mitigating the Differential Fault Attack on Rocca

We discuss here a few probable strategies to avoid differential fault attack or make it computationally hard or impractical.

While the construction of Aegis family, Tiaoxin and Rocca are all based on the AES round function, the basic difference is in the generation of the keystream or ciphertext. The Aegis family of ciphers and Tiaoxin has an output function that includes a bitwise AND operation but Rocca uses the AES round function even in its ciphertext generation phase. It was observed in [15] that the ciphers which has the following two properties can be attacked using fault attacks:

- The ciphertext output functions contains one quadratic term and is otherwise linear.
- The internal state transitions contain linear paths across different stages and do not have external input.

Based on these observations a few countermeasures were suggested.

However, the same countermeasures cannot be applied to Rocca as the output function is different from the these ciphers. The output function of Rocca makes use of AES round function on a state register and a XOR with another state register. Based on these observations and considering that the speed of the cipher should not be compromised, we observed that the potentially useful strategies for preventing partial recovery of state information from leading to full state recovery or key recovery include the following:

- Using more than one state registers while encrypting the plaintext. For example changing $C_i^0 = P_i^0 \oplus R(S_i[1]) \oplus S_i[5]$ to $C_i^0 = P_i^0 \oplus R(S_i[1] \oplus S_i[3]) \oplus S_i[5]$ will restrict the attacker to obtain values of combinations of state register $S_i[1] \oplus S_i[3]$ instead of obtaining the value of a single state register $S_i[1]$ directly. This will increase the required number of faults required.

- State registers used in the keystream generation on which the AES round function R is applied should again be non-linearly mixed when the state is updated. This will prevent the attacker from obtaining information of a state register by applying faults at different time stamps
- It is always a safer option to modify the state update function during intialization phase to be non-invertible without the knowledge of the secret key. This will prevent a state recovery attack to lead to key recovery.

However, these mitigation strategies leaves room to determine if they introduce some vulnerabilities which can be exploited by other attackers.

5   Conclusion

In this paper we demonstrate a differential fault attack on Rocca under the nonce reuse scenario. We show that we can recover the complete internal state using 4×48 faults. Since the round update function is reversible, internal state recovery also allows key recovery. In this attack we have assumed that the adversary has the knowledge of the location of the fault induced. It would be interesting to study this attack in the model where the adversary has no knowledge of the location of the fault induced.

Acknowledgement. Takanori Isobe is supported by JST, PRESTO Grant Number JPMJPR2031, Grant-in- Aid for Scientific Research (B)(KAKENHI 19H02141) for Japan Society for the Promotion of Science, and Support Center for Advanced Telecommunications Technology Research (SCAT).

References

1. Bartlett, H., Dawson, E., Qahur Al Mahri, H., Salam, M., Simpson, L., Wong, K.K.H.: Random fault attacks on a class of stream ciphers. Secur. Commun. Netw. **2019**, 12 (2019)
2. Boneh, D., DeMillo, R.A., Lipton, R.J.: On the importance of checking cryptographic protocols for faults. In: Fumy, W. (ed.) EUROCRYPT 1997. LNCS, vol. 1233, pp. 37–51. Springer, Heidelberg (1997). https://doi.org/10.1007/3-540-69053-0_4
3. Berti, F., Guo, C., Pereira, O., Peters, T., Standaert, F.X.: TEDT, a leakage-resilient AEAD mode for high (Physical) security applications. In: IACR Transactions on Cryptographic Hardware and Embedded Systems, vol. 2020, num 1, pp 256–320 (2019)
4. Biham, E., Shamir, A.: Differential fault analysis of secret key cryptosystems. In: Kaliski, B.S. (ed.) CRYPTO 1997. LNCS, vol. 1294, pp. 513–525. Springer, Heidelberg (1997). https://doi.org/10.1007/BFb0052259
5. Blömer, J., Seifert, J.-P.: Fault based cryptanalysis of the advanced encryption standard (AES). In: Wright, R.N. (ed.) FC 2003. LNCS, vol. 2742, pp. 162–181. Springer, Heidelberg (2003). https://doi.org/10.1007/978-3-540-45126-6_12

6. Dey, P., Rohit, R.S., Sarkar, S., Adhikari, A.: Differential fault analysis on tiaoxin and AEGIS family of ciphers. In: Mueller, P., Thampi, S.M., Alam Bhuiyan, M.Z., Ko, R., Doss, R., Alcaraz Calero, J.M. (eds.) SSCC 2016. CCIS, vol. 625, pp. 74–86. Springer, Singapore (2016). https://doi.org/10.1007/978-981-10-2738-3_7

7. Dusart, P., Letourneux, G., Vivolo, O.: Differential fault analysis on A.E.S. In: Zhou, J., Yung, M., Han, Y. (eds.) ACNS 2003. LNCS, vol. 2846, pp. 293–306. Springer, Heidelberg (2003). https://doi.org/10.1007/978-3-540-45203-4_23

8. Jean, J., Nikolić, I.: Efficient design strategies based on the AES round function. In: Peyrin, T. (ed.) FSE 2016. LNCS, vol. 9783, pp. 334–353. Springer, Heidelberg (2016). https://doi.org/10.1007/978-3-662-52993-5_17

9. Khairallah, M., Bhasin, S., Chattopadhyay, A.: On misuse of nonce-misuse resistance: adapting differential fault attacks on (few) CAESAR winners. In: 2019 IEEE 8th International Workshop on Advances in Sensors and Interfaces (IWASI), pp. 189–193. IEEE (2019)

10. Khairallah, M., Hou, X., Najm, Z., Breier, J., Bhasin, S., Peyrin, T.: SoK: on DFA vulnerabilities of substitution-permutation networks. In: Proceedings of the 2019 ACM Asia Conference on Computer and Communications Security, pp. 403–414 (2019)

11. Nikolic, I.: Tiaoxin-346 (version 2.1). CAESAR competition. Available from https://competitions.cr.yp.to/round3/tiaoxinv21.pdf

12. Sakamoto, K., Liu, F., Nakano, Y., Kiyomoto, S., Isobe, T.: Rocca: an efficient AES-based encryption scheme for beyond 5G. IACR Trans. Symmetric Cryptology 2021(2), 1–30 (2021)

13. Sakiyama, K., Li, Y., Iwamoto, M., Ohta, K.: Information-theoretic approach to optimal differential fault analysis. IEEE Trans. Inf. Forensics Secur. 7(1), 109–120 (2011)

14. Song, L., Tu, Y., Shi, D., Hu, L.: Security analysis of subterranean 2.0. Des. Codes Crypt. 89(8), 1875–1905 (2021). https://doi.org/10.1007/s10623-021-00892-6

15. Wong, K.K.-H., Bartlett, H., Simpson, L., Dawson, E.: Differential random fault attacks on certain CAESAR stream ciphers. In: Seo, J.H. (ed.) ICISC 2019. LNCS, vol. 11975, pp. 297–315. Springer, Cham (2020). https://doi.org/10.1007/978-3-030-40921-0_18

16. Wu, H., Preneel, B.: AEGIS: a fast authenticated encryption algorithm (v1.1) CAESAR competition. https://competitions.cr.yp.to/round3/aegisv11.pdf

Differential Fault Attack on Lightweight Block Cipher PIPO

Seonghyuck Lim[1]([✉]) [iD], Jaeseung Han[1] [iD], Tae-Ho Lee[1] [iD],
and Dong-Guk Han[1,2] [iD]

[1] Department of Financial Information Security, Kookmin University,
Seoul, Republic of Korea
{seonghyeck16,jae1115,20141932,christa}@kookmin.ac.kr
[2] Department of Information Security, Cryptology, and Mathematics,
Kookmin University, Seoul, Republic of Korea

Abstract. With the recent development of Internet of Things (IoT) devices, related security issues are also increasing. In particular, the possibility of accessing and hijacking cryptographic devices is also increasing due to the rapid increase in usage of these devices. Therefore, research on cryptographic technologies that can provide a safe environment even in resource-constrained environments has been actively conducted. Among them, there are increasing security issues of side-channel analysis for devices due to their physical accessibility. The lightweight block cipher PIPO was recently proposed in ICISC 2020 to address these issues. The PIPO has the characteristic of providing robust security strength while having less overhead when using the side-channel analysis countermeasures. A differential fault attack is a type of side-channel analysis that induces fault in cryptographic operations and utilizes difference information that occurs. Differential fault attacks on the PIPO have not yet been studied. This paper proposed a single-bit flip-based differential fault attack on the lightweight block cipher PIPO for the first time. We show that simulations enable the recovery of the correct secret key with about 98% probability through 64 fault ciphertexts. Therefore, the PIPO does not provide security against differential fault attacks. When using the PIPO cipher on IoT devices, designers must apply appropriate countermeasures against fault-injection attacks.

Keywords: Side-channel analysis · Differential fault attack · Bit-sliced lightweight cipher · PIPO

1 Introduction

Side-channel analysis (SCA) is cryptanalysis that uses physical information, such as power consumption, electromagnetic emission, and sound that occurs while

This work was supported by Institute for Information & communications Technology Promotion (IITP) grant funded by the Korea government (MSIT) (No. 2017-0-00520, Development of SCR-Friendly Symmetric Key Cryptosystem and Its Application Modes).

J. H. Park and S.-H. Seo (Eds.): ICISC 2021, LNCS 13218, pp. 296–307, 2022.
https://doi.org/10.1007/978-3-031-08896-4_15

a cryptographic algorithm operates on real devices [9]. Numerous devices have been widely used worldwide with the recent development of Internet of Things (IoT) devices. Under these circumstances, malicious attackers are becoming more accessible to these devices and are naturally becoming able to attack them physically. Therefore, there is an increasing interest in side-channel security in this environment, and a variety of lightweight ciphers and SCA countermeasures are being studied. However, existing block ciphers are inefficient due to large time and memory overhead when countermeasure is applied. When operating lightweight ciphers in an IoT environment, it is not easy to provide side-channel security at the algorithm level. In ICISC 2020, the bit-sliced lightweight block cipher PIPO has been introduced to mitigate overhead [7]. PIPO is designed to respond to SCA effectively. When SCA countermeasures such as masking are applied, it has very little overhead and provides security strength similar to existing ciphers. Various cryptanalysis and optimization papers on the PIPO have been continuously introduced recently, leading to an increasing interest in the PIPO [8,10].

Differential fault attack (DFA) is a type of semi-invasive SCA that uses difference information that occurs when cryptographic algorithms operate on a device by inducing an artificial fault. DFA was first proposed by Biham et al. for DES in 1997 [1]. Subsequently, DFAs on various cryptographic algorithms such as AES were studied [2,3,5], and fault-injection techniques for practical attacks were developed in many ways [11,12,14]. DFAs on bit-sliced block ciphers have been studied, but the actual target is mostly lookup table-based implementations and few studies on bit-sliced implementations. In 2018, Sinha et al. proposed a DFA on RECTANGLE-80 implemented with the bit-slice technique [16]. They are based on forcing certain bits to zero or flipping certain consecutive bits or all bits in a word. And they observe the change in the scope of a brute force attack according to each attacker's assumption. The attacker's assumption with coercion and continuity, as discussed in the paper above, is a challenging problem, and the comparatively weak attacker's assumption has a limit in that the range of brute force attacks is enormous.

Our Contributions. Our contributions are twofold. First, we proposed a DFA logic on the recently introduced the lightweight block cipher PIPO for the first time. A random bit-flip at a specific byte position is used in the proposed attack. Experiments have shown that 64 ciphertexts can recover the correct secret key with overwhelming probability. The PIPO does not provide security against DFA. So it suggests the need to apply fault-injection countermeasure techniques in operating the PIPO in the real world. The second contribution is that the proposed attack process can be applied to perform DFAs on various bit-sliced block ciphers. Through this, we expect to contribute to the evaluation of DFA security against unverified bit-sliced block ciphers.

Organization. The remainder of this paper is structured as follows. In Sect. 2, we introduce the lightweight block cipher PIPO and DFA. Section 3 provides the

Table 1. Notation for the PIPO cipher

Parameter	Description
RK_r, c_r	r-round key and constant
S, R, R^{-1}	S-Layer, R-Layer, and Inverse R-Layer
Sb	S-Box operation
C, C^{ℓ}	Normal and fault ciphertexts
m, m^{ℓ}	Normal and fault S-Layer output
j, k	Matrix index of PIPO input/output ($j, k \in [0, 7]$)
a_{col}^j	j-column vector values of PIPO input/output
a_{row}^k	k-row vector values of PIPO input/output
x	S-Layer input
i	S-Box input difference
b_p	1-bit of intermediate value ($p \in [0, 63]$)
$\|\|$	Bit concatenation operation

methodology of the proposed DFA logic on the PIPO. Then, in Sect. 4, we evaluate the validity of the proposed attack with a simulation-based experiment and discuss the applicability of other bit-sliced block ciphers. Finally, we conclude the paper in Sect. 5.

2   Backgrounds

2.1   PIPO: Plug-In Plug-Out

The PIPO cipher is described in this section using the notation in Table 1. Han et al. introduced the PIPO a lightweight block cipher in 2020 [7]. It is an SPN-structured cryptographic algorithm that encrypts 64-bit fixed-size plaintexts and is designed for bit-sliced implementation. It is divided into PIPO 64/128 and PIPO 64/256 according to key size and consists of 13 rounds and 17 rounds, respectively. The PIPO has a simple structure in which round operations consisting of S-Layer, R-Layer, and AddRoundKey are repeated after key whitening, as shown in Fig. 1. The operational input and output forms of the PIPO can be expressed in the 8 × 8 matrix, as shown in Fig. 2. When 64-bit plaintexts are defined as $(b_{63}\|\|b_{62}\|\|...\|\|b_1\|\|b_0)$, It is stored in rows by 8-bits as follows:

$$a_{row}^k = (b_{8 \times k+7}\|\|b_{8 \times k+6}\|\|...\|\|b_{8 \times k+1}\|\|b_{8 \times k}), k \in [0, 7] \tag{1}$$

The S-Layer operation can be considered that the 8-bit S-Box operation is performed on a column basis in the matrix in Fig. 2 since the PIPO is a bit-sliced structure. When the bit slicing operation is defined as $BitS$, the S-Layer operation can be expressed as follows:

$$S(a) = BitS\left(Sb\left(a_{col}^0\right), Sb\left(a_{col}^1\right), ..., Sb\left(a_{col}^6\right), Sb\left(a_{col}^7\right)\right) \tag{2}$$

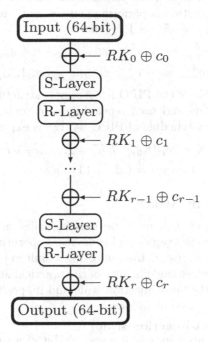

Fig. 1. Overall structure of the PIPO.

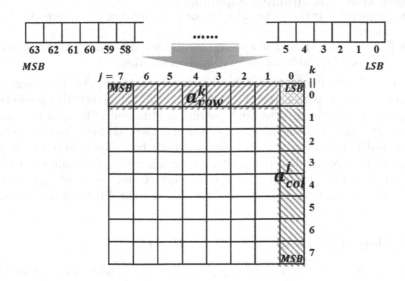

Fig. 2. Operational input and output form of the PIPO 64/128.

The R-Layer of the PIPO is a bit permutation that only uses bit-rotations in bytes. The R-Layer operation is performed on row units in Fig. 2, At this point, the rotation operation is performed as follows:

$$R(a) = (a_{row}^0 \lll 0, a_{row}^1 \lll 7, a_{row}^2 \lll 4, a_{row}^3 \lll 3$$
$$a_{row}^4 \lll 6, a_{row}^5 \lll 5, a_{row}^6 \lll 1, a_{row}^7 \lll 2) \tag{3}$$

Finally, the key schedule of the PIPO has a simple structure in which the secret key is divided by 64 bits and used repeatedly, and round constants are added for each round. The key schedule of PIPO 64/128 is expressed as follows:

$$K = K_1 \| K_0, \quad RK_i = K_{i \bmod 2} \oplus c_i$$
$$where \ i = 1, 2, ..., 13 \ and \ c_i = i \tag{4}$$

2.2 Differential Fault Attack

A DFA, which is a type of SCA, combines existing differential analysis with fault-injection attack. When the cryptographic device is operating, the attack exploits differece information that results from injecting a fault in the middle. The type of fault that arises determines the difficulty of the practical attack while performing a DFA. According to the fault-injection scale and its positioning capability, the fault model can be classified as follows:

- **Fault Model (fault-injection scale)**
  - `Bit Flip`: The attacker can flip a single-bit of a specific word
  - `Byte Error`: The attacker can change a single byte of a specific word into a random value.
  - `Word Error`: The attacker can change a single word into a random value.
- **Fault Model (positioning capability)**
  - `Chosen Position`: The attacker can specify exactly where the fault is injected.
  - `Random Position`: The attacker cannot specify exactly where the fault is injected. The faults occur in a random position.

With a smaller fault-injection scale, the attacker's assumption is stronger. Furthermore, when a specific position can be defined, the attacker's assumption is strong. Fault-injection attacks can be performed through techniques such as row-hammer attack, laser fault-injection, and electromagnetic fault-injection, etc. Bit flipping is difficult to induce with electromagnetic fault-injection technology, but it is possible to perform on powerful fault models with row-hammer attack and laser fault-injection. Through a low-hammer attack and laser fault-injection, this paper propose a bit-flip fault-based DFA logic on the PIPO at a reproducible level.

3 Differential Fault Attack on PIPO

In this section, we propose a DFA logic on the lightweight block cipher PIPO. The attack process is described based on the PIPO 64/128. The attack can be performed for the PIPO 64/256 by applying the same method for additional rounds.

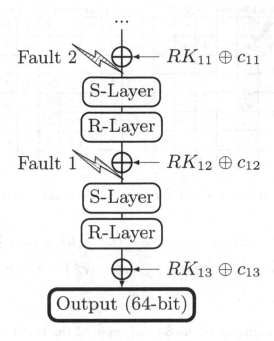

Fig. 3. Fault position of proposed DFA on the PIPO 64/128

3.1 Attacker's Assumption

The attacker can conduct encryption in the proposed DFA by obtaining a device with the PIPO operating with a fixed secret key. He or she can induce a fault in which a random single-bit is flipped at a specific byte position during the cryptographic operation and can monitor pairings of normal and fault ciphertexts.

3.2 Proposed DFA Scheme on PIPO

Since the PIPO 64/128 divides the secret key into two parts and uses it repeatedly, recovering two round keys can obtain a secret key completely. Thus, the proposed DFA recovers RK_{13} and RK_{12}, with a total of two attacks on the last round S-Layer input and the penultimate round S-Layer input, as shown Fault 1 and Fault 2 in Fig. 3. Each attack consists of four steps as follows:

STEP 1. Calculate the S-Layer I/O difference.

First, during the operation of the PIPO, the attacker is induced to flip a single-bit of a specific byte. This allows to acquire a pair of normal and fault ciphertexts. The normal and fault S-Layer output can be calculated using the acquired normal and fault ciphertext pairs. As a result, the attacker can calculate the S-Layer output difference $\Delta m \left(= m \oplus m^f \right)$ as shown in the following equation:

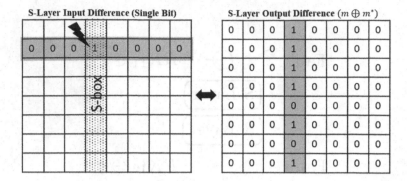

Fig. 4. Relation between S-Layer input difference and output difference

$$\Delta m = R^{-1}\left(C \oplus (RK_{13} \oplus c_{13})\right) \oplus R^{-1}\left(C^{\ell} \oplus (RK_{13} \oplus c_{13})\right)$$

$$= R^{-1}\left(C\right) \oplus R^{-1}\left(RK_{13} \oplus c_{13}\right) \oplus R^{-1}\left(C^{\ell}\right) \oplus R^{-1}\left(RK_{13} \oplus c_{13}\right) \quad (5)$$

$$= R^{-1}\left(C\right) \oplus R^{-1}\left(C^{\ell}\right)$$

When a certain single-bit of the S-Layer input of the PIPO is flipped, due to bit-sliced structural features, the S-Layer output difference occurs in a column containing that bit, as shown Fig. 4. Thus, the attacker can estimate the S-Layer input difference($= i$) depending on whether a specific column of the S-Layer output difference obtained by Eq. 5 is zero or not. When the attacker induced a random single-bit flip of tth $(0 \le t \le 7)$ byte and observed the difference in c^{th} $(0 \le c \le 7)$ column of the last round S-Layer output difference, the S-Layer input difference of that byte is 2^c and the S-Box input difference is 2^t.

STEP 2. Determining S-Layer input candidates.

The S-Box input values can be estimated according to pairs of S-Box input differences and output differences determined in **STEP 1**. The S-Box difference equation can be constructed as follows in terms of acquired values:

$$Sb\left(x_{col}^{j}\right) \oplus Sb\left(x_{col}^{j} \oplus i\right) = \left(m \oplus m^{\ell}\right)_{col}^{j} \quad (6)$$

Through the previous step, the attacker knows the values of i and $\left(m \oplus m^{\ell}\right)$ exactly. Thus, the S-Box difference table can be used to reduce the number of candidates for S-Box input$\left(= x_{col}^{j}\right)$ satisfying the Eq. 6. To determine the only one candidate, multiple difference information is required for the same S-Box. In other words, faults are required for multiple bits in the same column, i.e., the attack on multiple bytes. The attacker can specify the position of the fault-injected byte, and **STEP 1** allows us to find where the bit flip occurs. Thus, he or she can easily be filtering and collecting fault data that fits the conditions.

Theoretically, using three difference information to reduce a candidate, it is confirmed as only one candidate with a probability of about 89.1%. And using four difference information, a high probability of about 98.8% determines only one x_{col}^j candidate.

STEP 3. Calculate Round Key.

Repeat **STEP 1** to **2** to confirm S-Layer input in column units. Perform analysis on all columns. Determine all input bytes and calculate the last round key as follows:

$$RK_{13} = R\left(S\left(x\right)\right) \oplus C \oplus c_{13} \tag{7}$$

In the attack process, bit flip faults are required for all column positions in the S-Layer. That is, each of the eight columns must have a fault. And in the previous step, we confirmed that the faults of three or more byte positions uniquely determine one column with high probability. As a result, when the attacker performs an attack after filtering the ciphertext, it is possible to confirm RK_{13} with a probability of about 89.1% through 24 fault ciphertexts and 98.8% through 32 fault ciphertexts.

STEP 4. Confirm secret key.

For RK_{12} recovery, the attacker induces faults in penultimate round S-Layer input, as shown in Fault 2 in Fig. 3. The attack process is the same as the recovery of RK_{13}, resulting in only overhead for additional intermediate value calculations and no additional attack logic. Finally, the 128-bit secret key of PIPO 64/128 is completely restored by adding round constants to RK_{12} and RK_{13} obtained through the previous process and then concatenating them as follows:

$$K = (RK_{13} \oplus \texttt{0xd})\|(RK_{12} \oplus \texttt{0xc}) \tag{8}$$

4   Experiments and Discussion

4.1   Experimental Result

In this section, evaluation results are shown for the proposed DFA logic on the PIPO 64/128. This experiment is a simulation result and the experimental environment is shown in Table 2. We induced single-bit flip fault randomly for each byte of the last- and penultimate round S-Layer input and filtered the desired form of fault ciphertexts one by one based on **STEP 1** of Sect. 3. As a result of the attack, we were able to analyze the correct round key quickly within a second with 32 fault ciphertexts according to the proposed DFA process. Figure 5 shows the number of times to determine only one key out of 1000 attacks when the number of attack bytes is different. The number of faults ciphertexts used for each attack is ($8 \times \#$ *of attack bytes*). The experiments showed similar results to the theoretical predictions. It showed that when performing attacks on three to four bytes, the number of times determined by a single key was higher than 900 times, and a 100% success rate for more bytes.

Table 2. Experimental environment

Item	Configuration
CPU	Intel(R) Core(TM) i7-8700K CPU @ 3.70GHz
Memory	32.00G
OS	Window 10×64
Development platform	Microsoft Visual Studio 2017
Development language	C

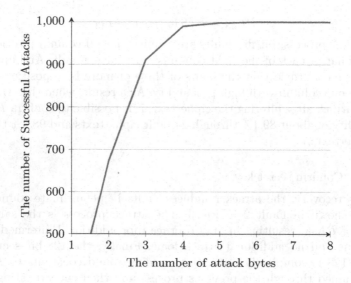

Fig. 5. The number of successful attacks according to the number of attack bytes (1000 times, considered successful when only one key is analyzed)

4.2   DFA on Bit-Sliced Block Ciphers

This section discusses the applicability of the proposed DFA logic to other bit-sliced block ciphers. Bit-sliced block ciphers include ROBIN, FANTOMAS [4], and RECTANGLE [17] etc. Although the S-Box input size and operational word units are different by ciphers. However, when representing intermediate values as matrices as shown in Fig. 2, bit-wise operations are performed per row, while S-Box operations are performed in units of columns. So if a single-bit of a specific byte in the S-Layer input is flipped, a 1-bit difference table for the S-Box can be built. The last round of each cipher is constructed as shown in Fig. 6. At this case, since ShiftRow and L-Layer are linear operations, secret key information is not required when calculating the output difference of the substitution layer, and it can be easily calculated through the inverse diffusion layer of the ciphertext difference. Therefore, it is possible to find the exact fault bit position by applying **STEP 1** of Sect. 3 equally to each cipher. And key candidates can be identified using multiple byte difference information and a difference table. As such, the proposed attack logic entails employing a 1-bit difference table and navigating for fault positions depending on the characteristics of the bit-sliced structure. As a result, it is easy to apply the proposed attack to various bit-sliced block ciphers.

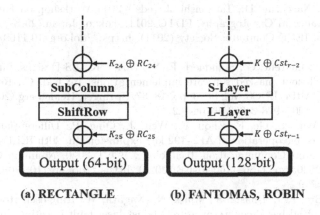

Fig. 6. Last round structure of RECTANGLE, FANTOMAS, and ROBIN

5 Conclusion

In this paper, we proposed a DFA logic on the lightweight block cipher PIPO for the first time and demonstrated the validity of the attack through simulation. With an overwhelming probability, the proposed DFA resulted in the accurate acquisition of the secret key for the PIPO 64/128 with 32 fault ciphertexts for each round, a total of 64 fault ciphertexts. When targeting PIPO 64/256, the proposed attack uses the same logic and performs additional attacks on two rounds. It just requires additional calculations for the intermediate values at this time, and no other logic is demanded, making it easier to apply. As a result, when the PIPO cipher is used in the real world, this paper recommends that the fault-injection countermeasure is used [6,13,15]. Because the suggested attack has a structure that is suited for attacking bit-sliced structures, we expect it to be applied in DFAs on various bit-sliced block ciphers. In the future, we plan to employ the proposed attack methodology for a variety of bit-sliced block ciphers. Because the proposed DFA logic is based on a single-bit flip model and must be able to specify a specific byte position, the attacker's assumption is rather strong. Thus, we plan to design an attack logic that alleviates the assumption of attackers, and verify the attack's validity to the real device through an actual electromagnetic fault-injection attack.

References

1. Biham, E., Shamir, A.: Differential fault analysis of secret key cryptosystems. In: Kaliski, B.S. (ed.) CRYPTO 1997. LNCS, vol. 1294, pp. 513–525. Springer, Heidelberg (1997). https://doi.org/10.1007/BFb0052259

2. Dusart, P., Letourneux, G., Vivolo, O.: Differential fault analysis on A.E.S. In: Zhou, J., Yung, M., Han, Y. (eds.) ACNS 2003. LNCS, vol. 2846, pp. 293–306. Springer, Heidelberg (2003). https://doi.org/10.1007/978-3-540-45203-4_23

3. Floissac, N., L'Hyver, Y.: From AES-128 to AES-192 and AES-256, how to adapt differential fault analysis attacks on key expansion. In: Breveglieri, L., Guilley, S., Koren, I., Naccache, D., Takahashi, J. (eds.) 2011 Workshop on Fault Diagnosis and Tolerance in Cryptography, FDTC 2011, Tokyo, Japan, 29 September 2011, pp. 43–53. IEEE Computer Society (2011). https://doi.org/10.1109/FDTC.2011.15

4. Grosso, V., Leurent, G., Standaert, F.-X., Varıcı, K.: LS-Designs: bitslice encryption for efficient masked software implementations. In: Cid, C., Rechberger, C. (eds.) FSE 2014. LNCS, vol. 8540, pp. 18–37. Springer, Heidelberg (2015). https://doi.org/10.1007/978-3-662-46706-0_2

5. Han, L., Wu, N., Ge, F., Zhou, F., Wen, J., Qing, P.: Differential fault attack for the iterative operation of AES-192 key expansion. In: 20th IEEE International Conference on Communication Technology, ICCT 2020, Nanning, China, 28–31 October 2020, pp. 1156–1160. IEEE (2020). https://doi.org/10.1109/ICCT50939.2020.9295779

6. He, W., Breier, J., Bhasin, S., Miura, N., Nagata, M.: Ring oscillator under laser: potential of pll-based countermeasure against laser fault injection. In: 2016 Workshop on Fault Diagnosis and Tolerance in Cryptography, FDTC 2016, Santa Barbara, CA, USA, 16 August 2016, pp. 102–113. IEEE Computer Society (2016). https://doi.org/10.1109/FDTC.2016.13

7. Kim, H., Jeon, Y., Kim, G., Kim, J., Sim, B.-Y., Han, D.-G., Seo, H., Kim, S., Hong, S., Sung, J., Hong, D.: PIPO: a lightweight block cipher with efficient higher-order masking software implementations. In: Hong, D. (ed.) ICISC 2020. LNCS, vol. 12593, pp. 99–122. Springer, Cham (2021). https://doi.org/10.1007/978-3-030-68890-5_6

8. Kim, H., et al.: Masked implementation of PIPO block cipher on 8-bit AVR microcontrollers. In: Kim, H. (ed.) WISA 2021. LNCS, vol. 13009, pp. 171–182. Springer, Cham (2021). https://doi.org/10.1007/978-3-030-89432-0_14

9. Kocher, P.C.: Timing attacks on implementations of Diffie-Hellman, RSA, DSS, and Other systems. In: Koblitz, N. (ed.) CRYPTO 1996. LNCS, vol. 1109, pp. 104–113. Springer, Heidelberg (1996). https://doi.org/10.1007/3-540-68697-5_9

10. Kwak, Y.J., Kim, Y.B., Seo, S.C.: Parallel implementation of PIPO block cipher on 32-bit RISC-V processor. In: Kim, H. (ed.) WISA 2021. LNCS, vol. 13009, pp. 183–193. Springer, Cham (2021). https://doi.org/10.1007/978-3-030-89432-0_15

11. Lim, H., Lee, J., Han, D.G.: Novel fault injection attack without artificial trigger. Appl. Sci. 10(11), 3849 (2020)

12. Roscian, C., Dutertre, J., Tria, A.: Frontside laser fault injection on cryptosystems - application to the AES' last round. In: 2013 IEEE International Symposium on Hardware-Oriented Security and Trust, HOST 2013, Austin, TX, USA, 2–3 June 2013, pp. 119–124. IEEE Computer Society (2013). https://doi.org/10.1109/HST.2013.6581576

13. Schneider, T., Moradi, A., Güneysu, T.: ParTI – towards combined hardware countermeasures against side-channel and fault-injection attacks. In: Robshaw, M., Katz, J. (eds.) CRYPTO 2016. LNCS, vol. 9815, pp. 302–332. Springer, Heidelberg (2016). https://doi.org/10.1007/978-3-662-53008-5_11

14. Seaborn, M., Dullien, T.: Exploiting the dram rowhammer bug to gain kernel privileges. Black Hat 15, 71 (2015)

15. Seo, H., Park, T., Ji, J., Kim, H.: Lightweight fault attack resistance in software using intra-instruction redundancy, revisited. In: Kang, B.B.H., Kim, T. (eds.) WISA 2017. LNCS, vol. 10763, pp. 3–15. Springer, Cham (2018). https://doi.org/10.1007/978-3-319-93563-8_1
16. Sinha, S., Karmakar, S.: Differential fault analysis of rectangle-80. IACR Cryptol. ePrint Archive, p. 428 (2018). https://eprint.iacr.org/2018/428
17. Zhang, W., Bao, Z., Lin, D., Rijmen, V., Yang, B., Verbauwhede, I.: RECTANGLE: a bit-slice lightweight block cipher suitable for multiple platforms. Sci. China Inf. Sci. **58**(12), 1–15 (2015). https://doi.org/10.1007/s11432-015-5459-7

Learning-based Side-Channel Analysis on PIPO

Ji-Eun Woo[1], Jaeseung Han[1], Yeon-Jae Kim[1], Hye-Won Mun[1],
Seonghyuck Lim[1], Tae-Ho Lee[1], Seong-Hyun An[1], Soo-Jin Kim[1],
and Dong-Guk Han[1,2]([envelope])

[1] Department of Financial Information Security, Kookmin University,
Seoul, Republic of Korea
{dnwldms928,jae1115,duswo0024,qwerty25879,seonghyeck16,20141932,
ashtree,suzin22,christa}@kookmin.ac.kr
[2] Department of Information Security, Cryptology, and Mathematics,
Kookmin University, Seoul, Republic of Korea

Abstract. As the global IoT market increases, the importance of security in the IoT environment is growing. So, studies on lightweight cipher techniques are actively underway for limited environments. In ICISC 2020, PIPO, a bitslice lightweight cipher that can effectively apply a countermeasure considering side-channel analysis, was proposed. In this paper, we propose Deep Learning-based profiled and non-profiled Side-Channel Analysis for PIPO. In profiled attack, we use an 8-bit model instead of 1-bit model that considered the bitslice characteristic of S-Box output. Although an each bit of S-Box output is distributed across the power trace, the 8-bit model has shown high training performance with 98% accuracy, and was able to derive right key successfully. In non-profiled attack, we propose a labeling technique suitable for the bitslice characteristic and show the excellence of our proposed labeling through experiments. Also, we expect that these characteristics will apply to other bitslice block ciphers as well as PIPO.

Keywords: Side-channel analysis · Deep learning · PIPO · Block cipher

1 Introduction

Recently, with the development of the Internet of Things (IoT), IoT devices, such as wearable biometric sensors and smart home devices, have increasingly become common in daily life and are widely used worldwide. However, IoT devices have limitations, such as the size of the hardware and power consumption. To implement encryption in such a limited environment, studies on lightweight block

This work was supported by Institute for Information & communications Technology Promotion (IITP) grant funded by the Korea government (MSIT) (No. 2017-0-00520, Development of SCR-Friendly Symmetric Key Cryptosystem and Its Application Modes).

J. H. Park and S.-H. Seo (Eds.): ICISC 2021, LNCS 13218, pp. 308–321, 2022.
https://doi.org/10.1007/978-3-031-08896-4_16

ciphers are increasing. However, these lightweight block ciphers may be vulnerable to Side-Channel Analysis.

Side-Channel Analysis (SCA) is an technique that recovers secret information by using side-channel information(e.g., power consumption, sound, and electromagnetic leaks) generated while encryption is performed on the target devices. In addition, SCA that uses the power consumption can be classified as profiled SCA and non-profiled SCA.

Profiled SCA creates a profile using a device that is very similar to a target device and finds secret information by matching the power traces obtained from the target device with the created profile, e.g., Template Attacks [1]. Non-profiled SCA derives secret information through statistical analysis of the power traces obtained when encrypting with the same secret keys and random plaintexts on the target device, e.g. Correlation Power Analysis (CPA), Differential power analysis (DPA) [3].

Furthermore, as deep learning techniques advance, studies on deep learning-based SCA are also increasing. Deep learning-based SCA derives secret information by training neural networks such as Multi-Layer Perceptron (MLP) and Convolution Neural Network (CNN) with intermediate values corresponding to side-channel information. In the case of profiling SCA, the intermediate values of the attack traces on target devices are derived using the trained neural network. In non-profiling SCA, the secret key is determined by the training performance of the neural network for each guessed key.

In this work, we propose deep learning-based profiled and non-profiled SCA on bitslice lightweight block cipher PIPO-64/128. In profiled SCA, we show that the neural network trained well by extracting features of power traces when we use an ID leakage model as label. Although the 1-bit model of S-Box output is considered when analyzing bitslice block cipher, we show that features are well extracted even using our model. In non-profiled SCA, we propose the improved labeling method on bitslice block cipher. And we demonstrate the excellence of our proposed labeling by comparing it to existing.

2   Background

2.1   PIPO: Bitslice Lightweight Block Cipher

PIPO (Plug-In Plug-Out) is a bitslice lightweight block cipher with a Substitution Permutation Network (SPN) structure proposed in 2020 [2]. It provides excellent performance in 8-bit AVR software with a bitsliced implementation. PIPO supports a 64-bit block size and uses an S-Box with 8-bit input and output. There are two variants of PIPO based on different key sizes (PIPO-64/128, PIPO-64/256), as shown in Table 1.

Table 2 shows the definition of notations used throughout this paper. For PIPO-64/128, the master key K is split into two 64-bit subkeys K_0 and K_1, i.e., $K = K_1 || K_0$. The round keys are then defined as $RK_r = K_{r \bmod 2}$ where $r = 0, 1, \cdots, 13$. Similarly, for PIPO-64/256, the master key K is split into four

Table 1. Types of PIPO

	Master key size	The number of rounds
PIPO-64/128	128-bit	13
PIPO-64/256	256-bit	17

64-bit subkeys K_0, K_1, K_2, and K_3, i.e., $K = K_3 \| K_2 \| K_1 \| K_0$, and the round keys are $RK_r = K_{r \bmod 4}$ where $r = 0, 1, \cdots, 17$.

Table 2. Definition of notations

Notation	Definition
$\oplus$	XOR (eXclusive OR) operator
$\gg$	Right shift operator
$\&$	AND operator
$\|$	Bitwise concatenation operator
$m \bmod n$	The remainder when m is divided by n
K	Master key
RK_r	r-th Round Key
S_i	i-th byte of S-Layer output
$s_{i,j}$	j-th bit of S_i

Each round consists of non-linear S-Layer, linear R-Layer, and Key Addition. The structure of PIPO is shown in Fig. 1.

Specifically, the non-linear S-Layer applies a bitslice implementation. Block ciphers in a bitslice structure can process multiple S-Box operations in parallel without table reference, since S-Box is implemented as a bitwise logical operation. Therefore, for 8-bit input and output of S-Box both are stored in different registers and operated in parallel, so as shown in Fig. 2, the operation is performed by storing the i-th input bits of each S-Box in the i-th byte ($0 \leq i \leq 7$).

2.2   Supervised Learning Using Multi-Layer Perceptron

Multi-Layer Perceptron (MLP) is a feed-forward neural network with multiple layers, and each layer has multiple perceptrons [4]. It forms a fully connected structure in which each perceptron of the previous layer and the perceptrons of the next layer are all connected. As shown in Fig. 3, MLP consists of an input layer, hidden layers, and an output layer. MLP can be learned through a data set given a large amount of data and corresponding labels (correct answer), which is called supervised learning [5]. The learning process is the following: Calculate the loss value between the label for the training data and the output value

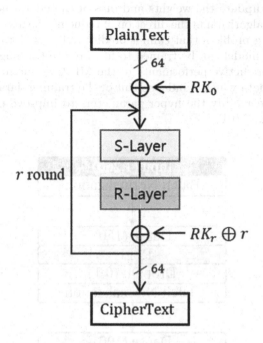

Fig. 1. PIPO structure

$$x = (x_{63}, x_{62}, x_{61}, \dots, x_2, x_1, x_0)$$

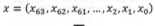

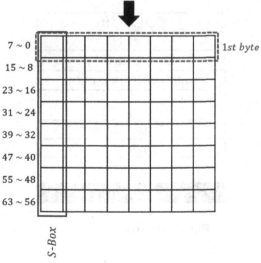

Fig. 2. S-Layer structure

of the MLP, and update the weights and bias of the neural network through a backpropagation algorithm in the direction of reducing the loss value. In this process, an overfitting problem that cannot predict well new data may occur, since a neural network model can be trained to fit only the training data. Therefore, to evaluate the predictive performance of the MLP, we monitor the overfitting using validation data which is independent of the training data [6]. If overfitting occurred, we then modify the hyper-parameters to improve the generalization performance of the MLP.

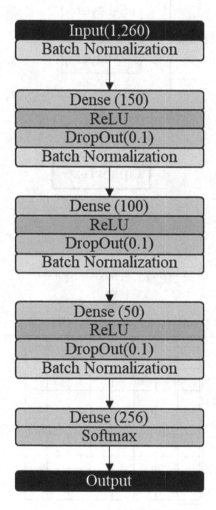

Fig. 3. The structure of MLP

2.3 Deep Learning-Based Profiled Side-Channel Attack

Profiled SCA is a technique of generating the profile through a profiling device which is similar the target device, then analyzing the secret information by matching the side-channel information of the attack target device with the profile of profiling device. In 2013, Martinasek et al. proposed Deep Learning-based profiled SCA (DL-based profiled SCA) [9]. The analysis process of DL-based profiled SCA is divided into profiling and attack phases. In the profiling phase, the neural network is trained by setting the input as the training traces and the output as the label about the target operation intermediate value. In the attack phase, the attack trace is input to the trained neural network and the intermediate value is restored through the output of the neural network. Martinasek et al. were set the label through the one-hot encoding of an intermediate value and performed DL-based profiled SCA for AES [9]. As above, in DL-based profiled SCA, typically, the one-hot encoding value of the intermediate value is used as a label.

2.4 Deep Learning-Based Non-profiled Attack

Non-profiled SCA is a technique for analyzing secret information using multiple side-channel information collected during the encrypting for the random plaintexts with the same secret key. In 2019, Benjamin proposed a Deep Learning-based non-profiled SCA (DL-based non-profiled SCA) [7]. The analysis process of DL-based non-profiled SCA is as follows. First, for each guess key, the neural network is trained by setting the input as the traces and the output as the label value for the target intermediate value. Then, since the label calculated by the right key is a value related to the traces, the neural network is well trained. However, since the label calculated by the wrong key is a value unrelated to the traces, the neural network is not well trained. We analyze the secret key by judging the guess key that trained the neural network best as the right key. In DL-based non-profiled SCA, we also prefer that the intermediate value of wrong keys have a low correlation with the intermediate value of the right key like the traditional non-profiled SCA, so it takes generally the output of the non-linear operation to the intermediate value. Timon was set the LSB or MSB of the S-Box output as the label and performed DL-based non-profiled SCA for AES [7].

3 DL-Based Profiled SCA on PIPO

3.1 Attack Scenario

Profiling Phase
The profiling phase is the process of training neural networks using power consumption collected during the encryption of PIPO-64/128. In this paper, a neural network is constructed using an MLP model. The PIPO S-Layer is implemented in parallel so that each byte of S-Box output is not all stored in the same register, but power consumption information is distributed. However, since an MLP has a

fully connected layer structure, it is expected that the features of the corresponding byte can be extracted even if the information is distributed. Therefore, to recover one byte of the first round key of PIPO-64/128, the power consumption should be set as the input of the neural network, and the output of the PIPO S-Layer is set as the label. In order to recover the entire first round key RK_0, we have to repeat this for all bytes.

Attack Phase
The attack phase is the process of finally recovering the key of PIPO-64/128 by putting the attack trace as an input into the trained neural network. By putting attack power consumption as input into one neural network obtained from the training phase, one byte of the output of the PIPO S-Box can be recovered. As shown in Fig. 4, the result of performing an inverse S-Box operation on the recovered S-Box output and an XOR operation with the plaintext is considered as the correct key. This process can be done on all bytes to recover the entire first round key RK_0, and the master key K can finally be recovered when both first and second round keys are found.

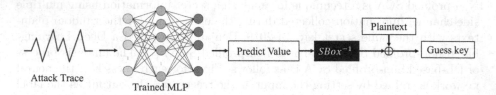

Fig. 4. Attack phase

Performance Metric
In order to evaluate whether the attack stage was well performed, the ratio of the number of correct guess keys among a total of 1,000 attack traces collected with random plaintexts and random keys is used as a performance metric. For example, if the attack phase is performed on 1,000 attack traces and 500 keys are matched, the success rate of the attack is 50%.

3.2   Experimental Result

In this section, we present our experiment results that apply DL-based profiled SCA for PIPO-64/128.

Experimental Environment
For the experiment, we obtain the power traces from PIPO-64/128 1st round S-Layer to R-Layer when encrypted 10,000 times with a random key and a random plaintext in the experimental environment as Table 3. Power traces were divided

into 9,000 profiling dataset and 1,000 attack dataset, and 10% of the profiling dataset was used as the validation data set for verification in the profiling phase.

We target S_i of first round, the output of S-Layer, and use the identity (ID leakage) model as our power model, so there are 256 classes. Thus, we set the number of the last node in neural network to 256. Also, label is target value's one-hot encoding value.

Table 3. Experimental environment

Target board	ChipWhisperer-lite
Target chip	Atmel XMEGA 128 (8-bit processor)
Sampling rate	29,538 MS/s
Tensorflow version	1.15.0
Keras version	2.3.1

MLP Architecture

This section describes the our MLP model used in the experiment. It has three hidden layers with 150, 100 and 50 nodes. also, activation function of the hidden layer used "ReLU" and the output layer used "Softmax". The number of nodes in the input layer is 1,260, which is the number of points in the power traces, and the number of nodes in the output layer is 256, the number of possible target values. Each hidden layer and input layer include a batch normalization and a dropout to prevent overfitting.

Table 4 shows our MLP architecture, and detail of hyperparameters are shown in Table 5.

Experimental Result

This section presents the experimental results when each byte of RK_0 is recovered. Figure 5 shows the training, validation loss(left) and the training, validation accuracy(right) of first byte of RK_0. In Fig. 5, The x-axis of the graph represents the number of epochs, and the y-axis represents the loss or accuracy. Also, the blue line is result of training and orange line is result of validation.

The maximum validation accuracy is 75%, and the correct guess rate when performing an attack on 1,000 attack data set is 72.8%. Table 6 shows the maximum validation accuracy and correct guess rate for RK_0. We can see that every byte has more than 60% validation accuracy, and the correct guess rate is similar. Therefore, RK_1 is recovered in the same way, the master key K for PIPO-64/128 can be recovered using RK_0, RK_1.

Due to the bitslice structure characteristics of the PIPO S-Layer, each bit of the S-Box output is distributed across the power traces. Nevertheless, it can be seen that the MLP model learns by extracting features by itself, even if the

Table 4. MLP on DL-based profiled SCA

Layer	Node (in, out)	Kernel initializer
Input	(1260, 1260)	–
Dense	(1260, 150)	He uniform
ReLU	(150, 150)	–
Dense	(150, 100)	He uniform
ReLU	(100, 100)	–
Dense	(100, 50)	He uniform
ReLU	(50, 50)	–
Dense	(50, 256)	He uniform
Softmax	(256, 256)	–

Table 5. Hyperparameters

Label	One-hot encoding (8-bit) of S-Layer output
Optimizer	Adam (learning rate = 0.001)
Batch size	32
Epochs	100
Loss function	Categorical cross entropy
Dropout	0.1

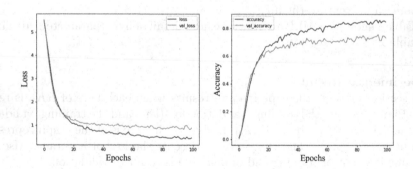

Fig. 5. Result of the first byte of RK_0

Table 6. Results of all bytes of RK_0

Byte	0	1	2	3	4	5	6	7
Maximum validation accuracy (%)	75	66	77	75	90	60	79	98
Correct guess rate (%)	72.8	67.4	76.8	71.8	87.1	56.4	78.3	97.1

label is composed using the 8-bit model of the S-Box output value rather than the 1-bit model. We expect to be applicable to not only PIPO but also other bitslice block ciphers.

4 DL-Based Non-profiled SCA on PIPO

4.1 Attack Scenario

Since PIPO-64/128 is also a block cipher using an S-Box, DL-based non-profiled SCA can be performed by similarly applying Timon's analysis [7]. The DL-based non-profiled SCA process is as follows.

- Set the input of the MLP to the power traces and the output to the label value (MSB or LSB, etc.) of the S-Box 1 byte output about the arbitrary guess key.
- After training is performed for all guess keys, the best-trained guess key is determined as the right key.

The learning metric uses the training loss value. That is, the guess key with the lowest final loss value is judged as the right key. Timon used the MSB or LSB value as the label value of DL-based non-profiled SCA for AES [7]. However, unlike AES, PIPO-64/128 is a bitslice block cipher. Therefore, in this paper, we propose a new labeling method considering the bitslice structure. Figure 6 shows the difference in the power trace of the general cipher and the bitslice cipher. In the general cipher, all bits of the S-Box output are exposed at a single time point.

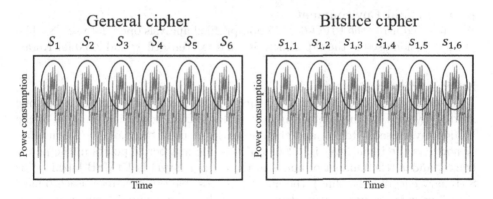

Fig. 6. General cipher's trace vs Bitslice cipher's trace

Therefore, in DL-based non-profiled SCA for general cipher, single-bit labeling or HW labeling in which multiple bits overlap is appropriate. However, in the traces of the bitslice block cipher, only a single-bit of the S-Box output is exposed at a single time point. In this case, the power information about each bit of the S-Layer output is data in an independent time point. Therefore, we propose binary encoding labeling that each single-bit is encoded as an independent label in DL-based non-profiled SCA for bitslice block cipher.

Algorithm 1. Binary encoded labeling algorithm

    Input : a 8-bit value x

   Output : a binary encoded label $y = (x_0, x_1, x_2, x_3, x_4, x_5, x_6, x_7), x_i \in \{0, 1\}$

1: **for** $i = 0$ to 7 **do**

2:    $x_i \leftarrow (x \gg i)$ & 1

3: **end for**

4: **Return** $y = (x_0, x_1, x_2, x_3, x_4, x_5, x_6, x_7)$

Algorithm 1 shows the proposed binary encoded labeling algorithm.

4.2 Experimental Result

In this section, we present our experimental results that apply DL-based non-profiled SCA for PIPO-64/128. For each labeling method, we derived the minimum number of traces required to DL-based non-profiled SCA and compared the performance of the methods.

Experimental Environment

We analyzed using the PIPO-64/128 non-profiled analysis open data set [8]. The library version used in the experiment is 2.6.0 for Tensorflow and 2.6.0 for Keras.

MLP Architecture

This section describes the our MLP model used in the experiment. It has one hidden layers, with the number of layer nodes is 200. Activation function of the hidden layer used "ReLU" and the output layer used "Sigmoid". The number of nodes in the input layer is 2,200, which is the number of points in the power traces, and x (the number of nodes in the output layer) is 1 (MSB labeling) or 8 (binary encoding labeling), the number of possible target values. Each binary encoding value is not independent of the other. For example, when let $y_1 = (0, 0, 0, 1), y_2 = (0, 0, 1, 1), y_3 = (1, 1, 1, 0)$, y_1 is closer with y_2 than y_3 because y_1, y_2 differ only one element but y_1, y_3 differ all element. Therefore, we did not apply one-hot encoding about labels in non-profiled SCA and the target of our MLP model is the regression problem. So we choose mean squared error as the loss function. Table 7 shows our MLP architecture, and detail of hyperparameters are shown in Table 8.

In our experiments, since the performance of the MSB labeling was better than LSB labeling, we focused on comparing MSB labeling with our proposed labeling method.

Table 7. MLP on DL-based non-profiled SCA

Layer	Node (in, out)	Kernel initailizer
Input	(2200, 2200)	–
Dense	(2200, 200)	He normal
ReLU	(200, 200)	–
Dense	(200, x)	He normal
Sigmoid	(x, x)	–

Table 8. Hyperparameters

Label	Binary encoding (8-bit), MSB of S-Layer output
Optimizer	Adam (learning rate = 0.0001)
Batch size	100
Epochs	1000
Loss function	Mean squared error

Experimental Result

We defined "number of traces required for analysis" is the number of traces when the right key has the lowest loss value. Figure 7 is the learning result of first byte of RK_0 on the binary encoding labeling neural network, and it is the result of learning with 60, 70, and 80 traces, respectively. The x-axis of the graph represents the number of epochs and the y-axis represents the loss value. In the graph, the black line is the wrong keys, the red line is the right key, and the blue line is some wrong key that has lower loss than the right key. At 60 traces, the analysis failed because there was some wrong key with a lower final loss than the right key, but at 70 traces, the analysis succeeded because the final loss of the right key was the lowest. Additionally, at 80 traces, the final loss of the right key decreased comparing a result of 70 traces. As such, we repeated the analysis with a trace of 10 units, and we find a minimum number of traces required for analysis by each labeling method. Table 9 shows the minimum number of traces by each binary encoding, and MSB labeling method in the first round key analysis. As a result, the average minimum number of traces for binary encoding is 86.75 and that of MSB is 153.75. Consequently, binary encoding labeling has minimum analysis traces that about 56.4% of MSB labeling.

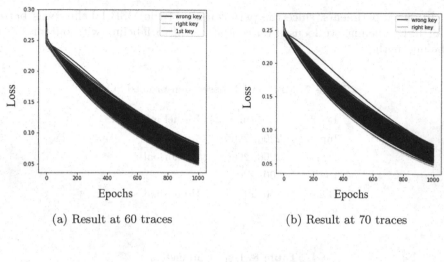

(a) Result at 60 traces   (b) Result at 70 traces

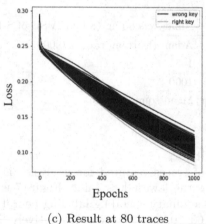

(c) Result at 80 traces

Fig. 7. Result of first byte of RK_0 on DL-based non-profiled SCA by binary encoding labeling

Table 9. Minimum number of traces required for analysis by each labeling method in RK_0

Label\Byte	0	1	2	3	4	5	6	7	Average
Binary encoding	70	90	90	100	100	100	70	70	86.75
MSB	170	160	190	160	130	140	120	160	153.75

5 Conclusion

In this paper, we propose deep learning-based profiled and non-profiled side-channel analysis for PIPO-64/128. For DL-based profiled SCA, the PIPO S-

Layer output's one-hot encoding value is used as a label. As a result, all bytes of first round key show a validation accuracy greater than 60% and up to 98%. In addition, the attack phase uses the ratio of the number of correct guess keys among a total of attack traces to evaluate attack performance. The ratio of correct guessing on attack dataset is up to 97%, which is similar to the validation accuracy. Thus, the right key could be recovered with an 8-bit model even though the S-Layer output was distributed across the power trace by bit slicing. On the other hand, for DL-based non-profiled SCA, we use binary encoding of PIPO S-Box output as the label. And the training loss value was used to evaluate the training performance. We show that when using binary encoding as the label, all bytes can be recovered with 100 power traces less than when using MSB label.

We expect that our experimental results can also be applied to (high-order) analysis on other block ciphers which are either bitslice-based or not. Thus, in future work, we plan to analyze other block ciphers using the proposed DL-based profiled SCA and DL-based non-profiled SCA.

References

1. Chari, S., Rao, J.R., Rohatgi, P.: Template attacks. In: Kaliski, B.S., Koç, K., Paar, C. (eds.) CHES 2002. LNCS, vol. 2523, pp. 13–28. Springer, Heidelberg (2003). https://doi.org/10.1007/3-540-36400-5_3
2. Kim, H., et al.: PIPO: a lightweight block cipher with efficient higher-order masking software implementations. In: Hong, D. (ed.) ICISC 2020. LNCS, vol. 12593, pp. 99–122. Springer, Cham (2021). https://doi.org/10.1007/978-3-030-68890-5_6
3. Kocher, P., Jaffe, J., Jun, B.: Differential power analysis. In: Wiener, M. (ed.) CRYPTO 1999. LNCS, vol. 1666, pp. 388–397. Springer, Heidelberg (1999). https://doi.org/10.1007/3-540-48405-1_25
4. Priddy, K., Keller, P.: Artificial Neural Networks: An Introduction. SPIE Tutorial Texts. SPIE Press (2005). https://books.google.co.kr/books?id=BrnHR7esWmkC
5. Reed, R.D., Marks, R.J.: Neural Smithing: Supervised Learning in Feedforward Artificial Neural Networks. MIT Press, Cambridge (1998)
6. Schaffer, C.: Selecting a classification method by cross-validation. Mach. Learn. **13**, 135–143 (1993). https://doi.org/10.1007/BF00993106
7. Timon, B.: Non-profiled deep learning-based side-channel attacks with sensitivity analysis. IACR Trans. Cryptogr. Hardw. Embed. Syst. **2019**(2), 107–131 (2019). https://doi.org/10.13154/tches.v2019.i2.107-131
8. TrusThingz: PIPO data set. https://trusthingz.org/index.php/pipo-data-set
9. Zeman, V., Martinasek, Z.: Innovative method of the power analysis. Radioengineering **22**, 586–594 (2013)

Constructions and Designs

Collision-Resistant and Pseudorandom Function Based on Merkle-Damgård Hash Function

Shoichi Hirose[✉][ID]

University of Fukui, Fukui, Japan
hrs_shch@u-fukui.ac.jp

Abstract. This paper presents a keyed hash function satisfying collision resistance and the pseudorandom-function (PRF) property. It is based on the Merkle-Damgård hash function. It is shown to satisfy collision resistance under the ideal assumption that the underlying compression function is a random oracle. It is also shown to be a secure PRF if the underlying compression function is a secure PRF against related-key attacks in two keying strategies. The novel feature of the proposed keyed hash function is its efficiency. It achieves the minimum number of calls to the underlying compression function for any message input. Namely, constructed with the compression function accepting a w-bit message block, it processes any $l(\geq 0)$-bit massage with $\max\{1, \lceil l/w \rceil\}$ calls to the compression function. Thus, it is more efficient than the standardized keyed hash function HMAC, which also satisfies both collision resistance and the PRF property, especially for short messages. The proposed keyed hash function, as well as HMAC, can be instantiated with the SHA-256 compression function.

Keywords: Hash function · Collision resistance · Pseudorandom function · Related-key attack · Provable security

1 Introduction

Background. Cryptographic hash functions are an important primitive in cryptography and are used for various applications such as message digest, message authentication, and pseudorandom generation. Among them, some interesting cryptographic schemes were recently constructed with a keyed hash function satisfying both collision resistance and the pseudorandom-function property simultaneously: compactly committing authenticated encryption with associated data (ccAEAD) [10,16] and hash-based post-quantum EPID signatures [8]. We call such a keyed hash function a collision-resistant and pseudorandom hash function.

It is also well known that a collision-resistant and pseudorandom hash function H directly instantiates computationally hiding and computationally binding string commitment. In the commit phase, for a message M, a sender chooses a key K uniformly at random, computes $\sigma \leftarrow H_K(M)$, and sends σ to a receiver.

© The Author(s), under exclusive license to Springer Nature Switzerland AG 2022
J. H. Park and S.-H. Seo (Eds.): ICISC 2021, LNCS 13218, pp. 325–338, 2022.
https://doi.org/10.1007/978-3-031-08896-4_17

In the open phase, the sender reveals M and K to the receiver. This scheme is computationally hiding since H is a pseudorandom function (PRF). It is computationally binding since H is collision-resistant: It is intractable to find a pair (M, K) and (M', K') such that $(M, K) \neq (M', K')$ and $H_K(M) = H_{K'}(M')$.

HMAC [4] is a collision-resistant and pseudorandom hash function, which is specified by NIST in FIPS PUB 198-1 [13] and by ISO in ISO/IEC 9797-2:2021 [20]. A drawback of HMAC is that it is not so efficient for short messages since it calls its underlying hash function twice.

Our Contribution. We present a new collision-resistant and pseudorandom hash function. It is a kind of Merkle-Damgård hash function $H^F : \{0, 1\}^{n/2} \times \{0, 1\}^* \to \{0, 1\}^n$ using a compression function $F : \{0, 1\}^n \times \{0, 1\}^w \to \{0, 1\}^n$, which is depicted in Fig. 1. H^F is regarded as a keyed function with its key space $\{0, 1\}^{n/2}$. It is based on MDP [18] and is very similar to Keyed-MDP (MDP keyed via IV). Thus, we call it KMDP$^+$.

H^F achieves the minimum number of calls to its compression function F under the assumption that a message input is fed only into the message-block input ($\{0, 1\}^w$) of its compression function. Namely, a message $M \in \{0, 1\}^*$ is processed with $\lceil |M|/w \rceil$ calls to the compression function if $|M| > 0$, where $|M|$ is the length of M. If $|M| = 0$, then M is processed with a single call to the compression function.

H^F is shown to be collision-resistant if F is a random oracle, that is, F is chosen uniformly at random: Any adversary needs $\Omega(2^{n/2})$ queries to F to find a colliding pair of inputs of H^F. H^F is shown to be a secure PRF if the compression function F used as a keyed function with its key space $\{0, 1\}^n$ is a secure PRF against related-key attacks [6] in two keying strategies. The proof uses the hybrid argument [15].

The construction is simple, and the techniques used for the security analyses are conservative. Nevertheless, as far as we know, KMDP$^+$ is the first keyed hash function satisfying collision resistance and the PRF property and achieving the minimum number of calls to its compression function for any message input. In addition, the SHA-256 compression function seems suitable for the instantiation of KMDP$^+$.

Related Work. An iterated hash function consisting of a compression function is called a Merkle-Damgård hash function [9,24]. Pseudorandom functions were first introduced by Goldreich, Goldwasser, and Micali [14].

Instantiated with a Merkle-Damgård hash function, HMAC is shown to be a secure PRF if its underlying compression function is a secure PRF in two keying strategies, keyed via the chaining value and keyed via the message [2]. AMAC [3] is also a hash-based PRF that calls its underlying hash function once. From its construction, it is easy to see that AMAC also satisfies collision resistance. However, due to its output transform such as truncation, SHA-256 does not seem suitable for the instantiation of AMAC with a sufficient level of collision resistance.

Bellare and Ristenpart [7] introduced the notion of multi-property preservation and presented the domain extension EMD shown to produce a hash function satisfying collision resistance, PRF property, and pseudorandom-oracle property (indifferentiability) from a compression function satisfying the corresponding property. Their construction assumes padding with Merkle-Damgård-strengthening and is not so efficient as our construction.

The domain extension MDP was presented by Hirose, Park, and Yun [18]. It is implicit in [18] that Keyed-MDP is also a collision-resistant and pseudorandom hash function. In terms of efficiency, though Keyed-MDP is very competitive with KMDP$^+$, the latter is still better than the former that assumes padding with Merkle-Damgård-strengthening.

A PRF based on a Merkle-Damgård hash function and achieving the minimum number of calls to its compression function was presented by Hirose and Yabumoto [19]. A Merkle-Damgård hash function achieving the minimum number of calls to its compression function was proposed and shown to satisfy indifferentiability [17]. We unify these two constructions and obtain KMDP$^+$.

The Merkle-Damgård hash function keyed via the initial value with prefix-free padding for message input is shown to be a secure PRF if the underlying compression function is a secure PRF [5]. Our proof on PRF is based on this proof.

Quite recently, Andreeva et al. [1] and Dodis et al. [11] presented similar domain extension schemes which outperform the Merkle-Damgård domain extension in terms of the number of calls to the underlying compression function. However, their domain extension schemes are not effective in processing a short message consisting of a few message blocks.

CMAC [25] is a CBC-MAC function designed by Iwata and Kurosawa [21, 22], which achieves the minimum number of calls to its underlying block cipher. It is not designed to satisfy collision resistance.

A distinguishing attack on the SHA-256/512 compression functions keyed via the chaining value was presented by Kuwakado and Hirose [23].

Organization. Section 2 gives notations and definitions. Section 3 describes the proposed keyed hash function. Section 4 shows the collision resistance of the proposed keyed hash function under the assumption that the underlying compression function is a random oracle. Section 5 shows that the proposed keyed hash function is a secure PRF if the underlying compression function is a secure PRF against related-key attacks in two keying strategies. Section 6 discusses the instantiation with the SHA-256 compression function and its efficiency. Section 7 gives a concluding remark.

2   Preliminaries

2.1   Notations

Let $\Sigma := \{0, 1\}$. Let $(\Sigma^n)^* := \bigcup_{i=0}^{\infty} \Sigma^{ni}$ and $(\Sigma^n)^+ := \bigcup_{i=1}^{\infty} \Sigma^{ni}$. Let $\varepsilon \in \Sigma^0$ be an empty sequence.

For a binary sequence $u \in \Sigma^*$, let $|u|$ be the length of u. For binary sequences $z_i, z_{i+1}, \ldots, z_{i+j} \in \Sigma^*$, let $z_i \| z_{i+1} \| \cdots \| z_{i+j}$ be their concatenation, which is also denoted by $z_{[i,i+j]}$ for simplicity.

Let $s \leftarrow S$ denote that s is assigned an element chosen uniformly at random from set S.

For integers a, b, and d, $a \equiv b \pmod{d}$ is denoted as $a \equiv_d b$.

A random function $\rho : \mathcal{D} \to \mathcal{R}$ is called a random oracle if, for any $x \in \mathcal{D}$, $\rho(x)$ is assigned an element chosen uniformly at random from $\mathcal{R}$.

2.2   Collision Resistance

Let $H^F : \mathcal{X} \to \mathcal{Y}$ be a hash function using a compression function F. The collision resistance of a hash function is often discussed under the assumption that its compression function is a random oracle.

Let $\mathbf{A}$ be an adversary trying to find a collision for H^F, that is, a pair of distinct inputs mapped to the same output. The col-advantage of $\mathbf{A}$ against H^F is defined as

$$\mathrm{Adv}^{\mathrm{col}}_{H^F}(\mathbf{A}) := \Pr[(X, X') \leftarrow \mathbf{A}^F : H^F(X) = H^F(X') \wedge X \neq X'].$$

It is assumed that $\mathbf{A}$ makes all the queries necessary to compute $H^F(X)$ and $H^F(X')$. Let $\mathrm{Adv}^{\mathrm{col}}_{H^F}(q)$ be the maximum col-advantage over all adversaries making at most q queries.

2.3   Pseudorandom Function

Let $f : \mathcal{K} \times \mathcal{X} \to \mathcal{Y}$ be a keyed function with its key space $\mathcal{K}$ and $f_K(\cdot) := f(K, \cdot)$. Let $\mathbf{A}$ be an adversary against f. The goal of $\mathbf{A}$ is to distinguish between f_K and a random oracle $\rho : \mathcal{X} \to \mathcal{Y}$, where $K \leftarrow \mathcal{K}$. $\mathbf{A}$ is given either f_K or ρ as an oracle and makes adaptive queries in $\mathcal{X}$. $\mathbf{A}$ outputs 0 or 1. The prf-advantage of $\mathbf{A}$ against f is defined as

$$\mathrm{Adv}^{\mathrm{prf}}_f(\mathbf{A}) := \left| \Pr\left[\mathbf{A}^{f_K} = 1\right] - \Pr\left[\mathbf{A}^{\rho} = 1\right] \right|,$$

where $\mathbf{A}$ is regarded as a random variable that takes values in $\{0, 1\}$. f is called a secure pseudorandom function (PRF) if no efficient adversary $\mathbf{A}$ has any significant prf-advantage against f.

The prf-advantage can be extended to adversaries with multiple oracles. The prf-advantage of adversary $\mathbf{A}$ with access to p oracles is defined as

$$\mathrm{Adv}^{p\text{-prf}}_f(\mathbf{A}) := \left| \Pr[\mathbf{A}^{f_{K_1}, f_{K_2}, \ldots, f_{K_p}} = 1] - \Pr[\mathbf{A}^{\rho_1, \rho_2, \ldots, \rho_p} = 1] \right|,$$

where $(K_1, \ldots, K_p) \leftarrow \mathcal{K}^p$ and $\rho_1, \ldots, \rho_p$ are independent random oracles.

2.4 PRF Under Related-Key Attack

Let $\mathbf{A}$ be an adversary against $f : \mathcal{K} \times \mathcal{X} \to \mathcal{Y}$. Let Φ be a set of functions from $\mathcal{K}$ to $\mathcal{K}$. $\mathbf{A}$ makes a Φ-related-key attack (Φ-RKA) [6]: $\mathbf{A}$ is given $g[K] : \Phi \times \mathcal{X} \to \mathcal{Y}$ such that $g[K](\varphi, X) := g(\varphi(K), X)$ as an oracle, where g is either f or a random oracle $\rho : \mathcal{K} \times \mathcal{X} \to \mathcal{Y}$ and $K \leftarrow \mathcal{K}$. $\mathbf{A}$ makes adaptive queries to the oracle and outputs 0 or 1. The prf-rka-advantage of $\mathbf{A}$ making a Φ-RKA on f is given by

$$\mathrm{Adv}_{f,\Phi}^{\mathrm{prf\text{-}rka}}(\mathbf{A}) := \left| \Pr[\mathbf{A}^{f[K]} = 1] - \Pr[\mathbf{A}^{\rho[K]} = 1] \right|.$$

f is called a secure PRF under Φ-RKAs if no efficient adversary $\mathbf{A}$ has any significant prf-rka-advantage.

The prf-rka-advantage of $\mathbf{A}$ with access to p oracles is defined as

$$\mathrm{Adv}_{f,\Phi}^{p\text{-}\mathrm{prf\text{-}rka}}(\mathbf{A}) := \left| \Pr[\mathbf{A}^{f[K_1],\ldots,f[K_p]} = 1] - \Pr[\mathbf{A}^{\rho_1[K_1],\ldots,\rho_p[K_p]} = 1] \right|,$$

where $(K_1, \ldots, K_p) \leftarrow \mathcal{K}^p$ and $\rho_1, \ldots, \rho_p$ are independent random oracles.

Lemma 1 ([19]). *For any adversary $\mathbf{A}$ against f taking at most t time and making at most q queries in total, there exists an adversary $\mathbf{A}'$ such that*

$$\mathrm{Adv}_{f,\Phi}^{p\text{-}\mathrm{prf\text{-}rka}}(\mathbf{A}) \leq p \cdot \mathrm{Adv}_{f,\Phi}^{\mathrm{prf\text{-}rka}}(\mathbf{A}').$$

$\mathbf{A}'$ *takes at most about $t + q \cdot \tau_f$ time and makes at most q queries, where τ_f is time required to compute f.*

3   Proposed Hash Function

Let $n > 1$ be an even integer and $w > 1$ be an integer. The proposed hash function KMDP$^+$ uses a compression function $F : \Sigma^n \times \Sigma^w \to \Sigma^n$. It also uses the following padding function:

$$\mathrm{pad}(M) := \begin{cases} M & \text{if } |M| > 0 \text{ and } |M| \equiv_w 0 \\ M \| 10^d & \text{otherwise,} \end{cases}$$

where d is the smallest non-negative integer satisfying $|\mathrm{pad}(M)| \equiv_w 0$. Notice that $\mathrm{pad}(\varepsilon) = 10^{w-1}$.

KMDP$^+$ is the hash function $\mathsf{H}^F : \Sigma^{n/2} \times \Sigma^* \to \Sigma^n$, which is described in Algorithm 1. It is also depicted in Figs. 1 and 2. To specify H^F, three fixed constants $IV, c_0, c_1 \in \Sigma^{n/2}$ are used. c_0 and c_1 are assumed to satisfy the following conditions: $c_0 \neq 0^{n/2}$; $c_1 \neq 0^{n/2}$; $c_0 \oplus c_1 \neq 0^{n/2}$.

For the PRF property, H^F is regarded as a keyed function with its key space $\Sigma^{n/2}$.

For H^F, the number of calls to its compression function F required to process an input message M is 1 if M is the empty sequence and $\lceil |M|/w \rceil$ otherwise.

Algorithm 1: The proposed hash function $\mathsf{H}^F : \Sigma^{n/2} \times \Sigma^* \to \Sigma^n$

---

  input : (K, M)
  output: $\mathsf{H}^F(K, M)$
  $M_1 \| M_2 \| \cdots \| M_m \leftarrow \mathtt{pad}(M);$ /* $|M_i| = w$ for $1 \le i \le m$ */
  $V_0 \leftarrow K \| IV;$
  for $i = 1$ **to** $m - 1$ **do** $V_i \leftarrow F(V_{i-1}, M_i);$
  if $|M| > 0 \wedge |M| \equiv_w 0$ **then** $V_m \leftarrow F(V_{m-1} \oplus (0^{n/2} \| c_0), M_m);$
  else $V_m \leftarrow F(V_{m-1} \oplus (0^{n/2} \| c_1), M_m);$
  return $V_m;$

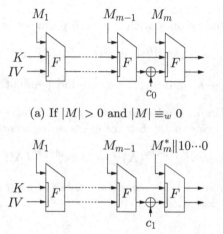

(a) If $|M| > 0$ and $|M| \equiv_w 0$

(b) If $|M| = 0$ or $|M| \not\equiv_w 0$. The last block M_m^* is incomplete: $1 \le |M_m^*| < w$.

Fig. 1. The proposed hash function. A message input M is divided into blocks of length w.

4 Collision Resistance

The collision resistance of H^F is discussed under the assumption that F is a random oracle. A pair of inputs (K, M) and (K', M') for H^F are colliding if $(K, M) \neq (K', M')$ and $\mathsf{H}^F(K, M) = \mathsf{H}^F(K', M')$. The following theorem implies that any adversary needs $\Omega(2^{n/2})$ queries to find a colliding pair of inputs for H^F.

Theorem 1. *For collision resistance of* H^F,

$$\mathrm{Adv}_{\mathsf{H}^F}^{\mathrm{col}}(q) \le q/2^{n/2-1} + q(q-1)/2^n.$$

Proof. Suppose that a colliding pair, M and M', are found for H^F. Namely, $\mathsf{H}^F(M) = \mathsf{H}^F(M')$ and $M \neq M'$. It is assumed that $|M| \le |M'|$ without loss of generality. Let $\mathtt{pad}(M) = M_1 \| M_2 \| \cdots \| M_m$ and $\mathtt{pad}(M') = M_1' \| M_2' \| \cdots \| M_{m'}'$.

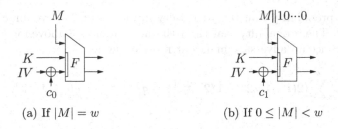

Fig. 2. The proposed hash function for at most a single-block message

(i) Suppose that $m = m' = 1$.

If $|M| < w$ and $|M'| < w$, or $|M| = |M'| = w$, then a colliding pair are found for F since $\mathrm{pad}(M) \neq \mathrm{pad}(M')$.

If $|M| < w$ and $|M'| = w$, then a colliding pair are also found for F since $c_0 \neq c_1$.

(ii) Suppose that $m = 1$ and $m' \geq 2$.

If $|M| < w$ and $|M'| \equiv_w 0$, then a colliding pair are found for F or an input for F such that the least significant $n/2$ bits of the corresponding output equals $IV \oplus c_0 \oplus c_1$.

If $|M| < w$ and $|M'| \not\equiv_w 0$, then a colliding pair are found for F or an input for F such that the least significant $n/2$ bits of the corresponding output equals IV.

If $|M| = w$ and $|M'| \equiv_w 0$, then a colliding pair are found for F or an input for F such that the least significant $n/2$ bits of the corresponding output equals IV.

If $|M| = w$ and $|M'| \not\equiv_w 0$, then a colliding pair are found for F or an input for F such that the least significant $n/2$ bits of the corresponding output equals $IV \oplus c_0 \oplus c_1$.

(iii) Suppose that $m \geq 2$ and $m' \geq 2$.

If $|M| \equiv_w 0$ and $|M'| \not\equiv_w 0$, or $|M| \not\equiv_w 0$ and $|M'| \equiv_w 0$, then a colliding pair are found for F or F wrt $c_0 \oplus c_1$. A pair of inputs (V_{i-1}, M_i) and (V'_{i-1}, M'_i) are called colliding wrt $c_0 \oplus c_1$ if $F(V_{i-1}, M_i) = F(V'_{i-1}, M'_i) \oplus c_0 \oplus c_1$.

Suppose that $|M| \equiv_w 0$ and $|M'| \equiv_w 0$. If $m = m'$, then a colliding pair are found for F. If $m < m'$, then a colliding pair are found for F or an input for F such that the least significant $n/2$ bits of the corresponding output equals IV.

Suppose that $|M| \not\equiv_w 0$ and $|M'| \not\equiv_w 0$. If $m = m'$, then a colliding pair are found for F. If $m < m'$, then a colliding pair are found for F or an input for F such that the least significant $n/2$ bits of the corresponding output equals IV.

Thus, a colliding pair for H^F implies

1. a colliding pair,
2. a colliding pair wrt $c_0 \oplus c_1$, or
3. an input mapped to an output whose least significant $n/2$ bits equals IV or $IV \oplus c_0 \oplus c_1$

for F. The probability that the j-th query induces 1 or 2 above for F is at most $2(j-1)/2^n$. The probability that the j-th query induces 3 above for F is at most $1/2^{n/2-1}$. Since an adversary makes at most q queries,

$$\sum_{i=1}^{q}(2(i-1)/2^n + 1/2^{n/2-1}) \leq q/2^{n/2-1} + q(q-1)/2^n.$$

$\square$

5   Pseudorandom-Function Property

We treat the compression function $F : \Sigma^n \times \Sigma^w \to \Sigma^n$ as a keyed function with its key space Σ^n in two keying strategies. In one strategy, a secret key is simply chosen uniformly at random from Σ^n. In the other strategy, it is chosen uniformly at random from $\Sigma^{n/2} \times \{IV\}(\subset \Sigma^n)$. To make the distinction clear, we denote the keyed compression function F in the latter keying strategy by $\tilde{F}$.

For both F and $\tilde{F}$, we consider $\{\mathsf{id}, \mathsf{x}_{c_0}, \mathsf{x}_{c_1}\}$-related-key attacks, where id is the identity permutation over Σ^n, and, for $b \in \{0,1\}$, x_{c_b} is a permutation over Σ^n such that $x \mapsto x \oplus (0^{n/2}\|c_b)$.

The following theorem implies that H^F is a secure PRF if both F and $\tilde{F}$ are secure PRFs under $\{\mathsf{id}, \mathsf{x}_{c_0}, \mathsf{x}_{c_1}\}$-related-key attacks.

Theorem 2. *For any adversary* $\mathbf{A}$ *taking at most* t *time and making at most* q *queries each of which has at most* ℓ *blocks after padding, there exist adversaries* $\mathbf{A}_1$ *and* $\mathbf{A}_2$ *such that*

$$\mathrm{Adv}^{\mathrm{prf}}_{\mathsf{H}^F}(\mathbf{A}) \leq \mathrm{Adv}^{\mathrm{prf\text{-}rka}}_{\tilde{F},\{\mathsf{id},\mathsf{x}_{c_0},\mathsf{x}_{c_1}\}}(\mathbf{A}_1) + (\ell-1)q\mathrm{Adv}^{\mathrm{prf\text{-}rka}}_{F,\{\mathsf{id},\mathsf{x}_{c_0},\mathsf{x}_{c_1}\}}(\mathbf{A}_2).$$

Both $\mathbf{A}_1$ *and* $\mathbf{A}_2$ *take at most about* $t+O(\ell q \tau_F)$ *time and make at most* q *queries, where* τ_F *is time required to compute* F.

Proof. Let $\mathsf{I}^c : \Sigma^n \times (\Sigma^w)^+ \to \Sigma^n$ be a keyed function specified in Algorithm 2. For an integer $k \geq 0$ and functions $\mu : (\Sigma^w)^* \to \Sigma^n$ and $\bar{\mu} : \Sigma^* \to \Sigma^n$, let $\mathsf{Hy}[k]^{\mu,\bar{\mu}} : \Sigma^* \to \Sigma^n$ be a function specified as follows: For $M \in \Sigma^*$ such that $\mathsf{pad}(M) = M_1\|\cdots\|M_m$,

$$\mathsf{Hy}[k]^{\mu,\bar{\mu}}(M) := \begin{cases} \bar{\mu}(M) & \text{if } m \leq k\,, \\ \mathsf{I}^{c_0}(\mu(M_{[1,k]}), M_{[k+1,m]}) & \text{if } m > k \wedge (|M| > 0 \wedge |M| \equiv_w 0), \\ \mathsf{I}^{c_1}(\mu(M_{[1,k]}), M_{[k+1,m]}) & \text{if } m > k \wedge (|M| = 0 \vee |M| \not\equiv_w 0). \end{cases}$$

Notice that $M_{[1,0]} = \varepsilon$.

Suppose that $\bar{\mu}$ is a random oracle and μ is a random oracle with a restriction that $\mu(\varepsilon)$ is chosen uniformly at random from $\Sigma^{n/2} \times \{IV\}$. Then,

$$\mathsf{Hy}[0]^{\mu,\bar{\mu}}(M) := \begin{cases} \mathsf{I}^{c_0}(\mu(\varepsilon), M_{[1,m]}) & \text{if } |M| > 0 \wedge |M| \equiv_w 0, \\ \mathsf{I}^{c_1}(\mu(\varepsilon), M_{[1,m]}) & \text{if } |M| = 0 \vee |M| \not\equiv_w 0, \end{cases}$$

which is equivalent to H^F. $\mathsf{Hy}[\ell]^{\mu,\bar{\mu}}$ works as a random oracle for any $M \in \Sigma^*$ such that $\mathsf{pad}(M)$ consists of at most ℓ blocks. Since every query made by $\mathbf{A}$ is assumed to consist of at most ℓ blocks after padding,

$$
\begin{aligned}
\mathrm{Adv}_{\mathsf{H}^F}^{\mathrm{prf}}(\mathbf{A}) &= \left| \Pr[\mathbf{A}^{\mathsf{Hy}[0]^{\mu,\bar{\mu}}} = 1] - \Pr[\mathbf{A}^{\mathsf{Hy}[\ell]^{\mu,\bar{\mu}}} = 1] \right| \\
&\leq \left| \Pr[\mathbf{A}^{\mathsf{Hy}[0]^{\mu,\bar{\mu}}} = 1] - \Pr[\mathbf{A}^{\mathsf{Hy}[1]^{\mu,\bar{\mu}}} = 1] \right| \\
&\quad + \sum_{k=1}^{\ell-1} \left| \Pr[\mathbf{A}^{\mathsf{Hy}[k]^{\mu,\bar{\mu}}} = 1] - \Pr[\mathbf{A}^{\mathsf{Hy}[k+1]^{\mu,\bar{\mu}}} = 1] \right|.
\end{aligned}
\tag{1}
$$

For the first term of the upper bound in Inequality (1), let $\mathbf{D}_0$ be a prf-rka-adversary against $\tilde{F}$. $\mathbf{D}_0$ runs $\mathbf{A}$ and simulates the oracle of $\mathbf{A}$ using its oracle. $\mathbf{D}_0$ outputs the output of $\mathbf{A}$. Let $\tilde{G}[\tilde{K}]$ be the oracle of $\mathbf{D}_0$, which are either $\tilde{F}[\tilde{K}]$ or $\tilde{\rho}[\tilde{K}]$, where $\tilde{K} \leftarrow \Sigma^{n/2} \times \{IV\}$ and $\tilde{\rho} : \Sigma^n \times \Sigma^w \to \Sigma^n$ is a random oracle. For the j-th query M made by $\mathbf{A}$ such that $\mathsf{pad}(M) = M_1 \| \cdots \| M_m$, $\mathbf{D}_0$ acts as follows:

– If $m = 1$, then $\mathbf{D}_0$ returns to $\mathbf{A}$

$$
\begin{cases}
\tilde{G}_{\tilde{K} \oplus (0^{n/2} \| c_0)}(M_1) & \text{if } |M| > 0 \wedge |M| \equiv_w 0, \\
\tilde{G}_{\tilde{K} \oplus (0^{n/2} \| c_1)}(M_1) & \text{if } |M| = 0 \vee |M| \not\equiv_w 0.
\end{cases}
$$

$\mathbf{D}_0$ gets $\tilde{G}_{\tilde{K} \oplus (0^{n/2} \| c_b)}(M_1)$ by asking (x_{c_b}, M_1) to its oracle for $b \in \Sigma$.
– If $m \geq 2$, then $\mathbf{D}_0$ returns to $\mathbf{A}$

$$
\begin{cases}
\mathsf{I}^{c_0}(\tilde{G}_{\tilde{K}}(M_1), M_{[2,m]}) & \text{if } |M| > 0 \wedge |M| \equiv_w 0, \\
\mathsf{I}^{c_1}(\tilde{G}_{\tilde{K}}(M_1), M_{[2,m]}) & \text{if } |M| = 0 \vee |M| \not\equiv_w 0.
\end{cases}
$$

$\mathbf{D}_0$ gets $\tilde{G}_{\tilde{K}}(M_1)$ by asking (id, M_1) to its oracle.

$\mathbf{D}_0$ implements $\mathsf{Hy}[0]^{\mu,\bar{\mu}}$ as the oracle of $\mathbf{A}$ if its oracle is $\tilde{F}[\tilde{K}]$. It implements $\mathsf{Hy}[1]^{\mu,\bar{\mu}}$ if its oracle is $\tilde{\rho}[\tilde{K}]$ since $\tilde{\rho}_{\tilde{K}}$, $\tilde{\rho}_{\tilde{K} \oplus (0^{n/2} \| c_0)}$, and $\tilde{\rho}_{\tilde{K} \oplus (0^{n/2} \| c_1)}$ are independent. Thus,

$$
\begin{aligned}
\left| \Pr[\mathbf{A}^{\mathsf{Hy}[0]^{\mu,\bar{\mu}}} = 1] - \Pr[\mathbf{A}^{\mathsf{Hy}[1]^{\mu,\bar{\mu}}} = 1] \right| &= \left| \Pr[\mathbf{D}_0^{\tilde{F}[\tilde{K}]} = 1] - \Pr[\mathbf{D}_0^{\tilde{\rho}[\tilde{K}]} = 1] \right| \\
&= \mathrm{Adv}_{\tilde{F}, \{\mathsf{id}, \mathsf{x}_{c_0}, \mathsf{x}_{c_1}\}}^{\mathrm{prf\text{-}rka}}(\mathbf{D}_0).
\end{aligned}
\tag{2}
$$

$\mathbf{D}_0$ takes at most about $t + O(\ell q \tau_F)$ time and makes at most q queries.

For the second term of the upper bound in Inequality (1), let $\mathbf{D}_k$ be a prf-rka-adversary against F for $k \in [1, \ell - 1]$. $\mathbf{D}_k$ runs $\mathbf{A}$ and simulates the oracle of $\mathbf{A}$ using its oracle. $\mathbf{D}_k$ outputs the output of $\mathbf{A}$. Let $G_1[K_1], \ldots, G_q[K_q]$ be the oracle of $\mathbf{D}_k$, which are either $F[K_1], \ldots, F[K_q]$ or $\rho_1[K_1], \ldots, \rho_q[K_q]$, where $K_i \leftarrow \Sigma^n$ and $\rho_i : \Sigma^n \times \Sigma^w \to \Sigma^n$ is a random oracle for $1 \leq i \leq q$. Notice that $\mathbf{A}$ makes at most q queries. For the j-th query M made by $\mathbf{A}$, let $\mathsf{pad}(M) = M_1 \| \cdots \| M_m$. Suppose that $m \leq k$. Then, $\mathbf{D}_k$ simulates $\bar{\mu}$ and returns $\bar{\mu}(M)$ to $\mathbf{A}$. Suppose that $m > k$. Let $\mathcal{J}$ be a set of integers such that

$$
\mathcal{J} = \{j' \mid \text{The } j'(<j)\text{-th query } M' \text{ of } \mathbf{A} \text{ satisfies } m' > k \text{ and} M'_{[1,k]} = M_{[1,k]}\},
$$

where $\text{pad}(M') = M_1' \| \cdots \| M_{m'}'$. Let $j^* \leftarrow j$ if $\mathcal{J} = \emptyset$ and $j^* \leftarrow \min \mathcal{J}$ otherwise. For the j-th query M of $\mathbf{A}$, $\mathbf{D}_k$ acts as follows:

- If $m = k + 1$, then $\mathbf{D}_k$ returns to $\mathbf{A}$

$$\begin{cases} G_{j^*}(K_{j^*} \oplus (0^{n/2} \| c_0), M_{k+1}) & \text{if } |M| > 0 \wedge |M| \equiv_w 0, \\ G_{j^*}(K_{j^*} \oplus (0^{n/2} \| c_1), M_{k+1}) & \text{if } |M| = 0 \vee |M| \not\equiv_w 0. \end{cases}$$

$\mathbf{D}_k$ gets $G_{j^*}(K_{j^*} \oplus (0^{n/2} \| c_b), M_{k+1})$ by asking $(\mathsf{x}_{c_b}, M_{k+1})$ to $G_{j^*}[K_{j^*}]$ for $b \in \Sigma$.
- If $m \geq k + 2$, then

$$\begin{cases} \mathsf{I}^{c_0}(G_{j^*}(K_{j^*}, M_{k+1}), M_{[k+2,m]}) & \text{if } |M| > 0 \wedge |M| \equiv_w 0, \\ \mathsf{I}^{c_1}(G_{j^*}(K_{j^*}, M_{k+1}), M_{[k+2,m]}) & \text{if } |M| = 0 \vee |M| \not\equiv_w 0. \end{cases}$$

$\mathbf{D}_k$ gets $G_{j^*}(K_{j^*}, M_{k+1})$ by asking (id, M_{k+1}) to $G_{j^*}[K_{j^*}]$.

In the process above, for the j-th query M, if $M_{[1,k]}$ is new, that is, $\mathcal{J} = \emptyset$, then $\mathbf{D}_k$ uses the new oracle $G_j[K_j]$ to compute the answer to the query. $\mathbf{D}_k$ implements $\mathsf{Hy}[k]^{\mu,\bar{\mu}}$ as the oracle of $\mathbf{A}$ if its oracles are $F[K_1], \ldots, F[K_q]$ since new K_j, which is chosen uniformly at random, is assigned to new $M_{[1,k]}$. $\mathbf{D}_k$ implements $\mathsf{Hy}[k+1]^{\mu,\bar{\mu}}$ if its oracles are $\rho_1[K_1], \ldots, \rho_q[K_q]$ since new $\rho_j[K_j]$ is assigned to new $M_{[1,k]}$ and $\rho_j(K_j, \cdot), \rho_j(K_j \oplus (0^{n/2} \| c_0), \cdot), \rho_j(K_j \oplus (0^{n/2} \| c_1), \cdot)$ are independent. Thus,

$$\left| \Pr[\mathbf{A}^{\mathsf{Hy}[k]^{\mu,\bar{\mu}}} = 1] - \Pr[\mathbf{A}^{\mathsf{Hy}[k+1]^{\mu,\bar{\mu}}} = 1] \right| = \text{Adv}_{F, \{\mathsf{id}, \mathsf{x}_{c_0}, \mathsf{x}_{c_1}\}}^{q\text{-prf-rka}}(\mathbf{D}_k). \tag{3}$$

$\mathbf{D}_k$ takes at most about $t + O(\ell q \tau_F)$ time and makes at most q queries.

From Inequality (1), Equalities (2) and (3), and Lemma 1, there exist adversaries $\mathbf{A}_1$ and $\mathbf{A}_2$ such that

$$\text{Adv}_{\mathsf{H}^F}^{\text{prf}}(\mathbf{A}) \leq \text{Adv}_{\tilde{F}, \{\mathsf{id}, \mathsf{x}_{c_0}, \mathsf{x}_{c_1}\}}^{\text{prf-rka}}(\mathbf{A}_1) + (\ell - 1) q \cdot \text{Adv}_{F, \{\mathsf{id}, \mathsf{x}_{c_0}, \mathsf{x}_{c_1}\}}^{\text{prf-rka}}(\mathbf{A}_2).$$

Both $\mathbf{A}_1$ and $\mathbf{A}_2$ take at most about $t + O(\ell q \tau_F)$ time and make at most q queries. $\qquad \square$

Algorithm 2: $\mathsf{I}^c : \Sigma^n \times (\Sigma^w)^+ \to \Sigma^n$

---

  input : $(U, X_1 \| X_2 \| \cdots \| X_x)$
  output: $\mathsf{I}^c(U, X_1 \| X_2 \| \cdots \| X_x)$
  $V_0 \leftarrow U$;
  for $i = 1$ **to** $x - 1$ **do** $V_i \leftarrow F(V_{i-1}, X_i)$;   /* $|X_i| = w$ **for** $1 \leq i \leq x$ */
  $V_x \leftarrow F(V_{x-1} \oplus (0^{n/2} \| c), X_x)$;
  return V_x;

Remark 1. Even if $\tilde{F}$ is a secure PRF, F is not necessarily a secure PRF. For example, suppose that $F(K_0\|K_1, X) = 0^n$ for any K_0 and X if $K_1 \neq IV$, where $|K_0| = |K_1| = n/2$. Then, F cannot be a secure PRF, while $\tilde{F}$ can be a secure PRF.

Even if F is a secure PRF, $\tilde{F}$ is not necessarily a secure PRF. For example, suppose that $F(K_0\|K_1, X) = 0^n$ for any K_0 and X if $K_1 = IV$. Then, $\tilde{F}$ cannot be a secure PRF, while F can be a secure PRF.

Remark 2. The actual key length of $\tilde{F}$ is $(n/2)$-bits. $\tilde{F}$ may be viewed as a tweakable keyed function with its key space $\Sigma^{n/2}$ and its tweak space $\Sigma^{n/2}$. A proof applying a hybrid argument under the sole assumption that $\tilde{F}$ is a secure tweakable PRF would give an upper bound containing $\ell q \cdot \mathrm{Adv}^{\mathrm{prf\text{-}rka}}_{\tilde{F}, \{\mathrm{id}, \times_{c_0}, \times_{c_1}\}}(\mathbf{A_1})$. It guarantees only $(n/4)$-bit security due to the simple guessing-key attack on $\tilde{F}$.

6 Discussion

6.1 Instantiation

KMDP$^+$ can be instantiated with the SHA-256 compression function together with, for example, the following constants:

$$IV = \texttt{510e527f 9b05688c 1f83d9ab 5be0cd19},$$

$$c_0 = \texttt{36363636 36363636 36363636 36363636},$$

$$c_1 = \texttt{5c5c5c5c 5c5c5c5c 5c5c5c5c 5c5c5c5c}.$$

IV is the second half of the initial hash value of the SHA-256 hash function [12]. c_0 and c_1 are taken from the constants $\texttt{ipad}$ and $\texttt{opad}$ of HMAC (Fig. 3) [13], respectively. For such c_0 and c_1,

$$c_0 \oplus c_1 = \texttt{6a6a6a6a 6a6a6a6a 6a6a6a6a 6a6a6a6a}.$$

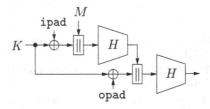

Fig. 3. HMAC using a hash function H. Both $\texttt{ipad}$ and $\texttt{opad}$ are fixed constants.

6.2   Efficiency

The SHA-256 compression function accepts a 512-bit message block. Thus, for KMDP$^+$ instantiated with the SHA-256 compression function, the number of calls to the compression function required to process an input message M is 1 if M is the empty sequence and $\lceil |M|/512 \rceil$ otherwise.

For HMAC [13], the amount of computation required to process an input message depends on the amount of computation required by its hash function. Here, we assume HMAC using SHA-256 [12]. The padding scheme of SHA-256 appends $10^* \| |M|_{64}$ to an input message M, where $|M|_{64}$ is the 64-bit binary representation of $|M|$. Thus, the number of calls to its compression function required to process M is $\lceil (M - 447)/512 \rceil + 4$.

$I^c(K, \mathsf{mdspad}(M))$ is an implementation of Keyed-MDP [18], where mdspad is padding with Merkle-Damgård strengthening. If $I^c(K, \mathsf{mdspad}(M))$ is instantiated with the SHA-256 compression function and mdspad is the padding scheme of SHA-256, then the number of calls to the compression function is $\lceil (M - 447)/512 \rceil + 1$. Thus, Keyed-MDP is very competitive with KMDP$^+$:

$$\lceil (M - 447)/512 \rceil + 1 = \begin{cases} \max\{1, \lceil |M|/512 \rceil\} & \text{if } 0 \le |M| \bmod 512 \le 447, \\ \lceil |M|/512 \rceil + 1 & \text{otherwise.} \end{cases}$$

7   Concluding Remark

We have proposed a collision-resistant and pseudorandom hash function based on Merkle-Damgård hashing. It achieves the minimum number of calls to its underlying compression function for any input. It can be instantiated with the SHA-256 compression function. Future work is to explore the PRF property of the SHA-256 compression function keyed via the chaining value against related-key attacks assumed for KMDP$^+$.

Acknowledgements. This work was supported by JSPS KAKENHI Grant Number JP21K11885.

References

1. Andreeva, E., Bhattacharyya, R., Roy, A.: Compactness of hashing modes and efficiency beyond Merkle tree. In: Canteaut, A., Standaert, F.-X. (eds.) EURO-CRYPT 2021. LNCS, vol. 12697, pp. 92–123. Springer, Cham (2021). https://doi.org/10.1007/978-3-030-77886-6_4
2. Bellare, M.: New proofs for NMAC and HMAC: security without collision-resistance. In: Dwork, C. (ed.) CRYPTO 2006. LNCS, vol. 4117, pp. 602–619. Springer, Heidelberg (2006). https://doi.org/10.1007/11818175_36
3. Bellare, M., Bernstein, D.J., Tessaro, S.: Hash-function based PRFs: AMAC and its multi-user security. In: Fischlin, M., Coron, J.-S. (eds.) EUROCRYPT 2016. LNCS, vol. 9665, pp. 566–595. Springer, Heidelberg (2016). https://doi.org/10.1007/978-3-662-49890-3_22

4. Bellare, M., Canetti, R., Krawczyk, H.: Keying hash functions for message authentication. In: Koblitz, N. (ed.) CRYPTO 1996. LNCS, vol. 1109, pp. 1–15. Springer, Heidelberg (1996). https://doi.org/10.1007/3-540-68697-5_1
5. Bellare, M., Canetti, R., Krawczyk, H.: Pseudorandom functions revisited: the cascade construction and its concrete security. In: Proceedings of the 37th IEEE Symposium on Foundations of Computer Science, pp. 514–523 (1996)
6. Bellare, M., Kohno, T.: A theoretical treatment of related-key attacks: RKA-PRPs, RKA-PRFs, and applications. In: Biham, E. (ed.) EUROCRYPT 2003. LNCS, vol. 2656, pp. 491–506. Springer, Heidelberg (2003). https://doi.org/10.1007/3-540-39200-9_31
7. Bellare, M., Ristenpart, T.: Multi-property-preserving hash domain extension and the EMD transform. In: Lai, X., Chen, K. (eds.) ASIACRYPT 2006. LNCS, vol. 4284, pp. 299–314. Springer, Heidelberg (2006). https://doi.org/10.1007/11935230_20
8. Boneh, D., Eskandarian, S., Fisch, B.: Post-quantum EPID signatures from symmetric primitives. In: Matsui, M. (ed.) CT-RSA 2019. LNCS, vol. 11405, pp. 251–271. Springer, Cham (2019). https://doi.org/10.1007/978-3-030-12612-4_13
9. Damgård, I.B.: A design principle for hash functions. In: Brassard, G. (ed.) CRYPTO 1989. LNCS, vol. 435, pp. 416–427. Springer, New York (1990). https://doi.org/10.1007/0-387-34805-0_39
10. Dodis, Y., Grubbs, P., Ristenpart, T., Woodage, J.: Fast message franking: from invisible salamanders to encryptment. In: Shacham, H., Boldyreva, A. (eds.) CRYPTO 2018. LNCS, vol. 10991, pp. 155–186. Springer, Cham (2018). https://doi.org/10.1007/978-3-319-96884-1_6
11. Dodis, Y., Khovratovich, D., Mouha, N., Nandi, M.: T5: hashing five inputs with three compression calls. Cryptology ePrint Archive, Report 2021/373 (2021). https://ia.cr/2021/373
12. FIPS PUB 180-4: secure hash standard (SHS) (2015)
13. FIPS PUB 198-1: the keyed-hash message authentication code (HMAC) (2008)
14. Goldreich, O., Goldwasser, S., Micali, S.: How to construct random functions. J. ACM 33(4), 792–807 (1986). https://doi.org/10.1145/6490.6503
15. Goldwasser, S., Micali, S.: Probabilistic encryption. J. Comput. Syst. Sci. 28(2), 270–299 (1984). https://doi.org/10.1016/0022-0000(84)90070-9
16. Grubbs, P., Lu, J., Ristenpart, T.: Message franking via committing authenticated encryption. In: Katz, J., Shacham, H. (eds.) CRYPTO 2017. LNCS, vol. 10403, pp. 66–97. Springer, Cham (2017). https://doi.org/10.1007/978-3-319-63697-9_3
17. Hirose, S.: Sequential hashing with minimum padding. Cryptography 2(2), 11 (2018). https://doi.org/10.3390/cryptography2020011
18. Hirose, S., Park, J.H., Yun, A.: A simple variant of the Merkle-Damgård scheme with a permutation. In: Kurosawa, K. (ed.) ASIACRYPT 2007. LNCS, vol. 4833, pp. 113–129. Springer, Heidelberg (2007). https://doi.org/10.1007/978-3-540-76900-2_7
19. Hirose, S., Yabumoto, A.: A tweak for a PRF mode of a compression function and its applications. In: Bica, I., Reyhanitabar, R. (eds.) SECITC 2016. LNCS, vol. 10006, pp. 103–114. Springer, Cham (2016). https://doi.org/10.1007/978-3-319-47238-6_7
20. ISO/IEC 9797-2:2021: information security - message authentication codes (MACs) - Part 2: mechanisms using a dedicated hash-function (2021)
21. Iwata, T., Kurosawa, K.: OMAC: One-key CBC MAC. Cryptology ePrint Archive, Report 2002/180 (2002). https://ia.cr/2002/180

22. Iwata, T., Kurosawa, K.: OMAC: one-key CBC MAC. In: Johansson, T. (ed.) FSE 2003. LNCS, vol. 2887, pp. 129–153. Springer, Heidelberg (2003). https://doi.org/10.1007/978-3-540-39887-5_11
23. Kuwakado, H., Hirose, S.: Pseudorandom-function property of the step-reduced compression functions of SHA-256 and SHA-512. In: Chung, K.-I., Sohn, K., Yung, M. (eds.) WISA 2008. LNCS, vol. 5379, pp. 174–189. Springer, Heidelberg (2009). https://doi.org/10.1007/978-3-642-00306-6_13
24. Merkle, R.C.: One way hash functions and DES. In: Brassard, G. (ed.) CRYPTO 1989. LNCS, vol. 435, pp. 428–446. Springer, New York (1990). https://doi.org/10.1007/0-387-34805-0_40
25. NIST Special Publication 800–38B: Recommendation for block cipher modes of operation: the CMAC mode for authentication (2005)

Forward Secure Message Franking

Hiroki Yamamuro[1(✉)], Keisuke Hara[1,2], Masayuki Tezuka[1], Yusuke Yoshida[1], and Keisuke Tanaka[1]

[1] Tokyo Institute of Technology, Tokyo, Japan
yamamuro.h.ab@m.titech.ac.jp
[2] National Institute of Advanced Industrial Science and Technology (AIST), Tokyo, Japan

Abstract. Message franking is introduced by Facebook in end-to-end encrypted messaging services. It allows to produce verifiable reports of malicious messages by including cryptographic proofs generated by Facebook. Recently, Grubbs et al. (CRYPTO'17) proceeded with the formal study of message franking and introduced committing authenticated encryption with associated data (CAEAD) as a core primitive for obtaining message franking.

In this work, we aim to enhance the security of message franking and propose forward security for message franking. It guarantees the security associated with the past keys even if the current keys are exposed. Firstly, we propose the notion of key-evolving message franking including additional key update algorithms. Then, we formalize forward security for five security requirements: confidentiality, ciphertext integrity, unforgeability, receiver binding, and sender binding. Finally, we show a construction of forward secure message franking based on CAEAD, forward secure pseudorandom generator, and forward secure message authentication code.

Keywords: Message franking · Forward security · Abusive verifiable reports

1 Introduction

1.1 Background

Message Franking. Billions of people use messaging services such as WhatsApp [22], Signal [19], and Facebook Messenger [11]. In these services, the security goal is end-to-end security: the third party including the service providers cannot compromise the security of messages. Keeping the messages secret from the service providers has recently led to the following problem: when the receiver receives malicious messages such as spam, phishing links, and so on, he/she attempts to report them to the service providers so that they could take measures against the sender. However, the service providers are not able to judge the reported messages were actually sent by the particular sender.

To tackle this problem, Facebook introduced the notion of message franking [12]. In message franking, the sender generates a commitment to a message,

J. H. Park and S.-H. Seo (Eds.): ICISC 2021, LNCS 13218, pp. 339–358, 2022.
https://doi.org/10.1007/978-3-031-08896-4_18

called a franking tag, along with a ciphertext generated using a secret key (which is shared with the receiver) and sends them to Facebook. Next, Facebook generates a cryptographic proof, called a reporting tag, from the franking tag using a tagging key (which is held by Facebook) and gives the ciphertext, the franking tag, and the reporting tag to the receiver. Then, the receiver decrypts the ciphertext using the secret key, gets the message and an opening of the franking tag, and verifies the validity of the franking tag. If the receiver wants to report a malicious message, he/she sends the reporting tag and the opening to Facebook in addition to the message. It enables Facebook to verify the specific sender actually sent the reported messages by validating the reporting tag using the tagging key.

Grubbs, Lu, and Ristenpart [13] initiated the formal study of message franking. They introduced committing authenticated encryption with associated data (CAEAD) as a core primitive for message franking. CAEAD is authenticated encryption with associated data (AEAD) that uses a small part of the ciphertext as a commitment to the message.

Forward Security. In general, most of cryptographic primitives are designed to be secure as long as their secret keys are not compromised. Thus, the exposure of secret keys is the greatest threat for many cryptographic schemes. Especially, if secret keys are compromised, the security of schemes is at risk not only after compromising but also in the past.

Forward security [9, 14] is one of the major solutions to address the exposure of secret keys, which ensures that compromise of the secret keys in the present does not influence the security of ciphertexts and tags generated in the past. Roughly, considering forward security, the lifetime of the system is divided into n time periods and secret keys are updated in each period so that any past secret keys cannot be calculated from the current secret keys. To date, forward security was defined in a digital signature scheme [3], a symmetric encryption scheme [4], and an asymmetric encryption scheme [5]. Recently, the definition of forward security has also been considered for practical cryptographic primitives, such as a non-interactive key exchange scheme [20], a 0-RTT key exchange protocol [8, 15], a 0-RTT session resumption protocol [2], and Signal protocol [1, 7].

In a message franking scheme, the exposure of secret keys causes malicious adversaries to decrypt and tamper with the past ciphertexts and forge the past reporting tags. Moreover, it also enables them to falsely report messages that were actually not sent and generate messages that fail verification. To avoid these problems, the challenge of achieving forward security in a message franking scheme is important.

1.2 Our Contribution

In this paper, we initiate the study on forward security for message franking. For capturing forward security, we firstly formalize key-evolving message franking, which includes two key update algorithms for a secret key and a tagging key, respectively.

Roughly, forward security in message franking guarantees the security of the ciphertexts and reporting tags generated with the past keys, even if the current keys are exposed. More precisely, we define forward security on key-evolving message franking for five security requirements: confidentiality, ciphertext integrity, unforgeability, receiver binding, and sender binding. Confidentiality and ciphertext integrity are the security notions for ciphertexts, while unforgeability, receiver binding, and sender binding are the security notions for reporting tags. Confidentiality guarantees that the information about the messages is not leaked from the ciphertexts and ciphertext integrity guarantees that the ciphertexts cannot be tampered with. Similar to the previous work on message franking [13], we adapt multiple-opening (MO) security for confidentiality and ciphertext integrity. MO security allows to securely encrypt multiple different messages under the same secret key. Unforgeability guarantees that reporting tags are not forged, receiver binding guarantees that the receiver is not able to report messages that were not actually sent, and sender binding guarantees that the sender is not able to send malicious messages that cannot be reported. See Sect. 3.1 for the details.

We show a construction of a key-evolving message franking scheme combining a CAEAD scheme with a forward secure pseudorandom generator (PRG) and a forward secure message authentication code (MAC) scheme. In a nutshell, we use a CAEAD scheme to generate ciphertexts and franking tags and decrypt them with a secret key updated by a forward secure PRG. Moreover, we use a forward secure MAC scheme to generate and verify reporting tags with an updated tagging key. See Sect. 4.2 for the details.

1.3   Related Work

As mentioned above, Grubbs et al. [13] introduced CAEAD as a core primitive for message franking. They provided two constructions of a CAEAD scheme: Commit-then-Encrypt (CtE) that combines a commitment scheme with an authenticated encryption with associated data (AEAD) scheme and Committing Encrypt-and-PRF (CEP) that uses a nonce-based PRG, a pseudorandom function (PRF), and a collision resistant PRF.

Dodis, Grubbs, Ristenpart, and Woodage [10] showed the attack against message franking for attachments. They also introduced encryptment, which is simplified CAEAD for design and analyse and provided an encryptment scheme using a hash function. Hirose [16] provided an encryptment scheme using a tweakable block cipher (TBC).

Leontiadis and Vaudenay [18] proposed a new security definition, called multiple-opening indistinguishability with partical opening (MO-IND-PO), which ensures confidentiality of unreported parts of the messages after reporting malicious parts. Chen and Tang [6] introduced targeted opening committing authenticated encryption with associated data (TOCE), which allows the receiver to report only the abusive parts of the messages for verification.

Huguenin-Dumittan and Leontiadis [17] introduced message franking channel, which is resistant to replay attacks, out-of-order delivery and message drops.

They provided a construction of a message franking channel using a CAEAD scheme and a MAC scheme.

Tyagi, Grubbs, Len, Miers, and Ristenpart [21] introduced asymmetric message franking (AMF) to achieve content moderation under the condition that the sender and receiver identities are hidden from the service providers. They provided a construction of an AMF scheme using an applied technique of a designated verifier signature scheme.

2   Preliminaries

2.1   Notation

For a positive integer n, we write $[n]$ to denote the set $\{1, \cdots, n\}$. For a finite set X, we write $x \xleftarrow{\$} X$ to denote sampling x from X uniformly at random and $|X|$ to denote the cardinality of X. For a string x, we write $|x|$ to denote the length of x. For an algorithm $\mathcal{A}$, we write $y \leftarrow \mathcal{A}(x)$ to denote running $\mathcal{A}$ on the input x to produce the output y. λ denotes a security parameter. A function $f(\lambda)$ is a negligible function if $f(\lambda)$ tends to 0 faster than $\frac{1}{\lambda^c}$ for every constant $c > 0$. $\mathsf{negl}(\lambda)$ denotes an unspecified negligible function.

2.2   Forward Secure Pseudorandom Generator

Definition 1 (Stateful Pseudorandom Generator [4]). *A stateful pseudorandom generator* $\mathsf{sPRG} = (\mathsf{Key}, \mathsf{Next})$ *is a tuple of two algorithms associated with a state space* $\mathcal{ST}$ *and a block space* $\mathcal{OUT}$ *defined as follows.*

- $St_0 \leftarrow \mathsf{Key}(1^\lambda, n)$: *The key generation algorithm* Key *takes as input a security parameter* 1^λ *and the total number of time periods* n *and outputs the initial state* St_0.
- $(Out_i, St_i) \leftarrow \mathsf{Next}(St_{i-1})$: *The next step algorithm* Next *takes as input the current state* St_{i-1} *and outputs a output block* Out_i *and the next state* St_i.

Definition 2 (Forward Security). *Let* $n \geq 1$ *be any integer. For a stateful pseudorandom generator* $\mathsf{sPRG} = (\mathsf{Key}, \mathsf{Next})$, *we define the forward security game between a challenger* $\mathcal{CH}$ *and an adversary* $\mathcal{A}$ *as follows.*

1. $\mathcal{CH}$ *generates* $St_0 \leftarrow \mathsf{Key}(1^\lambda, n)$, *sets* $i := 0$, *and chooses* $b \xleftarrow{\$} \{0,1\}$.
2. $\mathcal{CH}$ *sets* $i := i + 1$. *Depending on the value of* b, $\mathcal{CH}$ *proceeds as follows.*
   - *If* $b = 1$, $\mathcal{CH}$ *computes* $(Out_i, St_i) \leftarrow \mathsf{Next}(St_{i-1})$ *and sends* Out_i *to* $\mathcal{A}$.
   - *If* $b = 0$, $\mathcal{CH}$ *computes* $(Out'_i, St_i) \leftarrow \mathsf{Next}(St_{i-1})$ *and* $Out_i \xleftarrow{\$} \{0,1\}^\lambda$ *sends* Out_i *to* $\mathcal{A}$.
3. $\mathcal{A}$ *outputs* $d \in \{0,1\}$.
4. *If* $d = 1$ *or* $i = n$, $\mathcal{CH}$ *proceeds to the next Step, else repeats Steps 2 and 3.*
5. $\mathcal{CH}$ *sends* St_i *to* $\mathcal{A}$.
6. $\mathcal{A}$ *outputs* $b' \in \{0,1\}$.

In this game, we define the advantage of the adversary $\mathcal{A}$ as

$$\mathsf{Adv}_{\mathsf{sPRG},\mathcal{A}}^{\mathsf{FS\text{-}PRG}}(\lambda) := \left| \Pr[b' = b] - \frac{1}{2} \right|.$$

We say that sPRG is forward secure if for any PPT adversary $\mathcal{A}$, we have $\mathsf{Adv}_{\mathsf{sPRG},\mathcal{A}}^{\mathsf{FS\text{-}PRG}}(\lambda) = \mathsf{negl}(\lambda)$.

2.3 Forward Secure Message Authentication Code

Definition 3 (Key-Evolving Message Authentication Code [4]). *A key-evolving message authentication code scheme $\mathsf{FSMAC} = (\mathsf{Gen}, \mathsf{Upd}, \mathsf{Tag}, \mathsf{Ver})$ is a tuple of four algorithms associated with a key space $\mathcal{K}$, a message space $\mathcal{M}$, and a tag space $\mathcal{T}$ defined as follows.*

- $\mathsf{K}_0 \leftarrow \mathsf{Gen}(1^\lambda, n)$: *The key generation algorithm* Gen *takes as input a security parameter 1^λ and the total number of time period n and outputs the initial secret key K_0.*
- $\mathsf{K}_i \leftarrow \mathsf{Upd}(K_{i-1})$: *The key update algorithm* Upd *takes as input the current secret key K_{i-1} and outputs the next secret key K_i.*
- $(\tau, i) \leftarrow \mathsf{Tag}(\mathsf{K}_i, M)$: *The tagging algorithm* Tag *takes as input the current secret key K_i and a message M and outputs a tag τ and the current time period i.*
- $b \leftarrow \mathsf{Ver}(\mathsf{K}_i, M, (\tau, \hat{i}))$: *The verification algorithm* Ver *takes as input the current tagging key K_i, a message M, and a pair of a tag and a time period $(\tau, \hat{i})$ and outputs a bit b, with 1 meaning accept and 0 meaning reject.*

As the correctness, we require that for any $n, \lambda \in \mathbb{N}$, $M \in \mathcal{M}$, $\mathsf{K}_0 \leftarrow \mathsf{Gen}(1^\lambda, n)$, and $\mathsf{K}_i \leftarrow \mathsf{Upd}(K_{i-1})$ for $i = 1, \cdots, n$, $\mathsf{Ver}(\mathsf{K}_{\hat{i}}, M, \mathsf{Tag}(\mathsf{K}_{\hat{i}}, M)) = 1$ holds for all $\hat{i} \in [n]$.

Definition 4 (FS-sEUF-CMA Security). *Let $n \geq 1$ be some integer. For a key-evolving MAC scheme FSMAC, we define the forward secure strong existentially unforgeability under adaptive chosen message attack (FS-sEUF-CMA security) game between a challenger $\mathcal{CH}$ and an adversary $\mathcal{A}$ as follows.*

1. *$\mathcal{CH}$ generates $\mathsf{K}_0 \leftarrow \mathsf{Gen}(1^\lambda, n)$ and sets $i := 0$ and $S_t := \emptyset$ for all $t \in [n]$.*
2. *$\mathcal{CH}$ sets $i := i + 1$ and computes $\mathsf{K}_i \leftarrow \mathsf{Upd}(\mathsf{K}_{i-1})$.*
3. *$\mathcal{A}$ is allowed to make tagging queries. On tagging queries M, $\mathcal{CH}$ computes $(\tau, i) \leftarrow \mathsf{Tag}(\mathsf{K}_i, M)$, gives (τ, i) to $\mathcal{A}$, and appends $(M, (\tau, i))$ to S_i.*
4. *$\mathcal{A}$ outputs $d \in \{0, 1\}$.*
5. *If $d = 1$ or $i = n$, $\mathcal{CH}$ proceeds to the next Step, else repeats Steps 2 through 4.*
6. *$\mathcal{CH}$ sends K_i to $\mathcal{A}$.*
7. *$\mathcal{A}$ outputs $(M^*, (\tau^*, i^*))$.*

In this game, we define the advantage of the adversary $\mathcal{A}$ as

$$\mathsf{Adv}_{\mathsf{FSMAC},\mathcal{A}}^{\mathsf{FS\text{-}sEUF\text{-}CMA}}(\lambda) :=$$

$$\Pr[\mathsf{Ver}(\mathsf{K}_{i^*}, M^*, (\tau^*, i^*)) = 1 \wedge (M^*, (\tau^*, i^*)) \notin S_{i^*} \wedge 1 \leq i^* < i].$$

We say that FSMAC *is* $\mathsf{FS\text{-}sEUF\text{-}CMA}$ *secure if for any PPT adversary* $\mathcal{A}$, *we have* $\mathsf{Adv}_{\mathsf{FSMAC},\mathcal{A}}^{\mathsf{FS\text{-}sEUF\text{-}CMA}}(\lambda) = \mathsf{negl}(\lambda)$.

2.4   Committing Authenticated Encryption with Associated Data

Definition 5 (Committing Authenticated Encryption with Associated Data [13]). *A committing authenticated encryption with associated data (CAEAD) scheme* $\mathsf{CAEAD} = (\mathsf{Gen}, \mathsf{Enc}, \mathsf{Dec}, \mathsf{Ver})$ *is a tuple of four algorithms associated with a key space* $\mathcal{K}$, *a header space* $\mathcal{H}$, *a message space* $\mathcal{M}$, *an opening space* $\mathcal{O}$, *a ciphertext space* $\mathcal{C}$, *and a franking tag space* $\mathcal{B}$ *defined as follows.*

- $\mathsf{K} \leftarrow \mathsf{Gen}(1^\lambda)$: *The key generation algorithm* Gen *takes as input a security parameter* 1^λ *and outputs a secret key* K.
- $(C_1, C_2) \leftarrow \mathsf{Enc}(\mathsf{K}, H, M)$: *The encryption algorithm* Enc *takes as input a secret key* K, *a header* H, *and a message* M *and outputs a ciphertext* C_1 *and a franking tag* C_2.
- $(M', O) \leftarrow \mathsf{Dec}(\mathsf{K}, H, C_1, C_2)$: *The decryption algorithm* Dec *takes as input a secret key* K, *a header* H, *a ciphertext* C_1, *and a franking tag* C_2 *and outputs a message* M' *and an opening* O.
- $b \leftarrow \mathsf{Ver}(H, M, O, C_2)$: *The verification algorithm* Ver *takes as input a header* H, *a message* M, *an opening* O, *and a franking tag* C_2 *and outputs a bit* b, *with 1 meaning accept and 0 meaning reject.*

As the correctness, we require that for any $n, \lambda \in \mathbb{N}$, $M \in \mathcal{M}$, $H \in \mathcal{H}$, $\mathsf{K} \leftarrow \mathsf{Gen}(1^\lambda)$, $(C_1, C_2) \leftarrow \mathsf{Enc}(\mathsf{K}, H, M)$, *and* $(M', O) \leftarrow \mathsf{Dec}(\mathsf{K}, H, C_1, C_2)$, $M' = M$ *and* $\mathsf{Ver}(H, M', O, C_2) = 1$ *holds.*

Definition 6 (MO-IND Security). *For a CAEAD scheme* CAEAD, *we define the multiple-opening indistinguishability (MO-IND security) game between a challenger* $\mathcal{CH}$ *and an adversary* $\mathcal{A}$ *as follows.*

1. $\mathcal{CH}$ *generates* $\mathsf{K} \leftarrow \mathsf{Gen}(1^\lambda)$ *and sets* $S := \emptyset$.
2. $\mathcal{A}$ *is allowed to make encryption queries and decryption queries as follows.*
   - *On encryption queries of the form* (H, M), $\mathcal{CH}$ *computes* $(C_1, C_2) \leftarrow \mathsf{Enc}(\mathsf{K}, H, M)$, *gives* (C_1, C_2) *to* $\mathcal{A}$, *and appends* (H, C_1, C_2) *to* S.
   - *On decryption queries of the form* (H, C_1, C_2), *if* $(H, C_1, C_2) \notin S$, $\mathcal{CH}$ *gives* $\perp$ *to* $\mathcal{A}$. *Otherwise,* $\mathcal{CH}$ *computes* $(M', O) \leftarrow \mathsf{Dec}(\mathsf{K}, H, C_1, C_2)$ *and gives* (M', O) *to* $\mathcal{A}$.
3. $\mathcal{A}$ *sends* (H^*, M_0^*, M_1^*) *to* $\mathcal{CH}$, *where* $|M_0^*| = |M_1^*|$.
4. $\mathcal{CH}$ *chooses a challenge bit* $b \xleftarrow{\$} \{0, 1\}$, *computes* $(C_1^*, C_2^*) \leftarrow \mathsf{Enc}(\mathsf{K}, H^*, M_b^*)$ *and sends* (C_1^*, C_2^*) *to* $\mathcal{A}$.

5. $\mathcal{A}$ is allowed to make the same encryption and decryption queries as with Step 2 except that (H^*, C_1^*, C_2^*) cannot be queried in the decryption query.
6. $\mathcal{A}$ outputs $b' \in \{0, 1\}$.

In this game, we define the advantage of the adversary $\mathcal{A}$ as

$$\mathsf{Adv}_{\mathsf{CAEAD}, \mathcal{A}}^{\mathsf{MO\text{-}IND}}(\lambda) := \left| \Pr[b' = b] - \frac{1}{2} \right|.$$

We say that CAEAD is MO-IND secure if for any PPT adversary $\mathcal{A}$, we have $\mathsf{Adv}_{\mathsf{CAEAD}, \mathcal{A}}^{\mathsf{MO\text{-}IND}}(\lambda) = \mathsf{negl}(\lambda)$.

Remark 1. While Grubbs et al. [13] used the definition which guarantees that ciphertexts cannot be distinguished from random strings, our definition ensures that, for the two messages outputed by the adversary, it is hard to identify which message the received ciphertext is generated from. Similar to [6], we can construct a CAEAD scheme satisfying MO-IND security from an authenticated encryption with associated data (AEAD) scheme and a commitment scheme.

Definition 7 (MO-CTXT Security). *For a CAEAD scheme* CAEAD, *we define the multiple-opening ciphertext integrity* (MO-CTXT *security*) *game between a challenger* $\mathcal{CH}$ *and an adversary* $\mathcal{A}$ *as follows.*

1. $\mathcal{CH}$ generates $\mathsf{K} \leftarrow \mathsf{Gen}(1^\lambda)$ and sets $S := \emptyset$.
2. $\mathcal{A}$ is allowed to make encryption queries and decryption queries as follows.
   - On encryption queries of the form (H, M), $\mathcal{CH}$ computes $(C_1, C_2) \leftarrow \mathsf{Enc}(\mathsf{K}, H, M)$, gives (C_1, C_2) to $\mathcal{A}$, and appends (H, C_1, C_2) to S.
   - On decryption queries of the form (H, C_1, C_2), $\mathcal{CH}$ computes $(M', O) \leftarrow \mathsf{Dec}(\mathsf{K}, H, C_1, C_2)$ and gives (M', O) to $\mathcal{A}$.
3. $\mathcal{A}$ outputs (H^*, C_1^*, C_2^*).

In this game, we define the advantage of the adversary $\mathcal{A}$ as

$$\mathsf{Adv}_{\mathsf{CAEAD}, \mathcal{A}}^{\mathsf{MO\text{-}CTXT}}(\lambda) := \Pr[M^* \neq \perp \wedge (H^*, C_1^*, C_2^*) \notin S :$$
$$(M^*, O^*) \leftarrow \mathsf{Dec}(\mathsf{K}, H^*, C_1^*, C_2^*)].$$

We say that CAEAD is MO-CTXT secure if for any PPT adversary $\mathcal{A}$, we have $\mathsf{Adv}_{\mathsf{CAEAD}, \mathcal{A}}^{\mathsf{MO\text{-}CTXT}}(\lambda) = \mathsf{negl}(\lambda)$.

Definition 8 (R-BIND Security). *We say that a CAEAD scheme* CAEAD *satisfies the receiver binding* (R-BIND *security*) *if for any* $(H, M) \neq (H', M')$, $\mathsf{Ver}(H, M, O, C_2^*) = \mathsf{Ver}(H', M', O', C_2^*) = 1$ *never holds.*

Definition 9 (S-BIND Security). *We say that a CAEAD scheme* CAEAD *satisfies the sender binding* (S-BIND *security*) *if for any* $K \in \mathcal{K}$, $H \in \mathcal{H}$, $C_1 \in \mathcal{C}$, $C_2 \in \mathcal{B}$, *and* $(M', O) \leftarrow \mathsf{Dec}(\mathsf{K}, H, C_1, C_2)$, $\mathsf{Ver}(H, M', O, C_2) = 0$ *and* $M' \neq \perp$ *never holds.*

3   Forward Secure Message Franking

In this section, we introduce forward secure message franking. First, in Sect. 3.1, we define the syntax and its correctness of key-evolving message franking. Then, in Sect. 3.2, we provide forward security definitions for key-evolving message franking.

3.1   Syntax

In this section, we provide the syntax of a key-evolving message franking scheme. A key-evolving message franking scheme includes two additional algorithms for updating a secret key and a tagging key asynchronously.

Definition 10 (Key-Evolving Message Franking). *A key-evolving message franking scheme* FSMF *is a tuple of eight algorithms* (SKGen, TKGen, SKUpd, TKUpd, Enc, Tag, Dec, Ver) *associated with a secret key space* $\mathcal{SK}$, *a tagging key space* $\mathcal{TK}$ *a header space* $\mathcal{H}$, *a message space* $\mathcal{M}$, *an opening space* $\mathcal{O}$, *a ciphertext space* $\mathcal{C}$, *a franking tag space* $\mathcal{B}$, *and a reporting tag space* $\mathcal{T}$ *defined as follow.*

- $\mathsf{SK}_0 \leftarrow \mathsf{SKGen}(1^\lambda, n)$: *The secret key generation algorithm* SKGen *takes as input a security parameter* 1^λ *and the total number of time periods* n *and outputs the initial secret key* SK_0.
- $\mathsf{TK}_0 \leftarrow \mathsf{TKGen}(1^\lambda, n)$: *The tagging key generation algorithm* TKGen *takes as input a security parameter* 1^λ *and the total number of time periods* n *and outputs the initial tagging key* TK_0.
- $\mathsf{SK}_i \leftarrow \mathsf{SKUpd}(\mathsf{SK}_{i-1})$: *The secret key update algorithm* SKUpd *takes as input the current secret key* SK_{i-1} *and outputs the next secret key* SK_i.
- $\mathsf{TK}_j \leftarrow \mathsf{TKUpd}(\mathsf{TK}_{j-1})$: *The tagging key update algorithm* TKUpd *takes as input the current tagging key* TK_{j-1} *and outputs the next tagging key* TK_j.
- $(C_1, C_2, i) \leftarrow \mathsf{Enc}(\mathsf{SK}_i, H, M)$: *The encryption algorithm* Enc *takes as input the current secret key* SK_i, *a header* H, *and a message* M *and outputs a ciphertext* C_1, *a franking tag* C_2, *and the current time period* i.
- $(\tau, j) \leftarrow \mathsf{Tag}(\mathsf{TK}_j, C_2)$: *The tagging algorithm* Tag *takes as input the current tagging key* TK_j *and a franking tag* C_2 *and outputs a reporting tag* τ *and the current time period* j.
- $(M', O) \leftarrow \mathsf{Dec}(\mathsf{SK}_i, H, (C_1, C_2, \hat{i}))$: *The decryption algorithm* Dec *takes as input the current secret key* SK_i, *a header* H, *and a tuple of a ciphertext, a franking tag, and a time period* $(C_1, C_2, \hat{i})$ *and outputs a message* M' *and an opening* O.
- $b \leftarrow \mathsf{Ver}(\mathsf{TK}_j, H, M, O, C_2, (\tau, \hat{j}))$: *The verification algorithm* Ver *takes as input the current tagging key* TK_j, *a header* H, *a message* M, *an opening* O, *a franking tag* C_2, *and a pair of a reporting tag and a time period* $(\tau, \hat{j})$ *and outputs a bit* b, *with* 1 *meaning accept and* 0 *meaning reject.*

As the correctness, we require that for any $n, \lambda \in \mathbb{N}$, $M \in \mathcal{M}$, $H \in \mathcal{H}$, $\mathsf{SK}_0 \leftarrow \mathsf{SKGen}(1^\lambda, n)$, $\mathsf{TK}_0 \leftarrow \mathsf{TKGen}(1^\lambda, n)$, $\mathsf{SK}_i \leftarrow \mathsf{SKUpd}(\mathsf{SK}_{i-1})$, $\mathsf{TK}_j \leftarrow \mathsf{TKUpd}(\mathsf{TK}_{j-1})$ for $i, j = 1, \cdots, n$, $(C_1, C_2, \hat{i}) \leftarrow \mathsf{Enc}(\mathsf{SK}_{\hat{i}}, H, M)$, $(\tau, \hat{j}) \leftarrow \mathsf{Tag}(\mathsf{TK}_{\hat{j}}, C_2)$, and $(M', O) \leftarrow \mathsf{Dec}(\mathsf{SK}_{\hat{i}}, H, (C_1, C_2, \hat{i}))$, $M' = M$ and $\mathsf{Ver}(\mathsf{TK}_{\hat{j}}, H, M', O, C_2, (\tau, \hat{j})) = 1$ holds for all $\hat{i}, \hat{j} \in [n]$.

3.2 Security Definitions

In this section, we define forward security for five security notions: confidentiality, ciphertext integrity, unforgeability, receiver binding, and sender binding.

Confidentiality. Intuitively, confidentiality guarantees that the information of the messages is not leaked from the corresponding ciphertexts. More formally, we require that adversaries with the information of the current secret key cannot distinguish ciphertexts generated by the past secret key. We apply multiple-opening (MO) security [13] to confidentiality. MO security ensures that multiple ciphertexts, encrypted under the same secret key, whose opening is known do not endanger the security of other ciphertexts whose opening is not known. In MO security, the adversaries can make decryption queries in addition to encryption queries to learn the openings of the ciphertexts generated via encryption queries.

Definition 11 (FS-MO-IND Security). *Let $n \geq 1$ be some integer. For a key-evolving message franking scheme FSMF, we define the forward secure multiple-opening indistinguishability (FS-MO-IND security) game between a challenger $\mathcal{CH}$ and an adversary $\mathcal{A}$ as follows.*

1. *$\mathcal{CH}$ generates $\mathsf{SK}_0 \leftarrow \mathsf{SKGen}(1^\lambda, n)$ and sets $i := 0$ and $S_t := \emptyset$ for all $t \in [n]$.*
2. *$\mathcal{CH}$ sets $i := i + 1$ and computes $\mathsf{SK}_i \leftarrow \mathsf{SKUpd}(\mathsf{SK}_{i-1})$.*
3. *$\mathcal{A}$ is allowed to make encryption queries and decryption queries as follows.*
   - *On encryption queries of the form (H, M), $\mathcal{CH}$ computes $(C_1, C_2, i) \leftarrow \mathsf{Enc}(\mathsf{SK}_i, H, M)$, gives (C_1, C_2, i) to $\mathcal{A}$, and appends $(H, (C_1, C_2, i))$ to S_i.*
   - *On decryption queries of the form $(H, (C_1, C_2, \hat{i}))$, if $(H, (C_1, C_2, \hat{i})) \notin S_i$, $\mathcal{CH}$ gives $\perp$ to $\mathcal{A}$. Otherwise, $\mathcal{CH}$ computes $(M', O) \leftarrow \mathsf{Dec}(\mathsf{SK}_i, H, (C_1, C_2, \hat{i}))$ and gives (M', O) to $\mathcal{A}$.*
4. *$\mathcal{A}$ sends $(d, H^*, M_0^*, M_1^*, i^*)$ to $\mathcal{CH}$, where $|M_0^*| = |M_1^*|$.*
5. *If $d = 1$ or $i = n$, $\mathcal{CH}$ proceeds to the next Step, else repeats Steps 2 through 4.*
6. *$\mathcal{CH}$ chooses a challenge bit $b \xleftarrow{\$} \{0, 1\}$. If $i^* \geq i$, $\mathcal{CH}$ chooses $b' \xleftarrow{\$} \{0, 1\}$ and terminates. Otherwise, $\mathcal{CH}$ computes $(C_1^*, C_2^*, i^*) \leftarrow \mathsf{Enc}(\mathsf{SK}_{i^*}, H^*, M_b^*)$ and sends $(\mathsf{SK}_i, (C_1^*, C_2^*, i^*))$ to $\mathcal{A}$.*
7. *$\mathcal{A}$ outputs $b' \in \{0, 1\}$.*

In this game, we define the advantage of the adversary $\mathcal{A}$ as

$$\mathsf{Adv}_{\mathsf{FSMF}, \mathcal{A}}^{\mathsf{FS\text{-}MO\text{-}IND}}(\lambda) := \left| \Pr[b' = b] - \frac{1}{2} \right|.$$

We say that FSMF is FS-MO-IND secure if for any PPT adversary $\mathcal{A}$, we have $\mathsf{Adv}_{\mathsf{FSMF}, \mathcal{A}}^{\mathsf{FS\text{-}MO\text{-}IND}}(\lambda) = \mathsf{negl}(\lambda)$.

Ciphertext Integrity. Intuitively, ciphertext integrity guarantees that ciphertexts are not tampered with. More formally, we require that adversaries with the information of the current secret key cannot generate a new ciphertext which is correctly decrypted by the past secret key. Similar to the above confidentiality, we apply the MO security to ciphertext integrity.

Definition 12 (FS-MO-CTXT Security). *Let $n \geq 1$ be some integer. For a key-evolving message franking scheme FSMF, we define the forward secure multiple-opening ciphertext integrity (FS-MO-CTXT security) game between a challenger $\mathcal{CH}$ and an adversary $\mathcal{A}$ as follows.*

1. *$\mathcal{CH}$ generates $\mathsf{SK}_0 \leftarrow \mathsf{SKGen}(1^\lambda, n)$ and sets $i := 0$ and $S_t := \emptyset$ for all $t \in [n]$.*
2. *$\mathcal{CH}$ sets $i := i + 1$ and computes $\mathsf{SK}_i \leftarrow \mathsf{SKUpd}(\mathsf{SK}_{i-1})$.*
3. *$\mathcal{A}$ is allowed to make encryption queries and decryption queries as follows.*
   - *On encryption queries of the form (H, M), $\mathcal{CH}$ computes $(C_1, C_2, i) \leftarrow \mathsf{Enc}(\mathsf{SK}_i, H, M)$, gives (C_1, C_2, i) to $\mathcal{A}$, and appends $(H, (C_1, C_2, i))$ to S_i.*
   - *On decryption queries of the form $(H, (C_1, C_2, \hat{i}))$, $\mathcal{CH}$ computes $(M', O) \leftarrow \mathsf{Dec}(\mathsf{SK}_i, H, (C_1, C_2, \hat{i}))$ and gives (M', O) to $\mathcal{A}$.*
4. *$\mathcal{A}$ outputs $d \in \{0, 1\}$.*
5. *If $d = 1$ or $i = n$, $\mathcal{CH}$ proceeds to the next Step, else repeats Steps 2 through 4.*
6. *$\mathcal{CH}$ sends SK_i to $\mathcal{A}$.*
7. *$\mathcal{A}$ outputs $(H^*, (C_1^*, C_2^*, i^*))$.*

In this game, we define the advantage of the adversary $\mathcal{A}$ as

$$\mathsf{Adv}_{\mathsf{FSMF},\mathcal{A}}^{\mathrm{FS\text{-}MO\text{-}CTXT}}(\lambda) := \Pr[M^* \neq \perp \wedge (H^*, (C_1^*, C_2^*, i^*)) \notin S_{i^*} \wedge 1 \leq i^* < i :$$
$$(M^*, O^*) \leftarrow \mathsf{Dec}(\mathsf{SK}_{i^*}, H^*, (C_1^*, C_2^*, i^*))].$$

We say that FSMF is FS-MO-CTXT secure if for any PPT adversary $\mathcal{A}$, we have $\mathsf{Adv}_{\mathsf{FSMF},\mathcal{A}}^{\mathrm{FS\text{-}MO\text{-}CTXT}}(\lambda) = \mathsf{negl}(\lambda)$.

Unforgeability. Intuitively, unforgeability guarantees that reporting tags are not forged. More formally, we require that adversaries with the information of the current tagging key cannot generate a new reporting tag which is successfully verified by the past tagging key.

Definition 13 (FS-UNF Security). *Let $n \geq 1$ be some integer. For a key-evolving message franking scheme FSMF, we define the forward secure unforgeability (FS-UNF security) game between a challenger $\mathcal{CH}$ and an adversary $\mathcal{A}$ as follows.*

1. *$\mathcal{CH}$ generates $\mathsf{TK}_0 \leftarrow \mathsf{TKGen}(1^\lambda, n)$ and sets $j := 0$ and $S_t := \emptyset$ for all $t \in [n]$.*
2. *$\mathcal{CH}$ sets $j := j + 1$ and computes $\mathsf{TK}_j \leftarrow \mathsf{TKUpd}(\mathsf{TK}_{j-1})$.*
3. *$\mathcal{A}$ is allowed to make tagging queries. On tagging queries C_2, $\mathcal{CH}$ computes $(\tau, j) \leftarrow \mathsf{Tag}(\mathsf{TK}_j, C_2)$, gives (τ, j) to $\mathcal{A}$, and appends $(C_2, (\tau, j))$ to S_j.*
4. *$\mathcal{A}$ outputs $d \in \{0, 1\}$.*

5. If $d = 1$ or $j = n$, $\mathcal{CH}$ proceeds to the next Step, else repeats Steps 2 through 4.
6. $\mathcal{CH}$ sends TK_j to $\mathcal{A}$.
7. $\mathcal{A}$ outputs $(H^*, M^*, O^*, C_2^*, (\tau^*, j^*))$.

In this game, we define the advantage of the adversary $\mathcal{A}$ as

$$\mathsf{Adv}_{\mathsf{FSMF},\mathcal{A}}^{\mathsf{FS\text{-}UNF}}(\lambda) := \Pr[\mathsf{Ver}(\mathsf{TK}_{j^*}, H^*, M^*, O^*, C_2^*, (\tau^*, j^*)) = 1$$
$$\wedge \, (C_2^*, (\tau^*, j^*)) \notin S_{j^*} \wedge 1 \le j^* < j].$$

We say that FSMF is FS-UNF secure if for any PPT adversary $\mathcal{A}$, we have $\mathsf{Adv}_{\mathsf{FSMF},\mathcal{A}}^{\mathsf{FS\text{-}UNF}}(\lambda) = \mathsf{negl}(\lambda)$.

Receiver Binding. Intuitively, receiver binding guarantees that the receiver is not able to report messages which were not actually sent. More formally, we require that adversaries with the information of the current tagging key cannot generate two messages successfully verified by the past tagging key for a pair of franking tag and reporting tag.

Definition 14 (FS-R-BIND Security). *Let $n \ge 1$ be some integer. For a key-evolving message franking scheme FSMF, we define the forward secure receiver binding (FS-R-BIND security) game between a challenger $\mathcal{CH}$ and an adversary $\mathcal{A}$ as follows.*

1. $\mathcal{CH}$ generates $\mathsf{TK}_0 \leftarrow \mathsf{TKGen}(1^\lambda, n)$ and sets $j := 0$.
2. $\mathcal{CH}$ sets $j := j + 1$ and computes $\mathsf{TK}_j \leftarrow \mathsf{TKUpd}(\mathsf{TK}_{j-1})$.
3. $\mathcal{A}$ is allowed to make tagging queries. On tagging queries of C_2, $\mathcal{CH}$ computes $(\tau, j) \leftarrow \mathsf{Tag}(\mathsf{TK}_j, C_2)$ and gives (τ, j) to $\mathcal{A}$.
4. $\mathcal{A}$ outputs $d \in \{0, 1\}$.
5. If $d = 1$ or $j = n$, $\mathcal{CH}$ proceeds to the next Step, else repeats Steps 2 through 4.
6. $\mathcal{CH}$ sends TK_j to $\mathcal{A}$.
7. $\mathcal{A}$ outputs $((H, M, O), (H', M', O'), C_2^*, (\tau^*, j^*))$.

In this game, we define the advantage of the adversary $\mathcal{A}$ as

$$\mathsf{Adv}_{\mathsf{FSMF},\mathcal{A}}^{\mathsf{FS\text{-}R\text{-}BIND}}(\lambda) := \Pr[\mathsf{Ver}(\mathsf{TK}_{j^*}, H, M, O, C_2^*, (\tau^*, j^*)) = \mathsf{Ver}(\mathsf{TK}_{j^*}, H', M', O',$$
$$C_2^*, (\tau^*, j^*)) = 1 \wedge (H, M) \ne (H', M') \wedge 1 \le j^* < j].$$

We say that FSMF is FS-R-BIND secure if for any PPT adversary $\mathcal{A}$, we have $\mathsf{Adv}_{\mathsf{FSMF},\mathcal{A}}^{\mathsf{FS\text{-}R\text{-}BIND}}(\lambda) = \mathsf{negl}(\lambda)$.

Sender Binding. Intuitively, sender binding guarantees that the sender is not able to send malicious messages that cannot be reported. More formally, we require that adversaries with the information of the current tagging key cannot generate a ciphertext that are correctly decrypted but fail to verify by the past tagging key.

Definition 15 (FS-S-BIND Security). *Let $n \geq 1$ be some integer. For a key-evolving message franking scheme FSMF, we define the forward secure sender binding (FS-S-BIND security) game between a challenger $\mathcal{CH}$ and an adversary $\mathcal{A}$ as follows.*

1. *$\mathcal{CH}$ generates $\mathsf{TK}_0 \leftarrow \mathsf{TKGen}(1^\lambda, n)$ and sets $j := 0$.*
2. *$\mathcal{CH}$ sets $j := j + 1$ and computes $\mathsf{TK}_j \leftarrow \mathsf{TKUpd}(\mathsf{TK}_{j-1})$.*
3. *$\mathcal{A}$ is allowed to make tagging queries. On tagging queries of C_2, $\mathcal{CH}$ computes $(\tau, j) \leftarrow \mathsf{Tag}(\mathsf{TK}_j, C_2)$ and gives (τ, j) to $\mathcal{A}$.*
4. *$\mathcal{A}$ outputs $d \in \{0, 1\}$.*
5. *If $d = 1$ or $j = n$, $\mathcal{CH}$ proceeds to the next Step, else repeats Steps 2 through 4.*
6. *$\mathcal{CH}$ sends TK_j to $\mathcal{A}$.*
7. *$\mathcal{A}$ outputs $(j^*, \mathsf{SK}_i, H, (C_1, C_2, \hat{i}))$.*
8. *$\mathcal{CH}$ computes $(\tau, j^*) \leftarrow \mathsf{Tag}(\mathsf{TK}_{j^*}, C_2)$ and $(M', O) \leftarrow \mathsf{Dec}(\mathsf{SK}_i, H, (C_1, C_2, \hat{i}))$.*

In this game, we define the advantage of the adversary $\mathcal{A}$ as

$$\mathsf{Adv}^{\mathrm{FS\text{-}S\text{-}BIND}}_{\mathsf{FSMF}, \mathcal{A}}(\lambda) :=$$
$$\Pr[\mathsf{Ver}(\mathsf{TK}_{j^*}, H, M', O, C_2, (\tau, j^*)) = 0 \wedge M' \neq \bot \wedge 1 \leq j^* < j].$$

We say that FSMF is FS-S-BIND secure if for any PPT adversary $\mathcal{A}$, we have $\mathsf{Adv}^{\mathrm{FS\text{-}S\text{-}BIND}}_{\mathsf{FSMF}, \mathcal{A}}(\lambda) = \mathsf{negl}(\lambda)$.

4   Construction of Key-Evolving Message Franking

In this section, we show our construction of a key-evolving message franking scheme. First, in Sect. 4.1, we provide the formal description of our construction. Then, in Sect. 4.2, we give security proofs for our construction.

4.1   Construction

Let $\mathsf{sPRG} = (\mathsf{sPRG.Key}, \mathsf{sPRG.Next})$ be a stateful generator, $\mathsf{FSMAC} = (\mathsf{FSMAC.Gen}, \mathsf{FSMAC.Upd}, \mathsf{FSMAC.Tag}, \mathsf{FSMAC.Ver})$ a key-evolving MAC scheme, and $\mathsf{CAEAD} = (\mathsf{CAEAD.Gen}, \mathsf{CAEAD.Enc}, \mathsf{CAEAD.Dec}, \mathsf{CAEAD.Ver})$ a CAEAD scheme. We assume that outputs of sPRG can be used as secret keys of CAEAD. From these, we construct our key-evolving message franking scheme $\mathsf{FSMF} = (\mathsf{SKGen}, \mathsf{TKGen}, \mathsf{SKUpd}, \mathsf{TKUpd}, \mathsf{Enc}, \mathsf{Tag}, \mathsf{Dec}, \mathsf{Ver})$ in Fig. 1.

The correctness of the scheme immediately follows from the correctness of CAEAD and FSMAC.

SKGen($1^\lambda, n$)	TKGen($1^\lambda, n$)
$St_0 \leftarrow$ sPRG.Key($1^\lambda, n$)	$TK_0 \leftarrow$ FSMAC.Gen($1^\lambda, n$)
Output $SK_0 = (0, \epsilon, St_0)$	Output TK_0
SKUpd(SK_{i-1})	TKUpd(TK_{j-1})
Parse $SK_{i-1} = (i-1, Out_{i-1}, St_{i-1})$	$TK_j \leftarrow$ FSMAC.Upd(TK_{j-1})
$(Out_i, St_i) \leftarrow$ sPRG.Next(St_{i-1})	Output TK_j
Output $SK_i = (i, Out_i, St_i)$	
Enc(SK_i, H, M)	Tag(TK_j, C_2)
Parse $SK_i = (i, Out_i, St_i)$	$(\tau, j) \leftarrow$ FSMAC.Tag(TK_j, C_2)
$(C_1, C_2) \leftarrow$ CAEAD.Enc(Out_i, H, M)	Output (τ, j)
Output (C_1, C_2, i)	
Dec($SK_i, H, (C_1, C_2, \hat{i})$)	Ver($TK_j, H, M, O, C_2, (\tau, \hat{j})$)
Parse $SK_i = (i, Out_i, St_i)$	If CAEAD.Ver(H, M, O, C_2) $= 0$
If $\hat{i} \neq i$, Output $\perp$	Output 0
else $(M', O) \leftarrow$ CAEAD.Dec(Out_i, H, C_1, C_2)	else $b \leftarrow$ FSMAC.Ver($TK_j, C_2, (\tau, \hat{j})$)
Output (M', O)	Output b

Fig. 1. Construction of key-evolving message franking scheme.

4.2 Security Proof

In this section, we show that our construction of FSMF given in Sect. 4.1 satisfies security notions defined in Sect. 3.2.

Theorem 1 (FS-MO-IND Security). *If* sPRG *satisfies forward security and* CAEAD *satisfies* MO-IND *security, then* FSMF *satisfies* FS-MO-IND *security.*

Proof. Let $\mathcal{A}$ be a PPT adversary that attacks the FS-MO-IND security of FSMF. We introduce the following games $Game_\alpha$ for $\alpha = 0, 1$.

- $Game_0$: $Game_0$ is exactly the same as the game of FS-MO-IND security.
- $Game_1$: $Game_1$ is identical to $Game_0$ except that $\mathcal{CH}$ computes $Out_i \xleftarrow{\$} \{0,1\}^\lambda$ after computing $(Out'_i, St_i) \leftarrow$ sPRG.Next(St_{i-1}).

Let G_α be the event that $\mathcal{A}$ succeeds in guessing the challenge bit in $Game_\alpha$.

Lemma 1. *There exists a PPT adversary $\mathcal{B}$ such that* $|\Pr[G_0] - \Pr[G_1]| = 2 \cdot \text{Adv}_{\text{sPRG}, \mathcal{B}}^{\text{FS-PRG}}(\lambda)$.

Proof. We construct an adversary $\mathcal{B}$ that attacks the forward security of sPRG, using the adversary $\mathcal{A}$ as follows.

1. $\mathcal{B}$ sets $i := 0$ and $S_t := \emptyset$ for all $t \in [n]$.
2. Upon receiving Out_i from $\mathcal{CH}$, $\mathcal{B}$ sets $i := i + 1$.
3. $\mathcal{B}$ answers encryption queries and decryption queries from $\mathcal{A}$ as follows.
    - On encryption queries of the form (H, M), $\mathcal{B}$ computes $(C_1, C_2) \leftarrow$ CAEAD.Enc(Out_i, H, M), returns (C_1, C_2, i) to $\mathcal{A}$, and appends $(H, (C_1, C_2, i))$ to S_i.
    - On decryption queries of the form $(H, (C_1, C_2, \hat{i}))$, if $(H, (C_1, C_2, \hat{i})) \notin S_i$, $\mathcal{B}$ returns $\perp$ to $\mathcal{A}$. Otherwise, $\mathcal{B}$ computes $(M', O) \leftarrow$ CAEAD.Dec(Out_i, H, C_1, C_2) and returns (M', O) to $\mathcal{A}$.

4. When $\mathcal{A}$ outputs $(d, H^*, M_0^*, M_1^*, i^*)$, $\mathcal{B}$ returns d to $\mathcal{CH}$.

5. $\mathcal{B}$ receives St_i from $\mathcal{CH}$, sets $\mathsf{SK}_i = (i, Out_i, St_i)$, and chooses $g \xleftarrow{\$} \{0,1\}$.

6. If $i^* \geq i$, $\mathcal{B}$ sets $b' := g$, returns b' to $\mathcal{CH}$, and terminates. Otherwise, $\mathcal{B}$ computes $(C_1^*, C_2^*) \leftarrow \mathsf{CAEAD.Enc}(Out_{i^*}, H^*, M_g^*)$ and returns $(\mathsf{SK}_i, (C_1^*, C_2^*, i^*))$ to $\mathcal{A}$.

7. When $\mathcal{A}$ outputs g', if $g' = g$, $\mathcal{B}$ sets $b' := 1$, else $b' := 0$.

8. $\mathcal{B}$ returns b' to $\mathcal{CH}$.

We can see that $\mathcal{B}$ perfectly simulates the game $Game_0$ if $b = 1$ and $Game_1$ if $b = 0$ for $\mathcal{A}$. We assume that G_α occurs. Then, $\mathcal{B}$ outputs $b' = 1$ since $\mathcal{A}$ succeeds in guessing the challenge bit g in $Game_\alpha$. Thus, $\mathsf{Adv}_{\mathsf{sPRG},\mathcal{B}}^{\mathsf{FS\text{-}PRG}}(\lambda) = \frac{1}{2} \cdot |\Pr[b' = 1|b = 1] - \Pr[b' = 1|b = 0]| = \frac{1}{2} \cdot |\Pr[G_0] - \Pr[G_1]|$ holds.   □

Lemma 2. *There exists a PPT adversary $\mathcal{D}$ such that* $|\Pr[G_1] - \frac{1}{2}| = n \cdot \mathsf{Adv}_{\mathsf{CAEAD},\mathcal{D}}^{\mathsf{MO\text{-}IND}}(\lambda)$.

Proof. We construct an adversary $\mathcal{D}$ that attacks the MO-IND security of CAEAD, using the adversary $\mathcal{A}$ as follows.

1. $\mathcal{D}$ computes $l \leftarrow [n]$ and $St_0 \leftarrow \mathsf{sPRG.Key}(1^\lambda, n)$ and sets $i := 0$ and $S_t := \emptyset$ for all $t \in [n]$.

2. $\mathcal{D}$ sets $i := i + 1$, computes $(Out_i', St_i) \leftarrow \mathsf{sPRG.Next}(St_{i-1})$ and $Out_i \xleftarrow{\$} \{0,1\}^\lambda$ and sets $\mathsf{SK}_i := (i, Out_i, St_i)$.

3. $\mathcal{D}$ answers encryption queries and decryption queries from $\mathcal{A}$ as follows.
   - If $i = l$, on encryption queries of the form (H, M), $\mathcal{D}$ makes encryption queries of the form (H, M) to $\mathcal{CH}$, gets the result (C_1, C_2), returns (C_1, C_2, i) to $\mathcal{A}$, and appends $(H, (C_1, C_2, i))$ to S_i.
     On decryption queries of the form $(H, (C_1, C_2, \hat{i}))$, if $(H, (C_1, C_2, \hat{i})) \notin S_i$, $\mathcal{D}$ returns $\perp$ to $\mathcal{A}$. Otherwise, $\mathcal{D}$ makes decryption queries of the form (H, C_1, C_2) to $\mathcal{CH}$, gets the result (M', O), and returns (M', O) to $\mathcal{A}$.
   - If $i \neq l$, on encryption queries of the form (H, M), $\mathcal{D}$ computes $(C_1, C_2) \leftarrow \mathsf{CAEAD.Enc}(Out_i, H, M)$, returns (C_1, C_2, i) to $\mathcal{A}$, and appends $(H, (C_1, C_2, i))$ to S_i.
     On decryption queries of the form $(H, (C_1, C_2, \hat{i}))$, if $(H, (C_1, C_2, \hat{i})) \notin S_i$, $\mathcal{D}$ returns $\perp$ to $\mathcal{A}$. Otherwise, $\mathcal{D}$ computes $(M', O) \leftarrow \mathsf{CAEAD.Dec}(Out_i, H, C_1, C_2)$ and returns (M', O) to $\mathcal{A}$.

4. $\mathcal{A}$ outputs $(d, H^*, M_0^*, M_1^*, i^*)$.

5. If $d = 1$ or $i = n$, $\mathcal{D}$ proceeds to the next Step, else repeats Steps 2 through 4.

6. If $i^* \neq l$, $\mathcal{D}$ chooses $b' \xleftarrow{\$} \{0,1\}$, returns b' to $\mathcal{CH}$, and terminates. Otherwise, $\mathcal{D}$ returns (H^*, M_0^*, M_1^*) to $\mathcal{CH}$.

7. $\mathcal{D}$ receives (C_1^*, C_2^*) from $\mathcal{CH}$ and returns $(\mathsf{SK}_i, (C_1^*, C_2^*, i^*))$ to $\mathcal{A}$.

8. When $\mathcal{A}$ outputs g', $\mathcal{D}$ sets $b' := g'$ and returns b' to $\mathcal{CH}$

We can see that $\mathcal{D}$ perfectly simulates the game $Game_1$ for $\mathcal{A}$. We assume that G_1 occurs and $i^* = l$ holds or $i^* \neq l$ holds and the challenge bit matches the bit chosen randomly. Then, $\mathcal{D}$ succeeds in guessing the challenge bit in MO-IND security game. Since probability of $i^* = l$ is $\frac{1}{n}$ and probability that the challenge bit matches the bit chosen randomly is $\frac{1}{2}$, $\mathsf{Adv}_{\mathsf{CAEAD},\mathcal{D}}^{\mathsf{MO\text{-}IND}}(\lambda) = \left|\left(\frac{1}{n}\Pr[G_1] + \frac{n-1}{n}\cdot\frac{1}{2}\right) - \frac{1}{2}\right| = \frac{1}{n}\cdot\left|\Pr[G_1] - \frac{1}{2}\right|$ holds. □

Combining Lemma 1 and 2, We have

$$\mathsf{Adv}_{\mathsf{FSMF},\mathcal{A}}^{\mathsf{FS\text{-}MO\text{-}IND}}(\lambda) = \left|\Pr[G_0] - \frac{1}{2}\right|$$

$$\leq |\Pr[G_0] - \Pr[G_1]| + \left|\Pr[G_1] - \frac{1}{2}\right|$$

$$= 2\cdot\mathsf{Adv}_{\mathsf{sPRG},\mathcal{B}}^{\mathsf{FS\text{-}PRG}}(\lambda) + n\cdot\mathsf{Adv}_{\mathsf{CAEAD},\mathcal{D}}^{\mathsf{MO\text{-}IND}}(\lambda),$$

which concludes the proof of Theorem 1. □

Theorem 2 (FS-MO-CTXT Security). *If sPRG satisfies forward security and CAEAD satisfies MO-CTXT security, then FSMF satisfies FS-MO-CTXT security.*

Proof. Let $\mathcal{A}$ be a PPT adversary that attacks the FS-MO-CTXT security of FSMF. We introduce the following games $Game_\alpha$ for $\alpha = 0, 1$.

- $Game_0$: $Game_0$ is exactly the same as the game of FS-MO-CTXT security.
- $Game_1$: $Game_1$ is identical to $Game_0$ except that $\mathcal{CH}$ computes $Out_i \xleftarrow{\$} \{0,1\}^\lambda$ after computing $(Out_i', St_i) \leftarrow \mathsf{sPRG.Next}(St_{i-1})$.

Let G_α be the event that $\mathcal{A}$ succeeds in outputting the tuple $(H^*, (C_1^*, C_2^*, i^*))$ satisfying
$$M^* \neq\perp, (H^*, (C_1^*, C_2^*, i^*)) \notin S_{i^*}, \text{and } 1 \leq i^* < i$$
in computing $(M^*, O^*) \leftarrow \mathsf{Dec}(\mathsf{SK}_{i^*}, H^*, (C_1^*, C_2^*, i^*))$ in $Game_\alpha$.

Lemma 3. *There exists a PPT adversary $\mathcal{B}$ such that $|\Pr[G_0] - \Pr[G_1]| = 2\cdot\mathsf{Adv}_{\mathsf{sPRG},\mathcal{B}}^{\mathsf{FS\text{-}PRG}}(\lambda)$.*

Proof. We construct an adversary $\mathcal{B}$ that attacks the forward security of sPRG, using the adversary $\mathcal{A}$ as follows.

1. $\mathcal{B}$ sets $i := 0$ and $S_t := \emptyset$ for $t = [n]$.
2. Upon receiving Out_i from $\mathcal{CH}$, $\mathcal{B}$ sets $i := i + 1$.
3. $\mathcal{B}$ answers encryption queries and decryption queries from $\mathcal{A}$ as follows.
   - On encryption queries of the form (H, M), $\mathcal{B}$ computes $(C_1, C_2) \leftarrow \mathsf{CAEAD.Enc}(Out_i, H, M)$, returns (C_1, C_2, i) to $\mathcal{A}$, and appends $(H, (C_1, C_2, i))$ to S_i.
   - On decryption queries of the form $(H, (C_1, C_2, \hat{i}))$, if $i \neq \hat{i}$, $\mathcal{B}$ returns $\perp$ to $\mathcal{A}$. Otherwise, $\mathcal{B}$ computes $(M', O) \leftarrow \mathsf{CAEAD.Dec}(Out_i, H, C_1, C_2)$ and returns (M', O) to $\mathcal{A}$.

4. When $\mathcal{A}$ outputs d, $\mathcal{B}$ returns d to $\mathcal{CH}$.
5. $\mathcal{B}$ receives St_i from $\mathcal{CH}$, sets $\mathsf{SK}_i := (i, Out_i, St_i)$, and returns SK_i to $\mathcal{A}$.
6. When $\mathcal{A}$ outputs $(H^*, (C_1^*, C_2^*, i^*))$, $\mathcal{B}$ computes $(M^*, O^*) \leftarrow \mathsf{CAEAD.Dec}(Out_{i^*}, H^*, C_1^*, C_2^*)$. If $M^* \neq \bot$, $(H^*, (C_1^*, C_2^*, i^*)) \notin S_{i^*}$, and $1 \leq i^* < i$, $\mathcal{B}$ sets $b' := 1$, else $b' := 0$.
7. $\mathcal{B}$ returns b' to $\mathcal{CH}$

We can see that $\mathcal{B}$ perfectly simulates the game $Game_0$ if $b = 1$ and $Game_1$ if $b = 0$ for $\mathcal{A}$. We assume that G_α occurs. Then, $\mathcal{B}$ outputs $b' = 1$ since $\mathcal{A}$ succeeds in outputting the tuple $(H^*, (C_1^*, C_2^*, i^*))$ satisfying

$$M^* \neq \bot, (H^*, (C_1^*, C_2^*, i^*)) \notin S_{i^*}, \text{ and } 1 \leq i^* < i$$

in computing $(M^*, O^*) \leftarrow \mathsf{Dec}(\mathsf{SK}_{i^*}, H^*, (C_1^*, C_2^*, i^*))$ in $Game_\alpha$. Thus, $\mathsf{Adv}_{\mathsf{sPRG}, \mathcal{B}}^{\mathsf{FS-PRG}}(\lambda) = \frac{1}{2} \cdot |\Pr[b' = 1 | b = 1] - \Pr[b' = 1 | b = 0]| = \frac{1}{2} \cdot |\Pr[G_0] - \Pr[G_1]|$ holds. $\qquad \square$

Lemma 4. *There exists a PPT adversary $\mathcal{D}$ such that $\Pr[G_1] = n \cdot \mathsf{Adv}_{\mathsf{CAEAD}, \mathcal{D}}^{\mathsf{MO\text{-}CTXT}}(\lambda)$.*

Proof. We construct an adversary $\mathcal{D}$ that attacks the MO-CTXT security of CAEAD, using the adversary $\mathcal{A}$ as follows.

1. $\mathcal{D}$ computes $l \leftarrow [n]$ and $St_0 \leftarrow \mathsf{sPRG.Key}(1^\lambda, n)$ and sets $i := 0$ and $S_t := \emptyset$ for all $t \in [n]$.
2. $\mathcal{D}$ sets $i := i + 1$, computes $(Out_i', St_i) \leftarrow \mathsf{sPRG.Next}(St_{i-1})$ and $Out_i \leftarrow \{0, 1\}^\lambda$, and sets $\mathsf{SK}_i := (i, Out_i, St_i)$.
3. $\mathcal{D}$ answers encryption queries and decryption queries from $\mathcal{A}$ as follows.
   - If $i = l$, on encryption queries of the form (H, M), $\mathcal{D}$ makes encryption queries of the form (H, M) to $\mathcal{CH}$, gets the result (C_1, C_2), returns (C_1, C_2, i) to $\mathcal{A}$, and appends $(H, (C_1, C_2, i))$ to S_i.
     On decryption queries of the form $(H, (C_1, C_2, \hat{i}))$, if $i \neq \hat{i}$, $\mathcal{D}$ returns $\bot$ to $\mathcal{A}$. Otherwise, $\mathcal{D}$ makes decryption queries of the form (H, C_1, C_2) to $\mathcal{CH}$, gets the result (M', O), and returns (M', O) to $\mathcal{A}$.
   - If $i \neq l$, on encryption queries of the form (H, M), $\mathcal{D}$ computes $(C_1, C_2) \leftarrow \mathsf{CAEAD.Enc}(Out_i, H, M)$, returns (C_1, C_2, i) to $\mathcal{A}$, and appends $(H, (C_1, C_2, i))$ to S_i.
     On decryption queries of the form $(H, (C_1, C_2, \hat{i}))$, if $i \neq \hat{i}$, $\mathcal{D}$ returns $\bot$ to $\mathcal{A}$. Otherwise, $\mathcal{D}$ computes $(M', O) \leftarrow \mathsf{CAEAD.Dec}(Out_i, H, C_1, C_2)$ and returns (M', O) to $\mathcal{A}$.
4. $\mathcal{A}$ outputs d.
5. If $d = 1$ or $i = n$, $\mathcal{D}$ proceeds to the next Step, else repeats Steps 2 through 4.
6. If $i \leq l$, $\mathcal{D}$ terminates, else returns SK_i to $\mathcal{A}$.
7. When $\mathcal{A}$ outputs $(H^*, (C_1^*, C_2^*, i^*))$, if $i^* = l$, $\mathcal{D}$ returns (H^*, C_1^*, C_2^*) to $\mathcal{CH}$, else terminates.

We can see that $\mathcal{D}$ perfectly simulates the game $Game_1$ for $\mathcal{A}$. We assume that G_1 occurs and $i^* = l$ holds. Then, $\mathcal{D}$ successfully outputs the tuple (H^*, C_1^*, C_2^*) satisfying

$$M^* \neq \perp \text{ and } (H^*, C_1^*, C_2^*) \notin S$$

in computing $(M^*, O) \leftarrow \mathsf{CAEAD.Dec}(\mathsf{K}, H^*, C_1^*, C_2^*)$ in MO-CTXT security game. Since probability of $i^* = l$ is $\frac{1}{n}$, $\mathsf{Adv}_{\mathsf{CAEAD},\mathcal{D}}^{\mathsf{MO\text{-}CTXT}}(\lambda) = \frac{1}{n} \cdot \Pr[G_1]$ holds. □

Combining Lemma 3 and 4, We have

$$\mathsf{Adv}_{\mathsf{FSMF},\mathcal{A}}^{\mathsf{FS\text{-}MO\text{-}CTXT}}(\lambda) = \Pr[G_0]$$

$$\leq |\Pr[G_0] - \Pr[G_1]| + \Pr[G_1]$$

$$= 2 \cdot \mathsf{Adv}_{\mathsf{sPRG},\mathcal{B}}^{\mathsf{FS\text{-}PRG}}(\lambda) + n \cdot \mathsf{Adv}_{\mathsf{CAEAD},\mathcal{D}}^{\mathsf{MO\text{-}CTXT}}(\lambda),$$

which concludes the proof of Theorem 2. □

Theorem 3 (FS-UNF Security). *If* FSMAC *satisfies* FS-sEUF-CMA *security, then* FSMF *satisfies* FS-UNF *security.*

Proof. Let $\mathcal{A}$ be a PPT adversary that attacks the FS-UNF security of FSMF. We construct an adversary $\mathcal{B}$ that attacks the FS-sEUF-CMA security of FSMAC, using the adversary $\mathcal{A}$ as follows.

1. $\mathcal{B}$ sets $j := 0$ and $T_t := \emptyset$ for all $t \in [n]$.
2. $\mathcal{B}$ sets $j := j + 1$.
3. $\mathcal{B}$ answers tagging queries of the form C_2 from $\mathcal{A}$ as follows. $\mathcal{B}$ makes tagging queries of the form C_2 to $\mathcal{CH}$, gets the result (τ, j), returns (τ, j) to $\mathcal{A}$, and appends $(C_2, (\tau, j))$ to T_j.
4. When $\mathcal{A}$ outputs d, $\mathcal{B}$ returns d to $\mathcal{CH}$.
5. $\mathcal{B}$ receives K_j from $\mathcal{CH}$, sets $\mathsf{TK}_j = \mathsf{K}_j$, and returns TK_j to $\mathcal{A}$.
6. When $\mathcal{A}$ outputs $(H^*, M^*, O^*, C_2^*, (\tau^*, j^*))$, $\mathcal{B}$ returns $(C_2^*, (\tau^*, j^*))$ to $\mathcal{CH}$, else terminates.

We can see that $\mathcal{B}$ perfectly simulates the FS-sEUF-CMA security game for $\mathcal{A}$. We assumes that $\mathcal{A}$ successfully outputs the tuple $(H^*, M^*, O^*, C_2^*, (\tau^*, j^*))$ satisfying

$$\mathsf{Ver}(\mathsf{TK}_{j^*}, H^*, M^*, O^*, C_2^*, (\tau^*, j^*)) = 1, (C_2^*, (\tau^*, j^*)) \notin T_{j^*}, \text{and } 1 \leq j^* < j.$$

Then, $\mathcal{B}$ successfully outputs $(C_2^*, (\tau^*, j^*))$ satisfying

$$\mathsf{FSMAC.Ver}(\mathsf{K}_{j^*}, C_2^*, (\tau^*, j^*)) = 1 \text{ and } (C_2^*, (\tau^*, j^*)) \notin S_{j^*}$$

in FS-sEUF-CMA security game. Thus, $\mathsf{Adv}_{\mathsf{FSMAC},\mathcal{B}}^{\mathsf{FS\text{-}sEUF\text{-}CMA}}(\lambda) = \mathsf{Adv}_{\mathsf{FSMF},\mathcal{A}}^{\mathsf{FS\text{-}UNF}}(\lambda)$, which concludes the proof of Theorem 3. □

Theorem 4 (FS-R-BIND Security). *If* CAEAD *satisfies* R-BIND, *then* FSMF *satisfies* FS-R-BIND *security.*

Proof. Let $\mathcal{A}$ be a PPT adversary that attacks the FS-R-BIND of FSMF. We assume that $\mathcal{A}$ successfully outputs the tuple $((H, M, O), (H', M', O'), C_2^*, (\tau^*, j^*))$ satisfying

$$\mathsf{Ver}(\mathsf{TK}_{j*}, H, M, O, C_2^*, (\tau^*, j^*)) = \mathsf{Ver}(\mathsf{TK}_{j*}, H', M', O', C_2^*, (\tau^*, j^*)) = 1,$$
$$(H, M) \neq (H', M'), \text{and } 1 \leq j^* < j.$$

Then, $\mathsf{CAEAD.Ver}(H, M, O, C_2^*) = \mathsf{CAEAD.Ver}(H', M', O', C_2^*) = 1$ and $(H, M) \neq (H', M')$ holds. This contradicts the R-BIND security of CAEAD. Thus, Theorem 4 holds. $\square$

Theorem 5 (FS-S-BIND security). *If* CAEAD *satisfies* S-BIND, *then* FSMF *satisfies* FS-S-BIND *security.*

Proof. Let $\mathcal{A}$ be a PPT adversary that attacks the FS-S-BIND of FSMF. We assume that $\mathcal{A}$ successfully outputs the tuple $(j^*, \mathsf{SK}_i, H, C_1, C_2)$ satisfying

$$\mathsf{Ver}(\mathsf{TK}_{j*}, H, M', O, C_2, (\tau, j^*)) = 0, M' \neq \bot, \text{and } 1 \leq j^* < j$$

in computing $(\tau, j^*) \leftarrow \mathsf{Tag}(\mathsf{TK}_{j*}, C_2)$ and $(M', O) \leftarrow \mathsf{Dec}(\mathsf{SK}_i, H, C_1, C_2)$.

When $\mathsf{Ver}(\mathsf{TK}_{j*}, H, M', O, C_2, (\tau, j^*)) = 0$ holds, at least one of $\mathsf{CAEAD.Ver}(H, M', O, C_2) = 0$ and $\mathsf{FSMAC.Ver}(\mathsf{K}_{j*}, C_2, \tau) = 0$ holds.

If $\mathsf{FSMAC.Ver}(\mathsf{K}_{j*}, C_2, \tau) = 0$ holds, $\mathsf{FSMAC.Ver}(\mathsf{K}_{j*}, C_2, \mathsf{FSMAC.Tag}(\mathsf{K}_{j*}, C_2)) = 0$ holds. This contradicts the correctness of FSMAC.

If $\mathsf{CAEAD.Ver}(H, M', O, C_2) = 0$ holds, $M' \neq \bot$ and $\mathsf{CAEAD.Ver}(H, M, O, C_2) = 0$ holds in computing $(M', O) \leftarrow \mathsf{CAEAD.Dec}(Out_i, H, C_1, C_2)$. This contradicts the S-BIND security of CAEAD. Thus, Theorem 5 holds. $\square$

5   Conclusion

In this work, we propose forward secure message franking. Firstly, we formalize key-evolving message franking including additional key update algorithms. Then, we propose forward security for five security requirements. Finally, we show key-evolving message franking satisfying forward security based on committing authenticated encryption with associated data, forward secure pseudorandom generator, and forward secure message authentication code.

Our definition is based on CAEAD introduced by Grubbs et al. [13]. In [6,18], variants of CAEAD were also proposed. By applying forward secure PRG and forward secure MAC to these schemes as a similar manner to our construction, it seems that forward secure variants schemes are obtained.

Acknowledgements. A part of this work was supported by iJST OPERA JPMJO P1612, JST CREST JPMJCR14D6, JPMJCR2113, JSPS KAKENHI JP16H01705, JP17H01695, JP19J22363, JP20J14338, 21H04879.

References

1. Alwen, J., Coretti, S., Dodis, Y.: The double ratchet: security notions, proofs, and modularization for the signal protocol. In: Ishai, Y., Rijmen, V. (eds.) EURO-CRYPT 2019. LNCS, vol. 11476, pp. 129–158. Springer, Cham (2019). https://doi.org/10.1007/978-3-030-17653-2_5
2. Aviram, N., Gellert, K., Jager, T.: Session resumption protocols and efficient forward security for TLS 1.3 0-RTT. In: Ishai, Y., Rijmen, V. (eds.) EUROCRYPT 2019. LNCS, vol. 11477, pp. 117–150. Springer, Cham (2019). https://doi.org/10.1007/978-3-030-17656-3_5
3. Bellare, M., Miner, S.K.: A forward-secure digital signature scheme. In: Wiener, M. (ed.) CRYPTO 1999. LNCS, vol. 1666, pp. 431–448. Springer, Heidelberg (1999). https://doi.org/10.1007/3-540-48405-1_28
4. Bellare, M., Yee, B.: Forward-security in private-key cryptography. In: Joye, M. (ed.) CT-RSA 2003. LNCS, vol. 2612, pp. 1–18. Springer, Heidelberg (2003). https://doi.org/10.1007/3-540-36563-X_1
5. Canetti, R., Halevi, S., Katz, J.: A forward-secure public-key encryption scheme. In: Biham, E. (ed.) EUROCRYPT 2003. LNCS, vol. 2656, pp. 255–271. Springer, Heidelberg (2003). https://doi.org/10.1007/3-540-39200-9_16
6. Chen, L., Tang, Q.: People who live in glass houses should not throw stones: targeted opening message franking schemes. IACR Cryptology ePrint Archive, vol. 2018, p. 994 (2018). https://eprint.iacr.org/2018/994
7. Cohn-Gordon, K., Cremers, C.J.F., Dowling, B., Garratt, L., Stebila, D.: A formal security analysis of the signal messaging protocol. In: 2017 IEEE European Symposium on Security and Privacy, EuroS&P 2017, Paris, France, 26–28 Apr 2017, pp. 451–466. IEEE (2017). https://doi.org/10.1109/EuroSP.2017.27
8. Derler, D., Jager, T., Slamanig, D., Striecks, C.: Bloom filter encryption and applications to efficient forward-secret 0-RTT key exchange. In: Nielsen, J.B., Rijmen, V. (eds.) EUROCRYPT 2018. LNCS, vol. 10822, pp. 425–455. Springer, Cham (2018). https://doi.org/10.1007/978-3-319-78372-7_14
9. Diffie, W., van Oorschot, P.C., Wiener, M.J.: Authentication and authenticated key exchanges. Des. Codes Cryptogr. 2(2), 107–125 (1992). https://doi.org/10.1007/BF00124891
10. Dodis, Y., Grubbs, P., Ristenpart, T., Woodage, J.: Fast message franking: from invisible salamanders to encryptment. In: Shacham, H., Boldyreva, A. (eds.) CRYPTO 2018. LNCS, vol. 10991, pp. 155–186. Springer, Cham (2018). https://doi.org/10.1007/978-3-319-96884-1_6
11. Facebook: facebook messenger app (2016). https://www.messenger.com/
12. Facebook: messenger secret conversations technical whitepaper (2016)
13. Grubbs, P., Lu, J., Ristenpart, T.: Message franking via committing authenticated encryption. In: Katz, J., Shacham, H. (eds.) CRYPTO 2017. LNCS, vol. 10403, pp. 66–97. Springer, Cham (2017). https://doi.org/10.1007/978-3-319-63697-9_3
14. Günther, C.G.: An identity-based key-exchange protocol. In: Quisquater, J.-J., Vandewalle, J. (eds.) EUROCRYPT 1989. LNCS, vol. 434, pp. 29–37. Springer, Heidelberg (1990). https://doi.org/10.1007/3-540-46885-4_5
15. Günther, F., Hale, B., Jager, T., Lauer, S.: 0-RTT key exchange with full forward secrecy. In: Coron, J.-S., Nielsen, J.B. (eds.) EUROCRYPT 2017. LNCS, vol. 10212, pp. 519–548. Springer, Cham (2017). https://doi.org/10.1007/978-3-319-56617-7_18

16. Hirose, S.: Compactly committing authenticated encryption using tweakable block cipher. In: Kutylowski, M., Zhang, J., Chen, C. (eds.) Network and System Security - 14th International Conference, NSS 2020, Melbourne, VIC, Australia, 25–27 November 2020, Proceedings. Lecture Notes in Computer Science, vol. 12570, pp. 187–206. Springer (2020). https://doi.org/10.1007/978-3-030-65745-1_11

17. Huguenin-Dumittan, L., Leontiadis, I.: A message franking channel. IACR Cryptology ePrint Archive, vol. 2018, p. 920 (2018). https://eprint.iacr.org/2018/920

18. Leontiadis, I., Vaudenay, S.: Private message franking with after opening privacy. IACR Cryptology ePrint Archive, vol. 2018, p. 938 (2018). https://eprint.iacr.org/2018/938

19. Open Whisper Systems: Signal (2016). https://signal.org/

20. Pointcheval, D., Sanders, O.: Forward secure non-interactive key exchange. In: Abdalla, M., De Prisco, R. (eds.) SCN 2014. LNCS, vol. 8642, pp. 21–39. Springer, Cham (2014). https://doi.org/10.1007/978-3-319-10879-7_2

21. Tyagi, N., Grubbs, P., Len, J., Miers, I., Ristenpart, T.: Asymmetric message franking: content moderation for metadata-private end-to-end encryption. In: Boldyreva, A., Micciancio, D. (eds.) CRYPTO 2019. LNCS, vol. 11694, pp. 222–250. Springer, Cham (2019). https://doi.org/10.1007/978-3-030-26954-8_8

22. Whatsapp: Whatsapp messenger (2016). https://www.whatsapp.com/

New General Framework for Algebraic Degree Evaluation of NFSR-Based Cryptosystems

Lin Ding$^{(\boxtimes)}$ and Zheng Wu

PLA SSF Information Engineering University, Zhengzhou 450001, China
dinglin_cipher@163.com

Abstract. At CRYPTO 2017, Liu presented a general framework of iterative estimation of algebraic degree for NFSR-based cryptosystems, by exploiting a technique, called *numeric mapping*, and gave distinguishing attacks on Trivium-like ciphers, including Trivium, Kreyvium and TriviA-SC. This paper aims at further investigating algebraic degree estimation of NFSR-based cryptosystems from a new perspective. A new general framework for algebraic degree estimation of NFSR-based cryptosystems is formalized to exploit a new way of constructing distinguishing attacks. This illustrates that our new framework is more accurate than Liu's when estimating the upper bound on algebraic degree of NFSR-based cryptosystems. As result, the best known attack on the full simplified variant of TriviA-SC v2 is presented.

Keywords: Cryptanalysis · Nonlinear feedback shift register · Distinguishing attack · Trivium · Kreyvium · TriviA-SC

1 Introduction

In recent years, for constrained environments like RFID tags or sensor networks, a number of lightweight cryptographic primitives have been developed to provide security and privacy. Nonlinear Feedback Shift Register (NFSR) is widely used in the design of modern lightweight ciphers, such as Trivium [1], Grain v1 [2] and MICKEY 2.0 [3] which have been selected in the eSTREAM [4] portfolio of promising stream ciphers for small hardware, the authenticated cipher ACORN v3 [5] which has been selected as one of seven finalists in the CAESAR competition, the block cipher family KATAN/KTANTAN [6], and the hash function family Quark [7].

The well-known Trivium stream cipher, designed by De Cannière and Preneel in 2005, is a bit-oriented stream cipher in the eSTREAM project portfolio for hardware implementation, and has an exceptional structure which leads to good performance in both hardware and software. It has been studied extensively and shows good resistance to cryptanalysis, even after more than a decade of effort by cryptanalysts. Inspired by Trivium, some Trivium-like ciphers have

© The Author(s), under exclusive license to Springer Nature Switzerland AG 2022
J. H. Park and S.-H. Seo (Eds.): ICISC 2021, LNCS 13218, pp. 359–375, 2022.
https://doi.org/10.1007/978-3-031-08896-4_19

been successfully developed, e.g., Kreyvium [8] developed at FSE 2016 for the efficient homomorphic-ciphertext compression and TriviA-SC [9,10] developed as a component of the authenticated encryption cipher TriviA-ck. Trivium uses an 80-bit key and an 80-bit IV, while Kreyvium and TriviA-SC both use a 128-bit key and a 128-bit IV. These three ciphers all have 1152 rounds of initialization.

At CRYPTO 2017, Liu [11] presented a general framework of iterative estimation of algebraic degree for NFSR-based cryptosystems, by exploiting a new technique, called *numeric mapping*, and gave distinguishing attacks on Trivium-like ciphers, including Trivium, Kreyvium and TriviA-SC. The key idea is based on a simple fact. The advantage of this method is that it has linear time complexity and needs a negligible amount of memory. Nevertheless, the estimation bias of *numeric mapping* probably becomes larger as the number of iterated rounds increases, this estimation method still requires to be further investigated. In this work, Liu presented distinguishing attacks on 1035-round TriviA-SC v1, 1047-round TriviA-SC v2 and the full simplified variant of TriviA-SC, with time complexities of 2^{63}, 2^{61} and 2^{63}, respectively. After then, some new applications of the numeric mapping technique to other NFSR-based ciphers were published in [12–15].

Our Contributions. In this paper, we focus on formalizing a new general framework for algebraic degree evaluation of NFSR-based cryptosystems, to provide a new way of constructing distinguishing attacks. We first introduce a new notion, called *algebraic degree tuple*, which describes the algebraic degree of a multivariate Boolean function in each one of all variables. Based on this notion, a new technique, called *composite numeric mapping*, is proposed, which gives a new general idea for iteratively estimating the upper bound on algebraic degree of an NFSR. We prove that *composite numeric mapping* is at least as good as *numeric mapping*, and most likely better than it demonstrated by applications. Then a new general framework for algebraic degree estimation of NFSR-based cryptosystems is formalized, and an efficient algorithm is proposed and applied to Trivium-like ciphers. The effectiveness and accuracy of our algorithm is confirmed by the experimental results. More importantly, to the best of our knowledge, this is the first time that algebraic degree tuple is defined and used to exploit new cryptanalytic techniques, which gives a new view on cryptanalysis of NFSR-based cryptosystems. Our new framework is also potentially useful in the future applications to other cryptosystems that are not built on NFSR.

For a NFSR-based cryptosystem, our algorithm can give an upper bound on algebraic degree of any one internal state bit or output bit over a given set of initial input variables with any size, e.g., all the key and IV bits, or all the IV bits. It has practical time complexity and requires a negligible amount of memory. By using our algorithm, we first investigate the mixing efficiency of Trivium-like ciphers, when taking all the key and IV bits as initial input variables. The results show that the maximum numbers of initialization rounds of Kreyvium, TriviA-SC v1 and TriviA-SC v2 such that the generated keystream bit does not achieve maximum algebraic degree are at least 983, 1109 and 1110 (out of 1152), rather than 982, 1108 and 1108 obtained in [11], respectively. When taking all the IV bits as initial input variables, the result shows that the maximum number of initialization rounds of TriviA-SC v2 such that the generated keystream bit does not achieve maximum algebraic degree is at least 988 (out of 1152), rather than 987 obtained in [11]. In other cases, although we do not improve [11] in terms of the number of initialization rounds, tighter upper bounds on algebraic degree are mostly obtained. Take 793 rounds of Trivium as example, when taking all the IV bits as initial input variables, the upper bound on algebraic degree of the first output bit evaluated by our algorithm is 78, which is tighter than 79 by [11]. There results show that our new framework is more accurate than [11] when estimating the upper bound on algebraic degree of NFSR-based cryptosystems. All the results above are obtained on a common PC with 2.5 GHz Intel Pentium 4 processor within one second.

When taking a subset of all the IV bits as initial input variables, we apply our new framework to Trivium-like ciphers. As results, some new cubes which are as good as the results of [11] and can not be found by [11] are obtained. As for the full simplified variant of TriviA-SC v2, new distinguishing attack is found with time complexity of 2^{59}, which is the best known attack on the cipher. The result is listed in Table 1, and comparisons with previous works are made. It further illustrates that our new framework is more accurate than [11] when estimating the upper bound on algebraic degree of NFSR-based cryptosystems.

Table 1. Attacks on simplified variant of TriviA-SC v2

Cipher	# Rounds	Attack	Time compleixity	Reference
Simplified variant of TriviA-SC v2	Full	Distinguishing attack	2^{120}	[16]
	Full	Distinguishing attack	2^{63}	[11]
	Full	**Distinguishing attack**	$\mathbf{2^{59}}$	**Sect. 3.2**

To verify these cryptanalytic results, we make an amount of experiments on round reduced variants of Trivium-like ciphers. The experimental results show that our distinguishing attacks are always consistent with our evaluated results. They are strong evidences of high accuracy of our new framework. To facilitate the reader to verify our results, the supplementary materials are submitted together with our paper. They consist of the experimental results obtained by applying our algorithm to Trivium-like ciphers, including all the results on Trivium, Kreyvium, TriviA-SC v1 and TriviA-SC v2.

This paper is organized as follows. A new general framework for algebraic degree evaluation of NFSR-Based cryptosystems is formalized in Sect. 2. In Sect. 3, algebraic degree tuple evaluations of Trivium-like ciphers are given as applications to prove the effectiveness of our new framework. The paper is concluded in Sect. 4.

2 New General Framework for Algebraic Degree Evaluation of NFSR-Based Cryptosystems

2.1 A New Notion: *Algebraic Degree Tuple*

Denote $\mathbb{F}_2^n$ the n-dimension vector space over $\mathbb{F}_2$. Let $\mathbb{B}_n$ be the set of all functions mapping $\mathbb{F}_2^n$ to $\mathbb{F}_2$, and let $f \in \mathbb{B}_n$. The Algebraic Normal Form (ANF) of given Boolean function f over variables $x_1, x_2, \cdots, x_n$ can be uniquely expressed as

$$f(x_1, x_2, \cdots, x_n) = \bigoplus_{c=(c_1, c_2, \cdots, c_n) \in \mathbb{F}_2^n} a_c \prod_{i=1}^{n} x_i^{c_i}$$

where the coefficient a_c is a constant in $\mathbb{F}_2$, and c_i denotes the i-th digit of the binary encoding of c (and so the sum spans all monomials in $x_1, x_2, \cdots, x_n$). The algebraic degree of f, denoted by $\deg(f)$, is defined as $\max\{wt(c)\,|a_c = 1\}$, where $wt(c)$ is the Hamming weight of c. Thus, for a multivariate Boolean function, the degree of a term is the sum of the exponents of the variables in the term, and then the algebraic degree of the multivariate Boolean function is the maximum of the degrees of all terms in the Boolean function. Now, we define a new notion, called *univariate algebraic degree*, which describes the algebraic degree of a multivariate Boolean function in one of all variables.

Definition 1. Let $f(X) = \bigoplus_{c=(c_1, c_2, \cdots, c_n) \in \mathbb{F}_2^n} a_c \prod_{i=1}^{n} x_i^{c_i}$ be a multivariate Boolean function over n variables $X = (x_1, x_2, \cdots, x_n)$, the algebraic degree of f in one variable x_i $(i = 1, 2, \cdots, n)$, called *univariate algebraic degree*, is denoted by $\deg(f, x_i)$ and defined by

$$\deg(f, x_i) = \max_{a_c = 1}\{wt(c)\,|c_i = 1\}$$

In particular, denote $\deg(0, x_i) = -\infty$ and $\deg(f, x_i) = 0$ if the variable x_i does not appear in nonzero f.

Example 1. Let $x_t = x_{t-2}x_{t-7} \oplus x_{t-4}x_{t-5} \oplus x_{t-8}$ $(t \geq 9)$ be the update function of an NFSR with size 8. Then, iteratively compute

$x_9 = x_2x_7 \oplus x_4x_5 \oplus x_1,$
$x_{11} = x_2x_4x_7 \oplus x_1x_4 \oplus x_4x_5 \oplus x_6x_7 \oplus x_3,$
$x_{12} = x_3x_5x_8 \oplus x_2x_5 \oplus x_5x_6 \oplus x_7x_8 \oplus x_4,$
$x_{14} = x_2x_3x_7x_8 \oplus x_2x_5x_6x_7 \oplus x_3x_4x_5x_8 \oplus x_3x_5x_7x_8 \oplus x_1x_3x_8 \oplus x_1x_5x_6 \oplus$
$\quad\quad x_2x_4x_5 \oplus x_2x_5x_7 \oplus x_4x_5x_6 \oplus x_5x_6x_7 \oplus x_1x_2 \oplus x_2x_7 \oplus x_4x_7 \oplus x_7x_8 \oplus x_6$

It is easy to see that $\deg(x_9, x_1) = 1$, $\deg(x_{11}, x_1) = 2$, $\deg(x_{12}, x_1) = 0$, $\deg(x_{14}, x_1) = 3$ in Example 1.

Based on Definition 1, we define a new notion, called *algebraic degree tuple* as follows.

Definition 2. Let $f(X) = \bigoplus\limits_{c=(c_1,c_2,\cdots,c_n)\in\mathbb{F}_2^n} a_c \prod\limits_{i=1}^{n} x_i^{c_i}$ be a multivariate Boolean function over n variables $X = (x_1, x_2, \cdots, x_n)$, the **algebraic degree tuple** of f, denoted by $Tdeg(f, X)$, is defined by

$$Tdeg(f, X) = (\deg(f, x_1), \deg(f, x_2), \cdots, \deg(f, x_n))$$

Obviously, the algebraic degree of f is equal to the highest univariate numeric degree in the algebraic degree tuple $Tdeg(f, X)$, i.e.,

$$deg(f) = \max\{\deg(f, x_1), \deg(f, x_2), \cdots, \deg(f, x_n)\}$$

Recall Example 1, it is easy to see that $\deg(x_{14}) = 4$, while $Tdeg(x_{14}, X) = (3, 4, 4, 4, 4, 4, 4, 4)$. In fact, the algebraic degree of a multivariate Boolean function is the same as the degree of its term or terms having the highest degree and non-zero coefficient. However, in one variable, its corresponding univariate algebraic degree does not necessarily achieve the highest degree. Thus, it is clear that the multivariate Boolean function can be better characterized by its algebraic degree tuple than by the algebraic degree.

2.2 A New Technique: *Composite Numeric Mapping*

In this subsection, a new technique, called *composite numeric mapping*, is introduced, and a new general idea for iteratively estimating the upper bound on algebraic degree of an NFSR is given. It is a theoretical tool for algebraic degree estimation.

Before introducing our new technique, we have to define new computation models of upper bound on algebraic degree for $\oplus$ and $\cdot$ operations, since they are two fundamental operations in most NFSR-based cryptosystems, where the XOR of two internal state bits is computed in $\oplus$ and the AND of two internal state bits is computed in $\cdot$. Until now, the most classical computation models of upper bound on algebraic degree for $\oplus$ and $\cdot$ operations are $\deg(f \oplus g) \le \max\{\deg(f), \deg(g)\}$ and $\deg(f \cdot g) \le \deg(f) + \deg(g)$, respectively. They are the foundation of *numeric mapping* in [11]. More specifically, under *numeric mapping*, the algebraic degree of $f \oplus g$ has an upper bound $\mathbf{DEG}(f \oplus g) = \max\{\deg(f), \deg(g)\}$, and the algebraic degree of $f \cdot g$ has an upper bound $\mathbf{DEG}(f \cdot g) = \deg(f) + \deg(g)$. For simplicity, $\mathbf{DEG}(h)$ is called a super *numeric degree* of the composite function h in [11]. However, as for algebraic degree tuple, the trivial computation models have to be modified. The new computation models are described as follows.

Proposition 1. (New Computation Model of Upper Bound on Algebraic Degree Tuple for $\oplus$, denoted by $\widetilde{\oplus}$) Let $f(X)$ and $g(X)$ be two multivariate Boolean functions over n variables $X = (x_1, x_2, \cdots, x_n)$, $Tdeg(f\widetilde{\oplus}g, X) = (\deg(f\widetilde{\oplus}g, x_1), \deg(f\widetilde{\oplus}g, x_2), \cdots, \deg(f\widetilde{\oplus}g, x_n))$ gives an upper bound on algebraic degree tuple $Tdeg(f \oplus g, X)$, when the computation of $\deg(f\widetilde{\oplus}g, x_i)$ follows $\deg(f\widetilde{\oplus}g, x_i) = \max\{\deg(f, x_i), \deg(g, x_i)\}$.

It is clear to see that

$$\deg\left(f \oplus g, x_i\right) \leq \max\left\{\deg\left(f, x_i\right), \deg\left(g, x_i\right)\right\}$$
$$= \deg\left(f \widetilde{\oplus} g, x_i\right)$$

Since $\deg\left(f, x_i\right) \leq \deg\left(f\right)$ and $\deg\left(g, x_i\right) \leq \deg\left(g\right)$, we have

$$\deg\left(f \widetilde{\oplus} g, x_i\right) = \max\left\{\deg\left(f, x_i\right), \deg\left(g, x_i\right)\right\}$$
$$\leq \max\left\{\deg\left(f\right), \deg\left(g\right)\right\} = \mathbf{DEG}(f \oplus g)$$

Hence, the new computation model of upper bound on algebraic degree tuple for $\oplus$ operation ensures that the exact algebraic degree tuple of $Tdeg\left(f \oplus g, X\right)$ is always less than or equal to $Tdeg\left(f \widetilde{\oplus} g, X\right)$, i.e., $Tdeg\left(f \oplus g, X\right) \preccurlyeq Tdeg\left(f \widetilde{\oplus} g, X\right)$, where $Tdeg\left(f \oplus g, X\right) \preccurlyeq Tdeg\left(f \widetilde{\oplus} g, X\right)$ if $\deg\left(f \oplus g, x_i\right) \leq \deg\left(f \widetilde{\oplus} g, x_i\right)$ for all $1 \leq i \leq n$. Simultaneously, it also ensures that $Tdeg\left(f \widetilde{\oplus} g, x_i\right) \leq \mathbf{DEG}(f \oplus g)$ for all $1 \leq i \leq n$.

Denote $u_{\max} = \max\left\{\deg\left(f, x_i\right) | 1 \leq i \leq n\right\}$ and $v_{\max} = \max\left\{\deg\left(g, x_i\right) | 1 \leq i \leq n\right\}$. The new computation model of upper bound on algebraic degree tuple for $\cdot$ operation is described as follows.

Proposition 2. (New Computation Model of Upper Bound on Algebraic Degree Tuple for $\cdot$, denoted by $\widetilde{\cdot}$). Let $f\left(X\right)$ and $g\left(X\right)$ be two multivariate Boolean functions over n variables $X = (x_1, x_2, \cdots, x_n)$, $Tdeg\left(f \widetilde{\cdot} g, X\right) = (\deg\left(f \widetilde{\cdot} g, x_1\right), \deg\left(f \widetilde{\cdot} g, x_2\right), \cdots, \deg\left(f \widetilde{\cdot} g, x_n\right))$ gives an upper bound on algebraic degree tuple $Tdeg\left(f \cdot g, X\right)$, when the computation of $\deg\left(f \widetilde{\cdot} g, x_i\right)$ follows Table 2.

Table 2. The computation model of $\deg\left(f \widetilde{\cdot} g, x_i\right)$

-	$\deg\left(g, x_i\right) = -\infty$	$\deg\left(g, x_i\right) = 0$	$\deg\left(g, x_i\right) = v\left(v > 0\right)$
$\deg\left(f, x_i\right) = -\infty$	$-\infty$	$-\infty$	$-\infty$
$\deg\left(f, x_i\right) = 0$	$-\infty$	0	$v + u_{\max}$
$\deg\left(f, x_i\right) = u\left(u > 0\right)$	$-\infty$	$u + v_{\max}$	$\max\left\{u + v_{\max}, v + u_{\max}\right\}$

All cases in Table 2 can be easily checked, except one case when $\deg\left(f, x_i\right) = u\left(u > 0\right)$ and $\deg\left(g, x_i\right) = v\left(v > 0\right)$ are simultaneously satisfied. To verify the correctness of this case, a corollary is given and proved as follows.

Corollary 1. Let $f\left(X\right)$ and $g\left(X\right)$ be two multivariate Boolean functions over n variables $X = (x_1, x_2, \cdots, x_n)$, denote $u_{\max} = \max\left\{\deg\left(f, x_i\right) | 1 \leq i \leq n\right\}$ and $v_{\max} = \max\left\{\deg\left(g, x_i\right) | 1 \leq i \leq n\right\}$, if $\deg\left(f, x_i\right) = u\left(u > 0\right)$ and $\deg\left(g, x_i\right) = v\left(v > 0\right)$, then $\deg\left(f \cdot g, x_i\right) \leq \max\left\{u + v_{\max}, v + u_{\max}\right\}$.

Proof. Rewrite the function f as $f = x_i \cdot f_0 \oplus f_1$, where f_0 and f_1 denotes two derived functions over the remaining $n-1$ variables except x_i with $\deg(f_0) = u - 1$ and $\deg(f_1) \leq u_{\max}$. Similarly, rewrite the function g as $g = x_i \cdot g_0 \oplus g_1$, where g_0 denotes two derived functions over the remaining $n-1$ variables except x_i with $\deg(g_0) = v - 1$ and $\deg(g_1) \leq v_{\max}$. Thus, we have

$$f \cdot g = (x_i \cdot f_0 \oplus f_1) \cdot (x_i \cdot g_0 \oplus g_1) = x_i \cdot f_0 \cdot g_0 \oplus x_i \cdot f_0 \cdot g_1 \oplus x_i \cdot f_1 \cdot g_0 \oplus f_1 \cdot g_1$$

It is easy to see that

$$\deg(x_i \cdot f_0 \cdot g_0, x_i) \leq 1 + u - 1 + v - 1 = u + v - 1$$
$$\deg(x_i \cdot f_0 \cdot g_1, x_i) \leq 1 + u - 1 + v_{\max} = u + v_{\max}$$
$$\deg(x_i \cdot f_1 \cdot g_0, x_i) \leq 1 + u_{\max} + v - 1 = u_{\max} + v$$
$$\deg(f_1 \cdot g_1, x_i) \leq 0$$

Hence, we have

$$\deg(f \cdot g, x_i)$$
$$\leq \max\{\deg(x_i \cdot f_0 \cdot g_0, x_i), \deg(x_i \cdot f_0 \cdot g_1, x_i), \deg(x_i \cdot f_1 \cdot g_0, x_i), \deg(f_1 \cdot g_1, x_i)\}$$
$$= \max\{u + v_{\max}, v + u_{\max}\}$$

Since $deg(f) = u_{\max} = \max\{\deg(f, x_i) | 1 \leq i \leq n\}$ and $deg(g) = v_{\max} = \max\{\deg(g, x_i) | 1 \leq i \leq n\}$, we have

$$\deg(f \tilde{\cdot} g, x_i) = \max\{u + v_{\max}, v + u_{\max}\}$$

$$\leq \deg(f) + \deg(g) = \mathbf{DEG}(f \cdot g)$$

Thus, the new computation model of upper bound on algebraic degree tuple for $\cdot$ ensures that the exact algebraic degree tuple of $Tdeg(f \cdot g, X)$ is always less than or equal to $Tdeg(f \tilde{\cdot} g, X)$, i.e., $Tdeg(f \cdot g, X) \preccurlyeq Tdeg(f \tilde{\cdot} g, X)$, where $Tdeg(f \cdot g, X) \preccurlyeq Tdeg(f \tilde{\cdot} g, X)$ if $\deg(f \cdot g, x_i) \leq \deg(f \tilde{\cdot} g, x_i)$ for all $1 \leq i \leq n$. Simultaneously, it also ensures that $Tdeg(f \tilde{\cdot} g, x_i) \leq \mathbf{DEG}(f \cdot g)$ for all $1 \leq i \leq n$.

Based on these new computation models of upper bound on algebraic degree tuple for $\oplus$ and $\cdot$ operations, the upper bound on algebraic degree tuple of a composite function can be estimated by using the following new technique, called *composite numeric mapping*, and then estimating the upper bound on algebraic degree tuples of an NFSR can be easily done by iterative computation. Let $\mathbb{B}_n$ be the set of all functions mapping $\mathbb{F}_2^n$ to $\mathbb{F}_2$, let $f \in \mathbb{F}_2^n$ and $f(S) = \bigoplus_{c=(c_1,c_2,\cdots,c_m) \in \mathbb{F}_2^m} a_c \prod_{i=1}^{m} s_i^{c_i}$ be a multivariate Boolean function over m internal variables $S = (s_1, s_2, \cdots, s_m)$, let $X = (x_1, x_2, \cdots, x_n)$ be n initial input variables, let $D = (d_{i,j})_{i=1,2,\cdots,m, j=1,2,\cdots,n} \in \mathbb{Z}^{m \times n}$ satisfying $d_{i,j} \geq \deg(s_i, x_j)$ for all $1 \leq i \leq m$ and $1 \leq j \leq n$, we define the following mapping, called *composite numeric mapping* and denoted by **CDEG**,

$$\mathbf{CDEG} : \mathbb{B}_m \times \mathbb{Z}^{m \times n} \rightarrow \mathbb{Z}^n,$$

$$(f, D) \mapsto Tdeg\left(\underset{a_c=1, c=(c_1,c_2,\cdots,c_m) \in \mathbb{F}_2^m}{\widetilde{\bigoplus}} (s_1^{c_1} \tilde{\cdot} s_2^{c_2} \tilde{\cdot} \cdots \tilde{\cdot} s_m^{c_m}), X\right)$$

CDEG (f, D) gives an upper bound on algebraic degree tuple $Tdeg(f, X)$, called *composite numeric degree tuple* of f over variables X and denoted by **CNDT** $(f, X) = (\mathbf{CNDT}(f, x_1), \mathbf{CNDT}(f, x_2), \cdots, \mathbf{CNDT}(f, x_n)) = \mathbf{CDEG}(f, D)$. Hereinafter, **CNDT** (f, x_i) is called *univariate composite numeric degree* of f in one variable x_i for simplicity. Usually, we are more concerned with the smallest *univariate composite numeric degree* in the *composite numeric degree tuple* **CNDT** (f, X), denoted by **minCNDT** $(f, X) = \min\{\mathbf{CNDT}(f, x_i), 1 \leq i \leq n\}$, since it implies the best distinguishing attack on NFSR-based cryptosystems.

As demonstrated above, $\deg(f \oplus g, x_i) \leq \deg(f\widetilde{\oplus}g, x_i)$ and $\deg(f \cdot g, x_i) \leq \deg(f\widetilde{}g, x_i)$ simultaneously hold for all $1 \leq i \leq n$, and then we certainly have $Tdeg(h, X) \preccurlyeq \mathbf{CNDT}(h, X)$, where $Tdeg(h, X) \preccurlyeq \mathbf{CNDT}(h, X)$ if $\deg(h, x_i) \leq \mathbf{CNDT}(h, x_i)$ for all $1 \leq i \leq n$. Similarly, since **CNDT** $(f \oplus g, x_i) \leq \mathbf{DEG}(f \oplus g)$ and **CNDT** $(f \cdot g, x_i) \leq \mathbf{DEG}(f \cdot g)$ simultaneously hold for all $1 \leq i \leq n$, and then we certainly have **CNDT** $(h, x_i) \leq \mathbf{DEG}(h)$ for all $1 \leq i \leq n$.

Corollary 2. *The algebraic degree tuple of a multivariate Boolean function is always less than or equal to its composite numeric degree tuple. Simultaneously, each univariate composite numeric degree in the composite numeric degree tuple is always less than or equal to its numeric degree.*

Recall the Example 1. For $t = 16$, it is easy to compute $x_{16} = x_{14}x_9 \oplus x_{12}x_{11} \oplus x_8$. Then according to Definition 2, it has

$$Tdeg(x_{14}, X) = (\deg(x_{14}, x_1), \deg(x_{14}, x_2), \cdots, \deg(x_{14}, x_8)) = (3, 4, 4, 4, 4, 4, 4, 4)$$
$$Tdeg(x_9, X) = (\deg(x_9, x_1), \deg(x_9, x_2), \cdots, \deg(x_9, x_8)) = (1, 2, 0, 2, 2, 0, 2, 0)$$
$$Tdeg(x_{12}, X) = (\deg(x_{12}, x_1), \deg(x_{12}, x_2), \cdots, \deg(x_{12}, x_8)) = (0, 2, 3, 1, 3, 2, 2, 3)$$
$$Tdeg(x_{11}, X) = (\deg(x_{11}, x_1), \deg(x_{11}, x_2), \cdots, \deg(x_{11}, x_8)) = (2, 3, 1, 3, 2, 2, 3, 0)$$
$$Tdeg(x_8, X) = (\deg(x_8, x_1), \deg(x_8, x_2), \cdots, \deg(x_8, x_8)) = (0, 0, 0, 0, 0, 0, 0, 1)$$

Using *composite numeric mapping*, it has

$$\mathbf{CNDT}(x_{16}, X) = Tdeg((x_{14}\widetilde{}x_9) \widetilde{\oplus} (x_{12}\widetilde{}x_{11}) \widetilde{\oplus} x_8, X) = (5, 6, 6, 6, 6, 6, 6, 6)$$

It is easy to verify that **minCNDT** $(x_{16}, X) = \mathbf{CNDT}(x_{16}, x_1) = 5$ and **CNDT** $(x_{16}, x_1) < \deg(x_{16}) = 6$. This demonstrates that *composite numeric mapping* can exploit more useful information which is ignored by *numeric mapping*, and give more accurate estimation of the upper bound on the algebraic degree of the internal states of an NFSR.

2.3   A New General Framework for Algebraic Degree Evaluation of NFSR-Based Cryptosystems

A NFSR-based cryptosystem with internal state size of L usually consists of the update functions $G = (g_1, g_2, \cdots, g_L)$ and an output function f, where G are used to update the internal states and f is used to generate the output bit after a sufficient number of iterative rounds. By Corollary 2, the upper bound on algebraic degree tuple of each internal state bit or output bit of NFSR-based cryptosystems can be estimated, described in Corollary 3.

Corollary 3. *Denote by X the initial input variables of a NFSR-based cryptosystem, and let $G = (g_1, g_2, \cdots, g_L)$ and f be the update functions and output function respectively. Then the algebraic degree tuples of the updated bits and output bit are respectively less than or equal to their composite numeric degree tuples, i.e., $Tdeg\,(g_j, X) \preccurlyeq \mathbf{CNDT}\,(g_j, X)$, $1 \leq j \leq L$ and $Tdeg\,(f, X) \preccurlyeq \mathbf{CNDT}\,(f, X)$. Simultaneously, each univariate composite numeric degree in the composite numeric degree tuples of the updated bits and output bit is always less than or equal to the corresponding numeric degree, i.e., $\mathbf{CNDT}\,(g_j, x_i) \leq \mathbf{DEG}(g_j)$ and $\mathbf{CNDT}\,(f, x_i) \leq \mathbf{DEG}(f)$ for all $1 \leq i \leq n$ and $1 \leq j \leq L$.*

As shown in Corollary 3, *composite numeric mapping* gives a new general idea for iteratively estimating the upper bound on algebraic degree tuple of NFSR-based cryptosystems, and is at least as good as *numeric mapping*, and most likely better than it. The iterative estimation procedure is depicted in Algorithm 1.

In this algorithm, $S^{(t)} = \left(s_1^{(t)}, s_2^{(t)}, \cdots, s_L^{(t)}\right)$ denotes the internal state at time t with size L. The update functions $G = (g_1, g_2, \cdots, g_L)$ is written as vectorial Boolean functions from $\mathbb{F}_2^L$ to $\mathbb{F}_2^L$, where a few bits of input are updated and the rest bits are shifted. **CNMDegEst** is a procedure for estimating the upper bound on algebraic degree tuple using *composite numeric mapping*. The algorithm gives a composite numeric degree tuple $\mathbf{CNDT}\,(f, X)$ as output, which is an upper bound on algebraic degree tuple $Tdeg\,(f, X)$ of the output function f. This is based on the fact that, $Tdeg\,(g_j, X) \preccurlyeq \mathbf{CNDT}\,(g_j, X)$, $1 \leq j \leq L$ and $Tdeg\,(f, X) \preccurlyeq \mathbf{CNDT}\,(f, X)$.

Algorithm 1. CNMDegEst: Iterative Estimation of Upper Bound on Algebraic Degree Tuple of NFSR-Based Cryptosystems Using *Composite Numeric Mapping*

Require: Given the ANFs of the initial state $S^{(0)} = \left(s_1^{(0)}, s_2^{(0)}, \cdots, s_L^{(0)}\right)$, the ANFs of the update functions $G = (g_1, g_2, \cdots, g_L)$ and the output function f, and the set of initial input variables $X = (x_1, x_2, \cdots, x_n)$.

1: Set $D^{(0)}$ to deg $\left(S^{(0)}, X\right)$;
2: For t from 1 to N do:
3:     Compute $\mathbf{CNDT}\left(g_j\left(S^{(t-1)}\right), X\right) \leftarrow \mathbf{CDEG}\left(g_j\left(S^{(t-1)}\right), D^{(t-1)}\right)$ for all $1 \leq j \leq L$;
4:     $D^{(t)} \leftarrow \mathbf{CNDT}\left(G\left(S^{(t-1)}\right), X\right)$;
5: $\mathbf{CNDT}\,(f, X) \leftarrow \mathbf{CDEG}\left(f\left(S^{(N)}\right), D^{(N)}\right)$;
6: Return $\mathbf{CNDT}\,(f, X)$.

Complexity of Algorithm 1. Since the sizes of the ANFs of the update functions $G = (g_1, g_2, \cdots, g_L)$ and the output function f are constant and thus **CDEG** $\left(g_j\left(S^{(t-1)}\right), D^{(t-1)}\right)$ can be calculated in constant time, the time complexity of Algorithm 1 mainly depends on the values of N and L. Therefore, Algorithm 1 has a time complexity of $\mathcal{O}\left(N \cdot L\right)$. In the algorithm, it requires to store $D^{(t)}$ for $t = 1, 2, \cdots, N$, which leads to a memory complexity of $\mathcal{O}\left(L \cdot n \cdot N\right)$. When **CNDT** (f, X) is obtained, zero-sum distinguishers can be easily constructed.

Actually, we are more concerned with the smallest univariate composite numeric degree in the outputted composite numeric degree tuple **CNDT** (f, X), i.e., **minCNDT** $(f, X) = \min\{\textbf{CNDT}\left(f, x_i\right), 1 \leq i \leq n\}$, since it implies the best distinguishing attack on NFSR-based cryptosystems with time complexity of $2^{1 + \mathbf{minCNDT}(f, X)}$.

3   Algebraic Degree Tuple Evaluation of Trivium-Like Ciphers

In this section, we will refine and apply our new framework to Trivium-like ciphers, i.e., Trivium, Kreyvium and TriviA-SC to analyze the mixing efficiency of them and exploit distinguishing attacks on them.

3.1   The Algorithm for Algebraic Degree Tuple Estimation of Trivium-like Ciphers

In this subsection, we will present an efficient algorithm for algebraic degree tuple estimation of Trivium-like ciphers using *composite numeric mapping*, as depicted in Algorithm 2.

Algorithm 2. Algebraic Degree Tuple Estimation of Trivium-like Ciphers Using *Composite Numeric Mapping*

Require: Given the ANFs of the initial state $S^{(0)} = \left(A^{(0)}, B^{(0)}, C^{(0)}\right)$ (or $S^{(t)} = \left(A^{(t)}, B^{(t)}, C^{(t)}, K^*, IV^*\right)$), the ANFs of the update functions $G = (g_1, g_2, \cdots, g_L)$ and the keystream output function f, and the set of initial input variables $X = (x_1, x_2, \cdots, x_n)$.

1: Set $D^{(0)}$ to deg $\left(S^{(0)}, X\right)$;
2: For t from 1 to N do:
3:    For δ in $\{A, B, C\}$ do:
4:        **CNDT** $\left(g_\delta\left(S^{(t-1)}\right), X\right) \leftarrow \mathbf{CDEG}_{Tri}\left(g_\delta\left(S^{(t-1)}\right), D^{(t-1)}\right)$;
5:    Set $D^{(t)}$ using **CNDT** $\left(g_\delta\left(S^{(t-1)}\right), X\right)$ $(\delta \in \{A, B, C\})$ and $D^{(t-1)}$;
6: **CNDT** $(f, X) \leftarrow$ **CDEG** $\left(f\left(S^{(N)}\right), D^{(N)}\right)$;
7: Return **CNDT** (f, X).

Algorithm 2 is an application of Algorithm 1 to Trivium-like ciphers. Thus, its main process is similar to Algorithm 1, except two points required to be highlighted due to the special structure of Trivium-like ciphers. Firstly, all of the update functions $G = (g_1, g_2, \cdots, g_L)$, which are used to update all L internal state bits, are shifting operations except three quadratic functions. In other words, $D^{(t)}$ can be easily set when $\mathbf{CNDT}\left(g_\delta\left(S^{(t-1)}\right), X\right)(\delta \in \{A, B, C\})$ and $D^{(t-1)}$ are simultaneously obtained. Secondly, for estimating the upper bound on algebraic degree tuple more accurately, we exploit a new procedure $\mathbf{CDEG}_{Tri}$, a variant of $\mathbf{CDEG}$ specifically aiming at Trivium-like ciphers, to compute the composite numeric degree tuple of $g_\delta\left(S^{(t-1)}\right)(\delta \in \{A, B, C\})$ over initial input variables X. Note that the basic idea of procedure $\mathbf{CDEG}_{Tri}$ is similar to Lemma 4 of [11]. However, $\mathbf{CDEG}_{Tri}$ is based on *composite numeric mapping*, rather than *numeric mapping* used in [11]. An instance of $\mathbf{CDEG}_{Tri}$ for $\delta = A$ is depicted in Algorithm 3. The other two cases, i.e., $\delta = B$ and $\delta = C$, are similar and given in Algorithms 4 and 5 respectively in Appendix. The procedure $\mathbf{CDEG}_{Tri}$ is based on simple derivations, and can be easily verified.

Take $\delta = A$ for example. For $t \geq r_C + 1$, it has

$$
\begin{aligned}
& g_A\left(S^{(t)}\right) \\
&= \left(c_{r_C}^{(t)} \cdot c_{r_C+1}^{(t)}\right) \oplus \mathcal{L}_A\left(S^{(t)}\right) \\
&= c_1^{(t-r_C+1)} \cdot c_1^{(t-r_C)} \oplus \mathcal{L}_A\left(S^{(t)}\right) \\
&= \left[\left(b_{r_B}^{(t-r_C)} \cdot b_{r_B+1}^{(t-r_C)}\right) \oplus \mathcal{L}_C\left(S^{(t-r_C)}\right)\right] \cdot \left[\left(b_{r_B}^{(t-r_C-1)} \cdot b_{r_B+1}^{(t-r_C-1)}\right) \oplus \mathcal{L}_C\left(S^{(t-r_C-1)}\right)\right] \oplus \mathcal{L}_A\left(S^{(t)}\right) \\
&= \left[\left(b_{r_B}^{(t-r_C)} \cdot b_{r_B+1}^{(t-r_C)}\right) \oplus \mathcal{L}_C\left(S^{(t-r_C)}\right)\right] \cdot \left[\left(b_{r_B+1}^{(t-r_C)} \cdot b_{r_B+1}^{(t-r_C-1)}\right) \oplus \mathcal{L}_C\left(S^{(t-r_C-1)}\right)\right] \oplus \mathcal{L}_A\left(S^{(t)}\right) \\
&= \left(b_{r_B}^{(t-r_C)} \cdot b_{r_B+1}^{(t-r_C)} \cdot b_{r_B+1}^{(t-r_C-1)}\right) \oplus \left(b_{r_B}^{(t-r_C)} \cdot b_{r_B+1}^{(t-r_C)} \cdot \mathcal{L}_C\left(S^{(t-r_C-1)}\right)\right) \\
& \oplus \left(b_{r_B+1}^{(t-r_C)} \cdot b_{r_B+1}^{(t-r_C-1)} \cdot \mathcal{L}_C\left(S^{(t-r_C)}\right)\right) \oplus \left(\mathcal{L}_C\left(S^{(t-r_C)}\right) \cdot \mathcal{L}_C\left(S^{(t-r_C-1)}\right)\right) \oplus \mathcal{L}_A\left(S^{(t)}\right)
\end{aligned}
$$

Algorithm 3. $\mathbf{CDEG}_{Tri}\left(g_\delta\left(S^{(t)}\right), D^{(t)}\right)$ for $\delta = A$

If $t < r_C + 1$ then:
  Return $\mathbf{CDEG}\left(\left(c_{r_C}^{(t)} \cdot c_{r_C+1}^{(t)}\right) \oplus \mathcal{L}_A\left(S^{(t)}\right), D^{(t)}\right)$;
If $t \geq r_C + 1$ then:
  Return $\mathbf{CDEG}\left(h, D^{(t)}\right)$, where $h = \left(b_{r_B}^{(t-r_C)} \cdot b_{r_B+1}^{(t-r_C)} \cdot b_{r_B+1}^{(t-r_C-1)}\right)$

$$
\oplus \left(b_{r_B}^{(t-r_C)} \cdot b_{r_B+1}^{(t-r_C)} \cdot \mathcal{L}_C\left(S^{(t-r_C-1)}\right)\right) \oplus \left(b_{r_B+1}^{(t-r_C)} \cdot b_{r_B+1}^{(t-r_C-1)} \cdot \mathcal{L}_C\left(S^{(t-r_C)}\right)\right)
$$
$$
\oplus \left(\mathcal{L}_C\left(S^{(t-r_C)}\right) \cdot \mathcal{L}_C\left(S^{(t-r_C-1)}\right)\right) \oplus \mathcal{L}_A\left(S^{(t)}\right).
$$

Algorithm 2 gives a composite numeric degree tuple $\mathbf{CNDT}(f, X)$ of the output function f after N rounds over initial input variables $X = (x_1, x_2, \cdots, x_n)$ as output, which gives upper bounds on all n univariate algebraic degrees of the first output bit after N rounds of a Trivium-like cipher. When $\mathbf{CNDT}(f, X)$ is obtained, zero-sum distinguishers can be easily constructed, and then a distinguishing attack with time complexity of $2^{1+\min\mathbf{CNDT}(f,X)}$ can be obtained. Similar to Algorithm 1, the time complexity of Algorithm 2 mainly depends on the values of N and L. Since all of the update functions $G = (g_1, g_2, \cdots, g_L)$ are shifting operations except three quadratic functions for Trivium-like ciphers, Algorithm 2 has a time complexity of $\mathcal{O}(N)$. Similar to Algorithm 1, Algorithm 2 requires to store $D^{(t)}$ for $t = 1, 2, \cdots, N$. Since the number of initial input variables is constant for a given Trivium-like cipher, it leads to a negligible memory complexity of $\mathcal{O}(N)$.

3.2   Experimental Results

In general, the key and the IV are mapped to the internal state of the cipher by an initialization function which consists of a well-chosen number of iterative rounds without generating keystream bits. The security of the initialization function relies on its mixing properties, i.e., each key and IV bit should affect each internal state bit in a complex way. If the mixing is not perfect, then the initialization function may be distinguished from a uniformly random Boolean function. By using our algorithm, we will investigate the mixing efficiency of Trivium-like ciphers.

Table 3. New lower bound on the maximum number of rounds of not achieving maximum degree for Trivium-like ciphers with all the key and IV bits as initial input variables $(X = (K, IV))$

Cipher	# key + # IV	[11]		This paper	
		# Rounds	$\mathbf{DEG}(f)$	# Rounds	$\mathbf{minCNDT}(f, X)$
Trivium	160	907	158	907	**157**
Kreyvium	256	982	255	**983**	255
TriviA-SC v1	256	1108	254	**1109**	255
TriviA-SC v2	256	1108	254	**1110**	255

When Will the Key and IV Be Sufficiently Mixed? Taking all the key and IV bits as initial input variables X, we implement Algorithm 2 to Trivium-like ciphers including Trivium, Kreyvium and TriviA-SC. The results are listed in Table 3, and comparisons with previous results are made. The results show that the maximum numbers of initialization rounds of Kreyvium, TriviA-SC v1 and TriviA-SC v2 such that the generated keystream bit does not achieve maximum algebraic degree are at least 983, 1109 and 1110 (out of 1152), rather than 982, 1108 and 1108 obtained in [11], respectively. As for Trivium, although we do not improve the result of [11] in terms of the number of initialization rounds, tighter upper bound on algebraic degree is obtained. In detail, for 907 rounds of Trivium, the upper bound on algebraic degree of the first output bit evaluated by our algorithm is 157, which is tighter than 158 by [11]. There results show that our new framework is more accurate than [11] when estimating the upper bound on algebraic degree of NFSR-based cryptosystems. All results above are obtained on a common PC with 2.5 GHz Intel Pentium 4 processor within one second.

When Will the IV Be Sufficiently Mixed? Taking all the IV bits as initial input variables, i.e., $X = IV$, we apply Algorithm 2 to Trivium-like ciphers, to give new distinguishing attacks on these ciphers in the chosen IV setting. Here, the key is taken as parameter, that is, $deg(k_i, X) = 0$ for any key bit k_i. This is consistent with a distinguisher in the setting of unknown key. The results are listed in Table 4, and comparisons with previous results are made. The result shows that the maximum number of initialization rounds of TriviA-SC v2 such that the generated keystream bit does not achieve maximum algebraic degree is at least 988 (out of 1152), rather than 987 obtained in [11]. In other cases except TriviA-SC v1, although we do not improve the results of [11] in terms of the number of initialization rounds, tighter upper bounds on algebraic degree are mostly obtained. For 793 rounds of Trivium, the upper bound on algebraic degree of the first output bit evaluated by our algorithm is 78, which is tighter than 79 by [11]. For 862 rounds of Kreyvium, the upper bound on algebraic degree of the first output bit evaluated by our algorithm is 126, which is tighter than 127 by [11]. There results also show that our new framework is more accurate than [11] when estimating the upper bound on algebraic degree of NFSR-based cryptosystems. All results above are obtained on a common PC within one second.

Table 4. New lower bound on the maximum number of rounds of not achieving maximum degree for Trivium-like ciphers with all IV bits as initial input variables ($X = IV$)

Cipher	# IV	[11]		This paper	
		# Rounds	**DEG**(f)	# Rounds	**minCNDT** (f, X)
Trivium	80	793	79	793	**78**
Kreyvium	128	862	127	862	**126**
TriviA-SC v1	128	987	126	987	126
TriviA-SC v2	128	987	126	**988**	127

Furthermore, similar to [11], we also take a subset of IV bits as initial input variables X, and apply Algorithm 2 to Trivium-like ciphers. We consider an exhaustive search on the sets of input variables X which have size of around half of $\#IV$ and contain no adjacent indexes. Using Algorithm 2, we have exhausted all the cubes of size $37 \leq n \leq 40$ for Trivium, which contain no adjacent indexes, within half an hour on a common PC. The amount of such cubes is $\sum_{n=37}^{40} \binom{81-n}{n} \approx 2^{25}$. As for Kreyvium and TriviA-SC, we have exhausted all the cubes of size $61 \leq n \leq 64$ for them, which contain no adjacent indexes, in a few hours on a common PC. The amount of such cubes is $\sum_{n=61}^{64} \binom{129-n}{n} \approx 2^{30}$. As results, some new cubes which are as good as the results of [11] and can not be found by [11] are obtained, as shown in Table 6 in Appendix.

Table 5. Distinguishing attacks on the full simplified variant of TriviA-SC v2

Cipher	# Rounds	Size of cube	Time compleixity	Reference
Simplified variant of TriviA-SC v2	Full	-	2^{120}	[16]
	Full	63	2^{63}	[11]
	Full	**59**	$\mathbf{2^{59}}$	**This paper**

As for the full simplified variants of TriviA-SC, we have exhausted all the cubes containing no adjacent indexes of size 60 in a week on a common PC. The amount of such cubes is $\binom{69}{60} \approx 2^{36}$. Then we have also exhausted approximately one twentieth of all the cubes containing no adjacent indexes of size 59 in half a month on a common PC. The amount of such cubes is $\binom{70}{59}/20 \approx 2^{37}$. As results, new distinguishing attack on the full simplified variant of TriviA-SC v2 is found with time complexity of 2^{59}, which improves the attack in [11] by a factor of 2^4 and is the best known attack on the cipher. The result is listed in Table 5, and comparisons with previous works are made. The corresponding cube is listed in Table 7 in Appendix. These results clearly illustrate the superiority of our new framework, compared with [11].

4   Conclusions

A new general framework for evaluating the algebraic degree tuple of NFSR-based cryptosystems is exploited and formalized to provide a new way of constructing distinguishing attacks. This is based on a new technique called *composite numeric mapping*, which gives a new general idea for iteratively estimating the upper bound on algebraic degree tuple of NFSR-based cryptosystems. We prove that *composite numeric mapping* is at least as good as *numeric mapping*, and most likely better than it demonstrated by applications. Based on this new technique, an efficient algorithm for algebraic degree tuple estimation of NFSR-Based cryptosystems is proposed and applied to Trivium-like ciphers to prove the effectiveness of our new framework. To the best of our knowledge, this is the first time that the idea of estimating the algebraic degree of a cryptographic primitive in one variable is considered and explored into cryptanalysis. The new framework may help to give the cryptosystem designers more insight to choose the required number of iterative rounds, and we expect that our new framework could become a new generic tool to measure the security of NFSR-based cryptosystems. In the future, it would be interesting to work on converting distinguishing attacks to key recovery attacks, and applications to other NFSR-based cryptosystems.

Acknowledgements. The authors would like to thank the anonymous reviewers for their valuable comments and suggestions. This work was supported by the National Natural Science Foundation of China under Grant 61602514, 61802437, 61272488, 61202491, 61572516, 61272041, 61772547, National Cryptography Development Fund under Grant MMJJ20170125 and National Postdoctoral Program for Innovative Talents under Grant BX201700153.

Appendix

A   The Procedure $\mathbf{CDEG}_{Tri}$ for $\delta = B$ and $\delta = C$

The procedure $\mathbf{CDEG}_{Tri}$ in the two cases, $\delta = B$ and $\delta = C$, are described in Algorithms 4 and 5, respectively.

Algorithm 4. $\mathbf{CDEG}_{Tri}\left(g_\delta\left(S^{(t)}\right), D^{(t)}\right)$ for $\delta = B$

If $t < r_A + 1$ then:

   Return $\mathbf{CDEG}\left(\left(a_{r_A}^{(t)} \cdot a_{r_A+1}^{(t)}\right) \oplus \mathcal{L}_B\left(S^{(t)}\right), D^{(t)}\right)$;

If $t \geq r_A + 1$ then:

   Return $\mathbf{CDEG}\left(h, D^{(t)}\right)$, where $h = \left(b_{r_C}^{(t-r_A)} \cdot b_{r_C+1}^{(t-r_A)} \cdot b_{r_C+1}^{(t-r_A-1)}\right) \oplus$

$\left(b_{r_C}^{(t-r_A)} \cdot b_{r_C+1}^{(t-r_A)} \cdot \mathcal{L}_A\left(S^{(t-r_A-1)}\right)\right) \oplus \left(b_{r_C+1}^{(t-r_A)} \cdot b_{r_C+1}^{(t-r_A-1)} \cdot \mathcal{L}_A\left(S^{(t-r_A)}\right)\right)$

$\oplus \left(\mathcal{L}_A\left(S^{(t-r_A)}\right) \cdot \mathcal{L}_A\left(S^{(t-r_A-1)}\right)\right) \oplus \mathcal{L}_B\left(S^{(t)}\right)$.

Algorithm 5. $\mathbf{CDEG}_{Tri}\left(g_\delta\left(S^{(t)}\right), D^{(t)}\right)$ for $\delta = C$

If $t < r_B + 1$ then:

   Return $\mathbf{CDEG}\left(\left(c_{r_B}^{(t)} \cdot c_{r_B+1}^{(t)}\right) \oplus \mathcal{L}_C\left(S^{(t)}\right), D^{(t)}\right)$;

If $t \geq r_B + 1$ then:

   Return $\mathbf{CDEG}\left(h, D^{(t)}\right)$, where $h = \left(b_{r_A}^{(t-r_A)} \cdot b_{r_A+1}^{(t-r_A)} \cdot b_{r_A+1}^{(t-r_A-1)}\right) \oplus$

$\left(b_{r_A}^{(t-r_A)} \cdot b_{r_A+1}^{(t-r_A)} \cdot \mathcal{L}_B\left(S^{(t-r_A-1)}\right)\right) \oplus \left(b_{r_A+1}^{(t-r_A)} \cdot b_{r_A+1}^{(t-r_A-1)} \cdot \mathcal{L}_B\left(S^{(t-r_A)}\right)\right) \oplus$

$\left(\mathcal{L}_B\left(S^{(t-r_A)}\right) \cdot \mathcal{L}_B\left(S^{(t-r_A-1)}\right)\right) \oplus \mathcal{L}_C\left(S^{(t)}\right)$.

B   The Cubes Used in Our Attacks

Table 6. Some new cubes found by Algorithm 2 for Trivium-like ciphers

Cipher	# Rounds	Cube size	Cube
TriviA-SC v2	1046	62	0, 2, 4, 6, 8, 10, 12, 14, 16, 18, 20, 22, 24, 26, 28, 30, 32, 34, 36, 38, 40, 42, 44, 46, 48, 50, 52, 54, 56, 58, 60, 62, 64, 66, 68, 70, 72, 75, 77, 79, 81, 83, 85, 87, 89, 91, 93, 95, 97, 99, 101, 103, 105, 107, 109, 111, 115, 117, 121, 123, 125, 127
The full simplified variants of TriviA-SC	1152	63	0, 2, 4, 6, 8, 10, 12, 14, 16, 18, 20, 22, 24, 26, 28, 30, 32, 34, 36, 38, 40, 42, 44, 46, 48, 50, 52, 54, 56, 58, 60, 62, 64, 66, 68, 70, 72, 74, 76, 78, 81, 83, 85, 87, 89, 91, 93, 95, 97, 99, 101, 103, 105, 107, 109, 111, 113, 115, 117, 121, 123, 125, 127

Table 7. The cubes used in our distinguishing attack on the full simplified variant of TriviA-SC v2

Cipher	Cube size	Cube
The full simplified variant of TriviA-SC v2	59	0, 2, 4, 6, 8, 10, 12, 14, 16, 18, 20, 22, 24, 26, 28, 30, 32, 34, 36, 38, 40, 42, 44, 46, 48, 50, 52, 54, 56, 58, 60, 62, 64, 66, 68, 70, 73, 75, 77, 79, 81, 83, 85, 87, 89, 91, 93, 95, 97, 99, 101, 103, 105, 107, 109, 121, 123, 125, 127

References

1. Cannière, C.: TRIVIUM: a stream cipher construction inspired by block cipher design principles. In: Katsikas, S.K., López, J., Backes, M., Gritzalis, S., Preneel, B. (eds.) ISC 2006. LNCS, vol. 4176, pp. 171–186. Springer, Heidelberg (2006). https://doi.org/10.1007/11836810_13

2. Hell, M., Johansson, T., Maximov, A., Meier, W.: The grain family of stream ciphers. In: Robshaw, M., Billet, O. (eds.) New Stream Cipher Designs. LNCS, vol. 4986, pp. 179–190. Springer, Heidelberg (2008). https://doi.org/10.1007/978-3-540-68351-3_14

3. Babbage, S., Dodd, M.: The MICKEY stream ciphers. In: Robshaw, M., Billet, O. (eds.) New Stream Cipher Designs. LNCS, vol. 4986, pp. 191–209. Springer, Heidelberg (2008). https://doi.org/10.1007/978-3-540-68351-3_15

4. ECRYPT. The eSTREAM project. http://www.ecrypt.eu.org/stream/

5. Wu, H.: ACORN: a lightweight authenticated cipher (v3). CAESAR Submission (2016). http://competitions.cr.yp.to/round3/acornv3.pdf

6. De Cannière, C., Dunkelman, O., Knežević, M.: KATAN and KTANTAN — a family of small and efficient hardware-oriented block ciphers. In: Clavier, C., Gaj, K. (eds.) CHES 2009. LNCS, vol. 5747, pp. 272–288. Springer, Heidelberg (2009). https://doi.org/10.1007/978-3-642-04138-9_20

7. Aumasson, J.-P., Henzen, L., Meier, W., Naya-Plasencia, M.: QUARK: a lightweight hash. J. Cryptology **26**(2), 313–339 (2012). https://doi.org/10.1007/s00145-012-9125-6

8. Canteaut, A., et al.: Stream ciphers: a practical solution for efficient homomorphic-ciphertext compression. J. Cryptology **31**(3), 885–916 (2018). https://doi.org/10.1007/s00145-017-9273-9

9. Chakraborti, A., Chattopadhyay, A., Hassan, M., Nandi, M.: TriviA: a fast and secure authenticated encryption scheme. In: Güneysu, T., Handschuh, H. (eds.) CHES 2015. LNCS, vol. 9293, pp. 330–353. Springer, Heidelberg (2015). https://doi.org/10.1007/978-3-662-48324-4_17

10. Chakraborti, A., Nandi, M.: TriviA-ck-v2. CAESAR Submission (2015). http://competitions.cr.yp.to/round2/triviackv2.pdf

11. Liu, M.: Degree evaluation of NFSR-based cryptosystems. In: Katz, J., Shacham, H. (eds.) CRYPTO 2017. LNCS, vol. 10403, pp. 227–249. Springer, Cham (2017). https://doi.org/10.1007/978-3-319-63697-9_8

12. Ding, L., Wang, L., Gu, D., Jin, C., Guan, J.: Algebraic degree estimation of ACORN v3 using numeric mapping. Secur. Commun. Netw. **2019**, 1–5, Article ID 7429320 (2019). https://doi.org/10.1155/2019/7429320

13. Yang, J., Liu, M., Lin, D.: Cube cryptanalysis of round-reduced ACORN. In: Lin, Z., Papamanthou, C., Polychronakis, M. (eds.) ISC 2019. LNCS, vol. 11723, pp. 44–64. Springer, Cham (2019). https://doi.org/10.1007/978-3-030-30215-3_3
14. Ding, L., Wang, L., Gu, D., Jin, C., Guan, J.: A new general method of searching for cubes in cube attacks. In: Meng, W., Gollmann, D., Jensen, C.D., Zhou, J. (eds.) ICICS 2020. LNCS, vol. 12282, pp. 369–385. Springer, Cham (2020). https://doi.org/10.1007/978-3-030-61078-4_21
15. Kesarwani, A., Roy, D., Sarkar, S., Meier, W.: New cube distinguishers on NFSR-based stream ciphers. Des. Codes Crypt. **88**(1), 173–199 (2019). https://doi.org/10.1007/s10623-019-00674-1
16. Xu, C., Zhang, B., Feng, D.: Linear cryptanalysis of FASER128/256 and TriviA-ck. In: Meier, W., Mukhopadhyay, D. (eds.) INDOCRYPT 2014. LNCS, vol. 8885, pp. 237–254. Springer, Cham (2014). https://doi.org/10.1007/978-3-319-13039-2_14

Quantum Circuit

$T-depth$ Reduction Method for Efficient $SHA-256$ Quantum Circuit Construction

Jongheon Lee[1,2] (iD), Sokjoon Lee[2] (iD), You-Seok Lee[2] (iD), and Dooho Choi[3(✉)] (iD)

[1] Department of Information Security Engineering,
University of Science and Technology, Daejeon 34113, Korea
jheon85@ust.ac.kr

[2] Department of Computer Engineering (Smart Security), Gachon University,
Seongnam 13120, Korea
{jonghun0805,yslee}@etri.re.kr, junny@gacheon.ac.kr

[3] Department of AI Cyber Security, College of Science and Technology,
Korea University Sejong, Sejong 30019, Korea
doohochoi@korea.ac.kr

Abstract. In order to perform a quantum brute force attack on a crypto-system based on Grover's algorithm, it is necessary to implement a quantum circuit of the cryptographic algorithm. Therefore an efficient quantum circuit design of a given cryptographic algorithm is essential, especially in terms of quantum security analysis, and it is well known that T-$depth$ should be reduced for time complexity efficiency.

In this paper, we propose a novel technique to reduce $T-depth$ (and $T-count$) when some quantum circuits located in between two $Toffoli-gates$ are interchangeable with a controlled phase gate ($Controlled-P$ gate), and apply this technique to four types of quantum adders, resulting in a T-$depth$ reduction of about 33%.

We also present new SHA-256 quantum circuits which have a critical path with only 3 quantum adders while the critical paths of quantum circuits in the previous works consist of 7 or 9 quantum adders, and also apply our technique to the proposed $SHA-256$ quantum circuits and the included quantum adders. Among the previous results, the T-$depth$ of the circuit with the smallest $Width$ 801 was approximately 109,104. On the other hand, that of the proposed SHA-256 quantum circuit with the width 799 is 16,121, which is remarkably reduced by about 85%. Furthermore, the other proposed quantum circuit only requires 768 qubits which is the smallest $Width$ compared to the previous results to the best of our knowledge.

Keywords: SHA-256 · Quantum circuit · $T-depth$ · $Toffoli-gate$

1 Introduction

Hash algorithms were created to provide secure data transmission and data integrity in information and communication protocols. Hash algorithms can be used for digital signatures, keyed message authentication codes, random number

© The Author(s), under exclusive license to Springer Nature Switzerland AG 2022
J. H. Park and S.-H. Seo (Eds.): ICISC 2021, LNCS 13218, pp. 379–402, 2022.
https://doi.org/10.1007/978-3-031-08896-4_20

generation, key derivation functions, etc. [1]. In particular, the SHA-2 hash family, published in 2002, is designated as a hash function standard [2].

If a collision attack is performed on a hash algorithm, it is known that the attack succeeds if the operation is performed a number of times corresponding to half the length of the bit string constituting the output value due to the birthday paradox. $SHA-256$ provides 128-bit security strength against classical collision attack [1,2].

There have been many theoretical studies on hash functions such as $MD5$, SHA-1, and SHA-512, and in a quantum environment, it is known that the security strength of existing hash functions is halved when using Grover's algorithm [3]. Previous works dealt with several quantum attack algorithms and methods of implementing quantum circuits of the cryptographic algorithms that can perform pre-image attack, 2nd pre-image attack, and collision attack [4–6]. However, the circuits presented in the previous works have little details on implementation of the hash algorithm, and they are forms made intuitively rather than created by efficient quantum circuits, such as reducing $Depth$ or $Width$ (the number of qubits) of the circuits. That is, the circuit is inefficient to use the existing circuit as it is to verify whether the security strength is actually reduced by half.

Although there are various standardized hash families such as $MD5$, SHA-2, and SHA-3, we focus quantum design for SHA-2, since it is currently the most widely commercialized, such as SSL digital authentication and IEEE 1609.2-based wireless V2X communication. There are 6 algorithms totally in the SHA-2 hash family, and the structures of these algorithms are the same except for some constants and the number of rounds. Hence we concentrate on $SHA-256$ and designed quantum circuits in this paper. Before presenting the SHA-2 quantum circuit, we present the quantum adder circuits to be used in the SHA-2 quantum circuit. Since many additions are performed in SHA-2, it is essential to use an efficient quantum adder circuit. In general, in quantum circuits, as $T-depth$ ($Depth$ formed by T gates in critical path) and $Width$ increase, the computational complexity of quantum computing exponentially increases, which degrades circuit performance. We will present $T-depth$ and $T-count$ reduction methods that can be used in quantum adders and $SHA-256$ quantum circuits. In this paper, our contribution is threefold:

- We introduce a novel technique to be able to reduce T-$depth$. We show that if some quantum circuits located in between two Toffoli gates are interchangeable with a controlled phase gate, then T-$depth$ 6 is reduced to 4 or 5.
- We apply the above trick to four quantum adders - CDKM adder [7], VBE adder [8], TK adder [9], and HRS adder [10] - and so our improved adders have the effect of reducing the T-depth by about 33% compared to the previous adders.
- We propose a new SHA-256 quantum circuit design which has a critical path with only 3 quantum adders while the critical paths of quantuem circuits in the previous works consist of 7 or 9 quantum adders [5,6]. We use our improved adders in this new SHA-256 quantum circuit, and also this T-$depth$ reducing method is applied in the sub-circuits such as Maj, Ch in

the *SHA*-256 quantum circuit. One of our resulting circuit requires only 799 qubits and has 12,024 *Toffoli-depth* which is a huge reduction 67% compared to the previous work [6] with the smallest *Width* 801. Furthermore, the other proposed *SHA*-256 quantum circuit only requires 768 qubits that is the smallest *Width* of all the previous results to the best of our knowledge.

The rest of the paper is constructed as follows: Sect. 2 introduces some background for the *Toffoli*-gate and related works for the *SHA*-2 hash family and its quantum circuits. In Sect. 3, we propose a *T−depth* and *T−count* reduction method by gathering ideas from several papers. In Sect. 4, we apply this reduction method to quantum adder circuits. Section 5 presents the *SHA−256* quantum circuit made using these improved quantum adder circuits. We present a new design structure and apply the reduction method to the function blocks used in *SHA−256*. Finally, this section compares the amount of quantum resources with other existing quantum circuits. Section 6 mentions the conclusions and topics for further research in the future.

2 Background and Related Work

2.1 *Toffoli−Gate*

In classical circuits, *NAND* gates and *Fanout* gates form a universal set of gates for classical computation. In a quantum circuit, the *Clifford+T* set forms the standard universal fault-tolerant gate set [11]. $\{H, CNOT, T\}$ is a minimal generating set of the *Clifford+T* set. *Hadamard* gate (*H* gate), *NOT* gate (*X* gate), *T* gate, *P* gate ($=T^2$ gate), *Z* gate ($=T^4$ gate), and *Contorlled−NOT* gate (*CNOT* gate) belonging to *Clifford+T* are widely used and performed as follows. $\oplus$ stands for modulo-2 addition.

$$H : |x_1\rangle \rightarrow \frac{|0\rangle + (-1)^{x_1}|1\rangle}{\sqrt{2}} \quad X : |x_1\rangle \rightarrow |x_1 \oplus 1\rangle$$

$$T : |x_1\rangle \rightarrow e^{\frac{\pi i}{4}x_1}|x_1\rangle \qquad P : |x_1\rangle \rightarrow e^{\frac{\pi i}{2}x_1}|x_1\rangle \tag{1}$$

$$Z : |x_1\rangle \rightarrow (-1)^{x_1}|x_1\rangle \qquad CNOT : |x_1 x_2\rangle \rightarrow |x_1(x_1 \oplus x_2)\rangle$$

In the next section, we will deal with the circuit composed of *H* gate, *X* gate, *Z−rotation* gate (R_z gate (*T*, *P*, *Z* gate)), and *CNOT* gate. As the counterpart of *AND* gate in classical circuit, there is a *Toffoli-gate* in quantum circuit. A *Toffoli−gate* is a *doubly controlled NOT* gate (C^2NOT gate), and it causes a change in the remaining one value according to two input values among three input values. This gate can be decomposed into two *H* gates and one *doubly controlled Z* gate (C^2Z gate, Fig. 1).

$$C^2NOT : |x_1 x_2 x_3\rangle \rightarrow |x_1 x_2(x_3 \oplus (x_1 \wedge x_2))\rangle$$

$$C^2Z : |x_1 x_2 x_3\rangle \rightarrow (-1)^{x_1 x_2 x_3}|x_1 x_2 x_3\rangle \tag{2}$$

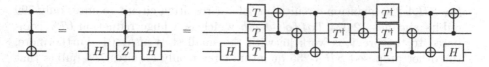

Fig. 1. A $Toffoli-gate$ with $T-depth$ 3 and $T-count$ 7 [12].

The phase of the output value from the C^2Z gate can be expressed exactly as $e^{\frac{\pi i}{4}4x_1x_2x_3}$. For x_1, x_2, $x_3 \in \{0,1\}$, the following expression holds [13].

$$4x_1x_2x_3 = x_1 + x_2 + x_3 - x_1 \oplus x_2 - x_2 \oplus x_3$$
$$- x_1 \oplus x_3 + x_1 \oplus x_2 \oplus x_3 \tag{3}$$

It can be seen that $4x_1x_2x_3$ consists of 7 operands. That is, C^2Z gate consists of 4 T gates and 3 $T^\dagger$ gates. T gates make phases $e^{\frac{\pi i}{4}x_1}$, $e^{\frac{\pi i}{4}x_2}$, $e^{\frac{\pi i}{4}x_3}$, and $e^{\frac{\pi i}{4}x_1\oplus x_2\oplus x_3}$. $T^\dagger$ gates create phases $e^{-\frac{\pi i}{4}x_1\oplus x_2}$, $e^{-\frac{\pi i}{4}x_2\oplus x_3}$, and $e^{-\frac{\pi i}{4}x_1\oplus x_3}$.

Meanwhile, the $Controlled\text{-}P^\dagger$ gate makes phase $e^{-\frac{\pi i}{4}2x_1\wedge x_2}$ $(=(-i)^{x_1\wedge x_2})$. Since $2x_1 \wedge x_2 = x_1 + x_2 - x_1 \oplus x_2$, it can be seen that $Controlled\text{-}P^\dagger$ gate consists of one T gate and two $T^\dagger$ gates. If $Controlled\text{-}P^\dagger$ gates exist on the two control lines of the $Toffoli\text{-}gate$, these two gates become a $C^2(-iX)$ gate composed of two T gates and two $T^\dagger$ gates [13] (Fig. 2).

$$x_1 + x_2 + x_3 - x_1 \oplus x_2 - x_2 \oplus x_3 - x_1 \oplus x_3 + x_1 \oplus x_2 \oplus x_3$$
$$- (x_1 + x_2 - x_1 \oplus x_2) \tag{4}$$
$$= x_3 - x_2 \oplus x_3 - x_1 \oplus x_3 + x_1 \oplus x_2 \oplus x_3$$

2.2 Quantum Adder Circuit

There are four types of quantum adder circuits covered in this paper: VBE adder, $CDKM$ adder, TK adder, and HRS adder [7,9,10,14]. These adders follow the ripple-carry form ($QRCA$, quantum ripple-carry adder), especially last adder is in-place constant-adder. Quantum resources used by each adder can be found in Table 1. In $SHA-256$, all adders are used in modular 2^{32}.

In the proposed $SHA-256$ quantum circuit, VBE adder and HRS adder are used only when adding the constant K_t [8,10]. As a result, it is possible to obtain the sum of 32-bit operands in modular 2^{32} with only 61 and 40 qubits in total, respectively.

$CDKM$ adder requires at least one work qubit (ancilla qubit) regardless of whether modular addition is performed. As $Toffoli-gate$ used in the adder is sequentially executed, $Toffoli-count$ is consistent with $Toffoli-depth$. Therefore, if you use a total of 5 work qubits, $T-depth$ can also be consistent with these values by using the Matroid Paritioning concept [15]. $Toffoli-depth$ is a measure used in [6], and is a concept used instead of $T-depth$. In the previous work, there are two main reasons for analyzing circuit resources with $Toffoli-depth$. One is that T gate is mostly used within $Toffoli-gate$, so even if the circuit

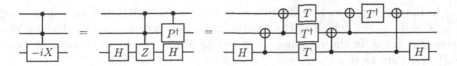

Fig. 2. A *doubly controlled* $(-iX)$ gate [13].

performance is expressed with relatively inaccurate *Toffoli−depth*, that is logically justified. The other is that they do not decompose quantum circuits down to *Clifford+T* gate sets to form basic-level circuits. That is, they omitted the *T−depth* and *T−count* reduction process. In this work, we will refer to both *Toffoli−depth* and more accurate *T−depth*.

  TK adder is a *QRCA* adder that does not use work qubits at all. Since fewer qubits are used, the *T−depth* is larger than other *QRCA* circuits. In the next section, we will provide a logic process that can reduce the *T−count* and *T−depth* of these four adder circuits. This process does not change *Toffoli−count* or *Toffoli−depth*.

2.3 Secure Hash Algorithm-2

Pre-processing Step. The *SHA*-2 hash algorithm consists of two main steps: a pre-processing step and a hash computation step [2]. In the first step, message padding and parsing are performed, and bits are added so that the length of the padded message is a multiple of 512 bits. The original message must be less than 2^{64} in length. That is, the length of the message must be able to be expressed in 64 bits. In this paper, it is assumed that the number N of 512-bit message blocks after the pre-processing step is 1. In *SHA−256*, there is a hash value update process after the main round function algorithm is executed 64 times. In this process, if N is 2 or more, an operation to copy the value is required. However, this cannot be done by the *No − cloning* theorem in quantum environment [16]. Therefore, it is necessary to assume that N is 1, and that's why the hash value update operation was omitted in previous studies [5,6]. The maximum length of the original message that can be handled by the *SHA−256* quantum circuit is 447 because the minimum length of the padding is 65 in one message block.

Hash Computation Step. In the hash computation step, a hash value (message digest) is created. Depending on the number of message blocks of the padded message, the entire algorithm iteration occurs. The main hash computation algorithm is repeated a total of 64 times each time this iteration is performed. In the main hash computation algorithm, all additions are performed in modular 2^{32} and are largely divided into message schedule algorithm and round function algorithm.

In the message schedule algorithm, 48 W_t ($t = 16, ..., 63$) are created by using W_t ($t = 0, ..., 15$), which is the existing 16 32-bit words composed of padded message values. In the message schedule algorithm, two logical functions $\sigma_0(x)$ and $\sigma_1(x)$ are used.

The initial hash value $H^{(0)}$ is a 256-bit constant value and is assigned to eight 32-bit internal variables a, b, c, d, e, f, g, h used in the round function algorithm. Four logical functions Maj, Ch, $\Sigma_0(x)$, $\Sigma_1(x)$ are used in the round function algorithm. A total of 64 32-bit words $K_0, K_1, ..., K_{63}$ are added sequentially for each round. The quantum circuit implementation for each internal function is introduced in the Sect. 5.

$$
\begin{aligned}
W_t &= M_t^{(1)} \quad 0 \leq t \leq 15 \\
&= \sigma_1(W_{t-2}) + W_{t-7} + \sigma_0(W_{t-15}) + W_{t-16} \quad 16 \leq t \leq 63 \\
where \quad & \sigma_0(x) = ROTR^7(x) \oplus ROTR^{18}(x) \oplus SHR^3(x), \\
& \sigma_1(x) = ROTR^{17}(x) \oplus ROTR^{19}(x) \oplus SHR^{10}(x)
\end{aligned}
\tag{5}
$$

$$
\begin{aligned}
& h = g, g = f, f = e, e = d + T_1, d = c, c = b, b = a, a = T_1 + T_2 \\
& where \quad T_1 = h + \Sigma_1(e) + Ch(e, f, g) + K_t + W_t, T_2 = \Sigma_0(a) + Maj(a, b, c), \\
& Maj(x, y, z) = (x \wedge y) \oplus (x \wedge z) \oplus (y \wedge z), Ch(x, y, z) = (x \wedge y) \oplus (\neg x \wedge z), \\
& \Sigma_0(x) = ROTR^2(x) \oplus ROTR^{13}(x) \oplus ROTR^{22}(x), \\
& \Sigma_1(x) = ROTR^6(x) \oplus ROTR^{11}(x) \oplus ROTR^{25}(x)
\end{aligned}
\tag{6}
$$

After the 64th round iteration is completed, the intermediate hash value $H^{(i-1)}$ is added to the values of $a, ..., h$ and updated to the value $H^{(i)}$. Since we assumed N = 1 earlier, i = 1. Finally, we get the 256-bit hash value $H^{(1)} = H_0^{(1)}||H_1^{(1)}||...||H_7^{(1)}$. If you look at Fig. 3, you can see the procedure of the $SHA-256$ algorithm.

$$
\begin{aligned}
H_0^{(1)} &= H_0^{(0)} + a, H_1^{(1)} = H_1^{(0)} + b, H_2^{(1)} = H_2^{(0)} + c, H_3^{(1)} = H_3^{(0)} + d, \\
H_4^{(1)} &= H_4^{(0)} + e, H_5^{(1)} = H_5^{(0)} + f, H_6^{(1)} = H_6^{(0)} + g, H_7^{(1)} = H_7^{(0)} + h
\end{aligned}
\tag{7}
$$

In the classic $SHA-256$ circuit, the critical path is a section in which 7 operands are added using 6 adders to produce the output value $T_1 + T_2$ [17]. Through repeated execution, $T_1 + T_2$ is updated 64 times and is continuously allocated to the internal variable a. Studies to reduce the time taken by this critical path in classical circuits have been conducted in several papers [17,18].

$SHA-256$ **quantum circuit** [4–6] presented quantum cryptosystem circuit implementations to investigate the security strength of the various cryptosystems. Among them, the resources used for the $SHA-256$ quantum circuit can be seen in Table 2. We implemented the circuit based on the $Clifford+T$ set as in previous studies. In [5], the $CDKM$ adder [7] was used for throughout the $SHA-256$ quantum circuit, and the quantum circuit implementation of each internal function was briefly presented. Round function algorithm and message

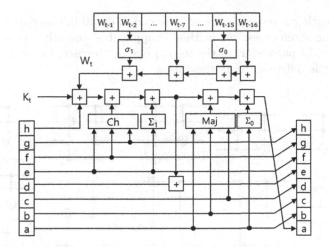

Fig. 3. Round function and message schedule algorithm in $SHA-256$.

schedule algorithm were processed in parallel, and $T-depth$ and $T-count$ were optimized by performing $T-par$ for the entire circuit [15].

In [6], $SHA-256$ quantum circuit implementation was presented in 4 versions, and $CDKM$ adder and $QCLA$ adder were used as adders [7,19]. As mentioned earlier, in this study, only $Width$ and $Toffoli-depth$ for each version were mentioned without performing $T-depth$ and $T-count$ reduction (optimization).

In the quantum circuit we present, the round function and message schedule algorithm are processed in parallel. Unlike previous works, it is not implemented with only one adder, but as a hybrid version in which several types of adders are placed in appropriate positions. For accurate comparison with previous papers, both $T-depth$ and $Toffoli-depth$ are written in Table 2.

3 $T-Depth$ and $T-Count$ Reduction Method

In the fault-tolerant model, it is known that implementing the T gate among the gates of the $Clifford+T$ set is much more difficult than all other gates and that the $T-depth$ determines the circuit runtime [20–22]. Therefore, many studies have been conducted on $T-depth$ and $T-count$ reduction to reduce and optimize quantum circuit construction costs [13,15,23,24]. We will use the matroid partitioning concept in [15] and modify the optimization subroutines in [24]. We will deal with a quantum circuit with a subcircuit between two $Toffoli-gates$.

If there are two $Toffoli-gates$ in the quantum circuit, their relative positions exist in ten cases [25] (Fig. 4). Three of these cases will be dealt with in this paper. The three cases we will cover are when both the control lines and the target line are shared, only the control lines is shared and only the target line is shared. The other seven cases are not covered in detail in this paper. In fact, for the remaining seven cases, our method is applicable similarly to the three cases we will cover. In particular, in the second and sixth cases, we should apply our method a little different from other cases.

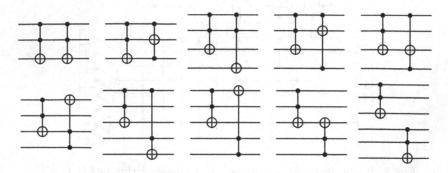

Fig. 4. Ten cases of relative positions for two $Toffoli\text{-}gates$ [25]. Of these, only three cases (first, third and ninth cases) are dealt with in this paper. For the remaining seven cases, our method can be applied similarly to the three cases we will cover.

3.1   Three Cases Where Our Method is Applied

Case 1) Both control lines and a target line are shared. Assume that two $Toffoli\text{-}gates$ share control lines and a target line and a subcircuit named A exists between these two gates as shown in Fig. 5. Now we create $Controlled\text{-}P^\dagger$ gate and $Controlled\text{-}P$ gate on the right side of $Toffoli\text{-}gate$ on the left side of the circuit. Since these two gates have an inverse operation relationship with each other, it is self-evident to constitute an identity circuit. Now consider $Controlled\text{-}P$ gate and the existing subcircuit A. If these two partial circuits are commutative, The $Controlled\text{-}P$ gate will be moved to the left of $Toffoli\text{-}gate$ on the right side of the circuit. That is, if exchange is possible as shown in Fig. 5, due to the matroid partitioning concept of [15], the total $T\text{-}depth$ can be reduced from 6 to 4, and the total $T\text{-}count$ can be reduced from 14 to 8. Let the basis variables corresponding to each line be x_1, x_2, x_3 [15]. As we saw in the previous section, these basis variables are the components of phase in the $R_z(\theta)$ gate. It can be seen that the $T\text{-}count$ can be reduced to 8 through Eq. (8).

$$(x_1 + x_2 + x_3 - x_1 \oplus x_2 - x_2 \oplus x_3 - x_1 \oplus x_3 + x_1 \oplus x_2 \oplus x_3)$$
$$+ (-x_1 - x_2 + x_1 \oplus x_2) + (x_1 + x_2 - x_1 \oplus x_2)$$
$$+ (-x_1 - x_2 - x_3 + x_1 \oplus x_2 + x_2 \oplus x_3 + x_1 \oplus x_3 - x_1 \oplus x_2 \oplus x_3) \quad (8)$$
$$= (x_3 - x_2 \oplus x_3 - x_1 \oplus x_3 + x_1 \oplus x_2 \oplus x_3)$$
$$+ (-x_3 + x_2 \oplus x_3 + x_1 \oplus x_3 - x_1 \oplus x_2 \oplus x_3)$$

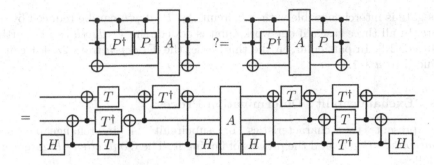

Fig. 5. Case 1) Both control lines and a target line are shared.

Case 2) Control lines are shared but a target line is not. Figure 6 shows the case where the control lines are shared but the target line is not. *T−depth* and *T−count* can be reduced through the same process. If there is a *Toffoli−gate* with an off-control part, As in the figure below of Fig. 6, a *P* gate or $P^†$ gate is created.

Case 3) A target line is shared but control lines are not. In the third case, we drew Fig. 7 using three *Toffoli−gates*. Unlike the previous two cases, this third case is a method applicable even when three or more *Toffoli−gates* exist. In this case, the control lines are not shared among *Toffoli−gates*, so the *T−depth* cannot be reduced with the same logic as in the previous two cases. Looking at Fig. 7, the rightmost *Toffoli−gate* maintains *T−depth* 3 and *T−count* 7 without any conversion. If *Controlled−P* gates and subcircuits A_1 and A_2 are interchangeable, the *T−depth* of the rightmost *Toffoli−gate* can be shared. That is, *T* gates and $T^†$ gates of these three gates are placed on the same time line to make *T−depth* 3. *T−count* does not change in this case. It is possible to reduce the *T−depth* from $3n$ to $2n + 1$ for n (≥ 2) *Toffoli−gates*. In fact, if a *Controlled−P* gate is made on control lines of the rightmost *Toffoli−gate* and

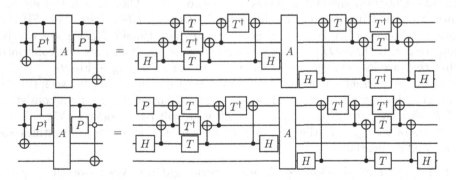

Fig. 6. Case 2) Control lines are shared but a target line is not.

this gate is interchangeable with subcircuit A_2, $T-depth$ can be reduced by one more. In all three cases, if one work qubit is added, the $T-depth$ can be further reduced [13]. In particular, in the third case, the $T-depth$ from $2n + 1$ can be reduced to $n + 1$.

3.2   Exchangeability Determination Process

We present the characteristics of subcircuit A interchangeable with $Controlled-P$ gate and the process of finding it. The $Controlled-P$ gate works as follows.

$$Controlled - P : |x_1x_2\rangle \rightarrow e^{\frac{\pi i}{4}2x_1 \wedge x_2} |x_1x_2\rangle \qquad (9)$$

It can be seen that x_1 and x_2, which are basis variables corresponding to each wire, are maintained as they are, and $i^{x_1 \wedge x_2}$ is generated. That is, in order for subcircuit A to be exchangeable with $Controlled-P$ gate, the above operation must be possible as it is. That is, the global phase $i^{x_1 \wedge x_2}$ should be generated even after passing through the subcircuit A first.

Let's take a simple example. An $Off-controlled-NOT$ gate is obviously interchangeable with the $Controlled-P$ gate. This is because one gate has an off-control part and the other has an on-control part. It can also be known from the Eq. (10).

$$x_2 \rightarrow -x_1 \oplus x_2 \Longrightarrow$$
$$x_1 + x_2 - x_1 \oplus x_2 \rightarrow x_1 - x_1 \oplus x_2 - (x_1 \oplus -(x_1 \oplus x_2)) = x_1 + x_2 - x_1 \oplus x_2 \qquad (10)$$

As it can be seen from Eq. (10) and Fig. 8, after passing through the $Off-controlled-NOT$ gate, x_2 is converted to $-x_1 \oplus x_2$, so after passing through the $Off-controlled-NOT$ gate, when passing through the $Controlled-P$ gate, we can make $i^{x_1 \wedge x_2}$. That is, these two gates are commutative.

As another example, consider the $SWAP$ gate. This gate is a gate that has the effect of swapping the positions of the two wires. Therefore, it can be seen intuitively that it is interchangeable with the $Controlled-P$ gate. This $SWAP$ gate can consist of three $CNOT$ gates. Since these three $CNOT$ gates can be replaced with three $Off-controlled-NOT$ gates, so it can also be confirmed that they are interchangeable by the previous example (Fig. 8, Fig. 9).

Now, we present a method to determine the exchangeability between subcircuit A and $Controlled-P$ gate. It was mentioned earlier that a circuit consisting of H gate, X gate, R_z gate, and $CNOT$ gate will be considered. We will use variants of the optimization subroutines in [24]. The following subroutines are executed sequentially.

1) X gate cancellation by X gate propagation. We move all X gates in A to the right through X gate propagation [24]. If there is a $CNOT$ gate in A and the target line is shared with the X gate, transform it into an

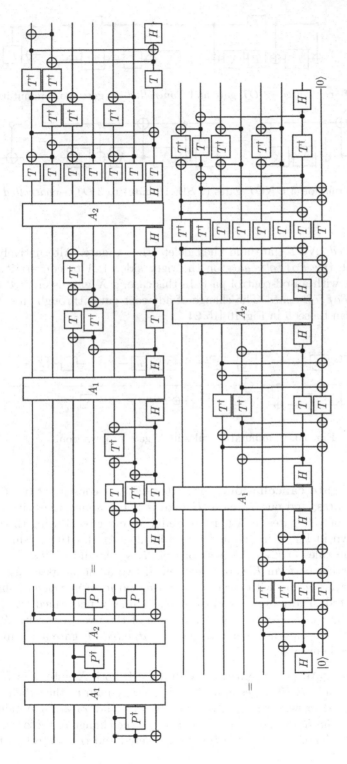

Fig. 7. Case 3) A target line is shared but control lines are not.

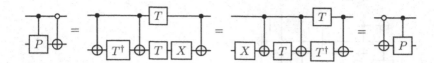

Fig. 8. $Off-controlled-NOT$ gate and $Controlled-P$ gate are commutative.

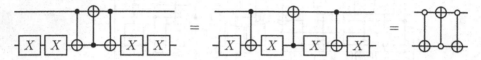

Fig. 9. Transformation 3 $CNOT$ gates (1 $SWAP$ gate) to 3 $Off-controlled-NOT$ gates

$Off-controlled-NOT$ gate and then delete the X gate. Alternatively, it is combined with the $Toffoli-gate$ on the right side of A to convert it into a $Toffoli-gate$ with an off-control part. In this case, a X gate is created on the right side of $Toffoli-gate$. The change of adjacent gates through this X gate propagation can be seen in Fig. 10 [15, 24].

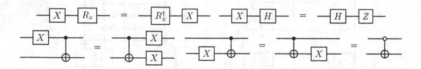

Fig. 10. Commutation rules in X gate propagation.

2) $Hadamard$ **gate cancellation.** $Controlled-P$ gate consists of two $CNOT$ gates, two T gates, and one $T^\dagger$ gate. H gate is not commutative with T gate [13,15]. Therefore, H gates in A must be reduced and erased using the circuit identities shown in Fig. 4 in [24] and Fig. 8 in [26]. At this time, using Fig. 5 in [24] and the rules of [27], the positions of R_z gates and $CNOT$ gates are changed to further perform H gate reduction. If two adjacent gates are placed in an inverse relationship with each other during position movement, they are obviously deleted. The movement of all gates is finally performed for H gate reduction. If the $Controlled-P$ gate shares one of the two wires with H gate, that is, if all H gates are not removed, then $Controlled-P$ gate and subcircuit A are not interchangeable.

3) $Z-rotation$ **gate** $(R_z(\theta)$ **gate) cancellation** If both X gates and H gates are all deleted, only $R_z(\theta)$ gates and $CNOT$ gates remain in the subcircuit A. We are interested in whether the basis variables x_1 and x_2 are maintained or not. Therefore, the $R_z(\theta)$ gates that do not affect the change of these two basis variables can be ignored. If the $R_z(\theta)$ gate is deleted and the control parts and target parts of adjacent $CNOT$ gates each share lines, they are also deleted because they are inversely related to each other.

4) Discrimination between $CNOT$ gates. Now, in the subcircuit A consisting of the remaining $CNOT$ gates, a $CNOT$ gate with a control part on one of the two lines where the $Controlled-P$ gate exists and a target part on the third line may remain. Again, since it does not cause any change in the basis variables, it can be ignored. In the opposite case, A is not an interchangeable circuit with a $Controlled-P$ gate because it causes a change in the basis variable corresponding to the lines.

Let's take a concrete example with Fig. 11 and the basis variables corresponding to each line be x_1, x_2, x_3, and x_4. Through X gate propagation, the X gate is combined with the $CNOT$ gate to become an $Off-controlled\ NOT$ gate. Then, H gate cancellation is performed. We can clear all H gates on the first and second lines. Now, only $R_z(\theta)$ gates and $CNOT$ gates remain on the first and second lines. The $CNOT$ gate connected to the first and fourth lines in the middle of the circuit can also be ignored. The H gate in the 3rd line also can be ignored because it has no effect on the basis variables x_1 and x_2. As a result, only 3 $CNOT$ gates remain and x_2 is changed to $x_2 \oplus x_4$. Since the basis variables x_1 and x_2 do not appear in the first and second lines, this subcircuit A in the example is not interchangeable with the $Controlled-P$ gate.

Although subcircuit A is not interchangeable with the $Controlled-P$ gate, it does not prevent subcircuit A's $T-depth$ from being reduced. You can see that there is no gate on the first wire of subcircuit A'. That is, subcircuit A is interchangeable with T gate. When using the T gate, $T-depth$ can be reduced to 4 as when using the $Controlled-P$ gate, but $T-count$ cannot be reduced to 8.

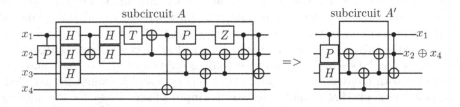

Fig. 11. (Example) Subcircuit A that cannot be commutative with $Controlled-P$ gate but with T gate.

We mentioned earlier that for the second and sixth cases in Fig. 4 we should apply our method a little different from other cases. That is, T gate and $T^\dagger$ gate should be used instead of $Controlled-P$ gate and $Controlled-P^\dagger$ gates (Fig. 12). $Controlled-P$ gate cannot be used due to the existence of H gates constituting $Toffoli-gates$. As mentioned earlier, T gate and H gates are not commutative. So to avoid wires with H gates, we use T gate and $T^\dagger$ gate instead.

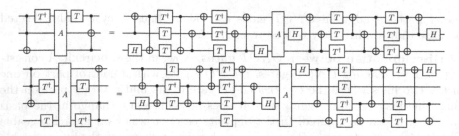

Fig. 12. The second and sixth cases in Fig. 4. In both cases, $T-depth$ is reduced from 6 to 4 like other cases. But $T-count$ can not be reduced to 8.

Consider a *triply controlled NOT* gate (C^3NOT gate, Fig. 13). This gate can be decomposed into 4 *Toffoli − gates* [28]. Looking at the middle figure of Fig. 13, it seems that it is not easy to reduce $T-depth$ to 8 due to the presence of H gates. However, in the wire at the bottom of the figure, the two H gates constituting the different *Toffoli − gates* are adjacent to each other, so they are removed. Therefore proper arrangement of *Controlled−P* gates and *Controlled−P†* gates in the circuit results in a C^3NOT gate with $T-depth$ of 8. This result is the same as Fig. 9 in [15] using the matroid partitioning concept. For every $k \geq 3$ if there are $k − 2$ qubits in arbitraty states, then a *controlled NOT* gate with k control parts (C^kNOT) can be made of $4(k − 2)$ *Toffoli − gates* by Lemma 7.2 in [28]. Applying our method, C^kNOT gate can be a gate where $T-depth$ is $8(k − 2)$.

3.3   Remark and Cautions

One might wonder why it doesn't cover the case where a single *Toffoli−gate* is alone. As mentioned in the introduction, we aim to create an efficient quantum cryptosystem circuit to verify security strength. A typical quantum attack algorithm used in this case is Grover's algorithm [3]. In this case, Grover's algorithm uses the *phase kick − back* technique. If there is only one *Toffoli−gate* and it is combined with *Controlled−P†* gate, *phase* -i occurs and it cannot be removed. A quantum circuit that cannot maintain the input phases $+\frac{1}{\sqrt{2^n}}$ for the number n of bits of the superposed input value cannot be used in Grover's algorithm. Therefore, when modifying the circuit to reduce $T-depth$ and $T-count$, we must take care that the phase $+\frac{1}{\sqrt{2^n}}$ of each state is maintained after passing through all gates in quantum cryptosystem circuit. So as mentioned later, our technique cannot be applied to a *Toffoli−gate* alone among *Toffoli−gates* of quantum adder circuits.

There are a few things to keep in mind when using the above method. First, If the subcircuit A is complex, we need to repeat steps 2, 3, and 4 several times

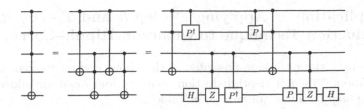

Fig. 13. A *triply controlled NOT* gate's $T-depth$ can be reduced from 12 to 8.

to know the exchangeability. In case of a $CARRY$ gate used in HRS adder [10], it is impossible to delete all H gates at once because it consists of many $Toffoli\text{-}gates$. Of course, $Toffoli\text{-}gates$ in A that share control lines with the $Toffoli\text{-}gates$ on either side can be neglected because they do not cause changes in basis variables x_1 and x_2.

Second, after subcircuit A and *Controlled-P* gates swap places, *Controlled-P* gate is sometimes changed to *Controlled-$P^\dagger$* gate. That is, in this case, one of the basis variables x_1 and x_2 is negated. This can also be combined with the right $Toffoli\text{-}gate$ to reduce $T\text{-}depth$.

Lastly, if subcircuit A has a special shape, then $Toffoli\text{-}gates$ on both sides can be reduced to one. For example, assume that two $Toffoli\text{-}gates$ share both two control lines and one target line. At this time, suppose that subcircuit A is a $CNOT$ gate that uses one of two control lines of the $Toffoli\text{-}gates$ as a target line and the fourth line as a control line. Then two $Toffoli\text{-}gates$ can be reduced to one $Toffoli\text{-}gate$ having a different control line (Fig. 14, [10]). That is, there is a situation in which the $Toffoli\text{-}count$ can be decreased. In this case, $T\text{-}depth$ can be reduced from 6 to 3 instead of 4. There are various other situations in which $Toffoli\text{-}count$ can be reduced (Fig. 14, [25,29,30]).

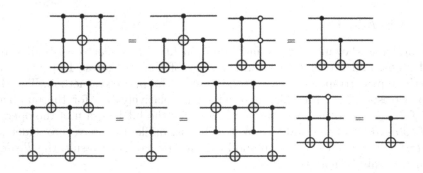

Fig. 14. $Toffoli\text{-}count$ reduction rules [25,29,30].

4   Application 1: Applying $T-depth$ and $T-count$ Reduction Technique to Quantum Ripple-Carry Adder

Now we apply the technique presented in the above section to some quantum adders. About 33% of T-depth reduction occurs in four quantum adders. These changed T-$depth$ values can be seen in Table 1.

4.1 $CDKM$ Adder

First, let's take a look at the $CDKM$ adder. As can be seen from Figure 6 in [7], all $Toffoli-gates$, except for one, can be paired by two and share two control lines and one target line. In the central part of the circuit, the subcircuit is composed of X gate and $CNOT$ gate. Because they share the target line, these two gates can be turned into Off-$controlled-NOT$ gate. Because the situation corresponds to case 1, we can reduce the $T-depth$ using our method (Fig. 5). We cannot use the above method for a $Toffoli-gate$ lying alone below the center of the $CDKM$ adder circuit.

4.2 VBE Adder

The VBE adder consists of $CARRY$ function blocks and SUM function blocks, and you can see the circuit in Figure 1 in [8] when one operand is a constant. In the $SHA-256$ quantum circuit to be mentioned in the next section, the VBE adder is used in a situation where one of the two operands is a constant. There is only one $Toffoli-gate$ in the $CARRY$ function block below the center of the VBE adder we will use. In $CDKM$ adder and VBE adder both, there is one $Toffoli-gate$ that we cannot apply the above method to, respectively. Therefore, the $T-depth$ reduction rates are slightly less than 33%.

4.3 TK Adder

TK adder is shown in Fig. 5 and Fig. 7 in [9]. TK adder consists of a total of 4 steps, and the first step consists only of $CNOT$ gates. The second and fourth steps correspond to the second case of the proposed method. The third step corresponds to the third case which is relatively free for the number of $Toffoli-gates$ in the above method. Also, for the bit length n of the operand, $Toffoli-count$ of this adder is 4n−6. That is, unlike the above two adders, for all $Toffoli-gates$ the above method can be applied. As a result, the $T-depth$ reduction rate is more than 33%.

4.4 HRS Adder

The design of HRS adder is much more complicated than those of the three adders above [10] (Fig. 15). Unlike VBE and $CDKM$ adders, there is no need to use clean work qubits. Instead, we can use borrowed dirty qubits, i.e. qubits

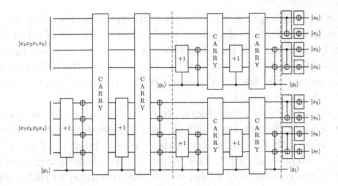

Fig. 15. The HRS adder for n $= 8$. The operand x and The constant a are added to calculate the sum s in mod 2^8. This circuit has three layers. In the last layer, it consists of $CNOT$ gates and NOT gates, and execution is decided according to the value of a. For example, if the value of least-significant bit a_0 is 0, $CNOT$ gate and NOT gate located at the top are not executed.

in arbitraty states. Therefore, the length of the circuit is long so that the states of dirty borrowed qubits are the same after the operation is finished. As it is designed using a divide-and-conquer scheme and module 2^{32} addition is performed, it consists of a total of 5 layers. In the last layer, any $Toffoli-gate$s are not used. The above $T-depth$ reduction technique cannot be applied to 6 $Toffoli-gate$s in each layer. Of the 408 $Toffoli-gate$s constituting $Toffoli-detph$, 384 $Toffoli-gate$s belong to the first case of the above method. Therefore, the $T-depth$ reduction rate is less than 33% like the first two adders.

Based on the above method, VBE adder and $CDKM$ adder with reduced $T-depth$ and $T-count$ are circuits with $T-depth$ and $T-count$ optimized by the matroid partitioning concept [15]. However, TK adder and HRS adder cannot be circuits optimized for $T-depth$ in the above way. This is because the circuits presented in [9,10] are circuits in which $Toffoli-count$ can be reduced. That is, since $Toffoli-count$ is not optimized, it cannot be said that $T-depth$ is optimized even if our $T-depth$ reduction method is used. In both, there are sections where there are three or more $Toffoli-gate$s that share both control lines. The $Toffoli-count$ reduction (optimization) technique is not covered in detail in this paper. It seems that a $T-depth$ optimized circuit can be obtained if the $T-depth$ reduction technique is used in the circuit that $Toffoli-count$ ($Toffoli-depth$) is optimized.

5   Application 2: Using Reduced Quantum Adders in Our New Quantum $SHA-256$ Circuit

5.1 $SHA-256$ Quantum Circuit Implementation

Now, we configure the $SHA-256$ quantum circuit using the above four adders with reduced $T-depth$. In Fig. 16, you can see the internal function blocks composing the $SHA-256$ quantum circuit we present. Work qubits are not shown in the figure. In case of the Maj function block, the circuit of [7] is used as it is. On the other hand, the Ch function block is our newly created function block, which consist of 1 $CNOT$ gate and 1 $Toffoli-gate$. Both function blocks do not use work qubits and have $Toffoli-depth$ of 1. These function blocks can be seen in more detail in Fig. 17.

Σ_0, Σ_1, σ_0, and σ_1 function blocks receive a 32-bit string as an input value and output a 32-bit string respectively. Since these quauntum circuits can be constructed using only $CNOT$ gates in the reverse direction of the PLU decomposition [4], $T-depth$s are all 0. The output values of these four function blocks are all used as the operands of addition and then restored to their original input values through the inverse operation in quantum circuit. Since they consist only of $CNOT$ gates, they do not significantly affect the performance speed of the circuit. For example, in the case of σ_0 function block, this quantum circuit with $Depth$ 50 can be made by using a total of 193 $CNOT$ gates. Although 20 swapping occurs, we do not change the swapping process to 3 $CNOT$ gates because we only need to change the positions of the lines. If it is converted to 3 $CNOT$ gates, a total of 253 $CNOT$ gates are required.

There are three main ideas introduced when designing the $SHA-256$ quantum circuit. We introduced a path balancing technique that makes some operations run in the next round. And instead of making T_1 first, we made $d + T_1$ first to reduce the length of the critical path of the entire circuit. In addition, the $T-depth$ is reduced as much as possible by providing enough work qubits to all adders performing in parallel.

In our proposed quantum circuit, we perform a total of 11 additions and 1 subtraction per round. This subtraction is used to restore the values of the internal variables e, f, g in the circuit. Subtraction will use the subtractor version of TK adder and $CDKM$ adder, so $T-depth$ and $T-count$ are not different from each adder. In the classical circuit, T_1, which is commonly required for $d + T_1$ and $T_1 + T2$, is made first, but in our quantum circuits, $d + T_1$ is made as quickly as possible. If you look at Fig. 18, you can see that W_t is used twice as an operand. In the round function algorithm, 8 adder circuits and 1 subtractor circuit are used, and in the message schedule algorithm, 3 adder circuits are used. Both algorithms are processed in parallel. In t-th round, the adder circuit with a long vertical line located to the left of Fig. 18 is to add W_{t-1}, so it is one of the adders constituting the round function algorithm.

The adder circuits used in the proposed circuit are VBE adder, $CDKM$ adder, TK adder and HRS adder mentioned in the previous section. In the previous works, only one adder circuit was used to construct each $SHA-256$ quantum circuit. We present circuits with reduced $Width$ or T-depth by arranging several types of adder circuits in appropriate positions.

There are two circuits presented by us. Our two proposed circuits are named $SHA-Z1$ and $SHA-Z2$, respectively. $SHA-Z1$ consists of a total of 768 qubits, and one HRS adder and eleven TK adders are used. If you look at Fig. 18, constant K_t is added using HRS adder at the front, and two TK adders

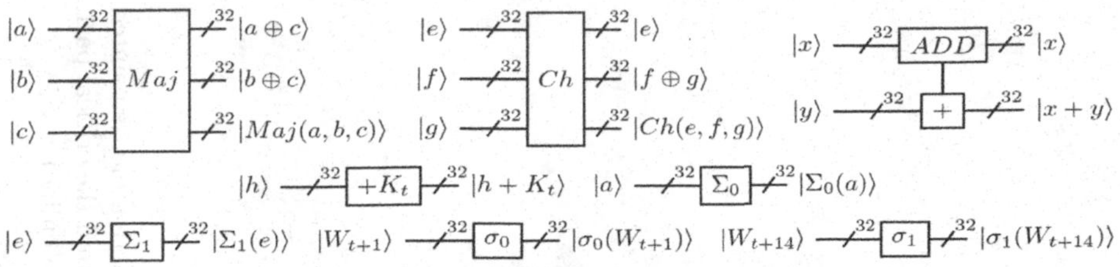

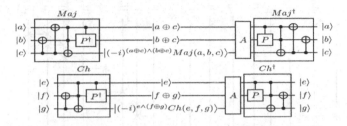

Fig. 16. Function blocks in $SHA-256$ quantum circuit. In Maj and Ch function blocks, phases are not indicated ($(-i)^{(a\oplus c)\wedge(b\oplus c)}$ and $(-i)^{e\wedge(f\oplus g)}$).

Fig. 17. Maj function block and Ch function block in $SHA-256$ quantum circuit. In the $SHA-256$ circuit, the qubits' states of each wire are maintained after passing through subcircuit A.

are located in the same time slice. The remaining nine TK adders are grouped into four and five for parallel processing. Of the 768 qubits, 256 qubits are used to represent the internal variables $a, ..., h$ in the round function algorithm, and 512 qubits are used in the message schedule algorithm. When we use the HRS adder, we can use idle qubits in the message schedule algorithm as the borrowed dirty qubits. HRS adder and TK adder don't use clean work qubits at all. Recall that T-$depth$s are not optimized for the HRS adder and TK adder to which our T-$depth$ reduction technique is applied. Therefore, $Toffoli$-$depth$ and T-$depth$ of this SHA-256 circuit can be further reduced.

$\quad SHA-Z2$ is a circuit with a total of 799 qubits, which consists of one VBE adder and 11 $CDKM$ adders. 11 $CDKM$ adders are composed of 2 $CDKM$ adders using only 1 work qubit and 9 $CDKM$ adders using 5 work qubits. Compared with the previous version, the HRS adder is replaced by the VBE adder and two $CDKM$ adders that uses 1 work qubit are located in the same time slice. The remaining 9 $CDKM$ adders using 5 works qubits are located in second and third time slices (Our quantum circuits consist of three time slices in one round, and the reason is that the critical path that determines the $T-depth$ consists of three adders). In this circuit design, there are a total of 31 work qubits. When VBE adder uses 29 work qubits, $CDKM$ adders operating in the same time slice uses 1 work qubit each. Since VBE adder performs addition in the modular 2^{32} and adds constants, therefore 32-bit addition can be performed with a total of 61 qubits [8]. The remaining 9 $CDKM$ adders can be used in a form in which the $T-depth$ is reduced as much as possible by using 5 work

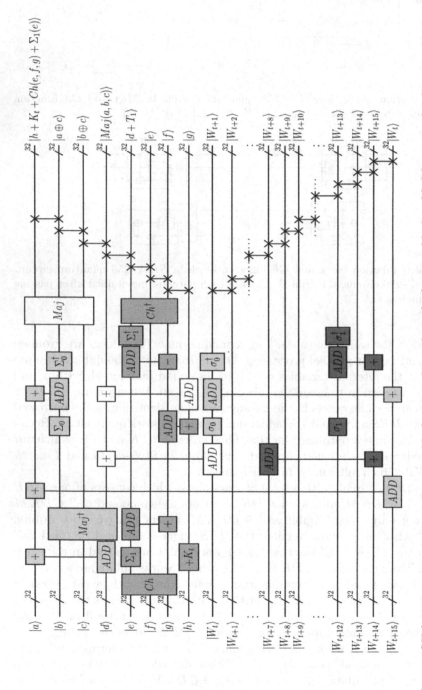

Fig. 18. $SHA-256$ quantum circuit. Function blocks painted in red are the function blocks added from round 2. Function blocks painted in green are added from round 3. Function blocks colored in blue constitute a critical path in one round. For each round the critical path consists of only 3 quantum adder circuits. Two-qubit gates at the end of each round are $SWAP$ gates. (Color figure online)

Table 1. Function block resources in SHA-256 quantum circuit. These T-$depth$ values are the results after our T-$depth$ reduction technique is applied. All quantum adders are performed in modular 2^{32}. HRS adder and VBE adder are only used when adding constant K_t. In HRS adder, 8 work qubits are borrowed dirty, that is, they are in arbitrary states.

	$Width$	$\#ancilla$	T-$depth$	$Toffoli$-$depth$
Maj	3	0	2	1
Ch	3	0	2	1
$\Sigma_0, \Sigma_1, \sigma_0, \sigma_1$	32	0	0	0
HRS adder	40	8	840	408
VBE adder	61	29	119	59
TK adder	64	0	191	93
$CDKM$ adder using 1 ancilla	65	1	123	61
$CDKM$ adder using 5 ancillas	69	5	61	61

qubits each. Since up to 5 $CDKM$ adders operate at the same time, the number of work qubits required in this time slice is up to 25. In fact, it is not necessary to use the method presented in the previous section for $T-depth$ reduction in the second and third time slices in SHA-$Z2$. This is because work qubits can be sufficiently provided. In this time, our method only reduces T-$count$.

A path balancing technique is introduced when constructing the proposed circuits. This technique repositions some operations so that they can be performed in the next round. In Fig. 18, the function blocks painted in red are the function blocks added from round 2. Function blocks painted in green are added from round 3. The upper area is the round function algorithm and the lower area is the message schedule algorithm. The message schedule algorithm starts from round 2 and gets the values of $W_{16}, ..., W_{63}$ through a total of 48 iterations. In the proposed circuit, the message schedule algorithm ends at round 50. That is, W_{16} is made in round 3 but not in round 2, and W_{63} is made in round 50. Of course, in the 50th round, the σ_0, its inverse function block and the $CDKM$ adder between them do not work.

On the other hand, the round function algorithm repeats up to the 65th round. Function blocks painted in red at the top of the circuit run from round 2 to round 65. The difference between the classic circuit and the proposed quantum circuit is that the classical circuit repeats 64 times for one message block, whereas the proposed quantum circuit repeats a total of 65 times. In the final 65th round, only the function blocks painted in red at the top are executed. In the final 65th round, there are 31 work qubits in our second proposed circuit, so all three additions use the $CDKM$ adder using 5 ancillas. After each round, the position of qubits is adjusted through swapping according to the hash algorithm.

In each round, the critical path can be composed of only three adders. That is, we design circuits to execute in parallel 3 out of 9 adders for each time slice in the round function algorithm. The critical paths of the quantum circuits

Table 2. $SHA-256$ quantum circuit resources comparison. Our two proposed circuits are named $SHA-Z1$ and $SHA-Z2$, respectively. When constructing our circuits, we used adder circuits with reduced T-depth to which the above technique was applied.

	$Width$	T-$depth$	$Toffoli$-$depth$	Used quantum adder
SHA-256 [5]	2402	70400	–	$CDKM$ [7]
SHA-$C1$ [6]	801	–	36368	$CDKM$ [7]
SHA-$C2$ & $C3$ [6]	853	–	13280	$QCLA$ [19]
SHA-$C4$ [6]	834	–	27584	$CDKM$ [7]
SHA-$C5$ & $C6$ [6]	938	–	10112	$QCLA$ [19]
SHA-$Z1$	768	78911	38360	HRS, TK
SHA-$Z2$	799	16121	12024	$VBE, CDKM$

created in previous studies [5,6] consist of 7 adders or 9 adders. Function blocks painted in blue are function blocks constituting a critical path with $T-depth$ that determines the performance of a quantum circuit. $SHA-Z1$'s critical path consists of one HRS adder, two TK adders, Ch function block's inverse and Σ_1 function block's inverse. On the other hand, $SHA-Z2$'s critical path consists of Ch and its inverse, Σ_1 and its inverse, one $CDKM$ adder using 1 ancilla and two $CDKM$ adders using 5 ancillas.

5.2   Quantum Circuit Resources Comparison

$SHA-Z1$ has been implemented with a smaller number of qubits than any previous circuits. $SHA-Z2$ has a smaller $Toffoli-depth$ than $SHA-C2$& $C3$ implemented as $QCLA$ with $Toffoli$-$depth$ $O(log\ n)$. Unfortunately, we could not make a circuit with $Toffoli-depth$ smaller than that of $SHA-C5$& $C6$ while using less than 900 qubits. If $QCLA$ is used in the proposed circuit, $Toffoli-depth$ can be less than 10000. However, in the proposed circuit, up to 5 adders are operated at the same time, so at least 265 work qubits will be required. Note that one $QCLA$ uses 53 work qubits for 32-bit module addition [19]. There may be improved $QCLA$ that requires less work qubits. If it exists, we can create much more efficient quantum circuits.

6   Conclusion and Future Work

We have proposed a novel method that reduces $T-depth$ when there are two $Toffoli-gates$ and subcircuit between them. By using this method, $CDKM$ adder, VBE adder, TK adder and HRS adder became circuits with reduced T-$depth$ by about 33%. And then these adders are placed appropriately for use in our SHA-256 circuit. Also we present new construction about $SHA-256$ quantum circuit so that the critical path consists of only 3 adders. This circuit's construction and performance are much better than $SHA-256$ circuits in previous works.

During this study, the necessity of reducing *Toffoli-count* emerged. It is expected that a *T-depth* optimized circuit can be made only by performing the *T-depth* reduction method on a circuit with optimized *Toffoli-count*. Under what conditions can the *Toffoli-count* be reduced when three or more *Toffoli-gates* share both control lines? *Toffoli-count* (or *Toffoli-depth*) optimization algorithm should be devised. There are previous studies that provided hints for implementing this algorithm [25, 29, 30].

We also don't know our proposed circuit design is optimized circuit construction in quantum environment. When we can use 799 qubits, is proposed circuit's *T−depth* is optimized? There may be more efficient circuit designs available for *SHA−256*. Finding or implementing a more efficient adder circuit that can be used for *SHA*-256 also could be a future research task. As mentioned previously, we need advanced in-place *QCLA* which the number of work qubits is reduced. Another candidates would be to build a multi-operand adder circuit specialized for *SHA−256* quantum circuit. Of course, the performance of this adder should be better than our proposed circuit. That is, *T−depth* of this adder must be less than *T−depth* of three consecutive adders that make up the critical path.

Acknowledgement. This work was partly supported by Institute of Information & communications Technology Planning & Evaluation (IITP) grant funded by the Korea government (MSIT) (⟨Q|Crypton⟩, No.2019-0-00033, Study on Quantum Security Evaluation of Cryptography based on Computational Quantum Complexity) and also partially supported by a Korea University Grant.

References

1. Forouzan, B.A., Mukhopadhyay, D.: Cryptography and Network Security. Mc Graw Hill Education (India) Private Limited, New York (2015)
2. NIST, FIPS PUB.: 180–4 Secure Hash Standard (SHS) (2015)
3. Grover, L.K.: A fast quantum mechanical algorithm for database search. In: Proceedings of the Twenty-Eighth Annual ACM Symposium on Theory of Computing (1996)
4. Jaques, S., Naehrig, M., Roetteler, M., Virdia, F.: Implementing Grover oracles for quantum key search on AES and LowMC. In: Canteaut, A., Ishai, Y. (eds.) EUROCRYPT 2020. LNCS, vol. 12106, pp. 280–310. Springer, Cham (2020). https://doi.org/10.1007/978-3-030-45724-2_10
5. Amy, M., Di Matteo, O., Gheorghiu, V., Mosca, M., Parent, A., Schanck, J.: Estimating the cost of generic quantum pre-image attacks on SHA-2 and SHA-3. In: Avanzi, R., Heys, H. (eds.) SAC 2016. LNCS, vol. 10532, pp. 317–337. Springer, Cham (2017). https://doi.org/10.1007/978-3-319-69453-5_18
6. Kim, P., Han, D., Jeong, K.C.: Time–space complexity of quantum search algorithms in symmetric cryptanalysis: applying to AES and SHA-2. Quantum Inf. Process. **17**(12), 1–39 (2018). https://doi.org/10.1007/s11128-018-2107-3
7. Cuccaro, S.A., et al.: A new quantum ripple-carry addition circuit. arXiv preprint quant-ph/0410184 (2004)
8. Beauregard, S., Gilles, B., José, M.F.: Quantum arithmetic on Galois fields. arXiv preprint quant-ph/0301163 (2003)

9. Takahashi, Y., Noboru, K.: A linear-size quantum circuit for addition with no ancillary qubits. Quantum Inf. Comput. **5**(6), 440–448 (2005)
10. Häner, T., Roetteler, M., Svore, K.M.: Factoring using 2n+2 qubits with Toffoli based modular multiplication. arXiv preprint arXiv:1611.07995 (2016)
11. Lidar, D.A., Todd, A.B.: Quantum Error Correction. Cambridge University Press, Cambridge (2013)
12. Amy, M., et al.: A meet-in-the-middle algorithm for fast synthesis of depth-optimal quantum circuits. IEEE Trans. Comput. Aided Des. Integr. Circuits Syst. **32**(6), 818–830 (2013)
13. Selinger, P.: Quantum circuits of T-depth one. Phys. Rev. A **87**(4), 042302 (2013)
14. Vedral, V., Adriano, B., Artur, E.: Quantum networks for elementary arithmetic operations. Phys. Rev. A **54**(1), 147 (1996)
15. Amy, M., Dmitri, M., Michele, M.: Polynomial-time T-depth optimization of Clifford+ T circuits via matroid partitioning. IEEE Trans. Comput. Aided Des. Integr. Circuits Syst. **33**(10), 1476–1489 (2014)
16. Nielsen, M.A., Isaac, C.: Quantum computation & quantum information, pp. 558–559 (2002)
17. Sun, W., et al.: Design and optimized implementation of the SHA-2 (256, 384, 512) hash algorithms. In: 2007 7th International Conference on ASIC. IEEE (2007)
18. Ahmad, I., Das, A.S.: Hardware implementation analysis of SHA-256 and SHA-512 algorithms on FPGAs. Comput. Electr. Eng. **31**(6), 345–360 (2005)
19. Draper, T.G., et al.: A logarithmic-depth quantum carry-lookahead adder. arXiv preprint quant-ph/0406142 (2004)
20. Buhrman, H., et al.: New limits on fault-tolerant quantum computation. In: 2006 47th Annual IEEE Symposium on Foundations of Computer Science (FOCS 2006). IEEE (2006)
21. Fowler, A.G., Ashley, M.S., Peter, G.: High-threshold universal quantum computation on the surface code. Phys. Rev. A **80**(5), 052312 (2009)
22. Fowler, A.G.: Time-optimal quantum computation. arXiv preprint arXiv:1210.4626 (2012)
23. Gidney, C.: Halving the cost of quantum addition. Quantum **2**, 74 (2018)
24. Nam, Y., et al.: Automated optimization of large quantum circuits with continuous parameters. NPJ Quantum Inf. **4**(1), 1–12 (2018)
25. Rahman, M.Z., Rice, J.E.: Templates for positive and negative control Toffoli networks. In: Yamashita, S., Minato, S. (eds.) RC 2014. LNCS, vol. 8507, pp. 125–136. Springer, Cham (2014). https://doi.org/10.1007/978-3-319-08494-7_10
26. Abdessaied, N., Soeken, M., Drechsler, R.: Quantum circuit optimization by Hadamard gate reduction. In: Yamashita, S., Minato, S. (eds.) RC 2014. LNCS, vol. 8507, pp. 149–162. Springer, Cham (2014). https://doi.org/10.1007/978-3-319-08494-7_12
27. Garcia, E., Juan, C., Pedro, C.P.: Equivalent quantum circuits. arXiv preprint arXiv:1110.2998 (2011)
28. Barenco, A., et al.: Elementary gates for quantum computation. Phys. Rev. A **52**(5), 3457 (1995)
29. Maslov, D., Gerhard, W., Michael, M.: Simplification of Toffoli networks via templates. In: IEEE Proceedings of 16th Symposium on Integrated Circuits and Systems Design, SBCCI 2003 (2003)
30. Miller, D., Dmitri, M., Gerhard, D.: A transformation based algorithm for reversible logic synthesis. In: Proceedings of 2003 Design Automation Conference (IEEE Cat. no. 03ch37451). IEEE (2003)

Efficient Quantum Circuit of Proth Number Modular Multiplication

Chanho Jeon, Donghoe Heo, MyeongHoon Lee, Sunyeop Kim, and Seokhie Hong[✉]

Institute of Cyber Security and Privacy (ICSP),
Korea University, Seoul, Republic of Korea
{cksgh419,dong5641,ope2527,shhong}@korea.ac.kr

Abstract. The efficient quantum circuit of Post Quantum Cryptography (PQC) impacts both performance and security because Grover's algorithm, upon which various attacks are based, also requires a circuit. Therefore, the implementation of cryptographic operations in a quantum environment is considered to be one of the main concerns for PQC. Most lattice-based cryptography schemes employ Number Theoretic Transform (NTT). Moreover, NTT can be efficiently implemented using the modulus $p = k \cdot 2^m + 1$, called Proth number, and there is a need to elaborate on the quantum circuit for a modular multiplication over p. However, to the best of our knowledge, only quantum circuits for modular multiplication of the general odd modulus have been proposed, and quantum circuits for specific odd modulus are not presented. Thus, this paper addresses this issue and presents a new optimized quantum circuit for Proth Number Modular Multiplication (PNMM) which is faster than Rines et al.'s modular multiplication circuit. According to the evaluation with commonly used modulus parameters for lattice-based cryptography, our circuit requires an approximately 22%–45% less T-depth than that of Rines et al.'s.

Keywords: CDKM adder · Proth number · Quantum circuit · Moduluar multiplication · Lattice · Number theoretic transform

1 Introduction

Public key cryptosystems such as RSA, DSA, and ECC operate on a signature and key exchange, and are the main factors in telecommunications and financial areas. Their security is based on the hardness of solving mathematical problems such as the integer factorization problem, discrete logarithm problem, and elliptic curve discrete logarithm problem. Although such problems require an at least sub-exponential time to solve on a classical computer, a quantum algorithm proposed by Peter Shor [7] in 1994 solves the discrete logarithm and integer factorization problem within polynomial time. This implies that the current cryptographic algorithms are unsecure against quantum algorithms on quantum computers.

© The Author(s), under exclusive license to Springer Nature Switzerland AG 2022
J. H. Park and S.-H. Seo (Eds.): ICISC 2021, LNCS 13218, pp. 403–417, 2022.
https://doi.org/10.1007/978-3-031-08896-4_21

As a substitute for classical public key cryptosystems, Post Quantum Cryptography (PQC) was designed to be resistant to attacks in a quantum computing environment. The National Institute of Standards and Technology (NIST) has been working on standardizing PQC. Various mathematical theories have been developed to prove the resistance of PQC, and the most commonly applied approach one is Lattice.

The security of lattice-based cryptography is based on Learning With Error (LWE), which uses lattice structures and errors to provide hardness. To increase the computational efficiency, LWE-based cryptography uses a new structure called Ring-LWE (RLWE). In RLWE-based cryptography, the adoption of NTT accelerates the polynomial multiplication considerably. Currently, five of the seven candidates for NIST PQC Round 3 are lattice-based cryptography. Among the five candidates, Kyber, Dilithium, and Falcon adopted NTT and outperformed the others. This indicates that an efficient implementation of NTT is an important research issue.

For the efficiency of NTT, RLWE-based cryptography uses $x^{2^m} + 1$ as a quotient polynomial and modulus p having the $2^{m+1} - th$ root. Because most of the computational complexity in NTT is the modular multiplication, a modular multiplication for the modulus p is the main factor determining the overall performance. In addition to the performance aspect, an efficient implementation of a modular multiplication also has a significant influence on a security analysis because attacks on RLWE-based cryptography require operations using the same modulus. However, to the best of our knowledge, only a modular multiplication quantum circuit for a typical odd modulus has been proposed [6], and an an optimized quantum circuit for PNMM, which often used in NTT, has not been proposed. Therefore, in this paper, we propose a quantum circuit for PNMM using the integer characteristics of the Proth number, and justify the performances by comparing the existing modular multiplication quantum circuit with our approach in terms of the T-depth and number of qubits.

The remainder of this paper is organized as follows. Section 2 describes the background necessary for this paper. Section 3 describes several gates required to implement PNMM and presents their implementations. Section 4 shows quantum circuits for each step of PNMM and provides the results of a T-depth evaluation. Finally, the last section summarizes the analysis results and presents future research topics.

2   Background

2.1   Proth Number

A natural number N is called a Proth number which is in the form of $N = k \cdot 2^m + 1$ where k is odd and $k < 2^m$. In particular, N is called a Proth prime if N is a prime number. Owing to its efficiency, a Proth prime is used as modulus for NTT.

Proth number N has a special property for a modular multiplication.

$$C = C_0 + 2^m C_1 \quad (0 \le C_0 < 2^m) \tag{1}$$
$$\Rightarrow kC = kC_0 + k \cdot 2^m C_1 \tag{2}$$
$$\equiv kC_0 - C_1 \pmod{N} \tag{3}$$

where C_0, C_1 represents lower m qubits of C and the remaining part respectively.

As in the case of Montgomery modular multiplication, PNMM can be applied within a special domain. It is possible to move an integer a to what is called Proth domain by multiplying k^{-1} on modular N. We denote an element on Proth domain as $\bar{a}$ moved from a. We set $\bar{x} = xk^{-1}$, $\bar{y} = yk^{-1}$. Then $k\bar{x} \cdot \bar{y} = kC \equiv kC_0 - C_1 \equiv xyk^{-1} = \overline{xy} \pmod{N}$. Within Proth domain, a modular multiplication can be executed using only 2 multiplications and some additions. At the end of the computations, the resulting values are returned to the original domain by multiplying with k.

2.2 CDKM Adder

Several quantum circuits are being studied for a cryptographic analysis, and many are designed for addition which is the most basic operation. Many adders such as VBE [9], CDKM [1], carry-lookahead [3], and ϕ adder [2] have been presented. Many improvements such as [8] have also been studied. In this paper, we use the CDKM adder which is an in-place adder using only one ancilla qubit. The CDKM adder consists of a combination of two gates, MAJ and UMA, which is implemented in different ways such as 2-cnot and 3-cnot version. The T-depth of a CDKM adder is $2n - 1$ when the number of qubits required to represent an input is n. In addition, when no carries occur or a carry is not delivered, a CDKM adder can be implemented by removing the gates affecting the MSB qubit from the original circuit, the depth of which is $2n - 2$.

2.3 Generic Quantum Modular Multiplication Circuit

In [6], Rines et al. describe a circuit that applies a modular multiplication with one fixed input in a general modulus p. In this study, we deal with the multiplication between two arbitrary inputs and apply it as a multiplication circuit with two arbitrary inputs. In addition, it is assumed that the adder uses a CDKM adder with one ancilla qubit. The outline of the quantum modular multiplication is as follows.

1. Compute the multiplication result of x and y
2. Divide $(x \cdot y)$ by p and obtain the remainder $x \cdot y \pmod{p}$ and quotient q.
3. To uncompute, $q \cdot p$ is calculated from the quotient q. We add $x \cdot y \pmod{p}$ to $q \cdot p$, thus making the output with value of $x \cdot y$. Finally, we uncompute the ancilla qubits which is the state of $x \cdot y$.

Here, $x \cdot y \pmod{p}$ is calculated using the above three processes, and the overall number of ancilla qubits requires a total of $\phi(n)+n+1$, where $\phi(n)$ qubits are used to store $x \cdot y$. In addition, n qubits are also used to store the modulus p used as a constant within the entire process, and the last 1 qubit is used by the CDKM adder. The toatl T-depth of multiplication, division, and uncomputation is $(3n^2 - 5n + 3\phi(n))$, $((5n - 3) \cdot (\phi(n) - n))$, $(3(\phi(n) - n)^2 - 2(\phi(n) - n))$ respectively, and the total T-depth is $(n^2 + 3\phi(n)^2 - 2\phi(n) - n\phi(n))$.

3   Quantum Circuit of Arithmetic

In this section, we present the quantum circuits of base operations for PNMM – Controlled CDKM Adder and Sign-Conversion, with their T-depth.

3.1   Controlled CDKM Adder

The controlled adder is a modified adder that determines whether an adder is applied according to the value of the control qubit. The Multiplication of two numbers a, b is generally calculated using summation of $a_i \cdot (b \cdot 2^i)$, where a_i is i-th bit of a. Therefore, each summation becomes a sort of a controlled adder which is applied according to a control qubit. Also, division introduced later in this paper uses a controlled adder in each loop. Thus we can know that the performance of controlled adder affects the performance of multiplication and division significantly. If all gates in the circuit are changed and thereby affected by the control qubit when converting the adder into a controlled adder, all $C^k NOT$ gates must be transformed into $C^{k+1} NOT$ gates. However, if the controlled adder is implemented in this way, all gates are controlled by the same control qubit, and thus the existing parallelized structure cannot be used. In addition, converting the $C^k NOT$ gate into a $C^{k+1} NOT$ gate leads to an increase in the number of ancilla qubits and $CCNOT$ gates, resulting in a significant degradation in performance. In the case of a controlled CDKM, the number of $CCNOT$ and $C^3 NOT$ gates increased, and the T-depth also increased to $9n + O(1)$ (Fig. 1). In this section, we provide a method for removing control qubits from multiple gates in a circuit and reducing the depth and number of ancilla qubits through a rearrangement and adjustment between gates.

Reverse Structure Optimization. Reverse structure optimization is a technique using some gate and its reverse gate on a same circuit. If gate A^{-1} exists with A in the same circuit, it is a circuit that does nothing. It can be used to reduce the number of gates that the control qubit affects in the controlled gate and applies an optimization in terms of the gate and depth. Figure 2 shows circuits that apply $Ctrl - A, Ctrl - B$, and $Ctrl - A^{-1}$ sequentially. The circuit is the same as a circuit that applying A, B, and A^{-1} or does nothing according to the value of the control qubit. Because a circuit that does nothing is the same as a circuit that applies A and A^{-1}, and a circuit that sequentially applies

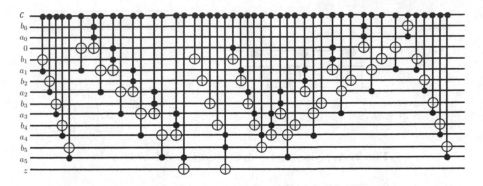

Fig. 1. Unoptimized quantum circuit of controlled CDKM adder

$Ctrl - A, Ctrl - B$, and $Ctrl - A^{-1}$ may be said to be the same as a circuit that applies $A, Ctrl - B$, and A^{-1}. Therefore, a circuit with a controlled gate corresponding to a reverse process on both sides can be optimized in terms of the gate cost and depth by deleting the control qubit of both sides (Fig. 3).

Gates in the controlled CDKM can be optimized by deleting the control qubits of both sides. It is known that the $CCNOT$ and C^3NOT gates perform as inverse functions for themselves. Therefore, circuits of $(CCNOT, Ctrl - B, CCNOT)$ and $(C^3NOT, Ctrl - B, C^3NOT)$ structures can be converted into circuits of $(CNOT, Ctrl - B, CNOT)$ and $(CCNOT, Ctrl - B, CCNOT)$, respectively.

Gate Rearrangement and Substitution. After applying a reverse structure optimization, it is possible to reduce the number of $CCNOT$ and C^3NOT gates remaining in the middle through a rearrangement and substitution between gates. If we change the order of remaining gate in the middle such that the gates operating on the same qubit can be collected, we can divide gates set into a type of $CCNOT + C^3NOT$ gate and $CNOT + CCNOT$ gate (Fig. 5).

The type of $CNOT + CCNOT$ gate can be simplified to proceed within three qubits, as shown in Fig. 6a. Figure 6a shows a circuit that changes (C, a, z) into $(C, a, z \oplus C \oplus C \cdot a)$. The addition of C and $C \cdot a$ values to the last qubit can be expressed by adding $C \cdot (a \oplus 1)$, which means that a $CNOT + CCNOT$ gate can be replaced with a $NOT + CCNOT + NOT$ gate (Fig. 6b). Depth increases from two $(CNOT, CCNOT)$ to three $(NOT, CCNOT, NOT)$ gates. However, there are many gates corresponding to type $CNOT + CCNOT$, and if each NOT gate on the left and right is applied in parallel, the overall depth is reduced.

Similarly, the type of $CCNOT + C^3NOT$ gate can be simplified to proceed within five qubits (Fig. 7a), and is a circuit that changes (C, a_0, a_1, a_2, z) into $(C, a_0, a_1, a_2, z \oplus C \cdot a_2 \oplus C \cdot a_0 \cdot a_1)$. Adding $C \cdot a_2$ and $C \cdot a_0 \cdot a_1$ values to the last qubit is equivalent to adding $C \cdot (a_2 \oplus a_0 \cdot a_1)$, which can be applied with

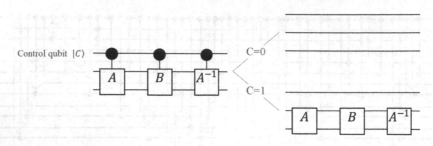

Fig. 2. Applying $Ctrl - A, Ctrl - B$, and $Ctrl - A^{-1}$

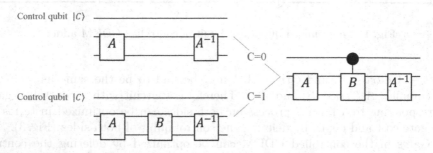

Fig. 3. Equivalent to $A, Ctrl - B$, and A^{-1}

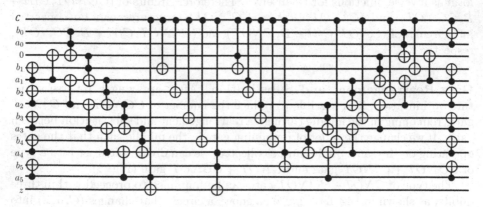

Fig. 4. Controlled CDKM adder circuit applying reverse structure optimization

three $CCNOT$ gates (Fig. 7b). Because one ancilla qubit and three $CCNOT$ gates are required to apply a C^3NOT gate, transforming $CCNOT + C^3NOT$ gate into three $CCNOT$ gates avoids the use of an unnecessary ancilla qubit and saves one $CCNOT$ gate.

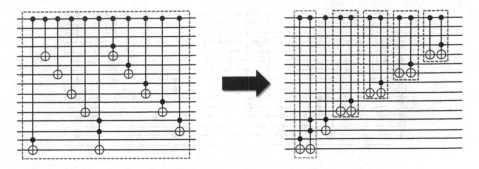

Fig. 5. Gate rearrangement

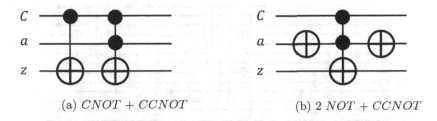

(a) $CNOT + CCNOT$ (b) $2\,NOT + CCNOT$

Fig. 6. Gate substitution from $CNOT + CCNOT$ to $2\,NOT + CCNOT$

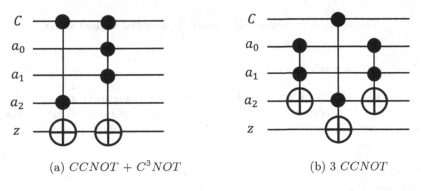

(a) $CCNOT + C^3NOT$ (b) $3\,CCNOT$

Fig. 7. Gate substitution from $CCNOT + C^3NOT$ to $3\,CCNOT$

Through reverse structure optimization and gate rearrangement and substitution, the T-depth of the controlled CDKM adder can be optimized to $3n + 1$ (Fig. 8). In addition, where a carry does not occur or does not need to be delivered, the T-depth can be reduced to $3n - 2$ by deleting one $CCNOT$ gate used for the carry transfer of the highest qubit and two $CCNOT$ gates next to it (Fig. 9).

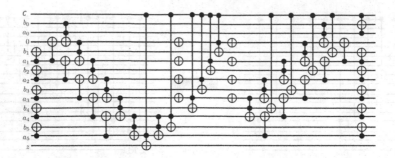

Fig. 8. Example circuit of optimized controlled CDKM adder when $n = 6$

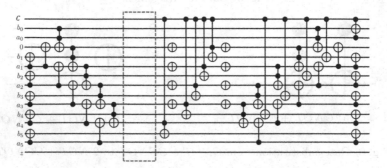

Fig. 9. No carry version of optimized controlled CDKM adder

3.2 Sign Conversion

If x is bit flipped in a binary, it will have the same value as $(-x - 1)$. Adding 1 to that value, it becomes $(-x)$, which is the number of inverted signs from the existing input. Consequently, a sign conversion was applied in accord with the following steps:

1. Bit flip
2. Increase by 1

In step 2, it is possible to apply a general quantum adder using ancilla qubits. However, there is also a circuit that does not use an ancilla qubit, borrows qubits containing random values, and increases by 1 as follows [4].

Increment. An increment is a gate that obtains $v + 1$ using input qubits that have a value of v and borrowed qubits (not ancilla qubits) that have an arbitrary value g, consisting of two subtractions and several gates. Two subtractions have an important position in the increment, and the subtraction used is a circuit that reverses the 2-CNOT version of the CDKM adder [1]. Subtraction is performed once between v and g, and once between g' which is bit flipped from g excluding LSB of g, twice in total. Let c be the value of LSB of g. Then we can get the

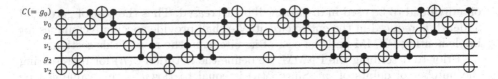

Fig. 10. Quantum circuit of increment

result $v - 2 \cdot c + 1$ after performing two subtractions. So $v + 1$ is obtained when c is 0, and $v - 1$ is obtained when c is 1.

To always obtain $v + 1$, place the $CNOT$ gate, which determines whether to bit flip v based on the value of c, before and after two subtractions (Fig. 10). When the controlled bit flip is applied by the $CNOT$ gate, v is converted into $-v - 1$ when c is 1, and the value of $-v - 1$ is then converted into $-v - 2$ after two subtractions. Going through the last controlled bit flip one more time, it can be seen that it becomes $v + 1$. When c is zero, the value is not converted by the controlled bit flip, and thus it can be confirmed that only two subtractions are performed and the value $v + 1$ is obtained. In the case of a controlled bit flip, only the $CNOT$ gate is used, and thus there are two subtractions that affect the actual T-depth, which is $4(n - 1)$ when the digit of the target qubit v is n.

4   Proth Number Modular Multiplication Circuit

In this section, we provide a quantum circuit for PNMM using the basic operations described in previous section, and compare it with the circuit for generic modular multiplication [6]. In the comparison, T-depth and the number of gates and qubits are mainly considered.

PNMM is a specific modular multiplication that outputs $kxy \pmod{p}$, where p is of the form $k \cdot 2^m + 1$, for two inputs x and y. To construct a circuit for PNMM, we split it into 4 phases as follows [Fig. 11]:

1. (*Multiplication*) Compute $C = xy$.
2. (*Setup*) Compute $kC_0 - C_1$ from $C = C_0 + 2^m C_1$.
3. (*Division*) Get the remainder $kC_0 - C_1 \pmod{p}$ and the quotient q using division.
4. (*Uncomputation*) Uncompute other values except for $kC_0 - C_1$.

Remark 1. As described in Sect. 2, PNMM must be executed on Proth domain. Thus, two input values x and y are actually of the form $x'k^{-1}$ and $y'k^{-1}$. In order to use PNMM in real systems, input values must be multiplied by k^{-1} before arithmetic operations and we multiply output values by k at the end of the computations.

Compared to generic modular multiplication, PNMM has one more phase, *Setup*. In this phase, we get the value $kC_0 - C_1$ which is equivalent to $kC \pmod{p}$ using 1 multiplication by k and 1 subtraction. Through *Setup*, the size of a dividend to be used in division will be decreased. Thus the cost of gates and T-depth is reduced in the entire circuit. We shall provide specific techniques for implementing PNMM and the cost of its circuit in the rest of this section.

Prior to describing the PNMM, we define the notation $\phi(n)$ for representing the number of qubits of xy. Since $\phi(n)$ is equal to $\lceil \log p^2 \rceil$, this value can be defined as below.

$$\phi(n) = \begin{cases} 2n - 1 & \text{if } n - 1 \leq \log p < n - \frac{1}{2} \\ 2n & \text{if } n - \frac{1}{2} \leq \log p < n. \end{cases}$$

4.1 Multiplication

Multiplication is calculated using $\sum a_i \cdot (b \cdot 2^i)$, and the controlled adder is used in multiplication because the value of a_t determines whether to add $(b \cdot 2^t)$. When the controlled adder is applied, $(b \cdot 2^t)$ is added, and thus no addition of the t LSB qubit is used. In addition, because $\sum_{i=0}^{t-1} a_i \cdot (b \cdot 2^i)$ is less than $(b \cdot 2^t)$, the addition of $\sum_{i=0}^{t-1} a_i \cdot (b \cdot 2^i)$ and $(b \cdot 2^t)$ is the addition of n MSB qubits, which can be expressed as follows (for convenience, d is defined as $\sum_{i=0}^{t-1} a_i \cdot (b \cdot 2^i)$)

$$|d\rangle_{n+t}|b \cdot 2^t\rangle_{n+t} \rightarrow |(d \gg t)\rangle_n|(d \bmod 2^t)\rangle_t|b\rangle_n|0\rangle_t$$
$$\rightarrow |(d \gg t) + b\rangle_n|(d \bmod 2^t) + 0\rangle_t|b\rangle_n|0\rangle_t$$
$$\rightarrow |(d \gg t) + b\rangle_n|(d \bmod 2^t)\rangle_t|b \cdot 2^t\rangle_{n+t}, \tag{4}$$

where $\gg$ denotes a right bitwise shift.

An n controlled CDKM adder is required for multiplication, and if $\phi(n) = 2n - 1$, a carry does not occur in the last controlled CDKM adder. Therefore the total depth is $(n - 1) \cdot (3n + 1) + (3n - 2)$ if $\phi(n) = 2n - 1$ and $(n - 1) \cdot (3n + 1) + (3n + 1)$ when $\phi(n) = 2n$. In conclusion, the T-depth is expressed as $(n - 1) \cdot (3n + 1) + (3 \cdot \phi(n) + 1) - 3n = 3n^2 - 5n + 3 \cdot \phi(n)$ for n and $\phi(n)$, .

4.2 Setup

The setup phase computes $kC_0 - C_1$ utilizing the multiplication $x \cdot y$ ($= C_0 + 2^m C_1$). During multiplication, C_0 represents the lower m qubits, and C_1 represents the remaining upper qubits. To obtain $kC_0 - C_1$, a process of adding kC_0 is applied after converting the sign of the upper qubit C_1. In this case, it is possible to reduce the number of ancilla qubits applied by adding $k_i \cdot C_0 \cdot 2^i$ instead a method of converting C_0 into kC_0 and adding kC_0. In addition, k is a value that is known prior to designing the circuit. Moreover, instead of using a controlled adder, the circuit is designed to apply the adder only when $k_i = 1$ and does not apply any gate when $k_i = 0$.

Because $0 \leq C_0 \leq 2^m - 1, 0 \leq C_1 \leq k^2 \cdot 2^m$, we can see that $-k^2 \cdot 2^m \leq kC_0 - C_1 \leq k \cdot 2^m - k$ is established. An ancilla qubit is needed to express the

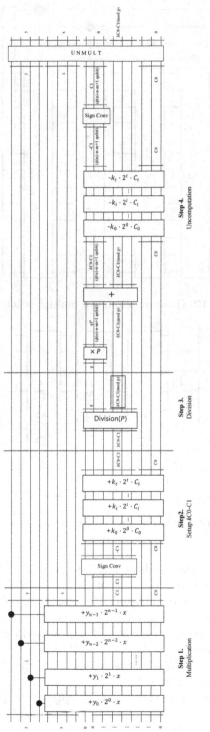

Fig. 11. Quantum circuit of proth number modular multiplication

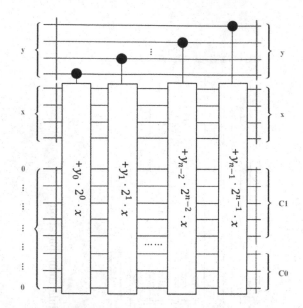

Fig. 12. Quantum circuit of multiplication

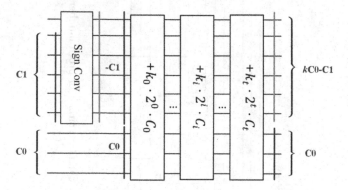

Fig. 13. Quantum circuit of setup $kC_0 - C_1$

sign of $kC_0 - C_1$, so put the ancilla qubit for the sign in the highest qubit of $kC_0 - C_1$. The total T-depth is the sum of the T-depth of the sign conversions of C_1 and the T-depth of add between $-C_1$ and $\sum k_i \cdot (C_0 \cdot 2^i)$. Because the adder is applied only if $k_i = 1$, the weight of k (i.e. the weight of p) is the main factor of the T-depth of *setup* phase. The T-depth used for a sign conversion is $4(\phi(n) - m - 1)$. Because $-C_1 + \sum k_i \cdot (C_0 \cdot 2^i)$ has a different computational complexity (T-depth) depending on the weight of p, the T-depth is calculated by assuming a full weight ($k_0 = 1, k_1 = 1, ..., k_{n-m-1} = 1$) with the maximum computational complexity. The maximum T-depth of $-C_1 + \sum k_i \cdot (C_0 \cdot 2^i)$ is thus $(n - m) \cdot (2\phi(n) - m - n)$.

4.3   Division

The *division* phase is the process of dividing $kC_0 - C_1$ by p, which is used as a modulus value, and obtaining the quotient and remainder (i.e. modular). Division is a structure through which a cycle using a controlled adder, which determines whether to add $2^i \cdot p$ by checking the value of the digit used as the sign of the qubit after subtracting $2^i \cdot p$, is repeated from the highest qubit to the lower qubit. However, with the proposed method, subjects $(=kC_0 - C_1)$ may be negative, and thus the method is modified to apply division even under situations in which subjects is negative using a controlled adder that adds $2^{\phi(n)-m} \cdot p$ according to the value of the highest qubit.

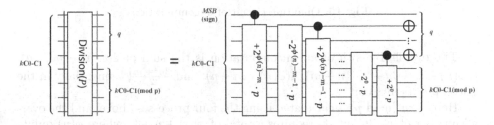

Fig. 14. Quantum circuit of division

The overall T-depth can be calculated by adding the T-depth of the first controlled adder and the set $(\phi(n)-n-m)$ of subtractions and controlled adders. Since the controlled adder used at this time is an adder that does not occur carry, the total T-depth is $(5n - 3) \cdot (\phi(n) - n - m) + (3n - 2)$.

4.4   Uncomputation

In *Uncomputation* phase, $q \cdot p$ $(\phi(n) - n - m + 1\ qubit)$ must first be generated using the quotient q calculated during the division. Using $p = k \cdot 2^m + 1$, there is no need to use an additional gate because $q \equiv q \cdot p\ mod\ 2^{\phi(n)-n-m+1}$ is always satisfied except for $\phi(n) = n + 2m$. Even in $\phi(n) = n + 2m$, because one LSB qubit of q affects the MSB of q with the $CNOT$ gate, generating $q \cdot p$ does not consume anything in terms of the T-depth in the *Uncomputation* phase. Here, $kC_0 - C_1$ $(\phi(n) - n - m + 1\ qubit)$ can be obtained by adding $kC_0 - C_1$ (mod p), remainder value obtained through division, to $q \cdot p$ $(\phi(n) - n - m + 1\ qubit)$. Thereafter, an uncomputation is applied through the reverse process of the previous setup and multiplication, and the remaining ancilla qubits except for the inputs x, y, and $k \cdot C_0 - C_1$ (mod p) corresponding to the output are returned to the existing $|0\rangle$ state.

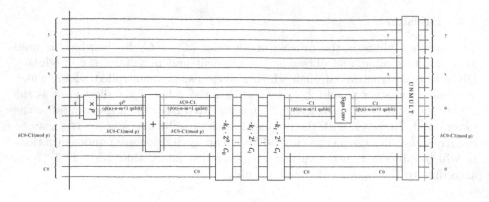

Fig. 15. Quantum circuit of uncomputation

The overall T-depth of an uncomputation is the sum of $2(\phi(n) - m - n)$, $(2\phi(n) - m - 3n + 2) \cdot (n - m)$, $4(\phi(n) - m - n)$, and $\frac{3n^2 + 5n}{2}$, sequentially in the uncomputation circuit.

Here, $kxy \pmod{p}$ is calculated using the four processes above, and the overall number of ancilla qubits requires a total of $\phi(n) + n + 2$, where $\phi(n)$ qubits are used to store xy; in addition, n qubits are also used to store the modulus p applied as a constant within the entire process, one qubit is used to represent the sign of $-C_1, kC_0 - C_1$, and the last qubit is used by the CDKM adder. In the *Setup* phase, before using a constant p, we use ancilla qubits concatenating to C_0 to compensate for the difference in the number of binary digits between $-C_1$ and $2^i \cdot C_0$ for CDKM adder. However because n qubits are sufficient, they are not added to the sum of the number of qubits required.

4.5   Experimental Result

For the purpose of implementing PNMM, an experiment was conducted by selecting a modulus that is frequently used in lattice-based cryptography with NTT. There are a total of five moduli p: $257, 769, 3329, 12289,$ and 8380417, and in that modulus, the depth of the existing modular multiplication and the depth of PNMM are compared. The experiment is conducted using Q|Crypton [5].

Table 1. The depth of a quantum circuit over modulus p commonly used for lattice-based cryptography

p	257	769	3329	12289	8380417
ModMul	6,822	9,424	13,585	18,502	49,987
PNMM	3,770	6,322	10,006	10,758	39,108
Rate($= \frac{\text{PNMM}}{\text{ModMul}}$)	0.553	0.671	0.737	0.581	0.782

As shown in Table 1, the depth of PNMM is smaller than the depth of the existing modular multiplication. The rate $(=\frac{PNMM}{ModMul})$ varies from 0.553 to 0.782, and indicates a reduction from 21.8% to 44.7% in depth compared to existing circuits. The experiment results also show that if a number with a small weight among the Proth numbers is used as the modulus, the difference in depth between the existing modular multiplication and PNMM may increase.

5   Conclusion

In this study, we attempted to optimize the quantum circuit of PNMM and provided the evaluation result of its T-depth and number of qubits. With a couple of moduli that are commonly used in lattice-based cryptography, the depth of the optimized circuit improved from 21.8% to 44.7% compared to the existing circuit. Because only a single extra qubit is used to represent the sign of a negative number during *Setup* and *Division* phases in our optimization circuit, there is no significant difference in the number of qubits required from the existing circuit. For further research, it would be interesting to reduce the number of ancilla qubits with no extra burden of T-depth. Moreover, implementing an optimization circuit for modular multiplication with one fixed input value is of interest because it is frequently used in NTT.

Acknowledgments. This work was supported by Institute for Information and communications Technology Planning and Evaluation (IITP) grant funded by the Korea government (MSIT) (No.2019-0-00033, Study on Quantum Security Evaluation of Cryptography based on Computational Quantum Complexity).

References

1. Cuccaro, S.A., Draper, T.G., Kutin, S.A., Moulton, D.P.: A new quantum ripple-carry addition circuit. arXiv preprint quant-ph/0410184 (2004)
2. Draper, T.G.: Addition on a quantum computer. arXiv preprint quant-ph/0008033 (2000)
3. Draper, T.G., Kutin, S.A., Rains, E.M., Svore, K.M.: A logarithmic-depth quantum carry-lookahead adder. arXiv preprint quant-ph/0406142 (2004)
4. Gidney, C.: Constructing large increment gates (2015). https://algassert.com/circuits/2015/06/12/Constructing-Large-Increment-Gates.html
5. Lee, S.: <Q|crypton>, the quantum security evaluation platform for cryptographic algorithms. In: PQCrypto 2021 (2021)
6. Rines, R., Chuang, I.: High performance quantum modular multipliers. arXiv preprint arXiv:1801.01081 (2018)
7. Shor, P.W.: Algorithms for quantum computation: discrete logarithms and factoring. In: Proceedings 35th annual symposium on foundations of computer science, pp. 124–134. IEEE (1994)
8. Van Meter, R., Itoh, K.M.: Fast quantum modular exponentiation. Phys. Rev. A **71**(5), 052320 (2005)
9. Vedral, V., Barenco, A., Ekert, A.: Quantum networks for elementary arithmetic operations. Phys. Rev. A **54**(1), 147 (1996)

Efficient Implementation

Grover on SM3

Gyeongju Song[1], Kyungbae Jang[1], Hyunji Kim[1], Wai-Kong Lee[2], Zhi Hu[3], and Hwajeong Seo[1(✉)] (iD)

[1] IT Department, Hansung University, Seoul 02876, South Korea
hwajeong84@gmail.com
[2] Department of Computer Engineering, Gachon University,
Seongnam, Incheon 13120, Korea
waikonglee@gachon.ac.kr
[3] Central South University, Changsha, China
huzhi_math@csu.edu.cn

Abstract. Grover's search algorithm accelerates the key search on the symmetric key cipher and the pre-image attack on the hash function. To perform Grover's search algorithm, the target algorithm should be implemented in a quantum circuit. For this reason, we propose an optimal SM3 hash function (Chinese standard) in a quantum circuit. We focused on minimizing the use of qubits and reducing the use of quantum gates. To do this, the on-the-fly approach is utilized for message expansion and compression functions. In particular, the previous value is restored and used without allocating new qubits in the permutation operation. Finally, we estimate the quantum resources required for the quantum pre-image attack based on the proposed SM3 hash function implementation in the quantum circuit.

Keywords: Quantum computer · Grover algorithm · SM3 hash function

1 Introduction

Quantum computers can solve specific problems in quantum algorithms much faster than classical computers. Two representative quantum algorithms that work on quantum computers are Shor's algorithm [1] and Grover's algorithm [2]. Shor's algorithm leads to vulnerability of Rivest-Shamir-Adleman (RSA) and elliptic curve cryptography (ECC), the most commonly used public key cryptography approaches. Integer factorization and discrete logarithm problems used in RSA and ECC are hard problems in classical computers. However, quantum computers using Shor's algorithm solve these hard problems within a polynomial time. To prevent this kind of attack, the National Institute of Standards and Technology (NIST) is working on standardizing post-quantum cryptography. In the standardization process, various post-quantum algorithms have been submitted. Grover's algorithm accelerates finding specific data in databases (i.e. brute force attacks). If $O(n)$ queries were required in a brute force attack, this

© The Author(s), under exclusive license to Springer Nature Switzerland AG 2022
J. H. Park and S.-H. Seo (Eds.): ICISC 2021, LNCS 13218, pp. 421–433, 2022.
https://doi.org/10.1007/978-3-031-08896-4_22

number can be reduced to $O(\sqrt{n})$ queries by using Grover's algorithm. In cryptography, Grover's algorithm lowers the n-bit security-level symmetric key cipher and hash function to $\frac{n}{2}$-bit (i.e. half) for key search and pre-image attack.

In recent years, there has been active research on how to optimize and implement symmetric key ciphers [3–13] and hash functions [14] as quantum circuits to minimize the quantum resources required for Grover's algorithm. In [15], quantum cryptanalysis benchmarking was performed by comparing resources required to attack public key cryptography, symmetric key cryptography, and hash function.

In quantum circuit optimization, it is important to reduce the number of qubits and quantum gates. The most important factor is to reduce the number of required qubits. As the number of qubits increases, quantum computers become more difficult to operate in a practical manner. International companies, such as IBM, Google, and Honeywell, are in the process of increasing the number of qubits for high computing quantum computers.

In this work, we focused on minimizing the number of qubits required to implement the SM3 hash function in a quantum circuit, while at the same time reducing the complexity of quantum gates. The existing message expansion function was divided into the first extension and second extension. The compression function was divided into the first compression and second compression, and then mixed and used. Through this method, the total number of qubits used was reduced by reusing the qubits used in the message. In the permutation operation, the value was returned through the CNOT-gate repetition rather than using a qubit to store the original value. Thus, we achieved an optimal quantum circuit of the SM3 hash function. In this paper, we used 2,176 qubits for storing the extended message (W_j ($j = 0, 1, ..., 67$)), 32 qubits for the T constant to be used for the update, and 256 qubits for the register update and output of the final hash value. We also used 32 qubits for permutation operations, 1 qubit for ripple-carry addition, and 224 qubits for AND and OR operations.

1.1 Contribution

- **First implementation of the SM3 hash function in a quantum circuit** To the best of our knowledge, this is the first implementation of the SM3 hash function in a quantum circuit. We obtained the optimal quantum circuit by minimizing the use of qubits and reducing the quantum gate complexity.
- **Efficient design of SM3 operations in a quantum circuit** We reduced the use of qubits by dividing the expansion function and compression function of the original SM3 hash function and mixing them. Permutation operations were also performed with minimum qubits.
- **Quantum resource estimation of Grover's search algorithm for the SM3 hash function** We evaluate quantum resources for the quantum pre-image attack on the SM3 hash function. A quantum programming tool, namely, IBM ProjectQ [16], was used to evaluate the proposed quantum implementation of SM3 hash function.

2 Related Work

2.1 SM3 Hash Function

The hash function completely changes the output value with only small changes in the input value, thus ensuring the integrity by detecting errors in a message. The hash function efficiently generates the hashed value, allowing it to be digitally signed and verified, and to generate and verify messages. The SM3 hash function is operated in units of 32 words, and it finally outputs a hash value of 256 bits. After increasing the message length using padding, the message expansion calculation is performed by Eq. 1 to expand the message to $W_0, W_1, ..., W_{67}, W_0', ..., W_{63}'$.

$$W_j \leftarrow P_j(W_{j-16} \oplus W_{j-9} \oplus (W_{j-3} \lll 15)) \oplus (W_{j-13} \lll 7) \oplus W_{j-6}$$
$$W_j' = W_j \oplus W_{j+4}, \ (16 \leq j \leq 67) \tag{1}$$

The message expansion function expands the message block $B^{(i)}$ to 132 words $(W_0, W_1, ..., W_{67}, W_0', ..., W_{63}')$. First, the existing message block $B^{(i)}$ is divided into 16 words $W_0, W_1, ...W_{15}$ and expanded to $W_{16}, ..., W_{67}$ using this. The expanded message makes $W_0, W_1, ...W_{67}, W_0', W_1', ...W_{63}'$ through the Eq. 1. The extended 132-word message is updated to registers A to H through the compression function. Registers A to H are 32 bits each, and initial values are stored. The final hash value is generated by performing the XOR operation to the updated register value with the previous register value through the compression function.

Algorithm 1. Compression function of the SM3 hash function.

Input: $W_0, W_1, \cdots, W_{67}, W_1', \cdots, W_{63}'$
Output: 32-qubits-register A, B, C, D, E, F, G, H after the message compression.
 1: **for** $j = 0$ to 63 **do**
 2:     $SS1 \leftarrow ((A \lll 12) + E + (T_j \lll (j \bmod 32))) \lll 7$
 3:     $SS2 \leftarrow SS1 \oplus (A \lll 12)$
 4:     $TT1 \leftarrow FF_j(A, B, C) + D + SS2 + W_j'$
 5:     $TT2 \leftarrow GG_j(E, F, G) + H + SS1 + w_j$
 6:     $D \leftarrow C$
 7:     $C \leftarrow B \lll 9$
 8:     $B \leftarrow A$
 9:     $A \leftarrow TT1$
10:     $H \leftarrow G$
11:     $G \leftarrow F \lll 19$
12:     $F \leftarrow E$
13:     $E \leftarrow P_0(TT2)$
14: **end for**
15: $V(i+1) \leftarrow ABCDEFGH \oplus V(i)$
16: **return** A, B, C, D, E, F, G, H

The compression function proceeds to $V^{(i+1)} = CF(V^{(i)}, B^{(i)}), i = 0, ..., n-1$ with the message of 132 words expanded in the message expansion function and previous 256-bit values as parameters. $SS1, SS2, TT1$, and $TT2$ are intermediate variables of 32 bits, and T in the $SS1$ update process contains the initial value of 32 bits. The FF and GG functions are Boolean functions that perform XOR, AND, and OR operations of parameters and output a value of 32 bits. FF and GG are used to update $TT1$ and $TT2$. Equation 2 is the calculation of FF and GG functions.

$$FF_j(X, Y, Z) = X \oplus Y \oplus Z, \ \ 0 \le j \le 15$$
$$FF_j(X, Y, Z) = (X \wedge Y) \vee (X \wedge Y) \vee (Y \wedge Z), \ \ 16 \le j \le 63$$

$$(2)$$

$$GG_j(X, Y, Z) = X \oplus Y \oplus Z, \ \ 0 \le j \le 15$$
$$GG_j(X, Y, Z) = (X \wedge Y) \vee (\neg X \wedge Z), \ \ 16 \le j \le 63$$

In the compression function, the last register value is stored by updating the register 64 times, and the final hash value of 256-bits is generated through an XOR operation with the register before the update.

2.2 Quantum Computing

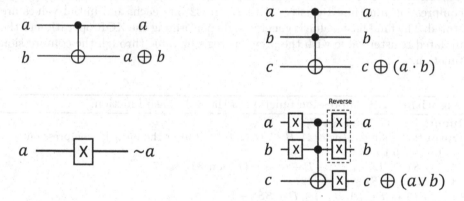

Fig. 1. CNOT gate, Toffoli gate, X gate, and OR gate in quantum gates.

Quantum computers utilize quantum mechanics phenomena, such as superposition and entanglement. A classical computer has bits, while a quantum computer has qubits that can superpose 0 and 1. In other words, a qubit has both values in the probability of being 0 and 1, and it is determined when it is measured.

As shown in Fig. 1, quantum circuits also have quantum logic gates, such as digital logic gates in digital circuits. The quantum gate can control the state of the qubit. The X gate is a quantum logic gate that corresponds to the NOT gate of a digital logic gate. The probability that the qubit state becomes 0 is changed to the probability that it is determined as 1. The CNOT gate represents an entangled state in which one qubit affects another qubit. It performs a NOT gate operation for the second qubit when the first qubit is 1. If the first qubit is 1, the NOT gate is applied to the second qubit. Otherwise, the second qubit is the output as it is. With the Toffoli gate, the states of two qubits affect the state of one qubit. If the first two qubits among the three qubits are 1, a NOT operation is performed for the third qubit. Otherwise, the value of the third qubit is not changed.

In addition, there is a Hadamard gate, which puts qubits in a superposition state, and a SWAP gate, which changes the state of two qubits. The Toffoli gate is an expensive gate. X gate and CNOT gate are relatively inexpensive in comparison with the Toffoli gate. Because quantum computers with a large number of qubits have not been developed, quantum circuits must be designed with consideration of resources, such as qubits and quantum gates.

There are platforms for quantum computing, such as IBM's ProjectQ, Qiskit, or Microsoft's Q#. These platforms provide quantum gates, a variety of libraries, and simulators. Through the Qiskit platform, it is possible to use real quantum processors in the cloud platform. Thus quantum computing technologies are actively being developed, including various quantum computing platforms and quantum languages.

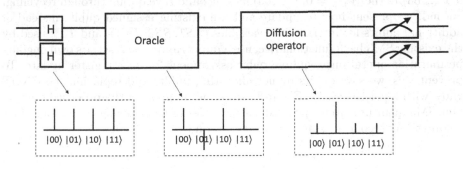

Fig. 2. Grover search algorithm (answer $x = 01$).

2.3   Grover Search Algorithm

Grover's search algorithm [2] is a quantum algorithm that searches a space with n elements to find the input data that generates the output of a particular function. On a classic computer, n searches are required to search an unsorted database. Because Grover's search algorithm can find the answer by searching for the $\sqrt{n}$, the time complexity is reduced from $O(n)$ to $O(\sqrt{n})$. In other words, Grover's algorithm threatens the symmetric key cryptography because it shortens the time required for brute force attacks.

Grover's search algorithm consists of oracle and diffusion operators, and its steps are carried out as follows. First, Hadamard gates are applied to qubits. The oracle function $f(x)$ returns 1 when x is the answer, and it inverts the phase of qubits representing the answer. Then, the diffusion operator amplifies the amplitude of inverted qubits through the oracle, increasing the probability of becoming the answer. Through repetition of the oracle and diffusion process, the probability of the answer is over the threshold. Finally, the value of x that exceeds the threshold becomes the answer. The overall structure of Grover's search algorithm when the answer $x = 01$ is shown in Fig. 2.

3 Proposed Method

3.1 SM3 Hash Function on Quantum Circuit

In the SM3 hash function designed in quantum circuits, we estimate the resource for applying Grover's algorithm based on a message padded with 512 bits. We propose a method of recycling message qubits by mixing the padded message with the message expansion function and the compression function. Two word messages $(W_j, W'_j \ (j = 0, 1, ..., 63))$ are included to update the register once with the compression function. First, we propose the method to update $W'_j \ (j = 0, 1, ..., 63)$ to the $W_j \ (j = 0, 1, ..., 63)$ message and save qubits through recycling. Second, we present how to update and use existing assigned qubits instead of additional qubits for intermediate variables $(SS1, SS2, TT1)$, and $TT2$ used by the existing SM3 hash function. Because a qubit cannot be reset, its own ongoing permutation operations require a qubit assignment for each register update. To prevent this, we save qubits by not allocating qubits and replacing the CNOT gates with repetitive tasks. Figure 3 shows the progress of the proposed system. Our SM3 quantum circuit proceeds in the order of first message expansion, first compression, second message expansion, second compression.

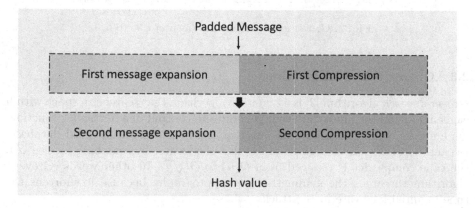

Fig. 3. System configuration for the proposed method.

3.2   Message Expansion

The original SM3 hash function outputs a hash function by expanding a message and then updating a register through a compression function. However, applying these methods to quantum circuits is inefficient, because 4,224 qubits are required only for message expansion. To solve this problem, we store the padded 512-bit message B in $W_0, W_1, ..., W_{15}$ and update $W_{16}, W_{17}, ..., W_{67}$ using permutation operations and CNOT gates. Updated values $(W_0, W_{17}, ..., W_{67})$ are used for the first compression function and then recycled to update $W_0', W_1', ..., W_{63}'$ in the second compression function without allocating additional qubits. Therefore, the message expansion function and the compression function are divided into the first message expansion function and the second message expansion function, the first compression function and the second compression function, which are used in combination.

Algorithm 2. First message expansion quantum circuit algorithm.

Input: $W_0, W_1, ..., W_{15}$.
Output: $W_{16}, W_{17}, ..., W_{67}$.
1: **Update:**
2:    **for** $i = 0$ to 31 **do**
3:        $W_{j-16}[i] \leftarrow \text{CNOT}(W_{j-9}[i], W_{j-16}[i]), \ j = 16, ..., 67$
4:        $W_{j-16}[i] \leftarrow \text{CNOT}(W_{j-3}[(i + 15)\%32], W_{j-16}[i]), \ j = 16, ..., 67$
5:    **end for**
6:    $Permutation_{p1}(W_{j-16})$
7: **for** $i = 0$ to 31 **do**
8:    $W_j[i] \leftarrow \text{CNOT}(W_{j-16}[i], W_j[i]), j = 16, ..., 67$
9:    $W_j[i] \leftarrow \text{CNOT}(W_{j-13}[(i + 15)\%32], W_j[i]), \ j = 16, ..., 67$
10:    $W_j[i] \leftarrow \text{CNOT}(W_{j-6}[(i + 15)\%32], W_j[i]), \ j = 16, ..., 67$
11: **end for**
12: **Update**(reverse)
13: **return** $W_{16}, W_{17}, ..., W_{67}$

Algorithm 2 is the first message expansion quantum circuit, which updates $W_{16}, W_{17}, ..., W_{67}$. In the first message expansion algorithm, W_j $(16 \leq j \leq 67)$ is generated using $W_{(j-16)}, W_{(j-9)}, W_{(j-3)}, W_{(j-13)}$ and $W_{(j-6)}$ $(16 \leq j \leq 67)$. Since qubits cannot perform simple allocation operations, CNOT gate operation values in lines 3 and 4 are stored in $W_{(j-16)}$. Because W_j is generated and the previous message value should not be changed, the update result value is stored in W_j, and the value of $W_{(j-16)}$, which is changed during the update process, is reversed and returned. The $Permutation_{P1}$ function in line 6 performs Eq. 4. Line 12 reverses lines 2 through 10.

In the second expansion function, the CNOT gate operation is performed on the message $(W_0, ..., W_{67})$ used in the first compression function, and a new message $(W_0', ..., W_{63}')$ is output. In this way, the qubit is reused. The message

---

Algorithm 3. Second message expansion quantum circuit algorithm.

Input: $W_k, W_{k+4}, \quad k = 0, ..., 63$.
Output: $W_t', \quad t = 0, ..., 63$.
1: **for** $i = 0$ **to** 31 **do**
2:     $W_j'[i] \leftarrow \text{CNOT}(W_j[i], W_{j+4}[i]), \quad j = 0, ..., 63$
3: **end for**
4: **return** $W_t', \quad t = 0, ..., 63$

$(W_0', ..., W_{63}')$ generated by the second expansion function is used by the second compression function.

3.3 Message Compression

The compression function uses an extended message to update the register. Both $W_0, ..., W_{63}$ and $W_0', ..., W_{63}'$ are required to use the compression function. After using $W_0, ..., W_{63}$, we reuse it as $W_0', ..., W_{63}'$ to reduce the use of qubits. The first expansion function is executed, and the obtained value $(W_0, ..., W_{63})$ is to run the first compression function. Then, the second expansion function is to generate the value $(W_0', ..., W_{63}')$ and performs the second compression function. Algorithms 4 and 5 are the first compression function and the second compression function, respectively.

Algorithm 4. First compression quantum circuit algorithm.

Input: 32-qubits-register A, B, C, D, E, F, G, H ,$W_0, ..., W_{63}$.
Output: 32-qubits-register A, B, C, D, E, F, G, H after the first compression.
1: **Update:**
2:     $T_j \leftarrow (T_j \lll j \bmod 32) \lll 7, \quad j = 0, .., 63$
3:     $value0 \leftarrow GG$
4:     $value1 \leftarrow FF$
5:     $E \leftarrow SS1$
6:     $A \leftarrow SS2$
7: $H \leftarrow TT2$
8: **return** A, B, C, D, E, F, G, H

$$SS1 = ((A \lll 12) + E + T_j) \lll 7, \quad j = 0, ..., 63$$
$$SS2 = E \oplus (A \lll 12)$$
$$TT1 = FF_j + D + A + W_j' \tag{3}$$
$$TT2 = GG_j + H + SS1 + W_j$$

The first compression function given in Algorithm 4 calculates the constants required for the register update. Using qubits as intermediate variables in quantum circuits consumes a lot of resources. Therefore, the calculation is performed in the register where the final value will be stored. In the first compression function, qubits of each 32-bit intermediate constant ($SS1, SS2, TT1,$ and $TT2$) are

---

Algorithm 5. Second compression quantum circuit algorithm.

Input: 32-qubits-register $A, B, C, D,$
$E, F, G, H, W_0', ..., W_{63}'.$

Output: 32-qubits-register $A, B, C, D,$
E, F, G, H after the second compression.

1: $D \leftarrow TT1$

2: **Update of first**
   compression (reverse)

3: $H \leftarrow Permutation_{p0}$

4: $Swap(D, H)$

5: $B \leftarrow B \lll 9$

6: $F \leftarrow F \lll 19$

7: $Swap(A, H)$

8: $Swap(B, H)$

9: $Swap(C, H)$

10: $Swap(D, H)$

11: $Swap(E, H)$

12: $Swap(F, H)$

13: $Swap(G, H)$

14: **return** A, B, C, D, E, F, G, H

---

stored. Constants $(SS1, SS2, TT1,$ and $TT2)$ are calculated by Eq. 3. In the first compression function, Boolean functions $(GG$ and $FF)$ are used to calculate the value. GG and FF are calculated as 2, and the final result is stored in the variables $(value0, value1)$ and used for calculating $TT1$ and $TT2$. The value of existing register E is not used after GG function and $SS1$ update. Therefore, the value of $SS1$ is calculated in the register E. Because the value of the existing register A is not used after the FF function, it is stored and used in the $SS2$ value register A. $TT2$ is updated with the extended message $(W_0, ..., W_{63})$ and the $SS1$ value stored in the register E. At this time, the value of register H is not used after $TT2$ operation. The $TT2$ value is stored in register H. As a result, the value of $TT2$ after the first compression function is stored in the register H. Since the extended message $(W_0, ..., W_{63})$ in the first message expansion function is not use after being used for the $TT2$ update in the first compression function. Thus, the first compression function is finished, and the message $(W_0', ..., W_{63}')$ is updated to the message $(W_0, ..., W_{63})$ through the second expansion function based on Algorithm 3. Finally, we use the updated message $(W_0', ..., W_{63}')$ to proceed with the second compression function(Algorithm 5).

$TT1$ updates with the extended message $(W_0', ..., W_{63}'$ and $SS2)$ stored in register A. We use the updated message $(W_0', ..., W_{63}')$ to proceed with the second compression function. $TT1$ updates with the extended message $(W_0', ..., W_{63}')$ and $SS2$ stored in register A. At this time, the value of register D is not used after the $TT1$ operation. The $TT1$ value is stored in register D. To update the register, the original A and E register values are required. Therefore, lines 2 to 6 of the first compression function are reversed. Then, register H is computed with the $permutation_{P1}$ operation and all registers are updated through a swap operation. A swap operation only changes the bit position. For this reason, there are no additional resources.

3.4 Hash Value

After the first expansion function is used, the first compression function, second expansion function, and second compression function are repeated 64 times in order. By completing the iteration, the updated registers $(A, B, C, D, E, F, G,$ and $H)$ are XOR with the previous registers $(A, B, C, D, E, F, G,$ and $H)$.

3.5 Permutation

In the SM3 hash function, there are two permutation functions $(P_0$ and $P_1)$. Equation 4 is the expression of P_0 and P_1.

$$P_0(X) = X \oplus (X \lll 9) \oplus (X \lll 17)$$
$$P_1(X) = X \oplus (X \lll 15) \oplus (X \lll 23) \tag{4}$$

The P_0 and P_1 permutation operations shift themselves and use the CNOT gate. If the operation value is saved, it is difficult to find the original qubit value, which causes problems in subsequent operations. In normal cases, original values of qubits should be stored and used qubits are used. However in the P_1 operation, a qubit is to store the value before the operation is allocated. Then, it can be used again in the next operation through the reverse operation. Therefore, a 32-bit storage qubit is allocated and used. In the P_0 operation, the stored qubit cannot be reused by the reverse operation. There is a problem that 32 qubits must be allocated every time, and the compression function update should be repeated. To solve this problem, if the same bit is counted twice as the CNOT gate, the counting is canceled. As a result, in P_0, the permutation operation is performed through the repeated use of the CNOT gate without allocation of a qubit. P_0 and P_1 are used in the compression function. Algorithm 6 represents a part of this operation, and Table 1 presents the state changes as the operation progresses.

When $A = a_{31}, ..., a_0$ is given, and a_0 is the most significant bit. The CNOT gate is executed in the order of $a_{31}, ..., a_{17}$. It is difficult to find the original a_{31} required in the calculation of a_{16}. Therefore, the operation to find the existing value is performed by repeatedly using the CNOT gate. Algorithm 6 computes a_{16} as part of $P0$. At this time, the CNOT gate is repeatedly used to use the original a_{31}, and the state change for each use is shown in Table 1. Because the XOR operation values of a_{16}, a_7 and a_{31} should be stored in a_{16}, they are calculated in order. Because the calculation is performed from a_{31}, the values of a_{16} and a_7 are preserved. In line 1, the XOR values of a_{16} and a_7 are stored in a_{16}. In line 2, the value of a_{31} is executed with the XOR operation. At this time, the XOR values of a_{31}, a_{22}, and a_{14} are stored in a_{31}. Because a_{22} and a_{14} are unnecessary values, we use the CNOT gate once more to cancel them. In line 4, the CNOT gate is used to neutralize the a_{14} value. In line 3, the CNOT gate is used to neutralize the a_{22} value. Because the XOR operation values of a_{22}, a_{13}, and a_5 are stored in a_{22}, only the a_{22} value is obtained by performing a_{13}, a_5, and the CNOT gate in lines 5 and 6.

Algorithm 6. Part of the P_0 calculation.

Input: a_{16}.
Output: $a_{16} \leftarrow a_{16} \oplus a_7 \oplus a_{31}$.
  1: $a_{16} \leftarrow \text{CNOT}(a_7, a_{16})$
  2: $a_{16} \leftarrow \text{CNOT}(a_{31}, a_{16})$
  3: $a_{16} \leftarrow \text{CNOT}(a_{22}, a_{16})$

  4: $a_{16} \leftarrow \text{CNOT}(a_{14}, a_{16})$
  5: $a_{16} \leftarrow \text{CNOT}(a_{13}, a_{16})$
  6: $a_{16} \leftarrow \text{CNOT}(a_5, a_{16})$

  7: **return** $a_{16} \leftarrow a_{16} \oplus a_7 \oplus a_{31}$

Table 1. Changes of states during Algorithm 6.

Line	Qubit	State
1	a_{16}	$a_{16} \oplus a_7$
2	a_{16}	$a_{16} \oplus a_7 \oplus a_{31} \oplus a_{22} \oplus a_{14}$
3	a_{16}	$a_{16} \oplus a_7 \oplus a_{31} \oplus a_{14} \oplus a_{13} \oplus a_5$
4	a_{16}	$a_{16} \oplus a_7 \oplus a_{31} \oplus a_{13} \oplus a_5$
5	a_{16}	$a_{16} \oplus a_7 \oplus a_{31} \oplus a_5$
6	a_{16}	$a_{16} \oplus a_7 \oplus a_{31}$

4 Evaluation

The proposed SM3 quantum circuit implementation was evaluated by using quantum emulator, namely, IBM ProjectQ. Among various compilers provided by IBM, the ProjectQ, quantum compiler can estimate the resources of implemented quantum circuits. It measures the number of Toffoli gates, CNOT gates, X gates, and qubits used in a quantum circuit.

We focused on optimizing the quantum gates and qubits for the implementation of the SM3 quantum circuit. One of important elements of a quantum circuit is making it work with minimal resources. Currently, the number of qubits available in quantum computer technology is limited, and it is efficient to reduce the quantum gate cost. Therefore, it can be used as an index to confirm the efficiency of the quantum circuit by comparing the quantum circuit resources of the SM3 quantum circuit proposed in this paper with other hash functions. First, in the proposed SM3 quantum circuits, the number of qubits to be used for message storage was reduced by mixing the expansion function and the compression function. By dividing the expansion function and the compression function into two, the message qubits used in the first compression function can be reused in the second compression function. Second, in the permutation operation, we found the original value with the CNOT gate without allocating a bit to store the original value. In this way, we reduced the number of qubits. Finally, Finally, it is implemented using minimal quantum gates. Based on this optimal quantum circuit, we can minimize the quantum resources required for Grover's search algorithm for the SM3 hash function.

Table 2. Quantum resources required for SHA2 and SHA3 quantum circuits and the proposed SM3 quantum circuit.

Algorithm	Qubits	Toffoli gates	CNOT gates	X gates	Depth
SHA2-256 [14]	2,402	57,184	534,272	–	528,768
SHA3-256 [14]	3,200	84,480	33,269,760	85	10,128
Proposed SM3	2,721	43,328	134,144	2,638	128,129

As far as we know, there have been no previous studies that implemented SM3 as a quantum circuit. Therefore, it is difficult to compare the implementation of our SM3 quantum circuit with other SM3 quantum circuits. As an alternative, we compare the quantum resources of SHA2-256 and SHA3-256 with SM3. Table 2 shows the amount of quantum resources used in the proposed SM3 quantum circuit and SHA[14]. SHA is a standard hash function announced by the National Institute of Standards and Technology (NIST) in the US. SHA2-256 and SM3 are calculated through a 512-bit message block and output a 256-bit hash value. SHA3-256 is a sponge structure, it outputs a hash value of 256 bits at all input lengths. When the available resources of a quantum computer reach the resources required for a hash function attack, it can be seen as the time when the security of the hash function can be broken. Therefore, the quantum resources of the optimized quantum circuit are used as an indicator to confirm the safety in the quantum computer. When SM3 was compared with SHA, it used more qubits than SHA2, but much fewer qubits than SHA3. In terms of quantum gates, much fewer quantum gates than SHA2 and SHA3 were used. In SHA2, X gate was not used, but more Toffoli and CNOT gates were used than in SM3. In quantum computers, Toffoli and CNOT gates are more expensive resources than X gates, so it was considered that more quantum gate resources were used.

5   Conclusion

In this paper, we implemented and optimized the SM3 hash function as a quantum circuit and estimated the required quantum resources. The quantum resources required for a quantum pre-image attack using Grover's search algorithm are determined according to the quantum circuit of the target hash function. Utilizing the proposed SM3 quantum circuits, Grover's search algorithm can be efficiently applied, and its performance was assessed by comparing it in terms of quantum resources with approaches proposed in other research. It is expected that the proposed implementation of the SM3 hash function in quantum circuits can be effectively applied to Grover's search algorithm.

Acknowledgment. This work was partly supported by Institute for Information & communications Technology Planning & Evaluation (IITP) grant funded by the Korea government(MSIT) (<Q|Crypton>, No.2019-0-00033, Study on Quantum Security Evaluation of Cryptography based on Computational Quantum Complexity, 40%) and this work was partly supported by Institute for Information & communications Technology Promotion(IITP) grant funded by the Korea government(MSIT) (No.2018-0-00264, Research on Blockchain Security Technology for IoT Services, 40%). Zhi Hu was partially supported by the National Natural Science Foundation of China (61972420, 61602526) and the Natural Science Foundation of Hunan Province (2020JJ3050, 2019JJ50827).

References

1. Shor, P.W.: Polynomial-time algorithms for prime factorization and discrete logarithms on a quantum computer. SIAM J. Comput. **26**, 1484–1509 (1997)
2. Grover, L.K.: A fast quantum mechanical algorithm for database search. In: Proceedings of the Twenty-Eighth Annual ACM Symposium on Theory of Computing, pp. 212–219 (1996)
3. Grassl, M., Langenberg, B., Roetteler, M., Steinwandt, R.: Applying Grover's algorithm to AES: quantum resource estimates. In: Takagi, T. (ed.) PQCrypto 2016. LNCS, vol. 9606, pp. 29–43. Springer, Cham (2016). https://doi.org/10.1007/978-3-319-29360-8_3
4. Langenberg, B., Pham, H., Steinwandt, R.: Reducing the cost of implementing AES as a quantum circuit. Techical report, Cryptology ePrint Archive, Report 2019/854 (2019)
5. Jaques, S., Naehrig, M., Roetteler, M., Virdia, F.: Implementing Grover oracles for quantum key search on AES and LowMC. In: Canteaut, A., Ishai, Y. (eds.) EUROCRYPT 2020. LNCS, vol. 12106, pp. 280–310. Springer, Cham (2020). https://doi.org/10.1007/978-3-030-45724-2_10
6. Anand, R., Maitra, A., Mukhopadhyay, S.: Grover on SIMON. Quant. Inf. Process. **19**(9), 1–17 (2020)
7. Jang, K., Choi, S., Kwon, H., Seo, H.: Grover on SPECK: quantum resource estimates. Cryptology ePrint Archive, Report 2020/640 (2020). https://eprint.iacr.org/2020/640
8. Jang, K., Kim, H., Eum, S., Seo, H.: Grover on GIFT. Cryptology ePrint Archive, Report 2020/1405 (2020). https://eprint.iacr.org/2020/1405
9. Schlieper, L.: In-place implementation of quantum-Gimli. arXiv preprint arXiv:2007.06319 (2020)
10. Jang, K., Choi, S., Kwon, H., Kim, H., Park, J., Seo, H.: Grover on Korean block ciphers. Appl. Sci. **10**(18), 6407 (2020)
11. Jang, K., Song, G., Kim, H., Kwon, H., Kim, H., Seo, H.: Efficient implementation of PRESENT and GIFT on quantum computers. Appl. Sci. **11**(11), 4776 (2021)
12. Song, G., Jang, K., Kim, H., Lee, W.-K., Seo, H.: Grover on Caesar and Vigenère ciphers. IACR Cryptol. ePrint Arch. **2021**, 554 (2021)
13. Jang, K., et al.: Grover on PIPO. Electronics **10**(10), 1194 (2021)
14. Amy, M., Matteo, O.D., Gheorghiu, V., Mosca, M., Parent, A., Schanck, J.: Estimating the cost of generic quantum pre-image attacks on SHA-2 and SHA-3 (2016)
15. Gheorghiu, V., Mosca, M.: Benchmarking the quantum cryptanalysis of symmetric, public-key and hash-based cryptographic schemes (2019)
16. Steiger, D.S., Häner, T., Troyer, M.: ProjectQ: an open source software framework for quantum computing. Quantum **2**, 49 (2018)

SPEEDY on Cortex–M3: Efficient Software Implementation of SPEEDY on ARM Cortex–M3

Hyunjun Kim[1], Kyungbae Jang[1], Gyeongju Song[1], Minjoo Sim[1], Siwoo Eum[1], Hyunji Kim[1], Hyeokdong Kwon[1], Wai-Kong Lee[2], and Hwajeong Seo[1(✉)]

[1] IT Department, Hansung University, Seoul 02876, South Korea
hwajeong84@gmail.com
[2] Department of Computer Engineering, Gachon University,
Seongnam, Incheon 13120, Korea
waikonglee@gachon.ac.kr

Abstract. The SPEEDY block cipher suite announced at CHES 2021 shows excellent hardware performance. However, SPEEDY was not designed to be efficient in software implementations. SPEEDY's 6-bit S-box and bit permutation operations generally do not work efficiently in software. We implemented SPEEDY block cipher by applying the implementation technique of bit-slicing. As an implementation technique of bit-slicing, SPEEDY can be operated in software very efficiently and can be applied in microcontroller. By calculating the round key in advance, the performance on ARM Cortex-M3 for SPEEDY-5-192, SPEEDY-6-192, and SPEEDY-7-192 are 65.7, 75.25, and 85.16 clock cycles per byte (i.e. cpb), respectively. It showed better performance than AES-128 constant-time implementation and GIFT constant-time implementation in the same platform. Through this, we conclude that SPEEDY can show good performance on embedded environments.

Keywords: Software implementation · SPEEDY · ARM Cortex–M3

1 Introduction

SPEEDY is a very low-latency block cipher designed for hardware implementation in high-performance CPUs. With gate and transistor level considerations, it has been shown that they can run faster in hardware than other block ciphers. The author of SPEEDY [1] provides reference code implemented in C. However, this software implementation does not show the superior performance like the hardware implementation. The performance of SPEEDY's software implementation has not been confirmed, but hardware-oriented block cipher is generally less efficient in software implementation than other software-oriented block ciphers. For this reason, efficient implementation should be considered for SPEEDY block cipher. In [2], Reis et al. shows that PRESENT can be implemented efficiently in software. PRESENT consists of a 4-bit S-box and a 64-bit permutation, which is

J. H. Park and S.-H. Seo (Eds.): ICISC 2021, LNCS 13218, pp. 434–444, 2022.
https://doi.org/10.1007/978-3-031-08896-4_23

far from being implemented in efficient software. However, they used a bit-slicing implementation of the S-box using new permutations and optimized boolean formulas instead of lookup tables, improving the best assembly implementation in Cortex-M3 by 8× than previous works. The implementation is close to competing with the software implementation of AES. In [3], Adomnicai et al. show a very efficient software implementation of GIFT using only a few rotations with a new technique called fix-slicing. It showed faster performance than the best AES [4] constant time at the time when it was reported that PRESENT [2] implementation 1,617 cycles were required in Cortex-M3 microcontrollers. Based on these studies, it is possible for a hardware-friendly cipher to implement in software efficiently. We expected that SPEEDY would be able to achieve sufficient performance in software through the previous technique. NIST's nominations for cryptographic standards include hardware and software evaluations, and ciphers with high performance in hardware and software are considered competitive over other ciphers. If the efficient implementation of SPEEDY's software is possible, it is thought that it will enhance the competitiveness of SPEEDY.

1.1 Contributions

We have achieved excellent performance by implementing SPEEDY in software on a 32-bit ARM processors. SPEEDY's 6-bit S-box and bit permutations seem to make the software implementation inefficient, but we use the bit-slicing implementation technique to resolve this issue. By implementing bit-slicing, all blocks of SPEEDY can be operated in a parallel way. It can also achieve constant time implementation, leading to the prevention of timing attacks. Bit-slicing technique is applied efficiently due to the bit permutation of the simple structure. The barrel shift of the Cortex-M3 maximizes these advantages. In ARM Cortex-M3, SPEEDY-5-192, SPEEDY-6-192, and SPEEDY-7-192 achieved 65.7, 75.25, and 85.16 clock cycles per byte, respectively. This is faster than the constant time implementation of GIFT-128 and AES-128 block ciphers in same architecture.

2   SPEEDY Algorithm

SPEEDY is a very low-latency block cipher. SPEEDY prioritizes speed and high security. It is primarily designed for hardware security solutions built into high-end CPUs that require significantly higher performance in terms of latency and throughput. A 6-bit S-box is used and 192 bits, which is the least common multiple of 6 and 64, is used as the block and key size considering the 64-bit CPU. 192 bits can be expressed in 32 rows of 6 bits each. SPEEDY Family consists of SPEEDY-5-192, SPEEDY-6-192, and SPEEDY-7-192 according to the number of rounds. It is noted that round 6 achieves 128-bit security, 7 round achieves 192-bit security, and round 5 provides a sufficient level of security for many practical applications. The SPEEDY-r-6ℓ an instance of this family with a block and key size of 6ℓ bits. It can be seen as a ℓ6 rectangular arrangement. The round function is as follows.

– SubBox (SB): SPEEDY's 6-bit S-box is based on NAND gates and is designed to be very fast in CMOS hardware while at the same time providing excellent cryptographic properties. S-boxes are applied to each row of states. The Disjunctive Normal Form (DNF) of S-box is as follows. In our implementation, the operation of DNF is followed, and S-box is performed by AND operation and OR operation.

$$y_0 = (x_3 \wedge \neg x_5) \vee (x_3 \wedge x_4 \wedge x_2) \vee (\neg x_3 \wedge x_1 \wedge x_0) \vee (x_5 \wedge x_4 \wedge x_1)$$
$$y_1 = (x_5 \wedge x_3 \wedge \neg x_2) \vee (\neg x_5 \wedge x_3 \wedge \neg x_4) \vee (x_5 \wedge x_2 \wedge x_0) \vee (\neg x_3 \wedge \neg x_0 \wedge x_1)$$
$$y_2 = (\neg x_3 \wedge x_0 \wedge x_4) \vee (x_3 \wedge x_0 \wedge x_1) \vee (\neg x_3 \wedge \neg x_4 \wedge x_2) \vee (\neg x_0 \wedge \neg x_2 \wedge \neg x_5)$$
$$y_3 = (\neg x_0 \wedge x_2 \neg x_3) \vee (x_0 \wedge x_2 \wedge x_4) \vee (x_0 \wedge \neg x_2 \wedge x_5) \vee (\neg x_4 \wedge \neg x_2 \wedge x_1)$$
$$y_4 = (x_0 \wedge \neg x_3) \vee (x_0 \wedge \neg x_4 \wedge \neg x_2) \vee (\neg x_0 \wedge x_4 \wedge x_5) \vee (\neg x_4 \wedge \neg x_2 \wedge x_1)$$
$$y_5 = (x_2 \wedge x_5) \vee (\neg x_2 \wedge \neg x_1 \wedge x_4) \vee (x_2 \wedge x_1 \wedge x_0) \vee (\neg x_1 \wedge x_0 \wedge x_3)$$

– ShiftColumns (SC): The j-th column of the state is rotated upside by j bits. In hardware implementation, ShiftColumnsdms is free with simple wiring, but additional operation is required in software.

$$y_{[i,j]} = x_{[i+j,j]}$$

– MixColumns (MC): A cyclic binary matrix is multiplied to each column of the state. In hardware, it can be implemented only with XOR gate, but similar to ShiftColumns, the additional operation is required in the software implementation. $\alpha = (\alpha 1, ..., \alpha 6)$ is the parameterized value for each version

$$y_{[i,j]} = x_{i,j} \oplus x_{[i+\alpha_1,j]} \oplus x_{[i+\alpha_2,j]} \oplus x_{[i+\alpha_3,j]} \oplus x_{[i+\alpha_4,j]} \oplus x_{[i+\alpha_5,j]} \oplus x_{[i+\alpha_6,j]}$$

– AddRoundKey (AK): The 6ℓ-bit round key k_r is XORed to the whole of the state.

$$y_{[i,j]} = x_{[i,j]} \oplus k_{r[i,j]}$$

– AddRoundConstant (AC): The 6ℓ-bit constant c_r is XORed to the whole of the state. round constants are chosen as the binary digits of the number $\pi - 3 = 0.1415....$

$$y_{[i,j]} = x_{[i,j]} \oplus c_{r[i,j]}$$

Encryption operates in the order of $A_k \rightarrow SB \rightarrow SC \rightarrow SB \rightarrow SC \rightarrow MC \rightarrow A_c$ in one round, and operates in the order of $A_k \rightarrow SB \rightarrow SC \rightarrow SB \rightarrow A_k$ in the last round. In the decoding, an inverse operation is performed in the reverse order. In the first round, it operates in the order of $A_k \rightarrow InverseSB \rightarrow InverseSC \rightarrow InverseSB \rightarrow A_k$, and from the next round, it repeats in the order $A_c \rightarrow InverseMC \rightarrow InverseSC \rightarrow InverseSB \rightarrow InverseSC \rightarrow InverseSB \rightarrow A_k$.

3   Proposed Method

This chapter describes the proposed SPEEDY implementation method. First, looking at the round function of SPEEDY from a software implementation point of view, in the case of ShiftColumns, it is computed for free in hardware, but the bit permutation in a column unit is inefficient in software. A block of 6-bit does not fit the 8-bit, 32-bit, and 64-bit blocks used in typical processor architectures. Implementing SPEEDY in software is inefficient due to 6-bit S-boxes and bit permutations. As a solution to this, we used the bit-slicing technique. Due to the effect of this alignment, the round function can be implemented efficiently in software.

We show that SPEEDY can work well in an embedded environment by implementing it on ARM Cortex-M3 microcontrollers. In our implementation, the 32 blocks of 6 bits are converted to a bit-slicing representation and stored in 6 32-bit registers. As a result, the round function is able to execute 32 blocks in parallel. Specifically, ShiftColumns and MixColumns work efficiently with the Cortex-M3 barrel shifter. Since we modified the logical operation process of S-box, S-BOX operation operates using few instructions and implemented it efficiently. Considering the case where the key is used repeatedly, the RoundConstant value is calculated in advance with the round key, and AddRoundConstant is omitted.

3.1   SPEEDY on ARM Cortex–M3

The Cortex-M3 is ARM's family of 32-bit processors for use in embedded microcontrollers. It is designed to be inexpensive and energy-efficient, so it has very effective characteristics for implementing IoT services. Arithmetic and logic operations take one clock cycle. However, branches, loads, and stores can take more cycles. A distinctive feature is that it supports a barrel shifter. By using the barrel shifter, rotation or shift can be performed at no additional cost in arithmetic or logical operations. This microprocessor haves 16 32-bit registers, 3 of which are for program counters, stack pointers and link registers, for a total of 14 registers available to developers (R_0-R_{12}, R_{14}). The first thing to consider to increase computational performance is to minimize access to memory.

Therefore, in our implementation, the address value of the periodically used round key is stored in one register and used repeatedly, and the intermediate value of the operation is stored by fixing 6 registers. In order to operate without access to memory except for the AddRoundKey function, 7 temporary storage spaces were required for SubBox operation, and 6 temporary storage spaces were needed for ShiftColumns and MixColumns respectively. For the efficient operation, all 14 registers are used and the value stored in the ciphertext address is called once at the end. It is stored on the stack at the start of the operation and loaded at the end.

3.2   Using Bit-Slicing in SPEEDY

Bit-slicing was the first technique used by Biham [5] instead of lookup tables to speed up the software implementation of DES. The basic method of bit-slicing is to express n-bit data by 1 bit in n registers. In this way, multiple blocks can be processed in parallel with bitwise operation instructions. In the case of AES,

Table 1. Bit-slicing representation from using 6 32-bit registers $R_0, \ldots, R_5$ to process 8 blocks $b^0, \triangle\triangle\triangle, b^7$ in parallel where b_j^i refers to the j-th bit of the i-th block.

	Block0	Block1	Block2	Block3	$\cdots$	$\cdots$	Block28	Block29	Block30	Block31
R_0	b_0^0	b_0^1	b_0^2	b_0^3	$\cdots$	$\cdots$	b_0^{28}	b_0^{29}	b_0^{30}	b_0^{31}
R_1	b_1^0	b_1^1	b_1^2	b_1^3	$\cdots$	$\cdots$	b_1^{28}	b_1^{29}	b_1^{30}	b_1^{31}
R_2	b_2^0	b_2^1	b_2^2	b_2^3	$\cdots$	$\cdots$	b_2^{28}	b_2^{29}	b_2^{30}	b_2^{31}
R_3	b_3^0	b_3^1	b_3^2	b_3^3	$\cdots$	$\cdots$	b_3^{28}	b_3^{29}	b_3^{30}	b_3^{31}
R_4	b_4^0	b_4^1	b_4^2	b_4^3	$\cdots$	$\cdots$	b_4^{28}	b_4^{29}	b_4^{30}	b_4^{31}
R_5	b_5^0	b_5^1	b_5^2	b_5^3	$\cdots$	$\cdots$	b_5^{28}	b_5^{29}	b_5^{30}	b_5^{31}

128-bit plaintext is expressed in 8 registers and operates. Larger registers allow more blocks to be operated. They work more efficiently on processors using large registers. In the case of SPEEDY, since 192 bits are divided into 32 blocks of 6 bits each, it can be expressed with 6 32-bit registers. The 192-bit plaintext is relocated to bitslcicing representation as shown in Table a and stored in 6 32-bit registers. With this expression method, the blocks of SPEEDY can be operated in parallel in all functions and operate efficiently. In S-Box operation is performed by combining bitwise operators, and all operations are processed in parallel with 32 blocks. In particular, SC and MC operations can be operated very simply and quickly with the barrel shift operation of Cortex-M3.

In general, when rearranging the input into a bit-slicing representation, this can be done using the SWAPMOVE technique [6].

$$\text{SWAPMOVE}(A, B, M, n) :$$
$$T = (B \oplus (A \ll n)) \wedge M$$
$$B = B \oplus T$$
$$A = A \oplus (T \gg n)$$

However, SPEEDY block cipher could not make a bit-slicing representation using only SWAPMOVE. In a 32-bit processor, 192 bits of plaintext are stored in six segments. At this time, it is inefficient to rearrange the 6-bit blocks in a bit-slicing representation because they are stored in different spaces. Considering this, we implemented it in three steps to make the most of SWAPMOVE technology. There are 5 blocks of 6 bits that can be completely stored in one register. Therefore, SWAPMOVE technology is applied to the blocks of 0-th to 29-th indexes, and the rest are implemented by moving 1 bit at a time. First, as shown in Figure a, step 1 is arranged in 6-bit blocks, and in step 2, indexes 30 and 31 are rearranged by bit-slicing expression and rearranged by moving one bit at a time. Finally, in step 3, SWAPMOVE rearranges the blocks from the 0-th to the 29-th index.

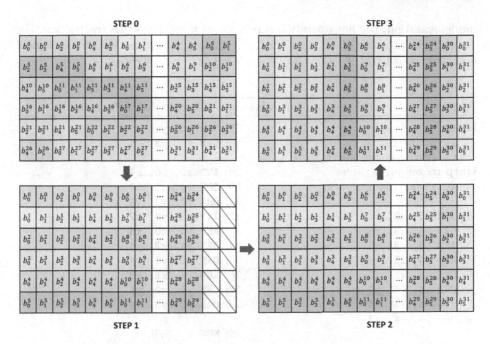

Fig. 1. Reorders plain text consisting of 32 blocks of 6 bits in 6 32-bit registers into a bit-slicing representation. A block of 6 bits is expressed as b_j^i, where i is the index of the block, and j is the position of the bit.

3.3 SubBox

SubBox layer operation is performed by combining logical operators instead of lookup table method. In the implementation of the expression by bit-slicing, 32 blocks of 6 bits can be operated in parallel by a combination of logical operators. It can be operated efficiently. Additionally, we use the rule of logical operators to reduce the number of logical operations. In this way, 8 instruction are reduced in the SubBox layer. The S-Box operation can be transformed into the following formula.

$$y_0 = x_3 \wedge (\neg x_5 \vee (x_4 \wedge x_2) \vee (x_1 \wedge ((\neg x_3 \wedge x_0) \vee (x_5 \wedge x_4))))$$
$$y_1 = x_5 \wedge ((x_3 \wedge \neg x_2) \vee (x_2 \wedge x_0) \vee (\neg x_5 \wedge x_3 \wedge \neg x_4) \vee (\neg x_3 \wedge \neg x_0 \wedge x_1))$$
$$y_2 = x_0 \wedge ((\neg x_3 \wedge x_4) \vee (x_3 \wedge x_1) \vee (\neg x_3 \wedge \neg x_4 \wedge x_2) \vee (\neg x_0 \wedge \neg x_2 \wedge x_5))$$
$$y_3 = x_2 \wedge ((\neg x_0 \wedge \neg x_3) \vee (x_0 \wedge x_4) \vee (x_0 \wedge \neg x_2 \wedge x_5) \vee (\neg x_0 \wedge x_3 \wedge x_1))$$
$$y_4 = (x_0 \wedge \neg x_3) \vee (\neg x_0 \wedge x_4 \wedge x_5) \vee ((\neg x_4 \wedge \neg x_2) \wedge (x_0 \vee x_1))$$
$$y_5 = x_2 \wedge (x_5 \vee (x_1 \wedge x_0)) \vee (\neg x_1 \wedge ((\neg x_2 \wedge x_4) \vee (x_0 \wedge x_3))$$

There is no Cortex-M3 assembly instruction corresponding to the $\neg$ operation or the operation $a \wedge \neg b$ used here. However, the operation of $a \vee \neg b$ can be performed with the ORN instruction as used in Algorithm a. For efficient implementation, the not operation is performed using the ORN instruction. For example, in the case of $(x_3 \wedge x_4 \wedge x_2) \vee (\neg x_3 \wedge x_1 \wedge x_0)$, use the rule of logical operators to convert it to $(x_3 \wedge x_4 \wedge x_2) \vee \neg((x_3 \vee \neg x_1) \vee \neg x_0)$.

Algorithm 1. bit-slicing implementations of S-box in ARMv6 assembly.

Input: input registers
    x0-x5 (r4-r9),
    temporal register t (r14)
Output: output registers
    y0-y5 (r1-r3, r10-r12)

```
 1: AND y3, x2, x4
 2: ORN y3, y3, x5
 3: AND y3, y3, x3
 4: AND y4, x5, x4
 5: ORN y5, x3, x0
 6: ORN y4, y4, y5
 7: AND y4, x1, y4
 8: ORR y0, y4, y3

 9: AND y3, x0, x2
10: ORN y4, x2, x3
11: ORN y3, y3, y4
12: AND y3, y3, x5
13: ORR y4, x5, x4
14: ORN y4, y4, x3
15: ORN y3, y3, y4
16: ORR y4, x0, x3
17: ORN y4, y4, x1
18: ORN y1, y3, y4

19: AND y3, x1, x3
20: ORN y4, x3, x4
21: ORN y3, y3, y4
22: AND y3, x0, y3
23: ORR y4, x3, x4
24: ORN y4, y4, x2
25: ORN y3, y3, y4
26: ORR y4, x0, x2
```

```
27: ORR y4, y4, x5
28: ORN y2, y3, y4

29: AND y3, x0, x4
30: ORR y4, x0, x3
31: ORN y3, y3, y4
32: AND y3, y3, x2
33: AND y4, x0, x5
34: ORN y4, x2, y4
35: ORN y3, y3, y4
36: AND y4, x1, x3
37: ORN y4, x0, y4
38: ORN y3, y3, y4

39: MOV t, #s0
40: ORR y4, x4, x2
41: ORR y5, x0, x1
42: ORN y4, y4, y5
43: ORN y4, t, y4
44: ORN y5, x3, x0
45: ORN y4, y4, y5
46: AND y5, x4, x5
47: ORN y5, x0, y5
48: ORN y4, y4, y5

49: AND t, x0, x3
50: ORN y5, x2, x4
51: ORN t, t, y5
52: ORN t, x1, t
53: AND y5, x1, x0
54: ORR y5, y5, x5
55: AND y5, y5, x2
56: ORN y5, y5, t
```

3.4 ShiftColumns

In the bit-slicing implementation, ShiftColumns can be implemented efficiently. In ShiftColumns, bits of the block are shifted in the column direction. In the bit-slicing representation, bits are converted into transposition in the row direction

---

Algorithm 2. bit-slicing implementations of ShiftColumns in ARMv6 assembly.

Input: input registers	2: MOV y1, x1, ROR #31
x0-x5 (r1-r3, r10-r12)	3: MOV y2, x2, ROR #30
Output: output register	4: MOV y3, x3, ROR #29
y0-y5 (r4-r9)	5: MOV y4, x4, ROR #28
1: MOV y0, x0	6: MOV y5, x5, ROR #27

---

because rows and columns are switched. Therefore, it can be implemented with rotation operation. 32 blocks are operated in parallel and can be implemented with 6 mov instructions. At this time, the value moved after rotation is stored in another register. And the value stored in the existing register is used again in the MC operation for operation.

3.5 MixColumns

In a bit-slicing implementation similar to ShiftColumns, the operation of Mix-Columns can be implemented efficiently. Since rows and columns are switched, rotate each row as much as a_i and perform XOR as shown below.

$$y[i] = x[i] \oplus (x[i] <<< a_0) \oplus (x[i] <<< a_1) \oplus (x[i] <<< a_2)$$
$$\oplus (x[i] <<< a_3) \oplus (x[i] <<< a_4) \oplus (x[i] <<< a_5)$$

For this operation, the value of $y[i]$ must be stored. As in Algorithm 3, this value reuses the value stored in the existing register in the previous SC process. Since the value stored in the existing register is the value before the SC operation, the additional rotation is required as much as the SC operation. This operation can be implemented with only the XOR instruction, since the rotation operation can be operated with a barrel-shifter. At this time, as a result of the SC operation, 32 blocks are operated in parallel with 36 EOR instruction.

3.6 AddRoundKey and AddRoundConstant

In the case of AC operation, the process of XORing each bit with a constant value is performed in the same way as in AR operation. Therefore, it is implemented to XOR the constant value and the round key value in advance. In consideration of the bit-slicing expression, the round key must also be packed in the same form, and as in Algorithm a, load and xor are each executed 6 times. When encryption starts after the key schedule operates first, the encryption process is calculated by omitting the AC process.

Algorithm 3. bit-slicing implementations MixColumns in ARMv6 assembly.

Input: input registers
    x0-x5 (r1-r3, r10-r12)
    y0-y5 (r4-r9)
Output: output registers
    y0-y5 (r4-r9)

1: EOR y0, y0, x0, ROR #31
2: EOR y0, y0, x0, ROR #27
3: EOR y0, y0, x0, ROR #23
4: EOR y0, y0, x0, ROR #17
5: EOR y0, y0, x0, ROR #11
6: EOR y0, y0, x0, ROR #6

7: EOR y1, y1, x1, ROR #30
8: EOR y1, y1, x1, ROR #26
9: EOR y1, y1, x1, ROR #22
10: EOR y1, y1, x1, ROR #16
11: EOR y1, y1, x1, ROR #10
12: EOR y1, y1, x1, ROR #5

13: EOR y2, y2, x2, ROR #29
14: EOR y2, y2, x2, ROR #25
15: EOR y2, y2, x2, ROR #21
16: EOR y2, y2, x2, ROR #15

17: EOR y2, y2, x2, ROR #9
18: EOR y2, y2, x2, ROR #4

19: EOR y3, y3, x3, ROR #28
20: EOR y3, y3, x3, ROR #24
21: EOR y3, y3, x3, ROR #20
22: EOR y3, y3, x3, ROR #14
23: EOR y3, y3, x3, ROR #8
24: EOR y3, y3, x3, ROR #3

25: EOR y4, y4, x4, ROR #27
26: EOR y4, y4, x4, ROR #23
27: EOR y4, y4, x4, ROR #19
28: EOR y4, y4, x4, ROR #13
29: EOR y4, y4, x4, ROR #7
30: EOR y4, y4, x4, ROR #2

31: EOR y5, y5, x5, ROR #26
32: EOR y5, y5, x5, ROR #22
33: EOR y5, y5, x5, ROR #18
34: EOR y5, y5, x5, ROR #12
35: EOR y5, y5, x5, ROR #6
36: EOR y5, y5, x5, ROR #1

---

4 Results

In this chapter, we compare the results for our implementation. The software was developed with Arduino IDE on the ArduinoDUE (AT91SAM3X8E) development board equipped with an ARM Cortex-M3 processor. The operating clock is 84 MHz, and it has 512 KB of flash memory and 96 KB of RAM. Performance comparison measured the average cycle when encrypting. Key scheduling is not taken into account as it is assumed that round keys are pre-computed and stored in RAM. We implemented SPEEDY-5-192, SPEEDY-6-192, and SPEEDY-7-192, and for comparison, AES-128 and GIFT-128 implemented in constant time in the same environment were compared together. In general, 128-bit blocks are encrypted, but since SPEEDY encrypts 192-bit blocks, the performance difference was compared based on cycle per byte (cpb) to compare other encryptions. And the key schedule was calculated in advance, and the average was measured when it was operated in ECB mode. As shown in Table 2, compared to the reference C implementation of SPEEDY-7-192, the speed difference was about 180 times. Although the optimization level of the reference C implementation is not performed in assembly level, it showed a noticeable high performance improvement. In addition, when comparing our implemented SPEEDY-6-192 with the same security level AES-128 and GIFT-128, the result of 75.2 cpb is 1.6× faster than 120.4 cpb of AES-128 and 1.3× faster than 104.1 cpb of GIFT-128. Considering that SPEEDY is designed to be hardware-friendly, this is a remarkable result.

Table 2. Comparison of SPEEDY implementation results and various constant-time implementation results on ARM Cortex-M3. The performance is evaluated in clock cycles per byte (cpb).

Implementation	Speed (cpb)	Block size
AES-128 encryption	120.4	128
GIFT-128 encryption	104.1	128
SPEEDY-7-192 encryption (reference)	15,407	192
SPEEDY-5-192 encryption (ours)	65.7	192
SPEEDY-6-192 encryption (ours)	75.2	192
SPEEDY-7-192 encryption (ours)	85.1	192

5   Conclusion

We implemented SPEEDY by applying the implementation technique of bit-slicing. For the case where the round key is calculated in advance, in ARM Cortex-M3, SPEEDY-5-192 achieves 65.7 cpb, SPEEDY-6-192 achieves 75.25 cpb, and SPEEDY-7-192 achieves 85.16 cpb, respectively. In the same environment, it showed better performance than 120.4 cpb of constant time implementation GIFT-128 and 104.1 cpb of constant time implementation AES-128. Through this, we showed that SPEEDY can be run very efficiently in software and can be applied in microcontrollers. The proposed technique is likely to be applicable to other processors, and in the future, we plan to implement other platforms (e.g. Cortex-M4). The proposed implementation is working in constant timing, which has an advantage against timing attacks. In the future work, we intend to apply an efficient masking technique for additional side-channel security.

Acknowledgment. This work was supported by Institute of Information & communications Technology Planning & Evaluation (IITP) grant funded by the Korea government (MSIT) (No. 2021-0-00540, Development of Fast Design and Implementation of Cryptographic Algorithms based on GPU/ASIC, 50%) and this work was partly supported by Institute for Information & communications Technology Promotion (IITP) grant funded by the Korea government (MSIT) (No. 2018-0-00264, Research on Blockchain Security Technology for IoT Services, 50%).

References

1. Leander, G., Moos, T., Moradi, A., Rasoolzadeh, S.: The SPEEDY family of block ciphers: engineering an ultra low-latency cipher from gate level for secure processor architectures. IACR Trans. Cryptographic Hardware Embed. Syst. **2021**, 510–545 (2021)
2. Reis, T.B.S., Aranha, D.F., López, J.: PRESENT runs fast. In: Fischer, W., Homma, N. (eds.) CHES 2017. LNCS, vol. 10529, pp. 644–664. Springer, Cham (2017). https://doi.org/10.1007/978-3-319-66787-4_31
3. Adomnicai, A., Najm, Z., Peyrin, T.: Fixslicing: a new GIFT representation: fast constant-time implementations of GIFT and GIFT-COFB on ARM cortex-M. IACR Trans. Cryptographic Hardware Embed. Syst. **2020**, 402–427 (2020)
4. Schwabe, P., Stoffelen, K.: All the AES you need on Cortex-M3 and M4. In: Avanzi, R., Heys, H. (eds.) SAC 2016. LNCS, vol. 10532, pp. 180–194. Springer, Cham (2017). https://doi.org/10.1007/978-3-319-69453-5_10
5. Biham, E.: A fast new DES implementation in software. In: Biham, E. (ed.) FSE 1997. LNCS, vol. 1267, pp. 260–272. Springer, Heidelberg (1997). https://doi.org/10.1007/BFb0052352
6. May, L., Penna, L., Clark, A.: An implementation of Bitsliced DES on the Pentium MMX^{TM} processor. In: Dawson, E.P., Clark, A., Boyd, C. (eds.) ACISP 2000. LNCS, vol. 1841, pp. 112–122. Springer, Heidelberg (2000). https://doi.org/10.1007/10718964_10

Author Index